S0-AFC-725

DRAMA *for Students*

DRAMA *for Students*

Presenting Analysis, Context and Criticism on Commonly Studied Dramas

Volume 3

David Galens, Editor

Dale Allender, English Instructor at West High School, Iowa City, Iowa, and liaison officer for Iowa Council of Teachers of English Language Arts, Advisor

Marie Slotnick, English Department Chair, Center Line High School, Center Line, Michigan, Advisor

Carolyn Tragesser, English Instructor, Moscow Junior High School, Moscow, Idaho, liason for National Council of English Teachers, Advisor

GALE

DETROIT • NEW YORK • LONDON

Drama for Students

Staff

Editorial: David M. Galens, *Editor.* Terry Browne, Christopher Busiel, Clare Cross, Tom Faulkner, John Fiero, David M. Galens, Carole Hamilton, Sheri Metzger, Daniel Moran, Terry Nienhuis, William P. Wiles, Joanne Woolway, Etta Worthington, *Entry Writers.* Elizabeth Cranston, Kathleen J. Edgar, Jennifer Gariepy, Dwayne D. Hayes, Kurt Kuban, Joshua Kondek, Tom Ligotti, Scot Peacock, Patti Tippett, Pam Zuber, *Contributing Editors.* James Draper, *Managing Editor.* Diane Telgen, *''For Students'' Line Coordinator.* Jeffery Chapman, *Programmer/Analyst.*

Research: Victoria B. Cariappa, *Research Team Manager.* Andy Malonis, Barb McNeil, *Research Specialists.* Julia C. Daniel, Tamara C. Nott, Tracie A. Richardson, Cheryl L. Warnock, *Research Associates.* Phyllis P. Blackman, Jeffrey D. Daniels, Corrine A. Stocker, *Research Assistants.*

Permissions: Susan M. Trosky, *Permissions Manager.* Kimberly F. Smilay, *Permissions Specialist.* Steve Cusack and Kelly A. Quin, *Permissions Associates.*

Production: Mary Beth Trimper, *Production Director.* Evi Seoud, *Assistant Production Manager.* Shanna Heilveil, *Production Assistant.*

Graphic Services: Randy Bassett, *Image Database Supervisor.* Robert Duncan and Michael Logusz, *Imaging Specialists.* Pamela A. Reed, *Photography Coordinator.* Gary Leach, *Macintosh Artist.*

Product Design: Cynthia Baldwin, *Product Design Manager.* Cover Design: Michelle DiMercurio, *Art Director.* Page Design: Pamela A. E. Galbreath, *Senior Art Director.*

Copyright Notice

∞™ This book is printed on acid-free paper that meets the minimum requirements of American National Standard for Information Sciences—Permanence Paper for Printed Library Materials, ANSI Z39.48-1984.

ISBN 0-7876-2752-6
ISSN 1094-9232
Printed in the United States of America

10 9 8 7 6 5 4 3 2 1

Table of Contents

The Study of Drama

We study drama in order to learn what meaning others have made of life, to comprehend what it takes to produce a work of art, and to glean some understanding of ourselves. Drama produces in a separate, aesthetic world, a moment of being for the audience to experience, while maintaining the detachment of a reflective observer.

Drama is a representational art, a visible and audible narrative presenting virtual, fictional characters within a virtual, fictional universe. Dramatic realizations may pretend to approximate reality or else stubbornly defy, distort, and deform reality into an artistic statement. From this separate universe that is obviously not ''real life'' we expect a valid reflection upon reality, yet drama never is mistaken for reality—the methods of theater are integral to its form and meaning. Theater is art, and art's appeal lies in its ability both to approximate life and to depart from it. By presenting its distorted version of life to our consciousness, art gives us a new perspective and appreciation of reality. Although, to some extent, all aesthetic experiences perform this service, theater does it most effectively by creating a separate, cohesive universe that freely acknowledges its status as an art form.

And what is the purpose of the aesthetic universe of drama? The potential answers to such a question are nearly as many and varied as there are plays written, performed, and enjoyed. Dramatic texts can be problems posed, answers asserted, or moments portrayed. Dramas (tragedies as well as comedies) may serve strictly ''to ease the anguish of a torturing hour'' (as stated in William Shakespeare's *A Midsummer Night's Dream*)—to divert and entertain—or aspire to move the viewer to action with social issues. Whether to entertain or to instruct, affirm or influence, pacify or shock, dramatic art wraps us in the spell of its imaginary world for the length of the work and then dispenses us back to the real world, entertained, purged, as Aristotle said, of pity and fear, and edified—or at least weary enough to sleep peacefully.

It is commonly thought that theater, being an art of performance, must be experienced—that is, seen—in order to be appreciated fully. However, to view a production of a dramatic text is to be limited to a single interpretation of that text—all other interpretations are for the moment closed off, inaccessible. In the process of producing a play, the director, stage designer, and performers interpret and transform the script into a work of art that always departs in some measure from the author's original conception. Novelist and critic Umberto Eco, in his *The Role of the Reader: Explorations in the Semiotics of Texts,* explained, ''In short, we can say that every performance offers us a complete and satisfying version of the work, but at the same time makes it incomplete for us, because it cannot simultaneously give all the other artistic solutions which the work may admit.''

Thus Laurence Olivier's coldly formal and neurotic film presentation of Shakespeare's *Hamlet* (in which he played the title character as well as directed) shows marked differences from subsequent adaptations. While Olivier's Hamlet is clearly entangled in a Freudian relationship with his mother, Gertrude, he would be incapable of shushing her with the impassioned kiss that Mel Gibson's mercurial Hamlet (in director Franco Zeffirelli's 1990 film) does. Although each of the performances rings true to Shakespeare's text, each is also a mutually exclusive work of art. Also important to consider are the time periods in which each of these films were produced: Olivier made his film in 1948, a time in which overt references to sexuality (especially incest) were frowned upon. Gibson and Zeffirelli made their film in a culture more relaxed and comfortable with these issues. Just as actors and directors can influence the presentation of drama, so too can the time period of the production affect what the audience will see.

A play script is an open text from which an infinity of specific realizations may be derived. Dramatic scripts that are more open to interpretive creativity (such as those of Ntozake Shange and Tomson Highway) actually require the creative improvisation of the production troupe in order to complete the text. Even the most prescriptive scripts (those of Neil Simon, Lillian Hellman, and Robert Bolt, for example), can never fully control the actualization of live performance, and circumstantial events, including the attitude and receptivity of the audience, make every performance a unique event. Thus, while it is important to view a production of a dramatic piece, if one wants to understand a drama fully it is equally important to read the original dramatic text.

The reader of a dramatic text or script is not limited by either the specific interpretation of a given production or by the unstoppable action of a moving spectacle. The reader of a dramatic text may discover the nuances of the play's language, structure, and events at their own pace. Yet studied alone, the author's blueprint for artistic production does not tell the whole story of a play's life and significance. One also needs to assess the play's critical reviews to discover how it resonated to cultural themes at the time of its debut and how the shifting tides of cultural interest have revised its interpretation and impact on audiences. And to do this, one needs to know a little about the culture of the times which produced the play as well as the author who penned it.

Drama for Students supplies this material in a useful compendium for the student of dramatic theater. Covering a range of dramatic works that span from the fifth century B.C. to the 1990s, this book focuses on significant theatrical works whose themes and form transcend the uncertainty of dramatic fads. These are plays that have proven to be both memorable and teachable. *Drama for Students* seeks to enhance appreciation of these dramatic texts by providing scholarly materials written with the secondary and college/university student in mind. It provides for each play a concise summary of the plot and characters as well as a detailed explanation of its themes and techniques. In addition, background material on the historical context of the play, its critical reception, and the author's life help the student to understand the work's position in the chronicle of dramatic history. For each play entry a new work of scholarly criticism is also included, as well as segments of other significant critical works for handy reference. A thorough bibliography provides a starting point for further research.

These inaugural two volumes offer comprehensive educational resources for students of drama. *Drama for Students* is a vital book for dramatic interpretation and a valuable addition to any reference library.

Source: Eco, Umberto, *The Role of the Reader: Explorations in the Semiotics of Texts,* Indiana University Press, 1979.

Carole L. Hamilton
Author and Instructor of English
Cary Academy
Cary, North Carolina

Introduction

Purpose of Drama for Students

The purpose of *Drama for Students* (*DfS*) is to provide readers with a guide to understanding, enjoying, and studying dramas by giving them easy access to information about the work. Part of Gale's "For Students" literature line, *DfS* is specifically designed to meet the curricular needs of high school and undergraduate college students and their teachers, as well as the interests of general readers and researchers considering specific plays. While each volume contains entries on "classic" dramas frequently studied in classrooms, there are also entries containing hard-to-find information on contemporary plays, including works by multicultural, international, and women playwrights.

The information covered in each entry includes an introduction to the play and the work's author; a plot summary, to help readers unravel and understand the events in a drama; descriptions of important characters, including explanation of a given character's role in the drama as well as discussion about that character's relationship to other characters in the play; analysis of important themes in the drama; and an explanation of important literary techniques and movements as they are demonstrated in the play.

In addition to this material, which helps the readers analyze the play itself, students are also provided with important information on the literary and historical background informing each work. This includes a historical context essay, a box comparing the time or place the drama was written to modern Western culture, a critical overview essay, and excerpts from critical essays on the play. A unique feature of *DfS* is a specially commissioned overview essay on each drama by an academic expert, targeted toward the student reader.

To further aid the student in studying and enjoying each play, information on media adaptations is provided, as well as reading suggestions for works of fiction and nonfiction on similar themes and topics. Classroom aids include ideas for research papers and lists of critical sources that provide additional material on each drama.

Selection Criteria

The titles for each volume of *DfS* were selected by surveying numerous sources on teaching literature and analyzing course curricula for various school districts. Some of the sources surveyed included: literature anthologies; *Reading Lists for College-Bound Students: The Books Most Recommended by America's Top Colleges;* textbooks on teaching dramas; a College Board survey of plays commonly studied in high schools; a National Council of Teachers of English (NCTE) survey of plays commonly studied in high schools; St. James Press's *International Dictionary of Theatre;* and Arthur Applebee's 1993 study *Literature in the Secondary School: Studies of Curriculum and Instruction in the United States.*

Input was also solicited from our expert advisory board (both experienced educators specializing in English), as well as educators from various areas. From these discussions, it was determined that each volume should have a mix of "classic" dramas (those works commonly taught in literature classes) and contemporary dramas for which information is often hard to find. Because of the interest in expanding the canon of literature, an emphasis was also placed on including works by international, multicultural, and women playwrights. Our advisory board members—current high school teachers—helped pare down the list for each volume. If a work was not selected for the present volume, it was often noted as a possibility for a future volume. As always, the editor welcomes suggestions for titles to be included in future volumes.

How Each Entry Is Organized

Each entry, or chapter, in *DfS* focuses on one play. Each entry heading lists the full name of the play, the author's name, and the date of the play's first production or publication. The following elements are contained in each entry:

- **Introduction:** a brief overview of the drama which provides information about its first appearance, its literary standing, any controversies surrounding the work, and major conflicts or themes within the work.

- **Author Biography:** this section includes basic facts about the author's life, and focuses on events and times in the author's life that inspired the drama in question.

- **Plot Summary:** a description of the major events in the play, with interpretation of how these events help articulate the play's themes. Subheads demarcate the plays' various acts or scenes.

- **Characters:** an alphabetical listing of major characters in the play. Each character name is followed by a brief to an extensive description of the character's role in the plays, as well as discussion of the character's actions, relationships, and possible motivation.

  Characters are listed alphabetically by last name. If a character is unnamed—for instance, the Stage Manager in *Our Town*—the character is listed as "The Stage Manager" and alphabetized as "Stage Manager." If a character's first name is the only one given, the name will appear alphabetically by the name.

  Variant names are also included for each character. Thus, the nickname "Babe" would head the listing for a character in *Crimes of the Heart,* but below that listing would be her less-mentioned married name "Rebecca Botrelle."

- **Themes:** a thorough overview of how the major topics, themes, and issues are addressed within the play. Each theme discussed appears in a separate subhead, and is easily accessed through the boldface entries in the Subject/Theme Index.

- **Style:** this section addresses important style elements of the drama, such as setting, point of view, and narration; important literary devices used, such as imagery, foreshadowing, symbolism; and, if applicable, genres to which the work might have belonged, such as Gothicism or Romanticism. Literary terms are explained within the entry, but can also be found in the Glossary.

- **Historical and Cultural Context:** This section outlines the social, political, and cultural climate *in which the author lived and the play was created.* This section may include descriptions of related historical events, pertinent aspects of daily life in the culture, and the artistic and literary sensibilities of the time in which the work was written. If the play is a historical work, information regarding the time in which the play is set is also included. Each section is broken down with helpful subheads.

- **Critical Overview:** this section provides background on the critical reputation of the play, including bannings or any other public controversies surrounding the work. For older plays, this section includes a history of how the drama was first received and how perceptions of it may have changed over the years; for more recent plays, direct quotes from early reviews may also be included.

- **For Further Study:** an alphabetical list of other critical sources which may prove useful for the student. Includes full bibliographical information and a brief annotation.

- **Sources:** an alphabetical list of critical material quoted in the entry, with full bibliographical information.

- **Criticism:** an essay commissioned by *DfS* which specifically deals with the play and is written specifically for the student audience, as well as excerpts from previously published criticism on the work.

In addition, each entry contains the following highlighted sections, set separate from the main text:

- **Media Adaptations:** a list of important film and television adaptations of the play, including source information. The list may also include such variations on the work as audio recordings, musical adaptations, and other stage interpretations.
- **Compare and Contrast Box:** an "at-a-glance" comparison of the cultural and historical differences between the author's time and culture and late twentieth-century Western culture. This box includes pertinent parallels between the major scientific, political, and cultural movements of the time or place the drama was written, the time or place the play was set (if a historical work), and modern Western culture. Works written after the mid-1970s may not have this box.
- **What Do I Read Next?:** a list of works that might complement the featured play or serve as a contrast to it. This includes works by the same author and others, works of fiction and nonfiction, and works from various genres, cultures, and eras.
- **Study Questions:** a list of potential study questions or research topics dealing with the play. This section includes questions related to other disciplines the student may be studying, such as American history, world history, science, math, government, business, geography, economics, psychology, etc.

Other Features

DfS includes "The Study of Drama," a foreword by Carole Hamilton, an educator and author who specializes in dramatic works. This essay examines the basis for drama in societies and what drives people to study such work. Hamilton also discusses how *Drama for Students* can help teachers show students how to enrich their own reading/viewing experiences.

A Cumulative Author/Title Index lists the authors and titles covered in each volume of the *DfS* series.

A Cumulative Nationality/Ethnicity Index breaks down the authors and titles covered in each volume of the *DfS* series by nationality and ethnicity.

A Subject/Theme Index, specific to each volume, provides easy reference for users who may be studying a particular subject or theme rather than a single work. Significant subjects from events to broad themes are included, and the entries pointing to the specific theme discussions in each entry are indicated in **boldface.**

Each entry has several illustrations, including photos of the author, stills from stage productions, and stills from film adaptations.

Citing Drama for Students

When writing papers, students who quote directly from any volume of *Drama for Students* may use the following general forms. These examples are based on MLA style; teachers may request that students adhere to a different style, so the following examples may be adapted as needed.

When citing text from *DfS* that is not attributed to a particular author (i.e., the Themes, Style, Historical Context sections, etc.), the following format should be used in the bibliography section:

"Our Town," *Drama for Students.* Ed. David Galens and Lynn Spampinato. Vol. 1. Detroit: Gale, 1997. 8–9.

When quoting the specially commissioned essay from *DfS* (usually the first piece under the "Criticism" subhead), the following format should be used:

Fiero, John. Essay on "Twilight: Los Angeles, 1992." *Drama for Students.* Ed. David Galens and Lynn Spampinato. Vol. 1. Detroit: Gale, 1997. 8–9.

When quoting a journal or newspaper essay that is reprinted in a volume of *DfS,* the following form may be used:

Rich, Frank. "Theatre: A Mamet Play, 'Glengarry Glen Ross'." *New York Theatre Critics' Review* Vol. 45, No. 4 (March 5, 1984), 5–7; excerpted and reprinted in *Drama for Students,* Vol. 1, ed. David Galens and Lynn Spampinato (Detroit: Gale, 1997), pp. 61–64.

When quoting material reprinted from a book that appears in a volume of *DfS,* the following form may be used:

Kerr, Walter. "The Miracle Worker," in *The Theatre in Spite of Itself* (Simon & Schuster, 1963, 255–57; excerpted and reprinted in *Drama for Students,* Vol. 1, ed. Dave Galens and Lynn Spampinato (Detroit: Gale, 1997), pp. 59–61.

We Welcome Your Suggestions

The editor of *Drama for Students* welcomes your comments and ideas. Readers who wish to suggest dramas to appear in future volumes, or who have other suggestions, are cordially invited to contact the editor. You may contact the editor via E-mail at: **david.galens@gale.com.** Or write to the editor at:

David Galens, *Drama for Students*
Gale Research
835 Penobscot Bldg.
645 Griswold St.
Detroit, MI 48226-4094

Literary Chronology

1856: George Bernard Shaw is born in Dublin, Ireland, on July 26.

1899: Noel Coward is born in Teddington-on-Thames, Middlesex, England, on December 16.

1905: *Major Barbara* has its first production at the Royal Court Theatre in London, England, on November 28.

1906: Lillian Hellman is born in New Orleans, Louisiana, on June 20.

1906: Clifford Odets is born in Philadelphia, Pennsylvania, on July 18.

1911: Tennessee Williams is born March 26, in Columbus, Mississippi.

1913: William Inge is born May 3, in Independence, Kansas.

1915: Arthur Miller is born in New York City on October 17.

1916: Peter Weiss is born November 8, in Nowawes, Germany.

1928: Edward Albee is born March 12, in Virginia.

1930: *Private Lives* has its first production at the Phoenix Theatre in London, England.

1930: Harold Pinter is born October 10, in Hackney, London, England.

1932: Athol Fugard is born in Middleburg, Cape Province, South Africa, on June 11.

1933: Joe Orton is born John Kingsley Orton in Leicester, England, on January 1.

1934: Edward Bond is born in Holloway, North London, England, on July 18.

1934: Amiri Baraka is born LeRoi Jones on October 7, in Newark, New Jersey.

1934: *The Children's Hour* is produced at the Maxine Elliot Theatre in New York City, on November 20.

1935: *Waiting for Lefty* has its first production on March 26, at the Longacre Theatre on Broadway.

1936: Sharon Pollock is born in Fredericton, New Brunswick, Canada, on April 19.

1940: David Rabe is born March 10, in Dubuque, Iowa.

1943: Sam Shepard is born in Fort Sheridan, Illinois, on November 5.

1945: August Wilson is born April 27, in Pittsburgh, Pennsylvania.

1947: David Mamet is born in Chicago, Illinois, on November 30.

1949: *Come Back, Little Sheba* is first produced by the Theatre Guild in Westport, Connecticut, on

September 12. It debuts on Broadway at the Booth Theatre on February 15, 1950.

1950: George Bernard Shaw dies in Ayot St. Lawrence, Hertfordshire, England, on November 2.

1953: *The Crucible* has its debut on Broadway at the Martin Beck Theatre, on January 22.

1955: *Cat on a Hot Tin Roof* has its first production on Broadway at the Morosco Theatre.

1962: *Who's Afraid of Virginia Woolf?* has its first production on Broadway at the Billy Rose Theatre, on October 13.

1963: Clifford Odets dies in Los Angeles, California, on August 14.

1964: *Dutchman* has its first production at the Off-Broadway Village South Theatre. It later moves to the Cherry Lane Theatre.

1964: *Entertaining Mr. Sloane* debuts at the New Arts Theatre in London, England. It moves to Broadway in 1965.

1964: *Marat/Sade* is first produced at the Schiller Theatre in West Berlin, Germany, on April 29. The play debuts on Broadway at the Martin Beck Theatre, on December 27, 1965.

1965: *The Homecoming* debuts at the New Theatre in Cardiff, Wales, on March 22; the production moves to the Aldwych Theatre in London's West End on June 3. The play has its American debut on Broadway at the Music Box Theatre on January 5, 1967.

1967: Joe Orton is bludgeoned to death by his lover, Kenneth Halliwell, on August 9, 1967, in London, England.

1971: *The Basic Training of Pavlo Hummel* has its first production on the Newman stage of Broadway's Public Theatre on May 20, 1971.

1971: *Lear* debuts on London's West End; the American debut is at the Yale Repertory Theatre, 1973.

1973: Noel Coward dies of a heart attack in Blue Harbour, Jamaica, on March 26.

1973: William Inge commits suicide on June 10, in Los Angeles, California.

1975: *American Buffalo* debuts in Chicago; the play debuts on Broadway in 1977.

1980: *Blood Relations* debuts at Theatre Three in Edmonton, Alberta, Canada, on March 12.

1980: *True West* has its first production Off-Broadway at the Public Theatre, December 23.

1982: *''Master Harold''. . . and the Boys* debuts in Newhaven, Connecticut, in March; the play moves to the Lyceum Theatre on Broadway, May 5.

1982: Peter Weiss dies in Sweden.

1983: *Fences* debuts as a staged reading at the Eugene O'Neill Theatre Center's National Playwright's Conference; a full production is staged at the Yale Repertory Theatre in 1985; the production moves to the Forty-sixth Street Theatre on Broadway in March, 1987.

1983: Tennessee Williams chokes to death in his suite at the Hotel Elysee in New York City on February 24.

1984: Lillian Hellman dies of cardiac arrest on June 30, in Martha's Vineyard, Massachusetts.

Acknowledgments

The editors wish to thank the copyright holders of the excerpted criticism included in this volume and the permissions managers of many book and magazine publishing companies for assisting us in securing reproduction rights. We are also grateful to the staffs of the Detroit Public Library, the Library of Congress, the University of Detroit Mercy Library, Wayne State University Purdy/Kresge Library Complex, and the University of Michigan Libraries for making their resources available to us. Following is a list of the copyright holders who have granted us permission to reproduce material in this volume of ***Drama for Students (DfS).*** Every effort has been made to trace copyright, but if omissions have been made, please let us know.

COPYRIGHTED EXCERPTS IN* DfS, *VOLUME 3, WERE REPRODUCED FROM THE FOLLOWING PERIODICALS:

Canadian Drama/L'Art Dramatique Canadien, v. 15, 1989. Reproduced by permission.—***Commonweal,*** v. CXIV, May 22, 1987. Copyright © 1987 Commonweal Publishing Co., Inc. Reproduced by permission of Commonweal Foundation.—***Critical Quarterly,*** v. 24, Winter, 1982. © Manchester University Press 1982. Reproduced by permission of Blackwell Publishers.—***Educational Theatre Journal,*** v. XX, March, 1968; v. 25, March, 1973; v. 25, December, 1973; v. 27, October, 1975. © 1968, 1973, 1975 University College Theatre Association of the American Theatre Association. All reproduced by permission of the Johns Hopkins University Press.—The ***Explicator,*** v. 43, Winter, 1985; v. 46, Summer, 1988; v. 54, Winter, 1996; v. 55, Winter, 1997. Copyright © 1985, 1988, 1996, 1997 Helen Dwight Reid Educational Foundation. All reproduced with permission of the Helen Dwight Reid Educational Foundation, published by Heldref Publications, 1319 18th Street, NW, Washington, DC 20036-1802.—The ***Hudson Review,*** v. XL, Autumn, 1987. Copyright © 1987 by the Hudson Review, Inc. Reproduced by permission.—***Modern Drama,*** v. 10, December, 1967; v. XXIV, 1981; v. XXV, December, 1982; v. XXIX, 1986; v. XXX, December, 1987; v. 36, March, 1993 © 1967, 1981, 1982, 1986, 1987, 1993, University of Toronto, Graduate Centre for Study of Drama. All reproduced by permission.—The ***Nation,*** v. 212, June 7, 1971. © 1971 the Nation magazine/the Nation Company, Inc. Reproduced by permission.—***New York,*** Magazine, v. 16, February 28, 1983. Copyright © 1997 K-III Magazine Corporation. All rights reserved. Reproduced with the permission of ***New York Magazine.***—The ***New Republic,*** v. 132, April 11, 1955. University Press of Florida, 1955. Copyright 1955 by the Board of Regents of the State of Florida. © 1980 the New Republic, Inc. Reproduced by permission of the ***New Republic.***—The ***New York Times,*** January 28, 1931; December 28, 1965; v. 130, December, 1980; February 22, 1997. Copyright 1931, © 1965, 1980; 1997 by the New York Times Company. Reproduced by permission.—

The ***New Yorker,*** v. XXVI, February, 1950; v. XLV, December 13, 1969. © 1969, 1977 by the New Yorker Magazine, Inc. Both reproduced by permission.—The ***Saturday Review of Literature,*** v. XI, March 2, 1935. Copyright 1935, renewed © 1962 Saturday Review magazine. Reproduced by permission of the ***Saturday Review,*** General Media Communications, Inc.—The ***Saturday Review,*** v. LIV, July 10, 1971; v. 4, April 2, 1977. © 1971, 1977 General Media Communications, Inc. Both reproduced by permission of the ***Saturday Review,*** General Media Communications, Inc.—***Theatre Journal,*** v. 40, March, 1988. © 1988 University College Theatre Association of the American Theatre Association. Reproduced by permission of The Johns Hopkins University Press.—***Time,*** New York, v. 124, July 23, 1984. Copyright 1984 Time Warner Inc. All rights reserved. Reproduced by permission from ***Time.—Times Literary Supplement,*** no. 4896, January 31, 1997. © The Times Supplements Limited 1997. Reproduced from the ***Times Literary Supplement*** by permission.

COPYRIGHTED EXCERPTS IN* DfS, *VOLUME 3, WERE REPRODUCED FROM THE FOLLOWING BOOKS:

Atkinson, Brooks. From ***Onstage: Selected Theater Reviews from The New York Times, 1920-1970.*** Edited by Bernard Beckerman and Howard Siegman. Arno Press, 1973. Copyright © 1973 by the New York Times Company. Reproduced by permission of the New York Times Company.—Beidler, Philip D. From ***American Literature and the Experience of Vietnam.*** University of Georgia Press, 1982. Copyright © 1982 by the University of Georgia Press. All rights reserved. Reproduced by permission.—Freedman, Morris. From ***The Moral Impulse: Modern Drama from Ibsen to the Present.*** Southern Illinois University Press, 1967. Copyright © 1967 by Morris Freedman. All rights reserved. Reproduced by permission of Southern Illinois University Press.

PHOTOGRAPHS AND ILLUSTRATIONS APPEARING IN* DfS, *VOLUME 3, WERE RECEIVED FROM THE FOLLOWING SOURCES:

An actor beats his bass drum playing the part of a Salvation Army worker in the show ***Major Barbara*** by George Bernard Shaw, photograph. Hulton-Deutsch Collection/Corbis. Reproduced by permission.—Baraka, Imamu Amiri (LeRoi Jones), photograph. Corbis-Bettmann. Reproduced by permission.—Bond, Edward, photograph by Jerry Bauer. © Jerry Bauer. Reproduced by permission.—Coward, Noel, photograph. AP/Wide World Photos. Reproduced by permission.—Edward Albee, standing outside of Boston's Colonial Theater where he is directing ***Who's Afraid of Virginia Woolf?,*** photograph. AP/Wide World Photos. Reproduced by permission.—***Fences*** by August Wilson, with James Earl Jones, photograph by Ron Scherl. Reproduced by permission of the photographer.—Movie still of Baraka's ***The Dutchman,*** with Shirley Knight and Al Freeman, Jr., Directed by Anthony Harvey, 1966, photograph. Continental Distributing Inc. Courtesy of The Kobal Collection. Reproduced by permission.—Movie still of Baraka's ***The Dutchman,*** with Shirley Knight, Directed by Anthony Harvey, 1966, photograph. Continental Distributing Inc. Courtesy of The Kobal Collection. Reproduced by permission.—Movie still of David Mamet's ***American Buffalo*** with Dustin Hoffman, Samuel Goldwyn Company, 1997, photograph by Brian Hamill. Samuel Goldwyn Company. Courtesy of The Kobal Collection. Reproduced by permission.—Movie still of David Mamet's ***American Buffalo*** with Dustin Hoffman, Dennis Franz, and Sean Nelson, 1997, photograph by Brian Hamill. Samuel Goldwyn Company. Courtesy of The Kobal Collection. Reproduced by permission.—Movie still of Joe Orton's ***Entertaining Mr. Sloane*** with Beryl Reid and Peter McEnery, Warner Brothers, 1969, photograph. Warner Brothers. Courtesy of The Kobal Collection. Reproduced by permission.—Movie still of Tennessee Williams's ***Cat on A Hot Tin Roof*** with Burl Ives, Elizabeth Taylor and Paul Newman, MGM, 1958, photograph. MGM. Courtesy of The Kobal Collection. Reproduced by permission.—Movie still of Edward Albee's ***Who's Afraid of Virginia Woolf?.*** Directed by Mike Nichols with Elizabeth Taylor and Richard Burton as Martha and George, Warner Brothers, April 28, 1966, photograph. UPI/Corbis-Bettmann. Reproduced by permission.—Movie still of Edward Albee's ***Who's Afraid of Virginia Woolf?.*** Directed by Mike Nichols with Elizabeth Taylor and Richard Burton as Martha and George, Warner Brothers, April 28, 1966, photograph. UPI/Corbis-Bettmann. Reproduced by permission.—From a theater production of Sharon Pollock's ''Blood Relations'' with Mike Curtis as Mr. Borden and Mary Sloane as the Actress, directed by Brenda Leadlay at the Guild Hall, Fall, 1997, photograph by John Tousigna. Reproduced by permission.—From a theatre production of Arthur Miller's ***The Crucible*** with Caroline Milmoe as Betty Parris, and Jenifer Landor as Abigail Williams, Royal Shakespeare Company tour, 1984, photograph. Donald Cooper, London.

Reproduced by permission.—From a theatre production of Athol Fugard's ***Master Harold . . . and the Boys*** with Ramolao Makhene as Willie, Duart Sylwain as Hally, and John Kani as Sam, Cottesloe Theatre/National Theatre, London, 1983, photograph. Donald Cooper, London. Reproduced by permission.—From a theatre production of Clifford Odets's ***Waiting for Lefty,*** photograph. Theatre Collection, Museum of the City of New York. Reproduced by permission.—From a theatre production of David Rabe's ***The Basic Training of Pavlo Hummel*** with Al Pacino and Jack Kehoe, directed by David Wheeler at the Longacre Theater, 1977, photograph. AP/Wide World Photos. Reproduced by permission.—From a theatre production of David Rabe's ***The Basic Training of Pavlo Hummel*** with Al Pacino, Tisa Chang, and Anne Miyamoto, directed by David Wheeler at the Longacre Theater, 1977, photograph. AP/Wide World Photos. Reproduced by permission.—From a theatre production of Edward Albee's ***Who's Afraid of Virginia Woolf*** with Diana Rigg and David Suchet at the Almeida Theatre, Islington, London, September, 1996, photograph by Robbie Jack. Robbie Jack/Corbis. Reproduced by permission.—From a theatre production of Edward Bond's ***Lear*** with Bob Peck as Lear, RSC, 1982, photograph. Donald Cooper, London. Reproduced by permission.—From a theatre production of George Bernard Shaw's ***Major Barbara.*** Directed by Michael Engler at the American Repertory Theatre and Institute for Advanced Theatre Training, January, 1990, photograph by Richard Feldman. AMERICAN REPERTORY THEATRE. Reproduced by permission of the photographer.—From a theatre production of Harold Pinter's ***The Homecoming*** with John Savident as Max, Terence Rigby as Joey, Jane Lowe as Ruth, and Harold Pinter as Lennie, Palace Theatre, Watford, 1969, photograph. Donald Cooper, London. Reproduced by permission.—From a theatre production of Noel Coward's ***Private Lives*** with Coward as Elyot, Gertrude Lawrence as Amanda, Adrienne Allen as Sibyl, and Laurence Olivier as Victor, September, 1940, photograph. Hulton-Deutsch Collection/Corbis. Reproduced by permission.—From a theatre production of Sam Shepard's ***True West*** directed by David Wheeler at the American Repertory Theatre and Institute for Advanced Theatre Training, April, 1992, photograph by Richard Feldman. AMERICAN REPERTORY THEATRE. Reproduced by permission of the photographer.—From a theatrical production of Lillian Hellman's ***The Children's Hour*** with Patricia Neal, Iris Mann, and Kim Hunter, photograph. Springer/Corbis-Bettmann. Reproduced by permission.—From a theatrical production of Lillian Hellman's ***The Children's Hour*** with Patricia Neal and Kim Hunter, photograph. Springer/Corbis-Bettmann. Reproduced by permission.—From a theatrical production of William Inge's ***Come Back, Little Sheba*** with Shirley Booth and Sidney Blackmer, photograph. Springer/Corbis-Bettmann. Reproduced by permission.—From a theatrical production of William Inge's ***Come Back, Little Sheba*** with Joan Lorring, Shirley Booth, and Sidney Blackmer, photograph. Springer/Corbis-Bettmann. Reproduced by permission.—Fugard, Athol, photograph. AP/Wide World Photos. Reproduced by permission.—Hellman, Lillian, photograph. AP/Wide World Photos. Reproduced by permission.—Inge, William R., photograph. The Library of Congress.—Mamet, David, photograph by Brigitte Lacombe. Grove/ Atlantic, Inc. Reproduced by permission.—Miller, Arthur, photograph. AP/Wide World Photos. Reproduced by permission.—Odets, Clifford, photograph. AP/Wide World Photos. Reproduced by permission.—Original painting of ***The Dead Marat,*** by Jacques-Louis David, 1793, photograph. Corbis-Bettmann. Reproduced by permission.—Orton, Joe, photograph. Archive Photos, Inc. Reproduced by permission.—Pinter, Harold, photograph. AP/Wide World Photos. Reproduced by permission.—Pollock, Sharon, photograph. © Sharon Pollock. Reproduced by permission of the author.—Rabe, David, photograph. AP/Wide World Photos. Reproduced by permission.—Shaw, George Bernard, photograph. AP/Wide World Photos. Reproduced by permission.—Shepard, Sam, photograph. © Archive Photos, Inc. Reproduced by permission.—The Actors' Workshop of Houston presents ***A Different Kind of Cat*** based on Tennessee Williams's ***Cat on A Hot Tin Roof.*** Directed by Manning Mpinduzi-Mott, November 8 to December 7, 1996, photograph. The Actors' Workshop of Houston. Reproduced by permission.—Weiss, Peter, photograph. AP/Wide World Photos. Reproduced by permission.—Williams, Tennessee, photograph by Alex Gotfryd. Reproduced by permission of the Estate for Alexander Gotfryd.—Wilson, August, photograph. AP/Wide World Photos. Reproduced by permission.

Contributors

Terry Browne: Professor in the School of Performing Arts, State University of New York, Geneseo. Entry on *The Homecoming.*

Christopher Busiel: Doctoral candidate, University of Texas, Austin. Entries on *The Basic Training of Pavlo Hummel* and *Who's Afraid of Virginia Woolf?*

Clare Cross: Doctoral candidate, University of Michigan, Ann Arbor. Entries on *Lear* and *Major Barbara.*

Tom Faulkner: Freelance writer, Royal Oak, MI. Entries on *Private Lives* and *Waiting for Lefty.*

John Fiero: Professor of Drama and Playwriting, University of Southwestern Louisiana. Entry on *The Children's Hour.*

Carole Hamilton: Freelance writer and instructor at Cary Academy, Cary, North Carolina. Entries on *Cat on a Hot Tin Roof* and *Dutchman.*

Sheri Metzger: Freelance writer, Albuquerque, NM. Entries on *Come Back, Little Sheba* and *Fences.*

Daniel Moran: Educator and author, Monmouth Junction, NJ. Entry on *American Buffalo.*

Terry Nienhuis: Associate Professor of English, Western Carolina University. Entries on *Entertaining Mr. Sloane* and *True West.*

William P. Wiles: Freelance writer, Rutland, VT. Entry on *Master Harold . . . and the Boys.*

Joanne Woolway: Author and educator affiliated with Oriel College, Oxford, England. Entry on *The Crucible.*

Etta Worthington: Freelance writer, Oak Park, IL. Entries on *Blood Relations* and *Marat/Sade.*

American Buffalo

DAVID MAMET

1975

Thorstein Veblen wrote that business wisdom, when reduced to its basest form, frequently resorts to "the judicious use of sabotage"—an idea that David Mamet explores in his *American Buffalo.* First performed in Chicago in 1975, the play made its way to Broadway in 1977. Although Mamet had already achieved some success with his *Sexual Perversity in Chicago* (1972) the response to *American Buffalo* was highly favorable, despite the occasional harsh review. Many critics applauded Mamet's ability to capture the cadences and ambiguities in everyday American speech: *Newsweek's* Jack Kroll, for example, remarked that "Mamet is someone to listen to. He's that rare bird, an American playwright who's a language playwright." Edwin Wilson, writing in the *Wall Street Journal,* stated that Mamet "has a keen ear for the idiosyncrasies and the humor of everyday speech." While some critics dismissed *American Buffalo* (like the *New York Daily News*'s Douglas Watt) as "a poor excuse for a play" and (like the *Christian Science Monitor*'s John Beaufort) "too superficial to waste time upon," most were enthusiastic about Mamet's look at the ways in which three petty crooks plan to steal a coin collection in the name of "good business."

Mamet's plays (and this one is no exception) are radically different from ones written in previous theatrical eras and periods. Characters rarely speak in full sentences and their language (depending on the topic at hand) is often a mix of half-thoughts and obscenities, making the plays—at times—difficult

to read. When performed, however, these seemingly inarticulate utterances yield a rhythm found in few other playwrights' work. ''Part of the fascination of the play,'' wrote *Women's Wear Daily*'s Howard Kissel, lies in ''noting how the same banal language takes on different colors as we perceive the changing relationships'' between the characters.

The conflict explored by Mamet here is the clash between business and friendship—between a man's ethics and desire to succeed in a world where so much of the population has subscribed to a shared myth of capitalism. As one character tells his younger friend, ''there's business and there's friendship''—two worlds which will be combined and then torn apart by the time the play is finished.

AUTHOR BIOGRAPHY

When asked by interviewer John Lahr to describe his youth in the *New Yorker,* Mamet remarked, ''My childhood, like many people's, was not a bundle of laughs. So what? I always skip that part of the biography.'' A quick review of his background, however, suggests the means by which Mamet has been able to so accurately depict the anger and idiom of American men. Born in Chicago, Illinois, on November 30, 1947, he was raised in a Jewish neighborhood on the city's South Side. His father, Bernard Mamet, was a labor attorney and (as Mamet has described him) an ''amateur semanticist.'' His mother, Lenore Silver, was a teacher. They divorced in 1958 and Mamet moved in with his mother and her new husband—whose violent temper is described in Mamet's essay, ''The Rake.'' At the age of fifteen, Mamet returned to live with his father and worked as a busboy at the Second City, Chicago's famous improvisational theater. Resisting his father's suggestion that he become an attorney, Mamet left Chicago to study theater and English at Goddard College in Vermont, where he received his bachelor of arts degree in 1969 (he also studied at the Neighborhood Playhouse School of the Theater from 1968-69).

After a teaching stint at his alma mater, Mamet returned to Chicago, where he worked at a number of different jobs (cab driver, cook, waiter) while trying to begin a career in the theater. After realizing that he was (as he described himself) a ''terrible'' actor, Mamet focused his artistic energies on playwriting and directing. His first success was *Sexual Perversity in Chicago* (1972) which was awarded the Joseph Jefferson Award for best new Chicago play of 1975; it was later produced off-Broadway in 1976. *American Buffalo* (1975) won the Drama Critics' Circle Award for best American play and prompted Clive Barnes, of the *New York Times,* to proclaim of Mamet, ''The man can write.''

Since then, Mamet has become a favorite with critics and audiences. He was awarded the Pulitzer Prize in 1984 for *Glengarry Glen Ross,* a searing and satiric look at real estate salesmen based, in part, on his own experience working as a telemarketer peddling worthless land. *Speed-the-Plow* (1988) caused a stir in the New York theater scene when the pop star Madonna was cast as its female lead, but the play was another success and was nominated (like *Glengarry Glen Ross*) for an Antionette (''Tony'') Perry Award. Greater controversy was caused by *Oleanna* (1992), Mamet's look at sexual harassment: the play culminates in a male professor assaulting a female student who has destroyed his career with sexual allegations. Other works include *The Cryptogram* (1994) and *The Old Neighborhood* (1997).

Despite his extensive success with drama, Mamet's talents are not limited to the theater. His screenplays for *The Postman Always Rings Twice* (1981), *The Verdict* (1982), *The Untouchables* (1987), *Hoffa* (1992), *The Edge* (1997), and *Wag the Dog* (1998; written with Hilary Henkin) have made him an in-demand presence in the world of major motion pictures. He has also written and directed four films: *House of Games* (1987), *Things Change* (1988), *Homicide* (1991), and the adaptation of his play *Oleanna* (1994). In addition, he has written collections of essays, a book on directing film, a book on acting, and two novels. Although playwriting is his foremost vocation, Mamet has proven himself to be a versatile and unpredictable force in the American literary scene.

PLOT SUMMARY

Act I

American Buffalo takes place in ''Don's Resale Shop,'' a secondhand junk store run by Don Dubrow,

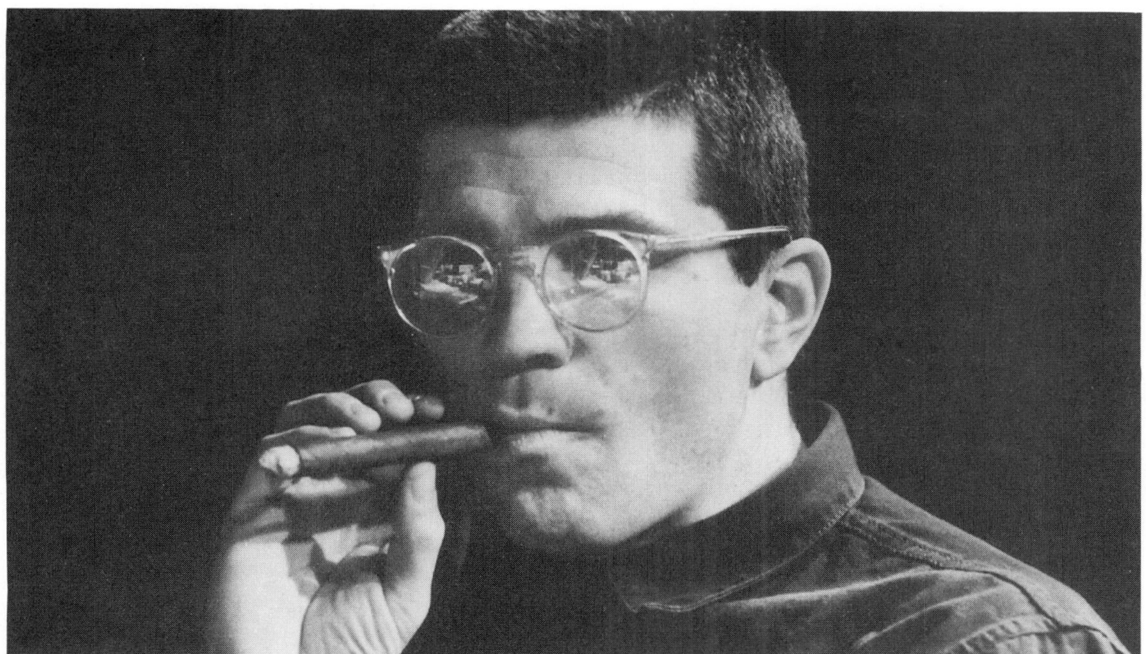

David Mamet

the play's protagonist. When the play opens, Don is instructing Bob, his young protege, in the art of "good business." Don offers pointers and advice which Bob accepts and echoes. The two discuss last night's poker game, held in the shop, and the virtues of Fletcher, a character who is never seen but who embodies all of the values that Don is trying to impart to Bob. Don offers other fatherly advice, such as, "*Never* skip breakfast," and, "it wouldn't kill you to take a vitamin." Their relationship, like that of a father and son, is thus established.

Their moment of quiet bonding is cut short when Teach, a friend of Don's, enters the shop and delivers an impassioned harangue about another friend of theirs, Ruthie, who begrudged him a slice of toast at the neighborhood diner that morning. Bob leaves to fetch the two men coffee from the same diner. Like Don, Teach offers his own personal wisdom on the topic of business and the need to keep it separate from friendship. (The "business" discussed in the play is always gambling or robbery.) When Bob returns, he speaks to Don about "the guy" he has been watching and informs him that he saw him put a suitcase in his car. Although Bob has forgotten to bring back Don's coffee, Don is delighted with Bob's information and sends him back to the diner to fetch the missing beverage.

Teach is suspicious about Don and Bob's conversation, and badgers Don into telling him about its subject. Don agrees and explains that a week ago, "the guy" came into the shop and offered him ninety dollars for a buffalo-head nickel that Don had mixed up in random pieces of junk. Deducing that the nickel must be worth much more (since "the guy" made a point of haggling him for the price), Don has decided to steal it back from him—along with any other coins he may have. He has enlisted Bob as his assistant and Bob has been watching "the guy's" house, which is around the corner from the shop. Later that night, Bob will steal the guy's coin collection.

Teach, however, decides that *he* should "go in" instead of Bob, who he calls a "great kid" but also an amateur who will not be able to complete a job as potentially complicated as this. Teach also refers to a past job where Bob, strung out on drugs, used a crowbar to break into a house. Although the details of this past caper are never revealed, the mention of it enrages Don, who tells Teach, "I don't want you mentioning that." Don feels that Bob is "trying hard" and that Teach should "leave him alone." Teach, however, is undaunted and tells Don that "simply as a business proposition" Don "cannot afford to take the chance" of using Bob for the job.

Don starts to waver on his previous stand and Bob returns from the diner. Don tells Bob to "forget about" the "thing." Bob tells Don he needs fifty dollars, which Don gives him. Although this is not spoken of openly until the end of the play, Bob is asking Don for money to support a drug habit. Bob exits, leaving Don and Teach to plan the robbery, which they do by looking in a guide to coins. ("You got to have a feeling for your subject," Teach explains.) While discussing how Teach will enter the house, Don becomes nervous about his partner's lack of preparation and decides to call Fletcher and have him work with them. Teach adamantly refuses, but Don insists that he "wants some depth." Teach reluctantly agrees and leaves the shop to go take a nap. He will return at 11:00 in order to carry out their criminal plans.

Act II

It is 11:15 that evening and Teach has not yet arrived. Don is also unable to reach Fletcher, whose phone line only offers him a busy signal each time it is called. Bob arrives (to the surprise of Don), asks him for more money and then offers him the sale of a buffalo-head nickel that he "got downtown." His actions here are clearly suspicious, but Don still feels guilty about shutting Bob out from the robbery; he therefore agrees to buy it on the condition that they look up its value in the coin-collector's guide. Bob, however, will not relinquish the coin and it is at this point that Teach enters, incensed at Bob's presence. Don scolds him for his tardiness, and Teach convinces Don to give Bob enough money to leave, which he does. Teach wonders about Fletcher's whereabouts, but Don tells him that Fletcher will arrive because "he said he'd be here."

In order to begin some "planning" and "preparation," Teach attempts to call "the guy" to make sure he is not home, but his nerves and incompetence cause him to keep dialing wrong numbers. Because Fletcher has still not arrived, Teach argues that they should complete the job themselves. Don, always loyal to his friends, wants to wait, but Teach convinces him that Fletcher cannot be trusted by telling a spurious story about Fletcher cheating during the previous night's poker game. Teach then takes a gun out of his pocket and the two argue over its necessity: Don feels that it is an unnecessary risk but Teach insists that it is a needed precaution.

As the tension between them rises, Bob returns; despite Teach's wishes, Don lets him in the shop. Bob tells them that Fletcher was mugged and is in the hospital with a broken jaw. Teach does not believe him and suggests to Don that Bob is in league with Ruthie or even Fletcher himself. Teach insists that Bob has gone behind their backs and performed the job with the others. Wanting to be sure he knows all the facts before making any accusations, Don asks Bob to name the hospital into which Fletcher has been admitted. Bob answers, "Masonic . . . I think" and Don calls there to check his story. Bob is nervous and becomes more frightened when he is asked about the buffalo-head nickel; he offers vague explanations for his having it. When Don's call reaches Masonic hospital and he is told that Fletcher was never admitted, he and Teach interrogate Bob, who insists on the validity of his story and that he just said "Masonic" because he "thought of it." Teach gives Bob one last chance to be honest and demands that he tell them "what is going *on,* what is set *up,* . . . and everything you know." When Bob proclaims his ignorance, Teach grabs a nearby object and hits him with it on the side of the head. Don looks away and tells Bob, "You brought it on yourself."

However, Ruthie then calls the shop and tells Don that Fletcher was, in fact, mugged and that he has been admitted to Columbus Hospital—not Masonic. As before, Don verifies this information with a phone call and the story is confirmed. Teach still grills Bob (whose mind becomes more foggy from the assault) about the nickel and gets a new story, specifically, that Bob bought it "in a coin store." Don, however, is finished with the job and tells Teach to leave the shop. Teach retorts with, "You seek your friends with junkies. You're a joke on the street, you and him," causing Don to physically attack him.

During the fracas, Bob gets Don's attention with a simple statement: "I missed him." When asked to explain, the two men learn that Bob had never spotted "the guy" that morning and that his entire report about him "leaving with a suitcase" was a lie. They also learn that Bob *did* buy the nickel in a coin store "for Donny." This infuriates Teach, who begins smashing the display cases in the shop while proclaiming, "There Is No Law. There Is No Right And Wrong. The World Is Lies. There Is No Friendship." Finally, he sits down and the three are still. Don sends Teach out to get his car so they can take Bob to the hospital. Bob looks at Don and apologizes for all the trouble he thinks he has caused, but Don tries to comfort him with, "You did real good. . . . That's all right."

Teach (Dustin Hoffman) and Don (Dennis Franz) confront Bob (Sean Nelson) about his buffalo nickel in a scene from the 1996 film adaptation, which was scripted by Mamet

CHARACTERS

Bob

Bob is Don's "gopher" and serves him in the dual capacities of coffee-fetcher and surrogate son. While he does listen patiently to all of Don's lessons on how to "do business," the audience also learns that he frequently borrows money from him to support a drug habit. Slow-witted and dull, he is not as talkative nor excitable as Don or Teach, but he does remain faithful to Don, even after he is assaulted by Teach on the grounds that he has betrayed their robbery scheme to other thieves.

Walt Cole

See Teach

Don Dubrow

The owner of Don's Resale Shop, Don is a seller of junk who plans the robbery which drives the play's plot. He is the "business associate" of Teach and a father figure to Bob. Early in the play,

MEDIA ADAPTATIONS

- *American Buffalo* was adapted as a film in 1996, starring Dustin Hoffman as Teach, Dennis Franz as Don, and Sean Nelson as Bob. Mamet wrote the screenplay and Michael Corrente directed. It is available from Samuel Goldwyn Home Video.

he tries to instruct Bob on how to be a ''stand-up guy,'' a conversation that reveals many of his values and assumptions. Using the never-seen Fletcher as his example, he explains that, to succeed, a man needs ''Skill and talent and the balls to arrive at your own *conclusions.*'' According to Don, ''Action talks and bullshit walks.'' Like Willy Loman in Arthur Miller's *Death of a Salesman,* Don believes that he understands exactly what qualities are needed for success in the world of ''business:'' he tells Bob, ''It's going to happen to you, it's *not* going to happen to you, the important thing is can you deal with it and can you *learn* from it.'' Although he appears headstrong when talking to Bob, his own need for lessons in loyalty is exposed when he allows Teach to convince him to cut Bob from the plan.

Teach

As his nickname suggests, Teach is a man who sees himself as a guru-like figure, dispensing parcels of wisdom to Don and Bob. He constantly offers platitudes which seek to instruct the others in the ways that ''business'' is conducted: ''A guy can be too loyal,'' ''Don't confuse business with pleasure,'' ''It's kickass or kissass,'' and ''You got to have a feeling for your subject'' are a few of the many ''rules'' he recites during the play. Teach subscribes to the notion that free enterprise is ''The freedom of the *Individual* to Embark on Any Fucking Course that he sees fit'' in order to ''secure his honest chance to make a profit'' and that, without such a code, ''we're just savage shitheads in the wilderness.'' Like Don, Teach believes himself to be adept in the world of deal-making and business. Yet his circumstances reveal his skills to be unprofitable.

Underneath Teach's ''lessons'' runs a current of anger at those who have succeeded in the fields of which he sees himself as an expert. When Don tells him that Ruthie and Fletcher won at last night's poker game because they are good card players, Teach ascribes their victories to cheating rather than skill. His anger at the world—and at his own meager place in it—culminates in the end of the play, when he smashes the display cases in the junk shop, shouting a new set of ''rules:'' ''There Is No Law. There Is No Right And Wrong. The World Is Lies. There Is No Friendship.''

THEMES

Friendship

When *American Buffalo* opens, Don is lecturing Bob on the importance of committing himself to the ''business'' deal they have made; Bob is supposed to be watching the target of their robbery but has instead returned to the junk shop. Don tells him, ''Action counts. Action talks and bullshit walks.'' After Bob apologizes, Don protests, ''Don't tell me you're sorry. I'm not mad at you.'' What the audience learns from this remark is that Don is genuinely interested in helping Bob become more astute in the ways of their own brand of business. He tells him that he should model himself after Fletcher, a ''standup guy'' and card shark who had to ''learn'' all he knows about becoming a success. Don impresses upon Bob the importance of attitude and intelligence when confronting the business world: ''Everything, Bobby: it's going to happen to you, it's *not* going to happen to you, the important thing is can you deal with it, and can you *learn* from it.''

Don's father-figure interest in Bob is implied through the advice he offers him on a number of topics. When he sends Bob to the diner to get coffee, he insists that he buy something for himself, since ''Breakfast is the most important meal of the day''; later, he urges Bob to take vitamins. His most important lesson, however, is what he tells Bob about friendship: ''There's lotsa people on this street, Bob, they want this and they want that. Do anything to get it. You don't have *friends* this life. . . .'' The implied end of this sentence—''is worth nothing''—reveals the high value Don places on friendship and people protecting each other from what he calls the ''garbage'' of the world. As the

TOPICS FOR FURTHER STUDY

- Look at some current bestsellers that offer their readers techniques for success in the workplace: are any of the values or assumptions suggested by their authors like those held by the characters in *American Buffalo?*
- Compare and contrast the business ideals of *American Buffalo*'s characters with those found in Arthur Miller's *Death of a Salesman.* How do characters in Miller's play (such as Willy, Ben, and Howard) offer the viewer attitudes about business similar to or different from those seen in Don and Teach?
- Compare and contrast Mamet's depiction of "good business" in *American Buffalo* with that seen in his *Glengarry Glen Ross:* how do both plays (when read together) seem to create a world where the American capitalist mythology is exaggerated?
- Samuel Beckett's *Waiting for Godot* concerns a pair of tramps who wait for a man named Godot who never arrives. How is Beckett's Godot like Mamet's Fletcher? How are Don and Teach like Vladimir and Estragon, Beckett's devoted but anxious tramps?

play proceeds, Bob is revealed to be a drug addict, frequently asking Don for money to support his habit—which Don "lends" him, preferring not to press him for explanations. By the end of the play, however, Don forsakes his friendship with Bob in the name of business—an action which causes him a great deal of shame, since he knows he has failed to follow his own advice. The last scene of the play shows their relationship being rebuilt and Don trying to make amends for his doubting the strength of Bob's devotion.

Like Don, Teach seems to hold up friendship as an absolute good. He enters the play cursing Ruthie, a mutual friend, for making a joke when he took a piece of toast off her plate at the diner. Her remark of "Help yourself" causes Teach to rage at her for forgetting all the times he has picked up the check: he tells Don, "All I ever ask (and I would say this to her face) is only she remembers who is who and not to go around with *her* or Gracie either with this attitude. 'The Past is Past, and this is Now, and so Fuck You.'" Ruthie's remark has hurt Teach because she has not lived up to the code of friendship that he assumes he embodies.

However, when Teach sees the chance to make "real classical money" in Don's robbery scheme, he immediately tries to talk Don into dismissing Bob. Hiding his avarice under the guise of "good business," Teach convinces Don that Bob, although Don's friend, is not a good candidate for such an operation: "A guy can be too loyal, Don. Don't be dense on this. What are we saying here? Business." When Don does remove Bob from the plan and their plot begins to turn awry, Teach suggests that Bob has betrayed them—a false implication which, nonetheless, is believed by Don until the final scene of the play, when he realizes that it is he who has betrayed Bob in the name of "good business."

Success and Failure

Don and Teach are small-time gamblers and thieves who constantly spout aphorisms that they think attest to their "business" savvy: "Things are not always what they seem to be," "You got to keep clear who your friends are," "Don't confuse business with pleasure" and "You got to trust your instincts" are only a few of their many saws. Don lectures Bob on "good business" and Teach tells Don that he should exclude Bob from the robbery because "as a *business* proposition" he "cannot afford" to have someone with his lack of experience break into a house.

Anyone watching the play, however, can see that their theory does not convert into practice. The viewer learns that a poker game took place last night in the shop, where Don ''did allright'' (very likely a euphemism) and Teach ended the game ''Not too good.'' When the game is discussed, Teach attributes his loss not to his own lack of skill but to Ruthie's cheating: ''She is not a good cardplayer,'' Teach asserts, because her ''partner'' is always ''going to walk around,'' presumably to glance at everyone's cards. (Teach later claims that Fletcher, last night's winner, cheats as well.) When Teach uses a collector's guide to quiz Don on what coins they should steal from their future victim's collection, Don shows his ignorance in this field by guessing that a certain coin is worth $18.60 instead of its actual worth of twenty cents. Later, when Teach tries to call the collector's house to be sure he is not home, he keeps transposing parts of the phone number, resulting in confusion and frustration instead of the ''planning'' and ''preparation'' he desires. Both Don and Teach have fully subscribed to the myths of ''business'' and how it should be practiced, but both are failures, since all of their knowledge resides in their adages instead of experience.

Deception

American Buffalo's plot is one that relies on implication and innuendo rather than concrete events. When the robbery is being arranged, Don and Teach have agreed to meet Fletcher at the junk shop at 11:00 that night. Bob has been told that he will not be involved and the two would-be criminals are satisfied that their planning will result in a successful ''shot.''

However, when Teach enters the shop after 11:15 and finds Bob there, the viewer (like the characters) becomes suspicious. Bob is trying to sell Don a buffalo-head nickel, much like the one they had originally planned to rob before Teach entered the play. Don is furious with Teach's tardiness, and Teach is equally furious at Bob's presence in the shop. Their tension grows when Fletcher does not arrive and cannot be reached by phone; Teach then begins insinuating that Bob, Fletcher, and Ruthie have stolen the coins themselves and that Bob has offered to sell the buffalo to Don because he needs some fast money. When Bob tells them that Fletcher was mugged and has been admitted to the hospital with a broken jaw, Don calls the hospital to check his story—and is told that Fletcher was never admitted. Convinced they are being hustled, Teach strikes Bob on the head. Don, Bob's former protector, mutters, ''We didn't want to do this to you.'' The viewer is now completely convinced that Bob has betrayed the two men.

This deception lies not between Bob and the two men, however, but between Mamet and the audience. The playwright leads the viewer to believe that Bob has betrayed Don and Teach and lied about Fletcher's absence. This is not the case: Ruthie calls Don and tells him the name of a different hospital to which Fletcher was admitted and the viewer learns that Bob did not steal the nickel from the intended victim's home. Because of their lust for ''business'' and assumption that everyone else holds these same cynical values, Don and Teach are eventually deceived by their own attitudes. Teach thus ends the play a speechless fool, and Don must then try to heal his friendship with Bob.

STYLE

Setting

American Buffalo takes place in Don's Resale Shop, a secondhand ''antique'' store (really a junk store) run by Don Dubrow. Although Mamet's script never describes the set in any detail, the play's scenic designers have always made a point of filling the stage with as much junk as possible: Clive Barnes (writing for the *New York Times*) called the Broadway set ''astonishing'' and described it as ''an agglomeration of trash that must have taken a team of assistants months to acquire.'' This same praise was even offered by critics who found fault with the play itself. For example, writing for the *Wall Street Journal,* Edwin Wilson found the play ''not heavy enough'' but the set to be a ''triumph of clutter.'' The set, therefore, serves as a way for a viewer to instantly create some assumptions about the characters, specifically, that they are lower class, small-time ''businessmen'' who spend their days surrounded by the debris of other people's success. As Frank Rich of the *New York Times* stated, the junk shop is a ''cage emblematic of the men's tragic sociological imprisonment.''

However, the setting does more than allow Mamet's trio a space in which to scheme their robbery; it allows the playwright to highlight the notion that the characters are living in a world of metaphorical ''junk.'' Throughout the play, Don and Teach give and receive lessons on such topics as honor, capitalism, and friendship—topics which are abandoned and left for ''junk'' when their robbery plan becomes threatened or when they fear they might miss their chance to make some easy money. Although they profess to have solid codes of ''business'' ethics, their desire to succeed pushes them into a world of moral ''junk.''

Symbolism

The item discussed throughout the play is a buffalo-head nickel that Don sells to a customer for ninety dollars. Deciding that the coin must be worth ''five times that'' because of the way the customer behaved when buying it, Don plans to rob the coin back from the customer (along with the rest of his coin collection) and sell it to another buyer for more money. Although Don and Teach's robbery is never executed, the coin remains an almost constant topic of conversation between them. Both view the nickel as a representation of the wealth for which they strive and both are certain that stealing the nickel (and the rest of the guy's coin collection) will bring them (as Don states), ''real classical money.''

Despite the glory they invest in it, however, the coin eventually comes to symbolize the degree to which the two men sacrifice the values in which they seem to so strongly believe at the start of the play. Like the real American buffalo, their friendship, ethics, and trust in each other vanishes—and, again like the real American buffalo, these things vanish due to an increasing fervor for riches and power. The beauty of the buffalo herd and the bonds of friendship are alike in their falling prey to capitalism and Teach's definition of ''free enterprise:'' ''The freedom . . . of the *Individual.* . . . To Embark on Any Fucking Course that he sees fit. . . . In order to secure his honest chance to make a profit.'' As he tries to explain this to Don, Teach echoes one of Mamet's authorial concerns: ''The country's *founded* on this.''

Dialogue

While all playwrights employ dialogue as their primary artistic tool, Mamet is exceptional in that his dialogue often hides—or reveals—a character's true thoughts or attitudes toward the subject at hand. The dialogue in *American Buffalo* is representative of Mamet's work in that it is highly fragmentary, filled with asides and pauses, and captures the rhythms and nuances found in everyday speech. Comparing the play's dialogue to elevator music, *Newsweek*'s Jack Kroll noted Mamet's ability to capture ''the dissonant din of people yammering at each other and not connecting.'' While the characters do talk to each other, they are just as often talking *at* each other as well, trying to bluff and sound their partners by using seemingly innocuous phrases. For example, when Teach fears that Don and Bob are concocting a robbery scheme without him, he tries to ''nonchalantly'' learn about it through a ''simple'' conversation in which Don does everything to avoid revealing his scheme.

In this conversation, Teach uses words in the same way a person uses a metal-detector on a beach: as the prospector searches for valuable metals, Teach probes his friend's mind to learn whether or not he has been cheated out of his ''shot.'' Both Teach and a prospector hope to find something valuable: a nugget of gold or the plan Don has hatched with ''the kid.'' Don tries to steer him away from the topic by asking him if he has enough money in his meter and being purposefully vague; Mamet's placement of pauses pinpoint when a character is formulating his next attempt to seek out or conceal information. A reader should also note that the lines in parentheses are meant to mark (according to Mamet), ''a slight change of the outlook on the part of the speaker—perhaps a momentary change to a more introspective regard.'' While other playwrights offer actors and readers numerous parenthetical adverbs before lines to suggest how they should be said, Mamet asks the actors and readers to consider each speaker's ''conversational goal'' and how—using only the most common words—he will try to achieve it. Once this is understood, the inflection and tone of each line should become more clear.

HISTORICAL CONTEXT

Although written in 1975, *American Buffalo* premiered on Broadway in 1977, in the midst of a theater season notable for its collection of odd—and, at times, disturbing—array of new characters. The winner of that year's Pulitzer Prize, Michael Cristofer's *The Shadow Box,* concerns the ends of three characters' lives as they wait for the deaths that their respective terminal illnesses will bring. Albert Innaurato's *The Transfiguration of Benno Blimpie* examines a frightening mother-son relationship, where the child is filled with food by his mother to compensate for her never having loved him. *The Last Meeting of the Knights of the White Magnolia,* by Preston Jones, looks at old-school southern racism as seen through a bigoted fraternal order. John Bishop's *The Trip Back Down* follows the slow decline of a racecar driver who attempts to find victory one last time. *Ashes* by David Rudkin, is a theatrical yet clinical report of a miscarriage. While the season did have its all-out comedies (such as Neil Simon's *California Suite,* the musical *Annie,* and a remake of *Volpone* titled *Sly Fox*), the New York scene offered audiences a great amount of dark drama.

The 1976-77 season also saw new plays by artists with solid theatrical reputations. Tennessee Williams's *Vieux Carre,* may have been reminiscent of his earlier work in its evocation of a seedy New Orleans populated with troubled souls, but the show closed after only seven performances. Harold Pinter (a playwright whom Mamet has praised throughout his career) offered puzzled theatergoers *No Man's Land,* a play keeping in-tune with other Pinter pieces and their blend of reality and absurdity.

Despite the intensity of the season, however, few audiences and critics were prepared for the brutality and verbal violence of *American Buffalo.* While other plays offered studies of bisexuality (Albert Innaurato's *Gemini*), insanity (Pavel Kohout's *Poor Murderer*) and wife-swapping (Michael Stewart and Cy Coleman's *I Love My Wife*), Mamet's play proved to be the most shocking, primarily due to its unadulterated use of obscenity. Writing in *The Best Plays of 1976-1977,* Otis L. Guernsey Jr. stated that Mamet ''has mastered a verbal instrument of high quality,'' but Guernsey also felt that the playwright uses this instrument ''to shock and alienate his audience with some of the foulest language ever heard on a stage.'' Thus, despite the fact that its plot is a relatively common one found in many genres, *American Buffalo* gained a certain notoriety for its use of honest street-talk; while this may not have been surprising in the cinema (*Dog Day Afternoon, One Flew Over the Cuckoo's Nest,* and *The Exorcist* were all recent blockbusters that made great use of visual and verbal obscenity), many people still felt that the content of drama would remain more ''refined.'' Since then, the theater world has largely accepted playwrights' use of ''foul language,'' but in 1977 the shock was felt among audiences and critics.

CRITICAL OVERVIEW

While Mamet's current reputation as an important American playwright is established and secure, *American Buffalo* was the first of his plays to receive intense critical attention. The play premiered on Broadway in February of 1977 (following its successful 1975 debut in Chicago) to reviews ranging as wide as the characters' emotional highs and lows in the play itself. Clive Barnes, writing for the *New York Times,* stated that although this play marked Mamet's first trip to Broadway, ''It will hardly be his last,'' for ''This man can write.'' Like Barnes, other admirers of the play called attention to Mamet's ability to recreate the rhythms of everyday speech heard in the conversations of his lowbrow characters. Likening the play to a ''jam session for jazz musicians,'' *Women's Wear Daily*'s Howard Kissel wrote that the ''fascination'' of the play lies in ''noting how the same banal language takes on different colors as we perceive the changing relationships'' of the characters. Similarly, Edwin Wilson (writing in the *Wall Street Journal,*) stated that ''the language, though limited, is extremely accurate'' and that Mamet ''has a keen ear for the idiosyncrasies and humor of everyday speech.'' Perhaps the greatest praise came from *Newsweek*'s Kroll, who likened Mamet to British playwright Harold Pinter (*The Homecoming*) but with his artistic ear ''tuned to an American frequency.''

Several reviewers, however, were shocked by Mamet's use of obscenity. For example, *Time*'s Christopher Porterfield described Mamet's dialogue as ''forlornly eloquent'' and praised his ''infallible ear for the cadences of loneliness and fear,'' but the critic also remarked that Mamet ''revels a bit too much in this scatology and blasphemy.'' He further suggested that if Mamet were to ''Delete the most common four-letter Anglo-Saxonism from the script . . . his drama might last only one hour instead of two.'' John Beaufort, writing in the *Christian Science Monitor,* called the play ''excessively foul-mouthed'' and remarked that its content (like its language) smacked of ''gratuitous sensationalism.'' (These charges against Mamet's dialogue were renewed when his *Glengarry Glen Ross* premiered in 1983.)

Like their opinions of Mamet's idiom, critics were also divided in their perception of *American Buffalo*'s themes and reflection of contemporary American life. For example, Irving Wardle, writing in the London *Times,* stated that a viewer ''would have to be tone deaf to miss the music, irony and virtuosity'' of Mamet's dialogue—but followed this compliment by describing the play as a ''suffocating tedium'' where the characters are ''at a standstill.'' The National Broadcasting Company's (NBC) Leonard Probst complained that ''the center of the play is missing''; The *Daily News* stated that Mamet ''promises much more than [he] delivers'' and labeled his work ''a poor excuse for a play.'' The *Wall Street Journal*'s Wilson wrote that Mamet's characters exist in a vacuum and that they ''are too rooted in their own junk, in their own pathetic schemes, in their own fake philosophy to speak for others.''

But these critics were not the only voices responding to Mamet's study in anger and shady business—several others praised Mamet for creating an almost allegorical tale of capitalism's dark side. Michael Billington, writing in the British *Guardian,* called *American Buffalo* a ''deeply political play'' and one that ''makes its points about society through the way people actually behave.'' Directly contradicting Wilson's remarks, Victoria Radin (of the *Observer,*) praised Mamet's ability to show the characters ''without patronage and with respect and even love for these little people'' who ''resemble the little person in all of us.''

American Buffalo's reputation has grown since its first performances. Now regarded as one of Mamet's most representative works, the play is still studied and discussed by scholars of modern American drama. In the *Dictionary of Literary Biography,* Patricia Lewis and Terry Browne suggested that the play epitomizes Mamet's style, since it ''does not rely on external plot or movement'' and offers a ''subtle development of character created out of inner movement and conflict.'' In his essay, ''David Mamet: The Plays, 1972-1980,'' Stephen H. Gale remarked that although the play is ''not sufficiently developed or epic enough to be as convincing as it might be,'' it is an important example of Mamet's career-long study of relationships. Perry Luckett, in *Magill's Critical Survey of Drama,* called *American Buffalo* an ''excellent example'' of Mamet's ''facility for urban speech'' and ability to detail ''the subtle manifestations of competition, trade, and the drive to acquire that he believes have nearly overwhelmed America.''

While critics have disagreed about *American Buffalo*'s relevance and weight, most concur with Kissel, who could be describing many Mamet plays when he writes, ''Generally in the theater the relationship between language and action is oversimplified—here the distance between the two is stimulating.''

CRITICISM

Daniel Moran

Moran is an educator specializing in literature and drama. In this essay, he examines the ways in which Mamet's play explores the characters' beliefs in ''The God of Business.''

William Butler Yeats's ''The Circus Animals' Desertion'' ends with the speaker stating that, since he cannot find a theme for his art, he must delve more deeply into his own experience to seek one: ''Now that my ladder's gone,/I must lie down where all the ladders start,/In the foul rag-and-bone shop of the heart.'' Like the speaker of Yeats's poem, the characters in David Mamet's *American Buffalo* are searching for satisfaction which they are sure will bring meaning to their lives in the form of financial success. And, again like the speaker of ''The Circus Animals' Desertion,'' the three men all lose hope that they will ever find it: their ''ladders'' of friendship and their shared myth of capitalism are systematically stripped away, until they are left pitiful, dejected, and lying like dogs in the ''foul rag-and-bone shop'' of their hearts.

To hint at the values and assumptions of the three men inhabiting the ''foul rag-and-bone shop'' of Don Dubrow's Resale Shop, Mamet's play contains an epigraph: ''Mine eyes have seen the glory of the coming of the Lord./He is peeling down the alley in a black and yellow Ford.'' These lines (attributed by Mamet to a ''folk tune'') equate God with the automobile—one of the foremost symbols of American capitalism and consumerism. Although the characters do not dress in expensive suits or carry briefcases, Mamet uses them to illustrate the ways in which members of the proletariat (lower class) have fully ingested and accepted the myths of American capitalism; as the play progresses, the characters are seen (in various ways) bowing down to the ''God of Business.'' This God, which dictates the way these petty thieves behave, allows them to excuse any betrayals or underhandedness in His name.

By the end of the play, however, the God becomes an angry one, as vengeful as any imagined by Jonathan Edwards (an eighteenth century theologian who spoke frequently of God's wrath toward sinners), and extracts a terrible payment. ''Business'' is an easy label to use in sugar-coating all kinds of deception, but if the God is invoked too often, He will demand great sacrifices from His

WHAT DO I READ NEXT?

- *Glengarry Glen Ross,* Mamet's 1983 look at the workings of a real-estate office, is an intense and unnerving glimpse into the lives of seven salesmen and the methods they use to "close" their deals with unsuspecting buyers of worthless land. The play was awarded the Pulitzer Prize and cemented Mamet's critical and commercial reputation.
- *Writing in Restaurants* (1986) is one of Mamet's collections of essays. In it, he offers his own highly-charged opinions of the theater, Hollywood, and himself.
- Although written in 1596 (almost 400 years before *American Buffalo*), Shakespeare's *The Merchant of Venice* also examines the ways in which different people think of "business" as a way to excuse their own aggression.
- Arthur Miller's 1949 drama *Death of a Salesman* examines the almost-insignificant role that an average American plays in the world of "big business" and how his self-delusion and desire for success eventually leads to his suicide.
- *The Theory of the Leisure Class* (1899) is a study of American beliefs in the myths of business and status. Written by Mamet's intellectual hero, Thorstein Veblen, the book offers an expository look at the values held by the characters of *American Buffalo.*
- Joel and Ethan Coen's screenplay of *Miller's Crossing* (1991), like *American Buffalo,* examines the differences between business and friendship—and how a single person attempts to straddle both sets of ideals.

believers. As "Don's Resale Shop" is a euphemism for "Don's Junk Store," "Good Business" is a euphemism employed by the characters to, as Mamet has described in an essay for the London *Times,* "suspend an ethical sense and adopt in its stead a popular accepted mythology and use that to assuage [their] consciences like everyone else is doing." What the play specifically examines is the way that one man—Don—becomes an acolyte of the God of Business to the point where he almost loses the one thing that gives his life *human* (rather than financial) meaning: his relationship with Bob.

The opening scene of the play establishes Don and Bob's relationship, which initially mirrors that of a teacher and student. Scolding Bob for not watching the house of the man they intend to rob, Don tells him "You don't come in until you do a thing" and that "Action counts." Bob keeps offering excuses until Don states, "I'm not mad at you." While a viewer may find this surprising due to the tone of Don's reprimands, a further conversation reveals that Don is genuinely interested in Bob's future and ability to operate in their low-class world of business: he tells Bob, "If you want to do business," then excuses "are not good enough." Bob must have "skill and talent and the balls" to arrive at his "own conclusions," or he will never succeed. Don invokes the God of Business in the form of Fletcher, an offstage gambler and minor business deity who embodies all of the values Don wants to impart to Bob: "You take him and put him down in some strange town with just a nickel in his pocket, and by nightfall he'll have that town by the balls. This is not talk, Bob, this is action."

According to Don, Fletcher "was not born that way," but he had to "learn" how to be a success, and this idea—that open eyes and intelligence will lead to financial success—is the crux of Don's myth and lesson: "Everything, Bobby: it's going to happen to you, it's *not* going to happen to you, the important thing is can you deal with it, and can you *learn* from it." (While Clive Barnes wrote in the *New York Times* that their relationship "may be homosexual," this seems both unlikely and irrelevant to the issue of friendship sacrificed for business that Mamet explores.) Unlike one based on business, their relationship offers returns not financial but emotional: Don offers Bob the idea that he can be a success and Bob offers Don his devotion and discipleship. Together, they mimic a father-son relationship that each of them is lacking in his life outside the junk shop.

When Teach enters the shop, however, the mood of the play changes from one of quiet bonding to one of fury. His opening harangue about a begrudged piece of toast reflects *his* ideas about friendship and its attendant duties:

> So Grace and Ruthie's having breakfast, and they're done. *Plates* . . . *crusts* of stuff all over . . . *so* on. Down I sit. 'Hi, hi.' I take a piece of toast off Grace's plate . . . and she goes 'Help yourself.' Help myself. I should help myself to a piece of toast it's four slices for a quarter. I should have a nickel every time we're over at the game, I pop for coffee . . . cigarettes . . . a *sweet roll,* never say a word. . . . But to have that shithead turn, in one breath, every fucking sweet roll that I ever ate with them into *ground glass* (I'm wondering were they eating it and thinking 'This guy's an idiot to blow a fucking *quarter* on his friends) . . . this hurts me, Don. This hurts me in a way I don't know what the fuck to do.

As with Don and Bob, Teach sees friendship as a form of give-and-take between its participants but with an important difference: Teach bases it not on emotional grounds, but material ones. While arguing about a piece of toast may seem trivial, Teach's monologue illustrates the degree to which he believes that friendship is a means of sharing *things* rather than emotions—a characteristic that will resurface later, when he convinces Don to cut Bob from the robbery plan. Ironically, Teach complains that there ''is not one loyal bone in that bitch's body,'' but later convinces Don to be disloyal to Bob so that Teach can become part of the robbery plot.

Teach's name reflects his assumptions about himself and what he sees as his knowledge of human nature and business. Throughout the play, he offers dozens of aphorisms that he uses to boost his own self-image. When looking through the coin collector's guide, he tells Don that there is ''one thing'' that makes ''all the difference in the world. . . . Knowing what the fuck you're talking about. And it's so rare, Don. *So* rare.'' His lament for the stupidity of the world, of course, naturally excludes himself as a part of it. Unlike the lessons of Don, which are carried out in practice until Teach begins to (as Don calls it) ''poison'' his mind, Teach's lessons are hollow and reflect his understanding not of real business, but the *myth* of American capitalism. ''You got to have a feeling for your subject,'' ''It's kickass or kissass,'' and ''You want it run right, *be* there'' may be theoretically true but are never practiced by Teach, whose legitimate ''job'' (if he even has one) is never alluded to by any of the characters. And almost as if to answer the charge of, ''If you're so smart, why aren't you rich,'' Teach has a stockpile of excuses for his low-class status, including the assertion that his companions cheat while playing cards. One of his most ludicrous excuses is voiced when he hears Don tell him how much old antiques are worth: he mutters, ''If I kept the stuff I threw *out* . . . I would be a wealthy man today. I would be cruising on some European yacht.'' Don simply replies with an ''Uh-huh,'' for he knows that despite all of the noise he makes, Teach is a junk shop Polonius (a wise counselor from William Shakespeare's *Hamlet,*) and an negative example of the ''action talks and bullshit walks'' philosophy.

While Teach's adages may be empty, he *is* flamboyant and convincing, and it is his skill as an orator that begins to corrupt Don, leading him to accept Teach's dictums. Although Don claims to know the difference between ''talk'' and ''action,'' he, too, has enough greed within him to begin believing Teach's ideas; the card game that took place the night before in the junk shop serves as the perfect metaphor for the way that Teach and Don begin to interact. Poker is a game combining business and friendship: one plays with his comrades but the ultimate goal is to win their money. The rewards are not emotional, but financial, and these are won by the means of being *un*friendly: bluffing, being secretive, and even cheating. Although Teach is a friend of Don's and obviously has some sort of shared past with him, he employs cardplaying skills—rather than sincerity—to edge his way into Don's plan and ultimately make him forsake Bob. Like Shakespeare's King Duncan (in *Macbeth*) who states, ''There's no art/To find the mind's construction in the face'' only to later be assassinated by the traitorous Macbeth, Don is adept at offering advice but less able to apply it to his own practices. This is especially true given that Don sees Bob—not himself—as the one in need of guidance.

Don is also not as distant from Teach as he might think. When telling the story of ''the guy'' who entered the shop and bought the nickel for ninety dollars, he brags of his business acumen, saying, ''he tells me he'll go fifty dollars for the nickel. . . . So I tell him (get this), 'Not a chance.''' He then tells Teach that the buyer's behavior suggested ''it's worth five *times* that'' and then begins

> "THE CHARACTERS IN DAVID MAMET'S *AMERICAN BUFFALO* ARE SEARCHING FOR SATISFACTION WHICH THEY ARE SURE WILL BRING MEANING TO THEIR LIVES IN THE FORM OF FINANCIAL SUCCESS."

to focus more on the buyer's personality rather than his wallet: "The next day back he comes and he goes through the whole bit again. He looks at *this,* he looks at *that.* . . . And he tells me he's the guy was in here yesterday and bought the buffalo off me and do I have some other articles of interest. . . . And so I tell him, 'Not offhand. . . .' He leaves his card, I'm s'posed to call him anything crops up. . . . He comes in here like I'm his fucking doorman. . . . He takes me off my coin and will I call him if I find another one. . . . Doing me this favor by just coming in my shop." Don's depiction of the buyer as a pompous con-artist who "takes him off" allows him to justify—to himself and to Teach—that the buyer deserves to be robbed. Rather than accept his lack of business sense, Don (like Teach) blames another for his being taken as a rube. *Not* stealing back the coin would simply be bad business.

It is this fear of being untrue to the God of Business that causes Don to accept Teach's terms. Although he insists that Bob is a "good kid" and deserves a "shot" at the robbery, Don is swayed by the siren song of Teach's capitalistic rhetoric: "A guy can be too loyal," Teach tells him. "Don't be dense on this." Urging Don not to "confuse business with pleasure," Teach begins a rapid-fire assault on Don's desire to remain faithful to Bob and brings up an incident when Bob had obviously failed them: "We both know what we're saying here. We both know we're talking about some job needs more than the kid's gonna skin-pop go in there with a *crowbar* ." Still faithful to Bob, Don becomes enraged at Teach's insinuation of Bob's drug use and states, "I don't want you mentioning that. . . . You know how I feel on that." When Teach offers an apology, Don remarks, "I don't want that talk only, Teach. You understand?. . . That's the only thing." Although he is firm in his protection of his ward, Don is already beginning to see the upcoming job as one in which business, not friendship, will have to be considered.

Teach remains undaunted: "All I'm saying, the job is beyond him. Where's the shame in this? This is not jacks, we get to go home we give everything back. Huh?. . . You take care of him, *fine.* (Now this is loyalty.) But Bobby's got his own best interests, too. And you cannot afford (and simply as a *business* proposition) you cannot afford to take the chance." When Don asks for a moment to consider this new idea, Teach becomes angry and resorts to sarcasm: "You don't even know what the *thing* is on this. Where he lives. They got alarms?. . . And what if (God forbid) the *guy* walks in? Somebody's nervous, whacks him with a table lamp—you wanna get touchy—and you can take your ninety dollars from the nickel shove it up your ass—the good it did you—and you wanna know *why?*. . . Because you didn't take the time to go first-class." Anyone sharing Don's belief in the "black and yellow Ford" of the American Dream would naturally want to "go first-class," and therefore Don agrees to cut Bob from the deal. When he informs Bob of his decision, Don gives him fifty dollars, which the viewer and Teach assume is for drugs but which Don feels too shameful to confront, since he had previously insisted to Teach that "the fucking kid's clean. He's trying hard, he's working hard." Thus, in a moment of guilt, Don has effectively paid off his conscience in order to follow Teach's ideals of business.

Like so many fictional crime-capers, however, the plan falls apart once everything is set in place and it is through this turning awry of the scheme that Mamet intensifies the previous Act's examination of business and friendship. Act Two begins at 11:15 that evening and Don is anxious over the fact that both Teach and Fletcher are missing. When Bob arrives, however, with a buffalo-head nickel to sell to Don, he becomes momentarily suspicious: he asks Bob if he saw Fletcher or Teach at the diner and Bob responds, "No. Ruth and Gracie was there for a minute." Don's reply— "What the fuck does that mean?"—hints at his fear of being swindled. When Teach enters, Don forces him to bear the brunt of his nervousness and scolds him for his tardiness. Teach, however, is annoyed at Bob's presence and fears that Don has weakened his commitment to their now-shared ideals; he asks Don where Bob got the nickel and implies, through his pauses, that all is not as it should be:

TEACH: And what was Bob doing here?

DON: He told you. He wanted to sell me the nickel.
TEACH: That's why he came here?
DON: Yes.
TEACH: To sell you the buffalo?
DON: Yes.
TEACH: Where did he get it?
DON: I think from some guy.
TEACH: Who? *Pause.*
DON: I don't know. *Pause.*
TEACH: Where's Fletcher?
DON: I don't know. He'll show up.

Although Don has already displayed a slight suspicion about the coin, he refuses to mention this to Teach for fear of betraying Bob. But since Teach is not as soft-spoken or loyal to anything except his God, he again (as he did in Act One) attempts to make Don have "the balls to face some facts" and offers his own interpretation of events: "You better wake up, Don, right now, or things are going to fall around your *head,* and you are going to turn around to find he's took the joint off by himself." Don still clings, however, to the shreds of loyalty and friendship left in his heart—until Teach begins working him from a different angle, explaining that Fletcher cheats at cards. The viewer knows that this story is false, but Don, in his anxious state, begins believing it because Teach is able to answer each of his protests against it: when Don asks him why he never exposed Fletcher as a cheat, Teach replies, "It's not my responsibility to cause bloodshed. I am not your keeper. You want to face facts, okay." Don is at his weakest here and again refuses to accept the notion that he may have been a dupe for another "business associate." And because he senses this about Don, Teach begins a fresh assault on all of the values that Don has tried to uphold for the entire play:

> I don't fuck with my friends, Don. I don't fuck with my business associates. I am a businessman, I am here to do business, I am here to face facts.
>
> (Will you open your eyes?. . .) The kid comes in here, he has got a certain coin, it's like the one *you* used to have . . . the guy you brought in doesn't show, we don't know where *he* is. (*Pause*)
>
> Something comes down, some guy gets his house took off. (*Pause*)
>
> Fletcher, he's not showing up. All right. Let's say I don't know why. Let's say *you* don't know why. But I know that we're both better off. We are better off, Don.

Like Othello, Don has been convinced by the "plausibility" of one who plays upon his most secret fears, and while Teach is no Iago (the villain in Shakespeare's *Othello,* who turns the title character against his wife), he is able to use language to transform the opinions and previously-held values of his "superior." Earlier in the Act, Teach defines "free enterprise" as "The freedom . . . of the *Individual.* . . . To Embark on Any Fucking Course that he sees fit. . . . In order to secure his chance to make a profit." Here, Teach is a hell-for-leather caricature of capitalism, "embarking" on a "course" founded on innuendo and insinuation in order to "make a profit," disregarding Don's concerns over loyalty to Fletcher and protection of Bob.

Teach, however, does not exist in a vacuum, and in order to demonstrate the prevalence and ubiquity of his mythology, Mamet engages in a daring theatrical maneuver at the climax of his play. When Bob returns to tell Don that Fletcher was mugged and is in the hospital with a broken jaw, Teach insists that he is lying and Don—now unable to trust anyone except the man who has been filling him with half-truths for the last half hour—calls the hospital to verify the story. When he is told that Fletcher was not admitted, he and Teach begin grilling Bob about the nickel and Fletcher's absence. The audience is completely convinced at this point that Fletcher, Bob, and possibly Grace and Ruthie have plotted against Don and Teach. Bob can offer no answers to any of their questions and Teach finally is possessed by the God of Business, punishing he whom has doubted His powers:

TEACH: I want you to tell us here and now (and for your own protection) what is going *on,* what is set *up* . . . where *Fletcher* is . . . and everything you know.
DON: (*sotto voce*) I can't believe this.
BOB: I don't know anything.
TEACH: You don't, huh?
BOB: No.
DON: Tell him what you know, Bob.
BOB: I don't know it, Donnie. Grace and Ruthie . . .
TEACH: (*grabs a nearby object and hits Bob viciously on the side of the head.*) Grace and Ruthie up your ass, you shithead; you don't fuck with us, *I'll* kick your fucking head in.

Although a viewer would not condone Teach's action here, he can certainly appreciate his frustration at being betrayed. Even Don, Bob's former protector, states to Bob, "You brought it on yourself."

But this is the moment where the entire play finds its meaning and where Mamet lays down his winning hand: Ruthie then calls and says that Fletcher *was* admitted to the hospital—which is verified when Don calls a different hospital from the one he had tried before. Bob then tells the men, "I missed him"—which they discover means that he never

Dustin Hoffman as Teach in a scene from the film adaptation

saw the buyer leave his house on a vacation earlier that day, as he reported. Bob made up the story to win back the good graces of Don, after he scolded him that morning for abandoning his post. Furthermore (and unbelievable as it may seem), he *did* buy the buffalo-head nickel ''in a coin store,'' as he originally claimed, ''For Donny.'' The very fact that the audience is shocked by these revelations reveals the degree to which *they*—like Teach and Don—have accepted the myth of business, for if a viewer of the play assumes that Bob has been lying, he can see just how much the notion of the ''dog eat dog'' world has affected his attitudes and assumptions. As the philosopher Friedrich Nietzsche said, ''When you look into the abyss, the abyss looks back into you.''

Teach's response to this revelation is a physical manifestation of his intellectual and moral outrage. Brandishing a dead-pig-sticker he toyed with earlier in the play, he begins smashing everything in the shop, proclaiming a series of newfound adages. Unlike his earlier ones, however, these are formed from his own despair and humiliation at discovering that his myth of the God of Business is just that—a myth: ''My Whole Cocksucking Life. The Whole Entire World. There Is No Law. There Is No Right And Wrong. The World Is Lies. There Is No Friendship. Every Fucking Thing. Every God-forsaken Thing.'' He continues his ranting and ultimately concludes that, although he is ''out there every day,'' there is ''nothing out there.'' The ''nothing'' here is the emptiness of his own rhetoric and all of his accepted wisdom. Earlier he preaches to Don that without the ideals of free enterprise, ''We're just savage shitheads in the wilderness.'' Now, however, he knows that his God of Business is an invention and that, when all of the aphorisms are laid bare, ''We all live like the cavemen.'' He exits the play apologizing to Don for wrecking his shop and wearing a paper hat that he makes to protect himself from the rain. Despite his former beliefs and convictions, he is now (in his comical cap) the dunce of his own myth.

While Don waits for Teach to return with his car so they can take Bob to the hospital, he and Bob resume the quiet conversational tone which was interrupted by Teach. Bob is apologetic and repeatedly says, ''I'm sorry. I fucked up.'' But rather than return to his stance from the beginning of the play, Don consoles him with, ''No. You did real good. . . . That's all right. . . . That's all right.'' Don knows that he should have taken his own advice, such as when he told Bob, ''Things are not always what they seem to be'' and that he must now try to heal the physical and emotional wounds caused by his forsaking friendship for the God of Business. As Mamet said in the *New Theatre Quarterly,* Don "undergoes recognition in reversal—realizing that all this comes out of his vanity, that because he abdicated a moral position for one moment in favor of some monetary gain, he has let anarchy into his life and has come close to killing the thing he loves." Don has almost left his friend to the same fate as the real American buffalo, which moved in herds of their own comrades but whom were also destroyed by the wave of capitalism and Teacher-defined "free enterprise" that swept the country. He is back in the "foul rag-and-bone shop" of his heart and must now rebuild his friendship with Bob if he is ever to find another "ladder" again. The "black and yellow Ford" has crashed, leaving the three men staring at the wreckage.

Source: Daniel Moran, for *Drama for Students,* Gale, 1998.

"MAMET'S USE OF LANGUAGE MUST BE REGARDED AS AN ACHIEVEMENT. IF THE VOCABULARY OF MEN SUCH AS BOBBY, TEACH AND DONNY IS IMPOVERISHED, MAMET'S RENDERING OF IT REMINDS US THAT VOCABULARY IS ONLY ONE OF THE RESOURCES OF LANGUAGE."

Jack V. Barbera

Barbera argues in this essay that, despite characters who lack true intellect, Mamet's play is a work of high intellectual content that adroitly chronicles a facet of American existence.

David Mamet, currently an associate director of Chicago's Goodman Theater, was born in Chicago in 1947 and grew up on the city's South Side. He attributes his sense of dramatic rhythm in part to a job during his high-school years as busboy at Second City, the famous Chicago improvisational cabaret. After several years in New England attending college and working at various theaters as a house manager and actor, Mamet returned to his native city and a series of odd jobs which included a stint teaching theater classes at the University of Chicago. Some of his plays were staged at small Chicago theaters during the early '70's—including the St. Nicholas Theater of which Mamet was a founding member and first artistic director. The title of my essay is a pun on the title of a play for which Mamet received the Joseph Jefferson Award (best new Chicago play) in 1974, and later an Obie Award, *Sexual Perversity in Chicago.* So there is some reason to associate him with that city! It is the setting of many of his plays, including the one I shall examine here. For *American Buffalo* Mamet again received an Obie, and it was named the best play in 1977 by the New York Drama Critics' Circle.

I say the setting of *American Buffalo* is Chicago, but in the text of the play the scene specified is "*Don's Resale Shop. A junkshop,*" and the city is not mentioned. There are telltale signs of locale however. The traveler from New York to Chicago still encounters verbal differences: "soda" becomes "pop," for example, and "bun" becomes "sweet roll." So a Manhattan audience attending *American Buffalo* knows Teach is not from the Big Apple when he vividly complains: "But to have that shithead turn, in one breath, every fucking sweet roll that I ever ate with them into *ground glass* . . . this hurts me, Don." And a Chicago audience, when it hears a passing reference to "Lake Shore Drive," knows the setting is, as it were, the neighborhood. A sophisticated Chicago audience also recognizes the allusion in the following bit of dialogue:

> TEACH: (. . . *Indicating objects on the counter*) What're *these*?
> DON: Those?
> TEACH: Yeah.
> DON: They're from 1933.
> TEACH: From the thing?
> DON: Yeah. (*Pause*) . . .
> TEACH: They got that much of it around?
> DON: *Shit* yes. (It's not that long ago.) The thing, it ran two years, and they had (*I* don't know) all kinds of people every year they're buying everything that they can lay their hands on that they're going to take it back to Buffalo to give it, you know, to their aunt, and it mounts up.

The "thing" that ran two years was the 1933 World's Fair held in Chicago in celebration of the city's 100th anniversary. Although it took place during the Great Depression, the Century of Progress Exposition was so popular it was held over for another year and attracted 100 million people.

Aside from the few specifically Chicago allusions in *American Buffalo,* Don's Resale Shop could be located in any number of large American cities. What is important is not Chicago, but a particular kind of urban American subculture—urban because one does not imagine a character like Teach, his staccato manner, in rural Kansas, say, or Mississippi. And one is more likely to imagine a junkie like Bobby in an urban setting. But it is the characters' street language which is worth examining for a moment, because it has stirred controversy among the critics. Gordon Rogoff concluded that, "With friends like [Mamet] . . . words don't need enemies," and Brendan Gill wrote of the play's "tiresome small talk," which attempts "in vain to perform the office of eloquence. . . ." Jack Kroll, however, praised the "kind of verbal cubism" in which Mamet's characters speak, saying the playwright "is someone to listen to . . . an American playwright who's a language playwright" and who is "the first playwright to create a formal and moral shape out of the undeleted expletives of our foul-mouthed time."

I find myself in tune with Kroll. In any assessment of *American Buffalo* Mamet's use of language must be regarded as an achievement. If the vocabulary of men such as Bobby, Teach and Donny is impoverished, Mamet's rendering of it reminds us that vocabulary is only one of the resources of language. Teach does have an eloquence when expressing his sense that he has been abused. Galled by Grace and Ruthie, he tells Don:

> Only (and I tell you this, Don). Only, and I'm not, I don't think, casting anything on anyone: from the mouth of a Southern bulldyke asshole ingrate of a vicious nowhere cunt can this trash come.

This sentence, so politely diffident at first, lets fall its invective in a rain of hammering trochees. It is marvelous invective, more vivid than that in James Stephens's "A Glass of Beer," and ironic to boot, for in the most vulgar language Teach has denounced as "trash" Grace's sarcastic remark, "'Help yourself.'" Teach is constantly undercutting himself this way, as when he says, again referring to Grace and Ruthie, "The only way to teach these people is to kill them." In Act 2, Don does not want him to take a gun on a robbery, and Teach replies that of course the gun is not needed:

> Only that it makes me comfortable, okay? It helps me to relax. So, God forbid, something inevitable occurs. . . .

The urban nature of the language in *American Buffalo* is a matter not just of its street vulgarity, or expressions such as "skin-pop" and "He takes me off my coin . . . ," but also of an abbreviation characteristic of urban pace. One of my Mississippi students told me she had a job in Manhattan which required her to answer the telephone saying, "Hello, this is so-and-so of the such-and-such company." A typical caller responded, "I like your accent honey, but could you speed it up?" Teach telescopes "probably" into "Prolly," and utters such staccato sentences as: "He don't got the address the guy?", and, "I'm not the *hotel,* I stepped out for coffee, I'll be back one minute." Such elliptic expression is a matter not of Mamet's invention, but of his ear for how some of us speak these days. On the Dick Cavett ETV show (Mamet appeared on November 29, 1979 and January 16, 1980), Mamet mentioned entering an elevator and hearing a woman say, "Lovely weather, aren't we?"

Besides the play's language, a second critical issue which has resulted in opposing assessments of *American Buffalo* is that of its content, or lack of it. Gill complained, in the review I have already mentioned, that the play provides the meager and familiar message "that life, rotten as it is, is all we have." And in a review in *America,* Catharine Hughes found that what happens in the play "too often seems much ado about very little." Before I proceed with a defense of *American Buffalo* as being of intellectual interest, and as going beyond the "message" Gill found in it, a capsule of the plot seems in order.

In his late forties, Don Dubrow is conversing with the much younger Bob about a man Bob is supposed to watch. Four major motifs emerge from their conversation: friendship, looking out for oneself, business, and being knowledgeable. Teach enters Don's junkshop and, while Bob is getting coffee, learns of Don's plan to rob the man Bob has been watching. After the man spotted a buffalo-head nickel in Don's shop and purchased it for ninety dollars, Don concluded it must be worth much more and that the man must have other valuable coins. Teach talks Don into cutting him in on the robbery, and convinces him Bobby is too young and, as a junkie, too unreliable to be part of it. That night the plan goes awry and Teach, in anger and frustration, "*hits* BOB *viciously on the side of the head.*" This unjust attack stirs Don against Teach, and restores the solicitude toward Bobby we noticed in Don at the start of the play. Even in this low-life ambiance, in effect, there is some decency. Though all three characters are losers, the friendship between Don and Bobby is something of worth.

It is in the relationships, tensions and contradictions in the patter of Don and Teach, concerning the motifs I mentioned, that the ''content'' of this play resides. Take the motif of business. Don tells Bobby that in business deals intentions are not good enough: ''Action talks and bullshit walks.'' And a bit later he defines business as ''common sense, experience, and talent.'' This soon turns into, ''People taking *care* of themselves.'' But if business is looking out for oneself, what is the relation between business and friendship? In passing, Don and Bobby have been discussing a business deal between Fletch and Ruthie. It seems that Fletch purchased some pig iron from Ruthie and made such a profit on it that Ruthie felt cheated. Was it unfair of Fletch to profit so much from a friend? Don, who defends Fletch, saying, ''That's what business *is,*'' and ''there's business and there's friendship, Bobby . . .'', goes on to say, ''what you got to do is keep clear who your friends are, and who treated you like what.'' But that is clearly what Ruthie has done, and that is why she is angry with Fletch and feels he stole from her. Later we learn that when Don imagines the nickel he sold for ninety dollars must be worth much more, he feels *he* was robbed—so much for ''That's what business *is.*'' Contradictions and elaborations on ''business'' continue through the play. A funny definition of free enterprise will stand as a last example:

TEACH: You know what is free enterprise?
DON: No. What?
TEACH: The freedom . . .
DON: . . . yeah?
TEACH: Of the *Individual* . . .
DON: . . . yeah?
TEACH: To Embark on Any Fucking Course that he sees fit.
DON: Uh-huh . . .
TEACH: In order to secure his honest chance to make a profit. Am I so out of line on this?
DON: No. . . .
TEACH: The country's *founded* on this, Don. You know this.

Of course the individuals in this case see fit to embark on robbery. Part of Mamet's intent in *American Buffalo* is to expose the shoddiness of the American business ethic by having his low-lives transparently voice it. He said as much in an interview with Richard Gottlieb:

> ''The play is about the American ethic of business,'' he said. ''About how we excuse all sorts of great and small betrayals and ethical compromises called business. . . . There's really no difference between the *lumpenproletariat* and stockbrokers or corporate lawyers who are the lackeys of business,'' Mr. Mamet went on. ''Part of the American myth is that a difference exists, that at a certain point vicious behavior becomes laudable. [*New York Times,* January 15, 1978].''

Mamet got the idea of an identical ethical perversity existing at both ends of the urban economic spectrum from Thorstein Veblen (1857–1929)—the American sociologist, economist, satirist, and sometime Chicagoan. In considering the relation between Veblen's thought and *American Buffalo,* one should start with Veblen's *Theory of the Leisure Class* (1899). His theory of the leisure class is related to his theory of business enterprise in that Veblen saw businessmen as involved with the pecuniary and predatory interests of ownership, rather than with the industrial and social interests of production. Teach is a good example of a Veblen ''lower-class delinquent,'' and Veblen's ideas of emulation, and of the snob appeal of what is obsolete, are relevant to the play—the latter, especially, as it applies to collecting rare coins and World's Fair memorabilia.

That Mamet is justified in expecting an audience to accept his play's small-time criminals as representative of American businessmen is arguable. One way of understanding the play's title mainly applies to them as members of a marginal class of society. In a review of the play for the *Nation,* Harold Clurman wrote: ''Look at the face of the coin, as reproduced on the show's playbill. The buffalo looks stunned, baffled, dejected, ready for slaughter. The animal is antiquated, and the would-be robbers are a mess. The combination is symbolic.'' Don and Teach and Bobby are as antiquated and out-of-it as the American buffalo or bison (successful American businessmen may or may not be ethical, but they are not marginal). We must admit that Don and Teach and Bobby are dumb. They are not even streetwise, though Don and Teach may think they are. Fletch probably is streetwise—consider the pig-iron deal, or the fact that he won at cards in the game in which Don and Teach lost. They admire and resent his success, and feel they have been cheated. They are envious of anyone who is knowledgeable and successful, such as the man who purchased the coin. Knowledge, an important motif in the play, is the key here. ''One thing. Makes all the difference in the world,'' says Teach. And when Don asks, ''What?'', he replies, ''Knowing what the fuck you're talking about. And it's so rare, Don. *So* rare.'' Of course Teach does not know what he is talking about, as we learn in the routines about which coins are valuable, where the man would keep his coins, how to get into his house, and what to do about a safe.

This contradiction leads us to the other way of understanding the title, a way which applies to the characters as representatives of the business class as well as representatives of a class of urban marginal crooks. For "buffalo" read the slang verb "to intimidate." It is because he does not know anything that Teach must try to buffalo Don. And it is common for businessmen to buffalo the public: "The windfall profits tax will dry up America's oil," and "If you don't buy this laxative no one will love you." Fletch evidently can buffalo successfully; Standard Oil can; Teach cannot (aside from Don, who buys his line, "Send Bobby in and you'll wind up with a broken toaster"). But to buffalo is as American as to bake an apple pie. Notions of the American way—democracy and free enterprise—become corrupted when they enter the look-out-for-number-one rationalizations of crooks and unethical businessmen. Down-and-outs in a democracy may feel they have been cheated because "all men should be equal." Knowledge creates divisions among people, divisions of power and wealth, but such divisions can seem undemocratic, un-American. So robbing and cheating are attempts to restore justice. Or, "In America one is free to make a fortune for himself" turns into Teach's definition of free enterprise. My modest conclusion is that in satirizing such corrupt notions Mamet *has* written a play of intellectual content.

Source: Jack V. Barbera, "Ethical Perversity in America: Some Observations on David Mamet's *American Buffalo*" in *Modern Drama,* Volume XXIV, no. 3, 1981, pp. 270–75.

Gordon Rogoff

While finding Mamet's knack for dialogue admirable, critic Rogoff complains that Mamet's play apes crime films from the 1940s and 1950s without the benefit of those dramas' clever storylines. Rogoff acknowledges that Mamet achieves his dramatic goals—although those goals are too modest for the critic's tastes.

David Mamet is apparently listening to America's lower class. The news he brings back in his new play, *American Buffalo* (at the Ethel Barrymore Theatre on Broadway), is that Americans living on the dark underside of small business and petty crookery speak of macho frustrations almost entirely in four-letter words. If the news doesn't seem new or persuasive, that may be because we have heard more antiseptic versions of it on big and little screens, where—with a little soap in their mouths—*American Buffalo*'s trio of charmless deadbeats would be more at home.

Robert Duvall's Walter Cole (known as Teacher) is the latest in a long line of Stanley Kowalskis trying to mimic the language they think businessmen use. Some of the linguistic turns are cleverly heard: Teacher-Kowalskis do like to say words like *averse, deviate, instance;* and they love to talk about planning, preparation, business propositions, and facing facts. Duvall's performance has as much body in it as it does dirty English, but it is more an expert impersonation of an archetype than an enactment of an authentic event.

How could it be otherwise? Mamet is imitating a hundred Bogart, Cagney, Robinson, and Brando movies, and he's not bad at the job. His dialogue has some of the vivacity missing from those movies. They were better at plot, however; and they didn't always treat Bogart and company like dummies. In *The Maltese Falcon,* Wilmer wasn't bright, but he had dignity. Mamet patronizes his trio: he is out to kill and get laughs. Modest ambitions, modestly achieved.

Source: Gordon Rogoff, "Albee and Mamet: The War of the Words" in *Saturday Review,* Volume 4, no. 13, April 2, 1977, pp. 37.

SOURCES

Barnes, Clive. "Stage: Skilled 'American Buffalo'" in the *New York Times,* February 17, 1977.

Beaufort, John. Review of *American Buffalo* in the *Christian Science Monitor,* February 23, 1977.

Billington, Michael. Review of *American Buffalo* in the *Guardian,* June 29, 1978.

Gale, Stephen H. "David Mamet: The Plays, 1972-1980" in *Essays on Contemporary American Drama,* Max Huber, 1981, pp. 207-23.

Guernsey, Otis L. Jr., Editor. *The Best Plays of 1976-1977,* Dodd, Mead, 1977, p. 14.

Jones, Nesta and Steven Dykes. *File on Mamet,* Methuen Drama, 1991, pp. 20-29.

Kissel, Howard. Review of *American Buffalo* in *Women's Wear Daily,* February 17, 1977.

Kroll, Jack. "The Muzak Man" in *Newsweek,* February 28, 1977.

Lahr, John. "Fortress Mamet" in the *New Yorker,* November 17, 1997, pp. 70-82.

Lewis, Patricia and Terry Browne. ''David Mamet'' in *Dictionary of Literary Biography,* Volume 7: *Twentieth Century American Dramatists,* Gale (Detroit), 1981, pp. 63-70.

Luckett, Perry. ''David Mamet'' in *Magill's Critical Survey of Drama: Volume 3,* Salem Press, 1985, pp. 1234-37.

Mamet, David. *American Buffalo,* Grove, 1976.

Mamet, David. Passage from interview in *New Theatre Quarterly,* February 1988.

Mamet, David. Interview in the London *Times,* June 19, 1978.

Porterfield, Christopher. ''David Mamet's Bond of Futility'' in *Time,* February 28, 1977.

Probst, Leonard. Review of *American Buffalo* for NBC-TV, February 16, 1977.

Wardle, Irving. Review of *American Buffalo,* in the London *Times,* June 29, 1978.

Watt, Douglas. ''Stuck in a Junk Shop'' in the *Daily News,* February 17, 1977.

Wilson, Edwin. ''A Phlegmatic American Buffalo'' in the *Wall Street Journal,* February 23, 1977.

FURTHER READING

Bigsby, C. W. E. and Christopher Bigsby. *Modern American Drama: 1945-1990,* Cambridge, 1992.

This book offers a survey of American theatrical trends since World War II.

Dean, Anne. *David Mamet: Language As Dramatic Action,* Fairleigh Dickinson University Press, 1990.

This book offers an overview of Mamet's career, including analysis on such famous works as *American Buffalo* and *Glengarry Glen Ross.*

Kernan, Alvin B., Editor. *The Modern American Theater,* Prentice-Hall, 1967.

Although Mamet is not examined in this collection of essays, Kernan's introductory essay is an overview of American theater containing several points that could easily be applied to Mamet's work.

Mamet, David. *True and False: Common Sense for the Actor,* Pantheon Books, 1997.

This short book is Mamet's guide to acting, which may prove useful when trying to imagine how scenes in his work are meant to be performed.

The Basic Training of Pavlo Hummel

DAVID RABE

1971

David Rabe's *The Basic Training of Pavlo Hummel* was the first American play of stature to deal with the experience of the Vietnam War. At least one historian of the Vietnam era, Philip Beidler writing in *American Literature and the Experience of Vietnam,* found that Rabe made ''the most important contributions to the dramatic literature of Vietnam during the period 1970-75.'' After being rejected by numerous regional and experimental theaters, the play was first produced professionally in 1971 at the Public Theatre by Joseph Papp's New York Shakespeare Festival, one of the country's most prestigious production organizations. Rabe's professional debut was a success: *Pavlo Hummel* enjoyed a run of 363 performances and received predominantly enthusiastic critical response. Clive Barnes of the *New York Times* acclaimed Rabe as a ''new and authentic voice of our theatre.'' For this play, Rabe received the *Village Voice*'s Obie Award for distinguished playwriting, and a Drama Desk Award for most promising playwright.

From trying to keep a journal during his military service in Vietnam, Rabe found that his experience there defied description, exceeding the capabilities of ''language as mere symbol,'' as he wrote in his introduction to *Two Plays: The Basic Training of Pavlo Hummel and Sticks and Bones.* Unwilling to bring his ''full sensibility to bear upon all elements'' of the experience, Rabe ''skimmed over things and hoped they would skim over me.'' In Rabe's depiction, the Vietnam experience is a ''sur-

real carnival of death,'' reflected in Pavlo's extremely confused state of mind, and in the mood of expressionism throughout the play. *The Basic Training of Pavlo Hummel* is not strictly an anti-war play; its author believes that war is inevitably a part of what he calls the ''eternal human pageant.'' Instead, Rabe examines the process of basic training as an American rite of passage, using his metaphor to illustrate the coercive power of the institution. Rabe himself called military basic training a metaphor for the ''essential'' training by which society reshapes all individuals.

AUTHOR BIOGRAPHY

David Rabe was born March 10, 1940, in Dubuque, Iowa, the son of a high school teacher who later became a meatpacker, and a department store worker. He was educated at Catholic institutions for whom he also played football. He earned his B.A. from Loras College in 1962. Rabe went to Villanova University in Philadelphia for a master's degree in theatre but was drafted before he completed the program of study. From 1965 to 1967 he served in the U.S. Army, with eleven months of duty in Vietnam. Rabe—like his character Pavlo Hummel—was assigned to hospital duty, and though he did not engage in combat, he witnessed fighting at close range. His experience in Vietnam—particularly his shock at the youth and inexperience of the soldiers dying there—provided the substance for his early theatrical successes.

As he recalls in the introduction to *Two Plays: The Basic Training of Pavlo Hummel and Sticks and Bones,* Rabe says that when he returned from Vietnam it was six months before he thought seriously of writing; he began only when he realized ''there was nothing else to do with the things I was thinking.'' Rabe returned to Villanova to complete his master's degree, afterwards holding a variety of jobs, including feature writer for the *New Haven Register* and assistant professor at Villanova. In 1969 he married Elizabeth Pan, a laboratory technician. The couple had a son, Jason, but the marriage ended in separation. (Rabe later married actress Jill Clayburgh in March, 1979.)

Rabe made an impressive theatrical debut in 1971, with the professional productions of his plays *The Basic Training of Pavlo Hummel* and *Sticks and Bones.* The plays were received enthusiastically as challenging explorations of America's involvement in Vietnam written by a soldier who had served there. The success of these two plays assured Rabe's place in the contemporary American theatre, a reputation later cemented by *Streamers* (1976), widely considered to be his most accomplished play. The three plays are taken collectively as Rabe's ''Vietnam trilogy,'' although they were not conceived or executed as a cohesive cycle.

Rabe's Vietnam plays are full of dark humor and stark images, expressing with lyrical and symbolic language the rage of alienated characters. The most well-known of Rabe's other dramatic works are *In the Boom Boom Room* (1973), about the humiliation and exploitation of a female go-go dancer, and *Hurlyburly* (1984), a bitter comedy about the Hollywood entertainment industry. Rabe's other works include the plays *The Orphan* (first produced 1974), *The Crossing* (a one-act, produced at Villanova around 1963 and professionally in 1976), and *Goose and Tomtom* (written 1978, produced 1982).

In addition to adapting several of his own works to film (including *Streamers*), Rabe has written screenplays for the films *I'm Dancing as Fast as I Can, Casualties of War,* and others. The many honors Rabe has received during his playwriting career include an Obie Award, a Drama Desk Award, and a Drama Guild Award—all for *Pavlo Hummel.* He has also won an Antionette (''Tony'') Perry Award for Best Play (for *Sticks and Bones*), a New York Drama Critics Circle Award for Best American Play (for *Streamers*), as well as a Rockefeller grant and a Guggenheim fellowship.

PLOT SUMMARY

Act I

The play opens with the title character, Pavlo, in a Vietnamese brothel with the prostitute Yen. Pavlo brags about his various escapades as a soldier, but underneath his bravado he appears insecure and edgy. A grenade is tossed through the window; Pavlo picks it up and attempts to throw it back out, but it explodes, mortally wounding him. Ardell enters, a black soldier in a ''strangely unreal'' uniform who serves as Pavlo's alter ego throughout the play (only Pavlo can see or hear Ardell). Ardell's

David Rabe

entrance triggers for the dying Pavlo a flashback of his army life; this jumbled series of recollections constitute the fragmented action of the play.

The action goes back in time to Pavlo's arrival at boot camp. There he encounters Sergeant Tower, the imposing drill sergeant (''I'm bigger than my name''), who immediately isolates Pavlo for ''looking about at the air like some kinda fool'' and makes him do push-ups; this initiates a pattern which is repeated throughout the play.

Though Pavlo desperately wants to identify as part of a group, his quirky individualism gets him in trouble not only with Tower but with the other recruits as well. Two of these men, Kress and Parker, are working in a furnace room and are particularly dissatisfied with their situation. Their comments reveal that Pavlo has quickly developed a bad reputation; Kress in particular curses the army for ''stickin' me in with weird people'' and wishes that Hummel would die. When Kress and Parker leave, Pavlo tries to please the squad leader, Pierce, by reciting the General Orders, to ''see if I'm sharp enough to be one a your boys.'' When the whistle for company formation is blown, however, Pavlo ignores it, and is again reprimanded by Tower. Pavlo is then confronted by a group of trainees who accuse him of stealing a soldier's wallet and consequently give him a ''blanket party'' (that is, they cover him in a blanket and collectively beat him).

The end of basic training arrives, and when the scores of the final proficiency tests are announced, Kress and one other soldier have been held back. They will be ''recycled'' (sent back for eight more weeks of training), while the rest of the men are sent home until they receive their assignments. Pavlo tells Kress ''I feel sorry for you'' and asks him several questions. Kress feels he is being taunted, so he attacks Pavlo and can only be subdued with great difficulty.

Pavlo, having blurted out previously that he plans to kill himself, swallows an entire bottle of aspirin; his life is on the line as the other men attempt to revive him. The act closes with a monologue of Ardell's in which he tells Pavlo, ''Ain't doin' you no good you wish you dead, 'cause you ain't, man.'' Ardell transforms Pavlo by putting the latter in his dress uniform and sunglasses, preparing him for his trip home.

Act II

The act opens on an address by the Captain to the platoon regarding the commencement of bombing campaigns against North Vietnam. The troops scatter at the end of this speech, and the scene changes immediately to Pavlo's arrival at the home of his half-brother, Mickey. The relationship between Pavlo and Mickey is somewhat strained. Pavlo appears anxious to prove himself as Mickey provokes him by refusing to believe Pavlo is in the army and stating that "Vietnam don't even exist." Pavlo lies about his relationships with the other men in his platoon, claiming "I got people who respect me."

Pavlo's frustrations at home continue as he unsuccessfully attempts to track down an old girlfriend, Joanna, whom he suggests might have killed herself out of despair (in reality, she is now married). Pavlo is then thwarted in his attempts to get his mother to reveal to him the identity of his father. Instead, Mrs. Hummel is fixated on a story about a coworker learning of her son's death in Vietnam; "I know what to expect," she says to Pavlo, a foreshadowing of Pavlo's own demise.

Interspersed with these scenes of home life are glimpses of Pavlo with his platoon. The scene then shifts fully to Vietnam, where Pavlo, despite his protests, has been posted as a medic at a mobile hospital. The setting of the field hospital—where Pavlo cares for the crippled Sgt. Brisbey—is juxtaposed against the setting of Mamasan's brothel, where Pavlo meets Jones and has his first sexual experience with the prostitute Yen. The scene of Pavlo and Yen's lovemaking is interspersed with another of Sergeant Tower's lectures to the platoon, this one about the care of their M-16 rifle: "You got to have feelin' for it, like it a good woman to you. . . ." Pavlo marches away from his bed as the rest of the troops move out, and the scene changes back to the hospital. Brisbey is obviously depressed about his condition. ("Some guys, they get hit, they have a stump," he says. "I am a stump.") Brisbey hints at a desire to commit suicide, asking for Pavlo's rifle to "save you from the sin of cruelty," but Pavlo refuses, attempting to dissuade Brisbey from his suicidal thoughts.

The setting of the field hospital is juxtaposed against a scene of Parham, a young Black PFC, attempting to cross a dangerous field under orders. Parham is wounded and cries for a medic; instead he is discovered by two Viet Cong who torture him for information, then kill him. Pavlo arrives with Ryan, and in attempting to remove Parham's body from the field, Pavlo is wounded. Ryan returns to retrieve Pavlo, as a body detail removes Parham; these actions are juxtaposed against a series of addresses by Sergeant Tower to his troops. A series of short scenes follow dramatizing Pavlo being wounded two more times. Pavlo begins agitating to be sent home; instead, he is given the Purple Heart and sent back to duty.

At Mamasan's brothel, Pavlo is quarreling with Sergeant Wall over the attentions of Yen, "the whore I usually hit on." Pavlo assaults Wall, who leaves and returns moments later, throwing in the grenade which kills Pavlo. Ardell and Pavlo have their final interaction as Pavlo is sealed in his coffin. Pavlo admits that in the end, the cause for and the circumstances under which he died are "all shit." This serves as the play's final pronouncement on not only war, but the human condition more broadly, as Ardell slams Pavlo's coffin shut and exits the stage.

CHARACTERS

Ardell

An African American soldier in a "strangely unreal" uniform who functions as Pavlo's alter-ego throughout the play. Only Pavlo can see or hear Ardell, and Rabe uses the device of this character to depict Pavlo's extremely confused state of mind. Ardell moves in and out of the fragmented action, creating a mood of expressionism throughout the play. Ardell allows the audience a glimpse into Pavlo's interior character at crucial moments in the play; he also provides a point of transition between scenes. At the close of the first act, Ardell tells Pavlo, "Ain't doin' you no good you wish you dead, 'cause you ain't, man." Ardell transforms Pavlo by putting the latter in his dress uniform and sunglasses, preparing him for his trip home. Similarly, the play ends with Ardell and Pavlo having their final interaction. As Pavlo is sealed in his coffin, Ardell prompts him to admit that in the end, the cause for and the circumstances under which he died are "all shit." Ardell slams Pavlo's coffin shut to conclude the play.

Sergeant Brisbey

A soldier at the field hospital in Vietnam who has been crippled by a land mine. He is extremely depressed about his condition and hints strongly that he wants to kill himself, asking Pavlo for a gun.

Burns

A trainee who plays craps with Pierce. He claims to have seen Pavlo steal from one of the other

MEDIA ADAPTATIONS

- There are no media adaptations of *The Basic Training of Pavlo Hummel* available. Rabe's two other well-known Vietnam plays, however, have been adapted. *Sticks and Bones* was produced for CBS in 1972, although the network withdrew support for the play and left the choice of whether to air it or not to their affiliates. *Streamers* was made into a film in 1983, directed by Robert Altman.

men. He and Kress are the two trainees who fail basic training.

The Corporal

Second in command of Pavlo's platoon, he leads the trainees in drills occasionally. Pavlo is envious of him because he has already seen combat in Vietnam.

Grennel

A soldier who serves in the field hospital with Pavlo.

Hendrix

A combat-seasoned soldier and therefore a person with some authority over the trainees. He is close to the Corporal and keeps lookout while the Corporal hustles Pavlo at pool.

Hinkle

A trainee; he speaks with a deep Southern drawl. It is his wallet that Pavlo is accused by the other men of stealing.

Mrs. Hummel

Pavlo and Mickey's mother; she suffers from mental illness. Mrs. Hummel's story about a co-worker learning of her son's death in Vietnam is a foreshadowing of Pavlo's own death; "I know what to expect," she says to Pavlo. Pavlo tries, unsuccessfully, to get his mother to reveal to him the identity of his father; Mrs. Hummel cannot understand why Pavlo doesn't remember her whispering his father's name to him when he was a child of three.

Michael Hummel

See Pavlo Hummel

Mickey Hummel

Pavlo's half-brother, considered weird, even by Pavlo's standards; Pavlo says of him that he "don't give a rat's ass for nothin' or nobody." The relationship between Pavlo and Mickey is somewhat strained; Mickey provokes Pavlo by refusing to believe he is in the army, and stating, "Vietnam don't even exist."

Pavlo Hummel

A teenager estranged from his family who seeks companionship and meaning in his life. Pavlo's desperate desire to belong cements his ties to the U.S. Army; he remains, however, a misfit who steals from his fellow soldiers and attempts suicide to get attention. Pavlo's confused state of mind is reflected in the play's expressionistic structure and in the characterization of Ardell, whom only Pavlo sees or hears. Pavlo wants to become a model soldier, but he is inept at his training. He sees himself as an effective fighting machine, but as Rabe points out in a note to the play, the only talent Pavlo reveals is "a talent for jumping into the fire." Seasoned by his experience in Vietnam, Pavlo becomes the kind of soldier who can brag, "I'm diggin' it man. Blowin' people away. Cuttin' em down." This comment exemplifies a kind of character degeneration, a substitution for Pavlo's lack of meaningful human contact.

Jones

An American soldier Pavlo meets in Mamasan's brothel in Vietnam. More experienced not only at war but at sex, he facilitates Pavlo's first sexual encounters with the prostitute Yen. He provides Pavlo with an extremely frank introduction to Vietnam: "You gonna be here and you gonna sweat. And you gonna be here and you gonna get V.D.!"

Kress

A trainee, large and muscular, "with a constant manner of small confusion as if he feels always that something is going on that he nearly, but not quite, understands." He is from New Jersey and is unpleasantly surprised to be so cold all the time at the

Georgia base. Kress is one of two trainees who fails basic training the first time, for which he holds a grudge against Pavlo. When Pavlo tells him ''I feel sorry for you, Kress,'' he thinks Pavlo is taunting him, and he responds with a physical attack.

Mamasan

An older Vietnamese woman and keeper of the brothel where Pavlo meets his fate.

Captain Miller

Pavlo's commanding officer at the field hospital, who first attempts to talk Pavlo out of his request for a transfer, then grants the request. Pavlo shows him a lack of respect because he is an R.O.T.C. officer rather than ''regular army.'' (There is also a Captain who addresses Pavlo's platoon at the end of basic training; the same actor plays all the officers.)

Jay Charles Johnson Parham

A young African American Private First Class who is wounded and cries for a medic; instead he is discovered by two Viet Cong who torture him for information, then kill him.

Parker

A trainee, small, wears glasses. At first, he is somewhat more sympathetic to Pavlo than the other trainees; he tells Kress not to ''knock that ole boy'' because ''Hummel's gonna keep us laughin'.'' Like the other men, however, Parker does not believe Pavlo when he denies having stolen from them.

Pierce

A trainee who acts as a squad leader. He is older than the other men in the squad and has a bit more life experience. While many of the trainees resent Pierce, Pavlo tries hard to please him. Pierce, meanwhile, likes Pavlo enough to try to keep him out of trouble with the other men.

Ryan

Pavlo's partner on patrol in the Vietnamese jungle.

Mrs. Sorrentino

The mother of Pavlo's former girlfriend, Joanna; she appears only as a voice when Pavlo speaks to her on the phone. She hangs up on Pavlo because he is acting strangely and grows violent when he learns Joanna is unavailable.

Sergeant Tower

Pavlo's African American drill sergeant in boot camp, a tough officer who states ''I am bigger than my name.'' Tower's name and military authority are also reflected in the drill sergeant's tower which dominates the play's set, giving him a literally central position in the play. Pavlo is fascinated by Tower, a near archetypal figure of masculine power who personifies the perfect solider in Pavlo's mind. Although Pavlo passes his basic training, however, he can never really live up to Tower's own standards and is constantly being reprimanded by the Sergeant.

Sergeant Henry Wall

A friend and visitor of Brisbey's at the Vietnamese hospital, ''middle-aged, gray-haired, chunky.'' His name somewhat describes his personality, as he is unmoved by Brisbey's shows of emotion. Later, Wall is drunk and behaving lewdly in the brothel; he and Pavlo fight. Humiliated, Wall leaves the brothel and returns moments later, throwing the grenade that kills Pavlo.

Yen

(Pronounced ''Ing.'') A Vietnamese girl who is a prostitute in Mamasan's brothel. Pavlo fights with Sergeant Wall over her and is killed as a result.

THEMES

Change and Transformation

''I'm different than I was!'' Pavlo brags to his half-brother, Mickey, during a visit home following his basic training. ''I'm not the same anymore. I was an asshole. I'm not an asshole anymore.'' This somewhat desperate statement, however, proves to be much more an expression of desire than a statement of fact, as Pavlo demonstrates by lying to Mickey about being respected and liked among his fellow army trainees. Pavlo does not succeed in

TOPICS FOR FURTHER STUDY

- What is a conscientious objector? Research the experience of conscientious objectors during the Vietnam war; you might examine Gerald R. Gioglio's *Days of Decision: An Oral History of Conscientious Objectors in the Military during the Vietnam War* (Broken Rifle Press, 1988). Why does Sgt. Brisbey ask Pavlo in the hospital, "you're not a conscientious objector, are you? So you got a rifle." How does the perspective of a conscientious objector compare to Pavlo's feelings about the war, or, based on what you might know from other sources, to those of Rabe?
- Many playgoers are surprised by the fact that Pavlo is not killed at the front but in a whorehouse after an argument that is ultimately meaningless. Research American casualties in the war; was it common for soldiers to be killed away from combat? What do the circumstances of Pavlo's death contribute to Rabe's depiction of the full experience of Vietnam?
- Tragedy, in its classical form, usually involves some act of self-recognition on the part of the primary character near the play's conclusion. What, if anything, does Pavlo seem to learn as a character throughout the course of the play? Compare his awareness while living to the symbolic dialogue he has with Ardell after his death.
- Research perceptions of the Vietnam war at home in the United States and how they developed as the war progressed. Consider Mickey's response to Pavlo's stories about basic training. What is the significance of Mickey's taunt, "Vietnam don't even exist"?

developing meaningful human relationships, nor does he seem capable of learning from his mistakes. He is generally incapable of change, expressing self-awareness only symbolically in his conversations with Ardell after the grenade explodes.

Death

True to the theme of a protracted and bloody military conflict, death pervades every aspect of Rabe's play. Mrs. Hummel is obsessed with a story about a coworker learning of her son's death in Vietnam. Her comment "I know what to expect" is a foreshadowing of Pavlo's own death, but Pavlo is not engaged enough to respond to this warning nor to his mother's accusation "I know what you're trying to do." Indeed, Pavlo by this time has already attempted suicide, but in an almost offhanded way, only expressing abstractly to Ardell a desire to "be bone." Later, Pavlo may receive his first real intimations of mortality from attending to Sergeant Brisbey in the field hospital. Although Pavlo's enthusiasm for combat fades a bit each time he is wounded, he continues to act carelessly and is unprepared for the possibility of his own death. The struggle to comprehend violence and death remains a theme throughout Rabe's trilogy of Vietnam plays.

Duty and Responsibility

The theme of duty pervades *Pavlo Hummel.* Pavlo wants to serve well, to do his military duty, but in this pursuit he cannot stop himself from breaking the army's rules. It makes more sense to him, for example, to practice handling his rifle on his own, rather than respond to the whistle for company formation. Sgt. Tower is incredulous, saying Pavlo must be "awful stupid, because all the good soldiers is out there in that formation like they supposed to when they hear that whistle."

Pavlo does not understand that the primary duty of the soldier is to obey, that without this collective discipline, the men cannot depend on one another in combat. While Rabe has stressed repeatedly that *Pavlo Hummel* is not an anti-war play in the strictest sense, the conclusion of the play does challenge directly (at least in the context of Vietnam) the idea of war as a soldier's patriotic duty to his country. As Pavlo is sealed in his coffin, Ardell prompts him to admit that in the end, the cause for and the circumstances under which he died are "all shit."

Human Condition

The play's perspective on the human condition is a fairly bleak one. The absurdity of human existence is highlighted strongly, especially by Sgt. Brisbey who, for example, tells Pavlo about a soldier whose hand was blown off, "and he kept crawlin' round lookin' for his fingers. Couldn't go home without 'em, he said, he'd catch hell." Sgt. Brisbey's anecdote about the explorer Magellan symbolizes a central theme of the play: Magellan, according to Brisbey, wanted to know the depth of the ocean on which he was sailing, so he dropped a rope of two hundred feet over the side of his ship. "He thinks because all the rope he's got can't touch bottom, he's over the deepest part of the ocean. He doesn't know the real question. How far beyond all the rope you got is the bottom?" This concept—the existential question of just how low a human being can sink, is also reflected in Pavlo's story about swimming in the Hudson River as a child, when he became disoriented and was fighting his way toward the bottom, thinking he was swimming upward. In both of these images is also reflected the confusion of existence—not only do human beings suffer, but, much of the time, they also lack a basic understanding of their situation.

Revenge

The climax of the action in *Pavlo Hummel* is an act of revenge: Sgt. Wall throws the grenade which kills Pavlo, in revenge for having been beaten and humiliated by him in the Vietnamese brothel. An analogous scenario marks the end of the first act, when Kress attacks Pavlo because he thinks the latter is taunting him. As Pavlo continues to yell obscenities at Kress, Pierce intervenes: "You gotta learn to think, Hummel. . . . You beat him; you had ole Kress beat and then you fixed it so you hadda lose. You went after him so he hadda be able to put you down." Thus, while there is no rational excuse for Sgt. Wall's brutal act of vengeance at the brothel, Pavlo is established as a character who often goes too far, pushing others into doing him harm. It is part of the complex psychology of his character, and of Rabe's play in general, that the audience is not allowed to perceive Pavlo as an unwitting victim of violence.

Rites of Passage

As a teenager estranged from his family and seeking companionship and meaning in his life, Pavlo has a desperate desire to belong; this need cements his ties to the U.S. Army. Pavlo wants to become a model soldier, but he is inept at his training. He sees himself as an effective fighting machine, but he remains a misfit who steals from his fellow soldiers and attempts suicide to get attention. The army training as a rite of passage is a journey to nowhere: the army has not fostered Pavlo's individuality nor his manhood—nor does it act as a surrogate family. The play suggests that those who look to an external institution to provide a rite of passage will ultimately be betrayed.

STYLE

Realism and Expressionism

While *Pavlo Hummel* struck audience members as a realistic portrayal of an American soldier's experience in Vietnam, this fact should not obscure the manner in which Rabe's play breaks from the form of theatrical realism. The interior dialogue between Ardell and Pavlo (continuing even after Pavlo's death) gives the play its psychological complexity, in a manner associated with expressionism (conversely, the psychology of characters in realism is revealed externally, through their actions). Rabe writes in his introduction to the play that it was primarily the influence of producer Joe Papp which caused him to refashion his essentially linear, realistic play during the course of rehearsal, giving it the expressionistic structure it was eventually to have (Rabe's career later moved more strongly toward realism).

Rabe has described in interviews his careful bridging of two styles, acknowledging that in *Pavlo Hummel* he "set up a framework in the play that *wasn't* realistic" but yet tried "to keep *Pavlo* as close to the facts . . . the graphicness of the events, as I could," (as he described his process in *Vietnam,*

Pavlo (Al Pacino) plays billiards with his fellow soldiers in a scene from a 1977 Broadway production

We've All Been There). Much of the realistic quality *Pavlo Hummel* does have is a reflection of Rabe's application of his own military experience onto the events and language of the play. Rabe's dramatic influences reflect his integration of varying theatrical styles: he calls Arthur Miller (author of *Death of a Salesman,* known for realistic plays on social issues) his favorite American playwright, but also acknowledges the influence of the Absurdist playwrights Eugene Ionesco (*The Bald Prima Donna*), Jean Genet (*The Balcony*), and Samuel Beckett (*Waiting for Godot*).

Plot Construction

Ultimately, Rabe's play achieves thematic unity not through telling a linear story from beginning to end but through the complex relationships which develop between scenes. Rather than simply building to Pavlo's death as a conclusion, the play stages the death twice, once at the very beginning and then repeated near the end. The audience thus knows Pavlo's death is inevitable and will watch the play differently than they would if its plot depended more upon an element of suspense.

Writing of the relationship between scenes in the play, *Critical Quarterly*'s Richard Homan called Rabe's technique "collage," through which, for example, the playwright "suggests the incompatibility of Pavlo's military way of life with his civilian life through the juxtaposition of scenes and speeches from both lives in simultaneous settings." Beidler, writing in *American Literature and the Experience of Vietnam,* similarly identified a quality of Rabe's dramatic style that he called "pastiche," and he believed more strongly than Homan in its effectiveness; Beidler found the play "inexhaustible," "a collection of master images."

Characterization

Because the action of *Pavlo Hummel* does not unfold in a fully realistic or linear form, Rabe's characters are often seen as something other than real people. Homan commented that while effective, Rabe's collage "allows only for personifications; character development and sustained dramatic conflict are impossible." Pavlo does have genuine complexity as a character, however, and many of Rabe's other portrayals—especially of the trainees and military characters like Sgt. Tower—are considered vivid and engaging. Edith Oliver was among the critics who found Rabe's characterizations to be a strength of his work, writing in the *New Yorker:* "For all its factual background, the play is not a documentary but a work of the imagination, and its drama, scene by scene, lies in what it reveals about the characters, whatever their circumstances."

Theatrical Space

Rabe's play makes use of multiple spaces on the stage with fluid changes between them and the interweaving and occasional overlapping of scenes. The sparse, abstract set design allows for rapid changes between scenes by merely suggesting different locales on different parts of the stage. The setting both facilitates the movement of scenes in Rabe's distinct dramatic structure and is itself an element of the play's expressionism. Dominating the sparse set, for example, is the drill sergeant's tower, which remains a pervasive image throughout the play (visible even during scenes set elsewhere than the boot camp).

HISTORICAL CONTEXT

Decades of civil conflict in Vietnam paved the way for the entanglement of the United States in the war in Indochina. Soon after the end of World War II, the guerrilla forces which had resisted Japan in the north turned their energies against the colonial power of France, the current occupying force in Vietnam. The Democratic Republic of Vietnam was established in Hanoi with Ho Chi Minh as president. In July, 1954, after years of escalating military conflict, the French and Ho's communist forces signed an agreement calling for an armistice and the temporary division of the country with French authority consolidated around Saigon in the southern half of the country. In 1963, southern military leaders, with the support of the U.S., overthrew the government of Ngo Dinh Diem.

The new military government that took Diem's place was weak, however, and by late 1964, South Vietnam was in virtual chaos. The administration of U.S. President Lyndon Johnson, fearing a total collapse of the Saigon regime, began to deploy American combat forces in the South in the hopes that a display of U.S. might would dissuade the communists from attempting to conquer South Vietnam. Hanoi, however (with support from the Soviet Union, China, and other socialist countries), stepped up their military campaign against the government of South Vietnam. In early 1968 Hanoi launched the Tet Offensive, a major series of attacks throughout the South. Though communist casualties were high, the offensive was a tactical success in that it made clear the might and commitment of the guerilla army. The Tet Offensive also succeeded in increasing antiwar sentiment in the United States and persuading President Johnson to halt further escalation of U.S. troop levels in South Vietnam.

By 1971, the gradual U.S. withdrawal from Vietnam accelerated with President Richard Nixon's announcement that the offensive combat role of American troops was at an end. The number of American soldiers in Vietnam had peaked at 543,000 in April, 1969; by January, 1972, the number was down to 139,000, and dropping steadily. American troops were also increasingly less involved in direct combat; while American war deaths had peaked at 14,592 for the year 1968, this number dropped to 1,380 for 1971. The withdrawal was part of the U.S. government's strategy of "Vietnamization"—that is, to return the military initiative to the South Vietnam Army. U.S. involvement in the war continued to be significant, however, particularly in the continuing bombing campaigns against the North and in the use of modern high-tech weapons (five of every six helicopter missions flown during 1971, for example, were piloted by Americans).

In 1971, the South undertook an ambitious campaign in the neighboring country of Laos. For some time, the communist forces had used this region as a staging area for attacks against the South; the southern initiative was an attempt to destroy the North Vietnamese supply routes along the Ho Chi Minh trail. Southern forces achieved some early victories, but as the campaign pushed farther into Laos it stalled. U.S. involvement in the effort remained selective; a base at Khe Sanh, for instance, was reactivated in January, 1971, to support the attack on Laos but was evacuated on April 6 of that year, a symbol of continuing U.S. disentanglement from the Indochina war.

The complexities of Cold War diplomacy remained a factor throughout the war in Vietnam. With President Nixon indicating a change in American policy towards China (a "thawing" of U.S.

COMPARE & CONTRAST

- **1971:** Reintegration into American society proves a difficult process for many Vietnam veterans. Denied the kind of celebration which marked the end of World War II, many American soldiers return from Vietnam with a great deal of shame, finding they have been rejected by their society. Many people who do not support U.S. involvement in Vietnam blame the soldiers who fought there for the tragedy of the war.

  Today: While Vietnam veterans continue to struggle with such legacies of the war as unemployment, homelessness, and mental illness, Americans have more widely addressed the need to welcome vets back into the fold of society. A national monument erected in Washington, D.C., along with numerous parades and other events, have publicly acknowledged the sacrifice of American soldiers in Vietnam.

- **1971:** Vietnam is the first ''televised war,'' and the first in which the press operates practically free of external restraints. Television makes Vietnam more vivid to the American public—it is dubbed ''the living room war''—with the result that it serves to fuel the growing opposition to the war.

  Today: War, along with seemingly every other aspect of human existence, is ever-more rigorously documented by television and the other media. The Cable News Network (CNN) sets new standards with their close coverage of the war in the Persian Gulf. Americans are thrilled by images of missile attacks and other high-tech military gadgetry; the media coverage fosters American public support for the war.

- **1971:** The Vietnam war remains for the most part unaddressed in American literature, drama, and film; the topic is widely considered, as Barbara Hurrell wrote, ''box office poison.''

  Today: Works like Rabe's *Pavlo Hummel* have created an opportunity for other writers and artists to address the war seriously and insightfully. A much wider body of art concerning the American experience in Vietnam has come into being in the last twenty-five years. Some of these works—like the films *The Deer Hunter, Coming Home, Apocalypse Now,* and *Platoon*—are widely considered American classics.

- **1971:** Defense Department analyst Daniel Ellsberg releases the ''Pentagon Papers'' to the press, documenting the decisions which led the U.S. into the Vietnam quagmire. The publication of these secret papers fuels further protest against American involvement in Vietnam.

  Today: While support for the U.S. military has not necessarily decreased, a larger portion of the American people believe in their right to know more about the actions of their government.

---

relations with that communist government), the North Vietnamese began to fear the possibility of an Indochina deal being made behind their back. China, however, hastened to state publicly that there was no question of its seeking a deal with the United States.

The Soviet Union, meanwhile, surpassed the United States as the global superpower, self-confidently increasing its military strength and political influence throughout the world (for example, signing new treaties with Egypt and India). America's belief in its need or ability to fulfill a global military role had been declining since it first realized it was unlikely to win the Vietnam war. This, combined with continuing domestic problems, resulted in a snowballing loss of national willpower.

At home in the United States, meanwhile, 1971 was a year of both success and failure for the peace movement. Peace leaders stressed that despite the withdrawal of American troops, the geographic scope of the Vietnam struggle had enlarged. American casualties might be replaced by South Vietnamese ones, they argued, but this fact did not alter the inherent immorality of the war. Two hundred thousand demonstrators attended an anti-war rally at the Capitol in Washington, D.C., while 156,000 people gathered for a similar demonstration in San Francisco. Additional groups continued to join the anti-war coalition, but the movement remained divided over strategy, with a split between those who simply protested U.S. participation in Vietnam and mainline peace organizations with a more inclusively pacifist strategy.

American society was rocked in 1971 by the actions of Daniel Ellsberg, a Defense Department analyst and consultant who had gradually changed his mind about the war while witnessing the failure of the "pacification" program in the Vietnamese countryside. Ellsberg released to the press a collection of "Pentagon Papers" documenting the decisions which led the U.S. into the Vietnam quagmire. As a result, he was indicted by a federal grand jury for unauthorized possession of national documents and later for the more serious charges of theft of government property and conspiracy. Publication of the documents, and news coverage of Ellsberg's case, fueled further protest against American involvement in Vietnam.

CRITICAL OVERVIEW

Reviews of *The Basic Training of Pavlo Hummel* upon its opening were largely enthusiastic, commenting on both the play's artistry and Rabe's promise as an up and coming playwright. Edith Oliver, reviewing the play for the *New Yorker,* called it "an astonishing accomplishment." Clive Barnes of the *New York Times* acclaimed Rabe as a "new and authentic voice of our theatre." Similarly, George Oppenheimer of *Newsday* highlighted Rabe's "new and striking talent." Henry Hewes, summing up the 1971 theatrical season for the *Saturday Review,* called Rabe "possibly the most promising playwright" of the year. "[I]mmensely gifted" is how Charles Michener described Rabe in a *Newsweek* article.

Pavlo Hummel has continued, since its initial production, to captivate many critics. In a 1982 article for the *New York Times,* Mel Gussow referred to the play as "searing." Philip Kolin, in his book *David Rabe: A Stage History and a Primary and Secondary Bibliography,* observed: "As long as the spectre of Vietnam haunts us so will *Pavlo.*"

Pavlo Hummel, however, has had its detractors. Walter Kerr's review for the *New York Times* was decidedly mixed, finding both promise and disappointment in the play. Rabe's work, he wrote, "is like a current of air on a very hot night that teases us and then goes away. It lacks a discovery." Stanley Kauffmann found little significance in *Pavlo Hummel,* calling it "one more good-hearted sentimental undergraduate play about the horrors of war . . . using stale expressionist fantasy and even staler rhetoric." To Kauffmann, the praise Rabe received was endemic of "professional yea-saying by theater critics" who lack "rigorous" judgment and refuse to write anything critical of the American theatre. Richard Homan was among critics who found that Rabe's "collage" technique merely renders characters as stereotypes or personifications; he called Rabe's treatment of his theme in *Pavlo Hummel* "crude." Similarly, Richard Watts of the *New York Post* found Rabe's title character a "ridiculous" creation and observed that "I felt Pavlo never really developed as a character."

Although critics differ in their assessments of the effectiveness of Rabe's dramatic technique, they are in stronger agreement that *Pavlo Hummel* was one of the first works of real significance regarding the American experience in Vietnam. Oliver wrote that Rabe's play "makes everything else I've seen on the subject seem skimpy and slightly false." *Newsweek*'s Jack Kroll found *Pavlo Hummel* "the first play to deal successfully with the Vietnam War and the contemporary American army." Harold Clurman, writing in the *Nation,* referred to other theatrical portrayals of Vietnam as "commonplace," with their "sham stage hyperbole," but found that in *Pavlo Hummel* "the sense of real men at war is present." He commented: "It is the first play provoked by the Vietnam disaster which has made a real impression on me." Not finding Rabe's treatment as genuine as did Clurman, *Time*'s Horace Judson, somewhat enigmatically, called the play "an antiwar cartoon, but a good one." Writing in his book *Uneasy Stages: A Chronicle of the New York Theatre, 1963-73,* John Simon found *Pavlo Hummel* "the best play about the war so far," but also criticized it, stating that it "often manages to stretch beyond the breaking point."

Pavlo Hummel, along with Rabe's other Vietnam plays, marked a transition from a time when the subject of Vietnam was, as Barbara Hurrell wrote, ''considered box office poison.'' The success of Rabe's early plays considerably opened up the possibility for other writers and artists to treat seriously the painful experience of the Vietnam war. To Hurrell, however, much of the treatment of Vietnam appeared superficial; she observed that ''it is not clear that the times are entirely receptive to such penetrating artistic inquiries as Rabe's trilogy.'' From Rabe's writing on Vietnam there is much to learn, Hurrell believed. The ''shadows'' cast by Rabe's characters, she commented, ''are reminiscent of the plight of the nation itself, which in a self-destructive momentum devoid of acceptable goals, was embroiled in a war many did not accept as necessary, under conditions many did not accept as real.''

Not surprisingly, critics of Rabe's work have continued to focus their attention primarily on the lingering effect his plays have had upon American perceptions of the Vietnam experience. Beidler found that in Rabe's ''trilogy'' of Vietnam plays, ''the principle of bring the war home evolved into a central thematic issue.'' The play brings home the Vietnam conflict ''in the fullness of its commingled banality and terrifying waste.'' On this bewildering ''landscape of death'' Pavlo's basic training serves as existential metaphor; it is ''the means whereby he learns, as the author notes, 'only that he is lost, now how, why, or even where.''' In his Vietnam plays, Richard Homan wrote, ''Rabe chooses a situation in which the horror of violence can be juxtaposed with the assumptions of everyday life. In the first two plays he tends to personify normal life in his civilian characters and the horror in his military characters with a resulting sense of ridicule toward both.'' Homan concluded that Rabe's Vietnam trilogy ''illustrates that violence on a personal scale, or on a national scale through military involvement, is a way of evading what troubles us most.''

Many critics have been pleased by the seeming absence of a strong ideological slant in Rabe's Vietnam plays. Catharine Hughes commented in *Plays, Politics, and Polemics* that ''unlike most of those who have written antiwar plays, Rabe refuses to grind the axe, to present pure victims and pure monsters.'' Rather than appearing as anti-war propaganda, Rabe's plays seem to critics to be true to experience. Michener wrote in *Newsweek* that experience, ''not ideology, is clearly the motherlode for Rabe's writing. Faithfulness to experience is what gives his plays their bite—and their comic edge.'' Rabe has said that ''I felt at the time that his rage and the rage of a lot of vets was such that they couldn't just come back and explain it; you had to make an experience of it somehow.''

CRITICISM

Christopher G. Busiel

Busiel is a Ph.D. candidate at the University of Texas, Austin, specializing in modern drama and theatre. In this essay he discusses Rabe's play in the context of differing conceptions of what constitutes an ''antiwar'' play.

Although *The Basic Training of Pavlo Hummel* dramatizes the senseless death of a young man in Vietnam, David Rabe has emphasized repeatedly that he did not intend his play to be received as an ''antiwar'' work. Certainly, the play is critical of the reasons that countries engage in wars and that young men go to fight in them. Pavlo's enthusiasm for the military is drawn strongly into question, as Ardell forces him at the play's conclusion to confront the reason for his death:

ARDELL: You tell it to me: what you think of the cause? What you think a gettin' your ass blown clean off a freedom's frontier? What you think a bein' R.A. Regular Army lifer?
PAVLO: (*softly, with nearly embarrassed laughter*) Sheeeeee . . . ittttt. . . . Oh, lord . . . oh . . .
ARDELL: Ain't it what happened to you? Lemme hear it.
PAVLO: Shit!
ARDELL: And what you think a' all the ''folks back home,'' sayin' you a victim . . . you a' animal . . . you a' fool?. . .
PAVLO: They shit!

This is strong commentary, punctuated by Ardell slamming shut the lid of Pavlo's coffin. Significantly, though, Pavlo scorns not just ''the cause'' and the enthusiasm with which he (and many other young soldiers) went off to Vietnam but also the ''folks back home'' who might view Pavlo as a victim of American involvement in the war. This complex perspective is true to Rabe's own definition of *Pavlo Hummel* as something other than an antiwar play. The distinction for Rabe rests not so much on content as the intended result of a play, or any other work of art. Rabe has written in his introduction to *Two Plays* that ''in my estimation,

WHAT DO I READ NEXT?

- Herr, Michael. *Dispatches* (1977). A highly personal, dramatic narrative, written by a journalist who was sent to Vietnam with the assignment of writing a monthly column from there. Eric Schroeder, in his book of interviews with American writers, *Vietnam, We've All Been There,* called it "the best book written about Vietnam."
- Rabe's *Sticks and Bones* (1971), which focuses on the painful homecoming of David, a blinded and embittered Vietnam veteran. David's family is unable to sympathize with his experience, a symbolic presentation by Rabe of American society's refusal to acknowledge the horrors of the war.
- Rabe's *Streamers* (1976), considered by many critics to be Rabe's most accomplished play. It is often grouped together with Rabe's *Pavlo Hummel* and *Sticks and Bones* as his "Vietnam Trilogy." The entire play takes place in an army barracks where troops await transport to Vietnam. Three soldiers—two white, one black—have an uneasy camaraderie which is disrupted by the intrusion of a embittered black soldier, leading to the eruption of violence.
- Eric Schroeder's *Vietnam, We've All Been There: Interviews with American Writers* (1992) takes its title from Michael Herr's *Dispatches,* highlighting how the Vietnam war, as Schroeder writes, "refused to remain a foreign conflict in a strange country far away; it came home in ways that we're still trying to work out." Included in the text, along with the chapter "David Rabe: 'A Harrowing Audience Experience,'" are interviews with novelists Norman Mailer and Robert Stone, poet Bruce Weigl, journalist/authors like John Sack, and others.

---

an 'antiwar' play is one that expects, by the very fabric of its executed conception, to have political effect."

Rabe not only rejects the idea that he intended his early Vietnam plays to have a political effect but more generally denies such a possibility for the theatre: "to think a play can have immediate, large-scale political effect is to overestimate vastly the powers that plays have." To Rabe, classifying his early plays as "antiwar" would serve only to narrow their impact to "the thin line of political tract," and thereby diminish their richness. Rabe believes that war is inevitably a permanent part of what he calls the "eternal human pageant," along with such elements as family, marriage, youth, and crime; therefore, the subject of war can (and should) be treated with as complex a perspective as these other topics. "A play in which a family looks bad," Rabe explains, "is not called an 'antifamily' play."

When *Pavlo Hummel* premiered in 1971, the subject of Vietnam was, as Barbara Hurrell wrote in the *Journal of American Culture,* "considered box office poison." (Even two years later, after the tremendous success of Rabe's first two plays, CBS withdrew its support for the broadcast of a television version of Rabe's *Sticks and Bones,* fearing that audiences would find it offensive.) Writing about Vietnam was still largely the realm of the journalist, as Robert Asahina observed in *Theatre:* "In the light of this apparent success of journalism in spearheading opposition to the war by making it 'more vivid' to the American public, it is scarcely surprising that conventional playwrights should have remained virtually silent about Vietnam."

When the American theatre did address the war, as in the Open Theatre presentation *Viet Rock,* it tended to be by "empt[ying] the stage of its literary content" (Asahina) in experimental, non-representational, and highly polemical productions. Rabe almost single-handedly broke this mold, opening up the possibility both for more complex treatments of Vietnam in the conventional theatre, and more broadly, for other writers and artists to treat seriously the painful experience of the Vietnam war. The Vietnam-themed film work of writer/director Oliver Stone (*Platoon, Born on the Fourth of July*) hardly seems possible without Rabe's innovations.

In the context of the American theatre's treatment of Vietnam , most critics found *Pavlo Hummel* astonishing, the first work of real significance regarding the American experience of the war. Harold Clurman, writing in the *Nation,* referred to other theatrical portrayals of Vietnam as ''commonplace,'' with their ''sham stage hyperbole,'' but he found that in *Pavlo Hummel* ''the sense of real men at war is present.'' Clurman commented: ''It is the first play provoked by the Vietnam disaster which has made a real impression on me.'' In the *New Yorker,* Edith Oliver wrote that Rabe's play ''makes everything else I've seen on the subject seem skimpy and slightly false.'' *Newsweek*'s Jack Kroll found *Pavlo Hummel* ''the first play to deal successfully with the Vietnam War and the contemporary American army.''

While critics seemingly responded merely to the literary quality of Rabe's writing, the praise they heaped upon *Pavlo Hummel* nevertheless had political implications. In praising Rabe's play, the critics simultaneously rejected other theatrical treatments of Vietnam, specifically the more polemical, ''antiwar,'' productions based on a belief that theatre *can* effect political change, or at least significantly alter political consciousness. Pleased by the seeming absence of a strong ideological slant in Rabe's Vietnam plays, Catharine Hughes commented in *Plays, Politics, and Polemics* that ''unlike most of those who have written antiwar plays, Rabe refuses to grind the axe, to present pure victims and pure monsters.''

The complexity of this perspective rests on the enigmatic character of Pavlo, who on the one hand accepts what he has been told about Vietnam (responding to the question ''Soldier, what you think a the war?'' with the simple reply: ''It's being fought''), but on the other expresses a personal enthusiasm for his participation, which does not allow audiences to see him as a misled victim. ''I'm diggin' it, man,'' he brags. ''Blowin' people away. Cuttin' 'em down. . . . It ain't no big thing.''

Again, Rabe's rejection of the idea of an ''antiwar'' play stems from a lack of faith in theatre's ability to affect the course of society. He commented in an interview in *Vietnam, We've All Been There: Interviews with American Writers,* ''The theater's expertise is not developed like the machinery of the media and the facility to use it. You just don't have the access—your ideas just don't reach the same numbers of people. The tremendous amount of skill and brainpower that goes into advertising, and governmental advertising, is so huge that a play barely makes a bubble.'' But by reaching a mainstream audience in a well-respected off-Broadway theatre, Rabe certainly made a ''bubble'' larger than that made by the more experimental and polemical Vietnam productions. Rabe has allowed the label ''confrontational'' to be applied to his plays, and if they are not ''antiwar'' in a strict sense, they nevertheless forced audiences to confront a war far from home and remote in thought. In short, Rabe can be credited with ''bringing the war home'' to a sizable audience. Indeed, as Philip Beidler wrote of Rabe's ''trilogy'' of Vietnam plays in *American Literature and the Experience of Vietnam,* ''the principle of bring the war home evolved into a central thematic issue.''Rabe has recounted the need for this kind of intervention, drawing from his own personal experience. ''Like Pavlo,'' he observed in *Vietnam, We've All Been There,* ''at the time I was drafted, unless you were fairly politically astute, there was no war.'' In *Pavlo Hummel,* this perspective may be presented most clearly in Mickey, who taunts Pavlo, ''Vietnam don't even exist.'' Upon his return from Vietnam, Rabe discovered a ''tremendous indifference at home'' that changed his entire perspective, forcing him ''to view the whole thing as decadent, really corrupt.'' Another kind of awareness about Vietnam, equally disturbing to Rabe, was that of the politically active war protester.

As he told Robert Berkvist in the *New York Times,* ''people kept trying to tell me what the war was about—they were the ones interested in debating the war but who didn't want to hear about the war itself. They weren't interested in any kind of evidence of, say, a Vietcong atrocity.'' In *Vietnam, We've All Been There,* Rabe commented that he ''was against the war ultimately, but I was never comfortable with the antiwar movement.'' Thus, Rabe's writing on Vietnam trod a careful line, forcing audiences to confront the tragedy of a war to which many had not yet faced but challenging the politically aware to adopt a more complex perspective on America's involvement in Vietnam.

Rabe told Berkvist, ''All I'm trying to do is *define the event* for myself and for other people. I'm saying, in effect, 'This is what goes on,' and that's all.'' Certainly, Rabe's Vietnam plays served a very personal end, as writing did for so many Vietnam veterans, allowing them a means to address the repressed trauma of their experience. Rabe attempted to keep a journal during his military service in Vietnam but found that his experience there defied description, exceeding the capabilities of ''language as mere symbol.'' He observed in *Vietnam, We've All Been There,* ''you knew you were not going to get it; it was larger and bloodier than anything you were going to put down.'' To Rabe, this inability to represent in a realistic manner the full experience of Vietnam nullified the value of certain types of writing. Rabe has said that ''I felt at the time that . . . the rage of a lot of vets was such that they couldn't just come back and explain it; you had to make an experience of it somehow.''

Theatre, by its very nature a tangible, shared experience among performers and an audience, proved to be for Rabe the appropriate art form. He created in *The Basic Training of Pavlo Hummel* a theatrical event audiences and critics found truer to experience than the polemical ''antiwar'' plays which had preceded it. Rabe's play, therefore, might have lacked a kind of political impact, but it made a different kind of impact through the perspective with which he addressed the experience and complex psychology of a soldier killed in Vietnam. The complexity of his first play ensured that years later, *Pavlo Hummel,* unlike *Viet Rock* and other works of the Vietnam era, has not faded from public memory. The play remains not just a significant work of the contemporary American theatre but specifically an enduring and complex examination of an unpopular war, the legacy of which still haunts American society.

Source: Christopher G. Busiel, for *Drama for Students,* Gale, 1998.

Phillip D. Beidler

Beidler discusses Rabe's ''Vietnam Trilogy'' (which also includes the plays Sticks and Bones *and* Streamers*) calling* The Basic Training of Pavel Hummel *''a mad pastiche of the American experience in Vietnam.'' The critic terms Rabe's contributions vital to literature concerning Vietnam.*

In the most important contributions to the dramatic literature of Vietnam during the period 1970–75—David Rabe's *The Basic Training of Pavlo Hummel* and *Sticks and Bones,* the first two plays in what,

"RABE NOT ONLY REJECTS THE IDEA THAT HE INTENDED HIS EARLY VIETNAM PLAYS TO HAVE A POLITICAL EFFECT BUT MORE GENERALLY DENIES SUCH A POSSIBILITY FOR THE THEATRE"

with the addition of *Streamers* in 1977, would become a major trilogy—the principle of bringing the war home evolved into a central thematic issue. Similarly . . . , the attempt to explore the effects of Vietnam on actual American life would also come to suggest the degree to which the war's horror had been implicit in the American character from the outset, a collective tragedy waiting to happen, a prophetic curse hiding at the heart of a whole mythology of culture.The range and ambition of Rabe's endeavors are suggested in the two plays by the large formal challenges he poses for himself. In both *The Basic Training of Pavlo Hummel* and *Sticks and Bones,* he deals in visions of pure hackneyed Americana, opts for the mode of the almost oppressively quotidian and familiar. In the first, he works (as he will again in *Streamers*) the old American ground of boot camp and barracks, the world of *See Here, Private Hargrove* and *Sands of Iwo Jima* and *No Time for Sergeants,* and later on of Ernie Bilko and even Beetle Bailey. In the second, his broad-ranging debts to domestic and popular lore are equally evident. The blinded veteran, David, returns to his family, including Ozzie the father, Harriet the mother, and Rick the younger brother, who hops about with a snapshot camera and asks plenty of vaguely cute, witless questions. At issue in these plays, then, is not only the experience of Vietnam but also the nature of what passes for reality in America, and how the war is precisely the function of a culture holding fast, against a whole accumulation of geopolitical evidence to the contrary, to a sentimental, even banal complacency in some idiot sense of its own goodness and right.

The size of the risk is repaid again and again by the enduring quality of the accomplishment. *Pavlo Hummel* and *Sticks and Bones* bring the war home in all the immediacy of spectacle and even affront that modern drama in its greatest strength can

Pavlo with Yen (Tisa Chang) in the brothel where he will meet his doom

produce. In these plays, like a sore or a boil or an encysted anger that can no longer be kept in, Vietnam spills its hot burden across the whole reach of our collective existence as a people.

Pavlo Hummel is a mad, inexhaustible pastiche of the American experience of Vietnam in the fullness of its commingled banality and terrifying waste. It is a collection of master images. The play opens with Pavlo in a Saigon bar, stinking, foul-mouthed, high-school drunk. . . . Then, like all drunks feeling sorry for themselves in a strange place, he begins to tell the usual sad story, sloppy, stumbling persiflage about lost love and other confidings. . . . Appropriately, just as he has begun to spill his guts in a figurative sense, a grenade is thrown into the bar. Pavlo gets his real chance. In an enactment of the worst fear of every GI in the war, he wakes up dead. . . . (pp. 112–14)

Afoot on the landscape of death, and accompanied by Ardell, the black comrade who serves as his slangy, irreverent GI Virgil, he now voyages in retrospect through the last stage of the American life that has eventually brought him to his moment of second-rate apotheosis. With him, we get to see the basic training as the *basic* training of Pavlo Hummel, the means whereby he learns, as the author notes, "only that he is lost, not how, why, or even where." If he has time to work up a talent, it is only the one he already has "for leaping into the fire."...

Source: Phillip D. Beidler, "In the Middle Range, 1970–75" in his *American Literature and the Experience of Vietnam,* University of Georgia Press, 1982, pp. 85–136.

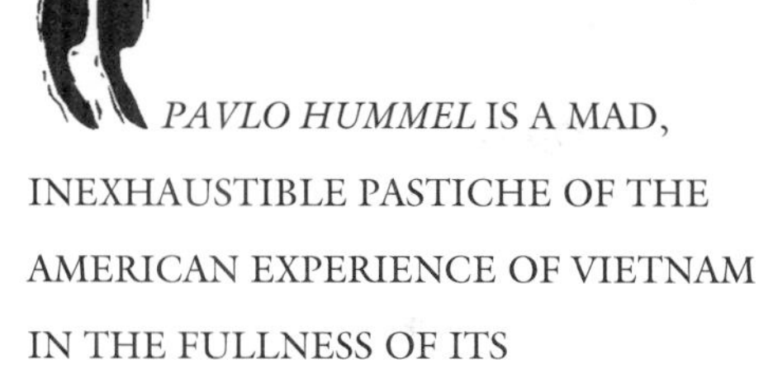

"*PAVLO HUMMEL* IS A MAD, INEXHAUSTIBLE PASTICHE OF THE AMERICAN EXPERIENCE OF VIETNAM IN THE FULLNESS OF ITS COMMINGLED BANALITY AND TERRIFYING WASTE."

Henry Hewes

In this review of the play's original production, Hewes praises The Basic Training of Pavel Hummel *as an "impressively authentic" piece of theatre.*

At the Public's Newman Theatre, *The Basic Training of Pavlo Hummel* has been given a superb production by director Jeff Bleckner and a disciplined cast headed by William Atherton in the title role. The play is little more than a story told in flashbacks, in which we see Pavlo's basic training and his career in Vietnam. Although it tells us very little about Vietnam, it paints an impressively accurate picture of the military life and its pathetic waste of men and boys. The basic-training phase of the action features a jazzy first sergeant, nicely played by Joe Fields, who catches the ironic humor of an experienced soldier having fun dehumanizing recruits into reasonably efficient dogs with the conditioned reflexes that give them a chance for survival in a shooting war.

A second irony in the play is that Pavlo does survive the shooting, but eventually loses his life in a brothel. Here Pavlo encounters another soldier with the girl he wants, and instead of waiting his turn viciously attacks and humiliates his rival. The soldier responds by throwing a grenade into the brothel. There is a flaw in all this, because we are not able to connect Pavlo's sudden sadistic behavior with his Army experience. And although the play includes a chorus character, the significance of the action, beyond a vague suggestion that war is a tragedy of meaningless accidents, fails to emerge. On the other hand, it might have required a wrenching of the material to make this important point clearer. And to wrench the material could have poisoned the honesty of this impressively authentic new play.

Source: Henry Hewes, review of *The Basic Training of Pavel Hummel* in *Saturday Review,* Volume LIV, no. 28, July 10, 1971 , p. 36.

Harold Clurman

Clurman reviews The Basic Training of Pavel Hummel*'s original production, finding the work a stirring representation of the war in Vietnam. Beyond terming the play as "good" or "bad," the critic praised Rabe's work for creating a vivid impression of the horror of the war.*

I understood little more than half of what was spoken or shouted by the actors in David Rabe's, *The Basic Training of Pavlo Hummel* (Public Theater). But though I gathered the impression that much of its text was well written, I was not troubled by missing so many of its lines. The pace had to be hectic, the scenes had to overlap, the sounds needed to be raucous: here was inferno.

It is supposedly a simple matter to write or stage a play depicting the horrors of war. That is not so. People screaming in agony, bodies flung about, wounds inflicted, harsh words yapped, ruthless cruelty on all sides nearly always become commonplace and boring in the usual anti-war play or picture. They are piteous preachments thundered at us in sham stage hyperbole; we do not believe them. This is not the case with *Pavlo Hummel.* The staging is largely stylized (without artiness), the gunfire is not deafening, no blood spurts out from the injured, but the sense of real men at war is present. We come to know the human abjectness of it all. It is haunting in its personal challenge.

Pavlo Hummel is a dumb kid who doesn't wish to go to war but once there he wants to fight it "like a man." He prefers combat duty to work as a hospital orderly. He's a fool, almost crackers, an amalgam of the innocent vices and stupid virtues of the universal unknown GI. He's good-natured and atrocious. Around him are the other clumps of recognizable humanity, reduced to the point where they lose any identity except that of soldiers, food for slaughter, self-killers, ridiculous and terrible, victims who are also venomous. War makes them

"*PAVLO HUMMEL* IS THE FIRST PLAY PROVOKED BY THE VIETNAMESE DISASTER WHICH HAS MADE A REAL IMPRESSION ON ME. —HAROLD CLURMAN"

so; they are totally immersed in a "planet" where everything has turned to filth.

The First Sergeant bellows a spiel of oaths and exhortations which are projected like bullets: they cause laughter and hurt. The phantomlike enemy is fierce and unfathomable. The savagery of "our" men is visited upon one another almost as much as on those of the opposite side. At the end of the play it is a shock and yet no surprise when we see that Pavlo Hummel has not been killed by an enemy raid but by a drunken U.S. sergeant who vied with Hummel over a girl inmate of a cat-house. The murder has nothing to do with the issues of the war, but much to do with war itself.

Is then *The Basic Training of Pavlo Hummel* a "good" play? The answer hardly concerned me. It strikes home as very few "better" plays do. It is the first play provoked by the Vietnamese disaster which has made a real impression on me. The author, David Rabe, was there, and we are there with him. The large cast—notably William Atherton, Joe Fields, Albert Hall, Lee Wallace, Bob Legall—is excellent throughout in type and performance, and the direction by Jeff Bleckner has the right overall sweep and smash and is often truly felt in detail. The setting by David Mitchell solves a knotty scenic problem with forceful simplicity.

Source: Harold Clurman, review of *The Basic Training of Pavel Hummel* in the *Nation,* Volume 212, no. 23, June 7, 1971 , p. 73.

SOURCES

Barnes, Clive. Review of *Pavlo Hummel* in the *New York Times,* May 21, 1971, p. 25.

Berkvist, Robert. "If You Kill Somebody . . ." in the *New York Times,* December 12, 1971, sec. 2, p. 3.

Clurman, Harold. Review of *Pavlo Hummel* in the *Nation,* Vol. 212, June 7, 1971, p. 733.

Geis, Deborah. "'Fighting to Get Down, Thinking It Was Up': A Narratological Reading of *The Basic Training of Pavlo Hummel*'" in *David Rabe: A Casebook,* edited by Toby Silverman Zinman, Garland (New York), 1991, pp. 71-83.

Hewes, Henry. "Taps for Lenny Bruce" in the *Saturday Review,* July 10, 1971, p. 36.

Homan, Richard L. "American Playwrights in the 1970s: Rabe and Shepard" in *Critical Quarterly,* Vol. 24, no. 1, 1982, pp. 73-82.

Hughes, Catharine. *Plays, Politics, and Polemics,* Drama Book Specialists (New York), 1973.

Judson, Horace. "Rags of Honor" in *Time,* April 24, 1972, p. 66.

Kauffmann, Stanley. "Sunshine Boys" in the *New Republic,* May 26, 1973, p. 22.

Kerr, Walter. "He Wonders Who He Is—So Do We" in the *New York Times,* May 30, 1971, sec. 2, p. 3.

Kroll, Jack. "This is the Army" in *Newsweek,* June 14, 1971, p. 70.

Marranca, Bonnie. "David Rabe's Vietnam Trilogy" in *Canadian Theatre Review,* Vol. 14, 1977, pp. 86-92.

Michener, Charles. "The Experience Thing" in *Newsweek,* December 20, 1971, p. 58.

Oliver, Edith. Review of *Pavlo Hummel* in the *New Yorker,* May 29, 1971, p. 55.

Oppenheimer, George. "Stage: Salute to Pavlo" in *Newsday,* May 21, 1971, p. A1.

Patterson, James A. "David Rabe" in the *Dictionary of Literary Biography* Volume 7: *Twentieth-Century American Dramatists,* edited by John MacNicholas, two parts, Gale (Detroit), 1981, pp. 172-78.

Rabe, David. Introduction to *Two Plays: The Basic Training of Pavlo Hummel and Sticks and Bones,* Viking (New York), 1973, pp. ix-xxv.

Schroeder, Eric. *Vietnam, We've All Been There: Interviews with American Writers,* Praeger (Westport, CT), 1992.

Silver, Lee. "*Pavlo Hummel* Opens at the Public/Newman" in the *New York Daily News,* May 21, 1971, p. 64.

Simon, John. *Uneasy Stages: A Chronicle of the New York Theatre, 1963-73,* Random House, 1975.

"Talk of the Town: Rabe" in the *New Yorker,* November 20, 1971, pp. 48-49.

Watts, Richard. "An Innocent in Vietnam" in the *New York Post,* May 21, 1971, p. 31.

Werner, Craig. "Primal Screams and Nonsense Rhymes: David Rabe's Revolt" in *Educational Theatre Journal,* Vol. 30, 1978, pp. 517-29.

FURTHER READING

Asahina, Robert. "The Basic Training of American Playwrights: Theater and the Vietnam War" in *Theatre,* Vol. 9, no. 2, Spring, 1978, pp. 30-47.

This article places Rabe's "Vietnam Trilogy" in the context of other dramatic works concerning Vietnam. Asahina feels that journalism controlled the public perception of the war and that dramatists of the era tended either to ignore it or to write strictly polemical plays against it. He examines how Rabe's "Vietnam Trilogy" broke with this pattern and dealt with the war in more complex, artistic terms.

Beidler, Philip D. *American Literature and the Experience of Vietnam,* University of Georgia Press (Athens), 1982.

Beidler states his study is "about the literary ways in which people have tried to talk about an experience called Vietnam." Like other historians and critics, Beidler's interest in the Vietnam War includes its deep effects upon American culture at home; speaking of the soldiers who served there he says, "Ineluctably theirs, the experience of Vietnam would have to become ours." Finding that in Rabe's "trilogy" of Vietnam plays, "the principle of bring the war home evolved into a central thematic issue," Beidler calls Rabe's first two plays "the most important contributions to the dramatic literature of Vietnam during the period 1970-75."

Contemporary Literary Criticism, Gale, Vol. 4, 1975; Volume 8, 1978; Volume 33, 1985.

This resource compiles selections of criticism; it is an excellent beginning point for a research paper about Rabe. The selections in these three volumes cover much of Rabe's playwriting career with material on *Pavlo Hummel* contained in each of them.

Gilman, Owen W., Jr., Editor. *America Rediscovered: Critical Essays on Literature and Film of the Vietnam War,* Garland (New York), 1990.

The essays in this collection, rather than focusing on individual authors, treat in depth a specific topic concerning literature and film of Vietnam. The essays include J. T. Hansen's "The Helicopter and the Punji Stick: Central Symbols of the Vietnam War," Marilyn Durham's "A Dual Perspective: First-Person Narrative in Vietnam Film and Drama," and David J. DeRose's "Vietnam and Sexual Violence: The Movie."

Hurrell, Barbara. "American Self-Image in David Rabe's Vietnam Trilogy" in the *Journal of American Culture,* Vol. 4, 1981, pp. 95-107.

Hurrell stresses the importance of Rabe's early work in bringing the Vietnam war home to American audiences, making the subject of the war a legitimate one for writers and artists. She highlights the transformational role of Rabe's own Vietnam experience, for while his upbringing in Iowa "shaped Rabe's basic images of America, his experience in Vietnam added the other ingredients necessary to fuel the creative force behind the Vietnam plays he later produced." Hurrell finds in all three of Rabe's Vietnam plays "exposition of the gulf between the self and the other as represented in the Vietnam conflict."

Kolin, Philip C. *David Rabe: A Stage History and a Primary and Secondary Bibliography,* Garland (New York), 1988.

This minutely detailed resource contains a biography of Rabe and a stage history of his plays. It also lists more than 1300 writings by and about Rabe, with evaluative annotations of many of them. The stage history of *Pavlo Hummel* is discussed on pp. 43-51.

Zinman, Toby Silverman, Editor. *David Rabe: A Casebook,* Garland (New York), 1991.

Contains a 1990 interview with Rabe and numerous other sources, including Deborah Geis's article "'Fighting to Get Down, Thinking It Was Up': A Narratological Reading of *The Basic Training of Pavlo Hummel.* "

Other Sources on the Vietnam War:

Hundreds of book-length studies have been written about various aspects of America's involvement in the Vietnam War. General studies include Maurice Isserman's *The Vietnam War* (Facts on File, 1992), John Devaney's *The Vietnam War* (F. Watts, 1992), Ray Bonds's *The Vietnam War: The Illustrated History of the Conflict in Southeast Asia* (Crown, 1983), and Kathlyn Gay's *Vietnam War* (Twenty-First Century Books, 1996). Many books focus on the perspectives of individual soldiers who served in Vietnam, such as Kim Wilenson's *The Bad War: An Oral History of the Vietnam War* (American Library, 1987), Al Santoli's *Everything We Had: An Oral History of the Vietnam War, by Thirty-Three American Soldiers Who Fought It* (Random House, 1981), and Kathryn Marshall's *In the Combat Zone: Vivid Personal Recollections of the Vietnam War from the Women Who Served There* (Penguin, 1988). Many of the book studies, like Rabe's *Sticks and Bones,* focus on the pain many American soldiers experienced during readjustment to home life; these include Steve Trimm's *Walking Wounded: Men's Lives during and since the Vietnam War* (Ablex, 1993) and Richard Severo's *The Wages of War: When America's Soldiers Came Home, from Valley Forge to Vietnam* (Simon & Schuster, 1989). Other specialized studies include Daniel C. Hallin's *The "Uncensored War": The Media and Vietnam* (Oxford University Press, 1986), Andrew Martin's *Receptions of War: Vietnam in American Culture* (University of Oklahoma Press, 1993), and Wallace Terry's *Bloods: An Oral History of the Vietnam War, by Black Veterans* (Random House, 1984). In 1985, an international team of journalists and media professionals produced *Vietnam, a Television History,* a thirteen-part documentary on America's involvement in Vietnam. It is widely available in libraries.

Blood Relations

SHARON POLLOCK

1980

Blood Relations was first produced in 1980 at Theatre 3 in Edmonton, Alberta, Canada. This was not the play's first appearance on stage, however, as Sharon Pollock often extensively revises her plays, even after the first couple of productions. The previous version was produced as *My Name Is Lisabeth* in 1976 at Douglas College with Pollock herself playing the role of Lizzie Borden. After significant revision, she renamed the play *Blood Relations* and staged it as a new work in 1980.

The play is based on historical fact: the 1892 double murder of Lizzie Borden's father and stepmother, a crime for which Lizzie herself was charged. The crime shocked the Massachusetts community of Fall River, as well as the whole nation, and citizens read with fascination reports of the trial. Lizzie was acquitted but the crime was never solved, and her innocence was questioned by the public. In contemporary times, the figure of Lizzie Borden has achieved iconic status. Many perceive her as an early feminist who did not shy from acting and thinking as an individual. It has often been theorized that, if Lizzie did in fact commit the murders, her actions were based on self-preservation, an attempt to escape from an abusive family situation.

Some reviewers of *Blood Relations* challenged Pollock for writing a work that failed to adequately confront feminist concerns, instead choosing to direct the play towards a more general political agenda. Pollock's work appears to be ''more involved with studies of oppression in general and political processes in particular than . . . in specific struggles of women,'' said S. R. Gilbert in *Contemporary Dramatists.*

Blood Relations was the first full-length play Pollock produced. A published version of it, released in 1981, won her the Governor General's Award, the first time such an award was made for a piece of dramatic literature.

Controversy often followed *Blood Relations,* specifically in 1982 and 1983, when Pollock sued a television station for damage to her literary reputation when it decided to drop her play and develop its own script. The case was settled out of court.

AUTHOR BIOGRAPHY

Sharon Pollock was born on April 19, 1936, in Fredericton, New Brunswick, Canada. Named Mary Sharon Chambers, she was the daughter of a physician and politician. Her mother died when she was sixteen, evidently a suicide. She studied at the University of New Brunswick but dropped out to marry Ross Pollock, a Toronto insurance broker, with whom she had five children before the marriage ended.

Pollock then became involved in theatre in New Brunswick and later moved on to Calgary, Canada. In 1971, after having worked as an actress, she began to write plays. Her first work to be staged was *Walsh,* which was produced in 1973. The play examines the Canadian government's treatment of Native North Americans. Like *Walsh,* her subsequent work often deals with political themes. *The Komagata Maru Incident,* which was first produced in 1976, addresses the issue of racism.

Blood Relations was first produced in 1980 (although an early version of the play was produced in 1976 under the title *My Name Is Lisabeth*) and signaled a shift in Pollock's drama towards the individual as seen in family and social relationships. The play earned Pollock a Governor General's Literary Award, the first time a published dramatic work received such an honor. A second Governor General's Award came to Pollock for *Doc,* produced in 1984. This play later evolved into *Family Trappings* and is based on autobiographical material about Pollock's family. Other productions of Pollock's work include *Fair Liberty's Call,* which premiered at the Stratford Festival in 1993, and *Saucy Jack,* performed first at the Garry Theatre in Calgary, where she is founder and artistic director.

Pollock's other literary honors include the Canada Australia Literary Award (1987) for her body of work, the ACTRA Nellie Drama Award for National Radio, and a Golden Sheaf Award for writing for television.

Pollock has not limited her activity solely to creating her dramas; she has taught playwriting at a number of Canadian universities and has worked as a director. She has been chairperson of the Advisory Arts Panel of Canada Council, headed the Playwright's Colony at the Banff Centre for Fine Arts, and has been associate director for both the Stratford Festival Theatre and the Manitoba Theatre Centre. In addition to the contemporary stage, she has written for radio and television. She has also written numerous dramatic works for children.

PLOT SUMMARY

Act I

The play opens on a late Sunday afternoon in the parlor of the Borden house in 1902, in Fall River, Massachusetts. Miss Lizzie enters with tea for the Actress, who protests she doesn't like the tea and toast routine while Lizzie puzzles over the proper way to pour tea. Lizzie worries that Fall River is a little boring for the Actress. She says she is there to see Lizzie. She gives a report about how her rehearsals are going. She reports hearing children in the alley singing a little song about Lizzie killing her parents. Lizzie asks if she defended her. The Actress reports she closed the window. They put on a record and dance as the Actress tries to figure out if Miss Lizzie looks jowly, a comment made in news reports during the trial. The Actress complains that Lizzie never tells her anything, when Lizzie fails to respond to the question of whether she committed the crime or not.

Lizzie wonders aloud whether part of the Actress's success is due to her connection with an infamous accused murderess such as herself. The Actress bristles at this, but Lizzie says that, ten years after the events, people still talk about her and the crime. Lizzie complains that Emma keeps asking, ''did you?'' The Actress starts to imitate Emma, carrying on both sides of an imaginary conversation with Lizzie's older sister.

Sharon Pollock

The Actress says she wants to know the truth. Lizzie suggests they play a game in which the Actress will play Miss Lizzie and Lizzie will play Bridget, the maid the family had in 1892.

The action shifts to Lizzie's murder trial that took place ten years before. The Defense questions Lizzie as Bridget, and she describes the Borden family, including the visit of Harry, Mrs. Borden's brother. This recollection dissolves to another flashback to the Borden home. Harry has arrived, and it is clear that the purpose of his visit is money, either for himself or his sister, who is Mr. Borden's second wife. Lizzie had Harry thrown out the last time he visited. He wonders what Bridget is doing with bread crusts. She says they are for Lizzie's pigeons, and Harry says Lizzie prefers animals to people. The Actress, now playing Lizzie, appears and Harry slips off to split wood.

After Bridget reports a conversation between Mr. Borden and his brother-in-law, Lizzie calls Harry a stupid bugger, flustering Bridget with her foul language. Lizzie voices her concern that Harry is only visiting to connive more money out of her father. Emma appears, complaining of the noise that has kept her from sleep. Emma indicates she's heard Lizzie's bad language. Emma doesn't want to deal with the reality of the family farm, which is in financial ruin, or Harry's schemes to get more of their father's money. Lizzie tries to make her talk about it.

Mrs. Borden, the girls' stepmother, comes down for breakfast and questions Bridget about Harry's appearance and whether Lizzie knows he's here. She comes to the conclusion that Lizzie is really quite spoiled. There is obvious tension between Mrs. Borden and Lizzie revolving around Mr. Borden's money. Mr. Borden appears and they discuss Lizzie and a widower, Johnny MacLeod, who is interested in her. Her father pressures Emma to talk with Lizzie. She goes off in a huff, unwilling to be the family mediator and communicator.

The scene shifts to Dr. Patrick and Lizzie talking outdoors, where she flirts with him, inviting him to run off with her, although he is married. Harry passes by and tells Lizzie to come in for lunch, even though they have just finished breakfast.

The scene shifts and Bridget and Lizzie talk about the expectation that Lizzie should get married and have a home of her own. Meanwhile Harry reports to Mrs. Borden that Lizzie has been consorting with the doctor. Mrs. Borden and Harry gang up on Mr. Borden, saying he can't control his own daughter. Mr. Borden says he'll talk with her.

The scene returns to the courtroom, and Lizzie recalls how she never was quite good enough as a girl, supposing that she never got at birth that magic formula for being a woman. The Defense returns and questions whether Lizzie could have delivered the ax blows that killed her parents.

The scene switches to a conversation between Borden and Lizzie as he tries to persuade her to see the widower MacLeod. "He's looking for a housekeeper not a wife," Lizzie contends. Mrs. Borden joins in and they talk of Lizzie leaving the house and the dowry she'll receive if she marries. Mr. Borden slaps Lizzie. Her stepmother reminds her that she is financially dependent on her father and that she can't hope to inherit a third of his estate when he dies.

Harry and Mr. Borden talk, revealing Harry's business. He wants the fallow farm put in Mrs. Borden's name and leased to him. Harry will conduct horse auctions and have buggy rides on the property, giving Borden twenty percent. What they are unaware of is Lizzie's presence, and she confronts her father. Borden's anger erupts and he directs it at the pigeons Lizzie keeps. Taking the hatchet Harry has brought in from splitting wood, Borden smashes it into the table. Ax in hand, Borden says he is going to take care of the birds. The act ends back in the present with Lizzie saying she loved the pigeons.

Act II

The action returns to Lizzie and the Actress's re-enactment. It is the following day. Emma tells Lizzie she is going away for a few days. Lizzie accuses Emma of running away from things. Lizzie underscores the reality—Harry is getting the farm signed over to their stepmother and will be living there. They will be essentially cut out of their father's will, left to subsist on only a small allowance.

The scene returns to the courtroom. The Defense reappears and questions Lizzie about what happened on that day, and she recalls going for a walk, eating pears, coming back, finding her Papa dead, and calling for Bridget.

The scene shifts back to that day. Mrs. Borden comes down for breakfast and soon Mr. Borden joins the table. Harry pops in and gets an invitation to go to town with Borden. Lizzie, knowing they plan to sign papers in town, tries to persuade her father not to go.

The scenes fades to another talk between Dr. Patrick and Lizzie. Lizzie says she could die if she wanted. They walk, and she is going to show him her birds but the cage is empty She asks him whom he would save if he could only save one of two people dying from an accident. Then she asks if he met Attila the Hun and could kill him, would he? He says he would fight in a war but is uncomfortable with this line of questioning. She launches into an attack on her stepmother but she doesn't get the support she wants and accuses Patrick of being a coward.

The scene turns to Mrs. Borden and Lizzie, who talks about her father killing her birds with an ax. Mrs. Borden is uncomfortable and decides to go upstairs. Lizzie asks her to carry her clean clothes upstairs and put them in her room. Mrs. Borden starts up the steps, and Lizzie follows, describing how she would kill someone, as they exit.

Lizzie comes back with a hatchet concealed in her basket of clothes and appeals to Bridget for help, coaching Bridget to say that someone broke in and killed Mrs. Borden.

The scene changes, and Mr. Borden is home. Lizzie talks about how much she loves him and the ring she once gave him. She encourages him to sleep and when he does, approaches him with the hatchet. The stage darkens.

Back in the present, Emma and Lizzie discuss the Actress. Emma considers the relationship "disgraceful." Emma again asks her sister if she did it. Annoyed by her sister's repeated inquiries, Lizzie threatens Emma with "something sharp." If she is guilty, Lizzie states, then Emma is guilty as well because Emma raised her and taught her everything. The play ends with the Actress deciding Lizzie did commit the murders. Lizzie, however, points her finger at the Actress and the audience.

CHARACTERS

The Actress

The Actress is Lizzie's friend and, by all appearances, lover. It is at her request that the tale of Lizzie's past is re-enacted. Once the flashbacks begin, the Actress assumes the role of Lizzie. In this capacity, she recreates the events leading up to the murders. Basing her assumptions on what she knows of the family's history, the facts of the murders, and her own personal knowledge of Lizzie's personality, the Actress pieces the past together. She arrives at the conclusion that Lizzie did commit the murders as a means to escape the claustrophobic life that her family—and society—imposed upon her.

Abigail Borden

She married Mr. Borden, a widower with two young girls, and she has never had a good relationship with Lizzie. She would rather not deal with her stepdaughter at all. When she is forced to confront Lizzie, she is harsh and critical, telling the girl that she must do what is expected of her (get married, move out, and have a family of her own) if she wants to progress in the world. Abigail is manipulative, jealous, and, like her brother, Harry, scheming. She sees Lizzie as a threat to the lifestyle that she wants for herself. Unlike her husband, who is stern with Lizzie because he is confounded by her, Abigail's animosity is rooted in dislike and jealousy.

Andrew Borden

Mr. Borden is the man of the house and therefore the one with power. He makes the decisions. Yet he is nagged by his wife and badgered by Lizzie, in their running feud over her future. He prefers not to deal with Lizzie if he can help it. He is pleasant to her if she is being good, but when he is exasperated with her, he can explode, as he does when he attacks her pigeons with the hatchet. His confusion with his daughter's behavior leads him to avoid her when possible and brutalize her when he is cornered by her. While he is not a physical threat to Lizzie's survival, his deal with Harry will effectively terminate the small amount of freedom Lizzie enjoys. For this reason his death is rationalized by Lizzie (and the Actress playing her in the dream thesis portions) as necessary for her own survival.

Emma Borden

Emma is Lizzie's older sister. Since her mother's early death, Lizzie has essentially been raised by her sister. Emma is a kind and loving person, but she is also meek and non-confrontational. She refuses to face facts, preferring to let any problems work themselves out over time. When Lizzie exhorts her sister to help her put a stop to Harry's plans, Emma refuses and instead goes off to visit some friends at the beach. While she loves her younger sister, Emma does not understand Lizzie. Like the Actress, Emma also believes that her sister committed the murders. She, however, cannot grasp the circumstances that might explain why her sister would commit such a crime.

Miss Lizzie Borden

Lizzie is the play's central character, the axis around which the play events occur. Ten years after the murder of her parents, a crime for which she was accused and later acquitted, she lives with her sister Emma. In both the play's present and in the flashback sequences, Lizzie is a headstrong, slightly eccentric woman. She has very firm beliefs about living her life by her own rules. Contrary to the expectations placed on women in the late 1800s, Lizzie has no desire to marry and become a glorified domestic servant to a man she does not love. She wishes to follow her own path and, like the pigeons she kept, soar above the confines of the earth.

In the play's present, ten years after the murders, Lizzie has evolved into something of a legend in her hometown. There are still whispers of her guilt, and her obvious sexual relationship with the Actress give further credence to the town gossip that she is an antisocial freak, an aberration of nature. True to her belief that people should be allowed to pursue their own interests regardless of what others think, there is a part of Lizzie that relishes her outlaw status. By living her life publicly without shame or apology, she is showing others like her that it is okay to be yourself.

Pollock allows the audience to view the character of Lizzie from two unique perspectives in the play. The first is the actual Lizzie who entertains the Actress in her home during the play's present time frame. The second Lizzie is presented in the flashback sequences. In these scenes, Lizzie is portrayed by her friend the Actress, an outsider to the events that took place ten years prior.

Dr. Patrick

Patrick is Lizzie's closest ally. He frequently visits her, going on long walks during which the two discuss their escape fantasies. While he is sympathetic to Lizzie's hopes and dreams, he does not fully understand her or her need for personal freedom. He responds to Lizzie's flirtation and intellectual ponderings, but when she challenges him in a mental game about the value of life—and the possibility of taking life—he has no real answer. In the courtroom sequences, he also plays the part of the Defense, arguing for Lizzie's innocence.

Harry Wingate

Harry is Lizzie's step uncle and the catalyst for her decision to murder her parents. He arrives at the Borden home to convince Lizzie's father to sign away ownership of the family farm to his wife, Harry's sister. Harry will then run the farm as an auction site. The deal that Harry and her father arrive at convinces Lizzie that she will be slowly eliminated from the family, her means of support cut off. Knowing that, once in control of the family's resources, her stepmother will force her out of the house and into a marriage that she does not want, Lizzie knows that she must act to preserve her life. Harry is little more than a two-dimensional conniver whose presence is more or less a wake up call to Lizzie.

THEMES

Truth

The question is raised what is truth? The Actress asks, "Did you do it?" A question to which Lizzie does not—or cannot—respond. Emma asks her regularly, a litany each day. "Did you—did you—did you?" And Lizzie is again mute. Throughout the play there are more questions raised than answered. The audience would expect empirical evidence, and the play produces the Defense attorney who questions the suspect and her maid. But their authenticity, their authority are in question because the events are being recounted by Lizzie. By presenting the evidence of the case through the memory of the accused, there is no certainty that the events portrayed are real or are figments of Lizzie's imagination.

Although it is based on an actual event, Pollock goes beyond the historical facts to delve into the mind and motivation of her central character. While the end results are the same—Borden and his wife are dead and Lizzie has been acquitted of the crime—Pollock raises questions as to the actual path taken to reach those results. She forces the audience to question their own assumptions and conclusions about the truth of things, about why things may have happened as they did.

Sacredness of Life

"Is all life precious?" Lizzie questions Dr. Patrick. She really isn't looking for an answer from him because she rejects immediately the affirmative response he offers. She cannot accept that the life of that "fat cow" (her stepmother) is precious, so she pursues the question further. She poses an ethical enigma to the Doctor. If he could only save one of two people injured and dying from an accident, whom would he choose? Would it be the bad person or the one trying to be good?

Lizzie focuses her questioning in a way that leaves the Doctor uncomfortable. In the same way, the spectator may become uncomfortable because it is clear that Lizzie is rationalizing the murder of her parents to preserve a way of life for her and her sister. In Lizzie's mind murder becomes logical and acceptable. An analogy is made to puppies on the farm who must be done away with because they aren't quite right. This is presented to further rationalize Lizzie's assumption that bad elements must be removed so that regularity (in this case her personal freedom) can be maintained.

When Lizzie's pigeons are killed, it is clear something important in Lizzie has been violated. The birds' deaths are symbolic of the fate that awaits her and her sister if they allow Borden and his wife to go forward with their plans. She cannot stand by without any response. The puppy that is not quite right—who is a threat to normalcy—and is killed becomes the people who are obviously sick and must also be removed. This allows the audience to understand Lizzie's way of thinking and, in some way, understand her motives for violence.

Women's Roles

Lizzie's father wants her to consider Johnny MacLeod as a husband. MacLeod is a neighbor who is a widower with three young children and is looking for a wife. With his daughter already in her thirties, Borden is worried that Lizzie will never go out on her own. The only solution for her is to marry. It's only natural, he tells her.

Lizzie resists, saying she won't be around when MacLeod comes to call. "He's looking for a housekeeper and it isn't going to be me," Lizzie says to her father. Her stepmother sees nothing wrong with such a domestic arrangement. That's essentially what happened with her. She came and married Lizzie's father, who had two young children, and cared for them. In exchange, she received a nice house to live in, food to eat, and companionship.

But this is not what Lizzie wants from life. She just can't fit into the mold society offers her. She complains to her father, "You want me living life by the Farmer's Almanac; having everyone over for Christmas dinner; waiting up for my husband; and serving at socials." This is not a life with which Lizzie can ever become comfortable.

It's not her fault, Lizzie tells the Actress at another moment. Somehow she didn't get that magic formula that is stamped indelibly on the brain, the formula for being the socially–acceptable version of a woman. "Through some terrible oversight . . . I was born . . . defective."

Lizzie even begs her father to let her go to work with him and learn how to keep books. He refuses. That's not a woman's place, he tells her. She responds that he can't make her do anything she doesn't want to do. Her stepmother urges her as well

TOPICS FOR FURTHER STUDY

- Research the O.J. Simpson murder trial. How was that case similar to the Lizzie Borden case? How was it different?
- Investigate the facts of the actual Lizzie Borden murder case. How consistent are the facts with the way the material is presented in the play? What do you think Pollock was trying to communicate?
- Look up the concept of documentary theatre. Come up with a list of essential elements for this approach. How well does *Blood Relations* fulfill these requirements?
- Research recent crime cases in which women were acquitted for violent crimes that they most obviously had committed. What are the similarities between these cases and the Lizzie Borden case that is presented in *Blood Relations?*
- Investigate the history of women's rights in the U.S. Make a timeline of the major events. If Lizzie Borden had been living today, how might her situation have been different?

to consider MacLeod, reminding her that her father is taking care of her. Lizzie volunteers to leave but, with no means to earn a living that isn't a possibility. Her stepmother tells her, ''You know you got nothing but what he gives you. And that's a fact of life. You got to deal with the facts. I did.''

All that Lizzie can see is that she is entitled to a third of what her father has. She thinks this only fair. But she has no right. Her stepmother says that her father is going to live a long time and indicates she won't be included in the will. ''Only a fool would leave money to you.''

So even though Lizzie is proud and defiant, she is without any real power. She is not supposed to be out walking and talking with married men, as she does with Dr. Patrick. She is without any money other than what is doled out to her. She has no right other than the birthright of her body. She can marry and have children. This is not a choice Lizzie could ever accept.

While contemporary women have many choices in deciding their life course, this was not the case in the late 1800s. Women were second-class citizens expected to fulfill specific—limited—roles in society. While Lizzie is spoiled, she is also prepared to work to preserve her independence. She offers to work in her father's office but that option is denied to her. Presented with the choice of conforming to a way of life she abhors (an arranged marriage with MacLeod) or living as little more than a servant (to her stepmother and step-uncle), Lizzie decides to actively alter her and her sister's fate.

There are many examples of Lizzie's desire to act and live independently—to stretch beyond the boundaries of traditional women's roles— in the play. This is illustrated by her open relationship with the Actress, a relationship that appears to be homosexual in nature. Such activity was scandalous in the nineteenth century; respectable women were not supposed to be overtly sexual—especially not with each other. While this is strong evidence of Lizzie's quest for independence, Pollock's most powerful statement lies in the murder itself: Lizzie is willing to kill to earn her personal freedom.

STYLE

Dream Thesis

Pollock has labeled Lizzie's re-enactment of the 1892 murder ten years prior as the ''dream thesis.'' The play avoids realism and defies logical time progression. There aren't clear entrances and exits. The actors weave in and out of the present and past. There are three real characters on stage, Lizzie, the Actress, and sister Emma. The others are pulled up from the memories of the 1892 event. This gives the scenes with Borden, his wife, Harry, and Dr. Patrick a hazy, hallucinatory quality; they are the ghosts of Lizzie's memory.

To make these sequences more surreal, the flashbacks are not played in a straightforward fashion. Events from the present, the trial, and the days leading up to the murder are jumbled together—representative of the randomness of dreams and memories. The ambiguity of the play increases when Lizzie proposes playing a game in which the Actress will play her. And so as the dream progresses, the audience is unable to keep a distance. There is always a question of what is real and what is not. As the two women assume their roles in the reenactment, the boundaries between Lizzie and the Actress fade. And then it is unclear who is the real Lizzie.

This approach provides the opportunity to consider the fluidity of truth, or perhaps the idea that there are many sides to truth and therefore many truths. The dream sequence is part of the structure that incorporates a play within a play, where action and conflict are happening on different levels.

By having the Actress re-live Lizzie's past, to perceive the events as Lizzie did, Pollock encourages the audience to do the same, to view Lizzie's life through the eyes of an outsider to the family. This technique effectively illuminates for the viewer the personal path that Lizzie took to the murders.

Documentary Theatre

The roots of documentary theatre go back to 1925 and the work of Erwin Piscator. According to Robert C. Nunn in *Canadian Literature,* this approach ''forgoes the traditional emphasis of dramatic theatre on the timelessness of the human condition in favour of an emphasis on the human situation unfolding in a specific historical context.'' It's an attempt to get at the truth that can be hidden by the existence of fact.

Documentary theatre is a way to look at how performers relate to the audience and how performance relates to reality. Techniques that are used include dreams, reflections, monologues, and flashbacks that are laced throughout the work. ''These break into the action,'' said Peter Weiss, a German dramatist known for his connection with the Theatre of Cruelty. As Weiss wrote in *Theatre Quarterly,* ''causing uncertainty, sometimes creating a shock-effect, and showing how an individual or a group are affected by the events portrayed. Laying bare the inner reality as opposed to external trappings.''

Blood Relations successfully jars the audience away from their comfortable understanding of truth and raises questions that are not answered in the play, questions that are meant to play over in the viewer's mind after the drama has ended.

Symbolism

Blood Relations weaves in two important images: the hatchet and the pigeons. Viewers are introduced to these images early in the play. The birds are brought up when the crusts of bread that Bridget has for them are seen and their importance to Lizzie is made known. The birds represent the part of Lizzie that can fly, that can be free. This is seen in her flirtatious talk with Dr. Patrick and her fantasies of stepping off to Boston with him. Like the birds, however, which are caged, Lizzie also is tied down. And Lizzie also is fed the crusts. The birds' link to Lizzie is further illustrated when Borden kills them. Just as he literally cuts them to pieces, he figuratively ''cuts'' Lizzie off from the life she desires, shattering her dreams.

The hatchet is a sharp–edged implement that clarifies and separates. Harry wields it, as does Mr. Borden. This symbol of masculinity and control is usurped, however, when Lizzie takes the hatchet to both her stepmother and father. In addition to being the instrument of liberation from her oppressive parents, the hatchet gives Lizzie value and a place in the community. She is more than just an old spinster; she is the one who took the ax and killed her father and stepmother, a source of tremendous talk even ten years after it occurred. The hatchet is symbolic of Lizzie's ability to transcend the patriarchy that she felt enslaved her.

HISTORICAL CONTEXT

The 1970s were an important time for the women's movement. Although women received the right to vote in the 1920s, most of society's advantages still resided with men. The women's advocacy group the National Organization of Women (NOW) was formed in 1966 and a few years later the feminist movement was given an important media voice with the debut of *Ms.* magazine. The women's movement had its highest profile in the years from 1972 to 1982, when an attempt to pass a constitutional

COMPARE & CONTRAST

- **1892:** Lizzie Borden is arrested for the brutal murder of her father and stepmother, a murder which left the community aghast. Later an all-male jury acquits Lizzie of the murders.

  Today: Sports hero O. J. Simpson is accused of the brutal slaying of his estranged wife Nicole Simpson and her friend Ron Goldman. Media coverage of the trial is enormous, and the proceedings are dubbed ''The Trial of the Century.'' Despite a preponderance of evidence implicating Simpson, he is acquitted. He is later found responsible for Nicole and Ron's deaths in a civil case, which establishes his liability in terms of money owed to Goldman's family. Despite the civil trial results, many consider him a murderer who escaped justice through the deceit and trickery of his skilled defense attorney, Johnny Cochran.

- **1890s:** A rash of mergers and buyouts result in the formation of trusts, which are designed to reduce competition. This results in major increase of wealth for a few individuals, while the real wages of workers increase so slightly that they remained on the verge of financial ruin.

  Today: Microsoft, a multi–billion dollar computer software company, has successfully eliminated or reduced most of its competition, making chairman Bill Gates one of the wealthiest men in the world. Microsoft is under investigation for charges that it has violated antitrust laws created to prevent market monopolies.

- **1976:** The first Michigan Womyn's (the intentional misspelling removes the word ''man'' from the gender title) Festival convenes, bringing women together from all over the country. The event attracts mostly gay women and makes the lesbian community quite visible.

  1980: The beginnings of the AIDS epidemic calls attention to political concerns of the gay and lesbian communities.

  Today: Ellen Morgan, the main character in the popular sitcom *Ellen,* comes out as a lesbian, as does the actress playing her, Ellen DeGeneres. Although there is significant protest from conservative religious movements, the show continues on prime time television. Gays continue to fight for equal rights and for the right to marry same sex partners.

---

amendment addressing the issue of equal rights for women was underway. The Equal Rights Amendment (ERA) was passed by both houses of Congress. The only hurdle was the requirement that the amendment be ratified by three–quarters of the states in America. A strong opposition movement, fueled by irrational fears that women would lose special privileges and would have to go to war and share public washrooms with men, gathered steam. The opposition was successful and the ERA was defeated.

In the Supreme Court, however, a victory for women was won in 1973 in the historic *Roe vs. Wade* case. This legal precedent established the right of an American woman to have an abortion. Some power was left in the hands of the individual states, which could place some limitations on the procedure. It was, however, a victory for feminists and, in essence, gave women the right of control over their own bodies.

The success of the forces that opposed the ERA represented a growing movement of conservatism in the U.S. It was that movement that resulted in the election of Ronald Reagan as president in 1980. He represented a broad base of Americans who had survived the massive changes in the 1960s and 1970s and believed that the government shouldn't be bothered with assuring the rights of all peoples. Reagan arrived on the political scene at a time when the economy was floundering and America's position of power in the world seemed threatened by numerous enemies. If government withdrew from certain areas of life, this conservative movement asserted, the economy would flourish and everyone would be better off.

Reagan's campaign had promised support for the family. What became clear was this was not support for women's issues but rather an attempt to keep women in traditional domestic roles. This position turned a blind eye to certain sociological realities: namely that many more marriages were ending in divorce and that there was a significant increase in single–parent families. For many women's activists, the 1980s served as an era during which their dedication to independence was renewed.

Struggles for freedom were also occurring on the world front in 1980. A significant event in Poland foreshadowed the eventual breakdown of the communist dictatorship that controlled the Soviet Union and Eastern Europe. Shipyard workers in Poland went on strike to protest a rise in meat prices. Their stand unified the majority of workers in the country who had grown uneasy with the way the government ran their lives. The spirit of protest spread to the general population of Poland. The slogan ''Solidarity'' was adopted to exemplify the working-class's unity. Ultimately the strikers' demands were met, including the release of jailed dissidents. This event gave Polish citizens a foothold in controlling their rights. The strikers were eventually able to gain control of the government and their leader, Lech Walesa, became Poland's new president.

Also in 1980, former Beatle John Lennon was shot to death by a disturbed fan, Mark David Chapman, shocking the world and ending for good any fantasies that the Beatles, who had gone their separate ways in the early 1970s, would reunite. Lennon's death stirred a continuing debate about gun control that was given further strength when John Hinckley attempted to assassinate President Reagan a short time later.

CRITICAL OVERVIEW

Pollock's early plays quite clearly were focused on making a comment about society, earning her the label of social playwright. ''With *Blood Relations* people who don't like social comment plays seem to think I've 'moved' considerably and I'm finally beginning to concentrate on character, that I've learned a few character traits and maybe they can expect some 'better' work from me,'' Pollock once said in an interview in *The Work: Conversations with English-Canadian Playwrights.*

Although not well-known in the U.S., Pollock has an impressive reputation in her native Canada. Jerry Wasserman of the *University of Toronto Quarterly,* labels her one of the ''two finest living [Canadian] playwrights.'' Richard Paul Knowles seemed in agreement when he wrote in *Atlantic Provinces Book Review* that ''Sharon Pollock is one of only a handful of playwrights in Canada who have put together a solid and developing body of work over a number of active years in the theatre, and of that handful she is one of the best.''

Some critics have been disappointed in what they perceive as a lack of clear feminist focus in *Blood Relations.* According to S. R. Gilbert, the play ''does not adequately explore issues of women in Victorian (or modern) society.''

Pollock commented on how male reviewers failed to see any connection with feminism in this work, with some seeing the play as a mystery play while others as perhaps a psychological study of a woman. ''It's only women who see it making a statement about women today,'' the playwright noted.

Pollock's claim that *Blood Relations* does have a feminist message has been echoed by many women critics. ''In many ways the play epitomizes the strengths and originality of theatre about women imprisoned in a man-ordered universe,'' said Ann Saddlemyer in *Rough Justice: Essays on Crime in Literature,* ''but at the same time . . . it speaks beyond this framework to explore even more far-reaching concerns of time and spirit.'' The structure of the play has received a good deal of attention and credit is given to Pollock for her effective use of the dream thesis.

Paul Matthew St. Pierre, writing in *Canadian Writers since 1960,* praised Pollock for her ability to reach audiences in ''imaginatively and strikingly unconventional manners.'' The critic lauded her for the use of the dream thesis in which the past is called up with the assistance of the Actress. St. Pierre claimed that this technique creates far more dramatic suspense than the actual physical action of the ax. ''This technical accomplishment, more than anything else, is the source of the play's triumph.''

The structure of *Blood Relations* allows for the ambiguity that is interwoven throughout the play.

A scene from the 1997 Guild Hall production of Pollock's play. The Actress (Mary Sloane) playing the part of Lizzie, takes an ax to Mr. Borden (Mike Curtis)

Nowhere does the play state in absolute terms that Lizzie is guilty (although the Actress's perception, playing Lizzie in the dream thesis, seems to indicate so). And the court acquits her. But then there's the Actress who arrives at the conclusion, after playing the role of Lizzie, that she is guilty.

A basic question that resounds throughout the play is ''did she?'' The play remains ambiguous and never really fully answers this. According to Saddlemyer, Pollock successfully reframes that question by pointing the finger (and ultimately the hatchet) at the viewer and asking, in Lizzie's shoes, what would you do?

Mary Pat Mombourquette noted in the *International Encyclopedia of Theatre* that Pollock is not one to let the audience off the hook. Passivity is not allowed. ''Instead she demands that the audience acknowledge that the act of judging makes them active participants in the theatrical event.''

Pollock, in the interview in *The Work,* entertained the thought that there may be more to the story, and that she has another play to write that takes off where *Blood Relations* ends. That play, she stated, will examine what happens to the woman who is unable to kill her father or mother, or even herself. That play will be ''about women and madness.''

Pollock has been labeled a regional playwright, living and working on the western coast of Canada. This is a label she both accepts with pleasure, looking askance at New York and London for acceptance, and one that she resists. Diane Bessai, in her introduction to *Blood Relation and Other Plays,* thinks the label is limiting, stating that ''few playwrights practicing the craft in Canada today have her range and technique.''

CRITICISM

Etta Worthington

Worthington is a playwright and educator. In this essay she examines the victimization experienced by Lizzie Borden in Pollock's play.

Long before she was arrested for the murder of her parents, Lizzie Borden was more than likely thought of as an eccentric personality around Fall

WHAT DO I READ NEXT?

- *Trifles* is a play by Susan Glaspell, written in 1916, with some interesting parallels to Pollock's work. It's the story of a farm woman arrested for murdering her husband. When looking for clues to prove her guilt, investigators find a canary dead of a broken neck.
- Eugene O'Neill's *Desire under the Elms* is a look at an explosive family situation, also involving a farm and which relative will inherit the land. Like *Blood Relations,* the play involves a stepmother and a violent act that tears the family apart.
- Another Sharon Pollock work, *Saucy Jack,* deals with a historical murder case. First produced in 1993, this play explores the story of Jack the Ripper.
- *The Angel of Darkness* (1997) by Caleb Carr deals with a forensic psychologist tracking a murderous governess. The novel deals with common nineteenth century perceptions of female roles and the often sociopathic lengths to which a woman wishing to live independently resorted.
- Henrik Ibsen's *A Doll's House* was written in 1879 and shocked the theatre world when its female protagonist, Nora, rejects the role that society expects of her and strikes out on her own.

River, Massachusetts. Even within her family she had a reputation. Her father avoided bringing up uncomfortable topics with her. He seemed to be afraid of what she might say or do. Harry, her stepmother's brother, would creep around, trying to avoid her, claiming Lizzie loved animals but ''what Miss Lizzie doesn't love is people.'' And her stepmother avoided her when she could, complaining of Lizzie to anyone who would listen; ''The truth is she's spoilt rotten.''

Yet in spite of this seeming display of power, Lizzie is essentially impotent. Her influence over people only extends to trivial matters. When it comes to exerting her will to attain something that is truly important to her, she is powerless. Within the social structure of the late-nineteenth century, Lizzie is at the mercy of female stereotypes. This headstrong, peculiar young woman, who was accused of killing her parents with a hatchet, is in fact a victim of the conservative era in which she lived.

Pollock's *Blood Relations* shows us a woman who is trapped in a body and an assumed role for which she is not suited. Confiding in her friend the Actress, Lizzie acknowledges that somehow she didn't get that special something that brands one as a socially-acceptable woman at birth. Lizzie puzzles over whether it was because her natural mother died at birth. Whatever the cause, she knows that she is different; she does not fit the mold.

Her isolation from social norms is highlighted when her father attempts to arrange a marriage between her and a local widower. She tells Borden that she tries to do what he expects of her, ''but I don't want to get married. I wouldn't be a good mother.''

It's only natural to be interested in a man, her father tells her, mistaking her talks with the married Dr. Patrick as some kind of love interest. But Lizzie's interaction with the doctor is removed from romance; she seeks his company because he is willing to listen to—and at times participate in—her ideas, hopes, and dreams. Unfortunately, Lizzie has no one else with whom she can relate (and, despite his willingness, Dr. Patrick is not the kindred soul she seeks). She feels isolated within her own family and ill-suited to fulfill the role expected of her. She is a victim of her body, put in a woman's body without having the ''natural'' inclinations of a woman. Ten years after the murder, Emma nags Lizzie about her relationship with the Actress, implying that they are lesbians. ''People talk,'' Emma tells Lizzie, who, it is clear, cares very little what others think of her behavior (and may even relish her scandalous reputation as a murderous lesbian). The proper Emma, however, is horrified with her sister's action and finally bursts out, "It's . . . disgraceful!"Lizzie Borden lives a life that others might consider enviable. Even her stepmother envies her, jealously complaining about the trip to Europe her father had given her. And although she is well provided for, she *is* the victim of abuse. While Lizzie appreciates the material comforts her family provides her, what she really craves is acceptance for who she is and encouragement to live her life as she feels she must. Yet her family—and the community at large—are too entrenched in subscribing to "normal" and "acceptable" female behavior to ever allow such freedom. Instead, Lizzie's family is often frustrated with her stubborn eccentricity, and they are unsure of how to interact with her. Borden vacillates between avoiding and ignoring her, to favoring her with gifts, to outright brutality when she tries his patience excessively.

This is illustrated in a flashback when Lizzie overhears Harry's scheme to have the farm signed over to his sister, Lizzie's stepmother. Lizzie bursts in on the men, Harry slinks off, and she demands to see what her father has hastily stuffed in his pocket. "What are you doing with the farm?" she demands. He insists it's not any of her business, but she presses him and tries to grab the papers from his pocket. He slaps her. Harry returns with a hatchet that Borden grabs and announces that he's going to eliminate the problem of the birds. "No," Lizzie pleads. These pigeons are more important to her than the humans who people the house. Borden realizes how vital the birds are to Lizzie. By destroying them he is consciously trying to wound her. It is possible that his intentions are to shock her into more acceptable behavior, but it is equally logical to assume that his act is one of pure malevolence. In any event, the birds' deaths have a profound affect on Lizzie. Not only did she love them as pets, the pigeons, and their capacity for flight, were a symbol of the freedom for which Lizzie yearned.

Borden's brutality is so stark and dramatic that we question the singularity of his act; this is not the first time that Lizzie's father has cruelly attacked her way of life. We understand, then, her attempts to please her father, her proclamations that she is trying to be good. Behind her tough guy act, Lizzie is a woman who has for years had to dodge the explosive, brutal anger of her father. She fears him and what he might do.

Borden forms the cornerstone of the dysfunctional family in the play. But in addition to the brutal, distant and controlling father, there is the conniving and bitter stepmother. She feels that Borden spoils his daughters—especially Lizzie. When she is ineffective at changing her husband's behavior, she schemes with her brother to gain control of the farm and gradually squeeze the girls out of Borden's financial support. So it is Harry that reports to Borden that people in the town are talking about him and that it's bad for business. "If a man can't manage his own daughter, how the hell can he manage a business—that's what people say."

Mrs. Borden brings all her resentment to bear on Lizzie. She has suffered, marrying a man and having to mother his two children (and have none of her own). She feels that Lizzie presence is undermining her own happiness, spoiling what would otherwise be a good life.

Emma is brought into the triangle when her father asks if she has talked to Lizzie about entertaining MacLeod. Emma has, despite Mrs. Borden's claims of mothering the girls, essentially raised Lizzie herself and has been made to feel responsible for her. It's not a role she enjoys, but she continues to look after her younger sister. But she complains as well. When pressed to influence her sister's thoughts on marriage, Emma indicates her unwillingness to get involved. "Then why don't you tell her?" she bursts out. "I'm always the one that has to go running to Lizzie telling her this and telling her that, and taking the abuse for it!"

Lizzie makes a valiant but unsuccessful attempt to solicit Emma's support in her opposition to Harry's scheme to take over the farm. Although it is highly unlikely that the two of them allied against their father would have had much impact, Lizzie still feels that she has to take a stand. Emma, however, chooses to sneak off to visit friends at the beach for a few days to avoid any confrontation. Lizzie feels betrayed and misunderstood, since the loss of the farm impacts Emma's future as much as it does hers.

Emma is less fretful of the future, trusting that things will somehow work themselves out. She prefers to avoid confronting her problems. As she tells Lizzie: "If I want to tell a little white lie to avoid an altercation in this house, I'll do so. Other people have been doing it for years." Lizzie pushes Emma away from her, recalling the experience of finding her birds dead and her father's callous attitude. "He didn't care how much he hurt me and you don't care either. Nobody cares.'' Unable to find comfort and support within her own family, Lizzie feels victimized and alienated.

But as she stated in *The Work,* Pollock sees Lizzie's problems as more than just her family. ''As soon as you start dealing with the politics of the family, it's not so easy to know who the bad guys are . . . *Blood Relations* is a play in which the woman is in conflict, not with her father—she loves her father—but with the society around her.'' While it is clear that her family could offer her more in the way of support, it is also evident that their subscription to social mores prevents them from endorsing the kind of life Lizzie wishes to lead. Lizzie is ultimately a victim of her times and her society.

Lizzie has ideas in her head of how she wants to live her life. What is clear is that she will never succumb to the pressure to marry even though it—and motherhood—were the only real roles for women at the end of the nineteenth century. When her father points out that marriage is a natural thing, she asks him if, because she does not want to marry, she is unnatural. It's a question to which he does not want to respond. If his daughter is, by biological definition, a woman and yet also not a *woman* by social definition, then the whole social order is in question. It is more than Borden can comprehend.

Lizzie tries to explain to her father what she wants. ''I want out of all this . . . I hate this house. I hate . . . I want out. Try to understand how I feel. . . . Why can't I do something?. . . I could go into your office. . . . I could . . . learn how to keep books?''

This question of course has no answer. Her father tells her that women do not work in offices. He begs her to think sensibly. As the daughter of a wealthy respectable community member, he and society expect her to function as a responsible and appropriate woman. And living apart from her family, or working outside the home, does not fit into the narrow constraints of society's expectations.

The double edged sword is this: even if she were allowed to strike out on her own, Lizzie has no real property rights. She can own property, and have her ''own'' life, only as connected to a male family member, whether father, husband, or brother. She demands as her right a third of the farm, but her stepmother makes it clear that she has no rights—neither society nor her family will give her any.

The only future she can envision is one in which her father has passed on, and she continues to live in this house with her intolerable stepmother and step uncle Harry. She foresees her sister obediently waiting on their stepmother while she, Lizzie, will just sit alone, isolated, in her room. This future is intolerable to her. She strolls and chats with Dr. Patrick, the one person with whom she can engage in fantasy of life with a bit of freedom. And although she may chat about going off to Boston, she counters that with talk about death, even her own: ''If I wanted to die—I could even do that, couldn't I?''

"POLLOCK'S *BLOOD RELATIONS* SHOWS US A WOMAN WHO IS TRAPPED IN A BODY AND AN ASSUMED ROLE FOR WHICH SHE IS NOT SUITED."

Dr. Patrick is flustered and tries to ease her out of her depression by discussing a fantasy they have shared about going to Boston. But this doesn't deter Lizzie from considering death, either for herself or someone else, as a solution to her problems. When she is with Dr. Patrick she allows herself the fantasy that she is free, that she could do this or that. But on this particular day, that fantasy is crushed when she has to confront again the brutal killing of her pigeons. She has reached the point where fantasy is no longer satisfying. She must take action in deciding her future.

What follows, or what may have followed, may seem like a premeditated and cold-blooded criminal act. The facts that are known for certain are these—both Borden and his wife were killed by blows from an ax. The defense proclaimed Lizzie innocent. The court believed Lizzie's story and found her not guilty. Ten years later, however, the question still lingers. Her sister Emma and her lover, the Actress, badger her for the truth. Did she do it?

Lizzie doesn't answer. On the surface it might appear that Lizzie is a criminal. But the surface as Pollock shows it in *Blood Relations* is a blurred area. The story is recalled as a kind of waking dream. Lizzie's experiences from that past are recalled by an outsider to the events, the Actress. It is unclear whether the story related is the truth or what the Actress assumes to be the truth. The facts of Lizzie's life offer a plausible motive for her to have committed the crime, but because she remains mute on the subject, the audience is left to ponder her actual involvement.

Lizzie was brutalized by her father, her family, and a society that insisted she act in a way that was inconsistent with her nature. There was no escape, or so it seemed to her. She was the victim, something we understand as the play ends and Emma again begs to know the truth. The Actress, arriving at her conclusion, says "Lizzie, you did." "I didn't," Lizzie responds. Pointing at the Actress and then the audience, she states, "You did."

The question at the center of *Blood Relations,* according to Ann Saddlemyer in *Rough Justice,* is "which is the greatest crime: imprisonment of the soul, or life at any price?" The evidence presented in Pollock's play seems to confirm Lizzie's acceptance of the latter. Realizing that to continue living in her parents' house meant a slow death of her ideals and the imprisonment of her independence, Lizzie chose to take action. Born in an era unwilling to accept a woman as a unique individual and misunderstood by her family, she saw herself as a victim. To Lizzie it was her parents' life or her own. Her final gesture, an accusatory finger pointed at the audience, is a call for the viewer to look at their own prejudices and preconceptions of what is "normal," what is "acceptable." While modern society has made great strides in accepting behavior that was once considered odd or antisocial, there are still many people who are persecuted because society at large cannot understand them. In accusing the audience of the crime, Lizzie is saying that, by imposing strict roles for women, nineteenth century society was just as guilty of the Borden murders as the woman who picked up the ax.

Source: Etta Worthington, for *Drama for Students,* Gale, 1998.

Susan Stone-Blackburn

Stone-Blackburn discusses Pollock's play from a feminist perspective. She also explores how the play fits into the category of metadrama—works that, in the critic's words, "examine the conventions . . . of dramatic representation itself."

In her introduction to a new collection of feminist essays on contemporary women's theatre, Lynda Hart reminds us of Marilyn Frye's analogy between women and stagehands. In the foreground of our collective world view, Frye observes, is "Phallocratic Reality," constructed by men and presented as objective reality. The analogue is dramatic realism, which depends on sustaining the onstage illusion of reality. In both cases, attention is not to stray to the background. Women's experience in the one instance and offstage reality in the other are kept in the dark, while men's experience and onstage action are illuminated. Feminism moves our focus of attention to the background, as does theatre that challenges the conventions of realism. Hart speaks of "a shift in the last decade" of feminist criticism "towards rigorous exploration of the language of representation itself". [*Making a Spectacle,* University of Michigan Press, 1989] The dramatic analogue would be metadrama, those plays about drama and theatre that examine the conventions—the language—of dramatic representation itself.

Feminism and metadrama intersect in the role-playing of Sharon Pollock's *Blood Relations.* The character of Lizzie Borden is created at the point of intersection. Her character is defined both by the social role-playing that was imposed on her by family and the rest of society in 1892 and by the Actress' 1902 performance as Lizzie, when she imaginatively creates Lizzie's part in the ax murders. The first kind of role-playing is a feminist concern; the second is metadramatic.

The part of the play that recreates the events of 1892 presents the independent, strong-minded Lizzie in contrast with her mousy older sister Emma. Except that she is not married, Emma is what society, represented by the senior Bordens, expects of a woman. "Emma's a good girl," as her father says. Lizzie rebels against the role she is expected to play. She struggles against the role of the dutiful daughter, alternately pleading with and raging at her father. She is contemptuous of the expectation that she will pose as eligible and alluring when she has no wish to become a dutiful wife and mother. Her flirtation with the married Catholic doctor is carried on out of boredom and defiance, not because she is attracted to him, as her father assumes, but because she can amuse herself and annoy her family without running the risk of being pushed into marriage with him. Lizzie's hatred of dependence and her individuality cannot be accommodated in her society. Her father, whom she loves, approves of her only when she wears a mask that horrifies her, when she pretends things she doesn't feel, when she reflects her father's idea of femininity.The first act closes on a highly theatrical depiction of Mr. Borden's slaughter of Lizzie's birds. Act II opens on the subject of death, not directly Lizzie's reflections on her father's destruction of the birds she loved, but her memory of her father drowning a puppy during one of her childhood stays at the family farm. The puppy was "different," Lizzie reflects—as she is "different"—and "different" things are killed. The atmosphere of death is pervasive from this point on.

Mr. Borden's destruction of Lizzie's birds recalls Jean's destruction of Julie's bird in *Miss Julie.* Pollock keeps the outcome of Strindberg's play before us, as Lizzie considers the possibility of taking her own life. The trap tightens around Lizzie, as her prospects for further freedom are cut off by the transfer of her father's property to her stepmother. As death looms ever larger, the only options are Julie's—suicide—or murder. "I want to die, but something inside won't let me," Lizzie says. "Something inside says no." So the murders can be seen as an act of strength, an assertion of Lizzie's own value, of the repressed woman's right to life.

Lizzie's parents portray traditional modes of thought. Mrs. Borden, whom Lizzie despises, is caught in the same trap as Lizzie, but she accepts it as inevitable. Mr. Borden is driven frantic by his inability to make his daughter conform to the only role for women he understands. He is bewildered and frustrated by her refusal to accept what he is convinced is best for her. Lizzie's murder of the senior Bordens can be taken as an attempt to destroy blind male authority and female acceptance of it.

In the part of *Blood Relations* that depicts events that take place in the Borden household in 1892, then, we are shown a woman who rebels against the social role expected of women; the role is so far from her sense of her true identity that she feels herself being destroyed by it; the role is a killer, and she reacts by becoming a murderer, enacting instead of suffering destruction. This fits Helene Keyssar's emphasis in *Feminist Theatre* on transformation rather than recognition as characteristic of feminist theatre. From the time of Aristotle, Keyssar observes, the recognition scene has been central to drama, but feminist drama presents metamorphosis in place of self-discovery. Lizzie Borden's transformation from repressed daughter to murderer, from victim of society to destroyer of paternal authority, is an instance of such transformation. The key development of the play is not a moment of self-recognition but rather Lizzie's decision to change, to seize power and strike out for freedom after a lifetime of powerlessness in which every possibility for freedom has been denied her.

" *BLOOD RELATIONS* IS A FEMINIST PLAY, BUT IT GOES BEYOND THE FEMINIST STUDY OF THE RESTRICTIONS OF WOMEN'S SOCIAL ROLES AND THE FEMINIST EMPHASIS ON THE POSSIBILITY FOR CHANGE."

Pollock's feminist exploration of social roles and their limitations is complex in a number of ways I do not propose to discuss in detail. Lizzie's Lesbian relationship with the Actress accounts for her rebellion against traditional courtship; her homosexuality is just one of the ways in which her individuality runs counter to the prescribed social role that stifles her. The contrast between Mrs. Borden, who is able to use the woman's role to her advantage, and her stepdaughters, who cannot, is instructive. And certainly it is noteworthy that it is the very strength of society's conviction that woman must be what popular belief dictates she is that acquits Lizzie in the murder trial. The Defense moves towards his concluding assertion of Lizzie's innocence with: "Gentlemen! If this gentlewoman is capable of such an act—I say to you—look to your daughters—if this gentlewoman is capable of such an act, which of us can lie abed at night, hear a step upon the stairs, a rustle in the hall, a creak outside the door?. . ."

Blood Relations is a feminist play, but it goes beyond the feminist study of the restrictions of women's social roles and the feminist emphasis on the possibility for change. These ingredients were in the early version of the play called *My Name is Lisbeth,* performed at Douglas College in 1976, a version that was judged wanting by Pollock and by others. The play that earned the first Governor General's award for drama and many productions across Canada and beyond is more — not only a feminist study of social roles but a sophisticated metadramatic exploration of role playing. The University of Calgary's collection of Sharon Pollock's manuscripts shows how she worked to create and strengthen the metadramatic impact of her play. In *My Name is Lisbeth,* there is no Actress, no 1902 frame, just the depiction of the events of 1892 in the Borden household. Later, the Actress and the role-playing device are introduced. Still later, the Actress' role is strengthened to the point at which it dominates the play. Even after she published the script in 1981, Pollock extended its metadramatic suggestions further in a production she directed.

In *Blood Relations,* Lizzie's choice of murder in response to the threat of self-destruction is portrayed by the Actress in 1902; we do not see a "direct" presentation of the events or characters of 1892, but rather what Pollock calls "a dream thesis"—all the characters of 1892 are imaginary. Miss Lizzie (the script's designation for the 1902 character), who has been tried and acquitted, will not say whether or not she committed the murders. The Actress comments on Miss Lizzie's awareness of the "fascination in the ambiguity. . . . If you didn't I should be disappointed . . . and if you did I should be horrified." If she didn't, Miss Lizzie is nothing more than "a pretentious small-town spinster," and the Actress is doubtful whether that is better than being a murderer (21). Certainly the ambiguity was central to Pollock's conception, which is reminiscent of Pirandello's *Right You Are (If You Think So)* and *Henry IV.* In a holograph note on the back of the penultimate page of a nearly final version of *Blood Relations,* Pollock wrote, "The ambiguity of her art is what keeps the Lizzie Borden legend alive." Historically, the ambiguity is maintained by the fact that although Lizzie was acquitted, no one else was ever convicted of the murders. In the play, Miss Lizzie's relationship with the Actress apparently depends on the fascination of that ambiguity. Metadramatically, the central ambiguity of the play is the relationship between Miss Lizzie and the Actress—not the sexual relationship, but their identities and their interaction in creating the events of 1892.

The device of the Actress' creation, under Miss Lizzie's guidance, of the circumstances that lead up to the murders, and then a gradual move into her part in such a way that the enactment of the murders is her own creation, produces the desired ambiguity. It also extends the exploration of role-playing with a construct that is overtly metadramatic. Like feminism which rejects conventional social roles, metadrama subverts dramatic conventions by calling attention to them, spotlighting the assumptions about the relationship between drama and life that underlie most dramatic performance. We have traditionally thought in terms of difference: actors play roles on stage, while offstage they revert to their true selves. Drama is about life, even if a play inevitably presents a perception of life rather than an imitation of life, as Richard Hornby argues in *Drama, Metadrama and Perception.* Metadrama is about our means of perception, about how we organize our experiences to present them in dramatic form; "it occurs whenever the subject of a play turns out to be, in some sense, drama itself." [*Drama, Metadrama and Perception,* Buckrell University Press, 1986] Much feminist drama, including *Blood Relations,* is about socially dictated gender roles. But *Blood Relations* is also about how we perceive role-playing itself. There is considerable use in the play of dreams, game-playing, images, all of which point to perception, rather than action, as central to the play. Most evident of all in this complex of non-naturalistic devices is the central device of role-playing, which raises questions of identity and reminds us "that all human roles are relative, that identities are learned rather than innate."

In the early stages of the Actress' adoption of Lizzie's role, she is tentative, guided by Miss Lizzie in her role of the maid Bridget to understand the family relationships and the situation. Miss Lizzie/ Bridget subtly corrects her mistakes and leads her towards an understanding of her role. As the Actress gains confidence in her role, Miss Lizzie, as Bridget, fades into the background. The Actress is never assigned a name of her own. She blends into Lizzie, both on stage as they change roles and in Pollock's designations in the script, where she is first THE ACTRESS, then LIZZIE and sometimes ACTRESS/ LIZZIE. Even before the role-playing is undertaken, Miss Lizzie has a line which begins to blur the line drawn between the two: "You look like me, or how I think I look, or how I ought to look . . . sometimes you think like me . . . do you feel that?" The Actress concurs: "Sometimes." The two can be seen to comprise one complete identity, each supplying something that is lacking in the other.

By Act II, the Actress is fully in control of her portrayal. Her Lizzie is now an independent creation, though we may not realize it as the drama unfolds. There are many reminders that Miss Lizzie and the Actress are role-playing in Act I, but there are fewer in Act II. The outlines of Lizzie's character are consistent with those developed under Miss Lizzie's guidance in Act I, but the Actress' performance of Lizzie's actions on the day of the murders is almost completely uninfluenced by Miss Lizzie/ Bridget, who is mostly absent from the stage during the buildup to the first murder. Bridget exits just after the beginning of Act II, reappears twice, briefly, instructing the Actress/Lizzie only once—"You mustn't cry"—before the Actress/Lizzie leads Mrs. Borden upstairs to her death.

Later, Miss Lizzie/Bridget appears unobtrusively just before the Actress/Lizzie picks up the ax to murder her father as he sleeps. Under Pollock's direction, the blackout that occurs just as the ax hesitates at the apex of its path was accompanied by a chilling scream. Who screams? One thinks of Bridget, horrified by Lizzie's deed. But could it be that Lizzie is horrified by the Actress' depiction of her as murderer of the father she loved? (Of course it could have been pure theatricality—just a scream, to underscore the horror of the moment.)

Because the Actress' portrayal of Lizzie as an ax murderer is so vivid and so psychologically convincing, and because our absorption in the unfolding events of Act II is virtually undisturbed by reminders that this Lizzie is an actress' creation—despite the theatricality of the blackout at the moment before the "onstage" murder — an audience is very likely to accept the truth of events as they have been portrayed. However, the end of the play provokes second thoughts on both the truth of the events just witnessed and the characterization of Lizzie as feminist heroine.

The characterization of Lizzie as a strong and independent woman in 1892 in undercut by the realization that in the frame play ten years later, Miss Lizzie still lives in the same house (which she had earlier longed to escape) and she still lives with her conventional sister Emma. Her dream of social prominence in a corner house on the hill remains unrealized, as does her alternate wish to live by herself on the family farm. Emma's concern about what people will think still intrudes on Miss Lizzie's life. Miss Lizzie has formed a bond with the unconventional Actress, but she is still chained to the old values, represented by Emma. Quite realistically, she has been unable to free herself entirely from the social role she might have hoped to escape with the death of the older Bordens—her transformation is limited. She is independent enough to maintain a socially unacceptable liason with the Actress, but hardly more independent than she was ten years earlier in her flirtation with the married doctor. Lizzie occupies a middle ground between Emma and the Actress on the scale ranging from social constraint to freedom from social role-playing. It is the Actress, the *professional* role player, who is freely unconventional, uninhibited, strong. And, as the last line of the play (Miss Lizzie's "I didn't. You did") reminds us, it is the Actress who enacted the murders, who might be said to have created a Lizzie strong enough to commit them.

In the final scene, Lizzie rebuffs Emma's persistent questioning about whether she committed the murders. In a sequence which Pollock originally placed early in the play but which gained power when she moved it to the end, Lizzie turns the spotlight on Emma: "Did you never stop and think that if I did, then you were guilty too?. . . It was you brought me up. . . . Did you ever stop and think that I was like a puppet, your puppet . . . me saying all the things you felt like saying, me doing all the things you felt like doing, me spewing forth, me hitting out. . . ." This speech suggests a parallel between the Actress' creation of Lizzie and Emma's creation of Lizzie, an assertion of psychological reality in which the differences between life and art fade into insignificance. And the implication that Lizzie is what Emma created is no more true or false than that she is what the Actress created. The Actress projects herself into a situation described by Lizzie and creates a Lizzie who murders her parents. Emma, Lizzie claims, created Lizzie to respond to a situation as Emma never dared to herself—as the Actress would respond. The good girl needs the feminist, which is why Emma stays with Lizzie, even though she has good reason to fear her. One might say that Emma deliberately absented herself from the home on the day of the murders, to give Lizzie more opportunity to act. A feminist reading would see how all three women share complicity in the murder—and the stage direction has the Actress looking at the audience when Lizzie concludes the play with "You did," which suggests an extension of complicity to the audience as well.

However, Lizzie is not necessarily either Emma's creation or the Actress'. She is ultimately an unknown. As Lizzie claims in trying to explain to her father that she cannot live simply as the reflection of what others want to see, "If no one looks in the mirror, I'm not even there, I don't exist!" Both Emma and the Actress as creators constitute a defense for Miss Lizzie, barriers to any claim she might make to autonomy, to self-definition—or to responsibility. But this recognition, interesting as it may be to us intellectually, carries relatively little dramatic impact. Dramatically, the truth is that "Lizzie" is a murderer. The murders are psychologically convincing, theatrically vivid. They are not realistically presented—the "onstage" murder is highly stylized, in fact, not actually depicted at all. But the drama is more powerfully convincing than the theoretical possibility of a different reality. The drama satisfies, leaving an audience incurious about the reality, despite the invitation in the play's conclusion to dismiss the staged events as just an imaginative construct of the Actress'. Lizzie's life remains an enigma, but the Actress' dramatic portrayal is vivid and arresting. The Actress outshines her subject, and the drama eclipses whatever the reality might have been. The art is more real than life.

Source: Susan Stone-Blackburn, ''Feminism and Metadrama: Role-Playing in *Blood Relations*'' in *Canadian Drama,* Volume 15, no. 2, 1989, pp. 169–78.

John Simon

Simon reviews Pollock's play, finding the work well-crafted and thought-provoking yet a less than diverting evening of theatre.

Sharon Pollock's *Blood Relations* is . . . quite routinely boring. Lizzie Borden may not be the most original subject for the stage (Elsie Borden might have been more interesting), but a woman who, as Miss Pollock plainly suggests, could ax her father and stepmother to death in 1893, and even in those pre-Alan Dershovitz days, get herself acquitted, is not likely, you would think, to yield an infinitely talky, monotonous, and in most ways unsurprising play. It is this most successful Canadian playwright's notion, however, that Lizzie was a lesbian feminist as well as a free and cultured spirit stifling in the burg of Fall River. When her father kept signing over more and more of her rightful inheritance to his crude wife and her cruder brother, and would not listen to reason, what else was Lizzie to do?

The play begins in 1903, showing us Lizzie and ''the Actress'' (presumably based on Nance O'Neil) together *chez* Lizzie, in the most discreetly conveyed flagrante delicto. This line is not pursued; instead, the two women act out a highly sanitized version of what happened back then, with the Actress playing Lizzie, Lizzie playing the Irish maid, the parents and an uncle playing themselves, and one other actor playing both Lizzie's married swain and her defense attorney. An awkward conceit, especially as some character is always skulking or lowering around the periphery, while the story lurches this way and that, and the revelations come thin and slow.

The language is genteel and civilized enough, though now and then somewhat anachronistic (''hooligan'' appears several years too early, and I doubt if in that time and place anyone would ''soak up the ambience''). But the serious prolepsis is in the characterization: ''To have murdered one's parents or to be a pretentious small-town spinster—which is worse?'' asks one or another of the Lizzies. The author's accusing finger, I'm afraid, points to the latter. I felt uncomfortably throughout that I was supposed to view the case as justifiable homicide. Under David Kerry Heefner's routine direction, and in a handsome production with a particularly apt set by Ron Placzek, all the actors are adequate, and both Lizzies, the mysterious Jennifer Sternberg and the extremely subtle Marti Maraden, outstanding.

Source: John Simon, ''Stages of Boredom'' in *New York,* Volume 16, no. 9, February 28, 1983 , p. 78.

SOURCES

Bessai, Diane. Introduction to *Blood Relation and Other Plays* by Sharon Pollock, NeWest Press, 1981, p. 8.

Gilbert, S. R. ''Sharon Pollock'' in *Contemporary Dramatists,* edited by James Vinson, St. Martin's Press, 1983, pp. 642-45.

Knowles, Richard Paul. ''Sharon Pollock: Personal Frictions'' in *Atlantic Provinces Book Review,* February-March, 1987, p. 19.

Mombourquette, Mary Pat. ''Blood Relations'' in the *International Encyclopedia of Theatre,* Volume 1: *The Plays,* edited by Mark Dady-Hawkins, St. James Press (Detroit), 1992, pp. 71-72.

Nunn, Robert C. ''Performing Fact: Canadian Documentary Theatre'' in *Canadian Literature,* Winter, 1984, pp. 51-56.

Pollock, Sharon. ''Canada's Playwrights: Finding Their Place'' in *Canadian Theatre Review,* Spring, 1982, pp. 34-38.

Saddlemyer, Ann. ''Crime in Literature: Canadian Drama'' in *Rough Justice: Essays on Crime in Literature,* edited by M. L. Friedland, University of Toronto Press, 1991, pp. 214-30.

St. Pierre, Paul Matthew, ''Sharon Pollock'' in *Canadian Writers since 1960,* second series, edited by W. H. New, Gale (Detroit), 1987, pp. 300-06.

Wallace, Robert, and Cynthia Zimmerman. *The Work: Conversations with English-Canadian Playwrights,* Coach House Press, 1982, pp. 114-41.

Weiss, Peter. ''The Material and the Models'' in *Theatre Quarterly,* January-March, 1971, pp. 41-43.

FURTHER READING

Langley, Winston E., and Vivian C. Fox, Editors. *Women's Rights in the United States: A Documentary History,* Greenwood Press, 1994.

This is an overview of the progress of women's rights in this country. The subject matter provides good background for understanding the circumstances of Pollock's female characters in *Blood Relations.*

Porter, Edwin H. *The Fall River Tragedy: A History of the Borden Murders,* King Philip Publishers, 1985.

Written by one of the reporters who covered the Borden murder case, this is a reprint of the book issued after trial. Reports say that all the books in the first pressing were bought up by Lizzie Borden.

Steele, Apollonia, and Jean F. Tener. *The Sharon Pollock Papers,* Canadian Archival Inventory Series, 1989.

An excellent overview of Pollock's work. This includes a critical essay on Pollock by Professor Denis Salter.

Zimmerman, Cynthia, Editor. *Playwriting Women: Female Voices in English Canada,* 1994.

This works studies six Canadian Women playwrights, including Pollock, and issues of feminism in their plays.

Cat on a Hot Tin Roof

TENNESSEE WILLIAMS

1955

Cat on a Hot Tin Roof, Tennessee Williams's third significant play (following *The Glass Menagerie* [1944] and *A Streetcar Named Desire* [1947]), was a huge commercial success, running for 694 performances on Broadway. It won Williams his third New York Drama Critics' Circle Award and his second Pulitzer Prize (his first being for *Streetcar*). Elia Kazan produced and directed the play in 1955 at the Morosco Theatre, after asking Williams to revise the third act to improve its dramatic progression. The published play script includes both the original version and the one revised for Kazan, appended by a preface in which Williams defends his original version. He continued to prefer the original, even after making further changes for a 1974 revival.

Cat on a Hot Tin Roof is rather loosely based on Williams's short story "Three Players of a Summer Game," a narrative that reveals the influence of D. H. Lawrence on the playwright's early work. *Cat on a Hot Tin Roof,* however, has all of the earmarks of Williams's unique dramas, involving as it does his emotionally biographical themes of ambivalence in sexual orientation, disaffection, and difficulty in maintaining intimate relationships. The play concerns a young man's disaffection and descent into alcoholism following the death of his college friend, and his wife's efforts to make him stop drinking so that he can take over his dying father's plantation.

Although criticized as being overly "violent" and maudlin, the powerful second act, in which the father, Big Daddy, confronts his alcoholic son, Brick, about the nature of his relationship with his friend, Skipper, is considered a hallmark of contemporary drama—Williams at his best. In that one long and vivid scene, the playwright portrays a profound relationship of mutual trust and respect, one that nevertheless fails to bridge the two men's weaknesses.

AUTHOR BIOGRAPHY

Tennessee Williams (born Thomas Lanier Williams on March 26, 1911) was the second child of a genteel southern belle and a traveling salesman who came from a long line of frontiersmen and glib politicians. Sickly and weakened by a life-threatening bout with diphtheria, the quiet child preferred books to sports, earning him the scornful nickname "Miss Nancy" from his robust father. Williams spent his early childhood in Tennessee in the rectory of his maternal grandfather, an Episcopal minister, mostly in the company of his older sister Rose and his domineering mother, Edwina. The conflict between his puritan maternal family and the cavalier sensuality of his father's side of the family warred within him for the rest of his life. This duality fueled his art with tension and plagued his life with bouts of mental breakdowns, addictions, and depression.

Williams's art reflected the emotional currents of his life: guilt over the deterioration of his schizophrenic sister Rose (who underwent one of the first prefrontal lobotomies to be performed in the United States), the masking of his own homosexuality (which he did not reveal publicly until 1970), and his addictions to alcohol and sleeping pills. In his plays, themes of cannibalism, rape, mutilation, sexual frustration, and twisted love disrupt the complacent southern decorum his troubled characters struggle to maintain.

Williams published his first short story at age seventeen and established himself as a cornerstone of Southern Gothic drama in his early thirties with *The Glass Menagerie* (1944), a nearly autobiographical version of Rose's stunted social coming out. For the next forty years he would produce a new play every two years, with his most acclaimed works appearing in the early half of this period. *A Streetcar Named Desire* (1947) and *Cat on a Hot Tin Roof* (1955) both won Pulitzer Prizes. In his heyday, Williams was the *enfant terrible* of contemporary theater; a gifted provocateur who delighted in shocking and titillating his audiences. Ill-health compounded by his addictions led to a complete mental and physical collapse in 1969, and his work, ever more lascivious, never recovered the vitality of his early plays. He died in 1983, eight years after the publication of his *Memoirs,* in which he revealed the intimate and sometimes sordid details of his tortured personal life.

Tennessee Williams

PLOT SUMMARY

Act I

Cat on a Hot Tin Roof takes place entirely in the bed-sitting room of the Pollitt plantation home in the Mississippi Delta. The plantation once belonged to a pair of bachelors, and it still shows evidence of their taste for "the Victorian with a touch of the Far East." Big Daddy had once worked for them as an overseer; now he owns the plantation and most of the land for miles around, having spent his life building it into a dynastic empire, "twenty-eight thousand acres of the richest land this side of the valley Nile." It is Big Daddy Pollitt's sixty-fifth birthday, and he is in an especially celebratory mood because he has just received the results of exploratory surgery: the pains in his stomach are not due to cancer as he had feared for three years but are merely the pangs of a spastic colon. However, Big Daddy and his wife, Big Mama (Ida Pollitt) have not been told the truth. The rest of the family knows that he does indeed have terminal cancer.

The action takes place in the upstairs bed-sitting room because Big Daddy's younger and favorite son, Brick, broke his ankle the night before while attempting to jump hurdles on the high school athletic track following a drinking bout.

Brick and his wife Maggie are getting ready for Big Daddy's birthday party when the first act opens. It becomes clear that Maggie resents the presence downstairs of her brother- and sister-in-law's brood of five "no-neck monsters" whose very existence are a reproach to Maggie, who has not produced the desired offspring with Brick. She wants and needs this proof of their readiness to take over the plantation, but Brick, who suffers from a disinterest in the plantation and apparently life itself, refuses to sleep with her. His disaffection stems from his unresolved relationship with Skipper, his best friend from college who died from drug and alcohol abuse.

Maggie recounts Skipper's downfall: he began drinking after Brick and he established their own pro football team. A spinal injury kept Brick home for a few away games, which Maggie attended with Skipper. After drinking together Maggie accuses Skipper of being in love with her husband. In response, Skipper attempts to prove his manhood to her in bed, but when he is unable to perform, he assumes that her accusation is right. Skipper abandons his career in pro football to succumb to the world of drugs and alcohol, which kills him. Her story momentarily snaps Brick out of his drunken reverie, and he swings his crutch at her head, barely missing her, and falls, as Maggie reminds him that she, unlike Skipper, is still alive.

They are interrupted by Dixie, one of Gooper and Mae's children. Dixie blurts out that Maggie is jealous because she can't have children. The scene closes with Maggie's announcement that the party guests are arriving.

Act II

Act II begins where Act I left off, with the arrival of Big Daddy, Reverend Tooker, Gooper, and Mae. Big Daddy expresses his lack of enthusiasm for the celebration in a single word, "Crap!" In walks the overweight Big Mama, who good-naturedly tolerates jokes at her expense. Gooper and Mae ostentatiously draw attention to Brick's drinking, which Brick affably ignores. None of the insincere birthday congratulations affect Big Daddy, but Big Mama bursts into sentimental tears—in her relief that Big Daddy does not have cancer. Big Daddy is relieved too but puts his positive feelings into interrogating Brick about the broken ankle, demanding to know if he broke it "layin' a woman."

Eventually the guests depart, leaving Big Daddy and Brick alone to talk. Brick would rather just drink until he feels the "click" that puts him into oblivion. But Big Daddy has a new lease on life, and he wants to have a frank talk with his beloved son. Big Daddy's confessions of sexual appetite and ease with a world of mendacity (lies and untruths) only disgust Brick, who tries to end the conversation. Big Daddy pursues the issue that he thinks may be bothering Brick, attempting to reassure his son that he will accept whatever kind of relationship Brick had with Skipper. But Brick is too defensive about the issue to appreciate his father's generosity.

Big Daddy then shocks Brick by announcing that it was Brick's rejection of Skipper that killed him (Skipper had called Brick to tell him about his episode with Maggie, but, unwilling to hear such a confession, Brick had hung up on his friend; the rejection was obviously too much for Skipper and the next Brick heard of his friend was the announcement of his death). The revelation of this truth leads Brick to retaliate with his own revelation: that Big Daddy does have cancer—and that all of the assembled party know it. These two men, who share a love for truth and a disdain for mendacity, are too mired in the pain of their private torments to attempt a connection with each other that might ease their respective suffering. The scene ends with Big Daddy's rage, condemning his family and all of the world as "lying dying liars."

Act III

[*There are at least three published versions of Act III. The one most often produced is the second version, which Williams revised at the request of producer/director Elia Kazan, who insisted that Big Daddy was too important a character to drop after the second act. The following summarizes Williams's original version. Williams defended it in the preface to the Broadway version as being truer to the character of Brick, who, Williams said, would have been unable to show the kind of dramatic progression that Kazan demanded for the Broadway production.*]

Again, no time elapses following the previous act. Everyone is asking where Big Daddy has gone, and Big Mama presumes he has gone to bed. After some prattling about the old man's resilience and Brick's drinking, the younger people get down to the important business at hand: Gooper, Mae, and Maggie want to tell Big Mama the truth about Big Daddy's cancer and then elicit her support in their competing plans to take over the plantation. The tension between Gooper and Mae on one hand and Maggie on the other comes to verbal blows as each sarcastically attempts to reveal the grasping designs of the other. Throughout the scene Brick blandly serves himself drinks and looks longingly out at the cool, detached moon.

Big Mama desperately appeals to Brick, saying that if he would only have a child, Big Daddy would happily leave the plantation to him. Brick fails to respond, but Maggie puts herself on the line with an astonishing announcement that she is pregnant. Gooper and Mae question her honesty while Big Mama runs to tell the news to Big Daddy. The scene ends with Brick and Maggie alone. She has locked up his liquor with the intention of returning it only after he has performed the duty necessary to ''make the lie true.'' The curtain falls as she turns out the light and gently embraces Brick.

CHARACTERS

Doctor Baugh

Doc Baugh's purpose in the play is to authenticate the fact that Big Daddy, does, indeed, have terminal cancer and not a ''spastic colon'' as Big Daddy has been led to believe. By ignoring the comments around him, Doc Baugh manages to stay out of the family's destructive squabbling; he simply explains the medical reality and leaves a hypodermic package of morphine to relieve Big Daddy's more severe pain when it inevitably comes.

Big Mama

See Ida Pollitt

Brother Man

See Gooper Pollitt

Doc

See Doctor Baugh

Lacey

Lacey is the Pollitts' good-natured black servant. Lacey and Sookey cackle at the family jokes and know enough to wait until after Big Daddy's fit of pique over Big Mama's ''horsin'' around to bring in the birthday cake and champagne.

Maggie the Cat

See Maggie Pollitt

Big Daddy Pollitt

Big Daddy is the center of attention in the Pollitt family, not only because he holds the position of patriarch but because he is dying and his property is up for grabs. Big Daddy has risen from the position of plantation overseer to the owner of the plantation. He thinks he has a spastic colon, ''made spastic by disgust'' by ''all the lies and liars . . . and hypocrisy'' that surround him. When Big Mama protests that she has loved Big Daddy, in spite of his ''hate and hardness'' for forty years, he responds with the exact words that Brick speaks to Maggie, ''Wouldn't it be funny if that was true.''

Big Daddy has been his own man for so long that he has not been ''infected by [the] ideas of other people.'' Thus, remarkable for the era in which the play takes place, Big Daddy does not judge Brick's relationship with Skipper as inappropriate. Unfortunately his acceptance comes too late for Brick, who continues to keep himself emotionally removed from everyone around him. Big Daddy genuinely loves Brick, offering his son the kind of unconditional love for which Brick respects his father. It is this unbounded trust for each other in a world of ''mendacity'' that ties the two men together and which not one other character in the play possesses

MEDIA ADAPTATIONS

- *Cat on a Hot Tin Roof* was adapted for film in 1958 by Metro-Goldwyn-Mayer (MGM). It was written (with Jame Poe) and directed by Richard Brooks and stars Paul Newman as Brick, Elizabeth Taylor as Maggie, and Burl Ives, who reprises his stage role, as Big Daddy. Both Newman and Taylor received Academy Award nominations for their performances. Taylor's is considered by many critics to be the definitive portrayal of Maggie the Cat. It is available on videotape from MGM/GBS Home Video.
- In 1976 Lawrence Olivier tried his hand at Big Daddy with Maureen Stapleton as Big Mama and the real-life husband and wife team of Robert Wagner and Natalie Wood as Brick and Maggie. Directed by Robert Moore.
- Jessica Lange was Maggie in a 1984 television production that also included David Dukes as Gooper, Tommy Lee Jones as Brick, and Rip Torn as Big Daddy. The production is available from MGM and Vestron home video.

or comprehends. Big Daddy's tragedy is not that he must die but that he dies thinking that Brick, just like all of the others, was going to lie about his cancer too.

Brick Pollitt

Brick has made a virtue of indifference, first as a football star admired from afar by family and friends, then as a dreamy alcoholic, hiding the truth of his complicity in his best friend's death behind a mask of indifference. Brick punishes himself and his wife, Maggie, whom he would rather have take the blame for Skipper's descent into drugs and alcohol. Brick imposes two punishments on himself and on his wife. One is drinking until he feels the ''click'' releasing him into the welcome oblivion of intoxication; he uses alcohol as a means of escape. The other is sexual abstinence.

Brick knows that his feelings for Skipper were ''pure an' true,'' and he claims disdain for a world that would have called him and Skipper ''fairies.'' But the real source of his guilt lies instead in remembering the night that Skipper called him, drunk, to confess, having been tricked by Maggie into believing himself a homosexual. Brick hung up on him. It was Brick's own rejection that caused Skipper's death, not an uncomprehending world. Brick fails to recognize his guilt until his father forces him to face it. Big Daddy loves Brick and loves the truth too. But Brick tragically misunderstands his father's motives and once more retaliates outward instead of accepting the truth. According to Williams, Brick suffers from ''moral paralysis:'' he cannot rise from the morass of his ''spiritual disrepair.''

Dixie Pollitt

Dixie is one of Mae's ''brood'' of children who run wild through the house and yard when not on display or performing vaudevillian songs as part of their parent's relentless drive to gain Big Daddy's attention and appreciation. Naturally, all of their antics fail to please. Dixie has overheard her parents discuss Maggie's failure to produce a child, and she taunts her aunt with this piece of information when Maggie reprimands her for misbehaving.

Gooper Pollitt

Big Daddy's eldest son. In his race against his brother Brick to win Big Daddy's approval and guarantee his claim on the estate, Gooper stoops quite willingly to calling attention to Brick's drinking problem and general indifference to Big Daddy. Gooper announces to the assembled birthday celebrants that he bets ''500 to 50'' that Brick does not even know what gift he bought for Big Daddy, knowing that Maggie bought the present since Brick himself would not bother. The older son hopes that by exposing Brick's disdain for their father, Big Daddy will transfer his allegiance to Gooper. But Big Daddy prefers his younger son's honest neglect over his elder son's obsequious fawning.

Ida Pollitt

Sincere, foolish, fat, always laughing ''like hell at herself,'' Big Mama's idea of fun (pulling the Reverend Tooker onto her lap when he extends his hand to help her up from the sofa) is not consistent with the kind of society to which Mae and Maggie aspire. Big Mama laughs the loudest at her husband's insults about her ''fat old body'' and general incompetence, but she often has to ''pick up or fuss with something to cover the hurt the loud laugh doesn't quite cover.'' She only lamely chastises Brick for drinking and expresses genuine concern for Maggie's childless plight.

Ida is ineffective at bringing her family around to her values of Christian love and forgiveness, loving and forgiving them so absolutely that they ignore her existence. Her laughter at her own expense, however, masks a tender and sincere soul, one that emerges poignantly when she learns that Big Daddy will die of cancer after all. In her genuine grief she gains a new dignity that she retains throughout the rest of the play.

Mae Pollitt

Mae flaunts the comfortable snobbery of the foolish. She is probably the driving force behind her impassive husband Gooper's persistence in securing Big Daddy's estate, despite Big Daddy's obvious scorn for his elder son. Mae's one shining moment was as the ''cotton carnival queen.'' Now she is squared off against Maggie for the role of future matriarch over Big Daddy's twenty-eight thousand acres of land—and the place in society such a role will accord her. Mae fights with everything she's got: by producing five children (the sixth is on the way) to guarantee the family line, by kissing up to Big Daddy and Big Mama, and by eavesdropping outside of Maggie and Brick's bedroom door in order to report Brick's drinking and sexual abstinence or any other gossip that might discredit their claim to the inheritance.

Maggie Pollitt

Maggie is a pretty southern woman who comes from a humble family and sees a slim but promising hope of getting ''something out of what Big Daddy leaves.'' She has a melodic southern drawl, an indulgent easy tolerance of her husband Brick's alcoholic distance but also a self-confessed ''hard'' edge, brought about her desperate situation. It is quite clear which holds the most importance to her between her love for Brick and her desire for a healthy portion of the Pollitt estate: she prefers the money, although she hungers for her husband's attentions as well.

Maggie calls herself a ''cat on a hot tin roof'' alluding to her precarious position with Brick, who will not sleep with her, and with her brother- and sister-in-law, who have the better claim on the Pollitt estate because of their brood of five ''no-neck monster'' children. Maggie, with the tenacity of an alley cat, intends to convince Brick to have sex with her to keep them in the running. The bow-and-arrow ''Diana trophy'' she won in an archery contest at Ole Miss is emblematic of her relationship with Brick and his family—she is the hunter. On stage Maggie is an elegant beauty, alternating between unabashed coquetry and vicious reproach: she is ''catty'' because, as she puts it, she's ''consumed with envy and eaten up with longing.''

Sister Woman

See Mae Pollitt

Sookey

Another black servant who serves the Pollitt family.

Reverend Tooker

The stage notes read that Tooker is ''the living embodiment of the pious conventional lie.'' Reverend Tooker spends his time at the birthday party dropping transparent hints about the various endowments other families have given to rival churches when their patriarchs died. His only purpose in sharing Big Daddy's birthday celebration seems calculated to garner his church a generous portion of the Pollitt estate. Tooker's nature is nakedly revealed when an unexpected pause in the general conversation catches him crassly joking to Doc

Baugh about the "Stork and the Reaper running neck to neck" in the Pollitt home.

THEMES

Truth versus Mendacity

A preoccupation with telling the truth, having the strength to accept the truth, and withholding the truth runs through *Cat on a Hot Tin Roof.* Big Daddy thinks he has just learned the truth when he is told, after extensive medical examinations, that he merely has a spastic colon and not cancer as he had feared. But this is not the truth; his worst fear is realized when Brick, in a moment of anger tells him that he is, in fact, dying. Brick has let out the big secret in response to Big Daddy's unveiling of Brick's secret truth—that Brick drove Skipper to the suicidal use of alcohol and drugs when he hung up on Skipper's attempt to "confess" his homosexual love for Brick. While Brick believed that the confession resulted directly from Maggie's jealous pressure upon Skipper, he also feared that he and Skipper's love would be misunderstood, even though it was the most "true" thing he had ever known.

Rather than face the truth of his role in his friend's death, Brick withdraws from the world, complaining that it is full of lies and liars ("mendacity"). His hatred for mendacity is a trait he shares with his father, Big Daddy, although the two men fail to recognize the extent to which their values correspond. Big Daddy has learned to live and thrive within a world of mendacity. Although he appears crass, he cares about Brick. While Big Daddy has learned to live with lies, his son cannot, turning to liquor to escape not only from liars but also from the horrible truth about Skipper's death. Brick gives no indication of the impact his discussion with Big Daddy has had on him; he remains aloof (and drunk) throughout the rest of the play. It becomes clear that Big Daddy, who lived with mendacity, had a healthier means of keeping himself true than does his son.

Homosexuality

When *Cat on a Hot Tin Roof* was first staged, its main theme was widely thought to be homosexuality. Williams denied this, and the play itself, after entering a more sexually permissive era, demands acknowledgment that homosexuality is not its central concern. Brick's love for Skipper, he insists—and both Maggie and Big Daddy affirm—was a platonic, non-physical love. That the physical aspect of their love is never resolved in the play indicates the discomfort and ambivalence over homosexuality that existed in the 1950s. Was Brick in love with Skipper, or was theirs the simple and profoundly deep love of friendship that Brick proclaims it to be? Brick had had a satisfactory relationship—sexual and otherwise—with Maggie until her jealousy of Skipper prompted her to disrupt the careful balance the three of them had achieved. Can two men who love each other also participate in a physical, sexual relationship without harming their status in society? This question reverberates in the play because the answer as to whether or not Brick and Skipper physically consummated their love is precluded by Skipper's death. Writers often "kill off" a character whose actions or presence contradict or threaten society's most cherished mores, thus raising a question without openly challenging the society with an explicitly stated answer.

Idealism

In this play, idealism opposes life itself, with its messiness and its impure combination of good and bad. When Brick tells Big Daddy that he drinks out of disgust with mendacity, he reveals that he is an idealist. Big Daddy explains to his son that he too feels surrounded by mendacity; it thrives in his family, in the church, in his clubs, even in himself, forcing him to make a pretense of liking it all. But Big Daddy is a realist—he keeps his ideals separate from his life. Big Daddy enjoys living: his idea of celebrating his new lease on life is to find a woman, "smother her with minks and hump her from hell to breakfast."

Brick, on the other hand, eschews sexual passion absolutely, looking up at the cool moon as a model of the ideal detachment he wants in his life and relationships. Brick's form of idealism is an escape from life. Maggie refuses to let him escape, however. She accuses him of feeling a passion for Skipper so "damn clean" and incorruptible that it was incompatible with life—"death was the only ice box where you could keep it," she tells him. Maggie defies Brick's sterile idealism, his death-

TOPICS FOR FURTHER STUDY

- Why does Maggie's announcement that she is pregnant seem like a viable solution to her? Will it solve her and Brick's problems?
- Research Southern Gothic literature. In what ways is *Cat on a Hot Tin Roof* exemplary of this genre?
- How have women's economic and social roles changed since the first production of *Cat on a Hot Tin Roof* in 1955? In what ways have they remained unchanged?
- What elements normally associated with the Antebellum (post-Civil War) South appear in the play? What more modern elements appear? Explain how elements from such diverse eras can coexist in this play.

in-life oblivion achieved through alcohol, and she demands that he cure it with life—by fathering a child.

STYLE

Symbolism

Symbolism is the use of objects to evoke concepts or ideas. Williams has often been accused of excessive symbolism in many of his plays. Obvious symbols in *Cat on a Hot Tin Roof* are the cat, the moon, and Brick's crutch; equally prevalent are the diseases of alcoholism and cancer.

Alcoholism and cancer are linked in *Cat on a Hot Tin Roof* as two diseases representing problems in the spiritual well-being of their victims. Brick embraces alcohol as a way to keep his guilty feelings from surfacing. At the same time, the alcohol has slowly begun to make a slave of Brick, just as cancer is slowly taking over his father. Alcoholism is a self-imposed form of death-in-life when its victims drink in order to achieve a state of oblivion, as Brick does. It is a disease that will ultimately lead to death as cancer does.

Big Daddy did not choose to have cancer, but his state of illness represents his life—apparently healthy on the outside yet rotting from within. He has all of the trappings of a successful man, but his marriage and family are not equal to his financial success, and his desire to celebrate life by draping a girl in mink and ''humping her from hell to breakfast'' has a ring of hollowness to it. He has become a shell containing little but disease, as has his son, who has constructed his own shell out of alcohol.

Brick has a broken ankle, itself a symbolic castration, and he hobbles to and fro on the stage using a crutch. The noise and commotion of the crutch draw attention to his constant trips for more liquor. Brick either drops the crutch or has it taken from him no fewer than five times in the first two acts. At different times, Maggie and Big Daddy each withhold the crutch from him in order to elicit a promise or a response, and once Brick refuses to sit with his mother, because he prefers to stay on his crutch. The crutch stands for an emotional scaffolding holding his spiritual and emotional self together, but it is all too clear that it is an inadequate support and can easily be toppled.

Brick avoids his family through drink, preferring the company of the cool, silent moon. In much of literature, the moon represents madness, but in this play it suggests the silent detachment that Brick desires. Yet in a way, his longing for the moon—serene but also inert and cold as death—is a form of madness, because it is a departure from living. Counterpoised against his longing for detachment (death) is Maggie the Cat's longing for life. Cats are

Big Daddy (Burl Ives) and Maggie (Elizabeth Taylor) regard the troubled Brick (Paul Newman) in a scene from the 1958 film adaptation

scrappy, self-sufficient, calculating. The cat is also a creature, Brick reminds Maggie, who can jump or be thrown from a considerable height and still land on its feet. Maggie is like an alley cat—a survivor—and she offers to share her skills with Brick.

Setting

There are several aspects regarding the setting of *Cat on a Hot Tin Roof* that bear scrutiny. The entire play takes place in an upstairs bed-sitting room of the Pollitt plantation. In other words, it is a room for sleeping as well as for living. This in itself is significant, since accepting one's sexuality, living with it, is one important theme of the play. In addition, the decor of the room and presumably of the rest of the home is also significant. In the ''Notes for the [Set] Designer,'' Williams explains that the home is decorated in ''Victorian with a touch of the Far East.'' These are two polar opposites in terms of the mood they represent. The Victorian era was known for its prim morals, at least on the surface. Women wore long dresses that covered them from neckline to ankle, although the dresses also accentuated and, in some cases even enhanced, the bust and posterior. The play takes place after the Victorian era, so this choice in style deliberately recalls the rigid morals and conflicting attitudes of an earlier time.

The "touch of the Far East" is another deliberate gesture. As Edward Said explained in his 1978 work, *Orientalism,* the Far East has long been associated with wantonness and sensuality. Williams emphasizes the significance of the manor's decor through allusions to the pair of bachelors, presumably a homosexual couple, who previously owned (and decorated) the mansion. Thus, as Williams explains in the set notes, the room evokes their ghosts, "gently and poetically haunted by a relationship that must have involved a tenderness which was uncommon." Williams wanted his scenery to evoke sensuality and also lend a mood of dignity and grace to his subject. Furthermore, the set has a dreamy, surrealistic atmosphere accomplished with soft lighting and a night sky instead of a ceiling, adding the dimension of timelessness.

HISTORICAL CONTEXT

Domestic Life in the 1950s

The year of *Cat on a Hot Tin Roof*'s debut, 1955, was an interesting time for male and female relationships; a pre-feminist/pre-gay rights era when ideas about alternative life styles were incubating, though not openly emerging. According to the era's social norms, there simply was no viable alternative for the traditional, mom, dad, and two children family pattern that was portrayed in television shows such as *Father Knows Best;* in reality, few American families came close to this idealized version of life.

The 1950s also saw young people begin to question the dictates of society; many began experimenting with drugs, dress, dance, and language that challenged convention—though in a rather tame way compared to the counterculture movement of the 1960s. Actor James Dean, a role model of disaffected arrogance and diffidence, starred in his two hit films in 1955, *East of Eden* and *Rebel without a Cause,* then died unexpectedly at the age of 24 in a car wreck that September. He was instantly catapulted from film star to mythic icon. Like Dean's popular film characters, it became hip to smoke with a squint, wear a black leather jacket, and stand apart from society in aloof judgement.

The Beats

Nineteen-fifty-five was also the time of literary introspection, black turtlenecks, and booze—all hallmarks of what became known as the Beat Generation. The Beats, however, did not include everyone, just a segment of mostly intellectual nonconformists. In 1955 poet Allen Ginsberg (aged 29) read "Howl" to an small but appreciative audience in Berkeley, California. The poem would become a landmark in Beat literature (along with Jack Kerouac's *On the Road*), contributing to the general "hipness" of the literary arts with its jazzy pastiche of the beat life executed in one long, breathless sentence. The phrase the "Beat Generation" had been introduced to the world in a 1952 *New York Times Magazine* article written by John Clellon Holmes, a writer on the periphery of the Beat movement. Holmes explained that for the Beat Generation "the valueless abyss of modern life is unbearable." This was the generation that grew up with the ever-present knowledge that "the bomb" would inevitably be dropped. Drinking and drugs were a common method of escape for a time. Cynicism and idealism fused into a posture of studied indifference—with an element of wistful hope.

Women in 1950s Culture

The majority of women in the 1950s wore gut-pinching girdles and accepted their role as homemakers. For a woman of this era to want a career was unique but to want a career *and* a family was unprecedented. Women were expected to choose one or the other, and most women chose (as they were expected to) the suburban home, two children, and a working husband (who counted on his wife to clean house, make dinner, and take care of the kids). Abortions could be obtained but not easily (in many U.S. states, the procedure was illegal); moreover, not wanting a child was considered a social crime. If a woman finished college, she was expected to have found a husband there, not a job. Most women had children very early in their marriages and lives, and they stayed home to raise them. If they felt disgruntled about their status, they had few avenues for expressing their complaints; women who were restless were seen as "neurotic" and in need of psychological treatment. A child was often seen as a solution to marital stress. It would give both parents

COMPARE & CONTRAST

- **1955:** In the United States, only 34% of women between the ages of 20 and 54 work outside of the home. Most married women are dependent upon their husbands' or fathers' financial support and women are expected to be full-time homemakers.

  Today: Nearly 80% of women between the ages of 20 and 54 work outside of the home. Women and men share almost equal wage earnings. In many families, both husband and wife work and share in the domestic duties.

- **1955:** Married women are expected to want, and to have, children. A woman who can not produce a child is seen as incomplete by society.

  Today: Families consist of many combinations of parents who work and care for children, and having children is no longer a must for women, although many women still feel biological and social pressure to bear a child.

- **1955:** Society has very strict prejudices regarding open homosexuality. Gay men are forced to hide or repress their sexual activity, leading to the phrase ''in the closet.''

  Today: Though there is still considerable prejudice, society is much more accepting and understanding of homosexual relationships. This open culture has led to many gays coming ''out of the closet'' and publicly proclaiming their sexuality. Many have been encouraged by famous role models such as singer Melissa Etheridge, actor Ellen DeGeneres, and politician Barney Frank.

something to focus on and make them face reality and their problems.

CRITICAL OVERVIEW

When *Cat on a Hot Tin Roof* opened at the Morosco Theatre in 1955 it starred Ben Gazzara as Brick, Barbara Bel Geddes as Maggie, and folk singer Burl Ives (in his first dramatic production) as Big Daddy. Reviewers considered the play a powerhouse of emotion and they recognized that Williams had broken out of the slump he had been in since his success with *A Streetcar Named Desire* in 1947. But they refused him unequivocal praise; instead, many of them chided Williams for toying around the edges of the play's ''real'' topic: homosexuality.

Walter Kerr, writing in the *New York Herald Tribune,* praised the performers only to accuse Williams of being ''less than candid,'' of mislaying or deliberately hiding the ''key'' to the play. Eric Bentley, in *New York* magazine, noted too much concern about how everyone is doing in bed and declared that a writer has a duty not to be vague and unequivocal about his true topic. Although, in a 1955 interview with Arthur Waters for *Theatre Arts,* Williams flatly denied that Brick was a homosexual, a few sentences later he admitted that Brick felt some ''unrealized abnormal tendencies'' at ''some time in his life.'' Of course, this interview could only serve to reaffirm a belief that Williams was ambivalent about the topic and that this ambivalence carried through to his play. Another fifteen years would pass before Williams would publicly discuss his own homosexuality, and his admission would do little to defray the commonly held opinion that *Cat on a Hot Tin Roof* fails to engage the topic of homosexuality forthrightly. When the play was revived nineteen years after its initial opening, in a more sexually liberated America, the furor over the topic of homosexuality had abated, and both the language and the Pollitts' dramatic problems seemed more quaint than shocking.

Reviews of the 1974 revival shifted in focus but were no less harsh than the 1955 reviews. John Simon wrote in *New York* that the play was ''worthy commercial fare, but not art,'' and he found fault with symbolism that recurred ''ad nauseum.'' Simon called Brick a ''nonentity,'' whose realization that the mendacity he hates is his own is made ambiguous by Williams's failure to explain whether Brick betrayed ''his friend or his homosexuality.'' Other critics also sought to resurrect the play from overemphasis on the theme of homosexuality, suggesting that the core theme is and always had been about truth. Roger Ashton recognized this in 1955, asserting in his review in the *New Republic:* ''Mr. Williams in this play is interested in something far more significant than one man's psychological makeup. He is interested in what may and may not be said about the truth as a motivating source in human life.''

From the very beginning, critics have focused on the play's violent passions and language. Marya Mannes in the *Reporter* called the 1955 *Cat on a Hot Tin Roof* a ''special and compelling study of violence.'' Richard Hayes of *Commonweal* found it little more than an expression of this violence, with no central organizing structure: he judged the play ''lacks almost wholly some binding integrity of experience.'' Robert Hatch writing for the *Nation* concurred, saying that, ''without love and hope, discussion of vice and virtue becomes academic.''

It is true that the play leaves several important questions unanswered, such as who will inherit the Pollitt plantation, whether Maggie will convince Brick to make the lie of her pregnancy true, and whether Brick will own up to his role in Skipper's death. In fact, director Elia Kazan had asked Williams to rewrite the third act to resolve what he felt was the play's flawed dramatic progression. Even with Williams's revisions to Act III, the play's narrative difficulties persisted. Nevertheless, critics had to admit that Williams had captured an intensity of feeling few others could accomplish. What the play may lack in narrative unity and progression it makes up for in lyric expressionism. The play is an aesthetic paradox: according to *New York Post* critic Richard Watts it is ''insistently vulgar, morbid, neurotic and ugly [but it] still maintains a quality of exotic lyricism.''

Despite the misgivings of the press, *Cat on a Hot Tin Roof* was a commercial success. It ran for 694 performances and won Williams his third New York Drama Critics' Circle Award and his second Pulitzer Prize. Today *Cat on a Hot Tin Roof* is counted as one of Williams's three significant contributions to American theater, along with *A Streetcar Named Desire* and *The Glass Menagerie.*

CRITICISM

Carole Hamilton

Hamilton is an English teacher at Cary Academy, an innovative private school in Cary, North Carolina. In this essay she discusses the possibility that the play centers not on homosexuality or truth but on the need for blessings conferred by a dying patriarch.

Many early critics argued that the central conflict of *Cat on a Hot Tin Roof* is Brick's struggle with homosexuality—his reluctance to either admit his own homosexual tendencies or to understand those of his friend, Skipper. These critics saw Maggie's desire for a child as an attempt to counterbalance Brick's ambivalence and win him back to his ''true'' sexual nature. Yet the play is not explicit in explaining his desires or true motivations. Walter Kerr, writing in the *New York Herald Tribune,* referred to Brick's ''private wounds and secret drives'' as ''a secret half-told'' about which Williams is less than candid. Williams defended himself against this accusation by asserting that ''The bird that I hope to catch in the net of this play is not the solution of one man's problem. I'm trying to catch the true quality of experience in a group of people, that . . . interplay of live human beings in the thundercloud of a common crisis.'' In other words, Williams denied that homosexuality per se was the central issue of *Cat on a Hot Tin Roof.* Whether or not homosexuality is central, Brick, who appears in every scene of the play, is clearly a pivotal character.

Benjamin Nelson, in his book *Tennessee Williams: The Man and His Work,* argued that the play was not at all about Brick's sexuality but about his idealism and ''tragic disillusionment.'' Brick tells Big Daddy that he drinks out of ''disgust'' with ''mendacity.'' *New Republic* critic Roger Ashton also suggested that the play is interested in ''truth as a motivating force in human life.'' Williams's corroborated this reading by saying in a 1957 interview, ''I meant for the audience to discover how people erect false values by not facing what is true to their natures, by having to live a lie.''

Certainly the characters in the play demonstrate an unusual preoccupation with telling or withholding the truth: about Big Daddy's cancer, about the true nature of Brick's relationship with Skipper, and about Brick's role in Skipper's death. If the play revolves around the revelation of truth or around the characters' ability to withstand or tell the truth, then

WHAT DO I READ NEXT?

- *King Lear,* William Shakespeare's tragedy about a king who disperses his kingdom to his daughters only to find that they cared more for his wealth than for him. He finds himself abandoned in his old age. Japanese director Akira Kurosawa reinterpreted the Lear story in his 1985 film *Ran,* which involves ancient Japanese royalty in a similar inheritance dispute. American author Jane Smiley adapted the Lear legend in her 1991 novel *A Thousand Acres.*
- John Updike's 1960 novel *Rabbit Run* concerns a disaffected salesman who abandons his alcoholic wife and their child to look for ''freedom,'' only to return, guilt-ridden and still dissatisfied.
- William Faulkner's character, Quentin Compson, who appears in his novels *The Sound and the Fury* and *Absalom, Absalom,* kills himself when he recognizes humankind's essentially evil nature.
- In his popular *Tales of the City* series Armistead Maupin offers touching and realistic vignettes of the homosexual lifestyle in San Francisco.
- Brett Harvey's *The Fifties: A Women's Oral History* (1993), recounts the stories of several women as they look back on their coming of age in 1950s America.

one expects that these issues will get resolved out at the end. In Big Daddy's case, they are. He receives the truth about his cancer from Brick, howls in rage at those who withheld this truth from him, then goes offstage, ostensibly to die. Unfortunately, this all takes place in Act II with a entire act left in the play. According to the ''truth'' reading, the third act would show how Brick resolves his relationship to truth and mendacity. This question is left unanswered, however, and a great deal of stage time is spent with Brick's inner thoughts hidden.

The final act, which Williams revised three times to total four versions, has received a great deal of criticism; the majority of negative criticism condemned the act as a poor ending to a powerful play. Many critics have argued that the heart of the play lies in the confrontation between Brick and Big Daddy and that once they say their piece to each other (in Act II), the story is essentially over. Yet the play meanders around and around in a contest between Gooper, Mae, and Maggie regarding the estate. Another reading of the play, one which takes into account the importance of the distribution of property in the play, helps to justify the actions of the final Act. The attention to the estate in Act III may not in fact be a flaw in balance but rather a continuation of an important conflict that actually frames and puts into context the central conflict between Brick and Big Daddy.

A clue to reconciling the secondary characters' conflict over the property with the friction between Brick and his father lies in the inscription Williams included on the title page of the play. It is from Dylan Thomas's poem, ''Do Not Go Gentle into that Good Night:''

> And you, my father, there on the sad height, Curse, bless, me now with your fierce tears, I pray. Do not go gentle into that good night. Rage, rage against the dying of the light!

Dylan's poem is an exhortation to fight against death, to live fully until the very last moment of life. The last two lines are often quoted when a person is dying. The phrase, ''rage, rage'' recalls Shakespeare's King Lear in his moment of madness preceding his death. His madness stems from his daughters' rejection of him once he has given them all of his wealth and property; he realizes that they care more for his kingdom and wealth than for him as a person. Wandering cold and alone, he shouts impotently against a storm, ''Rage! Blow!'' Like King Lear, Big Daddy also recognizes the inherent greed in his offspring, and in the moments before his death, he too rages impotently ("Lying dying liars!") while his children continue compete for his fortune.

The first two lines of the Thomas poem also bear relevance to Williams's play. These are the less frequently quoted lines and therefore deserve close attention. They read: "And you, my father, there on the sad height,/Curse, bless, me now with your fierce tears, I pray." Here is a request for the dying father to bless or to curse the child before dying. The presence of these lines on the title page attests to the importance of a dying patriarch's blessing or curse in the play. Much critical interest has focused on the son's errant behavior, his relationship to homosexuality, his drinking, and his concern for truth or mendacity, but few critics address the significance of the father's blessing to this emotionally taut play.

In some of the biblical stories of Genesis (stories with which Williams would have been intimately familiar growing up with his mother's religious family), the dying patriarch would call his sons around him in order to give them his blessing and confer on them his inheritance. Usually the first-born son would get all or most of the property, unless he had displeased his father or a younger son had distinguished himself in some important way. Thus it was that Joseph, the younger son of Judah, received his father's blessing because Joseph provided for the whole family during a famine. The dying Judah then blessed or cursed his other sons, one by one, according to their deeds.

The framing story of *Cat on a Hot Tin Roof* clearly involves the distribution of the dying patriarch's property. Maggie introduces the topic within the first three minutes of the play, and the final act is nearly consumed with Gooper and Mae's attempts to wrench the estate away from Brick and Maggie. In addition, the problem of distributing the estate does receive a kind of resolution. Although the patriarch himself does not perform the ritual, the matriarch, Big Mama, assumes his role; she literally uses Big Daddy's language ("I'm talkin' in Big Daddy's language now!"). She warns the greedy young people that nothing will be granted until Big Daddy dies, but at the same time, she indicates quite clearly that she intends for the plantation to go to Brick—on the condition that he "pull himself together and take hold of things."

The framing story openly involves the conferral of property, but the imparting of a blessing (or curse), as alluded to in the Dylan passage, is not made apparent. Big Daddy does not appear on his death bed, announcing his legacy and granting his blessings on Brick. Yet there is a moment when Big Daddy *tries* to confer his blessing: during the long duologue in Act II, when he persists, against Brick's wishes, to talk with his son. Big Daddy tries to "straighten out" his son ("now that *I'm* straightened out, I'm going to straighten out you!") during this talk. He does so in order to bless his son with his new-found philosophy of life.

> "THE CHARACTERS IN *CAT ON A HOT TIN ROOF* DEMONSTRATE AN UNUSUAL PREOCCUPATION WITH TELLING OR WITHHOLDING THE TRUTH."

Brick is a kind of prodigal son who started out as the apple of his father's eye. The star of his high school football team, he went astray when his friend Skipper died. Brick's descent into alcoholism makes him a weak candidate to manage the estate. He is the wayward son, still loved, but unable to assume his father's position because he is "throwing his life away" in drink. Mae and Gooper count on Brick's continued drinking, which will put Gooper in contention for the inheritance. They draw attention to Brick's alcoholism at every opportunity. Big Daddy refuses to give up on his son, however, just as Maggie and Big Mama continue to hope and to nag at Brick.

Unfortunately, Big Daddy is disrupted in his effort to transform Brick, an effort which might have led to a blessing and conferral of property. Big Daddy seems on the verge of blessing Brick's relationship toward Skipper, openly hinting that he would even accept a homosexual relationship ("I'm just saying I understand such . . ."). But Brick cuts him off in mid-sentence, entering into a crescendo of emotion that ends with the abrupt announcement that Big Daddy does, after all, have terminal cancer. This revelation is too much for the father to handle; he departs from the room and from the rest of the play (as Williams wrote it in his first and preferred version).

Does this reading of the play not suffer from the same problem that other readings have? That, in

A scene from A Different Kind of Cat, *an adaptation of Williams's play by the Actors Workshop of Houston*

finding the climax in the second act, the third act is superfluous? Although this interpretation does not resolve all of the structural ''problems'' of the play, it does come to terms with the main focus of the final act: the characters' preoccupation with the distribution of the estate. Furthermore, and rather significantly, the topic of blessings weaves its way through the final scene in a subtle, yet persistent manner.

Early in Act III, Maggie says of Big Daddy, ''Bless his sweet old soul,'' and Big Mama responds, ''Yais, bless his heart, where's Brick?'' In this simple exchange, the dying patriarch is blessed and the favored son is recalled, reminiscent of the French ritual saying when a king dies, ''le roi est mort; vive le roi!'' (the king is dead, long live the king!); the old ruler has died and now allegiance is placed with the heir to the throne.

Another blessing comes from the Reverend Tooker, who, as he departs, blesses the family (''God bless you all . . . on this place''). Although a poor representative of spiritual reverence, his blessing reminds the audience of another way of processing a family death—with greater spiritual feeling and compassion. Mae and Gooper represent the antithesis of benediction when they say that they ''have faith in prayer, but . . . certain matters . . . have to be discussed.'' Maggie sarcastically says ''Amen'' to Gooper's comment that a crisis ''brings out the best and the worst'' in a family.

The references to blessings in the final act may be slim and tangential, but they contribute to a more coherent appreciation of the play's dramatic progression. For one thing, they cast a more favorable light on Maggie, the character referred to in the play's title. She may be consumed with the thought of material wealth, but she also appears to genuinely love Brick, as she repeatedly claims. Brick declares that he is tired and ''wants to go to bed.'' Although the resolution of his lying in bed with Maggie is not revealed, it can be inferred. Twice Maggie has announced that it is her time to conceive, and Big Mama has pronounced that a child would force Brick to give up drinking and get his life in order. Her wish is the same as the one Big Daddy expresses in Act II before being interrupted by Brick. Big Daddy had wanted to bless his son, and his blessing, although unsaid, presumably may serve to grace his son's marriage bed and the creation of a child.

Source: Carole Hamilton for *Drama for Students,* Gale, 1998.

Jere Huzzard

Huzzard examines sex roles in Williams's play. The critic's primary theme is that of the sexual ambivalence that the male characters feel toward the female characters, particularly Brick and Big Daddy as they respond to their respective spouses.

Cat On A Hot Tin Roof is, among other related themes, clearly a play about the sexual ambivalence of males toward females. Even the minor characters for whom little or no conflict is presented, are to various degrees or in various ways epicene in nature; the preacher humorously so; the two former owners of the plantation (while they lived) openly and complacently so; and Brick's older brother and foil, shielded by his maternalistic wife's appalling (to Maggie at least) fertility, unconsciously so. (Witness how his and his wife's laments over Big Mamma's lack of affection for him are bluntly explained by the mother: "Gooper never liked Daddy"). Add to this revelation the at least rough similarity between Big Mamma's and Mae's deficient emotional and intellectual development, and Gooper, for what it matters, can be seen as a typically Oedipal son in an obliviously blissful marriage to a woman redolent of his mother if possibly more affectionate.

But there is far more substantial motivation in the play for Big Daddy's preference for Brick as favorite son and heir-apparent than Gooper's repressed hostility for the father, revealed by his transparent hypocrisy and insensitive greed. The reason for Big Daddy's persistent affection for Brick and his reluctance to disinherit him in spite of Brick's childless state and his increasingly irresponsible alcoholism lies in the subtle sexual affinities the father shares with his troubled son.

These affinities are quintessential to the meaning of the play, and Williams in his original version, before acquiescing to a revised third act for Broadway, takes great care to develop them not only through the action but even through form, by a canny (and I think heretofore unnoticed) use of parallel and finally, climactically, identical lines of dialogue.

As the action builds in the brutal second act, Big Daddy shocks his son by alluding to his knowledge of and tolerance for homosexual experiences. When Brick rejects his father's touching attempt to reassure him of his understanding, Big Daddy retaliates by accusing his son of a kind of self-righteous hypocrisy: "*You!*—dug the grave of your friend and kicked him in it!—before you'd face truth with him!" Brick retorts: "*His* truth, not *mine!*" Big Daddy summarily concedes the fine point of distinction as irrelevant. But to the reader, it is not irrelevant. Is Brick's assertion justifiable indignation of hysterical repression? Notwithstanding the validity of Williams' observation in his stage directions that "Some mystery should be left in the revelation of a character in a play," which version of the third act has the greater claim to artistic legitimacy depends on the answer to this question; and to answer the question the reader must not just

"*CAT ON A HOT TIN ROOF* IS CLEARLY A PLAY ABOUT THE SEXUAL AMBIVALENCE OF MALES TOWARD FEMALES."

follow the flow of the dialogue that constitutes the action of the play, but observe certain parallel constructions in that dialogue—parallelisms that clarify and extend the meaning of the play through such form. In short, Williams will not sacrifice either the verisimilitude of his action or the realism of his dialogue to give the reader a patently complete psychoanalysis of Brick, but he will reveal more depth of character and meaning to those who will notice the form as well as the function of his art.

To this purpose (and using the lesser example first), the reader should recall Maggie telling Brick how cool, detached, and indifferent he had always been in bed with her, while Big Daddy confesses how he slept with his wife till he was sixty and "never even liked her, never did!" Clearly both father and son had enjoyed a physical competency that surpassed their capacities for psychical union with females.

But far more dramatically, if the original version of the play is used, the reader can find father and son speaking an identical line of dialogue under identical situations: "Wouldn't it be funny if that was true?" That Brick, for the climactic last line of the play, should repeat verbatim to Maggie a line spoken by Big Daddy to Big Momma in the second act of the play is surely no coincidence. The point is not the precise degree of cynicism (unascertainable) contained each time in the line, but simply that the same line is spoken by both men in response to their respective wives' protestations of love.

The play ending with such a subtle parallelism casts a vast additional light (too obvious to be belabored here) on these two main characters, on their poignant relationship with each other and with their wives, and consequently on the play as a whole. The revised third act for Broadway, with its unrealistically sudden, Pollyanna ending, might make for better box office receipts, but Williams' original version attests far superiorly to his creative genius for rich and complex tragedy.

Source: Jere Huzzard, ''Williams's *Cat on a Hot Tin Roof*'' in the *Explicator,* Volume 43, no. 2, Winter, 1985 , pp. 46–47.

Eric Bentley

In this 1955 review, Bentley addresses claims that Cat on a Hot Tin Roof *is among the first dramas to deal with homosexuality. Despite some advances over his contemporaries, however, Williams—in Bentley's view—has not yet approached the subject in a direct or satisfactory manner.*

Cat on a Hot Tin Roof was heralded by some as the play in which homosexuality was at last to be presented without evasion. But the miracle has still not happened.

The cat of the title is the heroine, the roof her husband; he would like her to jump off, that is, find a lover. Driven by passions he neither understands nor controls, he takes to drink and envies the moon; the hot cat and the cool moon being the two chief symbols and points of reference in the play. The boy says he has taken to drink because ''mendacity is the system we live in.'' His father, however, explains that this is an evasion: the real reason is that he is running away from homosexuality. At this point, the author abruptly changes the subject to the father's mortal illness, and he never really gets back to it. One does not of course demand that he ''cure'' the boy, only that he present him: he should tell the audience, even if he does not tell the boy himself, whether a ''cure'' is possible, and, if not, whether homosexuality is something this individual can accept as the truth about himself. At present, one can only agree with the father that the story is fatally incomplete.

If some things in Mr. Williams' story are too vaguely defined, others are defined in a manner far too summary and definite. The characters, for example, are pushed around by an obsessively and mechanically sexual interpretation of life. ''How good is he (or she) in bed?'' is what everyone asks of everyone. Now it seems to me that there are people, even in the world of Tennessee Williams, who would not ask this question, especially not of those who are near and dear. And what does the query mean? A girl seems good in bed if you like *her;* otherwise, she seems bad in bed; and for most of us that is the heart of the matter. Mr. Williams, who apparently disagrees, sends his people to bed rather arbitrarily. The husband's friend, in the new play, goes there with the wife to prove he is not homosexual. She must have been seeing *Tea and Sympathy,* for she co-operates. In the circumstances we can hardly be surprised that he proves impotent; yet he reaches the startlingly excessive conclusion that he is homosexual; and kills himself. Surely the author can't be assuming that a man is either 100 percent heterosexual or 100 percent homosexual? One wouldn't know: the whole thing is disposed of so grandly in quick, if lengthy, narratives. It is perhaps characteristic that the plot depends for its plausibility upon our not questioning that if a man and woman come together *once,* a child will result.

Not all the characters are credible. If a girl has a hunch that her husband is homosexual, does she simply clamor for him to sleep with her? Not, certainly, if she is the kind of girl portrayed at the Morosco by Barbara Bel Geddes. Which brings me to the relation of play and production. It seems to be a relation of exact antithesis. When the curtain first goes up, Mr. Williams sends on stage a girl whose dress has been spilled on at dinner; but, so far as the audience can see, the dress is as spotless as it is golden and sparkling. It is the same with her personality and character. From the author: a rather ordinary girl, bornée, perhaps stupid, shabby genteel. From the production: Barbara Bel Geddes, the very type of non-shabby, upper-class gentility, wholesome as a soap ad. It is the same with other characters. Burl Ives may not be right for Williams' shocking vulgarian of a father, but his pleasantness certainly keeps (to use his own vocabulary) the audience from puking. Ben Gazzara may not seem Southern, or a football player, or a TV announcer (the problem husband is all three) but he is handsome and he can act neurotic intensity. It is the same with the whole evening: the script is what is called dirty, but the production—starting with the Mielziner set and its chiefly golden lighting—is aggressively clean.

So what is the function of Mr. Kazan's directing—to mislead? Reviewing my book of *NR* pieces in *The New Leader,* Mrs. Kazan says I attribute Machiavellian motives to unmotivated, intuitive acts. That is why I speak here of the function of the directing and not its intention, the result and not the motive. Obviously, the motive is to ''make the most of the play''; but the most has been made of *Cat on a Hot Tin Roof* at the cost, it seems to me, of some conflict with the script. Some directors are content to subordinate themselves to an author and simply try to make his meaning clear. Others bring in extra meanings at the cost of understanding or even obscuring some of the author's meanings. So mystifications and obfuscations take place without Machiavellian intention. And no one, I believe, would deny that Mr. Kazan belongs to the second school. Giving such a "clean" production to such a "dirty" script, he has persuaded some that the dirt is unimportant. The show looks wholesome; therefore, it is.

Not that one would prefer to see all this moral squalor spelled out in full natural detail, but that one must not expect unco-ordinated double vision to provide a clear picture. In the last act, while the script is resolutely non-comittal, the production strains for commitment to some sort of edifying conclusion. While nothing is actually concluded, images of edification are offered to our eyes. Barbara Bel Geddes is given an Annunciation scene (made of more golden light and a kneeling posture). At the very end, as I said last week, comes the outward form of that *Tea and Sympathy* scene without its content. And, in many places throughout, a kind of mutually frustrating activity has the effect of muffling the emotions that are supposed to sound out loud and clear. On the other hand, there are places where director and author stand together. These include all the comic bits. It should not escape notice that Williams is a very gifted humorist. Author and director join forces to help Mildred Dunnock, Pat Hingle, and Madeleine Sherwood create three of those superb tragi-comic portraits in secondary roles which are one of the chief attractions of current New York theatre. (I am thinking back to Eileen Heckart in *Picnic* and *Bad Seed,* Elaine Stritch and Phillis Love in *Bus Stop,* etc., etc.) Author and director are together, too, in the best scene of the play—a masterly piece of construction both as writing and as performance—a scene between father (Burl Ives) and son (Ben Gazzara) in which a new and better theme for the play is almost arrived at: that the simple old family relationships still mean something, that, in the midst of all the filth and incoherence and impossibility, people, clumsily, inconsistently, gropingly, try to be nice to each other. In that old goat of a father, there is even some residue of a real Southern gentleman. Anyhow, he is Mr. Williams' best male character to date.

Though I believe the new script is often too naturalistically sordid for theatre, and therefore has to suffer changes Kazanian or otherwise, it is also true that in many passages the writing has its own flamboyant theatricality. The humor, though compulsively "dirty," is, by that token, pungent and, in its effect, rather original. The more serious dialogue, though rhetorical, is unashamedly and often successfully so; the chief rhetorical device, that of a

"IF SOME THINGS IN MR. WILLIAMS' STORY ARE TOO VAGUELY DEFINED, OTHERS ARE DEFINED IN A MANNER FAR TOO SUMMARY AND DEFINITE."

repetition of phrase somewhat *a la* Gertrude Stein, is almost always effective. There is no one in the English-speaking theatre today who can outdo Mr. Williams' dialogue at its best: it is supple, sinuous, hard-hitting and—in cases like the young wife and the father—highly characterized in a finely fruity Southern vein. Mr. Williams' besetting sin is fake poeticizing, fake philosophizing, a straining after big statements. He has said that he only feels and does not think; but the reader's or spectator's impression is too often that he only thinks he feels, that he is an acute case of what D. H. Lawrence called "sex in the head." And not only sex. Sincerity and Truth, of which he often *speaks* and *thinks,* tend to remain in the head too—abstractions with initial capitals. His problem is not lack of talent. It is, perhaps, an ambiguity of aim: he seems to want to kick the world in the pants and yet be the world's sweetheart, to combine the glories of martyrdom with the comforts of success. If I say that his problem is to take the initial capitals off Sincerity and Truth, I do not infer that this is easy, only that it is essential, if ever Mr. Williams' great talent is to find a full and pure expression.

Source: Eric Bentley, review of *Cat on a Hot Tin Roof* in the *New Republic,* Volume 132, no. 15, April 11, 1955, pp. 28–29.

SOURCES

Ashton, Roger. "Correspondence: Back on a Hot Tin Roof" in the *New Republic,* April 25, 1955, p. 23.

Atkinson, Brooks. "Williams's Tin Roof" in the *New York Times,* April 3, 1955.

Bentley, Eric. "Tennessee Williams and New York Kazan" in the *New Republic,* reprinted in Bentley's *What Is Theatre?,* McLelland and Stewart, 1968, pp. 224-31.

Hatch, Robert. Review of *Cat on a Hot Tin Roof* in the *Nation,* April 9, 1955, pp. 314-15.

Hayes, Richard. Review of *Cat on a Hot Tin Roof* in *Commonweal,* June 3, 1955, pp. 250-51.

Kerr, Walter. "A Secret Half-Told in Fountains of Words" in the *New York Herald Tribune,* April 3, 1955, sec. 4, p. 1.

Mannes, Marya. "The Morbid Magic of Tennessee Williams" in the *Reporter,* May 15, 1955, pp. 41-42.

Nelson, Benjamin. *Tennessee Williams: The Man and His Work,* Obolensky, 1961.

Ross, Don. "Williams in Art and Morals: An Anxious Foe of Untruth" in the *New York Herald Tribune,* March 3, 1957, sec. 4, pp. 1-2.

Said, Edward. *Orientalism,* Pantheon, 1978.

Simon, John. "A Cat of Many Colors" in *New York,* August 12, 1974, pp. 48-49.

Waters, Arthur B. "Tennessee Williams: Ten Years Later" in *Theatre Arts,* July, 1955, pp. 72-73, 96.

Watts, Richard. "The Impact of Tennessee Williams" in the *New York Post,* March 25, 1955, p. 57.

FURTHER READING

Crandall, George W. *The Critical Response to Tennessee Williams,* Greenwood Press, 1996.

This volume contains full-text reprints of newspaper and magazine reviews of Williams's works.

Devlin, Albert J. *Conversations with Tennessee Williams,* University Press of Mississippi, 1985.

A selection of interviews spanning forty years covering topics from Williams's advice to young writers to frank discussions of his problems with drugs and alcohol.

Spoto, Donald. *The Kindness of Strangers: The Life of Tennessee Williams,* Little, Brown, 1985.

A thorough and scholarly biography of Williams that analyzes the correspondence between his tormented life and his equally anguished drama.

Williams, Tennessee. *Memoirs,* Doubleday, 1975.

An autobiographical account of Williams's personal life that includes much detail about his sexual exploits. The book is useful in the context it provides for much of the playwright's work.

The Children's Hour

LILLIAN HELLMAN

1934

Lillian Hellman's *The Children's Hour* premiered in New York at the Maxine Elliot Theatre, on November 20, 1934, with a cast of relatively unknown actors. The play was based on an essay the playwright had encountered titled ''Closed Doors; or, The Great Drumsheugh Case.'' It related the true story of two female teachers who were condemned by their community when a student alleged that they were having a homosexual affair. It was produced and directed by Herman Shumlin, for whom Hellman had been working as a script reader. Shumlin knew the risks of bringing the work of a novice playwright directly to the Broadway stage without an out-of-town tryout, but he had great faith in the play. From the outset, he was confident of the work's quality and felt that it needed little of the refinement and rewriting that is generally done during preview performances.

The risk paid great dividends. The play was a major commercial success and almost immediately earned the playwright a lasting place in the American theater. It remained on the boards at the Elliot for 691 performances, which, at the time, set the record for the longest single-venue run in theater history. Among other things, it earned Hellman about $125,000 and netted her further career opportunities, including a contract for writing the first film adaptation of the work.

The production was helped by its reviews, which were generally favorable. Some, like those of

Brooks Atkinson and Joseph Wood Krutch, did complain about the last part of the play, which they was felt was too melodramatic in its final array of coincidences and too heavy in its moralizing; but most critics found little to complain of and enthusiastically welcomed Hellman as one of Broadway's newest luminaries.

Because of its theme, *The Children's Hour* also gained some notoriety. Initially, it was banned in Boston, Chicago, and London. The flap over its content also scared off the Pulitzer Prize selection committee, which refused to attend a single performance of the play. The uproar and likely censorship by the Hays Office also forced Hellman to turn the central adult conflict into a standard love and jealousy triangle in her film adaptation, released in 1936 as *These Three.*

Ironically, it was the theme of the play that kept it relevant enough to lead to a revision and stage revival in 1952, at which time it also served as an oblique criticism of the hearings then being conducted by the House Un-American Activities Committee. By that time, Hellman had been blacklisted (forbidden employment for her political beliefs) in Hollywood, which added fuel to the continuing controversy over the play. It remained banned in Boston, but by 1962, when another screen adaptation was released, its frank if understated treatment of the lesbian theme no longer fanned the fires of moral outrage, allowing a much more objective assessment of Hellman's considerable achievement.

AUTHOR BIOGRAPHY

Lillian Hellman, born in New Orleans, Louisiana, on June 20, 1906, was the only child of Max and Julia Newhouse Hellman. Her paternal grandfather, Bernard Hellman, had emigrated from Germany in 1848 and settled in the city's Jewish community, where her father grew up. Her mother's family, from Alabama, had banking and other commercial interests in New York, where, in 1911, her father, a shoe merchant, moved the family when an embezzling partner forced him into bankruptcy.

While growing up, Hellman made annual treks to New Orleans to stay with her two spinster aunts. Her life in New Orleans was ethnically and culturally insulated from the more rustic (and conservative) life and values of the agrarian South, yet some contact with its traditions was inevitable and these values stayed with Hellman for her whole life. Her schooling was entirely northern, however. After high school, she briefly studied at New York and Columbia universities, but, in 1925, she took a job with a publishing firm as a reader and married Arthur Kober, a press agent. The couple went to Paris to edit the *Paris Comet,* an English-language magazine.

After returning to America, Hellman worked as a writer in Hollywood, where she met her lifelong friend, Dashiell Hammett, the mystery writer. She divorced Kober in 1932 and began work as a reader for the Broadway producer, Herman Shumlin. By then she had already collaborated on a play called *Dear Queen,* which was never produced or published.

In 1934, Hellman presented Shumlin with a draft of her play *The Children's Hour.* He was much taken with the play, yet, because of its frank content, he had to produce it with a cast of unknowns, a serious risk. The play opened at the Maxine Elliot Theater on November 20, 1934, becoming an immediate hit, lasting through 691 performances, and breaking all previous box office and attendance records.

The production turned Hellman into an overnight celebrity and earned her about $125,000, a considerable sum at the time. She also wrote a film adaptation for Samuel Goldwyn (the head of the powerful Metro-Goldwyn-Mayer studio) while working on another stage play, *Days to Come,* which, in 1936, turned into a Broadway flop.

After becoming deeply involved in anti-fascist groups and traveling to Europe to witness the atrocities in the Spanish Civil War, Hellman garnered a new triumph with her 1939 staging of *The Little Foxes.* She then advanced her anti-fascist views in *Watch on the Rhine* (1941) and the screenplay *The North Star* (1943). These works, bordering on propaganda, and her association with leftist organizations would eventually lead her into trouble when congressional committees, headed by Senator Joseph McCarthy, began investigating communism in America. By 1948, when she planned to adapt Theodore Dreiser's novel *Sister Carrie* to the screen, she had been put on Hollywood's infamous blacklist (a list of communists and communist-sympathizers who were considered ''unemployable'' due to their political beliefs), where she remained for almost twenty years.

Meanwhile, Hellman continued to write for the stage. Her 1946 play, *Another Part of the Forest,* was followed by *The Autumn Garden* (1951), an adaptation of French playwright Jean Anouilh's *L'Alouette* entitled *The Lark* (1955), a libretto for the Leonard Bernstein musical *Candide* (1956), *Toys in the Attic* (1960), and an adaptation of Burt Blechman's novel *How Much?* entitled *My Mother, My Father, and Me* (1963). Prompted in part by the deaths of friends, including, in 1961, Hammett and, in 1967, poet Dorothy Parker, Hellman turned to writing memoirs, completing three such books before her own death on June 30, 1984: *An Unfinished Woman* (1969), *Pentimento* (1973), and *Scoundrel Time* (1976).

Lillian Hellman pictured in her home in 1944

PLOT SUMMARY

Act I

The Children's Hour opens in the living room of a New England farmhouse that Martha Dobie and Karen Wright have converted into the Wright-Dobie School for girls. A sewing class and recitation are in progress, under the disconnected control of Mrs. Lily Mortar, Martha's aunt. Student Peggy Rogers reads aloud from Shakespeare, while most of the other girls, somewhat chaotically, carry on with other activities, including sewing, cutting hair, and parsing Latin verbs. Mary Tilford enters very tardily, carrying some discarded, wilted flowers with which to placate the easily flattered Mrs. Mortar. Mary is clearly willful and manipulative, but she seems no match for Karen Wright, who sees through her ploys easily.

Karen enters and quickly disabuses Mary of the belief that she can get away with her lying claim that she picked the flowers. After the other children are dismissed, Mary takes another tack, complaining about being blamed for everything, but Karen is not very sympathetic and announces that Mary is to be punished and is prohibited from leaving the school grounds for two weeks. Mary then falls to the floor, feigning a heart attack and sobbing that she is unable to breathe. Karen responds by sending Lily Mortar off to have Martha Dobie call Dr. Joe Cardin, Karen's fiance and Mary's uncle.

After Karen carries Mary out of the room, she and Martha discuss the troublesome girl, their problems with Martha's Aunt Lily, and Karen's marriage plans. Joe Cardin enters and almost immediately goes off to examine Mary. After Karen leaves, Martha and Lily talk, gradually working into a heated exchange when Martha suggests that her flighty and selfish aunt go to London at Martha and Karen's expense. In a fit of pique, Lily accuses Martha of being jealous of Dr. Cardin, calling Martha's feelings for Karen "unnatural." The loud altercation is overheard by two students, who are listening from the staircase outside.

Joe returns, announcing that there is nothing wrong with Mary. When he starts talking of his forthcoming marriage, Martha gets very upset and cries on his shoulder. Karen then returns and asks Martha to call in Mary and the two eavesdropping students. She decides to reassign the girls' rooms, hoping to counteract Mary's bad influence. When the girls are left alone, Mary forces the others to tell her what they overheard. She then decides to go to her grandmother's house with her incubating scheme to destroy Martha and Karen, and, as the act ends, she extorts money from one of the girls through physical intimidation.

Act II, Scene 1

The second act opens on the same night, in the living room at Mrs. Tilford's house, just as Mary arrives, having run away from the Wright-Dobie School. She is grilled by Mrs. Tilford's suspicious maid, Agatha, who is wise to child's devious ways. Agatha informs Mrs. Tilford of her grandchild's return; the grandmother follows up with her own interrogation. At first, she too is incredulous and dismisses the child's complaints of maltreatment at the hands of Karen and Martha as exaggerated nonsense. She believes Mary is simply being foolish and making an emotional mountain out of a mound of childish, irrational fears, and she is determined to make Mary return to the school. Desperate, the girl begins spinning a vicious web of innuendos and accusations, gradually arousing Mrs Tilford's doubts. The woman is finally convinced when Mary whispers her charges against Martha and Karen, who, she claims, have actively engaged in a lesbian affair. The scene ends with Mrs. Tilford on the telephone, talking first to Dr. Cardin and then to Mrs. Munn, the first of the parents to whom she will spread Mary's poisonous libel.

Act II, Scene 2

A few hours later, still in the living room at Mrs. Tilford's house, Agatha warns Mary to behave when Rosalie Wells comes to spend the night. Rosalie, Mary's schoolmate, has been taken from school, thanks to the slander passed on to the parents of the Wright-Dobie girls by Mrs. Tilford. Rosalie and Mary do not like each other, but Mary is able to intimidate the other girl because she knows that Rosalie had stolen a bracelet from Helen Burton. Threatened with exposure, Rosalie gives a solemn promise to support whatever Mary says.

Immediately thereafter, Dr. Cardin enters. Mrs. Tilford searches for a delicate way to convey what she believes about Karen and Martha, but before she can explain why she feels that Joe should not marry Karen, Martha and Karen come in to confront Mrs. Tilford with what they have discovered from one of the girls' mothers: that they are accused of being lovers. Joe sides with Martha and Karen, insisting that Mary face the women with her story, but Mrs. Tilford initially refuses to allow it, believing that Karen and Martha are the brazen liars. Joe persists, however, and the girl is brought in. Under questioning, her lies become very obvious, but, on the verge of being completely unmasked, she claims that it was Rosalie who witnessed the alleged sexual encounters of Martha and Karen. At the curtain, Rosalie confirms the story, fearful that Mary will carry out her threats to tattle on her.

Act III

The action returns to the school's living room in November, several months later. In the opening conversation between Martha and Karen, it is revealed that the two women had lost a libel suit brought against Mrs. Tilford. The pair are dejected, uncertain as to what to do. They have been ostracized by the small community, their reputations destroyed. After a grocery boy appears with a delivery and they are subjected to his smutty giggles, Lily Mortar arrives from her European tour. Selfish and insensitive, she is surprised that her niece, Martha, is less than delighted to see her. She does not try to understand the anger of Martha and Karen, which arises from Lily's failure to return to America to serve as a witness in the civil suit against Mrs. Tilford. Martha confesses that she always hated Lily, forcing the woman to leave just as Dr. Cardin arrives.

Joe at first insists that Karen marry him immediately and that they take Martha with them to Vienna, where he had gone to school. He admits that he does not really want to go to Europe but insists that it is their only option. After Martha leaves, Karen forces Joe to ask the question that she knows must trouble him—whether there is any truth behind the slander. Saddened by his lack of trust in her, Karen convinces Joe that they must put their relationship on hold and sends him away.

When Martha returns and learns what Karen has done, she confesses that, in fact, there is some truth in Mary's accusations, that her attraction to Karen has been physical, though she was unaware of it until Mary forced her to face herself honestly. Karen, very upset, sends Martha off to rest, but Martha, burdened with guilt for ruining Karen's life and her own self-discovery, shoots and kills herself.

Karen (Patricia Neal) and Martha (Kim Hunter), the targets of Mary's scheme

After Aunt Lily frantically rushes in to announce to the emotionally drained Karen what has happened, Agatha enters, begging that the contrite Mrs. Tilford be allowed an audience. Over Lily's objections, Karen agrees to see the woman. Mrs. Tilford then enters and explains that she has discovered the truth. She promises to make restitution, but Karen tells her that is too late, that Martha is dead, and that she plans to go away after Martha's funeral. Although she refuses to forgive Mrs. Tilford, at the end she allows her some hope that she and Joe can restore their relationship and that she will accept the older woman's financial help.

CHARACTERS

Agatha

A no-nonsense, middle-aged maid in the employ of Amelia Tilford. She is stern and straight-laced with Mary, who calls her ''stupid,'' although Agatha clearly sees through Mary's deceptions. Agatha's attempts to make the child into a ''lady'' are frustrated by Mrs. Tilford, who is deaf to the maid's common-sense observations. Agatha also attempts to support Matha and Karen in their efforts to convince Mrs. Tilford that Mary concocted her story to destroy the young teachers.

Aunt Lily

See Lily Mortar

Helen Burton

One of the girls at Karen and Martha's school, she plays a limited role. It is her bracelet that classmate Rosalie Wells ''borrows,'' an act which allows Mary to blackmail Rosalie into confirming Mary's lies about Karen and Martha. Helen is one of the first to be pulled out of the school when Mrs. Tilford begins spreading the fiction that Karen and Martha are lesbian lovers.

Dr. Joseph Cardin

Cardin, about thirty-five, is a relaxed and amiable doctor and Karen Wright's fiance. His casual dress reflects his warm, easy-going nature. He is also gracious and humorous and seems ideally suited to Karen. Like her, he recognizes that his cousin, Mary Tilford, is a spoiled but troubled child, which makes him a dangerous adversary for Mary because he has influence with her grandmother. However, when Mary poisons Mrs. Tilford's mind

MEDIA ADAPTATIONS

- *The Children's Hour* was first adapted to film in 1936, released under the title *These Three.* It was produced by United Artists and Goldwyn Pictures, directed by William Wyler, and written by Hellman, who was obliged to remove the lesbian theme entirely. The film features Miriam Hopkins as Martha Dobie, Merle Oberon as Karen Wright, Joel McCrea as Dr. Joe Cardin, and Alma Kruger as Mrs. Tilford. The film is available on video from Sultan Entertainment and through the Internet Movie Database (http://uk.imdb.com).
- The play was again adapted to film in 1961, released under alternative titles: *The Children's Hour* and *The Loudest Whisper.* It was produced by United Artists and the Mirisch Company, and again directed by William Wyler. The film stars Audrey Hepburn as Karen Wright, Shirley MacLaine as Martha Dobie, James Garner as Dr. Joe Cardin, and Faye Bainter as Mrs. Tilford. The film is available on video from MGM/UA Home Entertainment, Facets Multimedia, and through the Internet Movie Database.
- A 1995 documentary, *The Celluloid Closet,* based on a 1981 book by Vito Russo, examines gay themes (often subliminal) in motion pictures and covers the 1961 film version of *The Children's Hour.* Narrated by Lily Tomlin, the documentary was directed and produced by Rob Epstein and Jeffrey Friedman and features a host of celebrities offering commentary on the masked and open cinematic treatment of homosexuality. The documentary is available from Sony Classics and through the Internet Movie Database.

with her accusations against Karen and Martha, Mary is able to frustrate all his efforts to convince the old lady that her precious grandchild fabricated her story from pure spite.

Although Dr. Joe stands by Karen and Martha during the slander trial, he, too, finally falls victim to Mary's vindictive lies. After the trial, he is troubled by niggling doubts about the relationship of Karen and Martha. Although he sells his practice and makes plans to marry Karen and take her and Martha to Europe, his uncertainty finally causes him to accept Karen's suggestion that they break off their engagement. It is that act that prompts Martha's confessions about her real feelings and her resulting suicide. In the aftermath of Martha's death, there appears no real hope that Cardin and Karen can marry.

Catherine

Catherine is one of the students at the Wright-Dobie School. She appears only in the first scene, where she attempts to help Lois prepare for a Latin test. The Latin lesson contributes to the chaotic lack of discipline in Mortar's classroom, revealing Lily's incompetence as a teacher.

Martha Dobie

Karen Wright's friend and co-owner of their school, Martha is about the same age, twenty-eight. She is described as ''nervous'' and ''high strung'' and is certainly far less composed and self-assured than her friend. It quickly becomes obvious that she greatly depends on Karen's emotional stability and good sense to provide her with the confidence needed to make a go of their school. She is thus somewhat jealous of Dr. Cardin, who also places demands on Karen. On the surface, Martha seems pleased that Karen and Joe plan to marry and supports them, but her inner fears of an inevitable estrangement from Karen leads to a growing tension in the play.

Once Mary Tilford poisons her grandmother's mind against Martha and Karen, Martha must confront the possibility that her jealousy springs from a suppressed sexual longing for her friend. Although she joins Karen in the libel suit against Mrs. Tilford, she is finally unable to cope with her complex feelings, which include a strong sense of responsibility for Karen's breakup with Joe. After confessing that her love for Karen has included physical desire, she takes her own life.

Lois Fisher

Another of Karen and Martha's students, she receives Lain tutoring from Catherine at the play's opening, conjugating Latin in hectic counterpoint to Peggy Roger's reading of Portia's "quality of mercy" speech from Shakespeare's *Merchant of Venice* and Lily Mortar's languid criticism. Like Catherine, she plays no significant role in the rest of the drama.

Grocery Boy

The unnamed grocery boy makes a very brief appearance in the last scene, carrying a box of groceries into the school's living room. He is almost mute, but his puerile gawking and giggling are indicative of the damage done to the reputations of Karen and Martha as a result of Mary's accusations.

Dr. Joe

See Dr. Joseph Cardin

Lily Mortar

Hellman describes Lily Mortar as "a plump, florid woman of forty-five." She is Martha Dobie's aunt and teaches at the Wright-Dobie School. A self-centered woman, she lives in romanticized delusions of her past triumphs as an actress. She is also vain and very susceptible to flattery, an easy patsy for a conniving student like Mary Tilford. She refuses to grow old gracefully, dying her hair and dressing too fancifully for her reduced circumstances (and expanded waistline). She is also a thorn in the side of Karen and Martha, who find her pretensions and meddling very annoying. They finally are able to finance her trip to Europe but, for purely selfish and petty reasons, when she is needed home to support them in their civil suit against Mrs. Tilford, she fails to return until it is too late. Martha finally confesses to Lily that she has always hated her, but Lily seems impervious to her niece's feelings. At the end of the play, her concern for her own welfare seems to outweigh her self-righteous grief over Martha's death.

Evelyn Munn

One of the girls at the Wright-Dobie School, Evelyn is first encountered in the opening scene, in which she mangles Rosalie Wells's hair with a pair of scissors. Evelyn, who lisps, is relatively quiet and timid. With Peggy Rogers, she overhears the conversation between Martha Dobie and Lily Mortar; the overheard conversation becomes the keystone in the malicious arch of lies that Mary Tilford constructs. Like Peggy, Evelyn is a victim of Mary's intimidation, which, at the end of the first act, turns to physical abuse. When Mary attempts to extort money from Peggy, Evelyn tries to interfere and is slapped in the face for her efforts. She is one of the first children withdrawn from the school after Mrs. Tilford spreads Mary's slanderous accusations.

Peggy Rogers

A student at the Wright-Dobie School, Peggy, like Evelyn Munn, is easily intimidated by Mary Tilford. She appears in the opening scene, where, under Lily Mortar's tutelage, she tries to read Portia's famous speech on the quality of mercy. Unimaginative, she shows little interest in Shakespeare. Her grandest aspiration is to marry a lighthouse keeper.

Peggy is with Evelyn when they overhear the fateful conversation between Martha Dobie and her aunt. Thereafter the pair confide in Mary, who immediately puts her malicious scheme into operation by extorting money from Peggy, who was saving it for a bicycle.

Mrs. Amelia Tilford

A wealthy widow, Mrs. Tilford is a large, dignified woman in her sixties. She has been an influential supporter of the Wright-Dobie School, where her granddaughter, Mary, is enrolled. Although she is a fair and generous person, she lacks good judgment when it comes to matters concerning her granddaughter. She recognizes that Mary is both spoiled and manipulative, but she dotes on the child and is utterly blind to the girl's vicious nature.

Mrs. Tilford is a key player in the tragic direction of the play. Although she initially resists believing Mary's slander, she is finally convinced that the girl is telling the truth. She comes close to discovering the truth when Dr. Cardin and the accused women question Mary, but once Rosalie Wells perjures herself in support of Mary's lies, Mrs. Tilford completely accepts Mary's account. Indignant and self-righteous, she then attempts to have the school closed, in turn compelling Karen and Martha to engage her in a libel suit.

After the civil trial, she discovers the truth. She tries to undo the damage and atone for her actions, but her efforts come too late. With Martha dead and her relationship with Cardin destroyed, Karen gives the contrite and devastated matron little hope of personal redemption.

Mary Tilford

The spoiled granddaughter of Amelia Tilford, Mary is a problem child at the Wright-Dobie School. She appears "undistinguished," but she is clever and used to having her own way with her doting grandmother. She also attempts to manipulate everyone at the school, resorting to a variety of tricks, including flattery, feigned sickness, blackmail, physical intimidation, and whining complaints. Karen and Martha are not fooled by her behavior. They easily penetrate her lies and schemes and insist on disciplining her, but they do not really understand the depths of the girl's depravity.

Mary responds to her punishment by turning venomous. From Evelyn and Peggy, she learns of the conservation between Martha and her Aunt Lily in which the latter refers to the relationship of Martha and Karen as "unnatural." Mary uses this to poison her grandmother's mind against the women, leading her to believe that they are lesbians. It is her malicious slander that ruins the lives of Karen and Martha, for she is only exposed as a liar after it is too late to prevent Karen's breakup with Dr. Cardin and Martha's suicide.

Rosalie Wells

Rosalie, a student at the Wright-Dobie School, appears first in the hectic scene opening the play, having her hair badly trimmed by Evelyn Munn. Unlike Peggy and Evelyn, she is not cowed by Mary Tilford, whom she does not like. In fact, Karen and Martha plan to move Mary in with Rosalie, hoping that rooming with the stronger girl will put an end to Mary's troublemaking. But Mary finds out that Rosalie has stolen a bracelet from Helen Burton and threatens to expose her crime unless Rosalie does what Mary asks. As a result, Rosalie becomes a key character. She gives credibility to Mary's lies and convinces Mrs. Tilford that Mary is entirely truthful, making a reversal of the harm impossible.

Karen Wright

Karen Wright is Martha Dobie's close friend and partner in the Wright-Dobie School. She is twenty-eight, attractive, warm, and outgoing. She is admired and respected by her students, for whom she has a genuine affection. She is also an emotionally stable woman, at ease with herself and others. Martha is drawn to her because of her strength and stability, qualities that Martha admires because she cannot find them in herself. Dr. Joe Cardin, Karen's fiance, having a temperament much like Karen's, seems to love her more for her charm, gracious wit, and good looks than her emotional balance.

Although she tries to suppress her feelings, Martha fears the impending marriage of Karen and Cardin, believing that it will inevitably lead to an estrangement in her relationship with Karen. Karen and Joe both try to convince Martha that nothing will change, but she is too insecure to accept their reassurance.

Although Karen is a sensitive and caring person, she never detects any sexual desire in Martha's love for her. She has no such feelings herself, repressed or otherwise, thus she cannot fathom the complexity of Martha's jealousy. She loves Martha like a sister and is devastated both by Martha's confession and subsequent suicide. She is also emotionally crushed by the failure of the lawsuit against Amelia Tilford, which she had vigorously pursued. At the end of the play, her spirits simply sag into a kind of stoic acceptance of her fate, as is evidenced in her listless and mechanical final lines exchanged with Mrs. Tilford.

THEMES

Good and Evil

With the exception of Mrs. Tilford, it is a simple task to place the principal characters in *The Children's Hour* in the debit and credit columns of a moral balance sheet. The good, decent characters are Karen Wright, Martha Dobie, and Dr. Joe Cardin. The bad are Mary Tilford and Lily Mortar, who, though not in Mary's demonic league, is a vain and selfish parasite who cares only for her own welfare.

Mary is the more perplexing character because her viciousness seems to spring from some inner ugliness that can not be explained away by her class privilege or her grandmother's indulgence. As Karen remarks in the first act, she and Martha always talk of Mary as if the girl were an adult, as if she had never been blessed with childhood innocence. She is a pathological liar and manipulator, capable of any strategy that will satisfy her malicious desire to control everyone with whom she comes in contact.

TOPICS FOR FURTHER STUDY

- Research the fate of *The Children's Hour* in major cities, including Boston, Chicago, and London, where, in the 1930s, community standards led to a banning of the play's public performance.
- Research the question of libel and slander in American civil law. Relate your findings to the situation in the play.
- Read Maxell Anderson's adaptation of William Marsh's novel, *The Bad Seed,* comparing Mary Tilford with Rhoda Penmark, the child murderess of that work. How are the two girls similar? How are they different?
- Conduct a comparative investigation of the public response to the ''outing episode'' of the television sitcom *Ellen* and the furor raised over the lesbian theme in *The Children's Hour.*
- Research the relationship between the 1952 revival of *The Children's Hour* and the congressional (HUAC) investigations of domestic communism then in progress.
- Investigate current theory regarding the biochemical origins of criminal behavior and the psychopathic personality, relating your findings to Mary Tilford's character and behavior in *The Children's Hour.* Does Mary qualify as a sociopathic criminal?

She cows the other girls through intimidation, inspiring neither love nor respect, and when her influence over her classmates is threatened by Martha and Karen, she sets out to destroy them without a hint of remorse. Her feelings seem limited to fear and anxiety, in evidence only when she is threatened with exposure. Measured against her, Lily Mortar seems more oblivious than wicked or cruel.

Mary is the font of evil in the play, but her grandmother, Mrs. Tilford, is the sociopathic child's unwitting conspirator. Although she pampers her grandchild, Mrs. Tilford is a kind and good woman, but she is also self-righteous and very stubborn. Once convinced that she has uncovered the disturbing truth about Karen and Martha, she closes her mind to the possibility that Mary might have invented her tale. Until the very last she is wholly unaware of the fact that she is the main piece in Mary's evil chess game, a well-meaning pawn in the disguise of an imperious queen.

Clearly, like her spiritual mentor, Henrik Ibsen, Hellman is as concerned with evil arising from good intentions as with evil unalloyed. Virtue adrift from truth can become the ally of such evil and be every bit as destructive, as Mary, Karen, and Joe Cardin discover. Against such a powerful combination, the victim has almost no defense.

Guilt and Innocence

Hellman thus poses at least two perplexing questions with respect to guilt and innocence, the key figures being Mary and Mrs. Tilford. The girl convincingly demonstrates that the standard belief in childhood innocence should be held suspect, even if, as she later insisted, Hellman did not intend that Mary should be interpreted as so completely evil as she appeared on stage.

Once accepting the premise that malevolence can exist in the guise of innocence, Hellman asks the more troubling question of whether a person duped by evil can or should be exonerated for hurtful acts springing from a failure to penetrate evil's mask. It is a moral dilemma, with no simple solution, and is also the basis of the play's tragic force.

Atonement and Forgiveness

Because she is a moral woman, in the last part of *The Children's Hour,* after she has learned the truth, Mrs. Tilford seeks to atone for what she has done. She confesses that her role in the tragedy will trouble her all her remaining days, and she hopes to make matters right, but, when she finds out that Martha has committed suicide, she is crushed. She knows that full restitution is impossible.

In their final confrontation, Karen at first calls Mrs. Tilford ''old'' and ''callous,'' but finally holds out some hope that she will accept the matron's offer of help. She acknowledges that the woman has also been a victim of Mary's malice, harmed in an even more lasting way. Fully acknowledging her guilt, Mrs. Tilford promises Karen that she will see to it that Mary is never able to hurt another human being. That painful burden is part of her final penance, the crux of her ongoing atonement.

In contrast, Lily Mortar remains unrepentant for her failure to return from abroad to support Martha and Karen in their suit against Mrs. Tilford. Her self-vindicating vanity finally gives way to a tepid apology, but that only provokes Martha to confess that she has always hated Lily. There is no redemption for those who can not bear guilt, something that Lily Mortar is unable or refuses to do. Unlike Mrs. Tilford, she remains blind, unredeemed, and unforgiven.

Deception

Mary Tilford is a treacherous liar whose tactics are effective with her grandmother because she feigns reluctance to divulge what she ''knows'' and thereby makes her account credible. Mrs. Tilford is convinced in part because she believes that Mary is an innocent in such matters as lesbianism. Like an elfin Iago (a slanderous character from Shakespeare's play *Othello*), Mary is pragmatic, compounding her lies with fabricated details until her deception takes root as truth in Mrs. Tilford's mind. One of Hellman's major themes is that there is often no defense against deceit and slander and that the damage deception can do may be tragically irreversible.

Friendship

It is ironic that Martha and Karen are vulnerable to Mary's poison because they are very close friends. Together, they have fought hard to make a go of their school, and, with the support of Mrs. Tilford, they are on the brink of success when the venomous Mary destroys their dream.

The friendship of the two women, established when they were classmates in college, is very close, but it is clearly more self-defining for Martha than for Karen. Karen provides stability and verve for the more nervous and timid Martha, who seems to have more at stake in the friendship, even, perhaps, a suppressed sexual attraction. Martha finally admits to such guilty feelings just before taking her own life.

For Martha, Joe Cardin does pose the threat of some estrangement in her friendship with Karen. Despite the reassurances of both Joe and Karen, she obviously believes that their marriage will end (or at least greatly compromise) her close friendship with Karen. Her jealous fears prompt Mrs. Mortar to charge her with ''unnatural'' feelings, ultimately giving Mary a seed of truth from which to grow her evil plant.

STYLE

Setting

The Children's Hour employs two settings. The first, used in the opening and final acts, is the living and study room of the Wright-Dobie School for girls, located in a converted farmhouse about ten miles from Lancet, a rural town in Massachusetts. The second, used in both scenes of the second act, is the living room of Mrs. Tilford's house, presumably in the town of Lancet.

The setting plays a significant role in the play, for it posits a small-town attitude and closeness—a place where news travels fast—which is evident in the snickering of the grocery boy in the third act. The community ostracizes Karen and Martha, which helps create the oppressive atmosphere that makes Martha's suicide believable. Because the women are sensitive to their community's censure, they come to believe that their alleged behavior will follow them wherever they go, that they will be unable to escape from their notoriety.

Structure

The Children's Hour has a conventional, linear plot, consisting of three acts, the usual format employed by playwrights at the time. The formal divisions into acts and scenes is used to demarcate a change of time, but each formal segment also ends at a decisive moment, following the tradition of strong scene closures at the curtain. These elements all contribute to what is referred to as a well-made play. It is a time-honored technique, fundamental to melodrama, whether good or bad.

Within the structural design of the play, time is handled in a strict chronological order. The action covers a period of about eight months, opening in April and ending in the following November. A key event that occurs in the interval is the civil suit brought by Karen and Martha against Mrs. Tilford. It is not presented on stage, but its dreadful impact resonates throughout the last act of the play.

Realism

Hellman works entirely within the limits of the realistic problem play. *The Children's Hour* is very suited to the box set, with the invisible fourth wall through which an audience witnesses the work in progress. It uses no devices or techniques to dispel the total illusion of that reality.

From beginning to end, the characters behave and talk like real people in a situation that seems entirely credible. Their dialogue, although very focused and congruous, captures the idiom and cadences of real speech, and the action, though hardly typical, is wholly within the realm of the possible. Even Mary's psychopathic behavior, though not accounted for, is uncomfortably realistic and its results entirely plausible.

Foreshadowing

To maintain the complete illusion of reality, Hellman eschews the use of various theatrical devices and conventions. However, she prepares her audience to accept events as plausible from clues or hints preceding them. Hellman foreshadows actions largely through character revelation, particularly in the cases of Lily Mortar, Mary Tilford, and Martha Dobie.

Lily reveals her self-centeredness from the very beginning of the play. Her vanity is fed by the flattery of her students, and she proves to be easy prey for Mary. She lives on her imagined triumphs of the past, retreating from present obligations. Her failure to respond to Karen and Martha's request that she return from Europe to testify at the trial therefore becomes almost inevitable.

Mary's lies, cajoling flattery, feigned heart attack, and abusive treatment of her classmates all prepare the audience to accept her vicious slander against Karen and Martha as completely consistent with her character. Although Karen and Martha recognize that there is something seriously wrong with the girl, Mary easily dupes Lily Mortar and intimidates most of her classmates. Agatha, Mrs. Tilford's maid, and Dr. Cardin are also wise to Mary, but their counsel is ignored by the girl's grandmother once she is convinced that Mary could not have fabricated her damning story.

Martha's eventual disclosure of sexual attraction for Karen and her suicide are also partly foreshadowed by her behavior earlier in the play. Her nervous agitation and angry recrimination towards her aunt suggest a troubled soul. It is obvious that she fears estrangement from Karen, as is evidenced in her jealousy of Joe Cardin and her ambivalent feelings towards Karen and Joe's impending marriage. Mrs. Mortar's biting remark about the ''unnatural'' feelings that Martha has exhibited towards Karen and earlier friends also echoes through the play, bearing a grain of truth that erupts in Martha's confused confession of her feelings in the last act.

Irony

Hellman also uses irony in *The Children's Hour,* a device often employed by realists because it need not destroy the illusion of lifelike fidelity while contributing greatly to dramatic impact. Dramatic irony exists in scenes in which there is a discrepancy in the levels of knowledge of the characters or the characters and the audience (what the audience expects of the characters). Such scenes are often suspenseful, for the audience awaits an inevitable ''recognition,'' that moment at which a character is made aware of his or her ignorance. The effect can be devastating. The best example in *The Children's Hour* occurs in the third act, when Mrs. Tilford confronts Karen, completely unaware that Martha has killed herself. The disclosure breaks down all of Mrs. Tilford's reserve, for in that instant she realizes the irreversible damage she has caused and the guilt she must carry to the grave.

Irony in a lower key also exists at the end of the second act, when Rosalie Wells confirms Mary's claims that it was actually Rosalie who witnessed the lovemaking between Martha and Karen. The situation is doubly ironic, for Rosalie's credibility gains strength from the fact that she has been no friend to Mary and was deliberately chosen by Karen to become Mary's roommate because Mary seemed to have no influence over her. That Rosalie is being blackmailed by Mary is a fact known only to the two girls and the audience.

HISTORICAL CONTEXT

At the time that Hellman wrote *The Children's Hour,* in 1934, the United States was still mired in the economic doldrums of the Great Depression. Europe, too, was struggling with economic collapse, fomenting a political struggle between fascism and other economic/political systems that would finally erupt into World War II in 1939.

The chief figures in the political upheaval in Europe were Adolph Hitler in Germany, Josef Stalin in the Soviet Union, and Benito Mussolini in Italy, all of whom held expansionist dreams of world conquest. But there were other players, too. It was in 1934 that Austrian chancellor Engelbert Dollfuss sought to stem political opposition on the left by suppressing all political parties except his Fatherland Front, while in Bulgaria, supported by the king, fascists staged a coup and grabbed political control. Even France, a staunch democratic republic, stood on the brink of civil war because of political corruption condemned by factions representing both the extreme left and right. In Germany, meanwhile, the National Socialist Party (Nazis) conducted a blood purge, destroying dozens of party members accused of plotting to kill Hitler and eliminating Ernst Rohm and Gregor Stresser and their more radical wing of the Nazi Party.

Hellman, a cosmopolitan writer who had spent some time in Paris in the 1920s, was very concerned with what was happening in Europe in the 1930s. Her German-Jewish heritage and liberalism made her a dedicated anti-fascist, and she would, in succeeding years, give time, money, and artistic dedication to that cause, returning to Europe in 1937 to witness the loyalist struggle against Franco and the royalists in the Spanish Civil War. However, most of bread-line America was basically disinterested in the increasingly unstable political situation in Europe. Many still adhered to the isolationist policy that gained favor in the aftermath of World War I, believing that America should concern itself with solving it own problems before worrying about what was happening abroad. There was a strong ''America First'' movement determined to keep the United States free of new foreign entanglements.

The nation was also too busy trying to cope with poverty and unemployment. In order to solve the Depression's negative impact on writers, in 1934, as part of the Works Project Administration (WPA), the federal government, under the leadership of President Franklin D. Roosevelt, established the Federal Writers' Project, run by Henry G. Alsberg. It provided work for hundreds of writers, many of whom, from a conservative perspective, were much too radical. By that date, too, the Group Theatre had been in operation for three years, producing plays of ''social significance,'' some of which, like Clifford Odets's *Waiting for Lefty* (1935) and *Awake and Sing* (1935), advanced socialistic views. The new thirst for social consciousness in serious art helped diminish the reputation of playwrights like Eugene O'Neill, whose works largely ignored political issues while probing the human psyche and becoming increasingly autobiographical in content.

Although *The Children's Hour* lacks a political theme, it does indicate that Karen Wright and Martha Dobie have had to struggle to make a go of their school, hinting that the economic situation in America would put such a venture at grave risk. They have in fact had to depend on the support and good will of Mrs. Tilford, a very influential dowager. In general, however, the moral focus of the play transcends specific economic and political concerns. In some of her later works, notably *Watch on the Rhine* (1941) and *Another Part of the Forest* (1946), Hellman would evidence her political views.

The frank lesbian theme brought the play its notoriety, not the political views of its author. At the time, various groups, including federal, state, and local agencies, engaged in some form of censorship. An important example was the Hays Office, created in 1934 as a self-policing production code oversight agency by the Motion Pictures Producers and Distributors of American, Inc. (MPPDA) and headed by former Postmaster General Will H. Hays. Hellman, in deference to the dictates of the Hays Office, had to eradicate all traces of the lesbian theme in her film adaptation of the play.

CRITICAL OVERVIEW

Two versions of *The Children's Hour* have been staged. The original was used in the play's very successful premier at the Maxine Elliot Theatre in New York, starting on November 20, 1934. The play, produced and directed by Herman Shumlin, ran for a record-breaking 691 performances and immediately established Hellman's durable reputation. It also provoked considerable controversy.

The second version, staged in 1952, failed financially, although most critics and reviewers

COMPARE & CONTRAST

- **1930s:** The Great Depression brings great suffering to America, with attempts to blunt the hardship with the ''New Deal'' policies of President Franklin D. Roosevelt. Reforms include social welfare programs designed to alleviate the plight of the poor and dispossessed. Conservatives condemned such measures as socialistic, and some of the reforms were blocked by the Supreme Court as unconstitutional.

  Today: A fairly robust economy and nearly full employment contrast sharply with the conditions current in the Great Depression. Civil rights reforms and social welfare programs, some with a lineage that goes back to the liberalism of the 1930s, are now under attack from moderates and conservatives alike. Although it re-elected Democrat Bill Clinton president in 1996, the nation revealed its anti-liberal mood by installing a Republican majority in both houses of Congress.

- **1930s:** Private and public agencies exert powerful control over the arts. Common in theaters are ''bannings,'' particularly in cities like Boston, where the mayor, supported by religious groups, threatens to close down productions that violate the community's sense of moral decorum. In film, the Hays Office imposes strict regulations on movies, prohibiting nudity, suggestions of sex acts or seduction, any unconventional (passionate) kissing, and the use of profane or obscene language.

  Today: Although codes for rating films do exist, they serve largely as parental guides and not restrictions on what filmmakers can include in their art. Violent behavior, obscenity, nudity, and graphic sex are now common in R- and X-rated films. Commercial television avoids graphic nudity, sex, and language due to pressure from the religious right and fear of a drop in advertising revenue. The stage, however, freed itself from prevailing community standards even earlier, allowing nudity and vulgarity as early as the 1960s.

- **1930s:** In America, an open same-sex relationship is impossible. Most homosexuals remain ''closeted,'' knowing that public exposure would costs them their livelihoods and community acceptance. Branded as degenerates and perverts, many homosexuals bear a powerful sense of moral shame and self-loathing.

  Today: Many homosexuals have been ''outed'' in the gay liberation movement, and political correctness now argues that ''alternative orientations'' should be treated with respect equal to heterosexual ones, not just tolerated. Although some still view homosexuality as a perversion, there is little public condemnation of gays, and many celebrities, including political figures, have acknowledged their homosexuality. The AIDS crisis has contributed to the public awareness of the gay movement.

- **1930s:** Although public education is on the rise, many children attend sexually segregated private schools, some of which are very small and exclusive. Such institutions proliferate due to poor public school funding.

  Today: There are still some private, sexually segregated schools left, but the number has dwindled considerably, despite the fact that support for private education was for a time rekindled by the racial desegregation of public schools. The cost of private schooling has become prohibitive for most American families, some of which resort to home schooling as an alternative to public education.

praised it. Hellman, in addition to making minor revisions in the script, directed the production. It opened at the Coronet Theatre on Broadway on December 18, ran for 189 performances, and later went on the road to play in Chicago, a city that had originally banned the work. Controversy still surrounded the piece, but the grounds had shifted away from the lesbian theme to the work's relevance to the congressional anti-communist hearings then in progress. It was in 1952 that Hellman, already blacklisted in Hollywood, was subpoenaed to appear before the House Un-American Activities Committee (HUAC).

Much of the notoriety surrounding the first production was based on what at the time was perceived as its sensational content. Shumlin knew the play would shock the audience, and so did Lee Shubert, the Elliot's owner, who, Hellman recounts in her memoir *Pentimento,* complained during rehearsals that the production ''could land us all in jail.'' However, the New York authorities merely winked, though officials in Boston, Chicago, and London banned public performances of the play outright.

The critical judgments passed on the initial staging were mostly favorable. Reviewer Ide Gruber, in *Golden Book,* was quick to label it a ''powerful and gripping'' adult drama, ''well-written and well-acted.'' A few hailed Hellman a new genius of the ''well made'' play in the tradition of Ibsen and Anton Chekhov (*The Cherry Orchard*), touting, too, her courage as a writer willing to put her new career in harm's way with a frank treatment of a taboo subject. For Percy Hammond, writing in the *New York Herald Tribune,* the play had the power to make the audiences' ''eyes start from their sockets,'' in scenes moving ''so fast they almost tread upon one another's heels.''

Some major critics demurred praise, however. Negative assessments mostly focused on the third act. According to Joseph Wood Krutch, reviewing the play in the *Nation,* although the first two acts were compelling, the last act was ''so strained, so impossible, and so thoroughly boring that the effect is almost completely destroyed, and one is left to wonder that anything so inept was ever allowed to reach production.'' Other critics, including Brooks Atkinson and Stark Young, concurred, believing that the play was prone to melodramatic excess and engaged in too much postmortem moralizing following Martha's suicide. Even Hellman, in her ''Introduction'' to *Six Plays,* would later agree with that point, confessing that the last scene ''was tense and overburdened,'' but claiming, as a ''moral writer,'' that she could not avoid ''that last summing-up.'' Audiences, however, seemed far less troubled by the play's final moments than the critics were, and they continued to flock to the production. There could be little argument over the play's success.

In contrast, the 1952 revival of the play, with a run less than a third as long, fared better in reviews than as a profitable investment for its backers. One common theme of the reviews was the idea that the play had lost none of its forceful impact in the eighteen years separating the productions: its power, as John Beaufort asserted in a review in the *Christian Science Monitor,* ''to astound and appall.'' Even Brooks Atkinson, at best lukewarm in assessing the original version, found the work ''still powerful and lacerating'' in his *New York Times* column, ''At the Theatre.''

There were also new naysayers, including Eric Bentley, who, writing in the *New Republic,* complained that, on stage, everything seemed ''unreal, inorganic, unrelated,'' and that there was ''an absence of genuine passion.'' Bentley's bias against Hellman's work was based on his belief, advanced in *American Drama and Its Critics,* that the play was revised as a deliberate, ''quasi-liberal'' assault on McCarthyism. For Bentley, it represented ''a type of liberalism that has been dangerous'' but, by 1954, had become ''obsolescent.'' Yet other critics who saw a tie between the play's destructive scandal-mongering and McCarthy's witch hunt felt that the play had thereby gained a fresh vitality. For example, in *Variety,* Hobe argued that the play had ''acquired a stimulating new quality of contemporary significance.''

As Doris Falk asserted in her critical biography, *Lillian Hellman,* in the early 1950s ''the time was certainly ripe for the revival of *The Children's Hour* as a political play.'' Ultimately, however, the true worth of a play must rest on its intrinsic merits, not its relevance to some extraneous events. Although many earlier commentators on *The Children's Hour* tried to approach the play objectively, the furor surrounding it made a detached critical assessment very difficult. More recent scholarship, based on the play's text rather than performance, is not burdened with such extrinsic irrelevancies. On balance, *The Children's Hour* is now viewed as a remarkable maiden voyage in commercial theater, a work of extraordinary promise, but one that, as Jacob Adler said in *Lillian Hellman,* ''undeniably'' remains ''an apprentice work.'' For Adler and other critics, the play points clearly to what would become Hellman's dramatic hallmarks: strong characters, solid dramatic structure, and a moral epicenter that transcends its topical significance. It is the first of Hellman's "well made" thesis plays, on which her lasting reputation as the first important woman playwright in America largely rests.

CRITICISM

John W. Fiero

Fiero is a Ph.D. who teaches drama and playwriting at the University of Southwestern Louisiana. In this essay he discusses Hellman's play as both a "well made" play in the realistic tradition and as a tragedy built on a moral dilemma and pattern of development similar to that of William Shakespeare's Othello.

Lillian Hellman's *The Children's Hour* is a realistic thesis play, in a direct line of descent from the work of the great Norwegian playwright, Henrik Ibsen (*A Doll's House*). It is a fair example of the kind of serious play that has dominated the American theater through most of the twentieth century. Such plays deal with social issues or problems, usually using one or two families as the center of their thematic inquiry. While many very good plays were written in this tradition, a large number have suffered from their connection to past eras and now seem somewhat dated. William Inge's *Come Back Little Sheba* (1950) is an example, as is Robert Anderson's *Tea and Sympathy* (1953), both highly successful plays that are often considered too out of touch with contemporary times to merit commercial revival. In contrast, Hellman's *The Children's Hour* remains persistently relevant.

That is not to claim that the play is contemporary in its technique or its representation of prevailing social attitudes. It is not. Overt treatment of lesbianism, sensational in 1934, has lost virtually all its ability to shock an audience (homosexuality is discussed frankly and on a regular basis in contemporary pop culture). In that regard, Hellman's play is also long in the tooth, making it difficult to understand now why the play so offended officials outside New York. In fact, as Doris Falk remarked in her book *Lillian Hellman,* "it is ironic that this most outspoken and revolutionary play in its time should now seem so old-fashioned."

Nor did the play cut new artistic trails. Even before Hellman wrote the play, important dramatists like Eugene O'Neill (*Long Day's Journey into Night*) and Elmer Rice (*Street Scene*) had taken the American theater in new directions, in part as a reaction to the narrow dictates of the sort of realism to which, in *The Children's Hour,* Hellman remained wholly committed. Although some critics have carped about its melodramatic effects, Hellman's work carefully follows the formula of the well-made play. It is linear in plot, causal in its logic, and completely life-like in its characters' speech and behavior. Its principal theme, the destructive power of a malicious lie, is drawn out in the ritual recriminations at the end, perhaps too much so, but even that is characteristic of some of Ibsen's plays, *A Doll's House* (1879), for example, or *An Enemy of the People* (1882).

However, as is also true of Ibsen's best work, *The Children's Hour* seems to transcend the limits of its form and technique. From the outset, as is reflected in some reviews of the premier production, commentators found a tragic dimension in the play. "Tragedy" is a term often used as a synonym for "disaster," but at least some of the critics used it to describe the play's genre, in the Aristotelian sense of the word. (Aristotle outlined many of modern drama's techniques in his *Poetics.*) While complaining that producer/director Shumlin and Hellman "daubed" the play "with grease paint in the last quarter of a hour" (made it melodramatic), Brooks Atkinson's *New York Times* review named it "a pitiless tragedy."

The Children's Hour gains tragic weight because it encompasses a timeless moral dilemma. Specifically, it asks whether there is a sufficient defense against evil in the guise of truth or innocence. It is the same question addressed in William Shakespeare's *Othello,* and it gives the same perplexing and devastating answer: in some circumstances, no. In both plays, evil is accepted as a fact of life, vested in characters whose darkest motives are hidden, not just to other characters, but even to themselves. They are the plot drivers, working by guile to destroy those who have thwarted their will and deprived them of what they believe is their due.

Shakepeare's Iago and Hellman's Mary Tilford are not equivalent characters, of course, but they do share a narcissistic delight in their malicious manipulation of their victims. Both are also pragmatic and inventive, quickly and cleverly changing strategies to fit changing circumstances, as, for example, when, at the end of the second act, Mary, on the verge of exposure, extorts confirmation of her lies

WHAT DO I READ NEXT?

- *The Bad Seed,* Maxwell Anderson's 1955 stage adaptation of a novel by William Marsh, is a psychological study of a child murderess whose evil, disguised by a mask of innocence, is a genetic inheritance from her grandmother.
- *The Crucible,* Arthur Miller's 1953 drama based on the Salem Witch Trials of the seventeenth century, deals with the tragic havoc created by a vengeful girl and her compliant peers when they begin accusing many of Salem's citizens of witchcraft. By obvious implication, the work was an indictment of the investigations then being conducted by HUAC into alleged communist activities in America.
- *Othello,* William Shakespeare's great domestic tragedy, written around 1604, centers on the evil machinations of Iago, whose slanderous lies against the innocent Desdemona turn Othello, her husband, savagely against her and lead to her murder and Othello's suicide.
- *The Prime of Miss Jean Brodie,* Muriel Spark's 1961 novel (also adapted for the stage in 1966 and as a film in 1969) explores life in a Scottish girls' school in the 1930s with a focus on the eccentric teacher, Miss Brodie, and her damaging efforts to control the lives of her favorite students.

---

from Rosalie Wells. Also, just as Iago has his stooge, Roderigo, his "fool" who is also his "purse," so Mary has her unwitting dupes, like Peggy Rogers, from whom, at the end of the first act, she extorts money through physical intimidation.

Granted, such parallels are mostly superficial, but the common plot motif of a vicious lie that is accepted as truth—and its disastrous consequences—cannot be dismissed. Shakespeare works on a grander scale, of course. Othello, his protagonist, is a man of high station and repute. Hellman's protagonists, Karen Wright and Martha Dobie, though wholly decent people, are a pair of characters scratching at life, albeit valiantly. Furthermore, in *Othello* it is the titular character who believes the lie (that his wife, Desdemona, is cheating on him), acts on it (he murders his wife), and, when the truth is revealed, takes his own life. In *The Children's Hour,* it is Mrs. Tilford who believes and acts upon the lie. The chief victims of the slander are Karen and Martha. At the end, Karen may concede that Mary has harmed Mrs. Tilford more than anyone, but it is Martha who is dead and Karen who is left an emotionally-drained zombie, with neither friend nor fiance left to spark her into caring again. All she is able to do is hold out a glimmer of hope to Mrs. Tilford, in what many interpret as a consolation for those unable to confront what the subtext most likely conveys: complete desolation.

It is precisely because Karen and Martha are very ordinary people that arguments against their tragic stature might be raised. Many purists, approaching Aristotle's *Poetics* as an august, proscriptive document, scoff at the idea that real tragedy is possible in a modern, egalitarian society. Some, like Joseph Wood Krutch, insist that even if an elevated stature is not necessary, belief in man's basic nobility—his potential for greatness—is. In his famous essay, "The Tragic Fallacy" (reprinted in *Tragedy: Vision and Form*), Krutch argued that "a tragic writer does not have to believe in God, but he must believe in man," for tragedy is "the triumph over despair and confidence in the value of human life." For Krutch, modern psychology has done more than democracy has to diminish man's stature, for it has diligently worked to rob humankind of a tragic sense of life, of a residual faith in a compensatory justice that makes amends for human misery.

Playwright Arthur Miller, in his essay "Tragedy and the Common Man" (also printed in *Tragedy*), while admitting that modern tragedies are rare, claims they are not impossible. His defense of the unsung as suitable tragic figures seems as appropriate for Hellman's characters as it does for his own Willy Loman in *Death of a Salesman.* For Miller, an insistence that a tragic protagonist must hold an exalted rank is merely "a clinging to the outward forms of tragedy," not its spirit. Tragedy, as Miller sees it, arises as a "consequence of a man's total compulsion to evaluate himself justly." Moreover, a tragic flaw may be only "his inherent unwillingness to remain passive in the face of what he conceives to be a challenge to his dignity, his image of his rightful status." Like Willy, Karen and Martha are not passive; they fight, firm in the belief that it is within their power to control their own destinies and that there is recourse to justice. That they are defeated in their attempt "posits a wrong or an evil in . . . [their] environment." For Willy Loman, that wrong is the badly tarnished American Dream; for Martha and Karen, as for Othello, that wrong is a dreadful malice hidden in other characters, their tragic antagonists.

Compared to *Othello, The Children's Hour* offers a much dimmer tragic vision. It lacks the great intensity of Shakespeare's play, the passion and the majestic language, but it does have a similar pattern and moral base. In Hellman's play, passion is muted and held in check, not expressed in the raging frustration of a single character, as it is in *Othello.* At the end of Hellman's play, Karen Wright is icy and remote, but she is not blasted by grief. Strong feelings have simply been dispersed, dissipated in the off-stage suicide of Martha Dobie and the pathetic self-pitying behavior of Lily Mortar. Mrs. Tilford, the guilt bearer, is almost as pathetic in her hand-wringing search for atonement. These are but faint echoes of the grand death of the guilt-laden Othello, but they are echoes nonetheless.

Both *The Children's Hour* and *Othello* are morality plays, terrible in their implication that evil, through deceit, can defeat the unwary. Against evil, even the virtuous have no adequate defense, for evil wears a disarming mask and allies itself with the righteous. It appears as friendship in the "honest" Iago and childlike innocence in Mary Tilford and enlists the unwitting aid of characters who believe they are just, even if, as in Othello's case, that belief is within the tragic protagonist himself.

Curiously, in both plays, this moral center has often been obscured by other matters of less import. In *Othello,* it is interracial marriage while in *The Children's Hour* it is lesbianism, a taboo subject in 1934. Othello, the Moor, is an African, but his racial heritage has little outward importance, Iago's racial slurs and epithets notwithstanding. What matters is that it makes him vulnerable to self-doubt in his relationship with Desdemona. Latent fears about her sexual orientation affect Martha Dobie in an analogous way. Confronted and compounded with guilty feelings about Karen and Joe Cardin, these doubts overwhelm her with despair and lead to her suicide. Othello's blackness and Martha's sexual doubts simply mark them as susceptible to the evil genius of the villains in the respective plays, but they are matters that no longer carry much shock value. Paradoxically, as these elements become less and less sensational, the moral center in both works comes into a much sharper focus. In the case of Hellman's play, the only question is whether it can long survive the loss of that shock power, lacking as it does the grandeur of Shakespearean tragedy.

"LILLIAN HELLMAN'S *THE CHILDREN'S HOUR* IS A REALISTIC THESIS PLAY, IN A DIRECT LINE OF DESCENT FROM THE WORK OF THE GREAT NORWEGIAN PLAYWRIGHT, HENRIK IBSEN."

Source: John W. Fiero, for *Drama for Students,* Gale, 1998.

Philip M. Armato

Armato examines the concepts of good and evil as they pertain to the main characters of Hellman's play. Much as the playwright herself once asserted, the critic concludes that no character exemplifies outright good or evil but rather all possess measures of both.

Critics have often called *The Children's Hour* a melodrama. Those who have done so, see Karen Wright and Martha Dobie as "good" characters who are victimized by "evil" Mary Tilford. To Barrett H. Clark and Brooks Atkinson, Mary Tilford is a "monster." Even Hellman's most perceptive critic calls her "the embodiment of pure evil." If

Karen admonishes the troublesome Mary (Iris Mann) in a 1950s production of Hellman's play

The Children's Hour is the story of a ''sweet little teacher done to death by . . . [a] tyrannical child,'' then we must concur with Barrett Clark's reading of the play's ultimate meaning: ''. . . here is evil . . . make the best of it.''

With great patience, Lillian Hellman has defended her play against the attacks of those who have labelled it a melodrama. In a 1965 interview, for example, she said that it is wrong to view her characters as being entirely good or evil: ''You [the author] have no right to see your characters as good or bad. Such words have nothing to do with people you write about. Other people see them that way''. The interviewer reminded Hellman that in the preface to the 1942 edition of her plays she had said that *The Children's Hour* was about goodness and badness. To this she replied, ''Goodness and badness is different from good and bad people isn't it?'' Her assertions suggest that Hellman did not intend to portray a melodramatic conflict between two ''good'' teachers and an ''evil'' child when she wrote her play. To clarify the play's substance, we should ask what, within the world of the play, is good and what evil.

Playwrights seldom underestimate the dramatic value of the visual-aural impact at curtain rise. The opening of *The Children's Hour,* in a studyroom of the Wright-Dobie school, seems undramatic. Mrs. Lily Mortar, Martha Dobie's aunt, is sleeping, the students are sewing. The action which would catch the eyes of the audience is that of Evelyn Munn, ''using her scissors to trim the hair of Rosalie, who sits, nervously, in front of her. She has Rosalie's head bent back at an awkward angle and is enjoying herself.'' However, the audience sees this stark visual image of the infantile pleasure of exercising cruelty while hearing about mercy, for the first words are those of a student reciting Portia's famous speech in *The Merchant of Venice.* Portia's plea for mercy should make an exceedingly strong impression on the audience, for portions of it are interpolated six times between the dialogue of Mrs. Mortar and her pupils. The visual image of cruelty is juxtaposed with the words ''pity'' and ''mercy,'' which are repeated seven times during the opening moments of the play.

In *The Children's Hour* Hellman posits mercy as an ultimate good and merciless cruelty as an ultimate evil. But to understand the merciless world of Lancet and its cruelty, one must move beyond the notion that Mary Tilford is the embodiment of it.

The rancorous structure of interpersonal relationships in *The Children's Hour* is patterned after the structure of human association in the Venice of Shakespeare's *Merchant.* This can best be described as a victim–victimizer syndrome, the most concrete representation of which is the relationship between Antonio and Shylock. Antonio is convinced that his harsh treatment of Shylock is ''just,'' because the Jew's interest rates are harsh. As victim, Shylock suffers from spiritual agony, feelings of persecution, and desires revenge. If he is able to consummate his wish, Shylock will become the victimizer of the man who originally victimized him. That the victim–victimizer syndrome is finally self-destructive is seen in the courtroom scene, when each victimizer in turn is reduced to the position of victim. Shylock's demand for Antonio's life is turned against him when Portia reminds the court that an alien Jew must suffer the death penalty if he plots against the life of a Venetian citizen. The Duke and Antonio destroy the vicious circle by showing mercy to Shylock.

"IN *THE CHILDREN'S HOUR* HELLMAN POSITS MERCY AS AN ULTIMATE GOOD AND MERCILESS CRUELTY AS AN ULTIMATE EVIL."

In the first two acts of her play, Hellman develops three relationships which are characterized by the circular form and destructive content of the victim-victimizer syndrome; these pairs are: Karen Wright–Mary Tilford, Martha Dobie–Lily Mortar, and Amelia Tilford–Wright/Dobie. In *The Merchant,* a Jew who is socially inferior to a Christian is mistreated by the Christian and attempts to use the Duke—the land's highest authority—as a vehicle for his revenge. In *The Children's Hour,* an adolescent pupil who is socially inferior to an adult teacher is mistreated by the teacher and proceeds to use Lancet's most influential citizen—the powerful matron Amelia Tilford—as a vehicle for her revenge. Finally, in the much criticized third act, Hellman, like Shakespeare, posits mercy as the only solution to the moral dilemma which is created when we deal justly with each other.

Karen Wright's treatment of Mary Tilford has never been sensitively evaluated. No one has noticed that immediately preceding their initial confrontation, Hellman suggests that Karen is perhaps not as compassionate as a teacher of young children should be. For when Mrs. Mortar complains that one of her students does not "appreciate" Portia's plea for mercy, Karen replies: "Well I didn't either. I don't think I do yet." The harshness of her discipline will demonstrate the truth—on a far more literal level than she suspects—of her remark.

Mary Tilford's offense is a minor one. She attempts to excuse her tardiness by saying that she was picking flowers for Mrs. Mortar. The flowers, Karen knows, were "picked" from the top of a garbage can, and Mary's stubborn refusal to admit the truth convinces Karen that she must be punished. First, Mary is told to take her recreation periods alone for two weeks; then, that her Friend Evelyn will no longer be her roommate, and that she must now live with her enemy Rosalie. Mary is also ordered not to leave the grounds for any reason. Hellman emphasizes Karen's harshness by adding details—Mary is specifically forbidden participation in hockey and horse-back riding—and by one further prohibition. Mary hopes that Karen's rules apply only to weekdays; if so, she may still be able to attend an event she has been looking forward to, the boat-races on Saturday. Unfortunately, she is told that she cannot attend them. While these restrictions might not be extreme deprivation for an adult, they are so for a child.

Mary feels—and rightly—that she is being persecuted. From wanting to tell her grandmother "how everybody treats me here and the way I get punished for every little thing I do," she moves to a sense of her inner agony, objectified in her hysterical "heart problems," and finally to a rebellious attitude: "They can't get away with treating me like this, and they don't have to think they can." She sets out to take her revenge, as is the victim's wont. She accuses Karen and Martha of lesbianism, and persists in her lie. Her behavior is ugly, but has been provoked by Karen's earlier ugliness: she seeks an eye for an eye, a tooth for a tooth.

Karen's inability to deal compassionately with Mary Tilford is paralleled in Act I by Martha Dobie's attitude toward her aunt Lily. Karen and Martha decide that she must be relieved of her teaching duties, and literally thrown out of school. Their decision is just, for Mortar is a nuisance and an incompetent, yet they do not consider for a moment the effect such a dismissal may have on an old woman whose life has been the school. Again, justice is untempered by mercy, and again Hellman emphasizes the rigidity of the decision's administration. Martha not only tells Lily that she must leave, but makes fun of her—"We don't want you around when we dig up the buried treasure"—and threatens that "You ought to be glad I don't do worse." Mortar pathetically attempts to save face: "I absolutely refuse to be shipped off three thousand miles away. I'm not going to England. I shall go back to the stage. I'll write my agents tomorrow, and as soon as they have something good for me—.'' This is essentially a plea for mercy cast in a manner that will allow her to retain some semblance of dignity. The old crone is finished on the stage, her ''agents'' are imaginary, and if she does not leave until they find her a part, she will never leave at all, which is her wish. Her suggestion is brusquely rejected. As Karen isolates Mary, Martha exiles Mortar. Lily's reaction is the same as Mary's: ''You always take your spite out on me.'' As she exits, she casts toward Martha a ''malicious half-smile'' and the malice of revenge is realized when she refuses to testify on Martha's behalf at the libel trial.

In Act II, Karen and Martha suffer an ironic reversal of fortune; the victimizers become victims themselves. Amelia Tilford, an influential figure in the community of Lancet, misuses her authority over Karen and Martha just as surely as they had taken advantage of the weaker positions of Mary and Lily. When Mary tells Amelia that her two teachers are lesbian, the dowager immediately phones the parents of the children who are enrolled at Wright-Dobie and repeats the charges, thus destroying the school. When Karen and Martha come for an explanation, Amelia makes it clear that she does not want these two lepers in her house: ''I don't think you should have come here. . . . I shall not call you names, and I will not allow you to call me names. It comes to this: I can't trust myself to talk about it with you now or ever.'' Her condescension and her revulsion in the face of her visitors' suspected abnormality pervades the scene: ''This—this thing is your own. Go away with it. I don't understand it and I don't want any part of it.'' Ironically, Karen and Martha now suffer from the same humiliation and ostracism that they so rigorously inflicted on others.

To make the ironic parallel—and thus the lesson—even more explicit, Hellman shows Karen and Martha reacting just as Lily and Mary had. Both think that they are being unjustly persecuted: ''What is she [Amelia] trying to do to us? What is everyone doing to us?'' Both feel spiritual agony: ''You're not playing with paper dolls. We're human beings, see? It's our lives you're fooling with. *Our* lives.'' Finally, they feel the need for revenge: ''What can we do to you [Amelia]? There must be something—something that makes you feel the way we do tonight. You don't want any part of this, you said. But you'll get a part. More than you bargained for.''

In Act II, then, Hellman presents a change in relationships, but not a change in the structure of relationships. The rancorous victim-victimizer syndrome is as pervasive in this act as it was in the previous one, the difference being that relationships have now come full circle; those who mistreated others are now mistreated themselves. Clearly, Hellman implies that when one mistreats another, he plants the seeds of his own destruction. This insight is made even more explicit in the third act.

Martha admits to herself that she has always been physically attracted to Karen. Her attitude toward her self is just as harsh as it had been towards others—or as Amelia Tilford's attitude had been towards lesbianism. Indeed, Martha's rancorous attitude toward the imperfections of others is but a reflection of her own self-condemnation. Hellman is making the same crucial point that Sartre makes in *Dirty Hands,* when he has Hoederer say to Hugo, ''You, I know you now, you are a destroyer. You detest man because you detest yourself.''

As in the other two acts, there is a parallel action, but this time it is the difference that is instructive, not the similarity. Martha's self-condemnation is matched by a new-found self-disgust in Amelia Tilford. She discovers that Mary has lied about her two teachers, and realizes that her hasty phone calls have destroyed two people who are innocent of the charges. Her discovery propels her into the same kind of guilt and self-laceration that we have just seen driving Martha to suicide. Amelia begs Karen to allow her to ''do something'' for her so that she can in part expiate her sin. Karen extends mercy.

Hellman counterpoints Karen's new-found benevolence with the by now familiar infantile hostility of Lily Mortar, who protests against Amelia Tilford even setting foot in the school: ''With Martha lying there? How can you be so feelingless? . . . I won't stay and see it. I won't have anything to do with it. I'll never let that woman—.'' Martha's suicide, however, has for Karen been both harrowing and educative. Because of it she is, she tells Amelia, ''Not [young] any more.'' The brief statement implies that she feels sadness at the loss of her own innocence, but also suggests that Martha's death has introduced her to a new maturity. Her horror at the guilt that caused Martha's suicide leads her to sympathize with the plight of ''guilt-ridden'' Amelia. In the last moments of the play, she accepts Amelia's atonement and thereby extends compassion—the ultimate good in the world of the play.

MRS. TILFORD: You'll be all right?
KARAN: I'll be all right, I suppose. Goodbye, now. (*They both rise.*)
MRS. TILFORD: (*speaks, pleadingly*) You'll let me help you? You'll let me try?
KAREN: Yes, if it will make you feel better.
MRS. TILFORD: (*With great feeling.*) Oh, yes, oh, yes, Karen. (*Unconsciously* KAREN *begins to walk towards the window.*)
KAREN: (*Suddenly.*) Is it nice out?
MRS. TILFORD: It's been cold. (KAREN *opens the window slightly, sits on the ledge.*)
MRS. TILFORD: (*with surprise.*) It seems a little warmer now.
KAREN: It feels very good. (*They smile at each other.*)

Karen has destroyed the vicious circle that has characterized human relations; her compassion is the ultimate good in the world of the play.

The two traditional criticisms of *The Children's Hour's* last act are that Mary Tilford is the central interest of the play and so should not be missing at its conclusion; and that the final ''summing up'' (Hellman's words) is tedious. However, Mary Tilford is not the central interest of the play; a certain perverse structure of human relationships is. Moreover, if critics paid more attention to what Hellman is ''summing up,'' they would find that the conclusion of the play is a structurally necessary resolution, not a tedious reiteration of previous materials. Jacob H. Adler has noted that *The Children's Hour,* like *The Wild Duck,* ''ends not with . . . [a] suicide but with a brief discussion pinning down the issues as a result of the suicide.''

Works as diverse as Aeschylus' *Oresteia,* Shakespeare's *Measure for Measure,* and Melville's *Billy Budd* have dealt with the dichotomy between primitive justice and mercy. Although *The Children's Hour* is certainly a less monumental work of art than any of these, it is within its limits a wholly successful moral play. Hellman suggests that adults are too often ''children.'' While infantile revenge is matter of course in men's dealings with each other, Hellman shows a last-act discovery—Karen Wright's discovery of a more mature concept of compassion.

Source: Philip M. Armato, '''Good and Evil' in Lillian Hellman's *The Children's Hour*'' in *Educational Theatre Journal,* Volume 25, no. 4, December, 1973, pp. 443–47.

Anonymous

In this uncredited review, the critic offers a positive appraisal of the debut of The Children's Hour, *calling it a worthy ''contribution to the adult theatre.''*

THE CHILDREN'S HOUR IS NOT FOR CHILDREN BUT IS DECIDEDLY A CONTRIBUTION TO THE ADULT THEATRE."

Twenty or thirty years ago Miss Hellman's play, enthusiastically received in New York, would doubtless have been stopped by the police. As it is both engrossing drama and a serious and sincere study of abnormal psychology, this change may imply a certain progress in the public's discernment.

The piece shows the tragic effects on two young women school-teachers of poisonous gossip spread by a pestiferous little pupil—one of those ''problem'' children who can so disrupt the life of a boarding-school that prudent head-mistresses decline to admit them if they know the facts. The two young women, who have built up their school by years of patient work and self-sacrifice, are forced to close it, and although they are objectively innocent, one of the friends loses her fiancé, while the other, confessing that she has ''felt that way'' all along, finally kills herself.

There is an inherent difficulty in the double-headed nature of Miss Hellman's theme which is not successfully surmounted on the stage, although somewhat less apparent in the script. For two of the three acts, the spectator's interest is so centered on the schoolgirls themselves, and in particular the part of the pestiferous little girl—extraordinarily well played in the New York production—that the last act, which consists of retrospective moaning and moralizing, six months later, by the unfortunate teachers, comes as a decided anti-climax. Miss Hellman feels the need, evidently, of showing the tragic results of the child's unfounded accusations, but has not been able to do this without slowing up and clogging action which, up until the end of the second act, marches straight ahead. The play is not for children but is decidedly a contribution to the adult theatre.

Source: *Saturday Review of Literature,* March 2, 1935, pp. 523.

SOURCES

Atkinson, Brooks. Review of *The Children's Hour* in the *New York Times,* December 19, 1952, p. 35.

Atkinson, Brooks. ''The Play—*The Children's Hour,* Being a Tragedy of Life in a Girls' Boarding House'' in the *New York Times,* November 21, 1934, p. 23.

Beaufort, John. ''Tragic 'Children's Hour''' in the *Christian Science Monitor,* December 27, 1952, p. 4.

Bentley, Eric. ''Hellman's Indignation'' in the *New Republic,* Vol. CXXVII, January 5, 1953, pp. 30-31.

Bentley, Eric. ''The American Drama 1944-1954'' in *American Drama and Its Critics,* edited by Alan S. Downer, University of Chicago Press, 1965, p. 199.

Gruber, Ide. Review of *The Children's Hour* in *Golden Book,* Vol. XXI, February, 1935, p. 28A.

Hammond, Percy. ''The Theatres—'The Children's Hour,' a Good Play about a Verboten Subject'' in the *New York Herald Tribune,* November 21, 1934, p. 16.

Hellman, Lillian. *Pentimento,* New American Library, 1973, p. 127.

Hellman, Lillian. ''Introduction'' in *Six Plays,* Modern Library, 1960, pp. viii- ix.

Hobe. ''Plays on Broadway; *The Children's Hour*'' in *Variety,* December 24, 1952, p. 50.

Krutch, Joseph Wood. ''Drama; The Heart of a Child'' in the *Nation,* Vol. 139, December 5, 1934, p. 657.

Krutch, Joseph Wood. ''The Tragic Fallacy'' in *Tragedy: Vision and Form,* edited by Robert W. Corrigan, second edition, Harper & Row, 1981, pp. 227-37.

Miller, Arthur. ''Tragedy and the Common Man'' in *Tragedy: Vision and Form,* edited by Robert W. Corrigan, second edition, Harper & Row, 1981, pp. 168-70.

FURTHER READING

Adler, Jacob H. *Lillian Hellman,* Southern Writers Series, No. 4, Steck-Vaughn, 1969.

A 44-page pamphlet, this brief study gives much of its limited space to a discussion of *The Children's Hour.* The work also analyzes Hellman's artistic indebtedness to both Ibsen and Chekhov and the critical judgment that her plays often ''lapse into melodrama.''

Estrin, Mark W. *Lillian Hellman, Plays, Films, Memoirs: A Reference Guide,* G. K. Hall, 1980.

A primary source book for research, this is a recent annotated bibliography on Hellman, part of the ''Reference Guide to Literature'' series.

Falk, Doris V. *Lillian Hellman,* Frederick Ungar, 1978.

A critical biography gleaned from Hellman's work, this study presents a synopsis of each of Hellman's plays and also features discussions of ''theatricalism,'' realism, and the impact of the Depression and World War II on Hellman's craft.

Lederer, Katherine. *Lillian Hellman,* Twayne, 1979.

A useful bio-critical study of Hellman, this work provides an excellent base for further study of the playwright's work. It starts with a biography, then covers all of Hellman's plays and nonfiction. It also includes a chronology and selected bibliography.

Moody, Richard. *Lillian Hellman, Playwright,* Pegasus, 1972.

Both a biographical and critical study, the work covers all of the playwright's dramatic works. It includes a helpful summary of ''Closed Doors; or, The Great Drumsheugh Case'' (pp. 38-40) on which Hellman based her play.

Rollyson, Carl. *Lillian Hellman: Her Legend and Her Legacy,* St. Martins, 1988.

The most up-to-date, comprehensive and detailed biography of Hellman, this study stresses the playwright's complex character, especially her many contradictions as seen in her various affairs and feuds. Several photographs are included.

Roughead, William. *Bad Companions,* Duffield and Green, 1931.

This book includes the essay ''Closed Doors; or, The Great Drumsheugh Case,'' which provided Hellman with the idea and basic situation of *The Children's Hour.*

Turk, Ruth. *Lillian Hellman: Rebel Playwright,* Lerner, 1995.

A study designed for young adults, but useful for the general reader and recommended as a quick overview of Hellman's career. It includes several photographs and a brief bibliography of works suitable for younger researchers.

Wright, William. *Lillian Hellman,* Simon & Schuster, 1986.

Published two years after Hellman's death in 1984, this critical biography, attempting to tie the ''image'' of Hellman to the ''woman,'' draws an intimate and respectful picture of the playwright, despite the fact that she fought to obstruct Wright's research.

Come Back, Little Sheba

WILLIAM INGE

1949

Come Back, Little Sheba was to become William Inge's most popular play. But the Broadway production did not create an immediate ''smash hit.'' In his foreword to *Four Plays,* published in 1958, Inge observes that the play was popular with only about half of its reviewers and that its Broadway run was less than six months. Inge also reveals that he took a cut in royalties, and the cast took a cut in salary to keep the play running after the audiences dwindled within a few weeks of its opening. But in spite of the lukewarm reviews, *Come Back, Little Sheba* brought Inge several honors, including the George Jean Nathan Award and the Theatre Time Award.

At the time of its writing, Inge's play focused on subjects that were still controversial and not often discussed in public. Sexuality and pregnancy out of wedlock were shocking topics not usually portrayed in drama. Lola's pregnancy, which forced a shotgun wedding, was the type of scandal that families went to great effort to hide. This was also true of alcohol addiction. Membership in Alcoholics Anonymous was not a topic for casual conversation, and the kind of drunken scene Doc creates in Act II was a seventeen minute revelation for most audiences

Many critics attacked *Come Back, Little Sheba*'s use of symbolism, which they felt was too obvious. Most often Lola's dreams, Sheba the dog, and the blatant phallic symbolism of Turk's javelin were

singled out for such criticism. Other reviewers noted that the characters were either flat or too contrived—or boring and repetitive. But reviewers who praised the play often found that Inge's drama did accurately portray the suffering of ordinary people. In spite of the mixed nature of the reviews, most critics did agree on one topic, praising the performances of Shirley Booth as Lola, and Sidney Blackmer as Doc, which they felt transcended the material.

In the decades following *Come Back, Little Sheba*'s debut, the general consensus has been laudatory toward Inge's work. The play is now considered a groundbreaking achievement in the genre of domestic drama. While its subject matter has become common fodder fueling the mundane storylines of countless soap operas, *Come Back, Little Sheba* was among the first dramas to skillfully address the confluence of such topics as alcoholism, failed marriage, and broken dreams. While the play is sometimes referred to as dated and melodramatic, it is nevertheless valued as a prototype for realistic contemporary social theater.

AUTHOR BIOGRAPHY

William Inge, born May 3, 1913, was the fifth and last child born to Maude and Luther Inge. He was raised in Independence, Kansas, by his mother; his father was a salesman and was rarely at home. After graduating from the University of Kansas in 1935, Inge attended the George Peabody College for Teachers but left before completing a master of arts degree. After a brief period teaching English at a local high school, Inge returned to college to complete his master's program. He also worked as a drama critic, and it was during this period that he met noted playwright Tennessee Williams (*Cat on a Hot Tin Roof*), who encouraged him to write. Inge completed his first play, and, with the help of Williams, *Farther Off from Heaven* was produced in 1947.

Concurrent with his rising success as a writer, Inge began to address shortcomings in his character. He joined Alcoholics Anonymous in 1948, having already begun the process of Freudian analysis (a psychological practice designed to improve mental health) earlier. In 1949, he wrote *Come Back, Little Sheba,* which was produced on Broadway in 1950 and earned Inge the George Jean Nathan Award and Theatre Time Award. He scored another hit with *Picnic* (1952) which won the Pulitzer Prize for drama, the Outer Circle Award, the New York Drama Critics' Circle Award, and the Donaldson Award. Inge had two more Broadway hits in quick succession: *Bus Stop* (1955) and *The Dark at the Top of the Stairs*(1957), which was an expanded and revised version of *Farther Off from Heaven.*

Following this early success, however, Inge's subsequent plays, *A Loss of Roses* (1959), *Natural Affection* (1963) and *Where's Daddy?* (1966) were commercial failures, each closing after only a few performances. Inge had more success with his first attempt at screenwriting, *Splendor in the Grass* (1961), which earned him the Academy Award for Best Original Screenplay in 1961. Following this success, he moved to Los Angeles to concentrate on script writing—although he never repeated his early success.

Inge was deeply affected by negative reviews of his work. He struggled with depression and alcoholism for much of his life. Many of his plays focus on the complexity of family relationships and deal with characters who struggle with failed expectations, depression, and addiction. His death in 1973 from carbon monoxide poisoning was ruled a suicide.

PLOT SUMMARY

Act I, Scene 1

The scene opens with Doc entering the set, a cluttered and untidy downstairs kitchen and living room. Doc offers to prepare breakfast for the boarder, Marie, but she declines. When his wife, Lola enters, her disarray offers a distinct contrast to the other two character's neatness. She begins by telling Doc that she has again dreamed of her dog, Little Sheba, who was lost twenty years earlier, and she wonders if she'll ever find her lost pet. But Doc doubts that the dog will ever return. Both characters are nostalgic for a period more than twenty years earlier, when both were young and still dreaming of a different life. Lola was a popular beauty who longed for children before a botched midwife's delivery ended their infant's life and any hope of another child. Doc had planned on being a medical doctor before he was forced to marry and support a pregnant Lola; instead he became a chiropractor.

Lola applauds Doc for being sober a whole year. Doc then tells Lola that he will be at Alcoholics Anonymous that evening helping other people resist the urge to drink. When Lola asks Doc if he drank from disappointment, he responds that to stay sober he needs to forget the past. Doc leaves for work after noting that Marie is too nice a girl to waste time on a man like Turk.

Marie then thanks Lola for taking such good care of her. Lola wants to hear about Marie's romance with Turk, but the young man soon comes to pick up Marie. After she is left alone, an obviously lonely Lola tries to engage the postman, her neighbor, Mrs. Coffman, and the milkman in conversation. Lola finally turns to the radio for company when a messenger appears with a telegram for Marie. Lola cannot resist and steams it open to find that Marie's fiance, Bruce, will arrive the next evening.

As Lola is reading this message, Marie walks in to ask if she can complete her drawing of a seminude Turk in the living room. After quickly hiding the telegram, Lola watches Turk pose for Marie. When Doc returns, he is angry that Turk is seminude in front of Marie, but Lola assures him that it is for an art class. When Lola confesses to Doc the contents of the telegram, he is angry that she is so nosy. But Lola dismisses his concern and tells him that she is planning a wonderful dinner for Bruce, Marie, and the two of them. Just before Doc leaves the room, he tells Lola that if something happens to Marie, he will never forgive Lola. But he does not see the passionate kiss that Marie and Turk share after he has gone upstairs.

William Inge

Act I, Scene 2

When this second scene begins, it is clear that Lola has spent the day cleaning house. The rooms are neat and very clean. When Lola returns after borrowing silver polish from Mrs. Coffman, she asks Doc to show her some of his card tricks, and the two recall the happiness of their courtship. Lola observes that their youth has vanished like Little Sheba, and she regrets that she has gotten fat and slovenly. When Lola wonders if Doc regrets being forced to marry her, he replies that what's done is done and must be forgotten. Lola cheers him by doing the Charleston, but the mood is broken when Marie returns and casually makes fun of Lola's dancing.

Lola finally gives Marie the telegram announcing Bruce's arrival the next evening. When Marie goes into the next room, Lola watches her and Turk kissing. The two are engaging in some light-hearted sexual banter, and it is clear that their relationship has progressed beyond kissing. Doc is irritated at this spying, but Lola cannot see anything wrong with watching this bit of romance. After Doc leaves, Lola watches for a few more minutes, and then, when the couple leaves for a walk, Lola returns to the porch to call again to her lost dog.

Act II, Scene 1

It is the next morning, and Lola and Doc are at breakfast. Lola chats about Marie and Turk, but Doc tells Lola he would rather not talk. He says he did not sleep well and that he thought he heard a man's voice in the house when Marie returned after midnight. Doc walks into the living room and thinks that he hears a man's laugh coming from upstairs. He is forced to accept that Marie is not the virginal young women he had thought. A few moments later, Doc stumbles into Turk sneaking out the door. While Marie and Lola are getting the china for that evening's dinner, Doc goes into the kitchen and takes the bottle of liquor that has sat untouched for the last year. He wraps it in a coat and leaves the house. The scene ends with Lola telling Marie what a gentleman Doc is.

Act II, Scene 2

It is 5:30, and Lola is finishing her preparation for the dinner celebration. When Bruce arrives, Lola offers him a drink and goes into the kitchen to get the bottle. She discovers that the liquor is missing, and, understanding immediately that Doc is drinking, she calls his Alcoholics Anonymous mentor, Ed Anderson, for help. The scene ends with Marie and Bruce eating alone at the candle-lit table.

Act II, Scene 3

Lola awakens on the sofa the next morning. She calls Ed to come over, and after she hangs up, Doc tries to sneak into the house, pretending to be sober. When Lola confronts him, his anger, resentment, and disillusionment come out in a horrifying verbal attack directed toward Lola. Doc is so out of control that he takes a hatchet and chases Lola, telling her that he is going to cut off all her fat and accusing her of only cleaning house when a young man is due to visit. He collapses when Lola reminds him of how pretty she was when they first met.

At this point, Ed and another AA member, Elmo, arrive. They convince Doc to go with them to the hospital for treatment. After they leave, Mrs. Coffman, who came over when she heard the noise of the fight, also goes home. Lola is alone when Bruce and Marie arrive, announce they are to be married, and tell Lola that Marie is moving back home with Bruce. They are gone within minutes. Lola calls her mother and asks if she can come home, but it is clear that her mother says no.

Act II, Scene 4

It is one week later. Mrs. Coffman enters to ask if Lola would like to go to the relay races with her family, but Lola declines, since Doc is to come home that morning. After Mrs. Coffman leaves, Doc enters and apologizes to Lola for his behavior and begs her not to leave him. Lola tells him of a recent dream she had. She tells him that she now realizes that Little Sheba is gone forever. Both Lola and Doc understand that this story is an agreement to put the past behind them and move forward.

CHARACTERS

Ed Anderson

With Elmo, Ed is a member of Alcoholics Anonymous. Lola calls him frantic with worry when she discovers the bottle of alcohol is missing. She again calls him when Doc returns home drunk. It is Ed and Elmo who take Doc to the hospital.

Bruce

Bruce is Marie's hometown, clean-cut fiance. He provides the catalyst that finally moves Lola to clean house and prepare dinner when she eagerly anticipates his arrival. When he finally arrives, Bruce asks Marie to marry and move away with him.

Mrs. Coffman

Mrs. Coffman is the Delaney's German neighbor. In the first act, she has little time for gossip with Lola and tells her that she needs to keep busy. They are not friends, as is evidenced when Lola wonders if Mrs. Coffman might have killed Sheba. But when Mrs. Coffman hears Doc attack Lola in Act II, she goes next door to check on her neighbor and offer comfort. By the final scene a friendship is forming between the two women, and Mrs. Coffman again returns to ask Lola to accompany her family to the relay games.

Doc Delaney

Doc is a chiropractor. He had planned to go to medical school, but when Lola became pregnant, he married her and settled for chiropractic school instead. Doc is an alcoholic who has been sober for one year; he relies on Alcoholics Anonymous for support. He is disillusioned and disappointed at the loss of his only child, who died at birth, the loss of his medical career, and the loss of his wife's youth and beauty. Doc views Marie as the daughter he never had. His image of her is one of innocence and purity, but he lacks any fundamental ability to see her as she really is. Doc's denial of Marie's sexuality leads to yet another disappointment when he realizes that she is, in fact, having a sexual affair with Turk, although she has a boyfriend back home.

Doc's sobriety is fragile, and to cope with yet another disillusionment in his life, he once again returns to alcohol for support. When he returns home the next morning, Doc lashes out at Lola, calling her a slut and accusing her of being a fat and lazy burden who cost him the dreams of his youth. Doc grabs a hatchet and tries to attack Lola, but he is too drunk to do any harm. After a stay in the hospital to dry out, Doc again returns to Lola. In the final scene, he appears to have come to terms with his life as it is.

Lola Delaney

Lola's life is as full of disappointments as her husband's. But rather than drink to deal with depression, Lola sleeps excessively, often not waking until noon. She was pregnant when she and Doc married, and to avoid gossip, the couple allowed a midwife to deliver the baby. The infant died, and Lola was unable to conceive again. Lola's lost youth and beauty is symbolized by her lost dog, Sheba. Sheba is as irretrievable as Lola's beauty and Doc's dreams.

Lola has become fat and slovenly, and, in her boredom, she constantly accosts her neighbors and delivery people for conversation. She has no interest in housework or cooking, and instead, seeks escape through voyeurism. She encourages her young boarder's affair with Turk, leaving them alone and establishing opportunities for the two lovers to meet and then spying on them. Lola is so interested in Marie's love life that she secretly reads a telegram that announces the arrival of the girl's fiance, Bruce. It is unclear exactly where Lola's fantasies will lead, but she cleans the house to a nearly unrecognizable state and prepares a special dinner in anticipation of Bruce's arrival. Doc correctly understands Lola's role in what he considers to be Marie's fall from innocence, and his return to alcohol and his attack upon her appears to shock Lola into reassessing her life.

Elmo Huston

Like Ed Anderson, Elmo is a member of Alcoholics Anonymous. He helps Ed take Doc to the city hospital.

Marie

Marie is the Delaney's boarder. She is an art student and serves differing roles for both Doc and Lola. Doc envisions Marie as virginal and identifies her with the *Ave Maria* he hears playing on the radio. But Lola, who was once a beauty queen and popular with boys, identifies with Marie as a younger version of herself. Marie serves as the catalyst for the action in the play. Her fall from innocence results in Doc's return to drinking. She uses Turk to alleviate her boredom as she waits for Bruce to marry her. In the play's conclusion, she quite merrily runs off to marry Bruce, completely unaware of the near tragedy she has caused. At the time this play was written, Marie's open sexuality and her use of Turk as a sexual diversion would have been quite shocking to audiences.

MEDIA ADAPTATIONS

- *Come Back, Little Sheba* was adapted as a film in 1952. It was produced by Hal B. Wallace for Paramount Pictures and stars Shirley Booth as Lola, Burt Lancaster as Doc, Terry Moore as Marie, and Richard Jaeckel as Turk. Booth won an Academy Award for her performance.
- A made-for-television version was presented on NBC in 1977. The cast includes Lawrence Olivier, Joanne Woodward, Carrie Fisher, and Nicholas Campbell. It was produced by Granada Television.
- A musical adaptation titled *Sheba* opened in 1974 in Chicago. It starred Kay Ballard, George Wallace, Kimberly Farr, and Gary Sand.

Milkman

The milkman is another of Lola's objects of attention. Although she has been asked to leave a note telling him what she needs delivered, Lola repeatedly tries to engage him in conversation. It's a harmless flirtation for Lola, but causes a small delay for the milkman. However, he is charmed by her eagerness and clearly warms up to the short conversation.

Postman

The postman seems genuinely sympathetic to Lola's loneliness. He takes the time to come in and drink a glass of water with her and lingers long enough to exchange a few words. But when Lola tells him that her husband is a member of Alcoholics Anonymous, he seems almost uncomfortable with receiving this confidence. But after Lola presents him with a small toy for his grandchild, the postman cheerfully tells her that he will write her a letter if no one else does.

Turk

Turk is a stereotypical athletic stud. He throws the javelin, a clearly phallic symbol that reveals his purpose in the play. He poses for the art students, and Lola is excited at the prospect of seeing him nearly unclothed as he poses for Marie. He is interested in only one thing, and most of his time on stage is spent playing sexual games with Marie. Their banter is heavy with sexual import. Turk's departure in the morning after a night spent with Marie is witnessed by Doc and leads to his fall from sobriety.

THEMES

Addiction

At the time that *Come Back, Little Sheba* was first produced on Broadway, few people spoke openly about addiction. Alcohol abuse was, and remains, a common domestic problem, but families rarely spoke to outsiders about alcoholic family members. Membership in Alcoholics Anonymous was not a topic for the kind of casual conversation that Lola engages in with her milkman and postman.

Inge's play demonstrates how destructive alcohol can be. When Doc chases Lola with a hatchet in the second act, the audience is meant to feel horrified. The entire seventeen minute sequence of Doc's alcoholic breakdown is disturbing to watch, and when he is taken away to the psychiatric hospital, it is Inge's intention that the viewer feel both relief and disgust. Yet he also sought to illustrate to his audience the circumstances that lead to such addictions. While clearly showing the destructiveness of dependency, Inge seeks to foster understanding for why depressed people turn to alcohol for solace or escape.

Change and Transformation

The lives that Doc and Lola planned more than twenty years earlier have not come to fruition. Lola longs for her past happiness, for the time when she was young and beautiful and Doc was jealous of the other young men who also courted her. She wants to capture again the happiness of their early courtship and marriage and the anticipation of a baby. Instead, Lola has become fat and sloppy. Her appearance is careless and their house messy and dirty, and the children she longed for did not come. The baby died when Doc and Lola were forced to go to a midwife to avoid gossip about her premarital pregnancy. As a result of complications from that experience, Lola was unable to conceive again.

Doc also longs for the past. Before he was forced to marry and support a pregnant Lola, he planned on attending medical school and a subsequent career in medicine. Instead, he became a chiropractor, and, to forget the past, he also began to drink. The dissonance between Doc and Lola's youthful dreams and their unfulfilled present is the central conflict of the play. Their transformation from nostalgic longing to final acceptance is the work's thematic resolution.

Limitations and Opportunities

Doc drinks because he is disappointed and disillusioned at the loss of opportunity in his life. As a young man, he wanted to go to medical school and become a doctor. In place of his dream, however, he had to settle for less, becoming a chiropractor. The woman for whom he gave up his dream career has become fat and slovenly. Lola's hopes for a family and fulfilling marriage were dashed when their baby died at birth. Society prescribed that a woman's primary role was that of mother and wife. Unable to perform even this limited role, Lola sees no place for herself in postwar society. She is subsequently more interested in the lives of others who have a better chance of fulfilling these expectations—such as Marie and Turk or Marie and Bruce—than she is of her own. The play's resolution, with Doc and Lola finally coming to terms with their lot in life, offers the hope that they may finally transcend the disappointments in their lives and, together, discover new opportunities.

Loneliness

Lola spends her days trying to fill the time. She is lethargic and disinterested in keeping her home clean. She wants to sleep away half the day and fill the rest with idle gossip or voyeuristic pursuits; her primary pleasure comes from vicariously enjoying Turk and Marie's romance and cornering strangers into mindless conversations. Lola's loneliness is also evident in her invitation to cook dinner for Bruce and Marie, whose company she needs to assuage the emptiness in her life.

Memory and Reminiscence

Much of Inge's drama is centered on the time Lola and Doc spend dwelling on their past. Both remember the time when they were courting, when they were both happy and carefree. Lola remembers her beauty and how the boys all swarmed around her. She remembers Doc's jealousy and how much he loved her. Doc remembers his plans to go to medical school and his dreams of a brilliant career in medicine, but his membership in Alcoholics Anonymous has taught him that such memories are best forgotten. He tells Lola that the past is behind them and recites the AA prayer. It is important to note that when Doc is out of control and in a drunken rage, it is Lola's reminder of her past beauty that calms him and ends the danger. Inge clearly shows the couples' nostalgia as a refuge from the regret of their present circumstances. Their memories are an oasis to which they can retreat when their real lives become too depressing. That they are able to dispense with their reliance on such memories—an addiction as real and dangerous as Doc's drinking—represents a major turning point in their lives.

Sexuality

Marie's sexuality is the catalyst for Doc's return to drinking after a year of sobriety. Such overt sexuality was a new subject for the theatre; nice girls from good families did not engage in premarital sex as Marie so openly does. Those who did were the shameful objects of quickie marriages or back room abortions. Lola's early sexuality is seen by Doc as a bellwether to their later unhappiness; their premarital sex led to an unplanned pregnancy, marriage, and, ultimately, the loss of their dreams. Doc thus views such behavior as wrong and dangerous. When he is drunk, Doc accuses Lola of sexual impropriety. And now Marie, who is engaged to the nice boy back home, is having sex with Turk, a boy she does not love and who she has no intention of marrying. But Doc, who feels both sexual and paternal desires toward Marie, associates the young woman with the Virgin Mary. When he discovers that she is bedding a stereotypical jock whom she does not love, Doc's illusions are shattered, and he suffers a breakdown.

Sexuality in the 1950s was a taboo subject. There existed a great discrepancy between what was preached and what was practiced—as evidenced by Doc's participation in premarital sex and later condemnation of such behavior. Inge's use of sex in *Come Back, Little Sheba* is primarily as a tool to allow Doc to confront reality. His realization that a "virginal" woman such as Marie possesses carnal desire sends him into a tailspin, yet the realization also enables him to eventually deal with the mistakes of his past and face the consequences. For Lola, sex offers entertainment in the form of the lovemaking she witnesses between Marie and Turk. Doc's breakdown brings her to the realization that such behavior is unhealthy. She also understands that she must deal with reality and that sex must play a more personal role in her life.

TOPICS FOR FURTHER STUDY

- Research the history of Alcoholics Anonymous. Most people did not speak freely of addictions in 1950. Consider whether Inge's play breaks any new ground in its portrayal of an alcoholic's relapse and recovery.
- Some critics have criticized *Come Back, Little Sheba* for its lack of depth. Yet the play was very popular both on stage and as a movie. How do you account for its popularity?
- At the conclusion of this play, both Doc and Lola appear to have accepted the reality of their lives and both seem ready to move forward together. The dog, which had symbolized Lola's lost beauty and youth, is no longer the object of Lola's search. Explore the symbolism in the play and decide if you think that Inge relies too heavily on symbolism to carry his plot.
- Research the American post World War II experience. The early 1950s are often identified with isolation and repressed sexuality. In what ways do the Delaneys represent this repressed and inhibited ideal?

STYLE

Act

An act is a major division in a drama. In Greek plays the sections of the drama signified by the appearance of the chorus were usually divided into five acts. This is the formula for most serious drama from the Greeks to the Romans to the Elizabethan playwrights like William Shakespeare. The five acts denote the structure of dramatic action. They are exposition, complication, climax, falling action, and catastrophe. The five–act structure was followed until the nineteenth century when Henrik Ibsen (*A Doll's House*) combined elements into fewer acts. *Come Back, Little Sheba* is a two–act play. The exposition and complication are combined in the first act when the audience learns of Doc and Lola's disappointments, Doc's drinking

Marie (Joan Lorring) greets Doc (Sidney Blackmer) at the breakfast table in the original Broadway production

problem, and Marie's affair with Turk. The climax occurs in the second act when Doc begins to drink again. Doc's drunken return in Scene 2 provides the falling action, and the catastrophe occurs in this act when Doc and Lola are forced to recognize that they must live with the choices they have made and that the past cannot be changed.

Scene

Scenes are subdivisions of an act. A scene may change when all of the main characters either enter or exit the stage. But a change of scene may also indicate a change of time. In *Come Back, Little Sheba,* the second scene of Act I occurs later on the same day, and thus, indicates the passage of time in the play.

Setting

The time, place, and culture in which the action of the play takes place is called the setting. The elements of setting may include geographic location, physical or mental environments, prevailing cultural attitudes, or the historical time in which the action takes place. The location for Inge's play is the downstairs of an old house in a midwestern city; the time is post-World War II. The action occurs over a period of two days. The proceedings are further reduced to one set, the downstairs of the Delaney home. This narrows the focus to Doc and Lola's home, both literally and figuratively. The setting is the result of their life choices, the sum of their actions. It is the battleground upon which they must resolve their differences and move forward.

Plot

This term refers to the pattern of events. Generally plots should have a beginning, a middle, and a conclusion, but they may also sometimes be a series of episodes connected together. Basically, the plot provides the author with the means to explore primary themes. Students are often confused between the two terms; but themes explore ideas, and plots simply relate what happens in a very obvious manner. Thus the plot of *Come Back, Little Sheba*is the story of a husband and wife who find that their present is not commensurate with the dreams of their past. But the themes are those of loneliness, addiction, and lost opportunities.

Character

A person in a dramatic work. The actions of each character are what constitute the story. Character can also include the idea of a particular individual's morality. Characters can range from simple stereotypical figures to more complex multi-faceted ones. Characters may also be defined by personality traits, such as the rogue or the damsel in distress. ''Characterization'' is the process of creating a lifelike person from an author's imagination. To accomplish this the author provides the character with personality traits that help define who he will be and how he will behave in a given situation.

For instance, in the beginning of *Come Back, Little Sheba,* Doc is sober, although his evasive answers to Lola indicate he is not happy or even accepting of the life he is living. As the play progresses, it becomes clearer that Doc is in a great deal of emotional pain. He is using Marie's purity to represent all the lost opportunities in his life. When he realizes that she is not what he thought, he cannot deal with even one more disappointment in his life. These sequences define the character of Doc as a broken, disillusioned man. The traits Inge assigns to him identify him as such and his actions are therefore plausible to the audience.

Drama

A drama is often defined as any work designed to be presented on the stage. It consists of a story, of actors portraying characters, and of action. But historically, drama can also consist of tragedy, comedy, religious pageant, and spectacle. In modern usage, drama explores serious topics and themes but does not achieve the same level as tragedy. Drama is also applicable as a term to describe a storyline that is serious in nature and theme. *Come Back, Little Sheba* represents both definitions of the term.

Catharsis

Catharsis is the release of emotions, usually fear and pity. The term as first used by Aristotle in his *Poetics* to refer to the desired effect of tragedy on the audience. The final act of *Come Back, Little Sheba* is cathartic because the tension has been building as the audience has watched the affair of Marie and Turk progress, understanding of course, that its lack of concealment will lead to a climax when Doc realizes that Marie is not pure and virginal. When Doc finally explodes in rage at Lola, the audience also feels the eruption of this tension as a catharsis. For the audience, Doc, and Lola, this catharsis brings clearer understanding and, it is Inge's hope, change for the better.

Symbolism

Symbolism is the use of one object to replace another. It is an important tool in literature. The symbol is an object or image that implies a reality beyond its original meaning. This is different from a metaphor, which summons forth an object in order to describe an idea or a quality. For example, the dog Little Sheba is a symbol of Lola's lost youth. She searches for the dog, just as she searches for her lost beauty and youth. The javelin that he throws is a symbol for Turk's role in the play. He is a sexual plaything for Marie. The javelin is clearly identified with male sexual genitalia and sexuality. Likewise, Doc's idealized perception of Marie represents his desire to correct the mistakes of his past. He wants to believe that Marie will behave in a pure fashion and thus not suffer the fate that Lola has.

HISTORICAL CONTEXT

Post-World War II America was a period marked by the shift of populations from cities to suburbs. Thanks to the G.I. Bill (which provided government funding for the college education of men exiting the armed services), thousands of men who would never have been able to go to college found the way suddenly made easier. A building boom meant that those better educated men marry and the families could buy the new houses being built on tracts all across suburban America.

The decade also marked the beginning of a period of domestic perfection. Television would turn the postwar ideal of perfect families in perfect homes surrounded by perfect white fences into the national image. Unfortunately for many families, failure to live up to this ideal resulted in depression and despondency—much like Doc and Lola in *Come Back, Little Sheba.* Darkness was also evident in the political events of the decade. It was the beginning of Joseph McCarthy's "red scare" during which the House Un-American Activities Committee persecuted numerous American citizens suspected of communism. In Korea, early skirmishes signaled America's involvement in yet another war.

Despite the public emphasis on suburban existence, a large portion of America was still centered on a rural way of life. In Kansas, Inge's birthplace and the setting for *Come Back, Little Sheba,* there were fewer than one million people living in a state that serves as the exact geographical center of the U.S. By 1949, Kansas was still an agricultural center with one fourth of the nation's wheat grown there.

In cities across the nation, the women who had run factories and kept assembly lines running during World War II were out of men's slacks and once again back in aprons, domestically at work in their homes. By 1949, the baby boom of postwar America was well established. The emphasis, after years of depression followed by years of war, was on stability and family. Women lost the jobs they held during the war because war veterans needed work;

COMPARE & CONTRAST

- **1949:** Blue Cross Insurance programs cover thirty-seven million Americans, more than six times the number insured only ten years before.

  Today: Almost half of all Americans have no health insurance. In 1998, President Clinton and the U.S. Congress will once again consider a new health care package to ensure that all Americans have access to affordable health care.

- **1949:** Auto registrations show one passenger car for every 3.75 Americans.

  Today: Almost every American family has at least one automobile, with most owning two or three. The car has become an indelible symbol of life in America, with the majority of the population relying on the vehicles as their primary mode of transportation; autos have become personal statements, reflecting the personality and independence of their owners.

- **1949:** Tranquilizer drugs that eliminate anxiety and excitement without making users too drowsy are developed by Wallace Laboratories and by Wyeth Laboratories. The drug Valium becomes a common accessory for high-strung personalities.

  Today: Tranquilizers, anti-depressants, and other anti-anxiety drugs are heavily advertised in all publications and readily available to almost everyone. Valium has been supplanted in the public consciousness by such ''mental aids'' as Prozac and Halcion. Still more turn to illegal drugs such as marijuana for relaxation and stress relief.

- **1949:** The age of mass media begins; the nation now has more than one hundred television stations broadcasting in thirty-eight states. Five million homes have sets, but forty-five million homes still have radios.

  Today: Television sets occupy almost every home, with most domiciles having more than one set. Families that used to be grouped around the radio in the evening have been replaced by families that spread out in different rooms to watch programming on different sets. The internet becomes a new media venue for entertainment and information.

---

instead, women were returned to the domestic sphere they had occupied before the war. The role of wife and mother was repeatedly portrayed in the media as the highest aspiration for a woman in postwar society. When Lola laments early in the play that she does not know what she is supposed to do in a childless house, she is giving voice to the dark underside of that perfect American family. In the midst of a baby boom, what is a woman without children to do? Lola tells the audience that Doc does not want her working, but he is only repeating the natural order of domestic life.

Few women were working outside the home in this era, but women were beginning to become a stronger force in society. With production of consumer goods at an all time high, women as consumers were beginning to have more power. In addition, their wartime participation in the American work force had given them a taste of independence and pride in workmanship. The postwar years marked the beginnings of the women's movement that would flower in the ensuing decades. For many women, the 1950s reinforced the belief that they should have the same opportunities as men in both domestic and business situations. Yet due to the prosperity of the postwar business boom, many other women saw no reason to question the status quo. With increased money circulating in the economy, consumer spending was up and times were good.

A postwar production economy was trying to meet the demand for new cars, new washers, and the multitude of new items that television advertisements promised each family they would need. Auto manufacturer General Motors's profit in 1950 was nearly $636.5 million. The Gross National Product was $284 billion, a huge increase from 1940's $99 billion. The manufacture and sale of television sets also sharply increased to meet new demands. The acquisition of material goods was another symbol of the American Dream. If a family did not have a new home, new car, and completely modern new kitchen, then they were not living the good life.

CRITICAL OVERVIEW

When *Come Back, Little Sheba* opened on Broadway in February of 1950, it was to mixed reviews. Most critics cheered the performances of Shirley Booth and Sydney Blackmer in the lead roles. But all too many deplored the actors' waste in a play described as ''dramatic trivialities'' (Howard Barnes in *New York Theatre Critics' Reviews*) and ''underwritten to the point of barrenness'' (Brooks Atkinson in his second *New York Times* review two weeks after the play's opening). Barnes and Atkinson were not alone. *Commonweal*'s Kappo Phelan labeled Inge's drama ''a poor play on all counts,'' and in a review written for the *New Yorker,* Wolcott Gibbs called attention to the play's mix of ''realism and psychiatric claptrap.'' Yet not all critics hated the play; many liked it and many more had mixed reactions. Atkinson, in his first review for the *New York Times,* noted the play's topics as ''terrifyingly true'' and its story as ''straightforward and unhackneyed.''

The play's reception when it was released as a film in 1952 was similarly mixed. Booth's reprised performance was again noted as excellent, but critics still attacked the film, though in fewer numbers. The critic for *Theatre Arts,* Robert Hatch, complimented Booth's performance and said that Inge's play is an ''acute and compassionate statement of the horror implicit in wasted lives.'' Also noting the excellence of Booth's performance was Philip Hartung, whose review in *Commonweal* praised the play's ''repeated plea for compassion and understanding of one's fellow man.''

Come Back, Little Sheba was the first of four Broadway hits for Inge. But, this drama could not be described as a smash hit. It played for less than six months. Inge himself observed in the forward to the play that his work ''did good business for only a few weeks and then houses began to dwindle to the size of tea parties.'' Inge admitted that he took a cut in royalties and the actors took salary cuts to keep the play on stage. Yet based on *Come Back, Little Sheba*'s Broadway debut, Inge was voted the most promising new playwright by the Drama Critics Circle. And Booth and Blackmer each won Antionette (''Tony'') Perry Awards for their performances. The work was more successful financially as a film.

Inge's depiction of midwestern life provided a new setting for Broadway theater patrons. Prior to Inge's string of plays, most works focused on northeastern urban characters or the southern characters of Tennessee Williams. The topics portrayed in Inge's drama were also new to Broadway. The frank manner in which Inge presents alcoholism and addiction in the play was shocking to many viewers. And the audience would have also been horrified by the scene of Doc's drunken attack on Lola; domestic abuse, especially as it related to alcohol, was a subject discussed only in hushed whispers in the 1950s. Inge's depictions, however, opened the door for further dramatic discussion of the topics. In subsequent decades the matter become a popular topic for film and theater, with works such as *Lost Weekend* and *Leaving Las Vegas* presenting stark and realistic visions of addiction.

As with the topic of abuse, Inge innovated open portrayals of sex. One reviewer of *Come Back, Little Sheba, Catholic World*'s Euphemia Wyatt, found the scenes between Marie and Turk embarrassing. Certainly other members of the audience may have felt the same way. Marie makes only the slightest effort to be discrete as she sneaks Turk up to her bedroom after the Delaneys have gone to bed. Her sexual bantering with Turk offers no indication that she is embarrassed, only that she and Turk are interested in casual sex. In fact, Marie makes clear that Turk is being used as a diversion until she can marry her boyfriend back home. This was a shocking revelation in that many believed a woman should only have sex after marriage and, further, that the act serve only as a method of procreation. Addressing such topics may have earned Inge initial criticism, but by portraying them so realistically in his play he paved the way for a new contemporary theater. Later appraisals of Inge's work invariably include *Come Back, Little Sheba,* citing it as a seminal work of modern drama.

"INGE WAS AHEAD OF HIS TIME WHEN, THROUGH LOLA, HE POINTS OUT THE INEQUITIES BETWEEN WOMEN AND MEN."

CRITICISM

Sheri Metzger

Metzger is a professional writer who specializes in literature and drama. In this essay she discusses Inge's exploration of social preconceptions regarding marriage and success in postwar America. She concludes that Inge was ahead of his time in addressing inequities in the expected social roles of men and women.

When *Come Back, Little Sheba* made its first appearance on Broadway, many reviewers dismissed it as a boring domestic soap opera. Others focused on the psychological complexities of the two lead characters. But Jane Courant argued in *Studies in American Drama* that audiences should, instead, appreciate Inge's drama for its revolutionary exploration of social and cultural ideas. Courant noted that Inge "confronted sexual stereotyping, social conformity, and especially the cultural media that reinforced these values." Earlier, when Inge was still a drama critic for the *Saint Louis Star-Times,* he had criticized Hollywood films for creating only passive, accepting women.

Accordingly, said Courant, when Inge wrote *Come Back, Little Sheba* it was with the intent of creating a woman as rich and complex as any male character, who "coexisted with men as fully developed characters with strong physical and spiritual needs." Thus, Lola states early in the play, "When I lost my baby and found out I couldn't have any more, I didn't know what to do with myself." Lola is haunted by this loss, which she channels into her plaintive calls for her lost dog, Sheba. Doc, of course, is haunted by the loss of his career. When he was forced to give up his dreams of medical school, Doc also lost the economic and social prestige that came with the medical license.

Both their losses come at a point in postwar America where the baby boom signals the importance of family and a consumer-driven economy propels the prosperity of the nation. But the Delaneys have neither children nor prosperity. Courant declared that the "postwar American environment placed enormous value on social status and material success," and these values were "unabashedly proclaimed by the expanding electronic media, anxious to sell a vast array of consumer goods." In an early draft of *Come Back, Little Sheba,* Courant stated that Inge has Lola enter in Act I as the radio plays an ad for a cream to restore a woman's youth. Since the symbolism of Inge's play is so heavily focused on the loss of youth's beauty and promise, the connection to media influence is readily apparent.

The importance of media, especially Hollywood movies, is apparent in Lola's justification for watching Marie and Turk kissing. When Doc criticizes Turk and warns Lola that the young man is probably forcing Marie to kiss him, Lola replies that Marie "is kissing him like he was Rudolph Valentino." When Doc tries to stop his wife's description of Marie's and Turk's embrace, Lola replies that Doc thinks "every young girl is Jennifer Jones in *The Song of Bernadette.*" And in Lola's reply to Doc's accusation of spying, she compares what she is doing to watching actors kiss in a movie. Lola is unable to separate the reality of what Marie and Turk are doing from the beguiling images created in Hollywood. Courant argued that this exchange has different meanings for Lola and Doc. For Lola, "a fascinating movie is going on in her own home, and with no meaningful purpose in her own life, she passively accepts a role of observer with no notion of interfering." But Doc, "inappropriately places responsibility for Marie's behavior on his wife." Neither husband or wife seem aware that both are confusing illusion with reality.

Inge was ahead of his time when, through Lola, he points out the inequities between women and men. When Marie tells Lola that the female models in her art class can pose nude, but men must be covered, Lola is shocked at the inequity, and she exclaims, "If it's alright for a woman, it oughta' be for a man." But there is a double standard governing the behavior of men and women. This discrepancy is again noted when Doc automatically assumes Marie is pure and virginal, even identifying her with the Virgin Mary when he hears *Ave Maria;* but he naturally assumes that Turk is another debauched male, only interested in one thing—sex.

WHAT DO I READ NEXT?

- Published in 1953, *Picnic* is Inge's second Broadway play to be set in the Midwest. The play is concerned with the relationship between a sexually attractive man and a group of lonely women.
- *Bus Stop,* also by Inge, was published in 1955. Instead of a drama, Inge has used Kansas as a setting for a romantic comedy about a small group of people stranded in a snow storm. The happy ending of this play is not typical of Inge.
- *Look Homeward, Angel,* a 1929 novel by Thomas Wolfe, is also a realistic depiction of a family relationship, with the central character, Eugene, the son of an alcoholic.
- Edward Albee's 1962 play, *Who's Afraid of Virginia Woolf?,* examines the brutal and sometimes violent relationship between a husband and wife. As with Inge's play, broken dreams play a pivotal role in the story.
- *The Lost Weekend,* a 1945 film starring Ray Milland, and *Leaving Las Vegas,* a 1995 film starring Nicholas Cage, are uncompromising examinations of alcoholism and the destruction it brings.

The reality that Inge makes clear is that Marie is as sexually charged as Turk. Thus, the social implications of Inge's characterizations are important. The contrast between Doc and Turk is even more interesting. Doc is as sexually repressed as the illusion he creates about Marie. And Turk, whom Doc thinks of as a seducer of young virgins, is himself being used by the sexually liberated Marie. All of this reversed role-playing predicts the sexual revolution and women's rights movements that will explode in the 1960s. Inge's drama is nearly fifteen years ahead of its time. Given the potential for misunderstanding the playwright's intentions, it is little wonder that 1950 theatre critics provided such mixed reviews when *Come Back, Little Sheba* opened.

Marie has been the focus of much of the play's critical review. Her open sexuality and the easy manner in which she dismisses Turk when her fiance, Bruce, appears, is a incongruity for the cultural milieu in which Inge was writing. Marie does not easily fit into any grouping. She is neither pure nor tainted. And, she is more complex than she initially appears. For instance, when Marie first enters the stage she is described as wearing only a sheer dainty negligee. Marie seems genuinely unaware of Doc's infatuation with her or of the inappropriateness of her clothing. And yet, as she "starts dancing away from him," as the stage direction requires, there is a hint of flirtation. This is even more evident when Marie returns to the stage after she has dressed. After Lola kisses Doc goodbye, Marie jokes, "Aren't you going to kiss me, Dr. Delaney?"

Jordan Miller ignored this flirtation and the stage direction that Inge has supplied, and asserted in the *Kansas Quarterly* that Marie's role in Doc's fall is inadvertent. After first describing Marie as a "bubbly . . . classic stereotype of the oh-so-enthusiastic coed, eager to get her education in her own free way," Miller later referred to Marie as a complication to "Doc's trial." But Miller did not blame Marie for what happens to Doc and Lola; he blamed Lola. Miller excused Doc's infatuation with Marie by describing her as "the picture to Doc of the Lola that might have been," and so, "his infatuation with her is entirely understandable." Miller argued that Doc's enjoyment in Marie is to be expected in the face of Lola's appearance and he observed that "in Doc's vicarious enjoyment of Marie's fresh daintiness as a Lola substitute, as well as his intense pleasure at her very nearness, the conflict he is enduring within himself involving his loyalties to his repulsive wife is all the more obvious."

Blackmer and Booth as the troubled couple at the center of Inge's drama

Later, Miller excused Doc's fall from sobriety, as ''appropriate'' and ''effective.'' When he placed the blame for Doc's behavior on Lola, Miller assigned a meaning to the play that Inge never intended and, in fact, denied. Courant quoted an early article that Inge wrote for *Theatre Arts* in which he stated that Lola is ''childish rather than slovenly'' and that ''she possesses enough human warmth and compassion to make her his [Doc's] equal.''

Lola is more than a symbol of Doc's lost dreams or her own discarded hopes. And she is much more complex than Miller admitted when he described her as ''childish . . . [and] infantile,'' with an ''arrested emotional development.'' However, when Miller acknowledged that Lola is the ''picture of a thousand, of ten thousand women whose lives have descended to just such meaningless routines,'' he was articulating a social problem that Inge illuminates in this play. During World War II, women assumed many of the roles that men had traditionally held. Women worked in factories, on assembly lines, and in support of the war effort. When the war ended, and the men returned, women were fired to ensure employment for the returning veterans. Doc's insistence that Lola not work was all too common, but Inge's focus on the emptiness of her life illuminates the results of such actions. Lola has spent twenty years in the emptiness of her house. It is little wonder that she wants to sleep until noon or that she has little interest in cleaning her prison.

An interesting contrast is offered by Mrs. Coffman, who has seven children and a spotless home. Her house is not empty; she has the challenge of caring for a large family to fill her days. Lola, though, has nothing to fill her days. Lola's loneliness, manifested in her eagerness to gossip and chatter with whomever comes to her door, is clearly obvious. Her life is a ''meaningless routine,'' but it is because of a social standard that creates two distinct spheres for men and women. Doc works in the public sphere; the work is not the career he wanted, but it is a way to escape into the world. It is ironic that Doc has relegated Lola to the domestic sphere and an unfulfilled existence when his drinking is in reaction to his own unfulfilled dreams.

Source: Sheri Metzger, for *Drama for Students,* Gale, 1998.

William A. Henry III

In this review of a 1984 revival production of Come Back, Little Sheba, *Henry offers a favorable appraisal of the play and reaffirms Inge's place among America's best playwrights.*

When *Come Back, Little Sheba* opened on Broadway in 1950, critics hailed its author, William Inge, as an authentic voice of the plain people west of the Mississippi. He burnished his reputation for passionate simplicity with *Picnic* (winner of a 1953 Pulitzer Prize), *Bus Stop* (1955) and *The Dark at the Top of the Stairs* (1957). Never a master of plot or construction, Inge was incomparably tender, a poet laureate of adolescent sexuality and middle-aged longing. An honored place in theater history seemed assured. Then all went sour. Flop followed flop; drink and depression overtook him. When he committed suicide in 1973, the New York *Times* obituary appraised him as a man who had ''lost his gift.'' Gift there was, however, and after near oblivion, Inge is being rediscovered: last week the Roundabout Theater in New York City mounted a powerful *Come Back, Little Sheba,* the first major Manhattan production since its premiere. The Berkshire Theater Festival in Stockbridge, Mass., is currently staging *A Loss of Roses* with Elizabeth Franz and Shaun Cassidy. A musical version of *Bus Stop* and a West Coast stage revival of *Picnic* are pending, and Washington *Post* Drama Critic David Richards is writing an Inge biography.

Like all of Inge's best plays, *Sheba* is slight of plot but musky with atmosphere. An alcoholic chiropractor (Philip Bosco) and his slatternly wife (Shirley Knight) live in a dreary house in the Midwest, diverted from maudlin introspection only by their boarder, a sprightly college student (Mia Dillon). Doom seeps through every dusty curtain. Although the husband is supposedly recovered, it is apparent that he is looking for an excuse to take a drink. Although the college girl is beloved as a surrogate for the couple's baby daughter who died 20 years before, it is evident that she will, however inadvertently, add to the wreckage of the marriage. The title refers to the wife's calling for a lost puppy, yet it is clear that hers is in truth a *cri de coeur* for the unassuageable pain of growing old before she has even grown up. If this is the heartland, it is as seen by Freud: the husband lusts after the girl and fantasizes about her as the virtuous virgin that his wife was not; the wife acts kittenish even with the milkman; the girl selects lovers, then discards them. Middle age is portrayed as a time of aching sexual frustration, made more acute by the close-at-hand vision of youth. Some of Inge's kitchen-sink exposition seems dated and clumsy in its mix of naturalism and artifice. But *Sheba* remains a showcase for poignant acting. Knight attains a lumpish sweetness but does not sentimentalize her character as a victim. Bosco has little to do until his whisky-sodden storming, but radiates the disappointment that beclouds the house. Dillon blends coy charm with unhesitating selfishness. And as her beau of convenience, Kevin Conroy is boisterously funny yet pathetic, reveling in his self-image as "a brute," never realizing that it is he who is being overpowered. Inge did not transform his characters: they end where they began. But he understood them. In their interplay was genuine life, often blunted but ever resilient.

Source: William A. Henry III, "The Laureate of Longing" in *Time,* Volume 124, no. 4, July 23, 1984 , pp. 103.

Wolcott Gibbs

Gibbs reviews the original Broadway production of Come Back, Little Sheba, *awarding plaudits to the cast yet finding Inge's text short on substance. Despite his mixed feelings, Gibbs still finds several portions of the play fascinating and one scene in particular "genuinely shocking."*

"LIKE ALL OF INGE'S BEST PLAYS, *SHEBA* IS SLIGHT OF PLOT BUT MUSKY WITH ATMOSPHERE."

In the last scene of *Come Back, Little Sheba,* at the Booth, the forty-year-old heroine tells her husband about a dream she had the night before. She was, it seems, a spectator at a track meet, watching the javelin throw. At first, it appeared to her that the star performer was a young athlete who had stirred her powerfully in her waking life, not only by posing for a drawing in his running trunks but also by seducing a pretty student who happened to be boarding in her house. Rapidly, however, he turned into a succession of other young men, whose muscular physiques and fetching ways had appealed to her rather strongly, too. The confusion was finally resolved when this multiple personality was disqualified from further competition by her father, who chanced to be an official at the meet, and the event was won by her husband, who threw the javelin so high that it disappeared in the sky. The dream ended with her discovery of the body of her little dog, Sheba, who had run away one night and never come back and whom, in some mysterious way, she had come to identify with everything she had lost in life. It is doubtful whether so much elementary and perhaps slightly preposterous symbolism has ever been crowded into one dream before in the history of the theatre, and the fact that the author, William Inge, thinks enough of it to employ it as a sort of official key to the meaning of his play may partially explain why *Come Back, Little Sheba,* for all the true and touching things it has to say, is on the whole much less satisfactory than it ought to be.The story so conscientiously diagrammed by the dream is a fairly simple one. When the elderly hero was a young man, he had hoped to be a great doctor. However, a youthful romance with a girl somewhat beneath him had resulted in pregnancy and a hasty marriage, and he had been obliged to give up his medical studies and take to the science of chiropractic. When the child was born dead, the couple's frustration was complete, and by the time the play opens, he is a temporarily reclaimed drunkard, a member of Alcoholics Anonymous, and she is a hopeless slattern, indifferent to her own appearance and that of her house, and even unwilling to get up and cook his breakfast. Her only surviving interests, in fact, are popular radio programs; conversations with the deliverymen, especially if handsome; the love affair

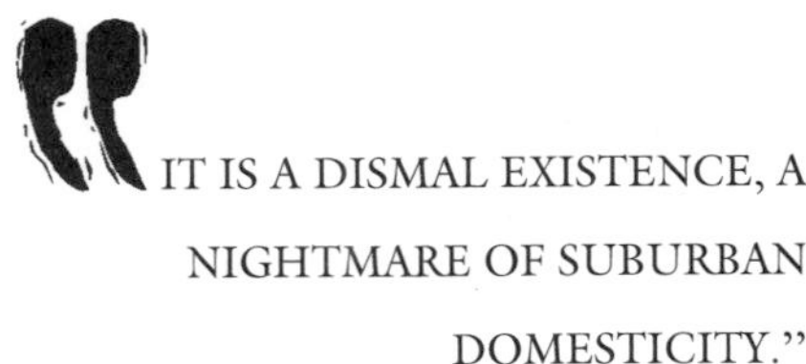

IT IS A DISMAL EXISTENCE, A NIGHTMARE OF SUBURBAN DOMESTICITY."

being conducted by her boarder, from which she obviously gets a strong vicarious excitement; and, of course, the loss of her dog. It is a dismal existence, a nightmare of suburban domesticity, but the unhappy pair are at least resigned to it until the husband, identifying the boarder with the daughter he never had, is infuriated by what he takes to be an attempt of his wife to debauch her and goes back to his bottle. There is a genuinely shocking scene in which, after reproaching her with ruining his life and turning their home into a bordello, he attacks her with a hatchet, but fortunately he falls down in a drunken stupor before any blood is shed. Nevertheless, the situation is still alarming, and everybody is rather relieved when two envoys from Alcoholics Anonymous come and take him away to a hospital. When he returns, a week later, he is naturally a chastened man, and the two are reconciled. It is apparently Mr. Inge's contention that since they have nothing but each other, they had better forget the past (there is some talk about getting a new dog to replace little Sheba) and try to make the best of things as they are. I found it rather hard to believe that conditions wouldn't be precisely as bad, if not worse, within a couple of months, but it is quite possible that I am underrating the power of good resolutions, made under great emotional tension, not to mention that of Alcoholics Anonymous.

Though I have a good many misgivings about the play, which strikes me as a peculiar mixture of effective realism and psychiatric claptrap, I have none at all about the performances given in it by Shirley Booth and Sidney Blackmer. Mr. Inge's heroine is an unusually taxing part, since she could readily seem only a silly and graceless woman, amply deserving everything her husband says about her, but Miss Booth achieves the difficult feat of arousing both pity and sympathy for her. It is a considerable accomplishment, calling for acting qualities, for a range of emotion, that I hadn't been aware she possessed. Mr. Blackmer's job is easier, long-suffering husbands and dipsomaniacs being among the few almost foolproof assignments the stage has to offer, but the transition between these two conditions certainly presents its problems, and I think he handles them admirably. Of the others, I especially liked John Randolph, as a physical-culture addict, and Olga Fabian, as a busybody living next door, and there were sound contributions by Joan Lorring, Lonny Chapman, and Daniel A. Reed. Howard Bay's set, described in the program as "an old house in a run-down neighborhood," has a fidelity to these specifications that would drive almost any man to drink.

Source: Wolcott Gibbs, "The Dream and the Dog" in the *New Yorker,* Volume XXVI, no. 1, February, 1950, pp. 68, 70.

SOURCES

Atkinson, Brooks. Review of *Come Back, Little Sheba* in the *New York Times,* February 16, 1950, p. 28.

Atkinson, Brooks. "Two Actors" in the *New York Times,* February 26, 1950, section 2, p. 1.

Barnes, Howard. "Good Acting Squandered" in the *New York Theatre Critics' Reviews,* Critics' Theatre Reviews, 1950, p. 350.

Burgess, Charles E. "An American Experience: William Inge in St. Louis 1943-1949" in *Papers on Language and Literature: A Journal for Scholars and Critics of Language and Literature,* Vol. 12, 1976, pp. 438-68.

Gibbs, Wolcott. "The Dream and the Dog" in the *New Yorker,* February 25, 1950, p. 66.

Hartung, Philip T. Review of *Come Back, Little Sheba* in *Commonweal,* December 26, 1952, p. 308.

Hatch, Robert. Review of *Come Back, Little Sheba* in *Theatre Arts,* December, 1952, p. 29.

Herron, Ima Honaker. "Our Vanishing Towns: Modern Broadway Versions" in *Southwest Review,* Vol. 51, 1966, pp. 209-20.

Inge, William. Introduction to *Four Plays,* Random House (New York), 1958.

Leeson, Richard M. *William Inge: A Research and Production Sourcebook,* Greenwood Press, 1994.

Lewis, Allen. "The Emergent Deans: Kingsley, Inge, and Company" in *American Plays and Playwrights of the Contemporary Theatre,* Crown (New York), 1965, pp. 143-63.

Miller, Jordan. "William Inge: Playwright of the Popular" in *Proceedings of the Fifth National Convention of the Popular Culture Association,* Bowling Green University Press (Bowling Green, OH), 1975, pp. 37-50.

Phelan, Kappo. "The State" in *Commonweal,*March 3, 1950, p. 558.

Sarotte, Georges-Michel. "William Inge: 'Homosexual Spite' in Action" in *Like a Brother, Like a Lover: Male Homosexuality in the American Novel and Theater from Herman Melville to James Baldwin,* Translated by Richard Miller, Doubleday, 1978, pp. 121-23.

Weales, Gerald. "The New Pineros" in *American Drama since World War Two,* Harcourt (New York), 1962, pp. 40-56.

Wyatt, Euphemia Van Renssalaer. Review of *Come Back, Little Sheba* in *Catholic World,* April, 1950, p. 67.

FURTHER READING

Courant, Jane. "Social and Cultural Prophecy in the Works of William Inge" in *Studies in American Drama,* Vol. 6, no. 2, 1991.

Courant is a professor at the University of California, Santa Cruz. Her critical reading of Inge is based on cultural-historical theory and seeks to examine the motivations and intents of Inge based on social influences. Her primary argument is that with the distance of several years and the events of the 1960s, it is easy to see how Inge was anticipating social change.

Inge, William. "The Schizophrenic Wonder" in *Theatre Arts,* May, 1950, pp. 22-23.

In this article, Inge is responding to the harsh criticism of the female characters in his play. He defends them by stating that critics are unable to "separate low morals from low incomes."

Leeson, Richard M. *William Inge: A Research and Production Sourcebook,* Greenwood Press, 1994.

This is a thorough critical overview of Inge's plays with information about reviews and critical studies.

McClure, Arthur F. *Memories of Splendor: The Midwestern World of William Inge,* Kansas State Historical Society (Topeka), 1989.

This book contains production information and photographs of Inge and his work.

Miller, Jordan. "William Inge: Last of the Realists?" in *Kansas Quarterly,* Vol. 2, no. 2, 1970, pp. 17-26.

Miller is a professor at the University of Rhode Island. Miller is from Kansas, and he finds that Inge's settings are very realistic and that he accurately portrays Kansas—and midwestern—life. In this article, Miller praises Inge's realistic portrayal of his characters.

Shuman, R. Baird. *William Inge,* Twayne (Boston), 1989.

This is a critical examination of all of Inge's plays.

Voss, Ralph F. *A Life of William Inge: The Strains of Triumph,* University of Kansas Press (Lawrence), 1989.

This is a critical biography of Inge's life.

The Crucible

ARTHUR MILLER

1953

Using the historical subject of the Salem Witch trials, Arthur Miller's play *The Crucible* (1953) presents an allegory for events in contemporary America. The Salem Witch Trials took place in Salem, Massachusetts in 1692, and were based on the accusations of a twelve-year-old girl named Anne Putnam. Putnam claimed that she had witnessed a number of Salem's residents holding black sabbaths and consorting with Satan. Based on these accusations, an English-American clergyman named Samuel Parris spearheaded the prosecution of dozens of alleged witches in the Massachusetts colony. Nineteen people were hanged and one pressed to death over the following two years.

Miller's play employs these historical events to criticize the moments in humankind's history when reason and fact became clouded by irrational fears and the desire to place the blame for society's problems on others. Dealing with elements such as false accusations, manifestations of mass hysteria, and rumor-mongering, *The Crucible* is seen by many as more of a commentary on ''McCarthyism'' than the actual Salem trials. ''McCarthyism'' was the name given to a movement led by Senator Joe McCarthy and his House Committee on Un-American Activities. This movement involved the hunting down and exposing of people suspected of having communist sympathies or connections. While those found guilty in McCarthy's witch hunt were not executed, many suffered irreparable damage to their

reputations. Miller himself came under suspicion during this time.

While *The Crucible* achieved its greatest resonance in the 1950s—when McCarthy's reign of terror was still fresh in the public's mind—Miller's work has elements that have continued to provoke and enthrall audiences. That the play works on a wider allegorical level is suggested by the frequency with which it has been performed since the 1950s and by the way that it has been applied to a wide number of similar situations in different cultures and periods. For example, Miller reported, in the *Detroit News,* a conversation he had with a Chinese woman writer who was imprisoned under the communist regime in her own country who said that "when she saw the play in 88 or 89 in Shanghai, she couldn't believe a non-Chinese had written it." The play speaks to anyone who has lived in a society where the questioning of authority and of the general opinion leads to rejection and punishment.

AUTHOR BIOGRAPHY

Arthur Miller was born on October 17, 1915, in New York City, the son of Isidore and Augusta Miller. His father lost his wealth during the Great Depression of the 1920s and the family, like many others, suffered economic hardship and could not afford to send him to college. Miller worked for two years in an automobile parts warehouse, earning enough money to attend the University of Michigan in 1934, where he studied history and economics. He graduated in 1938.

Benefitting from the U.S. Government's Federal Theatre Project, Miller began learning about the craft of the theatre, working with such skilled writers and directors as Clifford Odets (*Waiting for Lefty*) and Elia Kazan (the famous film and theatre director who later produced Miller's best-known work, *Death of a Salesman*). His first Broadway production, *The Man Who Had All the Luck,* opened in 1944 and ran for only four performances. After working as a journalist (work that included coverage of World War II) and writing a novel about anti-Semitism, Miller had his first real success on Broadway with *All My Sons* (1947); he followed this in 1949 with *Death of a Salesman.* Along with another early play, *A View from the Bridge,* and *The Crucible,* these are the plays for which Miller is best-known—though he has continued to write successfully, including a 1996 screenplay adaptation of *The Crucible* for a major motion picture.

In the 1940s and 1950s, because of his Jewish faith and his liberal political views, Miller was very much involved in contemporary debates that criticized the shortcomings of modern American society-particularly those dealing with inequalities in labor and race. It was also these political areas that were considered suspicious by Joseph McCarthy and his cronies, who sought to expose and erase Communism in America. Miller's association with people and organizations targeted by McCarthy's House Committee on Un-American Activities solidified his belief in the evils of blind persecution (while there may have been Communists who were bad people and a threat to America, this did not mean that all Communists were like-minded and posed a threat to the American way of life).

Earlier, Miller had written an adaptation of Henrik Ibsen's 1884 play, *An Enemy of the People,* which, according to his introduction, questioned "whether the democratic guarantees protecting political minorities ought to be set aside in time of crisis." As his later writing in *The Crucible* suggests, Miller did not believe that Communism was a threat that warranted the response provided by McCarthyism. U.S. authorities disagreed, however, and in 1954 when Miller was invited to Brussels to see a production of that play, the State Department denied him a visa. He then wrote a satirical piece called *A Modest Proposal for the Pacification of the Public Temper,* which denied that he supported the Communist cause. Nevertheless, he was called to appear before the House Un-American Activities Committee where, although his passport was conditionally restored, he nonetheless refused to give the names of people he had seen at Communist meetings. Because he refused to expose these people, Miller was found guilty of contempt of Congress in 1957.

In his personal life, Miller married Mary Grace Slattery in 1940; in 1956 they were divorced. In June 1956 he married Marilyn Monroe, the famous actress, and their marriage ended in 1961. Monroe subsequently committed suicide. Since 1962, Miller has been married to Ingeborg Morath, a photojournalist. He has four children, two each from his first and third marriages.

Arthur Miller

PLOT SUMMARY

Act 1

The play opens in Salem, Massachusetts, 1692, with the Reverend Samuel Parris praying over the bed of his daughter Betty. Abigail, his niece, enters with news from the Doctor that there is no explanation for Betty's inertia and disturbed state of mind. As their conversation progresses and he questions her, it is revealed that Betty has fallen into this state after her father found her in the woods dancing around a fire with Abigail, Tituba (Parris's slave from the island of Barbados), and other young women from the town. Parris warns Abigail that her reputation is already under suspicion as she has been dismissed from the service of Goody Proctor and has not been hired since. With the arrival of Goody Putnam, it is further revealed that her daughter Ruth is in a similar condition and that she was dancing in an attempt to communicate with her dead sisters.

Parris leaves to lead the recital of a psalm. Abigail reveals to Mercy, the Putnams' servant, that Mercy was seen naked. When Mary Warren, the Proctors' servant arrives, she suggests that they tell the truth and just be whipped for dancing, rather than risk being hanged for witchcraft. Betty wakes and tries to fly out of the window and then accuses Abigail of having drunk blood to make Goody Proctor die. Abigail warns them not to say any more.

When the farmer John Proctor arrives, Abigail's flirtation with him (which he resists) suggests that she has been sexually involved with him in the past. She tells him that it is all pretense and that Betty is just scared. Meanwhile, a psalm can be heard from below and at the phrase "going up to Jesus," Betty cries out. Parris and the others rush into the room, interpreting Betty's outburst as a sign that witchcraft is at work in the young woman. Rebecca Nurse, a wise old woman, comforts Betty. Parris has sent for Reverend Hale, who has past experience with witchcraft; Hale arrives with his many books. Tituba is questioned, and after a considerable amount of pressure, names women who she has seen with the Devil. Joining in the hysterical atmosphere, which is beginning to prevail, Abigail adds more names to the list, as does Betty.

Act 2

The setting shifts to the home of the Proctors. Elizabeth Proctor tells John that Mary, their servant, keeps going to the court to take part in the trial proceedings which have begun in the eight days that have elapsed between Acts 1 and 2. Elizabeth begs John to reveal to the investigators what Abigail told him about it all being pretense, but he is unwilling. She is suspicious that this is because he has feelings for Abigail. The servant Mary returns from the court and gives Elizabeth a rag doll which she made while at the court. In the following angry conversation between Mary and John (who threatens to whip her), she reveals that Elizabeth has been accused but says that she spoke against the accusation.

Hale arrives and questions the Proctors. To prove that they are Christian people, he asks John to recite the Ten Commandments. Revealingly, given his recent liaison with Abigail, John can remember them all except "Thou shalt not commit adultery," which Elizabeth supplies for him. Giles Corey and Francis Nurse arrive and report that their wives have been taken to prison. Ezekiel Cheever, the clerk of the court, arrives and, seeing the doll, lifts up its skirt to reveal the needle which Mary left in the stomach after knitting. This he connects with Abigail's recent falling to the floor with stomach pains which were found to be caused by a needle. Mary notes that Abigail sat next to her in court while she made the puppet. When the others have gone, Proctor insists that Mary must tell the court what Abigail has been doing, but she refuses, saying that she is too scared. Proctor throws her onto the ground.

Act 3

In the courtroom, tensions and long-standing battles among members of the Salem community are brought to the fore, as Corey accuses Putnam of trying to take his land (which, were he convicted, he would be forced to sell and which Putnam would gladly purchase). Later in the scene Corey accuses Putnam of persuading his daughter to make accusations against George Jacobs so that his land would also be forfeited.

Proctor and Mary arrive and Mary confesses that the testimonies were a fabrication. Proctor is told that Elizabeth is pregnant and cannot be sentenced. Proctor presents a petition from members of the town supporting Elizabeth, Rebecca Nurse, and Martha Corey, but he is accused by Governor Danforth of undermining the court. Danforth then demands that all the people who have signed the petition be arrested.

Abigail, with her friends, denies lying and acts as if she is being bewitched by Mary. Proctor angrily pulls her by the hair and, to avoid her having any hold over him, confesses to adultery with her. Abigail denies this, and when Elizabeth is brought in, she does the same, thinking to protect her husband. Hale believes Proctor, but Danforth does not. To distract the proceedings when they seem to be turning against her, Abigail points upwards and claims to see a great bird in the rafters which she interprets as Mary trying to hurt her. The other girls join in the accusation and Mary gives in and takes their side, accusing Proctor of being on the side of the devil. He is arrested along with Giles Corey. Hale leaves after denouncing the entire proceedings.

Act 4

Parris informs the investigators that Abigail has taken money from his safe and left town. He fears rebellion among his congregation, only a few of whom came to the church to hear John Proctor's excommunication. Hale reasons that the accused must be pardoned since they have not confessed and describes how: "There are orphans wandering from house to house; abandoned cattle bellow on the highroads, the stink of rotting crops hands everywhere, and no man knows when the harlot's cry will end his life." However, Danforth refuses to give in as twelve people have already been hanged; he speaks of his determination to extract a confession from Proctor.

Proctor and Elizabeth are left to talk alone. She informs him that while many have confessed, Rebecca Nurse still refuses to do so. She also reveals that Giles Corey refused to answer the charge and died under the pressure of huge stones that were placed on his chest in an effort to torture him into confessing. His final words were "more weight." In the presence of the investigators who then return, Proctor is on the brink of confessing. When Rebecca is brought in to hear him and, the investigators hope, learn from his example, he changes his mind, refusing to name others and finally tearing up his confession. As the prisoners are taken away to be hanged, Parris rushes after them, and Hale pleads with Elizabeth to intervene. But she will not. The play ends with Hale weeping.

CHARACTERS

Ezekiel Cheever

Cheever is a tailor and a clerk of the court who places great importance in his job, which he sees as a holy one. He is at once fearful, embarrassed, apologetic, and a little officious. He discovers the doll that Mary knitted for Elizabeth Proctor. Discovering a needle in the doll's stomach, he believes that Elizabeth is practicing some kind of witchcraft that has affected Abigail.

Giles Corey

An old man, Giles Corey is "knotted with muscle, canny, inquisitive, and still powerful. . . . He didn't give a hoot for public opinion, and only in his last years did he bother much with the church. . . . He was a crank and a nuisance, but withal a deeply innocent and brave man." Corey refuses to answer

MEDIA ADAPTATIONS

- The first film version of *The Crucible* was made in France in 1957. It stars Simone Signoret, Yves Montand, Mylene Demongeot, and Jean Debucourt. The film was directed by Raymond Rouleau and written by Jean-Paul Sartre.
- No further film adaptations were made until 1996, when Miller's own screenplay of his drama was put into production by Twentieth Century Fox. Directed by Nicholas Hytner, the film stars Daniel Day-Lewis as Proctor, Winona Ryder as Abigail, and Joan Allen as Goody Proctor. In his introduction to the Penguin edition of the screenplay, Miller pointed to the advantages of film: "There was the possibility of showing the wild beauty of the newly cultivated land bordered by the wild sea, and the utter disorder and chaos of the town meetings where the people were busy condemning one another to death for loving the Evil One. Now one could show the hysteria as it grew rather than for the most part reporting it only."
- Several versions of a sound recording of *The Crucible* in the Lincoln Centre for the Performing Arts, New York, Repertory Theater are available and are published by Caedmon.
- *The Crucible* has also been made into an opera with music by Robert Ward and libretto by Bernard Stambler. Recordings of the New York City Opera performance have been produced by Composers Recordings and Troy Albany Records.
- In 1995 Penguin Books produced an interactive multimedia CD-ROM which includes a searchable text of the play, hypertext annotations, video interviews, historical data, pictorial material, commentary, and a bibliography.

---

the charges levied against him and is crushed to death beneath heavy stones that are placed upon his chest by the inquisitors, who are attempting to torture a confession out of him. Because he neither admitted the charge nor denied it and risked being hanged, his property passed to his sons instead of the town. His refusal to cooperate and his disdain for the trials is illustrated in his last words before he dies beneath the stones: "More weight."

Deputy Governor Danforth

Danforth is described as a "grave man of some humor and sophistication that does not, however, interfere with an exact loyalty to his position and his cause." Contrary to the strong and proficient appearance he puts forth, however, he is revealed to be, at times, distracted and uncomprehending of the proceedings over which he presides. Although, like Hale, he is presented with considerable evidence that Proctor and the others are innocent, he refuses to grant them clemency. He argues that it would reflect badly on the court if he released prisoners after executing a number of people accused of the same crimes—regardless of their innocence. He is a stubborn man who sees no flexibility in the law and whose pride and position will not allow him to reverse a previous decision.

Goody Sarah Good

Goody Good is a ragged and crazy woman who seems to live on the edges of town life. Although past child-bearing age, she is thought to be pregnant. The fact that she is eventually jailed as a witch suggests how eager the townspeople are to condemn anyone who does not conform to the accepted norms of their community.

Reverend John Hale

Hale embodies many of the moral contradictions of the play: he is a man of integrity who, although at times misguided and overzealous, is willing to change his mind when confronted with the truth. Despite this admirable trait, he lacks the moral conviction to act against proceedings that will condemn innocents to death. He comes to realize that John Proctor is guilty of nothing more than adultery yet he lacks the courage to question the decisions of the court and the prevailing attitude of seventeenth century society. While his fair-mindedness and humanity deserve a measure of respect, Hale's inability to perceive—and endorse—the power in Proctor's stand for personal virtue leaves his character ignorant and weak.

Judge Hathorne

Hathorne is a "bitter, remorseless Salem judge" who has bigotted views although he appears courteous and respectful on the surface.

Marshall Herrick

Herrick seems to be the gentle and courteous side of law enforcement in Salem. He follows the law carefully, treats people gently, and has the respect of the townspeople. Despite this, he is still a participant in the inquisition that results in the executions of numerous residents.

Mercy Lewis

The Putnam's servant, Mercy Lewis is described as "a fat, sly, merciless girl." She quickly follows Abigail in her accusations and finds a power and confidence in accusation which contrasts with her usually fearful demeanor.

Francis Nurse

Nurse is a hard-working, honest member of the community who is shocked by his wife, Rebecca's arrest. Both he and his wife are shown to be kindly town elders who, before the accusations fly, are highly respected and liked by all. He is more or less an innocent bystander whose life is turned upside down by the hysteria that grips Salem.

Goody Rebecca Nurse

When Rebecca is accused of witchcraft it becomes clear that the town has lapsed into collective madness as she stands out uniquely as a woman of great wisdom, compassion, and moral strength. She is gentle and loving, deeply spiritual, and a mother of eleven children and twenty-six grandchildren. Her moral character and strong sense of her own goodness is evident in her adamant refusal to sign a confession. When she is brought into the room where John Proctor is about to sign his confession, her presence proves pivotal in Proctor's decision to take a stand for integrity and not sign the confession.

Betty Parris

Reverend Parris's daughter, Betty, is caught up in the fear and accusations which are generated after the girls are discovered dancing in the woods. It is not revealed whether her illness is feigned or if it is a genuine physical response to a traumatic situation, but it is clear that she is easily influenced and deeply affected by her experiences.

Reverend Samuel Parris

Parris, Salem's minister, and Abigail's uncle, is a weak character who appears to enjoy and to be protective of the status which his position brings. This aspect of his personality is evident in his dispute about whether the provision of his firewood should be take out of his salary or is extra to it. He is concerned with appearances, and, when interrogating Abigail about her dealings with witches in the opening scene, he seems to worry more about what these activities will mean to his reputation than Abigail's spiritual state. He continues to follow public opinion right to the end of the play, when he insists that Proctor's confession must be made publicly in order for it to be effective.

Goody Elizabeth Proctor

Although both her husband and Abigail remark on her coolness, Elizabeth is gentle and devoted to her family. Her goodness and dignity are evident in the way that she argues calmly against Hale and Danforth's accusations. Her loyalty to John is most clearly demonstrated when, thinking to protect him, she denies that he has committed adultery. Her acceptance of John's decision to recant his confession further illustrates her wisdom and her ability to grasp the wider issues of morality and personal integrity for which her husband is willing to die.

John Proctor

The central figure in the play, Proctor is an ordinary man, a blunt farmer who speaks his mind and is often ruled by his passions. It is revealed early in the play that he has had an adulterous affair with Abigail, who worked as his servant. Yet he clearly shows remorse for his act and is attempting to right his error; he is conciliatory with his wife, Elizabeth, and disdainful of Abigail's sexual advances.

When the accusations fly at the trials, he is determined to tell the truth, even if it means criticizing and antagonizing the investigators. His determination to expose Abigail's false accusations eventually leads him to admit his own adultery to the court. He is at his most self-aware in his final speech when he realizes the importance of maintaining his integrity. Explaining why he has recanted his confession, he cries: "Because it is my name! Because I cannot have another in my life! Because I lie and sign myself to lies! Because I am not worth the dust on the feet of them that hang! How may I live without my name? I have given you my soul, leave me my name!"

Goody Ann Putnam

Goody Putnam is "a twisted soul . . . a death-ridden woman haunted by bad dreams." The death of all of her children has affected her deeply. Her pain has been turned into a vindictiveness which is directed at Rebecca Nurse.

Thomas Putnam

Putnam is "a well-to-do hard-handed landowner" who attempts to benefit from the accusations made against other members of the community. Giles Corey accuses him of taking advantage of accused landowners' plights. Knowing that the convicted will be forced to sell their land for much less than it is worth, Putnam is all too eager to attain these properties at cut-rate prices. He has many grievances, and his vengeful, angry behavior seems to stem from his desire for power and possessions.

Tituba

Tituba is Reverend Parris's black slave and a native of the island of Barbados. She is suspected of black magic due to the traditions of Voodoo that were prevalent in her home country. She is genuinely fond of Abigail and Betty. The events bring out her superstitious nature, and her fears become uncontrolled, eventually degenerating into madness when she is in jail.

Susanna Walcott

Susanna Walcott is carried along by the hysteria of the other girls, enjoying the attention which they get from making accusations. Otherwise she is nervous and tense.

Mary Warren

Mary Warren is the Proctors' servant who seems timid and subservient but who finds a powerful role in a kind of people's jury in the courtroom. She occasionally dares to defy Proctor, particularly in her insistence that she must attend the hearings, but she is easily intimidated into at least partial submission. Proctor convinces her that she must expose Abigail's lies to the court, which she agrees to do. She becomes hysterical before the court, however, and soon joins Abigail in pretending that there is evil witchcraft at work. Her behavior in the court contributes, in part, to John Proctor's arrest.

Abigail Williams

In the character of Abigail are embodied many of the main issues of the play. Her accusations initially reveal a mischievous enjoyment in wielding power over other people's lives. But the fact that the events which they set in motion seem to far outweigh the initial mischief suggests that the community of Salem has embedded in its fabric elements of social corruption, moral disease, or unresolved and repressed feelings of anger and hostility. Abigail's actions should be seen as an effect rather than a cause of the town's accusatory environment.

It is noteworthy that, because her parents were brutally killed, she is without adults to whom she is close: Parris cares for her material needs, but there is no evidence that they are emotionally close or that he provides her with anything but the most basic of guidance. Her adulterous relationship with John Proctor might be seen as a craving for affection which, in the absence of family love, manifests itself in physical desire. Her eventual escape to Boston where it is reported she became a prostitute suggests the same craving for emotional love through physical intimacy. Abigail's apparent belief in witchcraft may have similar roots to her sexual neediness. It is psychologically plausible that she would need to find an alternative to the strict and, it seems, loveless Puritanism of her uncle, and that this would attract her to precisely the things—black magic, physical expression, and sexual conjuring—which the religion of her community forbids (she craved attention regardless of whether it was positive or negative attention). She is at once a frightening and pitiable character, malicious in her accusations and sad in her need for close human contact and attention.

THEMES

Politics

In the early 1950s, hearings at Senator Joseph McCarthy's powerful House Un-American Activi-

TOPICS FOR FURTHER STUDY

- What is your perception of the girls' allegations in the play? Do they really believe in witchcraft or are they fabricating the events?
- Is John Proctor a tragic figure? Compare his fate to that of such tragic literary figures as King Oedipus in Sophocles's *Oedipus Rex* and the title character in William Shakespeare's *Hamlet.*
- Examine the historical facts regarding the Salem Witch Trials and Joseph McCarthy's hearings. In what ways does Miller employ these facts in the service of his drama. How do the two historical events compare to each other?
- What purpose do Miller's authorial prose inserts in the text serve?
- Miller said that ''McCarthyism may have been the historical occasion of the play, not its theme.'' What other political and social events do you perceive the play addressing?

ties Committee had decided that the American Communist Party, a legal political party, was compromising the security of the nation by encouraging connections with Russia (America's ally during the Second World War but its enemy afterwards). Those who were sympathetic to the communist cause, or those who had connections with Russia, were summoned before the committee to explain their involvement, recant their beliefs, and name their former friends and associates in the communist cause. Miller himself had to attend a Senate hearing in 1957. He admitted that he had been to communist meetings—of writers—but refused to name anyone else. He denied having been a member of the Party and was eventually found guilty of contempt.

The McCarthy Committee's antagonism of innocent (and in most cases harmless) citizens—and politically-motivated persecution in general—is explored in *The Crucible* through the subject of witchcraft. Particularly, through the dramatization of events which took place in Salem, Massachusetts, in the seventeenth century. The town's hysteria at the beginning of the play has a direct parallel in the frenzy that communist ''witch-hunting'' caused in America in the 1950s. Further, John Proctor's trial, confession (obtained through antagonism and threats), and ultimate recantation conjures a scene similar to the ones that were played out in front of the House Un-American Activities Committee. By having his protagonist take a stand for his beliefs and his personal integrity, Miller displays a clear sympathy for those persecuted in McCarthy's inquisition. The playwright's message is one of personal and political freedom for every citizen.

The Crucible also examines political persecution as a tool for deflecting attention away from difficult problem areas. McCarthy's persecution of communist sympathizers did little to strengthen the fiber of American life (quite conversely, it added unwelcome suspicion and paranoia to many people's lives). To many, however, his actions made McCarthy look like an avenging hero for capitalism and diverted the American public's attention away from very real problems such as race and gender inequities. The investigators in Miller's play act in a very similar manner: They refuse to face the idea that their strict way of life may have led several young women to rebel (by, for example, dancing around a fire in the woods). Instead they blame the wayward girls' actions on the Devil and witchcraft. With this action they bond the community together in a battle against an outside evil that has corrupted their town. Unfortunately, in much the same way that McCarthy's persecution ultimately unraveled many American communities, the Salem Witch Trials end up destroying a way of life in the village.

Morals and Morality

The issues which *The Crucible* raises have general moral relevance, as well as being related directly to the situation in America at the time the play was written. As Dennis Welland has noted in his *Arthur Miller,* the play's moral is similar to those often found in the works of George Bernard Shaw (*Pygmalion, Major Barbara*). Shaw's morals often contend that wrong-headed actions—such as the witch trials—are often motivated by a lack of personal responsibility rather than based upon deliberate cruelty or malice. That is, rather than take a stand against proceedings they suspect are unjust, the townspeople of Salem go along with the trials. Welland stated: ''That is why Elizabeth quietly rejects as 'the Devil's argument' Hale's impassioned plea to her to help Proctor save himself . . . Elizabeth, like [George Bernard] Shaw's St Joan [in his play of that name], has learnt through suffering that 'God's most precious gift is not life at any price, but the life of spiritual freedom and moral integrity.' In Proctor's final recantation of his confession and his refusal to put his principles aside to save his life, we see the triumph of personal integrity in a world of moral uncertainty.''

Society

Paralleling Miller's exploration of individual morality is his portrayal of society's response to events within its community. In the girls' initial accusations and the frenzy that ensues, Miller demonstrates how peer pressure can lead individuals into taking part in actions which they know are wrong. And in the community's reaction to these accusations, he shows how easily stories can be taken out of context—and how people are blamed for crimes they haven't committed. Miller links the mass hysteria of Salem to the community's excessive religious zeal and very strict attitudes towards sex. Sexual relationships and other instances of physical expression seem on the surface to be repressed and the fact that the girls fear being whipped for dancing and singing suggests the strict codes of behavior under which they live.

Yet the town is not without its sexual scandal: Abigail and John Proctor's adulterous relationship is very much in the foreground of the play and is a factor in the unfolding of the tragic events. It may be that Miller is suggesting that such strict religious codes lead to the repression of feelings which eventually escape and find expression in forbidden forms of behavior. The mass hysteria of the young girls could be seen as an outbreak of sexual feelings and fantasies which have long been repressed.

Nicholas Hytner (*The Madness of King George*), the director of the 1996 film adaptation of *The Crucible* (for which Miller wrote the screenplay) pointed out this element when he noted in his introduction to the Penguin edition of the screenplay that ''a community that denies to its young any outlet for the expression of sexuality is asking for trouble.'' Through the events of the play, Miller seems to be warning against excessive religious (as well as political) fanaticism by showing the potential outbursts of feelings—and the disastrous results—which can occur if all forms of sexual expression are repressed.

STYLE

The Meaning in Miller's Title

The title *The Crucible* hints at paradoxical concerns which run throughout the play. On the one hand, a crucible, as a melting pot in which metals are heated to separate out the base metals from the valuable ones, could represent the spiritual improvement which can happen to human beings as a result of trials and hardship. On the other hand, a crucible is also a witches' cauldron in which ingredients are brewed together to be used in black magic. In this sense, Miller might be suggesting that good can even come out of attempted evil, as well as the normal and healthy challenges of Christian life. In this sense, the events in Salem are seen as a necessary evil which roots out evil at the very heart of the community and which brings about a kind of cleansing; the events in Salem had to occur so that they would not be repeated in subsequent times.

Prose Inserts

To understand how *The Crucible* might be performed, and to appreciate it as a text as well as a script, it is helpful to examine Miller's prose inserts, which explain the action which is taking place in the dialogue. In his directions, Miller leaves very little room for interpretation; in almost didactic terms, he spells out the background to the witch trials and fleshes out characters, focusing particularly on their motives and the psychological states that lead them to be swept along by the tragedy. For example, early in Act 1 Miller provides a quick thumbnail sketch of Thomas Putnam which explains his grievances about land and the way the town is run and gives details of his vindictive and embittered nature. This information helps the reader to appreciate Putnam's desire to gain land and status later on in the play; by giving this background information, Miller encourages the reader to feel little sympathy for the greedy old man when he and his wife carry on with the accusations which their daughter (herself an obviously disturbed child) helps to set in motion. For a viewer watching the play, these facets of Putnam's character must be conveyed by the actor, but for the reader or the actor, they provide a useful framework.

Language

Historical realism is suggested by the language which Miller employs for his characters' speech. It is the language of the seventeenth century East Coast settlers and is often highly conversational. The women's language is particularly rich in jargon: for example, Rebecca Nurse says that she will "go to God for you" which means that she will pray, and Mrs. Putnam says "mark it for a sign" which means that she thinks that something is a sign from God. By using this language, which is significantly out of time from contemporary standards, Miller establishes the historical distance of the events. This helps the reader or viewer to imagine the strict nature of society and the manner in which religion permeated nearly every facet of the villagers' lives.

Reported Speech

Because neither the events in the woods nor in the courtroom are actually seen in the play, this information is provided by characters' reports of what has happened. The viewer or reader must piece together an understanding of the events and of the vested interest of those reporting. This is particularly apparent in the very first scene where the audience must figure out why Betty is lying in bed in a catatonic state, why Tituba is trying to reassure herself and others that everything will be alright, and why Reverend Parris is so angry. When reading the text, it is helpful to ask not only who is speaking and to whom, but also what motives they have for describing things the way they do to this particular person and at this time.

HISTORICAL CONTEXT

Miller warns in the preface to *The Crucible* that "this play is not history," but it is certainly dependent on historical events for its story. It will be necessary in this section to deal with two periods of history: first the time of the Salem witch trials and second the time of McCarthyism in the 1950s when Miller was writing.

Marion Starkey's 1949 book, *The Witch Trials in Massachusetts* first generated interest in the events that took place in Salem, Massachusetts, in the seventeenth century. Those accused of witchcraft were hounded by representatives of their community (and the larger pressure of majority opinion) until they admitted their involvement, naming others involved in suspicious practices—although the majority of those accused and named were guilty of nothing more than behavior that did not conform to the societal norms of the time.

Despite what might be obvious to contemporary readers as free expression or eccentricity, these people were nevertheless prosecuted in Salem. Spearheaded by the crusade of the real-life Reverend Parris, twenty people were killed based on the suspicion that they had involvement with witchcraft. A good number of these people were killed for refusing to cooperate with the proceedings, having never confessed to any crimes. The Salem Witch Trials stand as an example of religious hysteria and mob mentality in American history.

Miller carefully uses this historical information as the basis for his play. The language of contemporary seventeenth century religious practice, which he frequently employs, demonstrates the thoroughness of his historical research into the customs of this period. For example, Parris points out at one point that "we are not Quakers." The Puritans disapproved of the Quakers because they believed that God could speak to individuals and inspire them to communicate on his behalf. Consequently, the Quakers avoided hierarchical forms of church government. The Puritans, in contrast, believed that God would only speak through his ordained ministers and accordingly placed great importance on their work. Further references include Abigail's comment about "these Christian women and their covenanted men" which reminds the audience that Puritans had to swear a solemn promise to accept the rules of the Church before they could become full members; and Proctor's criticism of Parris's fondness for highly decorated churches—"This man dreams cathedrals, not clapboard meetin' houses"; Puritans were not supposed to value this kind of decoration which was traditionally associated with other Christian denominations, particularly Roman Catholicism. *The Crucible* is steeped in the

COMPARE & CONTRAST

- **1600s:** Puritan settlers in New England, familiar with persecution, create tightly-knit communities where church and state are closely linked in the running of the society. In *The Crucible* Miller described the state which they created as ''a theocracy, a combine of state and religious power whose function was to keep the community together and to prevent any kind of disunity that might open it up to destruction by material or ideological enemies.''

  1953: Joseph Stalin, ruler of the Soviet Union since 1928, dies at the age of 73. Hostilities with the West continue and in the U.S. attempts are made through the House Committee on Un-American Activities to root out communists in America.

  Today: The end of the Cold War has seen the breakdown of a communist influence in Eastern Europe as well as the fragmentation of the Soviet Union into smaller independent states. Barriers between Russia and the U.S. have also largely disappeared and, although not allies, the two countries negotiate on matters such as world peace and world trade.

- **1600s:** Puritans in the seventeenth century believe in three different kinds of witchcraft: ''white magic'' which involves the use of charms and spells to bring good luck; ''black magic'' which utilizes spells and incantations to harm others; and Satanic servitude, which involves dedicating one's life in the service of the Devil. Whether or not witchcraft really exists, the effects of these beliefs on the community are great, and considerable fear is generated.

  1953: The Church of Scientology is founded in Washington D.C. by science fiction writer L. Ron Hubbard, who bases his philosophy on the belief that man is a free spirit who can achieve his true nature only by freeing himself from the emotional trappings of the past. Accusations that Scientology is not a true religion and that the organization uses intimidation tactics to extract money from its followers are widespread. Other controversial religious sects, including the Reverend Sun Myung Moon's Unification Church (commonly referred to as the Moonies), also form in the following decades.

  Today: Numerous cults and religious subsets exist all over the world. They are generally tolerated in free and liberal societies, but recent events involving mass suicides of such cults as the Branch Davidians in Waco, Texas, the Heaven's Gate group in California, and the nerve gas bombing by the Aum Shinrikyo (''Supreme Truth'') in Japan, have raised concerns about the influence of such cults, particularly on people who are young, impressionable, or socially isolated.

---

language and customs of seventeenth century east coast America.

Running parallel to these early events are those that took place in Miller's own time, on which the playwright symbolically comments through the story of the witch trials. Miller was interested in political issues, including communism, which had developed after the Second World War when Russia's communist government became a significant world power. In the early 1950s, hearings at Senator Joseph McCarthy's House Un-American Activities Committee had decided that the American Communist Party, a legal political party, was compromising the security of the nation by encouraging connections with Russia. Those who were sympathetic to the communist cause, or those who had connections with Russia, could be summoned before the committee to explain their involvement, recant their beliefs, and name their former friends and associates in the communist cause.

Of particular interest to the committee were those practicing communists in the artistic community. Reasoning that the most nefarious methods for converting Americans to communist beliefs would be through the films, music, and art that they enjoyed, McCarthy and his cohorts prosecuted a great many playwrights, screenwriters, and other artists. In a number of cases they were successful in "blacklisting" these artists—which meant that no one would purchase their services for fear of being linked to communism. This event had its highest profile in the Hollywood of the 1950s, when such screenwriters as Dalton Trumbo (*Spartacus*) and Ben Hecht (*Notorious*) were denied employment by major studios (although a great number of blacklisted talents continued to write using "fronts"—legitimate writers who would put their name on the blacklisted author's work). A number of Miller's contemporaries lost their livelihood due to these hearings, and the playwright himself was brought before the proceedings.

These themes are explored in *The Crucible* through the subject of witchcraft and social hysteria. In the town's hysteria at the beginning of the play lies a parallel to the frenzy that communist "witch-hunting" caused in America in the 1950s. And in John Proctor's trial, confession, recantation, and refusal to name his associates, are incidents which regularly occurred in front of the House Un-American Activities Committee. However, because of its broad sweep of moral themes, the play has also had a life beyond the immediate and specific historical circumstances for which it was written. For example, its themes have been applied to such diverse subjects as religious fanaticism in the late-twentieth century, child abuse accusations in the U.S. and in Europe, and political freedom in Eastern Europe and China. While McCarthyism had been Miller's inspiration, the play's themes address many different circumstances in which mob mentality overrides personal integrity and placing blame on scapegoats proves easier than confronting (and correcting) deep-rooted societal inadequacies. As long as such practices ensue, the play's historical context will continue to be revised and reapplied.

CRITICAL OVERVIEW

In its initial production in 1953, *The Crucible* received a mixed reception from drama critics, with many complaining that, while sturdy in its craftsmanship, the work was too obviously a morality play and lacked the adventurousness and innovation of his previous work. Critic Richard Hayes wrote in the *Commonweal:* "*The Crucible,* does not, I confess, seem to me a work of such potential tragic force as the playwright's earlier *Death of a Salesman;* it is the product of theatrical dexterity and a young man's moral passion, rather than of a fruitful and reverberating imagination. But it has, in a theatre of the small success and the tidy achievement, power, the passionate line—an urgent boldness which does not shrink from the implications of a large and formidable design." George Jean Nathan saw similar aspects of Miller's work, writing in his 1953 *Theatre Arts* review: "*The Crucible,* in sum, is an honorable sermon on a vital theme that misses because the sting implicit in it has been disinfected with an editorial tincture and because, though it contains the potential deep vibrations of life, it reduces them to mere superficial tremors."

In addition to being compared to *Death of a Salesman, The Crucible*'s debut also suffered due to the play's thinly veiled criticism of McCarthyism; many were too embarrassed or afraid to speak publicly or attend performances of the work. Nonetheless, it received numerous honors, including the Antoinette ("Tony") Perry Award and the Donaldson Award in 1953 as well as the Obie Award from the *Village Voice* in 1958.

The play reopened after the McCarthy era and has continued to be successful since then. In 1964 critic Herbert Blau noted that a competent production of the play virtually guaranteed good box office sales, and indeed it has been in almost continuous performance since the early 1960s. *The Crucible* is a particularly popular school text in both the U.S. and Britain. In *Modern Drama,* critic Robert A. Martin summed up the popularity of Miller's play when he noted that it "has endured beyond the immediate events of its own time. . . . As one of the most frequently produced plays in the American theater, *The Crucible* has attained a life of its own; one that both interprets and defines the cultural and historical background of American society. Given the general lack of plays in the American theater that have seriously undertaken to explore the meaning and significance of the American past in relation to the present, *The Crucible* stands virtually alone as a dramatically coherent rendition of one of the most terrifying chapters in American history."

Critic Henry Popkin also discussed the perpetual appeal of *The Crucible* in an essay in *College English.* While the critic did not see the depth of universality in human and political themes that

Martin wrote of, Popkin did express admiration for Miller's skill in creating human characters with whom audiences continue to identify. Explaining the play's appeal as a well-crafted drama, the critic wrote: ''*The Crucible* keeps our attention by furnishing exciting crises, each one proceeding logically from its predecessor, in the lives of people in whom we have been made to take an interest. That is a worthy intention, if it is a modest one, and it is suitably fulfilled.''

The 1996 film version of *The Crucible* won generally favorable reviews for its attention to detail. The adaptation was also lauded for the skill with which events such as the courtroom scenes, which are not depicted (only verbally reported) in the play, were successfully turned into large-scale crowd scenes which fully utilized the possibilities of film. Commenting on the durability of Miller's tale, Richard Corliss wrote in *Time* that ''*The Crucible* offers solid workmanship and familiar epiphanies.'' Yet the critic also noted that Hytner and his actors have provided new perceptions of the characters for a contemporary audience. Discussing the erotic energy of Winona Ryder's portrayal of Abigail, Corliss stated that ''Ryder exposes the real roots of the piece. Forget McCarthyism; *The Crucible* is a colonial *Fatal Attraction.*'' Reviewing the film for *Newsweek,* David Ansen saw the film's effectiveness emanating from the work's original themes, writing, ''Miller has revised his venerable opus, quickening its rhythms for the screen, but what works is what's always worked when this play is well produced: you feel pity, horror, moral outrage.''

CRITICISM

Joanne Woolway

Woolway is an educator affiliated with Oriel College in Oxford, England. In this essay she proposes that while Miller's play was aimed at criticizing a specific period in American history—the McCarthy trials of the 1950s—the work has relevance to modern society on a number of levels, particularly the topic of child abuse.

The theater critic Robert A. Martin wrote in *Modern Drama* that *The Crucible* ''has endured beyond the immediate events of its own time. If it was originally seen as a political allegory, it is presently seen by contemporary audiences almost entirely as a distinguished American play by an equally distinguished American playwright.'' His comments are misleading because they imply that a play cannot be ''distinguished'' if it is also political. What Martin seems to be assuming is firstly that a play must, in some sense, be ''timeless'' in order to be ''distinguished,'' and secondly, that a political play is, by its nature, only relevant within a limited historical and social context. I would argue that Miller's play is highly political, but that while it draws much of its impetus from a given historical situation—Joseph McCarthy's war against communist Americans—it also raises political questions which are valid in a range of social, cultural, and historical contexts.

The relevance of Miller's themes to modern audiences has been emphasized by the 1996 film production of *The Crucible,* directed by Nicholas Hytner (*The Madness of King George*) and adapted by Miller himself. In his introduction to the published edition of that screenplay, Miller commented, ''as we prepared to shoot the movie, we were struck time and again by its alarming topicality: it spoke directly about the bigotry of religious fundamentalists across the globe, about communities torn apart by accusations of child abuse, about the rigid intellectual orthodoxies of college campuses—there is no shortage of contemporary Salems ready to cry witchcraft. But the film's political agenda is not specific. *The Crucible* has outlived Joe McCarthy, and has acquired a universal urgency shared only by stories that tap primal truths.'' One of these areas—the topic of child abuse—particularly shows that Miller is keen to both root his writing in contemporary issues and at the same time challenge audiences by raising general questions about society, religion, and law.

Miller made many changes, mainly structural, to his play text when he adapted it for film. But the changes he made to one scene in particular also suggest his concern to make the screenplay topical. In an episode which is not in the original play, Ruth Putnam accuses Jacobs of having sent his spirit into her room and says that it laid on top of her and pressed down on her: ''He come through my window. . . . And then he lay down upon me . . . I could not take breath—his body crush heavy upon me. And he say in my ear, 'Ruth Putnam, I will have your life if you testify against me in court.''' Jacobs, taking her accusation more literally than it is intended, replies bemusedly, ''Why, Your Honor, I must

A scene from the 1984 Royal Shakespeare Company tour depicting Betty (Caroline Milmoe) and Abigail (Jenifer Landor)

have these sticks to walk with, how may I come through a window .''

The episode has undertones of child abuse—the accusation recalls recent cases in the U.S. and Britain where allegations of abuse have been made against members of a community which have later seemed to have been untrue. The play contains other elements which parallel these cases, particularly the scenes of collective hysteria, the speed with which gossip and rumors spread, and the inability of people to stop accusations once they have started. Miller's concern in supplying these topical references is not to suggest that such child abuse does not occur, but rather to point to the circumstances in a society from which these false claims might arise.

The society which is portrayed in *The Crucible* is one in which there is almost no outlet for creativity or imagination. Given this deficit, it is hardly surprising that the young women who gather in the woods to dance have strong imaginations which, when given any kind of outlet, take their imaginative stories to extremes and begin to believe—in one scene, for instance—that a large bird is indeed hovering in the roof of the courtroom. We know that

WHAT DO I READ NEXT?

- Shortly after *The Crucible* was published, and Miller was denied a visa to visit Brussels on the grounds of his supposed communist sympathies, he wrote a satirical piece called "A Modest Proposal for the Pacification of the Public Temper" in which denied that he supported the communist cause. The title is a reference to another satirical essay by Jonathan Swift, author of *Gulliver's Travels,* entitled *A Modest Proposal.*
- George Bernard Shaw's *Saint Joan* (1923) contains historical notes, a trial, confessions and recantations, and deals. The play deals with themes of social order and individual freedom similar to those examined in *The Crucible.*
- Marion L. Starkey's book, *The Witch Trials in Massachusetts* (Knopf, 1949), came out before *The Crucible* and was one of the first books to generate interest in the Salem Witch Trials. The text provides an interesting counterpoint to Miller's work, establishing the historical groundwork upon which he created his play.

their stories are fabrications, yet we can also appreciate that, to some extent, they believe what they are saying. The boundaries between fact and fiction are easily blurred when there are so few opportunities for expression. It is unclear at the beginning of the play as to the extent to which Betty Parris's illness is feigned. So too in the scene of Ruth's accusation in the film, the viewer's perception of Ruth's words lies within a grey area between an overactive imagination and a reality in which actual physical abuse may have occurred. This situation is similar to instances of mass delusion which are commonly identified in the behavior of religious cult members.

Director Hytner pointed to one possible cause of this collective delusion in his introduction: female adolescent hysteria. As he explained, "we worked from the premise that the source of the girls' destructive energy is their emergent sexuality, so the entire opening [with the girls ritually dancing around a fire] is designed to uncork the bottle of desire."

If we connect this emergent (and repressed) desire both to the excessively strict behavioral codes of Puritan religion in the seventeenth century and to the excessive demands of communities with extreme religious views, then the power of Miller's topical references to raise issues beyond their immediate setting becomes clearer. *The Crucible* is an indictment of society's attitudes towards religion and sexuality, I would argue, rather than an attempt to make a point about specific events in recent history.

In Miller's treatment of the character of Abigail, the distinction between individual malice and community disease is explained. The girl's behavior indicates her mischievous enjoyment of the power that accusations against others bring. But the events her allegations set into motion go beyond mere mischief, suggesting that the community of Salem has embedded in its fabric elements of social corruption, moral disease, or unresolved and repressed feelings of anger and hostility; Abigail's actions should be seen as a sign rather than a cause of these feelings. Because of her parents' brutal murder, she is without adults to whom she is close: Reverend Parris cares for her material needs but there is no evidence that they are emotionally close. Her adulterous relationship with John Proctor and her alleged fate as a prostitute in Boston might be seen as a craving for affection which, in the absence of family love, manifests itself in physical desire. Her apparent belief in witchcraft may have similar roots—in a need to find an alternative to the strict and, it seems, loveless Puritanism of her uncle, which attracts her to precisely the things—black magic, physical expression, and sexual conjuring—which the religion of her community forbids.

This commentary on collective guilt and responsibility adds further weight to Miller's critique of societies which do not maintain a balance between individual liberty and social organization. In his prose insert before the beginning of Act One in the original play text, Miller notes that the aim of a theocracy such as that found in Salem is to "keep the community together, and to prevent any kind of disunity that might open it to destruction by material or ideological enemies. It was forged for a necessary purpose and accomplished that purpose. But all organization is and must be grounded on the idea of exclusion and prohibition. . . . Evidently the time came in New England when the repressions of order were heavier than seemed warranted by the dangers against which the order was organized. The witch-hunt was a perverse manifestation of the panic which set in among classes when the balance began to turn toward greater individual freedom."

What Miller seems to be suggesting in both his play and screenplay is that examples of collective hysteria which lead to false accusations by a body of people who know those accusations to be untrue are not just examples of malicious slander but may also reveal deep-seated neuroses about sexual boundaries and individual freedoms caused by an excessive focus on prohibition and social acceptance. Where these fears cannot be expressed, and must instead be repressed, a perversion of normal social relations may occur. In the case of the Salem Witch Trials, Miller depicts this perversion in the form of extreme, and seemingly random, accusations against the ordinary people of a community. John Proctor sums up the suddenness and ease with which this corruption could be exposed when he cries out, "I'll tell you what's walking Salem—vengeance is walking Salem. We are what we always were in Salem, but now the little crazy children are jangling the keys of the kingdom, and common vengeance writes the law!"

But this is a criticism which could be made of any society; Miller's point is a timeless one, moving beyond the details of the Salem witch-hunts, and also beyond the topical allusions to cases of collective child abuse with which communities in the later twentieth century have become so involved. Whatever the historical context, both the play and film ask audiences to look inwards to the perversions, fears, and guilt which dominate their social and political life. In this sense, *The Crucible* is both timeless and deeply political.

Source: Joanne Woolway, for *Drama for Students,* Gale, 1998.

"MILLER'S PLAY RAISES POLITICAL QUESTIONS WHICH ARE VALID IN A RANGE OF SOCIAL, CULTURAL, AND HISTORICAL CONTEXTS."

Phillip G. Hill

In the following essay, Hill asserts that The Crucible *is undeserving of the negative comments that critics have made about it, and illustrates the play's strengths. Hill argues that* The Crucible, *"however short it may fall of being* the *great American drama, is nevertheless a thoroughly successful, provocative, and stimulating theater piece."*

The Crucible is too often spoken of as one of Arthur Miller's less successful plays. Its relative merits as compared with *Death of a Salesman* need not be argued here, but unquestionably the calumny that has been heaped upon it by well-meaning critics is little deserved—the play, however short it may fall of being *the* great American drama, is nevertheless a thoroughly successful, provocative, and stimulating theater piece. When competently performed, it can provide a deeply moving experience for the theater-goer.

The criticism of George Jean Nathan is perhaps typical. Nathan levels four principal charges at the play, [*The Theatre in the Fifties* (New York, 1953), pp. 105–109.] charges that in one form or another have been brought against it again and again by other critics. Nathan at least speaks from the advantageous position of having seen the play performed in New York, but too often it appears that wild charges are being flung at the play by critics who have never seen it staged—who have tried, perhaps inexpertly, to capture its full effectiveness from the printed page. This is a hazardous procedure at best, and in the case of *The Crucible* it has led to some gross distortions of what the play says and what it does. Let us examine each of Nathans' four charges and attempt to measure the validity of each.

In the first place, Nathan maintains that the power of the play is all "internal," that it is not communicated to an audience. If we take this criti-

"PLAYS ARE WRITTEN TO BE PERFORMED ON A STAGE, AND THE ULTIMATE TEST OF THEIR SUCCESS IS THEIR EFFECTIVENESS UNDER PRODUCTION CONDITIONS. *THE CRUCIBLE* STANDS UP VERY WELL TO THIS TEST."

cism to imply that the action occurs within the mind and soul of the protagonist, then of course the statement that the play's power is internal is accurate, but that this in any sense damns the play is belied by the large number of plays throughout dramatic literature that have their action so centered and that are regarded as masterpieces. Most of the plays of Racine can be cited at once in support of this contention, together with selected plays of Euripides, Shakespeare, and Goethe, to name but a few. That *The Crucible* does not communicate this power to an audience is an allegation regarding which empirical evidence is lacking, but the long lines at the box offices of most theaters that have produced it since it "failed" on Broadway constitute, at least in part, a refutation of the charge. At one recent production of which the writer has first-hand knowledge, all previous attendance records were broken, and experienced theater-goers among the audience testified that they had enjoyed one of the rare and memorable theatrical experiences of their lives. This hardly describes a play that fails to communicate its power to the audience, whatever the quality of the production may have been.

The second charge brought by Nathan against *The Crucible,* and one that is almost universally pressed by those who are dissatisfied with the play, is that it suffers from poor character development. To this charge even the most vehement of its supporters must, in all justice, admit some truth. Elizabeth Proctor is a Puritan housewife, an honest woman, and a bit straight-laced; beyond this we know little of her. John Proctor is an upright and honest farmer confronted by a challenge to his honesty; more can and will be said of the struggles within his soul, but the fact remains that the multi-faceted fascination of a Hamlet, an Oedipus, or even of a Willy Loman is indeed lacking. Danforth, on the other hand, is an all-too-recognizable human being: not at all the embodiment of all that is evil, but a conflicting mass of selfish motives and well-intentioned desires to maintain the status quo; not the devil incarnate, but a man convinced that a "good" end (maintaining the theocracy in colonial Massachusetts) can justify the most dubious means—in this case, the suborning of witnesses, the twisting of evidence, and the prostitution of justice. Reverend Hale, too, is a well developed and many-faceted character, a man who arrives upon the scene confident of his power to exorcise the Devil in whatever form he may appear, and who by the end of the play can challenge every value for which a hero ever died: "Life is God's most precious gift; no principle, however glorious, may justify the taking of it."

Still, it must be admitted that the principal power of *The Crucible* does not lie in its character development. The characters are entirely adequate for the purposes for which Miller designed them, and no immutable law requires that every play depend upon characterization for its success, but certainly there is some justice in suggesting that *The Crucible* exhibits only a moderate degree of character development.

Nathan's next point of criticism is one that was heard from many of the New York critics at the time of the play's original production, but that has ceased to have much potency since the McCarthy era has passed into history. It was loudly proclaimed in 1953 that *The Crucible* was essentially propagandistic, that it struck too hard at an isolated phenomenon, and that thus it was at best a play of the immediate times and not for all time. The thirteen years that have passed since this charge was leveled, and the continued success of the play both in this country and abroad in the interim, drain from the assertion all of the efficacy that it may once have appeared to have. From the short view inescapably adopted by critics themselves caught up in the hysteria of McCarthyism, the play may well have seemed to push too hard the obvious parallels between witch-hunting in the Salem of 1692 and "witch-hunting" in the Washington and New York of 1952. If so, then we have simply one more reason to be grateful for the passing of this era, for unquestionably the play no longer depends upon such parallels. A whole generation of theater-goers has grown up in these intervening years to whom the name McCarthy is one vaguely remembered from newspaper accounts of the last decade, and who nevertheless find in *The Crucible* a powerful indictment of bigotry, narrow-mindedness, hypocrisy, and violation of due process of law, from whatever source these evils may spring. Unquestionably, if the play were tied inextricably to its alleged connection with a political phenomenon now buried (a connection that Miller denied all along), it would even today not have a very meaningful effect upon its audiences. And yet it does.

The fourth charge against the play, and the one brought by the more serious and insightful of the critics dealing with *The Crucible,* is at the same time the most challenging of the four. For Nathan, together with a host of other critics, attacks the basic structure of the play itself, claiming that it ''draws up its big guns'' too early in the play, and that by the end of the courtroom scene there is nowhere to go but down. This charge, indeed, gets at the very heart of the matter, and if it can be sustained it largely negates further argument regarding any relative merits that the play might exhibit. I submit, however, that the charge cannot be sustained—that, indeed, the critics adopting such an approach reveal a faulty knowledge of the play's structure and an inaccurate reading of its meaning. Indeed, Miller appears to me to have done a masterful job of sustaining a central action that by its very nature is ''internal'' and thus not conducive to easy dramatic development, and of sustaining this central action straight through to its logical conclusion at the end of the play.

The term ''central action'' is being used here in what I take to be its Aristotelian sense: one central objective that provides the play's plot structure with a beginning, a middle, and an end; when the objective is attained, the play is over. This central action may be described in the case of *The Crucible* as ''to find John Proctor's soul,'' where the term ''soul'' is understood to mean Proctor's integrity, his sense of self-respect, what he himself variously calls his ''honesty'' and (finally) his ''name.'' Proctor lost his soul, in this sense of the term, when he committed the crime of lechery with Abigail, and thus as the play opens there is wanted only a significant triggering incident to start Proctor actively on the search that will lead ultimately to his death. That this search for Proctor's soul will lead through the vagaries of a witch-hunt, a travesty of justice, and a clear choice between death and life without honor is simply the given circumstance of the play—no more germane to defining its central action than is the fact that Oedipus' search for the killer of Laius will lead through horror and incest to self-immolation. Thinking in these terms, then, it is possible to trace the development of this central action in a straight-forward and rather elementary manner.

The structure of the play can conveniently be analyzed in terms of the familiar elements of the well-made play. The initial scenes involving Parris, Abigail, the Putnams, and the other girls serve quite satisfactorily the demands of simple exposition, and pave the way smoothly for the entrance of John Proctor. We learn quickly and yet naturally that a group of girls under Abby's leadership have conjured the Devil and that now at least two of them have experienced hysterical reactions that are being widely interpreted in terms of witchcraft. We also learn, upon Proctor's entrance, of the sexual attraction that still exists between him and Abby, and of the consummation of this attraction that has left John feeling that he has lost his soul. The inciting incident then occurs when Abby assures John that the girls' hysteria has ''naught to do with witchcraft,'' a bit of knowledge that is very shortly to try John's honesty and lead him inevitably to his death.

The rising action of the play continues, then, through the arrival of Hale, Abby's denunciation of certain of the Puritan women (taking her cue from Tituba's success) in order to remove any taint of guilt from herself, and eventually, in the next scene, to the accusation of witchcraft being directed at Elizabeth Proctor. The significant point here, however, is that the rising action continues through the bulk of the courtroom scene, as horror piles upon horror, accusation upon accusation, and complication upon complication, until the action reaches not a climax but a *turning point* when Elizabeth, who purportedly cannot tell a lie, does lie in a misguided attempt to save her husband. This act on her part constitutes a turning point because, from that moment on, Proctor's doom is sealed; no device short of a totally unsatisfactory *deus ex machina* can save him from his inevitable fate. The *central action* of the play is not yet completed however; Proctor has not yet found his soul, and even moderately skillful playing of the play's final scene can demonstrate quite clearly that this struggle goes on right up to the moment at which Proctor rips up his confession and chooses death rather than dishonor. Thus, this prison scene does not, as some critics have charged, constitute some sort of extended denouement that cannot possibly live up in intensity to the excitement of the courtroom scene, but rather the scene is, in technical terms, the *falling action* of the play, moving inevitably from the turning point to the climax.

This structural significance of the prison scene may be observed in a careful reading of the play, but it is more readily apparent in a competent production. Thus, it is the business of the actor playing Proctor to convey to the audience the fact that signing the confession and then refusing to hand it over to Danforth is not, as has so often been charged, a delaying action and an anti-climactic complication on Miller's part, but rather a continuing and agonizing search on Proctor's part for his honesty—for the course of action that will be truest to his own honor and will recover for him his lost soul. In a dilemma for which there is no simple solution, Proctor first sees the efficacy of Hale's argument, that once life is gone there is no further or higher meaning. Feeling that his honesty has long since been compromised anyway, Proctor seriously feels a greater sense of dishonor is appearing to "go like a saint," as Rebecca and the others do, than in frankly facing up to his own dishonesty and saving his life. On the strength of this argument, he signs the confession. Yet, as Proctor stands there looking at his name on the paper (and here the way in which the actor works with this property becomes all-important), we have a visual, tangible stage metaphor for the struggle that is going on within him. Proctor, unable fully to express the significance of his own plight, cries out:

> Because it is my name! Because I cannot have another in my life! Because I lie and sign myself to lies! Because I am not worth the dust on the feet of them that hang! How may I live without my name? I have given you my soul; leave me my name!

The audience must see that this cry for his "name" is still the same search that has been at the heart of the entire play, and that here it has reached not some kind of anti-climax, but rather *the* climactic moment of the play.

But in stating outright that his confession is a lie (and this is the first moment at which he says so in so many words), Proctor triggers in Danforth the one reaction that seals his own doom. For Danforth, however narrow-minded and bigoted he may be, does indeed believe in the fundamental fact of witchcraft, and he cannot allow a confession that is frankly and openly a lie:

> Is that document a lie? If it is a lie I will not accept it! What say you? I will not deal in lies, Mister!. . . You will give me your honest confession in my hand, or I cannot keep you from the rope. . . . What way do you go, Mister?

Thus stretched to the utmost on the rack of his dilemma, Proctor makes the decision that costs him his life but restores to him his soul: he tears up the confession. The denouement following this climactic moment consumes not a whole scene as has frequently been charged, but a mere twelve lines. Proctor is led out to die, and Elizabeth speaks the epitaph that once again, finally, sums up the central action and significance of the play: "He have his goodness now. God forbid I take it from him!"

Thus, a close structural view of *The Crucible* reveals that this fourth charge against it is also an unfair and inaccurate one. The play, however it may appear in the reading, does not, in performance, rise to a climax in the courtroom scene that cannot be equalled. Certainly the tension of the courtroom scene is great; certainly the prison scene, if poorly performed, could be a letdown. But in a competent performance the inevitable movement from the turning point toward a climax, technically called the "falling action" but certainly involving no falling interest or intensity, continues through the prison scene to that moment at which Proctor rips up his confession, after which a quick denouement brings us to a satisfactory, and at the same time stunning, conclusion.

The play is certainly not one of the great plays of all time. Still, it has been maligned unduly by a series of critics who apparently were either too close to their critical trees to see the theatrical forest or were relying on an inadequate understanding of the play's structure. That this structure is not immediately apparent to the reader, but rather must be brought out in performance, may suggest some degree of weakness in Miller's dramaturgy, but is certainly not a damning weakness in itself. Plays are, after all, written to be performed on a stage, and the ultimate test of their success is their effectiveness under production conditions. *The Crucible* stands up very well to this test.

Source: Phillip G. Hill, "*The Crucible:* A Structural View," in *Modern Drama,* Vol. 10, no. 3, December, 1967, pp. 312–17.

Brooks Atkinson

In the following review which originally appeared in The New York Times *on January 23, 1953, Atkinson outlines the plot of* The Crucible, *which he calls a "powerful play." Comparing it to Miller's* Death of a Salesman, *Atkinson argues that* The Crucible *"stands second . . . as a work of art," and maintains: "By the standards of* Death of a Salesman, *there is too much excitement and not enough emotion in* The Crucible.*"*

As drama critic for the New York Times *from 1925 to 1960, Atkinson was one of the most influential reviewers in America.*

Arthur Miller has written another powerful play. *The Crucible,* it is called, and it opened at the Martin Beck last evening in an equally powerful performance. Riffling back the pages of American history, he has written the drama of the witch trials and hangings in Salem in 1692. Neither Mr. Miller nor his audiences are unaware of certain similarities between the perversions of justice then and today.

But Mr. Miller is not pleading a cause in dramatic form. For *The Crucible,* despite its current implications, is a self-contained play about a terrible period in American history. Silly accusations of witchcraft by some mischievous girls in Puritan dress gradually take possession of Salem. Before the play is over good people of pious nature and responsible temper are condemning other good people to the gallows.

Having a sure instinct for dramatic form, Mr. Miller goes bluntly to essential situations. John Proctor and his wife, farm people, are the central characters of the play. At first the idea that Goodie Proctor is a witch is only an absurd rumor. But *The Crucible* carries the Proctors through the whole ordeal—first vague suspicion, then the arrest, the implacable, highly wrought trial in the church vestry, the final opportunity for John Proctor to save his neck by confessing to something he knows is a lie, and finally the baleful roll of the drums at the foot of the gallows.

Although *The Crucible* is a powerful drama, it stands second to *Death of a Salesman* as a work of art. Mr. Miller has had more trouble with this one, perhaps because he is too conscious of its implications. The literary style is cruder. The early motivation is muffled in the uproar of the opening scene, and the theme does not develop with the simple eloquence of *Death of a Salesman.*

It may be that Mr. Miller has tried to pack too much inside his drama, and that he has permitted himself to be concerned more with the technique of the witch hunt than with its humanity. For all its power generated on the surface, *The Crucible* is most moving in the simple, quiet scenes between John Proctor and his wife. By the standards of *Death of a Salesman* there is too much excitement and not enough emotion in *The Crucible* . . . .

FOR ALL ITS POWER GENERATED ON THE SURFACE, *THE CRUCIBLE* IS MOST MOVING IN THE SIMPLE, QUIET SCENES BETWEEN JOHN PROCTOR AND HIS WIFE."

After the experience of *Death of a Salesman* we probably expect Mr. Miller to write a masterpiece every time. *The Crucible* is not of that stature and it lacks that universality. On a lower level of dramatic history with considerable pertinence for today, it is a powerful play and a genuine contribution to the season.

Source: Brooks Atkinson, in a review of *The Crucible* (1953) in *On Stage: Selected Theater Reviews from The New York Times, 1920–1970* , edited by Bernard Beckerman and Howard Siegman, Arno Press, 1973, pp. 344–45.

SOURCES

Ansen, David. "One Devil of a Time" in *Newsweek,* December 2, 1996, p. 80.

Corliss, Richard. "Going All the Way" in *Time,* Vol. 148, no. 25, December 2, 1996, p. 81.

Hayes, Richard. Review of *The Crucible* in the *Commonweal,* Vol. LVII, no. 20, February 20, 1953, p. 498.

Interview with Arthur Miller in the *Detroit News,* October 26, 1996, p. 1C.

Martin, Robert A. "Arthur Miller's *The Crucible:* Background and Sources" in *Modern Drama,* September, 1977, pp. 279-92.

Nathan, George Jean. "Henrik Miller" in *Theatre Arts,* Vol. XXXVII, no. 4, April, 1953, pp. 24-26.

Popkin, Henry. "Arthur Miller's *The Crucible*" in *College English,* Vol. 26, no. 2, November, 1964, pp. 139-46.

Welland, Dennis. *Arthur Miller,* Oliver & Boyd, 1961.

FURTHER READING

Budick, E. Miller. "History and Other Specters in *The Crucible*" in *Arthur Miller,* edited by Harold Bloom, Chelsea House (New York), 1987.

Budick discusses the role of John Proctor and the questions of personal morality and integrity.

Herron, Ima Honaker. *The Small Town in American Drama,* Southern Methodist University Press (Dallas), 1969.

Herron discusses different portrayals of American small town life, focusing on *The Crucible* in her chapter on "The Puritan Village and the Common Madness of the Time."

Miller, Arthur. Introduction to his *The Crucible: Screenplay,* Viking Penguin, 1996.

In his introduction, Miller provides some insights into the production of the 1996 film adaptation of his legendary play. He also discusses the text as a work that would appeal to modern audiences, citing a number of contemporary issues that the play addresses.

Starkey, Marion L. *The Witch Trials in Massachusetts,* Knopf (New York), 1949.

This book came out before Miller's play and was one of the first works to generate interest in the Salem Witch Trials. Starkey works with documents about the trial, which were collected together in the 1930s, and draws parallels with the 1940s, including the atrocities in Nazi Germany.

Warshow, Robert. "The Liberal Conscience in *The Crucible*" in *Essays in the Modern Drama,* edited by Freedman and Morris.

Warshow discusses the character of Hale and questions of social control and individual freedom.

Dutchman

AMIRI BARAKA

1964

Dutchman, Amiri Baraka's shocking one-act play was first presented at the Cherry Lane Theatre in New York City in March, 1964. It won the Obie Award for best off-Broadway play, putting Baraka, who was actively contributing to five other plays at the time, into the public limelight. He was still in his Bohemian phase but would the following year divorce his white (Jewish) wife, move to Harlem, and change his name from LeRoi Jones to Amiri Baraka indicating his new Black Nationalist leanings. *Dutchman,* written just before this move, is a transitional piece. It carries elements of the dadaist poetry of his Bohemian stage, anti-racist sentiments, and the radical black consciousness-raising that would characterize much of his later work.

Dutchman is an emotionally charged and highly symbolic version of the Adam and Eve story, wherein a naive bourgeois black man is murdered by an insane and calculating white seductress, who is coldly preparing for her next victim as the curtain comes down. The emotionally taut, intellectual verbal fencing between Clay (the black Adam) and Lula (a white Eve) spirals irrevocably to the symbolic act of violence that will apparently repeat itself over and over again. Baraka's play is one of mythical proportions, a ritual drama that has a sociological purpose: to galvanize his audience into revolutionary action. *Dutchman* initially played to primarily white audiences, until Baraka moved it to a Harlem theater that he founded in order to reach, and to educate, his intended audience of the black

bourgeoisie. Ironically, the Harlem audiences labeled it a white-hating play and the play closed in Harlem due to lack of revenue. But Baraka was now fully established as the roaring black literary lion, and he continued his mission of black consciousness raising through a prolific output of drama, poetry, essays, and political activity.

AUTHOR BIOGRAPHY

Amiri Baraka was born Everett LeRoi Jones on October 7, 1934, to Anna Lois Russ Jones, a social worker, and Coyt Jones, a postal supervisor. Called LeRoi, he grew up in Newark, New Jersey, a gifted student who graduated from high school early and won a scholarship to Rutgers University. He transferred to the predominantly African American Howard University after only one year, however, because he felt too much like an outsider at Rutgers. But he felt equally uneasy at Howard because there, "They teach you how to pretend to be white." From university, Jones went into the Air Force, where he also faced racial oppression. Just as his stint at Howard had taught him about the "Negro sickness" of self-hatred, his experience in the armed forces taught him about the "white sickness" of hating others. Whites infected themselves with mental illness "by having to oppress, by having to make believe that the weird, hopeless fantasy that they had about the world was actually true." For Jones, the only positive aspect of military duty was the opportunity to read widely.

After his discharge, Jones settled in Greenwich Village, New York, becoming a Bohemian intellectual and part of the Beat literary movement that included writers such as Jack Kerouac (*On the Road*) and Allen Ginsberg (the epic poem "Howl"). Jones began coediting an avant-garde literary magazine with his Jewish wife, Hettie Roberta Cohen. But this period of relative literary tameness and cohabitation with white culture would soon end. Jones became increasingly militant in his crusade against white oppression, expressed in violent symbolism in his poetry, essays, and drama. In 1965, Jones gradually divorced himself from his integrated life, left his wife and two daughters, and became a public figurehead of black cultural nationalism. In Harlem, and later in Newark when his Harlem theater closed, he tried to put on "a play a week" in an effort to revitalize the black American identity or, as he put it, to "blow a million words into the firmament like black prayers to force change."

During the 1967 Newark riots Jones was arrested, beaten, and tried for incitement. His Black militant poem *"Black People!"* and an excerpt from a speech were read as "evidence," and he was sentenced to two and one-half years in prison; he later succeeded in having the sentence overturned in a retrial. Like Malcolm X, Jones was attracted to the Islamic religion. In 1967 he changed his name to Imamu (a title meaning "spiritual leader" that he soon dropped) Amiri (prince) Baraka (blessed one) as a mark of his new identity. But the strictures of the Black Muslims proved oppressive, and he shifted his allegiance to Kawaida, a spiritual doctrine based on seven principles of cultural responsibility (it is the doctrine behind the holiday Kwanzaa).

Baraka's collections of essays, *A Black Value System* (1970) and *Kawaida Studies: The New Nationalism* (1972) explain how adopting this system of cultural values would transform Black people and ultimately, America. He eventually broke with Kawaida, too, but remained a political activist for Black Nationalism. In 1974, he took another political turn and embraced communism. Shifts in the form of his artistic work paralleled these shifts in social consciousness: in theater he moved from the comparatively conventional form of *Dutchman* (1964) to the African pageantry of *Slave Ship* (1967) to the communist drama of *S-1* (1976).

Baraka remarried in 1966, taking Sylvia Robinson (who changed her name to Bibi Amina Baraka) as his new wife. The couple have five children together (in addition to the two children he had with Cohen). Baraka was elected to the Black Academy of Arts and Sciences in 1970. His other literary honors include: the Obie Award for Best American Off-Broadway Play, 1964, for *Dutchman;* a Guggenheim fellowship, 1965-66; second prize at the International Art Festival, Dakar, 1966, for *The Slave;* a National Endowment for the Arts grant in 1966; and a Doctorate of Humane Letters from Malcolm X College in Chicago (1972).

PLOT SUMMARY

Scene 1

Dutchman takes place "in the flying underbelly of the city:" in a subway train. Throughout the play, the audience is made aware of the setting through the roar of the train and the flashing lights as it speeds and slows and occasionally stops for passengers. Twenty-year-old Clay, a black man, is riding the train. At first, only his seat is visible. Before the action of scene gets underway, he exchanges a fleeting smile with an unknown face on the platform and then goes back to reading his magazine.

Lula, a thirty-year-old white woman with long red hair wearing a small, revealing dress, boards the subway, daintily eating an apple. After momentarily awaiting his acknowledgment of her presence, she takes the seat next to Clay. Her manner and mode of conversing with Clay swings from boldly flirtatious to oddly morose and aloof as they share more apples than Clay wants, and fence around the possibility of a sexual encounter. Some of her comments surprise him with their eerily insightful knowledge of his private life (''You tried to make it with your sister when you were ten''), while others seem downright psychotic (''You're a murderer, Clay, and you know it''). Lula claims that she only knows so much about Clay because he is a ''well-known type,'' that type being a socially ambitious black man.

She invites herself to the party to which she correctly guesses he's on his way, and he accepts her company, given that she has been actively seducing him. Despite the fact that her conversation is fraught with hostile racist comments and sudden lapses of attention, he allows this strange seduction and continues, with forced affability, to banter with her. She refers to him as ''the Black Baudelaire,'' ''My Christ. My Christ,'' and ''a black nigger.'' At the end of the scene she entreats him to ignore their separate histories and pretend to be ''anonymous beauties smashing along through the city's entrails''; then she yells, ''GROOVE!'' and the scene ends.

Scene 2

In the second scene, more seats are visible and other people are either sitting or boarding and disembarking from the train. Lula and Clay are oblivious of them. As the scene opens, they are discussing how they will act at the party. Lula describes a slow public seduction, which intrigues Clay. Along with the implicit promise of a sexual encounter, Lula also promises that they'll be eating apples along the way to her tenement apartment. As they continue to talk about Clay's ''manhood,'' Clay briefly notices the others on the subway, but soon he is once again submerged in his intense interaction with Lula, ignoring his surroundings.

Amiri Baraka (formerly LeRoi Jones)

Traces of morbidity in Lula's description of her home (''like Juliet's tomb'') give Clay pause. He asks her if she is an actress because she is so self-aggrandizing. She denies this, but warns him that she lies. Clay demands the whole story from her. She answers elliptically, mysteriously, saying that her life consists of ''apples and long walks with deathless intelligent lovers;'' Lula characterizes his life as ''change, change, change.'' She accuses Clay of being ''even too serious to be psychoanalyzed.''

A few more people board the subway and again, Clay notices them. Lula claims to know them all, then inexplicably asks if they frighten Clay because he is ''an escaped nigger.'' Struggling to maintain his composure in the face of another hostile jibe, Clay makes light of the comment, turning the conversation to plantations, the source of the blues. Lula launches into a hysterical blues song, during which she shudders rhythmically and bumps into the other passengers, punctuating her act with vicious profanity. In front of the shocked audience of passengers, she invites Clay to ''do the nasty.'' Clay is now desperately clinging to his dignity, yet he is still fascinated by her boldness. His conservative side wins, however, and he refuses her invitation to dance. She responds with a string of vicious insults: ''You middle class black bastard.

Forget your social-working mother for a few seconds and let's knock stomachs. Clay, you liver-lipped white man. You would-be Christian. You ain't no nigger, you're just a dirty white man.'' Her invectives turn into an insanely poetic entreaty to rebel: ''Get up and scream at these people. . . . Red train coughs Jewish underwear for keeps! Expanding smells of silence. Gravy snot whistling like sea birds. Clay. Clay, you got to break out. Don't sit there dying the way they want you to die.''

Even though Clay attempts—vainly—to stop Lula's behavior, the momentum of the situation is gathering force like a runaway train: it must end in violence. He tries to physically force her back into her seat, and she calls him an Uncle Tom. The other passengers laugh, and a drunk gets up and joins in her dance. Finally, Clay's anger rises, and he grabs her, calling her a ''dumb bitch.'' When he still cannot silence her, he slaps her face hard, twice. It is his turn to express the anger that he has held in check until now, but his anger is more heartfelt than Lula's has been.

In his speech Clay reveals that even in anger he is still holding a much more violent reaction in check. He'd kill them all ''wantonly'' if he could. But he cannot—it would do no good. Therefore, he demands, ''If I'm a middle class fake white man . . . let me be. And let me be in the way I want.'' He tells Lula that her sexual offer misses the mark. She knows nothing of the belly rub. Her having slept with black men does not make her an expert on black people. Whites who love jazz fail to recognize that what Bessie Smith and Charlie Parker are really saying to them is ''Kiss my ass!'' Clay sees murder as the only cure for the black neurosis, for ''If Bessie Smith had killed some white people, she wouldn't have needed that music. She could have talked very straight and plain about the world. . . . Just straight two and two are four. Money. Power. Luxury.'' Murder would make blacks sane, but it's safer to code one's anger. Furthermore, Clay explains, educating blacks is dangerous for whites, for when blacks finally understand the ''great intellectual legacy of the white man'' they'll be able to rationalize murder just as the whites have done.

Clay's impassioned speech sobers Lula; she tells him she's heard enough and agrees that they will not now enact ''that little pageant'' she had planned. But she isn't finished with him yet. As he reaches across her to retrieve his books, she plunges a knife into Clay's chest. His mouth works ineffectively as he dies. Now the complicity of the rest of the white world is made apparent as the passengers help Lula throw Clay's dead body from the train and then get off of the train themselves.

Lula busies herself with ''getting everything in order:'' straightening her purse, bag, dress. She scribbles quickly into a notebook and drops it in her bag, just in time to be ready for the young black man of about twenty who boards the train. The cycle begins again as Lula gives the young man a long, slow look. An old black conductor performs a brief soft shoe and greets the younger man. Lula stares at him down the aisle, and the conductor tips his hat as he leaves the train car. The curtain drops.

CHARACTERS

Clay

Clay is a twenty-year-old black man, or, according to Baraka, a Negro man. The distinction is that a Negro, according to the playwright's nominative system, is one who compromises his own identity in order to maintain a peaceful relationship with his white oppressors. Clay is a typical bourgeois black male, so predictably bourgeois that Lula is able to tell his life history by the evidence of his dress (a too narrow suit coat), his demeanor (decorous, tentative), and his style of speech (middle class, intellectual, full of pretensions).

Clay is at first attracted to the sexy, young woman who begins a taunting seduction of him and invites herself along to his friend's party. But her sudden mood swings and unexpectedly violent racist language shock him. Even so, he maddeningly humiliates himself in his attempts to maintain his composure at all costs and to match her violence with intellectual dexterity. For some reason he is intrigued by her, as though she is some kind of social test he desperately wants not to fail. But the sordid truth is that it is his very anxiety to prove himself worthy to *her* (white cultural) values that causes him to fail this test. For Clay, who dreamed in college of being a black Baudelaire (a famous French poet), is a member of the black bourgeoisie (upwardly mobile middle class), ''just a dirty white man,'' a white wannabe.

Clay recognizes the compromises he has made, yet shirks from committing the murder of whites that would absolve him of compromise. He takes refuge in the fortress of his words. He warns Lula, however, that the cultural conditioning of blacks could backfire, since they soon may be able to rationalize their murders as whites do. Lula's symbolic murder of him serves to quiet him, but it is also merely an extreme version of the social murder he submits to in prostituting his manhood by conforming to white values.

Lula (Shirley Knight) begins her dangerous seduction of Clay (Al Freeman, Jr.), in a scene from the 1967 film adaptation of Baraka's play

Conductor

The old conductor is the stereotypical ''Jim Crow'' or ''Uncle Tom'' black character (characters who would often dance and sing to delight whites) who seems content with his lowly station in relation to whites. His quick soft shoe shuffle before exiting the rail car is symbolic of the way blacks expressed their suppressed freedom through artistic forms such as dance, music, and song. Clay, like Baraka, found this sublimation of rage both impotent and self-delusional. But the reality is that, at the play's close, the conductor is alive while Clay is dead.

Lula

The caucasian Lula is a thirty-year-old femme fatale who alternately seduces and insults Clay. She is a mythical apple-offering Eve to his clumsy and naive Adam. Lula is the embodiment of western civilization, seductive and ferociously greedy, relentless, but also psychotic, lonely, trapped by her own cultural identity. There is never a sense, as there is with Clay, that a real beating heart lies behind her cultural armor. Instead, she is the mythical all-devouring female, mindlessly dispatching with Clay's manhood (and later his dead body) so that she can attend to her next victim. She is programmed to destroy, she simply follows the path, placing her feet ''one in front of the other.''

This process of oppression bores Lula, and she occasionally lapses into a daze and makes morbid comments on her fantasized seduction (''You'll call my rooms black as a grave. You'll say, 'This place is like Juliet's tomb'''). She lets loose strings of racist insults when Clay fails to succumb to her seduction and ''rub bellies'' with her in a crazy erotic dance. She cannot abide the brutal honesty of Clay's final speech, in which he is finally truthful about his fate and his reluctance to change it. But her irritation only reminds her of her duty, to dispatch with this victim and move on to the next.

Young Negro

Ostensibly Lula's subsequent victim. The young black man of about twenty boards right after Lula and the other passengers throw Clay's dead body off of the train. Like Clay, he carries some books, indicative of his intellectual ambitions. Like Clay,

MEDIA ADAPTATIONS

- Anthony Harvey directed a film version of *Dutchman* in 1967 that received little attention and played lightly at small theaters for a brief period. Al Freeman, Jr. played Clay and Shirley Knight portrayed Lula. Produced by Kaitlin Productions, Ltd. in association with the Dutchman Film Company. Available from San Francisco, California Newsreels.

too, Lula entices him with her gaze, and her mythical, ritual cycle of racial hostility begins anew.

THEMES

Race and Racism

Racial oppression and racial hatred lie at the heart of *Dutchman.* Yet this play is not a simplistic denunciation of racism but rather one long invective against one (in Baraka's view ineffective) solution to racism: assimilation. Clay is a representative of the form of assimilation practiced by many of the black middle class, a pursuit of white values and culture through ''white'' education. Clay carries a stack of books, and he wears the garb of the well-educated. Lula seems to hate Clay on sight, explaining that he is a ''type'' she has seen often. She infers that he has a black friend with a ''phony English accent.'' Clay, she tells him, looks like he is trying to grow a beard and has ''been reading Chinese poetry and drinking lukewarm sugarless tea.'' These are the trappings of the Bohemian intellectual, such as Baraka was himself at the time he wrote this play.

Lula hates Clay not just because he is black, but because of his obvious attempts to discard his racial heritage. She berates him for his meek acceptance of assimilation as a desirable goal, saying, ''Boy, those narrow-shoulder clothes come from a tradition you ought to feel oppressed by.'' When she taunts him that his grandfather was a slave who did not go to Harvard, he responds lamely that his grandfather was a night watchman. In other words, he tries desperately to distance himself from his slave heritage, even at the cost of remembering that he is black. As he states, he was the one student at a ''colored college'' whose role model was not Averell Harriman (a white American statesman) but Charles-Pierre Baudelaire, a white (French) poet. Clay wants to distinguish himself, but he limits himself to a superficial shift, choosing art over politics.

Clay also fails to recognize the irony that he is as deluded as the other students at the black college, who aspire not to be black leaders but white ones. It is left to Lula to clarify that he would have to be the *black* Baudelaire, and she chides him ''I'll bet you never once thought you were a black nigger.'' Clay's pretension is not about becoming an educated black; he actually seems to aspire to be white—or at least to so steep himself in white intellectualism that his color will not matter. Lula reminds him that he is black, and, when she calls him a murderer, it is apparent that it is his black self that he murders.

Violence and Cruelty

Clay steadfastly seeks to maintain his composure in the face of Lula's violent language and cruel reminders of his lowly status in society. The question becomes, how much cruelty will Clay tolerate before he stands up for himself, for the manhood Lula questions? The dramatic irony and symbolic tragedy of the play occurs in its final violence, when Lula stabs a knife into Clay as he reaches for his books to leave her. It is dramatic irony in the sense that he has finally made a stance and shown his manhood, but he fails to recognize that Lula intended all along to destroy him utterly. His tragic ending is symbolic of the violence of white oppression,

TOPICS FOR FURTHER STUDY

- Ironically, when Baraka moved *Dutchman* to a Harlem theater in order to reach a black audience, the play was quickly rejected by the audiences because they saw it as promoting hatred of whites. Is this a racist, white-hating play?
- Clay's reaction to Lula is infuriating because he desperately tries to maintain his composure, his "mask" of bourgeois pretensions, in the face of her ever-more vitriolic racist jibes. Why doesn't he simply ignore her, move to another seat, or ask her to leave him alone? What is the significance of his "fatal attraction" to her?
- When Clay finally reacts in outrage, his outburst proves cathartic to the audience as well as to himself. Aristotle in his *Poetics* suggested that catharsis is the objective of all tragedy: that feelings of pity and fear raised in the audience would be purged by the resolution of the tragedy. Over time, critics have debated what Aristotle meant by catharsis. Is it that the audience learns vicariously to avoid the problems that led to the downfall of the tragic hero? Is it that the balance of the audience's own emotions of pity and fear is restored through vicariously watching them resolved in the tragic hero? Or is it that the tragic hero serves as a scapegoat for feelings too strong for the audience to admit? Which of these readings seems to fit the cathartic experience of Baraka's emotionally demanding play?
- In *Dutchman,* Baraka suggests that Clay's pursuit of assimilation with American bourgeois culture, in the form of his intellectual pretensions, is a path of self-destruction. Baraka suggests an alternative: to develop a separate black value system and a new black aesthetic. He purposely built theaters and community centers to promote the cultural ideas of the Black Arts Movement. From a modern perspective, in what ways has this cultural and aesthetic movement of the 1960s succeeded? In what ways has it failed?

---

which regularly murders blacks in both a figurative as well as literal sense. The play's increasing dramatic tension leads to the final act of violence against Clay. In Baraka's value system, Clay deserves this violence for not using a more direct, and violent, means of bettering his life and silencing the likes of Lula.

Passivity

Intersecting the theme of violence and cruelty is the theme of passivity. Clay passively accepts a second-class role in society, a role that by its very definition can never produce excellence because it is a weak copy of the original, white culture. Black assimilation consists of adopting the values and norms of the oppressing society. This passive act of accepting the culture of the dominant power engenders a race of followers, not leaders. A black Baudelaire can never surpass Baudelaire's artistry because by adopting both the genre and the criteria for judging it, invention is stymied. The very impetus to invent is destroyed. No leader, political, artistic, or social, can emerge in a copycat society—nothing grows in a stagnant pond. The stagnation of black society in a sterile, white pond can only lead to a downward spiral in imagination, performance, and self-image.

At another level, Clay's passivity exists in resorting to words instead of action. He responds to Lula's taunts with sophisticated-sounding rebuttals. When he finally erupts in rage, it is apparent that his nonchalance had been a mask.

Sexism

Lula is a mythical, evil Eve, enticing Clay (Adam, who was made of clay) with sexual wiles and murderous intent. Like Eve, she eats and offers apples. In fact, she offers Clay so much of the fruit that he cannot eat any more. She is the Gorgon/siren/fury, the archetypal devouring female. She figuratively emasculates Clay, repeatedly challenging his ''manhood'' with verbal jibes; she then physically destroys him and throws his body off of the train. She is a sterile goddess, with hands as ''dry as ashes,'' luring him to her room as ''black as a grave,'' a dwelling that she promises will remind Clay of ''Juliet's tomb.'' She tempts Clay with sexual promise, murders him dispassionately with a quick stab, and then prepares herself for her next victim. She is actually bored by the endless cycle of her role; she has ''a gray hair for each year and type'' of man she's gone through. Lula belongs to the sisterhood of ''Crow Jane,'' or ''Mama Death,'' Baraka's idea of the siren muse who lures black artists to pervert their black artistry to fit the hollow, sterile criteria of white art.

STYLE

Allegory

Dutchman's stage directions suggest that the subway is ''heaped in modern myth.'' This phrase alerts the reader to the presence of allegorical meaning. Allegory presents an abstract idea in the guise of a concrete image and symbolic elements in the work point to the allegorical meaning. Thus the story of Clay and Lula holds more significance than the chance encounter of two individuals on a subway. Clues to the structure of the allegory, which is a kind of extended metaphor that organizes the story, exist in the symbols of the play: the apple, the subway, and the name, ''Clay,'' which seems to refer to Adam, who was made of clay; in this context, Clay is the black everyman.

In *Dutchman,* the key to the allegorical meaning of the relationship between Clay and Lula lies in the relationship between Adam and Eve. Eve (innocently or not, depending upon one's view), seduced Adam (with an apple, a symbolic element of that story) into partaking of forbidden knowledge. Lula seduces Clay sexually, partakes of apples with him, and then forces him to face the knowledge that his cloak of white, bourgeois values masks his social impotence; the knowledge is forbidden to Clay in the sense that it will shatter his illusions. In Baraka's allegory Lula personifies both white dominance and (Baraka's) disgust for black assimilation, while Clay personifies passive acceptance of low social status by blacks and their blind refuge-taking in the culture of their oppressor.

Symbolism

Symbolic images and names evoke associations that contribute to the meaning of a literary work. In *Dutchman,* the image of the apple, Eve's prop, threads throughout the play. Lula first walks onto the set daintily eating an apple. She offers one to Clay, and then offers more and more of them to him until he refuses another. Her bounty of apples suggests that their evil poison is so pervasive that Clay will never be able to avoid contaminating himself.

The name of the play is also symbolic, referring to the legendary ghost ship the *Flying Dutchman,* doomed to endlessly sail the seas leaving only death in its wake; the title also suggests a connotation to the Dutch slave ships that transported blacks to enslavement. In addition, Clay's name connotes a black Adam, one who is molded by white society, like clay. The accumulation of related symbols and the structure of the relationship between Clay and Lula confirms the significance of this reading.

The setting of *Dutchman* also carries symbolic weight. Baraka drew attention to the importance of the train's symbolism in the stage directions, where he characterizes the subway as ''heaped in modern myth.'' This is a play about the modern myth of black assimilation: limiting oneself to existence on the low-status paths of the ''flying underbelly of the city.'' The entire play takes place in a subterranean universe, a subway car hurtling towards its destination. The train slows down, stops to let passengers on and off, and then regains speed. There is a sense of movement and progress, but the train is actually repeating the same route over and over. Clay is merely following the ''track'' of white culture, sensing forward motion but in reality restricted to the underbelly, or lower class, of the thriving city above. Subway trains ferry people back and forth across the city, traveling the same short distances over and over again, following a repetitious daily schedule—the path is cyclical. Likewise, Lula's process of seducing and killing her victims is cyclical. She indicates that she has done this for years and has a ''gray hair for each year and type.''

Autobiographical Elements

At the time that Baraka wrote *Dutchman,* he was part of the Bohemian literary culture of Greenwich Village (the Beats) and was married to a white woman, with whom he coedited a literary magazine. Like Clay, he grew up in New Jersey and had aspirations as a poet. Baraka's real life was a successful version of Clay's, however; he awoke from his dream of assimilation in time to save himself from his protagonist's fate.

In the play, Clay screams at Lula, ''If I'm a middle-class fake white man . . . let me be. And let me be in the way I want.'' Only a year later Baraka would reject his entire white world—wife, children, and all—to start a new, black life in Harlem. To a certain extent, the play can be read as a trial of Baraka's assimilated period, in which he condemns himself through Lula's words and actions. The playwright symbolically kills off his passive, ''white'' self through this fictional account and is reborn in real life as the hero that Clay refuses (or is unable) to become.

HISTORICAL CONTEXT

Civil Rights in the 1960s

The year of *Dutchman*'s debut, 1964, was a tense year in the United States—especially for civil rights issues. Both violent and nonviolent protests occurred daily in contention of these issues. Although it had been nearly a decade since Rosa Parks, by refusing to vacate her bus seat to a white patron, sparked a series of bus boycotts that led to a wholesale Civil Rights Movement, legalized equal rights for blacks were still denied in practice. Sit-ins and other forms of nonviolent resistance took place to protest the reluctance of some businesses, schools, and communities to support the civil rights that had been made law by the Civil Rights Act.

The 1964 Civil Rights Act made provisions for fair voting, use of public facilities, education, and employment practices, essentially abolishing segregation; and the Equal Employment Opportunity Commission (EEOC) was appointed to ensure that all races had the same opportunities in securing employment. Yet these laws were frequently ignored—especially in southern states such as Alabama and Mississippi. Often, emotions reached such a pitch that riots ensued in major cities (notably Harlem and Philadelphia) where the demographics had shifted to a black majority for the first time in history. These ''race riots,'' in which blacks and whites hurled abuses both verbal and physical, would expand and persist virtually unabated for the next four years.

The summer before *Dutchman* debuted, Martin Luther King made his ''I Have a Dream'' speech at a civil rights rally in Washington, D.C. Then-president John F. Kennedy attempted to cancel the rally due to the threat of violence. King's protest was peaceful, however, and its success contributed to the enactment of the Civil Rights Acts in 1964. Of particular interest was equity in voting rights. To this end poll taxes, designed to discourage blacks who couldn't afford to vote, were outlawed. Northern civil rights workers often traveled to southern states to monitor elections and ensure that blacks were safe at the voting booths. Three such men traveled to Mississippi in 1964. On their way home, they were ruthlessly beaten and murdered by white supremacists, who were not brought to justice until the 1990s.

Baraka, being a political activist as well as a playwright, consciously used art as a means to achieve social justice. He was personally involved in race riots and on one occasion was arrested for the possession of firearms and incitement, although he denied the charge and was later acquitted. His play *Dutchman* participated in the discourse of hatred and violence of the times, taking a strong stand against one segment of the black population: those who attempted to assimilate with white culture at a time when many, Baraka included, felt the need for militant opposition to white oppression.

Black Arts Movement

In the course of defining a new, self-determined black population, blacks eschewed the terms ''negro'' and ''colored'' that were associated with racism and oppression and demanded to be called ''black'' or Afro-American (and later, African American). Both terms affirmed positive aspects over negative ones: intensifying color to the extreme—black—and underscoring the African heritage of former slaves. These two trains of thought merged in the search for a new ''black'' identity. Styles, language, and values from African cultures were adopted and sometimes freely adapted to formulate the style of the ''Afro-American.'' The phrase ''black is beautiful'' both acknowledged the aesthetic beauty of the black body and affirmed the value of black culture as the new black aesthetic as well.

Along with this dramatic shift in cultural identity came a shift in the assessment of black art. Although jazz had long been a black musical expression, it was considered more of a craft or practice than an acknowledged art form. Jazz became an art form in its own right, stepping out from the foster parentage of the (white) Bohemian cul-

COMPARE & CONTRAST

- **1964:** Tension over racism is at a peak, with numerous protests occurring in major urban centers. The 1964 Civil Rights Act is flagrantly ignored by many southern businesses, schools, and local governments. Although blacks now hold the same voting, working, and educational privileges as white Americans, they are sometimes actively (and illegally) barred from accessing these rights. The summer of 1964 is named ''Freedom Summer'' for the number of staged protest demonstrations that take place across the country in support of Civil Rights.

  Today: Minorities are assured their legal rights as United States citizens. Schools, voting places, and businesses are vigilant in upholding civil rights laws.

- **1964:** The Equal Employment Opportunity Commission (EEOC) is first established in 1964 to serve as a ''watchdog'' to assure that employers do not discriminate in hiring practices because of race, age, or gender. In 1965 President Johnson extends the reach of Equal Opportunity with an executive order for Affirmative Action requiring the active recruitment of minorities in employment and education.

  Today: Some Americans want to do away with Affirmative Action, suggesting that it encourages reverse discrimination and that the advances made in equal opportunity over the past thirty years render Affirmative Action unnecessary. Opponents to California Proposition 209 insist that Affirmative Action should remain in place to combat the ''glass ceiling'' of unequal pay and status that still afflicts minorities and women in the job market.

- **1964:** Race riots are widespread, with armed groups of whites and blacks openly fighting in the streets of urban areas such as Philadelphia and Harlem. On several occasions, the National Guard is called in to restore the peace. Race riots will occur in major cities such as Watts and Detroit over the next few years as the United States comes to terms with the implementation of the Civil Rights Acts.

  Today: While race riots are now rare, in 1992, three days of violent rioting ensued in Los Angeles after the acquittal of four policeman who were videotaped beating a black man, Rodney King, during a routine traffic arrest. Once again, the National Guard had to be called in to restore peace, and property damage mounted to millions of dollars. This incident awakened Americans to the fact that discrimination in police forces and other bureaucratic agencies continues to plague minority Americans. In 1997, a poll reported that over two-thirds of Los Angeles's residents still consider race relations problematic.

---

ture. African artifacts became collector's items as art objects rather than as anthropological oddities.

Baraka was at the forefront of the re-evaluation of black and African art forms. He wrote jazz criticism for avant-garde magazines and consciously promoted black artists in music, art, theater, religion, and cultural values by finding avenues to move them into the public forum. He established a community center called *Spirit House* in Newark to disseminate new ideas about black culture. He was the driving force behind what became known as the Black Arts Movement, which celebrated black and African culture, the black body and facial features, and urban and rural black dialects. The Black Arts Movement included the didactic purpose of raising consciousness about black art and culture. It was the American counterpart to Negritude, the Caribbean movement to honor the art, music, and language of black culture in that part of the world.

Baraka's own poetry was quite explicit about the reculturizing, political agenda of the Black Arts Movement. In a poem entitled ''Black Art'' from his 1966 collection *Black Arts* the final lines read, "Let the world be a Black Poem/And Let All Black People Speak This Poem/Silently/or LOUD." Baraka was considered the "high priest" of the Black Arts Movement, who, through theater, poetry, essays, and actions carried his message beyond the intellectual elite.

CRITICAL OVERVIEW

When *Dutchman* opened in 1964, white audiences hailed Baraka as the new black voice of the American theater. He had suddenly caught the public eye. *Playboy* magazine called him "the most discussed—and admired—Negro writer since James Baldwin." It was ironic that in calling whites to task for their racism, Baraka earned their admiration. Stephen Schneck explained in *Ramparts* that "The blase New York culture scene was titillated by his maledictions. . . . The more he attacked white society, the more white society patronized him. . . . The masochistic vein was a source of hitherto untapped appeal, big box office stuff, and LeRoi Jones was one of the very first to exploit it."

Baraka's fame landed him teaching positions at the State University of New York, Buffalo and Columbia University. Isabel Eberstadt, writing in the *New York Herald Tribune,* called him a "critic, a celebrity . . . a king of the lower East Side . . . a Rabid racist, who Hates whites, Hates Negroes . . . Hates intellectuals, Hates liberals." Eberstadt's was a positive review, like many of the early appraisals of the play. Others, however, were disturbed by the work's outspokenness. As Baraka continued to work the vein of anti-racist sentiment, the negative appraisal of his work was catalogued into the works that set the standard for literature in America.

Allan Lewis's 1965 book, *American Plays and Playwrights of the Contemporary Theatre,* called *Dutchman* a flawed dramatic structure, an "apostrophe to hate." *Native Sons: A Critical Study of Twentieth Century Negro American Authors,* Edward Margolies's 1968 work assessing twentieth century black literature, called Baraka's rage "monomaniacal obsessions . . . ideas tossed together in a whirlpool of hysteria." Many of his critics weighed the play in terms of its dramatic content, measuring against white dramatists who portrayed in-depth characters deep in conflict. Baraka's play was not about individuals but was a parable about society as a whole. John Ferguson, in a 1971 article in *Modern Drama,* expressed concern that "Lula is a symbol, but Clay is a person." Ferguson did recognize the play as a ritual drama, but he assessed it against the norms of classical Greek theater, which is not the genre that Baraka evokes.

Other critics saw the expression of Baraka's artistic anger as genius. In a survey conducted by *Negro Digest* in 1968 among thirty-eight African American writers, Baraka was named "the most promising black writer," "the most important living black poet," and "the most important black playwright" in America. According to drama scholar Hugh Nelson in *Educational Theatre Journal,* Baraka's work may contain flaws, but it "has the vital ability to suggest a multiplicity of meanings in a simple and direct action." In 1969, Darwin Turner recognized Baraka's social agenda and its success, writing in *Black American Literature: Poetry,* "Since 1964, Jones has concentrated on the use of literature—poetry and drama especially—as the force of revolution. To this end, he has revised his poetic style to make it more meaningful for community residents who have found little relevance in the traditional formal language of American poetry. His success is evidenced in the extreme popularity of his frequent public readings in community assemblies."

Certainly, Baraka had a profound effect on the black intellectuals of his day. Black playwright Ed Bullins, in an interview in *Negro Digest,* stated that "I didn't really find myself until I saw *Dutchman.* That was the great influence on my life. . . . [LeRoi] has changed theater in this country by creating or influencing or whatever he has done to black theater, which will have a great effect on the overall theater of this country." Writer Toni Cade (now Toni Cade Bambara) said that Baraka's plays of 1962-1964 *were* black theater. Poet/playwright Ntozake Shange also acknowledged her debt to Baraka, as did poet Sonia Sonchez and many others. The public acknowledged his artistic leadership in 1970, by electing him to the Black Academy of Arts and Sciences. He enacted, according to Theodore Hudson in *From LeRoi Jones to Amiri Baraka: The Literary Works,* "a gradual change from a subjective, tentative lyricist to an activist priest-poet" but continually "satirical, inventive in imagery, expressive, consummately in command of language, occasionally lyrical, partial to only a few symbol-images (his own), 'profane,' and disdainful of conventions of form and mechanics."

The seventies marked a turning point in critical work on Baraka's output, seeing a handful of serious scholarly works published about him, notably Hudson's work and Werner Sollors's *Amiri Baraka/ LeRoi Jones: The Quest for a ''Populist Modernism.''* Lloyd Brown's 1980 volume on Baraka in the Twayne author series describes him as worthwhile if not for his artistic merit, which he considers burdened with a certain amount of ''intellectual flabbiness,'' but for his politically involved art. ''He is a political weather vane.'' Supporters still steadfastly honored his contribution as an artist. C. W. E. Bigsby, writing in *The Second Black Renaissance: Essays in Black Literature,* called him ''the most important black writer of the 1960s.''

CRITICISM

Carole Hamilton

Hamilton is an English teacher at Cary Academy, an innovative private school in Cary, North Carolina. In this essay she discusses Baraka's concept of the ''Revolutionary Theatre'' as it applies to his early play, Dutchman.

A 1969 television interview with Baraka conducted by David Frost (on the syndicated program *The David Frost Show*) became heated and confrontational; Baraka clearly represented a threat (Frost introduced him as a ''provocative gentleman'') to white society and his message of self-determination for blacks was misunderstood as white hatred. From the beginning of the interview, when Frost asked Baraka if his play *Slave Ship* is a ''Get Whitey'' play, Frost seemed to expect a battle from Baraka. He got one, and in the process missed Baraka's key point: that the playwright's quarrel was not with white individuals, but with a white culture that does not recognize blacks. At the close of the interview, Frost got in the last word but failed to realize that Baraka had achieved his goal: to reach the black audience, not to convince the white interviewer. The final words of their verbal boxing match follow. Frost had just accused Baraka of being too extreme, of offending white people, and he compared Baraka to others interviewed on his program:

> Frost: I have had people on this stage like Jesse Jackson and Billy Taylor, people who have made a great deal of sense making the points you have made, and doing so without . . .
>
> Baraka: Let that be defined by your ability to understand what the world is about. You do not know, finally, what we are talking about. We are trying to use this media as a way to get to our own people. What you impose is in opposition to the truth. You don't understand. . . .What is important to me is the ability to talk to black people, not the ability to make you understand. Do you understand that? [Applause.]
>
> Frost: Yes, absolutely. But, on the other hand, what I was trying to say involved two things . . .
>
> Baraka: You're trying to grade my paper. You're trying to tell me I wasn't as good as Jesse Jackson or Billy Taylor.
>
> Frost: Right.
>
> Baraka: Yeah, but *who* wants to hear that? [Laughter. Applause.]
>
> Frost: I'll take that, yes. Seven out of ten for LeRoi Jones.

Besides the apparent animosity in the interview, Frost misunderstood Baraka's aim to discuss the need for a self-determined black population. In fact, instead of listening to and hearing Baraka, Frost treated him like a child, like one who should be admonished for behaving inappropriately. His demeanor towards Baraka simply reinforced Baraka's point: that white Americans feel privileges to judge and to condemn blacks according to a value system to which they alone hold the key. To Frost, Baraka was a madman, someone who simply made no sense. Baraka often faced this kind of assessment of his speech and writings, not because he was actually mad or incoherent, but because his mode of discussion did not fit into the prevailing and accepted (white) discourse, or way of communicating.

French philosopher Michel Foucault considered the control over discourse to be one of the key functions that protect the power (usually dictatorial in nature) of a society. Each society has rules and conventions that exclude the kind of discourse that would threaten its hold on power. Society will often define as mad those whose speech and actions do not conform to the standards and conventions of acceptable messages and modes of behavior. Defining nonconformists as mad makes it easier to ignore them, even to lock them up or have them ''cured'' by psychologists. ''Madness'' can run the gamut from complete incoherence to actions or speech that are merely unconventional (and therefore often threatening to ''normal'' society).

Baraka was often characterized as ''out of step'' with the rest of society—full of unprovoked, illogical anger. Why did he not follow the pacifist

WHAT DO I READ NEXT?

- The Baraka play published with *Dutchman* is called *The Slave.* It is a fable loosely based on Baraka's former marriage to a white woman that exposes the latent racism of liberal whites. His 1969 play *Slave Ship* moves away from the traditional American dramatic structure to the pageantry of African drama. It portrays the total "sense" experience of coming to America on a slave ship.
- Ralph Ellison's *Invisible Man* explores the emptiness of the assimilationist dream. The novel's protagonist discovers not only that his black skin makes him an invisible member of American society but that black leaders and educators actually encourage him to deny his heritage and make himself even more invisible.
- Black feminist playwright Ntozake Shange expressed her debt to Baraka's innovations in language and social revolution in the new black theater. Her 1975 play, *for colored girls who have considered suicide/when the rainbow is enuf,* portrays the plight of black women, doubly oppressed by whites and by black males, in a dramatic production that combines dance, music, poetry, and improvisation fused together into a new genre she calls the "choreopoem."
- Randall Dudley's 1969 poem "Booker T. and W. E. B." describes the schism between assimilationist thought, represented by Booker T. Washington and W. E. B. DuBois, and more ambitious efforts to improve the status of blacks in America.

---

road of Martin Luther King, or, as one interviewer asked him, stick to his poetry and leave politics alone? The anger and hatred expressed in his plays, which became more virulent after *Dutchman,* disturbed audiences white and black. Critics accused him of moving away from "legitimate" theater into radical politics. Oddly enough, societies also tend to attribute strange prophetic powers to the "mad," assuming that if one can separate the mere "noise" of the mad person from the "truth," then the lunatic may carry a legitimate message. Baraka was the madman, whose "strange" anger seems less strange after three decades. His perspective and his mode of discourse have been absorbed into the culture, and some of the changes for which he called, though by no means all, have been instilled in the culture as well.

Culture consists of the norms and ideals of society—its way of behaving, speaking, and expressing spiritual concepts. The youth of society are trained (both in and out of school) and indoctrinated into the society's mode of behaving, into being able to participate in the discourse of society, so that the person can function effectively, without being considered "mad." Cultural anthropologist Edward Said pointed out that controlling how its members act is one of the key functions of a society. It does so by encouraging some kinds of behavior and discourse and discouraging others. Said explained that one of the "possessions" of culture is the power to define and endorse certain practices. There are ranks and levels in society, and the way that one demonstrates one's rank or status is to practice the discourse of the rank in which one belongs . . . or wants to belong.

In *Dutchman,* Clay has sought his education in the discourse of white society: he has been "molded" by it, like clay. He displays his newly learned skill when he banters politely with Lula, since polite banter is one of the earmarks of the fully sophisticated member of intellectual American society. He tries to ignore her hostile remarks, because hostile remarks are not acceptable in sophisticated society, and because Lula is attractive to him and he wants to impress her. One could say that he has been "trained" to find her attractive and to think that "winning"

Lula's extroverted behavior climaxes with a loud dance in which she taunts Clay to join in her "GROOVE!"

someone like her would increase his social status. Clay is a tragic figure because his passive acceptance of her verbal abuse leads inevitably to his murder, and it is his cultural training that has made him a tragic "type."

As Baraka explained in an interview quoted in *Conversations with Amiri Baraka,* Clay's tragic flaw is his passivity; "He should be resisting that type of murder." Clay commits the crime that Baraka (in his 1962 essay, "The Myth of a 'Negro Literature',") condemned black artists for committing: being content "to cultivate *any* mediocrity, as long as that mediocrity was guaranteed to prove to America . . . that they were not really who they were, i. e., Negroes."

Baraka fought such an urge to mediocrity on many fronts—with his poetry, essays, and drama as well as through his political activities in black communities. Of these agendas, he considered the theater the most effective means, because it addressed the widest audience, including culturally ignorant blacks. In an essay called "The Revolutionary Theatre," he says that "what we show them must cause the blood to rush . . . cause their deepest souls to move.'' Furthermore, ''The Revolutionary Theatre, which is now peopled with victims, will soon be peopled with new kinds of heroes—not weak Hamlets debating whether or not they are ready to die for what's on their minds, but men and women (and minds) digging out from under a thousand years of 'high art' and weak-faced dalliance.''

This weak-faced dalliance is what the black bourgeoisie mistakenly adopted as they sought a way into cultured (white) society. Clay represents that form of foolishness, with his bookish pretensions and ''narrow-shouldered'' coat, a coat that does not fit his body. Clay wants to hide behind a mask of culture and to fit his body and mind into the image that white culture dictates. When Lula's taunts finally break through his controlled resistance, he shocks her, and himself, with his own hostility, yet it has been lurking there beneath the mask. He blurts out, ''Just murder would make us sane.'' But his own hostility surprises him, he has been trained to abhor hostility, and he recants, saying that no, he would rather not kill but be ''safe with my words, and no deaths.'' His retreat is his tragic flaw. He fails to struggle as Baraka intends to struggle.

During an interview (reprinted in *Conversations*) following the debut of *Dutchman,* Baraka was asked why not just stick to poetry? Citing the immediacy and potential reach of drama, he answered, ''You have to be involved, whether you say you are or not. I'm black. I have to be involved. When I walk down the street, a man doesn't say, 'There goes a cultured nigger.' He says, 'There's just another nigger.''' By this statement Baraka reveals the plight of the black in America, who is doomed no matter how much he absorbs of white culture. Furthermore, not realizing the futility of this mode of being, blacks attempting to assimilate must continually strive to accomplish what can never be achieved—to be completely accepted into white culture.

Against this bleak future, the Black Arts Movement proposed a startling alternative: to raise black culture up, to transform the perception of blacks to one in which black language, body image, and culture were beautiful. This ''black is beautiful'' movement in and of itself posed no real threat to white America. But Baraka had insight into the ways that culture changes; he knew that no real change occurs without revolution. To those who suggested nonviolent change, Baraka reminded them that changing themselves would not change the American system. The American culture allowed people to exist in social castes; its businesses took advantage of the masses of working poor.

"IN *DUTCHMAN,* CLAY HAS SOUGHT HIS EDUCATION IN THE DISCOURSE OF WHITE SOCIETY."

In his essay, ''The Last Days of the American Empire,'' Baraka explains that to change themselves without affecting white society would simply not do; it would feed into the oppressive, white program. He felt that what liberal whites wanted was for the ''black man somehow to be 'elevated' Martin Luther King style so that he might be able to enter this society . . . and join the white man in a truly democratic defense of this cancer, which would make the black man equally culpable for the evil done to the rest of the world.'' Baraka objected to this easy way out because it supported an unacceptable status quo: a society that takes advantage of its people must be destroyed. His plays were vehicles to convince black audiences that only a total destruction of the white American way would change their status. *Dutchman* served this end, and the plays that followed it made his point with more and more clarity and vehemence.

With an agenda of destroying white culture, why, then, does the play *Dutchman* end with Clay's murder instead of with Clay murdering Lula? Why not illustrate the revolution in success instead of chronicling one more failure to affect change? The answer lies in Baraka's purpose for Revolutionary Theatre. His drama, like his poetry, is designed to ''raise up/return, destroy, and create'' (in the words of his poem, ''Ka'Ba.'') He wanted to ''make an art that [would] call down the actual wrath of the world spirit.'' It was angry theater, designed to move his black audiences to action.

Baraka's was an effective, cleansing theater. Not only did it inspire his audiences to pursue political and social change, it also irretrievably changed the heart and purpose of American theater. At least as far as race goes. Ironically, latter-day productions of *Dutchman* were suppressed for a (superficially) different reason: some complained that the play has too many ''dirty'' words in it. As

Baraka said in a 1991 interview, "When you think about it, they are really throwing *Dutchman* off the train, aren't they?"

Source: Carole Hamilton for *Drama for Students,* Gale, 1998.

George Ralph

In this article, Ralph offers another meaning for the title of Jones's play, one that has a meaning more directly rooted in the vocabulary of theatre—and one that bears considerable significance to the events that transpire between Lula and Clay.

The relation of LeRoi Jones's careening subway car in *Dutchman* to two "Dutchman" ocean vessels—the legendary ghost ship *Flying Dutchman* and a slave ship of the Dutch East India Company—has been amply explicated. It is likely, however, that a further, purely theatrical reference may be intended. In stage practice the "dutchman" is a narrow band of muslin glued vertically onto two adjoining flats to give the appearance of a solid wall. In point of fact, little effort is required to pull the flats apart, breaking the "wall" and dispelling the illusion of solidarity.

Jones's set description indicates that an obviously flimsy theatricality is appropriate in the design of the subway car itself. "Or paste the lights, as admitted props, right on the subway windows," etc. Further, as metaphor, "dutchman" in its stagecraft function images the meretricious facade of civility and potential symbiosis in Clay and Lula's relationship. Both parties contribute to sustaining the false commonality. In its initial design, this commonality is the construct of white society: Lula. Sherley Anne Williams describes Lula's mastery of the situation in terms of ". . . her insistence that Clay conform to her view of him which brings about the outburst which leads to his death." But complicity in the form of employing the racial pseudo-accord as a disguise is the product of black culture: Clay. That is, ". . . the survival of the Black man in America . . . is predicated upon his ability to keep his thoughts and his true identity hidden."

The rending of the veneer, the dutchman, to reveal the irreparable breach is the climactic point of the drama. Goaded finally into abandoning his middle-class white-society guise, Clay exclaims that Lula cannot possibly know or identify with his experience, his being, his blackness. He proceeds to unburden himself in a vitriolic and impassioned diatribe against Lula and her kind. But she holds the knife. And, as she has established the terms of maintaining the deceptive dutchman, so it is she who calls for its laceration. She responds to Clay's verbal violence with "I've heard enough," and stabs him in the chest. She completes the gesture of rupture in her command to the other subway passengers: "Get this man off me!"

Jones's view of American social history suggests that such a "dutchman" has been imposed by whites, in that ". . . even the most liberal white man in America does not want to see the existing system really *changed.*" As in *Dutchman*'s subway, so in real-life America: the insubstantial, sham "dutchman" must be ripped apart. The only question is what side determines the time, method, and outcome. Jones has specified—in an essay written shortly after *Dutchman*'s premiere performance—that the "revolutionary theatre" is to facilitate the tearing of this artificial social fabric. His play's "dutchman" metaphor, then, can be seen as adumbrating both the task of a socially conscious theater and the future of American racist society.

Source: George Ralph, "Jones's *Dutchman*" in the *Explicator,* Volume 43, no. 2, Winter, 1985, p. 58.

Hugh Nelson

In this excerpt, Nelson compares Jones's play to the legend of the flying Dutchman. He also explains how the playwright employs facets of the legend to create both modern myth and contemporary truth.

Leroi Jones describes the setting for his short play, *Dutchman,* with a significant metaphor: "In the flying underbelly of the city. Steaming hot, and summer on top, outside. Underground. The subway heaped in modern myth." The play's title supplemented by these provocative hints and allusions would lead one to believe that the action might be illuminated by examining it in terms of the various renderings of the legend of "the Flying Dutchman." It is my feeling that Jones has made complex use of the "Dutchman" theme in converting it into modern myth. The two major figures, Clay and Lula, are not the colorless characters of allegory; their symbolic relationship as revealed by the "Flying Dutchman" legend is as powerfully ambiguous as their dramatic relationship in a human context.

The legend first appears in literature in Sir Walter Scott's *Rokeby* where the source of the curse which dooms ship and crew to endless voyage is given as a horrible murder committed on board. Scott provides a plausible explanation for the ship's wanderings in the form of a plague which breaks out among the crew following the murder, making the vessel unwelcome in any port of call. Captain Marryat's novel, *The Phantom Ship* (1839), adds a son seeking his father, the doomed captain. Richard Wagner's *Der Fliegende Hollander* (1843) makes some rather more significant additions and alterations. The curse in this case has been imposed by an angry Deity as a result of the Captain's presumption in swearing an oath to round the Cape even if it should take him an eternity to do so. The curse can be lifted only if the Captain finds a wife who is willing to sacrifice everything in his behalf through the purity of her love for him. In order to provide for this possibility, he is granted several days every seven years to search for such a maiden on dry land. Wagner's libretto centers around the Captain's discovery of such a maiden, his joy in her pledge of devotion to him, and his mistaken belief that she has been false to him. The curse is finally lifted when Senta, the maiden, leaps into the sea from a cliff in order to display her faithfulness; the ship sinks immediately and Senta and the Dutchman are seen flying up from the sea together to an appropriately epiphanic accompaniment in the orchestra.

It is clear that Jones' subway car bears more than a superficial resemblance to "the Flying Dutchman" and its doomed crew. He has set the first half of his play in a subway car empty but for the two central figures; during the second scene, other passengers file in gradually until, at the play's climax, the car is full. The empty car and the full car are both necessary to the play. The private drama becomes a public ritual. Without the drama, the ritual would be meaningless while the ritual adds a new and important dimension to the drama.

As a setting for a ritual murder, the New York subway needs no symbolic reinforcement, as recent subway violence clearly indicates. As the "underbelly" of the city, it is a place of darkness and potential danger, lonely, beyond recourse, crowded with humanity but massively impersonal. As an underground, it has almost automatic associations with the mysterious depths of body, mind, and society: with the physiologcial world of digestive and excretory processes, with the psychological world of suppressed wishes always threatening to erupt, and with the sociological "melting-pot" (in Jones' vision more a cauldron of discrete substances which will not mix) from which the subway draws its hot cargo and into which it throws it back again.

"AS IN *DUTCHMAN*'S SUBWAY, SO IN REAL-LIFE AMERICA: THE INSUBSTANTIAL, SHAM 'DUTCHMAN' MUST BE RIPPED APART."

The "Dutchman" image, however, if we take it seriously, draws attention to certain specific qualities of the subway. Like the doomed ship, it seems to operate either senselessly or according to some diabolical plan. It goes nowhere, never emerges from its darkness; reaching one terminus, it reverses itself and speeds back towards the other with brief pauses at identical stations rescued from anonymity only by a slightly different arrangement of defaced posters, bodies, and turnstiles. The doors open and shut mechanically. Anonymous men behind barred windows push identical tokens towards equally anonymous travelers. The subway is in fact a marvelous sample of the autonomy of the inanimate which confronts us everywhere in our mechanized society. Just as primitive man created myth to explain satisfactorily the apparent irrationality of nature, so his modern-day counter-part, the city-dweller, begins to feel again the need for myth to explain his own demonic and seemingly equally irrational inventions and artifacts. Thus, the subway in Jones' metaphor becomes a doomed ship under the control of an irremediable curse.

The same mechanism makes it possible to consider the passengers as the crew of this ship. The fact that they are not present in the opening scene and, more important, the fact that even when present they do not speak, makes them seem as unreal as the ghosts who walked the Flying Dutchman's decks. As a crew, they have no tasks, for their craft maneuvers through its tunnels without any need of their assistance. Though wraithlike, they do however exhibit intention through their hostility towards Clay and their role as Lula's accomplices. That they are or at least become accomplices is clear, and this leads to the next stage of the comparison. If the passengers are a species of crew then it is Lula and not Clay who is their captain. This relates her rather than Clay to the figure of the Dutchman.

This is a surprising discovery. If the "Dutchman" metaphor does in fact filter down to the level

"IT IS CLEAR THAT JONES' SUBWAY CAR BEARS MORE THAN A SUPERFICIAL RESEMBLANCE TO 'THE FLYING DUTCHMAN' AND ITS DOOMED CREW."

of character, then it is Clay, the Negro, whom we would expect to fill the symbolic role of the Captain. As a Negro, he lives under an automatic curse in a white society which, in Jones' view, promises to lift the curse only if he sacrifices his identity and converts his values to those of a materialistic and rationalistic culture. Working from the Wagnerian version of the legend, Lula would be the maiden through whom and in whom he can find release if she will love him and give herself to him totally. Jones' conclusion would then display the failure of any such redeeming love, and the inevitability of racial hatred and vengeance culminating in the murder of a victim. Clay is released from his curse only through death, and the cycle begins to repeat itself as Lula confronts her next victim in the play's final moments. . . .

Source: Hugh Nelson, ''LeRoi Jones' *Dutchman:* A Brief Ride on a Doomed Ship,'' in *Educational Theatre Journal,* Volume XX, no. 1, March, 1968, pp. 53–59.

SOURCES

Bigsby, C. W. E. ''Black Drama: The Public Voice'' in his *The Second Black Renaissance: Essays in Black Literature,* Greenwood Press, 1980, pp. 207-56.

Cade, Toni. ''Black Theater'' in *Black Expressions: Essays by and about Black Americans in the Creative Arts,* edited by Addison Gayle, Jr., Weybright and Talley, 1969, pp. 134-43.

Eberstadt, Isabel. ''King of the East Village'' in *New York Herald Tribune,* December 13, 1964, Sunday Magazine Section, p. 13.

Ferguson, John. ''*Dutchman* and *The Slave*'' in *Modern Drama,* February 13, 1971, pp. 398-405.

Frost, David. Television interview with LeRoi Jones on *The David Frost Show,* Group W Productions, Westinghouse Broadcasting Company (Los Angeles), 1969.

Hudson, Theodore R. *From LeRoi Jones to Amiri Baraka: The Literary Works,* Duke University Press, 1973.

Lewis, Allan. *American Plays and Playwrights of the Contemporary Theatre,* Crown, 1965.

Margolies, Edward. *Native Sons: A Critical Study of Twentieth Century Negro American Authors,* Lippincott, 1968.

Miller, James A. ''Amiri Baraka'' in *Dictionary of Literary Biography,* Volume 16: *The Beats: Literary Bohemians in Post-War America,* edited by Ann Charters, Gale (Detroit), 1983, pp. 3-24.

Reilly, Charlie, Editor. *Conversations with Amiri Baraka,* University Press of Mississippi, 1994.

Schneck, Stephen. ''LeRoi Jones, or, Poetics & Politics, or, Trying Heart, Bleeding Heart'' in *Ramparts,* July 13, 1968, pp. 14-19.

''A Survey: Black Writers' Views on Literary Lions and Values'' in *Negro Digest,* January, 1968, pp. 16-18.

Turner, Darwin T. *Black American Literature: Poetry,* Charles E. Merrill, 1969.

X, Marvin. ''An Interview with Ed Bullins: Black Theatre'' in *Negro Digest,* April, 1969, p. 16.

FURTHER READING

Harris, William J. *The Poetry and Poetics of Amiri Baraka: The Jazz Aesthetic,* University of Missouri Press, 1985.
Finds traces of jazz elements in Baraka's poetic output.

Lacey, Henry C. *To Raise, Destroy, and Create: The Poetry, Drama, and Fiction of Imamu Amiri Baraka (LeRoi Jones),* Whitson, 1981.
An explication of many of Baraka's works as they fit into an assessment of his development as an artist.

Nelson, Hugh. ''LeRoi Jones's *Dutchman:* A Brief Ride on a Doomed Ship'' in *Educational Theatre Journal,* Vol. 20, March 1968, pp. 53-58.
This essay describes the source of the *Flying Dutchman* motif in Baraka's play.

Olaniyan, Tejumola. *Scars of Conquest/Masks of Resistance: The Invention of Cultural Identities in African, African-American, and Caribbean Drama,* Oxford University Press, 1995.
A work of post-colonialist criticism by a leading scholar of African American studies that describes how the expressive and performative nature of drama by Wole Soyinka, Amiri Baraka, Derek Walcott, and Ntozake Shange constitutes black artists' move away from Eurocentric and Afrocentric norms and conventions.

Tomlinson, John. *Cultural Imperialism: A Critical Introduction,* John Hopkins University Press, 1991.

Explains the dynamics of the form of domination that occurs within the culture of societies, the form of domination that Baraka sought to rectify.

West, Cornel. *Race Matters,* Beacon Press, 1993.
A thorough description of the social and economic dynamics of racism.

Entertaining Mr. Sloane

JOE ORTON

1964

Entertaining Mr. Sloane was Joe Orton's first full-length play and it initiated a meteoric, three-year career that established him as one of the most significant writers of stage farce in the twentieth century. This exalted stature is now supported largely by two additional full-length plays—*Loot* (1965), and *What the Butler Saw* (produced posthumously in 1969)—and to a lesser extent by four one-act plays originally written for radio and television.

Entertaining Mr. Sloane opened in London in May of 1964 in a small "fringe" or off-Broadway-like theatre. Its unconventional subject matter, explicit sexual themes, and coarse humor drew contradictory reviews, as did Orton's plays throughout his career. However, by the end of June, 1964, the controversial nature of the play helped catapult it into a major London theatre and Orton's short but brilliant career was launched. The most persuasive early praise came from the extremely popular but very conventional playwright, Sir Terence Rattigan, whose craftsman-like and conventional "well-made" plays (dramatic works that have a distinct five act structure over which the plot logically unfolds) had dominated British commercial theatre from the 1930s until the late 1950s. Rattigan visited the production in its first week and ensured its transfer to a "West End" or Broadway-like theatre by investing a considerable amount of money in it himself. Controversial as the play was in both London and New York, *Entertaining Mr. Sloane*

also enjoyed a German production and was soon slated for a film adaptation.

Clearly influenced in his earliest work by fellow British dramatist, Harold Pinter (*The Homecoming*), Orton gradually forged a distinct comic style that distanced his work from Pinter. As critics still speak of certain plays as Pinteresque, they now also refer to a farce that turns grotesque, explicitly sexual, and purposefully shocking as Ortonesque.

AUTHOR BIOGRAPHY

Joe Orton was born John Orton in Leicester (pronounced "Les-tur"), England, an industrial city eighty miles northwest of London, on New Year's Day, 1933. The son of working-class parents—his father a gardener and his mother a factory worker—Orton was raised in a stable but emotionally barren and conventional middle-class suburban environment. His defiant homosexuality, unhappy home life, and emotionally distant relationship with his parents finally came together in the mid-1960s to produce an iconoclastic comic style that emerged in his first produced comedy-farce, *Entertaining Mr. Sloane*. Intent in this and all subsequent plays on questioning middle-class values, Orton specialized in suggesting that unconventional passions existed beneath conventional middle-class behavior and language.

As a teenager, Orton became devoted to amateur theatre, and after leaving school and losing a number of mundane office jobs, he quite surprisingly won a scholarship in 1951 to London's very prestigious Royal Academy of Dramatic Arts (RADA). There Orton met Kenneth Halliwell, his long-time lover and sometime collaborator. After Orton graduated from RADA in 1953, he worked briefly as an actor in repertory theatre and then joined Halliwell in virtual poverty as the two lived together and worked jointly on a number of bizarre, unpublished novels. It was under the guidance of the older and more sophisticated Halliwell that Orton discovered his interest in writing.

In 1962, however, Halliwell and Orton were imprisoned for six months for stealing and defacing dozens of books from a suburban London library. The two pranksters would alter the books, often with comically obscene illustrations, and then haunt the library to observe the reactions of browsing patrons. Prison was a turning point in Orton's life.

Joe Orton

As his biographer John Lahr put it in *Prick up Your Ears: The Biography of Joe Orton,* "Orton found [in prison] a focus for his anger and a new detachment in his writing."

As he refined his satiric attitude toward middle-class culture and discovered his flair for unconventional comedy, Orton became more confident as an independent writer and less tolerant of Halliwell's insecurity. His personal relationship with Halliwell deteriorated steadily as *Entertaining Mr. Sloane* initiated Orton's meteoric rise to artistic prominence and celebrity status. Within three years his play *Loot* (1965) became an enormous success, several one-act plays written for television bolstered and widened his reputation, and *What the Butler Saw* (produced in 1969) was completed in manuscript. Orton had even been commissioned to write a screenplay—*Up against It* (produced as a play in 1979 and later re-adapted as a stage musical by musician Todd Rundgren)—which was to be the follow-up to the Beatles's film *A Hard Day's Night.* Halliwell responded to Orton's sudden fame and increasing sexual infidelity with extreme jealousy, envy, and depression. On the night of August 9, 1967, as Orton slept, Halliwell bludgeoned him to death with nine blows from a hammer. Halliwell then took his own life with an overdose of sleeping pills. Despite a relatively small body of work produced during what would have been the early stage of his career, Orton's dramas have endured, finding new audiences with each subsequent decade since their creation.

PLOT SUMMARY

Act I

Entertaining Mr. Sloane begins with a dowdy, forty-ish woman named Kath showing her middle-class home to a prospective lodger, a street-wise and coarse twenty-year-old boy named Sloane whom she had met that afternoon in the public library. Kath almost immediately hints to Sloane that she is willing to have sex with him and reveals that she once had a young son out of wedlock whom she gave up for adoption. Sloane agrees to take a room in the house, revealing that he was himself brought up in an orphanage.

Kath's elderly father, Kemp, enters, and initially mistakes Sloane for his son, Ed. While Kath is in the kitchen, Kemp talks with Sloane and toasts crumpets (small cakes) over the electric logs in the fireplace. Eventually Kemp decides that he recognizes Sloane as the young hitchhiker who two years ago murdered Kemp's former boss. Kemp then stabs Sloane in the leg with the toasting fork. Kath returns from the kitchen, scolds her father for his uncivilized behavior and then ministers to Sloane's wound, insisting that Sloane remove his trousers so she can apply antiseptic and a bandage. While dressing Sloane's wound, Kath ignores the doorbell, expecting a nosy lady acquaintance who might spread rumors. She somewhat coyly attempts to seduce Sloane. Sending Sloane upstairs for a bath, Kath demands an explanation from her father, eventually sending him to Sloane's former lodging to collect the young man's belongings.

Kath's brother, Ed, then enters. A participant in some kind of vague ''business'' that sounds like it has underworld connections, Ed has come to get Kemp to sign papers that will commit him to an old folks home. Ed does not live in the same house with Kath and their father, but before his entrance he overheard the talk of the new tenant and now forbids Kath to take in Sloane. Ed already suspects the possibility of sexual relations between Kath and the new lodger and asserts that rumors of such behavior would hurt his reputation and livelihood.

Ed insists on meeting Sloane. When he does, Ed is immediately attracted to Sloane himself. The homosexual Ed dismisses Kath, interviews Sloane, and offers him a job as his personal chauffeur. As Sloane goes to eat, Ed tells Kath he will pay Sloane's rent. Ed leaves, and Kath is finally alone with Sloane, who has re-entered from the kitchen. Kath quickly seduces the willing Sloane on the living room sofa as the first act ends.

Act II

One morning, six months later, Kath enters from a shopping trip to find Sloane lying on the sofa wearing boots, leather trousers, and a white T-shirt. Sloane explains that he is resting while Eddie works on the car because Sloane has a hangover from a late night out with three of his male friends. As he fields Kath's probing questions about women, Sloane accuses her of jealousy and attempting to run his life, threatening to leave if she persists. Kemp enters looking for his pills but refuses Sloane's help in finding them. While Kemp babbles, Kath whispers to Sloane that she is pregnant. After Kemp leaves Sloane refuses to marry her. But to mollify Kath, Sloane turns over to her, as a token of his respect, a locket his mother had given him.

Ed enters and joins Kath in vying for Sloane's attentions. After Sloane exits to the kitchen, Ed intimates that he might fire Sloane from his chauffeur's job for joy-riding the previous night, but Kath says she needs her ''baby'' because Ed took away her other baby, the child she bore out of wedlock to Tommy, one of Ed's former friends. When Sloane re-enters, Ed traps him into admitting he was with a woman the night before. He counsels Sloane on the untrustworthiness of females. Sloane agrees to move out of the house and go with Ed once Sloane receives sufficient financial incentives.

Kemp enters and breaks his usual silence with his son because he wants to tell Ed about Kath's pregnancy, Sloane's crime, and about Sloane threatening and beating him. When Sloane returns and Kemp leaves the room, Ed confronts Sloane with Kemp's accusations concerning the pregnancy. Sloane claims that Kath threw herself at him. Sloane seems penitent, and Ed decides to forgive him if Sloane will promise to avoid women in the future. Before he leaves, Ed sides with Sloane against Kemp. Once alone with Kemp, Sloane menaces the old man before learning that the police have Sloane's fingerprints. Sloane then confesses the "accidental" killing of Kemp's former boss, attempting to win Kemp's silence. When Kemp threatens to go to the police, Sloane knocks the old man down behind the sofa and kicks him. When Kemp doesn't respond to Sloane's invitation to rise, Act II ends with the surprised Sloane calling for Ed rather than for Kath.

Act III

Ed enters, finds his father behind the sofa, and carries him upstairs to the old man's bedroom. When Ed returns, he reports that Kemp is dead. While Sloane is shocked and frightened, Kath seems oblivious to the seriousness of her father's condition. Ed revels in his new position of power. Sloane begins to pack to leave with Ed, but Ed pretends to be intent on forcing Sloane to face the authorities until Sloane lays his hand on Ed's knee, accepts responsibility for the killing, asks for forgiveness, and promises eternal devotion.

Kath returns screaming, having discovered Kemp's body and finally realizing that her father is dead. Ed convinces Kath that Kemp had been ill and coaches her about what she should say when the doctor arrives. Ed reminds her that if Sloane is tried for murder Kath will lose him, so Kath begins to see Kemp's death in a different light. Kath agrees to polish the stairs and put Kemp's new shoes on him, making it look like he slipped down the stairs. But when Sloane enters with his suitcase, Ed explains that Sloane is coming to live with him. Kath reveals her pregnancy and is shocked when she hears that Sloane has accused her of seducing him. She and Ed argue over Sloane's affections and which one of them is best for him. When Sloane is asked to choose between the two, he chooses to leave with Ed, claiming never to have cared for Kath. Ed cruelly forces Kath to look at herself in the mirror. She sees herself as attractive until Sloane corroborates Ed's assessment of her appearance and the situation in which she now finds herself.

Under these new circumstances, Kath announces that she will describe their father's death as murder and reveal what Kemp reported about the murder of his former boss. Faced with blackmail on both sides, Sloane slaps Kath and threatens her physically. In the struggle, Kath's false teeth fall out and roll under the sofa. Then Ed comes up with the idea of sharing Sloane, living with Sloane by himself six months of the year and then permitting Sloane to live six months with Kath. Kath will say that Kemp fell downstairs and Kath and Ed will exchange the locket that Sloane gave her whenever they trade Sloane. The play ends with Ed announcing that it has been a pleasant morning and with Kath sitting on the sofa eating a piece of candy.

CHARACTERS

Dadda

See Kemp

Ed

Ed vies with his sister Kath to be Sloane's sexual partner and ends up sharing him with her. Mean-spirited, self-centered, pompous, and domineering, Ed is the son of the aging Kemp and part of the mysterious "business" that employs Sloane as a chauffeur after Ed becomes sexually attracted to him. As a young man Ed was very active in sports, which his father admired, but a rift occurred one day between Ed and his father shortly after Ed's seventeenth birthday, when Kemp discovered Ed doing something unmentionable in his bedroom.

Now barely on speaking terms with his father, Ed arrives in the first act to procure Kemp's signature, presumably on papers that would commit his father to the kind of old-age home in which Orton's own father, William Orton, was eventually placed. When Kemp is accidentally killed by Sloane at the

MEDIA ADAPTATIONS

- *Entertaining Mr. Sloane* was adapted as a feature film by Canterbury Film in 1970. The screenplay was written by Clive Exton, produced by Douglas Kentish, directed by Douglas Hickox. Beryl Reid stars as Kath, Peter McEnery as Sloane, Harry Andrews as Ed, and Alan Webb as Kemp. This ninety minute film was made more widely available on VHS in 1980 by Thorn EMI Video, in 1989 by Warner Home Video, and in 1990 by HBO Video.
- *Prick up Your Ears* (1987), is a feature film based on John Lahr's biography of Orton. Produced by Andrew Brown and directed by Stephen Frears, the screenplay was written by Alan Bennett and stars Gary Oldman as Orton, Alfred Molina as Kenneth Halliwell, Vanessa Redgrave as Orton's agent, Peggy Ramsey, Julie Walters as Elsie Orton, the playwright's mother, and Wallace Shawn as the biographer John Lahr. The film was distributed in VHS format by Virgin Vision, and Samuel Goldwyn Home Entertainment.

end of Act II, Ed shows no remorse for the death of his father and throughout Act III seems only interested in preserving his sexual partnership with Sloane. Of all the characters, Ed asserts the most hypocritical concern for high moral values.

Eddie

See Ed

Kath

Kath competes with her brother Ed for Sloane's sexual favors. A frumpy, middle-aged woman with a raging sexual appetite, she lures Sloane into her home as a prospective lodger and then seduces him, as she apparently had seduced at least one man (Ed's ''mate'' Tommy) before. Kath then becomes pregnant by Sloane, just as she did by Tommy. Starved for affection, randy but determined to put on a coy demeanor, Kath refuses to see herself as she really is, pretending to be young, innocent, and respectable. In the case of Kemp's death, she comically and pathetically denies the reality of her father's condition as long as she possibly can. Superficially comical, Kath is perhaps, deep down, quite as cruel, vicious, and heartless as her brother. Orton's biographer, John Lahr, explained that Kath is ironically modeled on Orton's mother, Elsie, who professed an abhorrence of human sexuality and was herself, like Kath, the possessor of a complete set of false teeth.

Kemp

Kemp is the elderly father of Kath and Ed, the pathetic occupant, with Kath, of the household that Sloane joins. Hard of hearing and weak of eyesight, Kemp recognizes Sloane as the murderer of his former boss—a photographer who picked up the hitchhiking Sloane, photographed him, and then took Sloane for a burglar as Sloane got up in the night to destroy the incriminating photos. For the last twenty years Kemp has not been on consistent speaking terms with his son, Ed, but he breaks his silence in an attempt to accuse Sloane as a murderer and the culprit in Kath's pregnancy.

Stubborn and ignorant of his own vulnerability, Kemp challenges Sloane at the end of Act II, refuses to accept Sloane's appeal for silence, and dies after Sloane beats him. Kemp is probably the most ''decent'' character in the play and its only genuine victim. He is modeled after Orton's own father, who also was almost blind and referred to as ''Dadda.''

Sloane

Sloane is the sexually opportunistic, lower-middle-class young man who comes to the home of Kath and her father as a lodger, accidentally kills Kemp at the end of Act II, and ends up as an alternating sexual partner to the blackmailing brother and sister duo of Ed and Kath, living with one for six months and then the other for the next six months. A handsome, amoral, self-serving, aggressive, and potentially violent young man without much education but with considerable street smarts, Sloane is capable of turning nearly any situation to his own advantage. He either achieves his greatest victory at the end of the play or suffers his ultimate defeat, depending on how one interprets the play's last scene. As Lahr reported in *Prick up Your Ears,* Orton "saw himself as the physical prototype for Sloane," the most notable clue being the careful attribution to Sloane of the "delicate skin" that Orton was so vainly proud of in himself.

THEMES

Sex

Orton's most obvious subject in *Entertaining Mr. Sloane* is sexual appetite. With the exception of the aged Kemp, the characters are so preoccupied with their sexual needs that by the end of the play they appear completely self-centered, frighteningly insensitive, and almost subhuman.

Kath is the one most openly hunting for sexual satisfaction. Having met Sloane that afternoon in the library, she invites him to consider her home as an alternative to his present lodgings. When Sloane says in his fourth speech of the play, "I can't give you a decision right away," Kath says "I'd be happy to have you." The sexual pun on "have" is obvious, and Sloane gets the message. After a brief silence he says "are you married?" and the question is equivalent to "are you sexually available?" This is the fictional counterpart of the real-life "pickups" that Orton describes so explicitly in his writings in *The Orton Diaries.* In the pre-AIDS homosexual world, Orton was outrageously promiscuous to the point of obsession, and in the characters of *Entertaining Mr. Sloane* he portrayed a similar kind of sexual obsession.

Ed is the most circumspect in his expression of sexual needs, but the onset of his sexual interest in Sloane is as rapid as Kath's. When he first meets Sloane, Ed is intending to dismiss the prospective lodger from his sister and father's house, but Ed only gets the word "I" out of his mouth before he begins to assess Sloane as a potential sexual partner. Sloane reads the signals immediately and is "smiling" as Ed's conversation probes for information about Sloane's availability as a sexual partner.

Sloane, of course, is initially the sexual predator, par excellence, as he is willing to serve either sex and by Act II is out cruising for additional women. But with the death of Kemp, Ed and Kath surpass Sloane in darkly comic obsessiveness, for they show no concern for the passing of their father and immediately use the event to further their sexual claims on Sloane. As the third act unfolds, Ed and Kath have completely forgotten their newly deceased father and are jockeying for sexual supremacy with Sloane. As the play ends, the predatory Sloane becomes a thoroughly "kept" man, and Kath and Ed are comically reduced to a parody of sexual appetite: Ed callously ends the play with the incredibly incongruous line, "Well, it's been a

TOPICS FOR FURTHER STUDY

- Read John Lahr's biography of Orton, *Prick up Your Ears* (1978) or view the 1987 film version of the biography to gather more specific information on Orton's upbringing and relationship with his parents, family, and friends. Discuss how these relationships are reflected in the characters, plot, humor, and tone of *Entertaining Mr. Sloane.*
- View the film version of *Entertaining Mr. Sloane.* Compare it to your reading of the stage version and discuss the ways in which the film version either succeeds or fails to represent your experience of the play. Decide to what extent the differences between the two versions are related to the differences between the stage and film.
- Research the history of homosexuality on stage in twentieth century theatre to see how Orton's portrayal of homosexual behavior relates to the ground-breaking representations of homosexual characters in the 1960s and succeeding decades.
- Research the state of sexual permissiveness in the 1960s. You may also want to compare it to the relative openness about sexuality in the 1950s, 1970s, 1980s, and 1990s. Find specific examples that illustrate permissiveness (or the lack of it) and research explanations for why this openness should change from decade to decade.

An example of the forthright sexuality in Orton's play: Sloane (Peter McEnery) toys with Kath (Beryl Reid) in a scene from the 1970 film adaptation

pleasant morning'' and Kath settles on the sofa eating a piece of candy.

Appearance and Reality

If the intensity of these characters' sex drives makes them funny, what makes them even funnier is their attempt to hide their obsessions. While Kath is seducing Sloane, she generally pretends to be coy or describes her affections as ''motherly.'' When Sloane responds aggressively to her sexual hints, Kath pretends to be outraged (''Mr. Sloane—don't betray your trust'') while soon giving him all the ''go ahead'' signals he might need: ''I must be careful of you. Have me naked on the floor if I give you a chance. If my brother was to know. . . . Would you like to go to bed?'' Perhaps the most deftly comic treatment of Kath's hypocrisy occurs at the end of Act I when Kath greets Sloane in a transparent neglige and tells him ''I'm just at a quiet bit of knitting before I go to bed.'' She then realizes that she has only one knitting needle and must search in the junk of the living room to find its mate.

Ed's approach to masking his sexual rapacity is more subtle. After he's decided in his first interview with Sloane that he wants the young man as a sexual partner, Ed offers Sloane gifts to appeal to Sloane's mercenary interests. Whereas Kath tries to entice Sloane with the promise of sexual availability and motherly shelter, Ed is simply willing to buy Sloane's body, but like Kath, Ed wants to appear shocked when the conversation and action gets too explicit. Near the end of the first interview, Ed fantasizes about Sloane's undergarments—"do you wear leather . . . next to the skin? Leather jeans, say? Without . . . aah" and when Sloane gets explicit, finishing Ed's incomplete sentence with the fantasy Ed had in mind—"pants?"—Ed retreats into his pose—"Get away! (pause) The question is are you clean living? You may as well know I set great store by morals. Too much of this casual bunking up nowadays."

Sloane is more honest in his sexual behavior, but he also pursues his sexual interests with hypocrisy—most clearly when he's at a disadvantage and must pretend to be repentant in order to maintain his easy life. This happens first in the second act when Ed discovers that Sloane has used Ed's car to romance the hostess at one of the nighteries he's visited. Once caught, Sloane says "would you accept an unconditional apology. . . . It won't happen again. . . . I respect you." The humor of this comes from the audience's realization that Sloane respects no one and will always be an inveterate philanderer. Perhaps the only thing funnier is that Ed chooses to believe Sloane, against all evidence, because Ed's sexual need is so great.

In his initial interrogation of Sloane, Ed apologizes for Kath's behavior and when Sloane says, "she seems all right," Ed says, "you can't always go on appearances." Ed's rejoinder could be taken as Orton's abiding comic concern: what "appears to be" is usually a pose to hide one's real feelings—feelings which are usually dominated by sexual drives, self-interest, and the desire for power.

Morals and Morality

A more conventional playwright might turn this attempt to hide sexual obsession into a moral stance, permitting or even leading the audience to make judgments about the destructiveness and folly of this behavior. But Orton's thematic approach seems to be to attack conventionality itself, and while he revels in the comic hypocrisy of his characters he doesn't mean to suggest that their behavior ought to be "normal." For Orton, the obsession with normality is far worse than the obsession with sex, which he seems to find fairly innocuous. In fact, the obsession with normality not only causes the hypocrisy but perhaps also adds to the intensity of the rapacious sexual behavior as characters respond to the repression of their instinctive sexual needs.

As a victim in his personal life of conventional moral judgments about homosexuality, Orton seems to suggest that conventional notions of morality ought to be challenged in order to encourage fresh thinking and to break the complacent certainty of the middle class as to what is right and wrong. The most effective way to force this thought process on his audience is to present them with outrageous behavior, entice them to laugh at it, and then refuse to give the audience the satisfaction of a moralistic ending that would reinforce the status quo of conventional morality. At the end of *Entertaining Mr. Sloane* Kemp's death will go unexamined by the police, as will Sloane's earlier killing, and the sexual triangle that has been established might continue to satisfy the sexual needs of these characters indefinitely.

STYLE

Violence

Paradoxical as it might sound, the pivotal point in the comedy of *Entertaining Mr. Sloane* is the killing of Kemp at the end of Act II. This genuinely violent scene challenges the customary light tone of comedy and initiates the creation of that special "Ortonesque" quality for which Orton's plays would soon become famous.

As Kemp enters at the end of Act II, Sloane slams the door behind him and stalks the old man, who backs away and pathetically calls for Ed, the son he has barely spoken to for the last twenty years. Sloane wrenches Kemp's walking stick away from him, ordering Kemp to sit in a chair, and when Kemp attempts to leave, Sloane pushes him back into the chair and shouts "what you been saying about me?" Every time Kemp attempts to rise during the interrogation, Sloane pushes him back down and menaces him until Kemp reveals that the authorities have fingerprints from the crime scene where his former boss was killed. This information puts Sloane at a disadvantage, and he confesses to the killing in an attempt to gain Kemp's silence.

When it's clear that Kemp will not cooperate, Sloane turns vicious again, pushing Kemp back into the chair and once again taking his walking stick from him, this time throwing it out of reach. He twists Kemp's ear, saying ''you make me desperate. I've nothing to lose, you see.'' He knocks Kemp behind the sofa and kicks him repeatedly. This is not the ''safe'' physical violence where masters and servants from the comedies of Moliere or Shakespeare hand out beatings. This is genuine violence that threatens to replace laughter with serious apprehension and concern. It is only at the end of this violent scene that Orton permits the audience to laugh, coaxing out of them nervous laughter when Sloane finally prods the unconscious Kemp with a gentle kick of his boot and says, ''eh, then. Wake up. (Pause.) Wakey, wakey.''

Black Humor

This strange, Ortonesque sense of humor is generally referred to as ''black humor,'' the kind that attempts to shock the audience into laughing at what is essentially grotesque and horrifying. This dark humor receives its full expression in Act III when Kath, Ed, and Sloane respond to Kemp's death with varying forms of apathy, self-interest, and uncivilized human behavior.

Act III begins with Kath, Ed, and Sloane huddling over Kemp's body and Kath saying ''somebody fetch his tablets.'' However, in response to this request ''nobody moves'' and the stage picture immediately communicates both laughter and these characters' self-interest and lack of compassion. Ed soon exits with Kemp, and when Ed returns (fairly quickly) he reports that Kemp is dead (did Ed finish him off?). Ed's only concern now is how he can use the incident to gain control over Sloane. Though Kath may subconsciously suspect that Kemp is dead, she carries on as if her father is merely ill. She is darkly funny because her activities are so disconnected from her very recent concern for her father: she now does housecleaning, worries about Kemp getting toffee stuck in his teeth, and hums ''The Indian Love Call.''

The distressed Sloane is a figure of dark comic fun as the tables are turned on him and he frets about the possibilities of facing the law, but the grim humor really heats up when Sloane figures out how to extricate himself. Sloane tantalizes Ed by playing the role of penitent and subservient sexual slave—sitting beside Ed, Sloane lays a hand on Ed's knee and simply says ''I accept responsibility.'' Reassured in his power and control, Ed says, ''Good. Remove that hand, will you?,'' and the laughter comes from seeing Ed resume his pretense of strict morality while his father lies dead upstairs. The mutual posing—Ed as a wounded man of high moral fiber, Sloane as a genuine penitent—then leads to naughty double *entendre* that shocks the laughing audience into accepting both the characters' obsession with sexual pleasure and their indifference to the fresh corpse. ''I'd wear my jeans out in your service. Cook for you'' says Sloane, and Ed responds ''I eat out.'' Just before Kath enters screaming, having discovered Kemp's body, Ed and Sloane are talking in sexual code—''only women drink tea in bed'' says Ed and Sloane rejoinders, ''you bring me my tea in bed, then. Any arrangement you fancy.''

Kath puts a final touch on this dark laughter when she reveals her insensitivity to the death of her father. Initially, she appears genuinely concerned that her father has died, but the audience is shocked into laughter with lines from her such as, ''will I have to send his pension book in?'' and ''I shall never get in my black [dress]. I've put on weight since we buried mamma.'' Her self-interest, along with Ed's and Sloane's, is summed up perfectly by Ed's strangely comic line, ''I would never suggest deceiving the authorities under normal circumstances. But we have ourselves to think of.'' Kath's specific brand of self-interest is funny because in this final scene she is so changeable. She agrees to make Kemp's death seem like an accidental fall down newly polished stairs, reneges when she is rejected by Sloane, and then resumes the lie when Ed's plan for sharing Sloane makes the lie convenient again. It is moral flexibility like this that gives rich humor to lines like Kath's ''respect the truth always. It's the least you can do under the circumstances.''

Perhaps the most difficult laughter to assimilate in the final scene is Ed and Sloane's cruelty toward Kath. Ed forces Kath to face the reality of her middle-aged figure, dragging her in front of the mirror. When he says ''you've nothing to lure any man,'' she asks pathetically, ''is that the truth, Mr. Sloane?'' and Sloane casually answers, ''more or less.'' The audience is forced to laugh at both Sloane's unexpected bluntness and Kath's comeuppance. At the same time the audience feels sympathy for her, and in the background is always the reminder of her insensitivity to her father's death. It is this kind of multi-layered complexity of humor that gained Orton his stature as a significant figure in twentieth-century drama.

HISTORICAL CONTEXT

The Decriminalization of Homosexuality in England

The mid-to late-1960s are often thought of as an era of sexual permissiveness (a concept often labeled "free love"). During this time, many young people questioned what society had labeled sexually taboo. At times they openly flouted sexual convention in an attempt to force society to reevaluate and loosen established mores. Events often called "love-ins" encouraged casual sex with multiple partners. Many others resisted the free love movement and vocally criticized the permissiveness as evidence of a decline in moral standards. In *Entertaining Mr. Sloane* Orton gleefully challenges the status quo. His three main characters openly pursue heterosexual, bisexual, and homosexual satisfaction without being subjected to any moralistic judgment (at least within the fictional realm of the play).

The most inflammatory sexual pursuit of Orton's characters was the implied homosexual activity between Eddie and Sloane. Homosexuality had a long history of social and legal condemnation in England and the implicit sexual relationship between Sloane and Eddie as well as the real-life relationship between Orton and Kenneth Halliwell were still punishable offenses when *Entertaining Mr. Sloane* appeared in London in 1964. By Orton's death in 1967, however, British legislation responded to continued appeals for tolerance by decriminalizing homosexuality in private life, opening the door to even more permissive attitudes in subsequent decades.

The social and legal hostility toward homosexuality goes back at least as far as England's King Henry VIII, who initiated legislation enacted by Parliament in 1533 that made homosexual acts punishable by death. In 1861 life imprisonment was substituted for the death penalty and in 1885 the Criminal Law Amendment Act reduced the maximum penalty to two years with hard labor for homosexual acts that did not involve anal intercourse. It was under this legislation in 1895 that the famous British playwright Oscar Wilde was convicted and sentenced to prison for his affair with Lord Alfred Douglas. It was this same criminal code under which Orton was living and writing in the mid 1960s.

The turning point in the decriminalization of homosexuality began in 1954 when a government-appointed group called the Wolfenden Committee began research that would lead to a report in 1957 recommending in part that homosexual acts between consenting adults in private no longer be considered a criminal offense. Parliament initially rejected the recommendations involving homosexuality, and it took another decade for public sentiment to insist on the legal relief embodied in the Sexual Offenses Act of 1967. And even this law still included significant restrictions and exclusions. As a minor under the age of 21, Mr. Sloane's sexual activities in the play would still have made him and Eddie liable to prosecution, though in 1967 the sexual practices of Orton and Halliwell, as consenting adults in private, would have finally become safe from prosecution.

This liberalization, of course, was only the beginning of social and legislative reform. As Jeffrey Weeks points out in *Sex, Politics, and Society: The Regulation of Sexuality since 1800,* by 1965 the percentage of those favoring homosexual law reform in Britain had jumped from a figure of only 25% in 1957 to 63%. Of that number who favored reform, however, 93% remained convinced that homosexuality was "a form of illness requiring medical treatment." The Gay Rights Movement initiated in the United States in the late 1960s continued to question the old concept of sexual "normalcy," and even the AIDS crisis (a situation that many conservative and religious leaders proclaimed as a divine judgement that homosexuality was wrong) could not extinguish the increasing momentum for homosexual rights. In part through works such as Orton's, an openness toward sexuality helped foster growing acceptance of the homosexual orientation. Orton's success in introducing homosexual themes in his drama paved the way for similar portrayals in subsequent films (*Priscilla, Queen of the Desert*), television shows (*Ellen*), and nearly all other forms of popular culture.

Beatlemania

In early 1963, the Beatles were one of several bands performing in small nightclubs in their hometown of Liverpool, England, but by December of 1963 their first megahit, "I Want to Hold Your Hand" turned them into an international phenomenon. In 1964, the year that *Entertaining Mr. Sloane* debuted, the Beatles began their domination of the world's pop scene with their first trip to America for a tour and a landmark appearance on the *Ed Sullivan Show.* At these concerts, the predominantly teenage audiences erupted in hysterical screaming that all but drowned out the music. Reminiscent of the

COMPARE & CONTRAST

- **1964:** *Last Exit to Brooklyn* by American novelist Hubert Selby is published. A London court will convict Selby of obscenity but he will win a reversal on appeal. *Entertaining Mr. Sloane,* like all of Orton's unconventional and purposely provocative plays, was often charged with being obscene, and though his plays were never brought to court they were all subject to the censorship of the Lord Chamberlain.

  Today: The Theatres Act of 1968 abolished the Lord Chamberlain's role as official censor for stageplays and allowed a much more explicit treatment of sexuality on stage. In today's climate of increased sexual openness, Orton's plays might still seem shocking to some but would no longer be considered obscene except by a small minority.

- **1964:** Playwright John Osborne's *Inadmissible Evidence* is produced at London's Royal Court Theatre. In 1956, Osborne's *Look Back in Anger* had revolutionized British theatre, and though by 1964 Osborne's influence had begun to wane, he was still important enough to lead John Orton to change his name to Joe Orton to avoid being confused with the celebrated playwright of the 1950s.

  Today: After a long period of inactivity as a playwright in the 1970s and 80s, Osborne's last play, *Dejavu* (produced in 1992), attempted to rejuvenate his literary reputation but failed. Billed as a sequel to *Look Back in Anger, Dejavu* closed after a short run and Osborne died in 1994 without returning to his former glory. In 1971, distinguished British critic John Russell Taylor had written in *The Second Wave* that in *Entertaining Mr. Sloane* ''Orton managed to write the first solid, well-managed commercial play which belonged, specifically and unmistakably to the post-Osborne era.''

- **1964:** Richard Lester's *A Hard Day's Night* was released in August as a film vehicle for the phenomenally popular Beatles. Orton would himself be commissioned to write a script for the musical group, but his *Up against It* was rejected as not wholesome enough for the commercially successful lads from Liverpool.

  Today: The Beatles are a legendary part of music history and are influential to millions of listeners and musicians. Unlike many popular groups from the 1960s, the Beatles music sounds as fresh and contemporary today as it was when it was released. The band continues to attract new fans.

- **1964:** The ''Profumo Affair'' was still powerfully affecting the British psyche. Profumo had admitted to an adulterous affair with Christine Keeler, a 21 year-old model, and the scandal was laced with the suggestion of a possible breach of security since Miss Keeler had been having a simultaneous affair with a Soviet diplomat. The Profumo affair affected Britons for years as it revealed a disparity between surface respectability and the vaunted image of governmental integrity.

  Today: Sexual scandals of British figures in high places continue to occur, most recently among the British royal family itself, but they now seem less shocking as they are calmly assimilated by the tabloid hungry public. As John Lahr put it in *Prick up Your Ears,* ''in retrospect, the Profumo affair [now] seems trivial. The overreaction of the British public was a barometer of the society's nervousness about the future of its ruling Establishment. Sexuality represented a threat to the old order.''

adulation showered in earlier generations on figures like actor Rudolph Valentino, singer Frank Sinatra, and performer Elvis Presley, this hysteria was of some concern to those who thought the response indicated a serious breakdown in cultural values. Since the hysteria took its strongest form in women and teenage girls, many commentators saw the adulation as an unusually public expression of sexual longing. Others saw the enthusiasm as a distressing substitute for spiritual values, a concern that was exacerbated some years later when John Lennon casually suggested that the Beatles had become more popular than Jesus Christ. Still others interpreted the whole phenomenon as a dismissal of convention, established authority, and the status quo—a charge that was reinforced by the Beatles' unconventional clothes and androgynously long hair.

As the Beatles' popularity grew, they became known not only for their own music, which had become ambitious and adventurous in ways never imagined on the pop landscape, but as lightning rods for other areas of pop culture. With their considerable stature, the group made millions of people aware of obscure artists such as Peter Max, musicians like Ravi Shankar, and independent filmmakers such as Richard Lester (who directed the group's film debut, *A Hard Day's Night* and its follow-up *Help!*). More than any band before them, the Beatles became a pop culture entity whose compliments and endorsements could bring fame and fortune to the artist upon whom they were bestowed.

Orton's role as a champion of the unconventional soon brought him into contact with these famous musicians from Liverpool; it was no wonder that they should think of the iconoclastic author of *Entertaining Mr. Sloane* and *Loot* as the possible creator of their next film. In a personal interview described in Orton's diaries and quoted in Lahr's biography of Orton, a meeting between Orton and Paul McCartney revealed that McCartney, a rare theatre goer, had found *Loot* ''the only play he hadn't wanted to leave before the end.'' Commissioned in 1967 to write the screenplay for the follow-up to *Help!,* Orton came up with *Up against It.* The script was laced with cross dressing, murder, adultery, and imprisonment. The Beatles, however, eventually rejected this script as too unconventional even for their iconoclastic and controversial image. In 1991, musician Todd Rundren (who, with his band Utopia, once released an album of intentionally Beatlesque songs titled ''Deface the Music'') would resurrect *Up against It* as a stage musical, the results of which he released as an album titled *Second Wind.*

CRITICAL OVERVIEW

Entertaining Mr. Sloane has generally been overshadowed by what are now considered Orton's more mature and more clearly ''farcical'' plays, *Loot* and *What the Butler Saw.* However, when Orton's first full-length play premiered, eminent British playwright Terence Rattigan called it (in a letter to Orton quoted by Lahr) ''the most exciting and stimulating first play . . . that I've seen in thirty (odd) years' playgoing.'' And while reviewing the 1981 Off-Broadway revival of the play, *New Yorker* theatre critic Edith Oliver, while admitting the superiority of Orton's later efforts, exclaimed, ''but what a debut!''

As with all of Orton's purposefully shocking plays, *Entertaining Mr. Sloane* aroused violently mixed reactions in its initial production. Some reviews referred to him as a bright new figure in the theatre world while others blanched at the play's amorality, noting that the play's homicide (Kemp's death) was unaccompanied by any moral judgment. Still others, like the anonymous critic for the London *Times,* tried to ride the fence, saying ''the coarseness is sometimes offensive but it is characteristic of the offensive people who use it; it is theatrically valid.'' As Lahr pointed out in *Prick up Your Ears,* Orton ''enjoyed the hostility as much as the praise, bad reviews featuring [in his scrapbook] as prominently as raves.'' The most negative review for the initial production at the New Arts Theatre came from one W. A. Darlington, in the conservative *Daily Telegraph,* who asserted that ''not for a long time have I disliked a play so much as I disliked Joe Orton's *Entertaining Mr. Sloane.* I feel as if snakes had been writhing round my feet.'' As Lahr reported, Orton responded to this vitriol by writing his own mock condemnation of the play for the ''Letters to the Editor'' section of *The Daily Telegraph,* assuming the pseudonym of Mrs. Edna Welthorpe and declaring that she was ''nauseated by this endless parade of mental and physical perversion.'' As the war of opinions raged, Rattigan saw in Orton's first play the style of William Congreve (*Love for Love*) and Oscar Wilde (*The Importance of Being Earnest*). Rattigan put up half the money for a transfer from the production's small, fringe venue at the New Arts to the Wyndham

Theatre in the fashionable West End. There, Darlington reviewed the play a second time and found the characters still "shameless and repulsive in the extreme" but grudgingly admitted that his interest was this time "held throughout" (as quoted by Lahr).

Though the play continued to be very controversial during its run at the Wyndham, this major West-End production made Orton an overnight sensation. His play was soon slated for publication as the best new play of the year, and Orton was frequently labeled the year's most promising playwright. As Lahr summarized in his biography, "Orton, who had been surviving on three pounds a week until his first royalty check, found his weekly earnings to be as much as 239 pounds. The play was sold to Paris in August, and the next year to Spain, the United States, Israel, and Australia. It would be made into a film and a television play. Orton had arrived in the style of his comedy—with a vengeance." As Lahr further pointed out, Orton "relished the scandal" that *Entertaining Mr. Sloane* had provoked because it "proved the comic truth of his play: that the culture hid its violence behind a show of propriety."

The first American production of *Entertaining Mr. Sloane* opened on Broadway in October of 1965, attracting large preview audiences and the approval of established playwrights such as Edward Albee (*Who's Afraid of Virginia Woolf?*), Tennessee Williams (*Cat on a Hot Tin Roof*), and Peter Shaffer (*Equus*). The reviews for the American debut, however, were largely negative. Norman Nadel for the *World Telegram and Sun* said the play had "the sprightly charm of a medieval English cesspool," while John McClain of the New York *Journal American* suggested (as quoted by Lahr) that "if this is [England's] best play of any year they are in serious trouble." Howard Taubman of the *New York Times* called it "a singularly unattractive play." The production closed after thirteen performances. But the outraged Taubman continued his indictment of the play even after it closed, writing an essay in the Sunday *New York Times* that labeled *Entertaining Mr. Sloane* "nihilistic" and (in a blatant self-contradiction) "too insignificant to merit further belaboring." This prompted a response in the same paper a week later from Orton's director, Alan Schneider, who expressed confidence in the play's "ultimate vitality and durability in the history of contemporary drama."

The American vindication of *Entertaining Mr. Sloane* came in 1981 when an Off-Broadway revival succeeded where its earlier Broadway production had failed. *New York Times* reviewer Mel Gussow called the revival a "blissfully perverse comedy of bad manners," concluding that "today, posthumously, Orton's reputation is secure." Edith Oliver wrote in the *New Yorker* that this "first of Joe Orton's high comedies of lowlife" was "a minor classic." Referring to its 1965 Broadway flop, she added, "one wonders how so many people in New York could have failed to recognize its quality at once." And Robert Asahina, writing for the *Hudson Review* concluded that "*Entertaining Mr. Sloane* is still an insightful commentary on the sexual and social role confusion that is considerably more widespread now than when it was written."

Orton's first produced play has survived all of its controversial productions and continues to be revived in theatres around the world. Clearly less farcical than *Loot* and *What the Butler Saw, Entertaining Mr. Sloane* is now considered less typical of his style than Orton's last two major plays but still "Ortonesque" in its provocative content and style.

CRITICISM

Terry R. Nienhuis

Nienhuis is a Ph.D. specializing in modern and contemporary drama. In this essay he discusses the moral dimensions of comedy and their relevance to Orton's first full-length play, Entertaining Mr. Sloane.

The rebellious and comical style that Joe Orton is most famous (or infamous) for does not surface in its complete form until his last two major plays, *Loot* and *What the Butler Saw.* His first major play, *Entertaining Mr. Sloane,* however, ultimately embodies enough of the qualities noticed by his critics and seen throughout his works to illustrate the central artistic issue in Orton's drama. Is Orton a master satirist and farceur, a ground-breaking comic genius, or a disenchanted man-child metaphorically throwing rocks at the establishment?

Known now mainly for his wildly extravagant farce, Orton's absurd tendencies do not get liberated in *Entertaining Mr. Sloane* until Act III, most notably when—in the struggle with Sloane—Kath's false teeth fall out of her mouth and roll under the sofa. Up until this point in the play, Orton's comic skill is manifested mainly in bizarre situations and

WHAT DO I READ NEXT?

- *Loot* (1965) and *What the Butler Saw* (1969) are Orton's most famous plays and works that clearly show his mastery of stage farce.
- *Not in Front of the Audience: Homosexuality on Stage* (1992), by Nicholas de Jongh is a thorough and interesting history of the portrayal of homosexual characters in theatre.
- *The Orton Diaries,* (1986) edited by John Lahr, records the last eight months of Orton's life from December 1966 to August 1967, and includes entries from the diary Orton occasionally kept as an adolescent. Alarmingly explicit in its references to sexuality, these diaries create a portrait of Orton that helps the reader understand the audacious tone and themes of his plays.
- *The Room* (1957) and *The Birthday Party* (1958) are two plays by fellow British dramatist Harold Pinter that clearly influenced Orton's early work. *The Homecoming* (1965) is a Pinter play that also involves an ''intruder'' and sexual sharing.
- *The Importance of Being Earnest* (1895) by Oscar Wilde is a late nineteenth-century comedy of manners that set a brilliant standard for verbal wit that Orton perhaps comes close to matching. In a now widely quoted phrase used in a review of *Loot,* London theatre critic Ronald Bryden dubbed Orton the ''Oscar Wilde of Welfare State gentility.''
- *Not Now Darling* (1967) and *Run for Your Wife* (1983) by Ray Cooney are more conventional, commercial British farces that simply seek to entertain their audiences with fast-moving plots and jokes that resemble television sitcoms. While *A Little Hotel on the Side* (1894) or *A Flea in Her Ear* (1907) by the French ''Father of Modern Farce,'' Georges Feydeau, demonstrate how sex can be treated almost antiseptically in farce. *Hay Fever* (1925) or *Private Lives* (1930) by Noel Coward show classic British farce that focuses more on witty dialogue than sexual commotion.

---

strikingly incongruous dialogue. Until the end of Act II, Orton's comedy is fairly conventional in the sense that it follows the fairly standard models of the comic world.

Kath, for instance, is conventionally comic in the way she pretends to more refinement and propriety than she actually possesses. This is clear from the subtle but effective opening lines of the play when Kath is proudly showing off her ordinarily middle-class home as if it were a lavishly furnished mansion: ''This is my lounge . . . I should change the curtains. Those are our winter ones. The summer ones are more of a chintz.'' The audience laughs at this dialogue out of a sense of superiority because it immediately sees the disparity between Kath's pretensions and the reality of her life. And implicit in this laughter is a subtle moral judgment—that human beings ought to be honest with themselves and not give in to shallow aspirations for social status. In the rest of the play, Kath's comic posturing grows even funnier as she constantly attempts to hide her ravenous sexual appetite behind a facade of ''motherly'' affections. And for most of the play Ed generates much of the same kind of laughter for many of the same kinds of reasons.

Sloane, however, is a more disturbing figure in Orton's comic world because it is clear from the beginning that he is genuinely dangerous. He is not a clumsy pretender who is easy to see through, and his opportunism is not amateurish and silly; he is an adept conniver who appears able to get anything he wants, a potent force for potential evil who has killed once and will kill again. What's more, he is sociopathically devoid of conscience or morals; he sees any act as acceptable as long as it gets him what he desires.

"SLOANE IS A DISTURBING FIGURE IN ORTON'S COMIC WORLD BECAUSE IT IS CLEAR FROM THE BEGINNING THAT HE IS GENUINELY DANGEROUS."

Comedy thrives on the threat of pain and unhappiness, but in the classic comic world there is a tacit agreement with the audience that the pain and unhappiness will not be enduring or genuine. In fact, part of the audience's superiority as witnesses to a comedy is their understanding that the problems the characters are fretting over will eventually be solved and seem insignificant in the glow of the comic resolution. But when comedies get more "dark," as in Shakespeare's problem farces like *Measure for Measure* or in existentialist comedies such as Samuel Beckett's *Waiting for Godot,* the specter of real pain and unhappiness rises to threaten the typical reassurance of the comic world. Very few comedy writers can successfully include real and enduring pain—much less death—in their comic worlds because human beings take genuine pain and death very seriously and will have to consider themselves insensitive if they laugh at such subjects. Orton, of course, was well aware of the boundaries of comedy and purposely sought to upset this tacit agreement with the audience about ultimate safety, forcing his audience to laugh where he knew they would find their laughter ultimately uncomfortable.

This happens most notably in *Entertaining Mr. Sloane* when Kemp dies at the end of Act II. Nearly blind and deaf, physically weak to the point of "shuffling" when he walks, Kemp seems perhaps mentally impaired as well, "a slate off" as Sloane puts it. Victimized by his own children, Kemp is an outcast in his own house, soon bound for an old-folks home, and he ultimately strikes the audience as a pathetic figure, not suitable as an object of ridicule; laughter at Kemp's expense will make the audience seem cruel. But in forcing laughter on his audience Orton does not permit it to extend Kemp any sympathetic feelings. The height of Kemp's pathos perhaps comes in an exchange with Kath in Act I when he says "I'm all alone. . . . You don't love me. . . . I'm going to die, Kath. . . . I'm dying" and Kath angrily responds, "You've been at that ham haven't you?" The incongruity of her response is cruel but also irresistibly funny and the audience's complicity through their laughter tests the boundaries of comedy. These boundaries are more severely tested at the end of Act II when Kemp actually dies at the hands of the smoothly vicious Sloane. Kemp is the only one of the characters in the play who is concerned with conventional morality. When he recognizes Sloane as the murderer of his former boss, he is determined to notify the police, even when Sloane first bribes and then threatens him. When there's a question of justice to be met, Kemp refuses to be concerned with his own safety or with practicality, but Orton does not permit his audience to admire these qualities. Instead, in Kemp's death, Orton introduces genuine pain and injustice into his comic world and, by presenting the event in a humorous context, provokes unsettled feelings for many viewers.

Those critics who most admire Orton's work, like his biographer John Lahr, often see Orton as an accomplished satirist. They see him savagely attacking the hypocrisy of conventional middle class values and expertly demonstrating that beneath the facade of respectability and refined language the characters are frequently, if not exclusively, self-centered. Lahr illustrated this admiration for Orton by beginning his introduction to the collected plays with these words: "like all great satirists, Joe Orton was a realist. He was prepared to speak the unspeakable; and this gave his plays their joy and danger. He teased an audience with its sense of the sacred, flaunting the hard facts of life people contrived to forget. There were, for Orton, no 'basic human values.' Man was capable of every bestiality; and all moral credos were heroic daydreams, the luxury of affluence."

But satire in its highest form, like comedy, always entails a moral purpose, implicit as it might be in the hands of great artists. The classic satirists like Alexander Pope, Jonathan Swift, Moliere, or Richard Brinsley Sheridan used ridicule to point out a divergence from common sense or some rational norm. They hoped, through their attacks on the foolish and wayward to lure people back into the fold of sensible behavior. Pope, for example, hoped to reconcile warring families when he wrote *The Rape of the Lock* and Moliere was suggesting that idealism could be carried too far when he wrote *The Misanthrope.* Does Orton have a similar satiric purpose?

While Orton's supporters admire his wit and humor, a fairly significant number of Orton's critics have contended, as Lahr himself admits, that Orton had no moral purpose in his writing, that his comedy was "anarchic," to employ a commonly-used term, implying a complete denial of moral absolutes or belief in behavioral norms. These critics often offer alongside a clear appreciation for Orton's genius a tempering reservation about the ultimate artistic value of his work, often suggesting that his comedy reflects more of the adolescent's need for rebellion than the satirist's desire to reform.

Benedict Nightingale, for example, in *Encounter,* wrote that Orton's celebration of "the tripes, the glands and, of course, the genitals . . . [the] delight in the overthrow of reason and the breakdown of order . . . can, as I say, prove liberating, even exhilarating, in the theatre. [But] there is also something about its greedy, sticky-fingered hedonism that can only be called infantile." In another essay in the *New Statesman,* Nightingale put Orton's work in the larger context of the comic tradition, stating that while comedy can be cynical and cruel, it is rarely presented in such extremes as evidenced in Orton's work. Nightingale felt that the playwright had "an indiscriminate scorn for most things human, from institutions to affections." In this world neither reason nor concern for one's fellow human has a place, and the pursuit of one's singular pleasure is all that matters. As the critic summarized, "It is this gleeful nihilism that characterises Orton—this that makes him fascinating and, to me, repellent and suspect. Could it be that, as a promiscuous homosexual and onetime jailbird, he found it necessary to prove that the world's judges, coppers, civil servants, psychiatrists and sturdily married heterosexuals were no better than himself? If everyone else is bad, it's easier to live with one's own excesses. If everyone else is telling lies about themselves, one can at least congratulate oneself on one's honesty." Nightingale closed his assessment by stating that despite being "a sparkling comedian and a smirking hooligan," the critic saw "more complacent hedonism than reformist zeal in his work."

Martin Esslin, renowned theatre critic and author of the seminal book, *The Theatre of the Absurd* (1961), expressed similar reservations about the nihilistic qualities of Orton's world. In an essay entitled "Joe Orton: The Comedy of (Ill) Manners" in *Contemporary English Drama,* Esslin asserted that Orton's satiric attacks were "merely for the elation of having got away with it." Comparing Orton's work with the "savage indignation" of writers like Jonathan Swift, Esslin found that in Orton "rage is purely negative, it is unrelated to any positive creed, philosophy, or programme of social reform." Esslin suggested that "behind Orton's attack on the existing state of humanity in the West there stands nothing but the rage of the socially and educationally under-privileged . . . he articulates, in a form of astonishing elegance and eloquence, the same rage and helpless resentment which manifests itself in the wrecked trains of football supporters, the mangled and vandalized telephone kiosks and the obscene graffiti on lavatory walls." Comparing Orton's work to the ground-breaking dark comedy of Samuel Beckett, Esslin suggested that "this is neither the bitter laugh of which Beckett speaks, the laugh about that which is bad in the world . . . but the mindless laugh which . . . amounts to no more than an idiot's giggle at his own image in the mirror."

Finally, C. W. E. Bigsby, author of *Joe Orton* in the "Contemporary Writers" series, found Orton's art merely "a provocation, an act of revenge, a deliberate flouting of authority and flaunting of his own exhibitionist tendencies." And in what could perhaps equally be said of *Entertaining Mr. Sloane* Bigsby says of *Loot* "it was very clearly an act of public revenge for the humiliations society had inflicted upon him in an equally public way . . . it was a play that very deliberately set out to flout all normal standards of good taste."

Nightingale perhaps summed it up best: "as it is, we are left with a tantalizing, maddening blend of wit, the *agent provocateur* and the child hoodlum: enough to keep critical discussion and disagreement on the bubble for a long time."

Despite the mixed feelings of these critics, there are many others who perceive Orton's work as social reportage, a presentation, in the extreme, of middle class life as it truly exists beneath its homogenous veneer. While a certain amount of bitterness in the playwright's message is undeniable (as Bigsby contended), Orton's bile can be attributed to the incongruity of the lifestyle in which he was raised and, during his younger years, was prohibited to speak of. Orton sought to expose middle class conformity, to strip away the superficial normalcy so many sought to preserve. He wanted to show that humor and pain, farce and death, can often occur simultaneously. Above all, Orton targeted those who publicly claimed high morals while privately pursuing their whim despite the cost to others. By

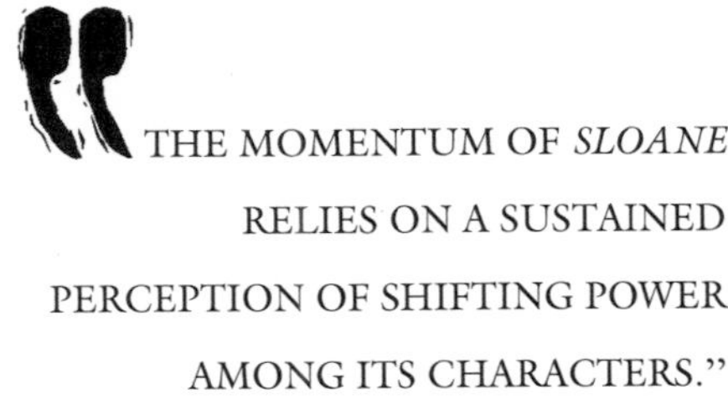

THE MOMENTUM OF *SLOANE* RELIES ON A SUSTAINED PERCEPTION OF SHIFTING POWER AMONG ITS CHARACTERS."

illustrating this hypocrisy with dark humor, forcing the audience to laugh (and often cringe) at such behavior, Orton hoped to strip away such superficiality in both his targets and even, perhaps, in his audiences.

Source: Terry R. Nienhuis, for *Drama for Students,* Gale, 1998.

Ben Brantley

Brantley reviews a 1997 production of Orton's play, praising the staging for preserving the playwright's clever wordplay while also enhancing the theatrical experience with new sensorial touches.

It isn't what most people would think of as a sexually tantalizing smell: floral, fruity and unquestionably synthetic, it is as welcome to the nostrils as a vinyl handkerchief. But for the blowzy, middle-aged Kath, played to pulpy perfection by Ellen Parker in the new revival of Joe Orton's *Entertaining Mr. Sloane,* this aerosol room freshener is just what's needed for seducing a strapping lad with the smoothest skin she's ever seen.

Smell, thank goodness, is not a sense that's much exploited in the theater. But when Ms. Parker's strawberry spray wafts into the audience at the Classic Stage Company, it feels ingeniously apt, an aromatic equivalent of what you've been hearing on stage. Orton's characters do indeed seem to speak the verbal equivalent of cheap air freshener: a canned amalgam of bourgeois pieties and dime-novel sentiments that never conceal the gamy lust and avarice beneath.

The appeal of this deliciously dark-minded comedy from 1964 rests more completely on language than do Orton's masterpieces of physical farce, *Loot* and *What the Butler Saw.* But the new Classic Stage production, directed by David Esbjornson, cleverly scales up the sensory experience of the show, carried out to the last garish, eye-popping detail of Narelle Sissons' sets and Michael Krass's costumes. And in so doing, it deftly mirrors the tacky social surfaces with which the characters overlay all manner of ungodly acts.

Indeed, Mr. Orton's amoral creatures can get away with absolutely anything—murder, sexual blackmail and one of the sickest me a trois in theater history—as long as there's an oily platitude at hand. This, after all, is a play in which the title character (Neil Maffin), after kicking an old man into insensibility, murmurs blandly, ''All this could have been avoided.'' And in which Kath speaks sweetly of her maternal instincts while planting a kiss on Sloane's lips that is anything but motherly.

The key to playing Orton's hypocrites—as opposed to, say, Moliere's or Wycherly's—is in never acknowledging any contradiction between word and deed. Fortunately, this is a fact of which Mr. Esbjornson's crackerjack four-member ensemble, rounded out by Brian Murray and George Hall, are acutely and enjoyably aware.

The pivot of the play is Sloane, a wastrel Adonis whom Kath, a girlish frump with delusions of gentility, brings home as a lodger. Never mind that he can't pay the rent; Mr. Sloane, as she will insist on addressing him, is most useful in other ways.

There are complications. Kath's geriatric father (Mr. Hall) doesn't like the intruder, whom he seems to remember in connection with a murder. And Kath's brother, Ed (Mr. Murray), a loutish businessman with a deep-felt nostalgia for the ''pure'' pleasures of boyhood athletics, hires the lad as a chauffeur, with the clear possibility of optional services.

There will be a death, a pregnancy and two violent assaults before the show is over. But the characters' Teflon dialogue can accommodate all this with the same chipper vapidity with which Kath describes those pretty tulips over by the municipal offices. In Orton's world, steeped on a daily brew of television, B-movies, tabloids and threadbare saws, denaturized language has become both anesthetic and ultimate defense.

Mr. Esbjornson's production occasionally flirts with a dangerous, self-conscious jokiness. But he understands that the momentum of *Sloane* relies on a sustained perception of shifting power among its characters, a process to which his actors are finely tuned.

Mr. Maffin, an atypically lanky, Nordic Sloane, turns his height into the perfect territorial weapon as he roams over the furniture like an overgrown cat. And he locates Sloane's essential passivity, molding himself into the wayward son, assaultive thug or sports-loving mate that each of the others expects him to be.

Mr. Murray plays his character's perversely righteous anger beautifully. Mr. Hall artfully suggests shrewdness and senility in one breath. But it is Ms. Parker's Kath, a faded butterfly of fluttering affectations and a spine of steel, who best embodies the Orton paradox. And when she primly says to Sloane, "Kiss my hand, dear, in the manner of the theater," she takes utter possession of the show.

Ms. Sissons' conception of what Kath coyly describes as "my lounge" is a lurid marvel of mixed floral patterns and textures, a set that somehow seems to assault the sense of touch as well as sight. The production gives off an almost palpable sense of physical surfaces.

The ways the characters run their fingers over upholstery and clothing take on an obsessive quality in which carnality and consumerism blend seamlessly. And when Kath talks about the smoothness of Sloane's skin, it is chillingly similar to the way she speaks of her newly repaired china shepherdess.

Obviously, for both Ed and Kath, whose calculating eyes belie their talk of rehabilitating their poor orphan boy, Mr. Sloane is just another material comfort, like a nice cigarette case or lawn gnome. For all his thuggish amorality, he is no match for this cast-iron culture of appearances. The gratifying strength of Mr. Esbjornson's production is its gleeful embrace of the premise that surface is indeed everything.

Source: Ben Brantley, "A Houseguest Inspires Not So Maternal Feelings" in the *New York Times,* February 22, 1997, pp. C13–14.

Bert Cardullo

Cardullo examines the aspects of Orton's play that qualify it as both a "wildly funny" farce and a "profoundly disturbing" social commentary. Discussed are such elements as Sloane's sexual malevolence and the Oedipal relationship that is hinted at between Kath and Sloane.

"SLOANE MAY AMUSE AS WELL AS DISTURB AUDIENCES, BUT THE VISION BEHIND *ENTERTAINING MR. SLOANE* IS WHOLLY DISTURBING."

In his introduction to *Joe Orton: The Complete Plays,* John Lahr wrote that "Sloane feels no guilt and his refusal to experience shame is what disturbs and amuses audiences. Sloane is a survivor whose egotism is rewarded, not punished." Sloane implies that he is egotistical, excessively self-loving, because he became an orphan at an early age: "It was the lack of privacy [in the orphanage] I found most trying. (*Pause.*) And the lack of real love." He has no relatives; his parents both died at the same time when he was eight years old. Sloane may amuse as well as disturb audiences, but the vision behind *Entertaining Mr. Sloane* (1964) is wholly disturbing.

The only husband and wife mentioned in the play are Sloane's parents—and they seem to have killed themselves. Kemp is Kath and Ed's father, but he and his son haven't spoken for 20 years, and his daughter treats him as if he were a naughty little boy. Kath and Ed allow Sloane to get away with killing their father in return for sexual favors: he will spend six months of the year with Kath and six months with Ed "as long as the agreement last." The first man Sloane killed was Kemp's boss, who was apparently a homosexual. Sloane says that the boss "wanted to photo me. For certain interesting features I had that he wanted the exclusive right of preserving. You know how it is. I didn't like to refuse. No harm in it I suppose. But then I got to thinking." Kath, at 41 or 42, is old enough to be Sloane's mother. In fact, she had a son when she was young by Tommy, Ed's best friend and lover at the time. She says to Sloane, "You're almost the same age as he would be." Kath gave the boy up for adoption and she and Tommy never married. The implication is that Sloane is her son. Sloane, Ed's new lover, gets Kath pregnant; they won't marry either, and she will probably give her baby up for adoption. Ed arranged the adoption of Tommy's son, and there is no reason to believe that he will not do the same for Sloane's—Ed refers to the baby Kath is carrying as "him."

Sloane's ego is rewarded, then, by other egotistical, unloved characters: all three substitute sex for love. It is no accident that the Kemp home stands alone in the midst of a rubbish dump—''it was intended to be the first of a row,'' says the old man. It is a home without love that begets a bastard who himself begets a bastard. John Lahr said that Orton, in his depiction of characters like Kath, Ed, and Sloane, ''was not being heartless, merely accurate'': in their rapaciousness, ignorance, and violence, these people are the representative products of our age. No wonder Orton has an old woman make ''a special trip [all the way from Woolwich] with her daughter in order to dump a bedstead'' outside the Kemp house: it is as if the woman is exhorting her daughter not to risk the marriage bed in times inhospitable to families and children, times peopled by the likes of this dwelling's occupants.

In her last conversation with Ed, Kath, wanting to spend time with Sloane that should be allotted to Ed according to their agreement, says, ''It deepens the relationship if the father is there [present at the birth of his child].'' Ed replies, ''It's all any reasonable child can expect if the dad is present at the conception. Let's hear no more of it.'' This is wildly funny. But it is also profoundly disturbing, because prophetic: writing a parody on the Oedipal theme in 1964, Orton foresaw at the same time the age of test-tube babies, sperm banks, single-parent families, and homosexual fathers and mothers.

Source: Bert Cardullo, ''Orton's *Entertaining Mr. Sloane*'' in the *Explicator,* Volume 46, no. 4, Summer, 1988 , pp. 50–51.

SOURCES

Asahina, Robert. Review of *Entertaining Mr. Sloane* in the *Hudson Review,* Winter, 1981-82, p. 568.

Darlington, W. A. Review of *Entertaining Mr. Sloane* in the *Daily Telegraph,* May 7, 1964.

Esslin, Martin. ''Joe Orton: The Comedy of (Ill) Manners'' in *Contemporary English Drama,* edited by C. W. E. Bigsby, Holmes & Meier, 1981, pp. 95-107.

Gussow, Mel. Review of *Entertaining Mr. Sloane* in the *New York Times,* May 21, 1981, p. C28.

''Hard to Define Triangle'' in the London *Times,* May 7, 1964, p. 20.

Lahr, John, editor. ''Introduction'' in *Joe Orton: The Complete Plays* Grove, 1976, p. vii.

Nadel, Norman. '''Entertaining Mr. Sloane' Opens'' in the *New York World-Telegram & The Sun,* October 13, 1965.

Nightingale, Benedict. ''The Detached Anarchist: On Joe Orton'' in *Encounter,* March, 1979, pp. 55-61.

Nightingale, Benedict. ''Orton Iconoclast'' in the *New Statesman,* July 18, 1975, p. 90.

Oliver, Edith. ''Re-enter Mr. Sloane'' in the *New Yorker,* July 6, 1981, pp. 51, 54.

Schneider, Alan. ''Mr. Sloane's Director Talks Back'' in the *New York Times,* October 31, 1965, section 2, p. X5.

Taubman, Howard. Review of *Entertaining Mr. Sloane* in the *New York Times,* October 13, 1965, p. 41.

Taubman, Howard. ''Aiming at Easy Targets'' in the *New Times,* October 24, 1965, section 2, p. 1.

Taylor, John Russell. ''Joe Orton'' in *The Second Wave: British Drama for the Seventies,* Methuen, 1971, p. 140.

Weeks, Jeffrey. *Sex, Politics, and Society: The Regulation of Sexuality since 1800,* Longman, 1981, p. 265.

FURTHER READING

Bigsby, C. W. E. *Joe Orton,* Methuen, 1982.
A sophisticated scholarly analysis of Orton's work that places *Entertaining Mr. Sloane* in the context of postmodernist thought. Difficult reading but essential for the advanced study of Orton's drama.

Charney, Maurice. *Joe Orton,* Grove Press, 1984.
In a chapter on *Entertaining Mr. Sloane,* Charney focuses on the characters' use of language as a way of hiding their true selves.

Dean, Joan F. ''Joe Orton and the Redefinition of Farce'' in *Theatre Journal,* December, 1982, pp. 481-92.
An article that examines the ways in which Orton altered the practice of stage farce to take it beyond the conventional boundaries of light entertainment.

Lahr, John. *Prick up Your Ears: The Biography of Joe Orton,* Knopf, 1978.
The definitive biography of Joe Orton, written by the son of the great comic actor, Bert Lahr (he played the Cowardly Lion in *The Wizard of Oz*). Very readable and an indispensable guide to any question involving Orton's life and work. Contains passages from the *The Orton Diaries.*

Nakayama, Randall S. ''Domesticating Mr. Sloane'' in *Theatre Journal,* May, 1993, pp. 185-96.
This article is a portrait of Orton that offers a different perspective from the one found in Lahr's biography.

Rusinko, Susan. *Joe Orton,* Twayne, 1995.
An accessible critical biography of Orton with a useful chapter on *Entertaining Mr. Sloane* that puts the play in the context of Orton's life and other works.

Sypher, Wylie. *Comedy,* Johns Hopkins, 1956.
A collection of three classic essays examining the theoretical (and moral) bases of comedy: George

Meredith's ''An Essay on Comedy,'' Henri Bergson's ''Laughter,'' and Sypher's own ''The Meanings of Comedy.'' Provides an excellent understanding of comedy in fiction, giving the reader a strong background with which to analyze Orton's work as it fits into the concept of comedy.

Fences

AUGUST WILSON

1983

The first staged reading of August Wilson's play *Fences* occurred in 1983 at the Eugene O'Neill Theatre Center's National Playwright's Conference. Wilson's drama opened at the Yale Repertory Theatre in 1985 and on Broadway at the 46th Street Theatre in 1987. *Fences* was well-received, winning four Antionette (''Tony'') Perry Awards, including best play. The work also won the New York Drama Critics' Circle Award, the Pulitzer Prize, and the John Gassner Outer Critics' Circle Award. Wilson was also selected as Artist of the Year by the *Chicago Tribune.*

Fences was a huge success with both critics and viewers, and it drew black audiences to the theatre in much larger numbers than usual. Because the play had four years of pre-production development before it opened on Broadway, Wilson had a chance to tighten and revise the action, watching his characters mature into lifelike creations. James Earl Jones played the role of Troy in the first staging of *Fences* on Broadway. Jones—and many black audience members—recognized and identified with Wilson's use of language to define his black characters. In an interview with Heather Henderson in *Theater,* Jones stated that ''Few writers can capture dialect as dialogue in a manner as interesting and accurate as August's.''

Reviewers also noted Wilson's ability to create believable characters. In his review for *Newsweek,* Allan Wallach noted that it is the men who dominate the script and bring it to life—singling out Jones, whom Wallach noted, is at his best ''in the bouts of drinking and bantering.'' It is Jones's performance that creates ''a rich portrait of a man who scaled down his dreams to fit inside his run-down yard.'' Clive Barnes, writing for the *New York Post,* said that Wilson provides ''the strongest, most passionate American dramatic writing since Tennessee Williams'' (*Cat on a Hot Tin Roof*). *Fences,* said Barnes, ''gave me one of the richest experiences I have ever had in the theater.''

AUTHOR BIOGRAPHY

August Wilson was born Frederick August Kittel, on April 27, 1945, in a ghetto area of Pittsburgh, Pennsylvania, known as ''The Hill.'' Wilson's white father, a German baker named August Kittel, abandoned the family when Wilson was a child. Wilson's mother, Daisy Wilson Kittel, worked as a cleaning woman to raise her six children. Later, after Wilson's mother had remarried, his stepfather moved the family to a white neighborhood where Wilson was subjected to unbridled racism. At age 15, Wilson dropped out of school after being falsely accused of plagiarism; after that episode, he continued his education on his own, with periods of extensive reading at the public library.

Wilson began his career writing poetry and short stories but switched to drama in 1978 when he was invited to write plays for a black theatre in Minneapolis-St. Paul. Several fellowships enabled Wilson to concentrate on writing plays as a full-time venture. Although his early efforts, *Fullerton Street* (1980), *Black Bart and the Sacred Hills* (1981), and *Jitney* (1982) received little attention, he gained recognition with his 1984 play, *Ma Rainey's Black Bottom,* which was accepted for a staged reading at the Eugene O'Neill Theatre Center's National Playwright's Conference in 1982. The following year, *Fences* was also presented at the O'Neill conference and in 1986 *Joe Turner's Come and Gone* became Wilson's third play to be produced at the conference.

Each of these plays followed their initial readings at the O'Neill with productions at the Yale Repertory Theatre and later stagings on Broadway. In 1987, *The Piano Lesson* opened at the Yale Repertory Theatre; *Two Trains Running* followed three years later. Wilson's *Seven Guitars* opened at the Goodman Theatre in Chicago in 1995. Wilson has stated that he envisions his plays as representative of the black experience in America, since each play is set in a different decade.

August Wilson in 1989

Wilson married for the first time in 1969, but the marriage ended after three years and the birth of a daughter, Sakina Ansari. He married for a second time in 1981; this marriage ended in 1990. Wilson has won several honors for his writing, including the New York Drama Critics' Circle Award, an Antionette (''Tony'') Perry Award, and a Pulitzer Prize for *Fences; The Piano Lesson* was also awarded a Pulitzer Prize in 1990. Several of his other works have been nominated for Tony Awards.

PLOT SUMMARY

Act I, scene i

The play opens with Troy and Bono engaged in their usual Friday night ritual of drinking and talking. Troy has made a formal complaint to his bosses that only white men are permitted to drive the garbage trucks for the waste disposal company at which both men work. The two men finish their discussion of work, and Bono asks Troy about a woman, Alberta, he suspects Troy of seeing. Troy denies that he would risk losing his wife, Rose, but Bono does not give up so easily and reminds Troy that he has been seen at Alberta's house when he said he was elsewhere.

Their conversation is interrupted by Troy's wife, Rose, who enters the yard. Their conversation about where to shop is interrupted by Lyons's entrance. Lyons is Troy's son by a previous marriage. He has come by because he knows that his father gets paid on Fridays; he is in need of a loan and asks his father for ten dollars. Troy pointedly notes that Lyons needs to get a job. Lyons's reply is that his father had no hand in raising him, and thus, he has no right to chastise or complain about how Lyons is living his life. Rose intervenes and gives Lyons the money.

Act I, scene ii

Rose is hanging clothes on the line. Troy enters and they begin to banter about Rose's habit of playing numbers (a form of betting, like a lottery). Troy thinks it foolish and a waste of money, but Rose finds this little bit of gambling to be a harmless diversion that occasionally offers a small reward. Their conversation moves to Troy's inquiry about the presence of their son, Cory. At that moment, Troy's brother, Gabriel, enters the yard. He is singing and carrying a bowl of discarded fruit and vegetables that he has picked up and is now attempting to sell. Gabriel was injured in the war and is now mentally disabled. Gabriel is worried that his older brother is angry that he has moved out and into his own place. As Gabriel exits, still singing, Rose reassures Troy that he has done all he can to care for his brother.

Act I, scene iii

Four hours later, Rose is taking the dried clothes down from the line. Cory enters and is directed by his mother to get into the house and start the chores that he ignored when he went to football practice. Troy enters the yard and after hearing that Cory is home, yells for his son to come out of the house. An argument ensues between father and son about Cory's concentration on football at the expense of his other obligations: school, chores, and a part-time job he has just quit. Troy demands complete control over Cory and insists that he quit football. Cory responds by asking his father why he doesn't like his son. Troy evades a direct answer, and, instead, he replies that his son is provided with a home and food because he, Troy, fulfills his responsibility to his family. The confrontation ends with Troy telling Cory to get back down to the supermarket and get his job back.

When Rose returns, Troy explains that he wants his son to do better than his father and to have a better job than that of a garbage man. Rose tries to soften Troy by reminding him that he missed his chance to be a professional athlete because he was too old, but Troy is unwilling to admit that she is right. The scene ends with Troy's declaration that he simply moves through life, existing from one Friday night to the next.

Act I, scene iv

It is another Friday night, two weeks later, and Cory is on his way to play football. He ignores Rose when she confronts him about the chores he has left undone and states that he'll do them later. Troy and Bono enter the yard after Cory leaves, and Troy announces that he has been made a driver. At that moment Lyons comes to repay the money he borrowed two weeks ago. Most of this scene is devoted to the issue of Cory's future.

Troy launches into an autobiographical story that explains much of his behavior. The audience learns about Troy's brutal father and that he has been on his own since he was fourteen. The audience also learns that Troy spent fifteen years in jail and that is where he met Bono. The scene ends with a confrontation between Troy and Cory, who has just entered the yard. Troy accuses Cory of lying and orders him to get his old job back and quit the football team.

Act II, scene i

Troy has just returned from bailing Gabriel out of jail. Bono is with him, and, in response to his friend's concern about Rose, Troy admits that he has been seeing another woman and that she is going to have his baby. Rose enters the yard as Bono is leaving. Troy realizes that with a child coming, he must accept responsibility for what he has done. He tells Rose that he is to be the father to another woman's child. His response to her anger and pain is an admission that the other woman offers an escape from his responsibilities. She makes him forget the endless repetition of his life for a few moments. The scene ends in a confrontation between Rose, Troy, and Cory that stops just short of physical violence.

Act II, scene ii

It is six months later, and it is clear that the relationship between Rose and Troy has been severed. Although Troy gives his wife his paycheck, he is spending almost all his time with Alberta. Troy and Rose argue, but their fight is interrupted by a phone call telling them that the baby has been born but that the mother has died. The scene ends with Troy yelling at death, vowing to build a fence around his house and those he loves to keep death away.

Act II, scene iii

Troy returns with the infant, who he has named Raynell, and he and Rose agree that she will raise the child, who should not be punished for her parents' sins.

Act II, scene iv

It is two months later and much has changed. Cory has graduated and is looking for a job, but Lyons tells him that jobs are scarce. Rose is busy with her church activities; she has found something to fill the space within that Troy had occupied before his deception. A brief conversation between Troy and Bono reveals that the two friends have drifted apart. Troy is a driver and Bono is still picking up the trash on a different route. After Bono leaves, Cory returns and there is a final argument between father and son. Clearly Cory blames Troy for his mother's pain and for his own disappointment. The argument turns violent when Cory attempts to strike at Troy with a baseball bat; he misses and Troy seizes the bat but stops just short of striking his son. In the end, Cory leaves the house for good, and Troy ends the scene with a taunt for death to come.

Act II, scene v

It is seven years later and the family has gathered for Troy's funeral. Cory arrives in his marine uniform. When he states that he will not go to Troy's funeral, his mother convinces him that he has an obligation to go. But it is the singing of Troy's favorite song with the child, Raynell, that really convinces Cory to put the past behind him. The scene ends with all the principal characters in the yard. Gabriel announces he has come to blow the trumpet for Troy's admittance to Heaven through St. Peter's gate. The horn's mouthpiece is broken, however, and instead Gabriel begins to dance and howl as the stage darkens.

CHARACTERS

Jim Bono

Bono is Troy Maxson's closest friend. They met while in prison and spent fifteen years together locked inside. Troy has been the leader whom Bono has willingly followed. They work together hauling garbage until Troy is promoted to driver. That event, combined with Troy's preoccupation with his pregnant mistress, serves to create the first serious discord between the two men in nearly thirty-four years of friendship. Bono is very concerned with Troy's dalliance with another woman and the risk it poses to his friend's marriage. Jim's wife, Lucille, is never seen on stage, but he speaks of her with obvious affection and admiration; she has tamed his wanderlust. Bono's positive relationship with Lucille demonstrates that a man has the ability to change the direction of his life.

Cory Maxson

Cory is the Maxsons' teenage son. When the play opens he is being actively recruited for a college football scholarship. His father feels that he is spending too much time at practice and ignoring his other responsibilities. Cory represents all the possibilities his father never had, but he also represents Troy's unmet dreams. Troy wants his son to achieve a future that does not include hauling garbage. Yet the father is unwilling to let the son attempt something that may bring him success; Troy is afraid that the world of white-dominated sports will only break Cory's heart.

When Cory quits his job to concentrate on football, his father retaliates by going to the coach and forbidding Cory to play. After a particularly heated confrontation, Cory leaves home. At the play's end, he returns after an absence of seven years for his father's funeral. Cory has spent the last six years as a Marine, but he is now considering a new direction that includes marriage and a new job.

Initially he does not want to attend his father's funeral, the chasm is too wide, and he believes his controlling father never loved him. He eventually realizes that he must put the past behind him, forgive his father, and attend the funeral.

Gabriel Maxson

Gabriel is Troy's brother. Troy has helped care for Gabriel since World War II during which his brother received a debilitating head injury. Gabriel's mental capacity has been diminished by the injury and left him believing that he is the archangel Gabriel. Troy used Gabriel's disability settlement to buy the house in which the family lives, and he continues to receive a part of Gabriel's monthly benefit checks as rent. When the play opens, Gabriel has just moved into his own lodgings. His life is filled with his singing and his expressed wait for St. Peter to call upon Gabriel to open the gates of heaven.

After bailing Gabriel out of jail several times, Troy finally has him committed to a mental hospital. At the play's end, it is Gabriel who brings some resolution as he calls for the gate of heaven to open and admit Troy. Gabriel attempts to blow a trumpet to herald Troy into heaven, finds that the mouthpiece is broken, and begins a jumping about and howling as the stage darkens.

Lyons Maxson

Lyons is Troy's thirty-four-year-old son from a previous marriage; he was raised by his mother after Troy was sent to jail, and he has little respect for his father's advice. He does, however, have need of his father's money, frequently arriving at the house on Troy's paydays. Lyons hopes for a career as a musician and is disinterested in any work that would interfere with his goal. Consequently, he is unemployed and is supported by his wife, Bonnie. Lyons knows little about his father, but when he hears that his father has been on his own since he was fourteen, Lyons is finally impressed enough to pay attention as his father speaks.

Raynell Maxson

Raynell is the child Troy fathered with his mistress, Alberta. When Alberta dies giving birth, he brings the three-day old infant home for Rose to raise. She is seven years old when her father dies, but she has come to represent all the family's hopes for a better future. In the final scene, it is Raynell and Cory's singing of their father's favorite song that helps heal the pain of Cory's angry memories of his father.

Rose Maxson

Rose is Troy's wife of eighteen years. She is ten years younger than him and a strong woman who is devoted to her husband. Her devotion ends, however, when Troy tells her of his affair with Alberta and his impending fatherhood. Rose wants the fence built around their house so that she can keep her family safe within its confines. She tries to mediate the conflicts that arise between Troy and his sons. It is Rose who loans money to Lyons, and it is Rose who tries to soften Troy's unconditional control over Cory's life. She is deeply wounded by Troy's affair and although they continue living in the same house, their loving relationship as husband and wife is over. Rose agrees to raise the child, Raynell, because she does not believe that the child should suffer for the sin of her parents. She substitutes religion for the companionship of marriage, and by the time Raynell is born, Rose has become an active member of her church. It is Rose who calls for family unity and healing at the play's end; she urges all the family members and friends to forgive and remember the good things about Troy.

Troy Maxson

Troy is the principal character. He is fifty-three when the play begins. He has led a hard life, raised by an abusive father and later jailed for robbery and murder. During the fifteen years he spent in jail, Troy became an accomplished baseball player. But after his release from jail Troy was too old to play in the newly-integrated major leagues. He is bitter and resentful at the opportunities lost because of the color of his skin and is desperate to protect Cory from the same sort of disappointment. Troy lives in the past and fails to recognize that the world has changed. His father was brutal and controlling, and although Troy loves Cory, he knows of no other way to bring up a son. Thus he repeats the mistakes of the previous generation.

Troy feels a need to control every element of his life and even declares that he will fight death if necessary. His affair with Alberta represents his attempt to escape the responsibility he feels for wife, son, and home. Unable to open up to those that he loves, Troy keeps much of his emotion inside, building imaginary fences between himself and his family and friends. While he realizes the financial responsibility of being the head of a family, he fails to grasp the emotional part of the job. Troy finally succeeds in isolating himself from his wife, his brother, his sons, and his friend.

THEMES

Death

In *Fences,* death is a character. Rather than the elusive unknown, death becomes an object that Troy attempts to battle. The unfinished fence that Troy is building around his home is completed only when Troy feels threatened by death. In one of the stories he tells, Troy relates how he once wrestled with death and won. When the simmering conflict between Troy and Cory finally erupts and the boy leaves his father's house for good, it is death that Troy calls upon to do battle. And in the last scene, it is death that unites the family and helps bring resolution to their lives. When the family meets again at Troy's funeral, they are finally given a chance to bury the pain and disappointments of their lives.

Duty and Responsibility

Troy Maxson is a man who assumes the responsibilities of father, husband, and provider. In addition, he looks after his disabled brother, Gabriel. Though he faces these responsibilities, he is also overwhelmed by them, seeking escape when it is offered to him. When it is revealed that Alberta, the other woman that Troy has been seeing, is pregnant, Troy responds that he is not ducking the responsibility of what he has done. He accepts the obligation he owes to both his wife and his mistress.

When Rose asks why Troy needed another woman, his reply is that Alberta was an escape from his responsibilities. She did not have a roof that needed fixing; her house was a place where he could forget that he was someone's husband, someone's father, someone's employee. Troy feels the weight of responsibility so heavily that he can see only endless weeks of labor, endless paychecks to be cashed, endless Fridays blending into one another. When Alberta dies giving birth, Troy assumes responsibility for the infant and brings her to his home. In turn, Rose agrees to raise and care for the child. In the end it is the responsibility each member of the family feels toward the others that brings resolution to the story.

Fences

Fences represent many different things in Wilson's drama. Rose thinks the partially built fence around the house will keep her loved ones safe inside. But for Troy, the fence is a way to keep unwanted intruders out. After Alberta's death, he completes the fence as a means to keep death from entering and hurting his loved ones. When Troy played baseball, he was never content to hit the ball into the stands. His hits always had to go over the fence. And yet, Troy builds a fence around Cory to keep him from his goals and desires. Troy's efforts at controlling his son create an imaginary fence that keeps the boy separate from his family for seven years. There are similar fences between Troy and his loved ones; in one way or another he has kept them separated from a part of himself.

When Troy tells his life story, it is a tale of penitentiary walls behind which he was a prisoner for fifteen years. Bono was also confined within these walls. By Act II, the walls of a mental hospital will separate Gabriel from his family. Troy also sees white America having a fence that keeps blacks contained, apart from the good life that whites enjoy. It is the fence that kept him from realizing his dreams and the fence that makes blacks garbage collectors while whites advance to better positions such as driver.

In the sense of physical setting, the fence around Troy's house also contains the action of the play. Everything takes place in the yard; all of the scenes and the dialogue occur within the boundaries of the fence.

Friendship

The friendship between Troy and Bono is the first relationship shown in the play. Their conversations provide a glimpse into Troy's thoughts. Bono has been following Troy's lead since they met in prison more than thirty years earlier. Troy has been a role model for Bono, but Bono serves as a conscience for Troy. It is Bono who first alerts the audience to Troy's extramarital affair, and it is Bono who questions the wisdom of Troy's actions. The friendship is tested when Troy is promoted to driver and put on another route. When questioned about his absence from Troy's house, Bono replies that it is the new job that keeps them apart. But there is also a hint that Troy's betrayal of Rose has changed the dynamics of their friendship.

Limitations and Opportunities

At the heart of Troy's unhappiness is his disappointment at not being able to play professional baseball. Troy became an accomplished ball player while in prison. He was good enough to play in the

TOPICS FOR FURTHER STUDY

- What is the nature of the conflict between Cory and Troy? Research the options for black athletes who were recruited by colleges in the 1950s. Do you find that Troy's reservations about Cory's future as a ballplayer have merit?
- Troy cannot read and so the oral tradition is an important means of communication for him. He tells his life story in Act I, scene iv. But he also tells part of his story through song. Research the role of storytelling as a part of the black experience. Consider also how the oral tradition has been replaced in many cultures by the printed page. Do you think that the oral tradition is a disappearing part of the American cultural experience?
- In *Fences,* Troy's description of the devil eventually evolves into a description of a white salesman who cheats his black customers because they are too afraid to question his pronouncements, and thus, they allow themselves to be cheated. Examine the commercial relationship between whites and blacks in the 1950s. Is Troy's cynicism justified by the facts?
- Early in Wilson's play, music and athletics are singled out the best opportunities for young black men to escape the ghetto existence of black urban life. Later, Cory joins the Marines, but is this an escape? In 1964, the United States is beginning a build-up of military strength in Vietnam, it will evolve into a war that will eventually be lost. What exactly did the military offer young black men? Research the role of the black soldier in Vietnam and consider if the percentage of blacks who died in that war represented an unequal sacrifice of life.

Negro leagues, but his true desire was to play major league ball. Troy felt he was excluded because, at the time, black players were still not accepted, but the story is more complex than Troy wants to believe. The fifteen years that Troy spent in prison made him too old for the major leagues. Troy ignores this argument, since to acknowledge that he was too old is to accept partial responsibility for not being able to play; it was his own actions that led to a fifteen year prison term, a period during which his youth slipped away. It is easier for Troy to blame a system that discriminates against black players than to admit that he lacked either the talent or the youth to play major league baseball.

Troy's son, Cory, also has the opportunity for a better life through athletics. But Troy is so bitter over his own lack of opportunity that he holds his son back from any success he might achieve. When Cory is recruited for a college football scholarship, it is his father who forbids Cory to play. Troy is unable to accept that his son might succeed where he had failed—and Cory accuses his father of just such a motivation. But it is more than a desire to control Cory's success that is at the heart of Troy's actions. He truly fails to see that the world has changed in the past twenty years. Black men are now playing professional sports with white men. The restrictions that kept the two races apart athletically have eased. A football scholarship would mean more than playing a sport; it would be an opportunity for education and a chance to advance to a better world.

Race and Racism

In a story that Troy tells in the play, the devil is represented as a white business owner who takes advantage of his black customers. The setting for *Fences* is just before the racial tensions of the 1960s erupt. Troy is a garbage man. He has noticed that only white men are promoted to driver, and, although he possesses no driver's license, Troy complains about the injustice of a system that favors one race while excluding another. Because he has complained, Troy is promoted, but the result is that he no longer works with his friends and the camaraderie of the workplace is lost. Troy also feels that his dream to play professional baseball was destroyed because he was a black player in a white world. Because he has spent a lifetime being excluded, Troy cannot see any advantage for his son when college recruiters come to watch Cory play football. Troy cannot trust the white man, the devil, and so, he forbids his son to play football.

STYLE

Act

A major division in a drama. In Greek plays the sections of the drama signified by the appearance of the chorus and were usually divided into five acts. This is the formula for most serious drama from the Greeks to the Romans to Elizabethan playwrights like William Shakespeare. The five acts denote the structure of dramatic action. They are exposition, complication, climax, falling action, and catastrophe. The five act structure was followed until the nineteenth century when Henrik Ibsen (*A Doll's House*) combined some of the acts. *Fences* is a two act play. The exposition and complication are combined in the first act when the audience learns of Troy's affair with another woman and of the conflict between father and son, the role sports plays in each man's life. The climax occurs in the second act when Troy must admit to having fathered a child with his mistress. The climax to the father-son friction also occurs in the second act when the conflict between Troy and Cory escalates, and Cory leaves his father's home for good. The catastrophe also occurs in this act when the players assemble for Troy's funeral and Cory is finally able to deal with his resentment and accept his father's failings.

Setting

The time, place, and culture in which the action of the play takes place is called the setting. The elements of setting may include geographic location, physical or mental environments, prevailing cultural attitudes, or the historical time in which the action takes place. The location for *Fences* is an urban city in 1957 America. The action occurs over a period of several months and then jumps ahead seven years for the last scene. The action is further reduced to one set, the yard of the Maxson home.

Character

A person in a dramatic work. The actions of each character are what constitute the story. Character can also include the idea of a particular individual's morality. Characters can range from simple stereotypical figures to more complex multi-faceted ones. Characters may also be defined by personality traits, such as the rogue or the damsel in distress. ''Characterization'' is the process of creating a life-like person from an author's imagination. To accomplish this, the author provides the character with personality traits that help define who he will be and how he will behave in a given situation. For instance, in the beginning of *Fences* Troy seems to accept the responsibilities he has acquired. He appears content with his marriage and comfortable in providing for his family and caring for Gabriel. As the action progresses, however, it becomes clear that Troy yearns for escape from these responsibilities. He finds this escape with Alberta but at the cost of his marriage.

Conflict

The conflict is the issue(s) to be resolved in the play. It usually occurs between two characters, but it can also occur between a character and society (as it does in Arthur Miller's *The Crucible*). Conflict serves to create tension in a plot—it is often the motivating force that drive a plot. For instance, in *Fences* there is a clear conflict between Cory's desire to play footfall and the disappointments that his father felt when his dreams of success in professional sports were never realized. There is also conflict between Troy and his wife when she discovers that he has fathered a child with another woman. And finally, Troy's disappointment in sports represents the conflict between a largely white-dominated organization, professional sports, and a talented black man who feels he has been cheated and deprived of success. This conflict provides one of the fences that isolates black athletes from opportunities available to white Americans.

Metaphor

Metaphor is an analogy that identifies one object with another and ascribes to the first object the qualities of the second. For example, the fence is a metaphor for the walls that confine Troy and Bono to prison. There are fences (though unseen) between Troy and his family. It is also a metaphor for the white society that confines blacks and restricts their opportunities. In this drama, baseball is also a metaphor for Troy's life. His successes are hits over the fence, but his failures are strike-outs.

Plot

This term refers to the pattern of events. Generally plots should have a beginning, a middle, and a conclusion, but they may also be a series of episodes connected together. Basically, the plot provides the author with the means to explore primary themes. Students are often confused between the two terms; but themes explore ideas, and plots simply relate what happens in a very obvious manner. Thus the plot of *Fences* is the story of a black family divided by the loss and anger of past and present disappointments. But the themes are those of family unity and love and racial intolerance.

HISTORICAL CONTEXT

Professional Athletics

By 1957, the year in which *Fences* is set, black athletes had become an integrated part of professional and college sports, at least on the surface. The all-white teams of the World War II—and previous—years began to include blacks in 1947 when Jackie Robinson became the first black to play professional baseball since the color line was drawn in the 1890s. But the change still did not bring the same opportunity and equality as blacks might have hoped. Black leagues began to falter and disappear as more blacks began to support the now integrated ball teams. Troy Maxson, who had played in the Negro Leagues, found the change to integrated leagues had come too late; he was now too old to play professional ball.

The Negro Leagues had been financial disasters for players; salaries were inadequate to support a family. But, ten years after integration, the major leagues did not prove to be a financial bonanza for black players either. The huge salaries that were to become the hallmark of professional sports in the 1980s and 1990s simply did not exist in the late 1950s. The picture for college athletics was also different for blacks than for whites. Black players were not always permitted to live in campus housing, and when they traveled to games, black athletes were sometimes refused accommodations at hotels where the team was staying. Instead, black players were dropped off at the YMCA or lodged with black families. Given this knowledge, it is little wonder that Troy is suspicious of the recruiters who want to seduce his son with college scholarships and the possibility of a career in professional sports.

Employment

When the flood of immigrants poured into the United States at the beginning of the twentieth century, they found opportunity and employment in factories, offices, and small business. The white work force was plentiful and employers took advantage of the availability of the eager new citizens, who came expecting that hard work would make it possible to marry, raise a family, and live the American Dream. But for blacks, who were also moving into large northern cities in huge numbers, the American Dream remained an elusive possibility, just beyond their grasp.

Troy admits that had he not been able to use his brother's disability benefit, he would not have been able to purchase a home, even though he had been working hard for nearly twenty years. With the availability of a large white work force, blacks were too often the last hired and the first fired. In addition, many black workers lacked the training necessary to get ahead. The job of hauling garbage is available to blacks, but even within that job, there is a division of work by race. White employees drive trucks; black employees load the garbage. Troy cannot read and does not have a driver's license, but he breaks through the color barrier to win a driver's job because he complains that there are no black drivers. The union, which protects his job when he complains, is the one ally the black workers have.

Housing

Because of limited job opportunities, most blacks did not earn enough money to own their own homes. But in 1957 the American Dream became a reality for many white families. In the post-war economy, home ownership for whites was booming. The World War II G.I. bill had made it possible for returning servicemen to go to college. These better educated men found successful careers that brought a higher standard of living than the previous generation had known. This resulted in an explosion of new home building, the creation of suburbs, and ultimately, the exodus of whites from the inner city. Few blacks could afford the new homes that were going up on development sites all across the country. Instead, many urban blacks lived in the same kind of ghetto in which Wilson himself had been born. The front yard of the Maxson home is a rarity for most black families who often lived in huge inner-city apartment buildings.

COMPARE & CONTRAST

- **1957:** Ku Klux Klansmen accuse Alabama grocery-chain truck driver Willie Edwards, 25, of having made remarks to a white woman and force him at pistol point to jump to his death from the Tyler Goodwin Bridge into the Alabama River. It was Edwards's first day on the truck route.

  1985: Philadelphia police try to dislodge members of MOVE, an organization of armed blacks. They firebomb a house from the air on May 13 and the fire spreads to adjacent houses, killing 11 and leaving 200 homeless.

  Today: A black woman, previously on public assistance, organizes a million woman rally in Philadelphia. This variant on the 1996 million man march on Washington D.C. draws more than one million black women in a show of strength and solidarity.

- **1957:** The Motown Corporation is founded in Detroit, Michigan, by entrepreneur Barry Gordy Jr., 30, who invests $700 to start a recording company whose ''Motown Sound'' will figure large in popular music for more than two decades.

  1985: *The Color Purple,* a film based on Alice Walker's novel, is a top grossing box office success for star Whoopi Goldberg and director Steven Spielberg.

  Today: *Rosewood,* a film based on actual events that occurred in 1927, examines the massacre that destroyed a small Florida town after a white woman falsely accuses a black man of sexual assault.

- **1957:** Ghana becomes the first African state south of the Sahara to attain independence.

  1985: South Africa declares a state of emergency July 20, giving police and the army almost absolute power in Black townships. The country's policy of apartheid has kept blacks as second-class citizens for decades.

  Today: For the first time, South Africa is ruled by the racial majority (blacks) led by Nelson Mandela, who languished in white-run prisons during the last 27 years of apartheid rule.

- **1957:** The first U.S. civil rights bill since Civil War reconstruction days, passed by Congress September 9, establishes a Civil Rights Commission and provides federal safeguards for voting rights. Many Southerners oppose the bill.

  1985: The Gramm-Rudman-Hollings Act signed by President Reagan mandates congressional spending limits in an effort to eliminate the federal deficit.

  Today: Welfare reform results in a loss of services, including food stamps, public assistance, and medical care for many of the nation's poorest citizens. The reform is intended by politicians to be a mechanism that will force welfare recipients into the job force. But the change is seen by the many organizations that assist the poor as a misdirected effort that will punish the nation's already disadvantaged children.

Racism

The 1950s still revealed an America with two races, separated by color and economic barriers. Blacks and whites attended different schools, lived in different neighborhoods, and received different benefits from their citizenship. Before the advent of forced busing in the 1960s, most blacks attended schools in poorer neighborhoods. Because schools are funded by a complicated system of bonds supported by taxes, black schools (in neighborhoods that collected lower taxes) received less money and thus had smaller resources with which to pay salaries, maintain buildings, or buy new equipment. The result was that students at predomi-

James Earl Jones as the failed baseball player Troy Maxson, a role he originated

nately black schools received a sub-standard level of education.

Other areas of inequality included suffrage and justice. Blacks were not encouraged to vote; in fact, many areas discouraged blacks from voting by instituting difficult competency exams as qualifiers. Whites were not required to pass these exams. Accordingly, blacks had little input into the political decisions that shaped their lives. Blacks also suffered unequal treatment under the law. Many could not read the contracts they signed or were too intimidated to protest. In addition, blacks often became the victims of discrimination under criminal statutes. Ignorance of their legal rights meant that blacks often languished in jail. In some cases, blacks were lynched by unruly mobs who were sometimes sanctioned by a law enforcement organization that looked the other way. The civil unrest of the 1960s was a direct result of these injustices.

CRITICAL OVERVIEW

When *Fences* first opened on Broadway in March of 1987, Wilson had already spent four years in preproduction revisions to his play. James Earl Jones, who won a Tony Award for his performance in the Broadway production, had first played Troy Maxson in the Yale Repertory Theatre production two years earlier. His ease and interpretation of an already familiar character were evident to reviewers who hailed Jones's performance. Allan Wallach, in his *Newsday* review, said that Jones gave this role ''its full measure of earthiness and complexity.'' Jones, said Wallach, was at his best when Troy is drinking and laughing with his friends; his ''performance is at its heartiest in the bouts of drinking and bantering.'' Wallach also singled out Wilson's ability to capture the ''rhythms of his characters'' who gather in the yard of the Maxson home, a yard that ''becomes a rich portrait of a man who scaled down his dreams to fit inside his run-down yard.'' Wallach's review is an acknowledgment of Wilson's strength in ''depicting a black man forced to come to terms with an unfeeling white world.'' However, Wallach also found that the scenes where Troy interacts with his family sometimes fell to conventional family fare.

Reviewer Clive Barnes offered no such distinction in his review that appeared in the *New York Post.* Barnes called *Fences* a play that ''seems to break away from the confines of art into a dense, complex realization of reality.'' *Fences* is a play that makes the audience forget it is in a theater, thinking instead that they are witnessing a real family drama. Barnes also singled out Jones for praise in a role that left the reviewer ''transfixed.'' But Wilson was also praised for writing drama ''so engrossing, so embracing, so simply powerful'' that he transcended an effort to label him a black playwright. Instead, Wilson's ability to tell a story makes such labels, in Barnes's opinion, ''irrelevant.'' Barnes also praised the play for its historic relevance and cited the lessons Troy learned while in prison and his experience playing baseball. Barnes declared that Wilson has created "the strongest, most passionate American dramatic writing since Tennessee Williams." Barnes's review contained no reservations. He praised the actors, noting that Jones's performance was not the only excellent one of the production and offered equal approval for the staging and setting. The sum total of these elements resulted in what Barnes described as "one of the richest experiences I have ever had in the theatre."

Edwin Wilson's praise of *Fences* was just as full of compliments as that of Barnes and Wallach. In his *Wall Street Journal* review, Wilson stated that with *Fences,* the author had demonstrated that he can "strike at the heart, not just of the black experience, but of the human condition." Troy is a character who is multi-dimensional; his complexity reveals a man "with the full measure of his shortcomings as well as his strengths." The audience witnesses the characters' depth of ambition, their frustration, and their pain, according to this reviewer. As did other reviewers, Wilson also noted the exceptional quality of the setting and the staging. *Fences,* said Wilson, is "an especially welcome and important addition to the season."

CRITICISM

Sheri Metzger

Metzger is a professional writer with a specialty in drama. In this essay she discusses Wilson's metaphoric use of baseball in portraying the life of his lead character, Troy Maxson.

The most prevalent image in August Wilson's *Fences* is baseball. It is the sport that defines Troy Maxson's life and provides the measure of his success. Indeed, Wilson has constructed the play into nine scenes—or innings—to emphasize the connection. According to Christine Birdwell in *Aethlon,* the innings correspond to the seasons of Troy's life. In some innings Troy is the hero who wins for his team, his family. These are the innings defined by Troy's success: his early success as a great hitter for the Negro Leagues, his protest at work that wins him a promotion to driver, and his noble, responsible efforts to provide for his family. But some innings are losses for Troy (and his team): his misunderstandings and painful confrontations with his two sons, his institutionalizing of his brother Gabriel, his broken relationships with Rose and Bono, and the death of Alberta. In the ninth inning, when Troy is dead, his family gathers in the yard to remember Troy's wins and losses.

Birdwell noted that Wilson does not provide much information about the black baseball leagues in his play. The role baseball plays in framing Troy's strengths and weaknesses is more important than the history of the game itself. Instead the emphasis is on characterization. The audience learns that Troy was a good hitter and that his home run average far exceeded those of many white players. Nevertheless, the Negro League was not a source of viable income for its players; Troy could not have bought his home without the additional money from Gabriel's disability checks. In one of his complaints about the color line in baseball, Troy observes that he "saw Josh Gibson's daughter yesterday. She was walking around with raggedy shoes on her feet." He then compares Gibson's child to the child of a white major league player, and declares "I bet you Selkirk's daughter ain't walking around with raggedy shoes on her feet." The reference is clear: Negro League players cannot make enough money to support their families. The injustice rankles Troy whose bitterness at the slight baseball has shown him is evident throughout the play.

Besides his thirty-year friendship with Bono, the fifteen years that he spent in prison provided Troy with another benefit. It demonstrated to him that he had a talent, one that set him apart from other men, one that proved his worth. But, as Birdwell noted, baseball also proved a disappointment. For Troy, "the triumphs of the past have become bitter betrayals, and baseball now means lost dreams. Baseball had defined Troy, had given him meaning and status; now it has left him with nothing tangible."

Troy is so angry over his own lost opportunities that, by 1957, he cannot take pleasure in the fact that black men are finally able to play major league ball. Integration means nothing to him because it came too late to benefit *his* life. He complains that "if you could play ball then they ought to have let you play." Ability and not color should determine who plays baseball, but Troy recognizes that justice has been missing for black men. When he tries to explain his distrust of the white sport establishment to Cory, Troy observes that "the colored guy got to be twice as good [as the white player] before he get on the team." He also notes that although the leagues are now integrated, the black players sit on the bench and are not used. Cory has no personal

WHAT DO I READ NEXT?

- Maya Angelou's *I Know Why The Caged Bird Sings* (1969) offers an autobiographical look at the American black experience. This book provides a feminine perspective of the effects of racism.
- *The Wedding Band* (1966), a play by Alice Childress, examines racism and intolerance through the eyes of a couple who are trying to find acceptance for their interracial love affair. Because the subject was so controversial, the play was not produced until several years after it was written.
- *A Raisin in the Sun* (1959) by Lorraine Hansberry also explores segregation, racism, and the lack of economic opportunities that beset African Americans. The integration of white neighborhoods by minority families is still an important issue nearly forty years after this play was first produced.
- *The Color Purple* (1982) by Alice Walker is a fictional look at the effects of segregation and racism both within black culture and between blacks and whites. The novel (and Steven Spielberg's later movie adaptation) celebrate the strength of black women.
- Toni Morrison's *The Bluest Eye* (1970) examines what it means to grow up black and female in America. Morrison explores how white standards of beauty affect young black girls, and she looks at the nature of the relationship between black and white women.
- *The Piano Lesson,* another play by August Wilson, was first performed in 1987. This play probes the conflicts between traditional values and the need to change to better survive the future.

---

experience that corresponds to his father's. He has been playing football in high school and recruiters want him to play in college; he fails to see any lack of opportunity. Each man feels the other is blind to the truth, but both are centered in their own experience.

In a real sense, Troy has become blind to the changes of the past ten years, and it is this ignorance that provokes him to deny Cory's chance at succeeding. Too often, fathers use sons to achieve the success they feel they have been denied. But Troy has no desire to live vicariously through his son. Finally, in the eighth inning/scene, their opposing positions result in a confrontation that turns violent. After having been told by his father that he is earning strikes, Cory grabs a baseball bat and advances with the intent of swinging at his father. This is the strike-out about which Troy has been warning his son. Cory swings twice and misses, but Troy is stronger and seizes the bat, denying his son the third swing that may have resulted in a strike-out—or a hit.

Birdwell observed that in this scene, ''Wilson presents a reverse image of the traditional, treasured father-and-son backyard game depicted in films and on television. Instead father and son vie for the bat transformed into a weapon, and savage combat erupts.'' Baseball should provide fathers and sons with a bonding experience, with an opportunity for playful competition. But Cory cannot compete with Troy. Troy's need for control, a pattern he learned from his own brutal father, is too ingrained for him to soften his ways. Although he means the best for Cory, Troy's misdirected efforts result in the loss of his son. He will die without having ever seen Cory again.

The relationship that Troy forges with his wife, Rose, also proves to be limited by his experience in baseball. After eighteen years of marriage, Troy feels he needs to escape the confining walls of responsibility through an affair with another woman. The other woman, Alberta, is Troy's attempt to capture what has been lost, his youth. If Troy is now too old to play major league baseball, he is not too old to be attractive to other women. Birdwell insisted that Alberta "returns Troy to baseball's yesteryears, in which, according to Bono, 'a lot of them old gals was after [him],' when he 'had the pick of the litter.'"

While Troy might see another woman as a way to escape into the past, there is less opportunity for Rose to escape the pressures and responsibilities of life. The role women play in *Fences* is limited by the time period in which the play is set. In the 1950s, women were restrained by traditional roles and the division of private and public spheres. Men functioned in the public sphere; they left the home to go to jobs. In contrast, women primarily functioned in the private sphere of home and domestic chores. When Rose is confronted with Troy's infidelity, she may choose to remain in the marriage, but that choice does not signify that she is accepting or helpless. During her marriage, Rose has allowed Troy to fill her life. She tells Troy, "I took all my feelings, my wants and needs, my dreams . . . and I buried them inside you."

But Troy's betrayal forces Rose to reassess her position, according to Harry Elam in *May All Your Fences Have Gates*. This reassessment, noted Elam, means new avenues of freedom that "affirm rather than assault traditional gender limitations." Rose substitutes her church for her husband. When, at the end of the seventh inning/scene, Rose tells Troy that "this child got a mother. But you a womanless man," she is asserting her independence from her husband. Elam quoted Patricia Collins's argument that black women learn independence at church, but they also learn to subordinate their interests to the greater good of the African American community.

Rose has chosen to take the subservient role in marriage. She admits her complicity, but the audience is reminded that her options were few. Yet she is not an oppressed woman, and when Rose takes the infant Raynell and speaks the lines that end this scene, Elam noted that "the audience, particularly black female spectators, erupted with cheers and applause." Clearly, Rose is perceived by black women as a strong female character and not an oppressed figure. As Sandra Shannon noted in an essay in *May All Your Fences Have Gates,* Rose "evolves from a long-suffering heroine to a fiercely independent woman." This evolution is what audiences are cheering.

With *Fences,* Wilson created a play that explores the barriers that confine blacks. The title serves as a metaphor for all the fences that imprison

"BASEBALL DEFINES TROY MAXSON'S LIFE AND PROVIDES THE MEASURE OF HIS SUCCESS."

the Maxsons. The fence that surrounds the Maxson home is not the white picket fence of the 1950s American ideal. Their fence is not decor and it is not an enhancement—its purpose is strictly utilitarian. At the beginning of the play, Troy thinks he is building a fence to please Rose. She wants a fence that will keep all those she loves safe inside its walls. Later, after Alberta's death, Troy completes the fence to keep danger, death, outside its walls.

For most of the play's action, though, Troy is in no hurry to complete Rose's fence, after all, he has spent time in prison with fences limiting his movements. And when he played baseball, he was never content to just hit a home run into the stands; he felt that he had to transcend the boundaries of the stadium and hit a ball over the fence. For Troy, fences have been a restriction, and he's in no hurry to build another. Yet there are many fences that lie in Troy's way that he cannot control or hit a ball over. The mental hospital where Troy confines Gabriel provides one such fence, while another kind of fence—one between the living and the dead—is erected when Alberta dies. It is this latter enclosure that finally creates a sense of urgency in Troy.

The fence Troy completes, however, will fail to keep Cory inside. Although Troy has attempted to confine Cory within his authority, his son does escape. Yet when he returns, the audience learns that Cory is now bound within the confines of a far more strict institution, the military. Cory has escaped from his father's authority only to end up bound in the rule of the Marine Corps. With the Vietnam War looming only a few years away, the boundary created by the military is an especially dangerous one for black males.

The fences that would keep Cory from reaching his goals is not unlike the fences that limit Rose. In the last scenes of the play when Rose finally asserts herself, she is really only exchanging Troy's fence for the one offered by the church. Religion provides its own fences and limitations, and for Rose, who chooses not to break free of the institution of marriage, the church offers a haven within its institutionalized walls. Even Gabriel who is allowed a temporary escape from the mental hospital, ends the play with an effort to create an opening in the fence so that Troy might enter heaven. But for blacks, the most difficult fence to scale, the one that restricts their achievements, the one that steals opportunities, is the fence that whites erect to keep blacks in a place away from mainstream success. This is the fence that Wilson wants his audience to see. This is the fence against which blacks are forced to struggle.

In an interview that appeared in *In Their Own Words: Contemporary American Playwrights,* Wilson said that by the end of *Fences,* every character had been institutionalized, except Raynell; she is the hope of the future. Raynell stands within the confines of the fence that surrounds the yard, but the audience leaves with the perception that she will go beyond that barrier to achieve a better future than her father.

Source: Sheri Metzger for *Drama for Students,* Gale, 1998.

Richard Hornby

In this review, Hornby gives a positive appraisal of Wilson's work, deeming both the text and the production to be exemplary.

August Wilson's *Fences* deals with a black family living in ''a North American industrial city'' in the late 1950s. The father, Troy Maxson, is a former star baseball player of the Negro leagues who was too old to get into the majors when they at last opened up to blacks after World War II. He resents the false promise that sports held for him, and blocks his own son's promising career as a football player.

Troy's life has been filled with disappointment, oppression, and just plain bad luck: Raised in the South in billet poverty, he today cannot even read. As a youth, he served time in the penitentiary as result of a stabbing in a robbery he committed simply to get food. His brother received a head injury in the war that reduced him to a mental child, with only Troy to care for him. Troy holds down a job as a garbage collector, prevented by the color of his skin from getting promoted to driver. All these problems are ''fences'' that have held him in all his life.

Nevertheless, this is not a bitter play, but a warm and often comic view of black life in America. Troy has a wonderful, loving wife, and a strong friendship with his longtime co-worker, Jim Bono. Troy's relationships with his son, with another son by a previous marriage, and with his retarded brother Gabriel, are not always harmonious, but are always based on deep and genuine feeling.

All the action of the play, in nine scenes spread over eight years, takes place in the Maxsons' back yard. Many of the scenes appear on the surface to be mere slices of life, with nothing much happening, yet, like Chekhov, Wilson always keeps the plot subtly moving forward. Troy jokes and tells stories, rails against the ballplayers of the day—Jackie Robinson is just lucky, there were black teams he could not even have made in the old days!—banters with his wife, argues with his sons and brother, and procrastinates over repairing the back fence, the visible manifestation of the symbol that unifies the play. As with Chekhov, major events take place offstage: we hear how Troy eventually gets a promotion by going to his union, and how he drifts into an affair with a young woman (never seen) that nearly wrecks his marriage, and leaves him and his wife with another child to raise when the woman dies in childbirth.

The rift between Troy and his son widens; blocked from going to college on a football scholarship, and disgusted with his father's infidelity, the boy confronts Troy in the only overtly physical scene in the play. In this classic father-son *agon,* each has an opportunity to kill the other, but draws back. Tragedy averted, the son goes off to join the Marines, returning only for his father's funeral years later, confronting the many fences that have figured in their lives—''fences to keep people out, and fences to keep people in.''

James Earl Jones was superb in the lead role. He still has the physical strength and agility he had twenty years ago in *The Great White Hope,* and although, like the character he played in *Fences,* he shows his age, he also convinced you of his underlying athletic ability, which is so important to the role. When Troy insisted that he ''can hit forty-three home runs right now!'', Jones made you believe it. He also skillfully used his well-known, resonant voice with wide variations and contrasts, giving a rich, musical quality to the many stories—the play is full of long, set speeches—which were also enhanced by his ability for both physical and vocal mimicry, as he imitated the many real and imaginary characters he described. Jones is a wonderfully *precise* actor; the performance was full of telling detail, such as the way he would swig at a bottle of gin he was sharing with his friends, managing a big, fast swallow while fastidiously keeping the bottle from touching his lips. The role won him a Tony Award for the best performance of the year on Broadway, and one should add that he was lucky, these days, to have a role worthy of his talents to perform there.

Jones was supported by an excellent cast, especially Mary Alice, who brought ease, charm, and poignancy to the role of his wife, and Frankie R. Faison, who turned the tricky role of the retarded brother—which could easily have degenerated into something sentimental or, on the other hand, disgustingly clinical—into a performance that was deft and lyrical. Lloyd Richards directed with his usual skill and clarity, while James D. Sandefur designed the naturalistic yet evocative setting. The only flaw here was that, perhaps because it was in the inappropriate 46th Street Theatre, sightlines required the setting to be placed far downstage, which limited much of the blocking to one dimension.

Fences won the Pulitzer Prize for Drama, which it well deserved. Some of its excellence, however, derives from its being part of a whole school of contemporary black playwriting, by authors such as Lonne Elder III, Charles H. Fuller, Jr., and Leslie Lee. Many of their plays are better than anything written by fashionable white playwrights like Sam Shepard, David Mamet, or David Rabe, yet they have received less attention and are less likely to appear in anthologies or college courses in contemporary American drama. Influenced by Ibsen and Chekhov, they realistically depict life in black America with understatement, humor, and sadness. They also show the influence of jazz, especially the blues, whose lyrics combine comedy and pathos in giving voice to the problems of ordinary black people. The intense personal relationships that are the glory of black life are made vivid for all of us.

Source: Richard Hornby, review of *Fences* in the *Hudson Review,* Volume XL, no. 3, Autumn, 1987, pp. 470–72.

Gerald Weales

Weales reviews Fences, *commenting on the advances that Wilson has made since his previous play* Ma Rainey's Black Bottom. *Weales offers a positive review of the play.*

At the end of August Wilson's *Fences,* the Maxsons gather for the funeral of Troy, who has dominated the family and the play. His "mixed-up" brother Gabe, who had "half his head blown away" in World War II and who believes that he has been to heaven, unlimbers the trumpet he always carries "to tell St. Peter to open the gates." There is no mouthpiece, no trumpet blast. After three increasingly desperate tries, Gabe howls in anguish and frustration. Light pours across the scene. "That's the way that go!" he says, smiling his satisfaction.

"*FENCES* IS NOT A BITTER PLAY, BUT A WARM AND OFTEN COMIC VIEW OF BLACK LIFE IN AMERICA."

That's not really the way that go, meaning the play as a whole, but the effectiveness of the final scene is a reminder that Wilson stretches the limits of the realistic form his play takes (as he mixed songs and dramatic scenes in *Ma Rainey's Black Bottom*) and that the verisimilitude of his language cannot disguise the lyric qualities in his work. For the most part, *Fences* is a family play in an old American tradition—*Awake and Sing!, Death of a Salesman, A Raisin in the Sun*—in which the conflicts within the family are given definition by the social forces outside. Set in "a Northern American industrial city" (i.e., Wilson's Pittsburgh) in 1957, it uses the metaphor of the fence which Troy builds around his backyard as title to a play about the fences between husband and wife, father and son, black and white.

Troy Maxson is a black man in his early fifties, at once an authority figure and a garrulous, playful nice guy. James Earl Jones, in one of his best roles, joins the playwright in making Troy both attractive and threatening. Although he has the strength to buck the system, to get himself promoted from garbageman to driver, he sees the world in terms of his own past. He has become a variation on the tyrant father he ran away to escape. He has come to believe that a black man's only choice is between jail, where he spent some youthful years, and a steady job; he cannot see that there might be other possibilities in the 1950s, roads that were not open thirty years earlier.

A central prop in *Fences* is the baseball that hangs on a rope from the tree in the yard. Troy's device for batting practice, it is a constant reminder for him and for us of his greatest triumph and his greatest disappointment. Having learned to play

"FOR THE MOST PART, *FENCES* IS A FAMILY PLAY IN AN OLD AMERICAN TRADITION, IN WHICH THE CONFLICTS WITHIN THE FAMILY ARE GIVEN DEFINITION BY THE SOCIAL FORCES OUTSIDE."

baseball in prison, he went on to become a star in the Negro League but, despite his talent, the color line kept him out of the majors. Whether out of jealousy or to protect the young man, Troy refuses to sign the papers that would let his son go to college on a football scholarship, a destructive act that leads to a final confrontation between the two and a reenactment of the father-son conflict that sent Troy off on his own. He uses his sense of ownership and control (my house, my yard) not only to stifle his son's ambitions but to misuse his brother, whose disability payments bought the house, and his wife, whom he loves but to whom he brings the child of another woman. Sitting in the audience, one could sense who was on what side of which fence by the applause that accompanied the son's defiance and the wife's revolt, her acceptance of the child and rejection of Troy as husband. Troy fills the last scene even in his absence, and when his son, now a sergeant in the Marines, joins his half-sister in singing Troy's song about Blue that ''good old dog,'' acceptance of and forgiveness for what Troy and his world had made of him prepare the way for Gabe's bringing the light. What remains is Troy's strength, his sense of duty, and his odd vulnerability. ''That's the way that go!''

Source: Gerald Weales, review of *Fences* in the *Commonweal,* Volume CXIV, no. 10, May 22, 1987, pp. 320–21.

SOURCES

Barnes, Clive. ''Fiery 'Fences''' in the *New York Post,* March 27, 1987.

Birdwell, Christine. ''Death as a Fastball on the Outside Corner: *Fences*'s Troy Maxson and the American Dream'' in *Aethlon: The Journal of Sport Literature,* Vol. 8, no. 1, Fall, 1990, pp. 87-96.

Ching, Mei-Ling. ''Wrestling against History'' in *Theater,* Vol. 19, no. 3, Summer-Fall, 1988, pp. 70-71.

DeVries, Hilary. ''A Song in Search of Itself'' in *American Theatre,* Vol. 3, no. 10, January, 1987, pp. 22-25.

Elam, Harry J., Jr. ''Of Angels and Transcendence: An Analysis of *Fences* by August Wilson and *Roosters* by Milcha Sanchez-Scott'' in *Staging Difference: Cultural Pluralism in American Theatre and Drama,* edited by Marc Manfort, Peter Lang (New York), 1995, pp. 287-300.

Henderson, Heather. ''Building *Fences:* An Interview with Mary Alice and James Earl Jones'' in *Theater,* Vol. 16, no. 3, Summer-Fall, 1985, pp. 67-70.

Pereira, Kim. ''August Wilson'' in *Reference Guide to American Literature,* edited by Jim Kamp, third edition, St. James Press, 1994, pp. 919-21.

Shafer, Yvonne. ''Breaking Barriers: August Wilson'' in *Staging Difference: Cultural Pluralism in American Theatre and Drama,* edited by Marc Manfort, Peter Lang, 1995. pp. 267-85.

Wallach, Allan. ''Fenced in by a Lifetime of Resentments'' in *Newsday,* March 27, 1987.

Wilson, Edwin. ''Wilson's 'Fences' on Broadway'' in the *Wall Street Journal,* March 31, 1987.

FURTHER READING

Chalk, Ocania. *Pioneers in Black Sport,* Dodd, Mead (New York), 1975.

Chalk provides a detailed discussion of the complicated issue of integration in professional sports.

Elam, Harry J. ''August Wilson's Women'' in *May All Your Fences Have Gates,* University of Iowa Press, 1994.

Elam is a Professor of Drama at Stanford University. This essay is an examination of the role of women in Wilson's dramas.

Elkins, Marilyn. *August Wilson: A Casebook,* Garland (New York), 1994.

This narrow volume is a collection of essays that discuss Wilson's work within the context of historical and cultural influences.

Holway, John. *Voices from the Great Black Baseball Leagues,* Dodd, Mead, 1975.

This is a scholarly investigation of the Negro Leagues based on player interviews and an examination of sports reportage.

In Their Own Words: Contemporary American Playwrights, Theatre Communications Group, 1988.

This essay is the transcript of a March 1987 interview with Wilson in which he discusses several of his plays.

Nadel, Alan. *Essays on the Drama of August Wilson,* University of Iowa Press (Iowa City), 1994

This is a collection of essays on Wilson's dramatic work. There is also a comprehensive bibliography included.

Paige, Leroy "Satchel." *Maybe I'll Pitch Forever,* Doubleday, 1962.
Perhaps the best-known player from the Negro baseball leagues, Satchel Paige is considered to be one of the finest players to engage the game of baseball. This book is an autobiographical look at his career in the Negro Leagues.

Rogosin, Donn. *Invisible Men: Life in Baseball's Negro Leagues,* Atheneum (New York), 1983.
This book offers an overview of the social issues that led to the end of the great Negro Leagues.

Ruck, Rob. *Sandlot Seasons: Sport in Black Pittsburgh,* University of Illinois Press (Urbana), 1987.
This nonfiction text probes the history of sports in Pittsburgh, the city of Wilson's youth and the model for the urban setting of *Fences.*

Shannon, Sandra G. "The Ground on Which I Stand" in *May All Your Fences Have Gates,* University of Iowa Press, 1994.
Shannon is an Associate Professor of English at Howard University. Her essay examines the role of African American women in Wilson's dramas.

The Homecoming

HAROLD PINTER

1965

The Homecoming, now considered by many critics to be Harold Pinter's masterpiece, was not universally admired when it was first produced in England by the Royal Shakespeare Company at London's Aldwych Theatre, on June 3, 1965. Many critics, while praising the production directed by Peter Hall, found the play itself to be baffling and enigmatic in the extreme. Harold Hobson, critic for the *Sunday Times* and an early proponent of Pinter's, predicted that the play would ''suffer in the estimation of audiences who will perceive an aesthetic defect that does not exist, in the place of a moral vacuum that does.'' Despite numerous viewer reactions that verified Hobson's forecast, *The Homecoming* had a long run to packed houses in London before moving to the United States.

The Broadway opening of *The Homecoming* on January 3, 1967, at the Music Box Theatre was greeted with great excitement. Repeating its London success, the production had a long run in spite of some negative reviews, the most notable by Walter Kerr of the *New York Times.* In March *The Homecoming* won the Antionette (''Tony'') Perry Award as best play on Broadway and in May it was voted best new play on Broadway by the New York Drama Critics' Circle. It also received the Whitbread Anglo-American award for the best British play of the year. This sensational success established Pinter's reputation in New York, opening the door to widespread production of his subsequent work.

While baffled by the fact that the startling action of the play seemed to lack any *rational* explanations, both critics and audiences responded to Pinter's gift for dramatic suspense and sharp, biting comedy. *The Homecoming* does in fact deal with many themes, such as emotional impotence, Oedipal desires, personal loneliness and isolation, appearance and reality, and familial power struggles, to mention a few; and, audiences and critics alike sensed that there is a great deal more going on in the play than can be easily articulated. As John Russell Taylor put it in *Plays and Players* magazine, "The secret of the play does not lie in our providing a neat crossword-puzzle solution." Despite—and perhaps because of—the play's ambiguity, *The Homecoming* has remained a centerpiece in Pinter's canon. New productions of the play are frequent as actors, directors, and audiences attempt new interpretations of Pinter's work.

AUTHOR BIOGRAPHY

Harold Pinter was born in the northern borough of Hackney, a working-class section in London, England, on October 10, 1930. Pinter's father, Hyman (Jack) was a hard-working tailor of women's apparel and his mother, Frances, a homemaker. The Pinter family was part of the immigrant wave of Jews that arrived in London around the turn of the century. Pinter's forebears came from Poland and Odessa and brought with them a love of culture and learning. At the outbreak of World War II in 1939, Pinter was evacuated to a castle in Cornwall for a year where, away from his loving home for the first time, he suffered loneliness, bewilderment, separation, and loss—themes that recur in all his works. He also discovered just how sly and nasty a group of boys isolated from their families could be. Back in Hackney, where he spent most of the war years, he was constantly made aware of the impermanence of life.

Pinter attended Hackney Downs Grammar School from 1944 to 1948, where his talents were inspired by Joe Brearley, an English teacher. Pinter wrote for the school magazine and discovered a flair for acting in school productions. He also was one of a group who called themselves "The Boys," a sort of gang tied together by their common love for intellectual adventure. Along with other boyish pursuits, the group would often gather and argue about literature. Although the Boys were not immune from the desire for domination and the clashes brought about by sexual competition, many remained friends throughout their adult lives.

On leaving school, Pinter received a grant to study acting at the Royal Academy of Dramatic Art, but he soon became disenchanted with the academic process and left after two terms. In 1948 he was called up for national military service and declared himself a conscientious objector, a status that was denied him. He was tried and expected to go to prison but instead was fined thirty pounds by a sympathetic magistrate and released. In 1951 he resumed his acting education at the Central School of Speech and Drama. He then spent eighteen months touring Ireland with the theatrical company of Anew McMaster followed by the 1953 London season with the company of Donald Wolfit. Following this activity, he took on the stage name David Baron and began acting in provincial repertory theatres. During this acting stint, Pinter met actress Vivian Merchant, with whom he often worked. The couple were married in 1956.

On May 9, 1957, one of the Hackney "Boys," Henry Woolfe, asked Pinter to write a play to be produced six days later at Bristol University. Pinter, writing in the afternoons between morning rehearsals and evening performances, completed his first play, *The Room,* in four days. The production was a success and was subsequently entered in the *Sunday Times* student drama festival several months later. Harold Hobson, an influential drama critic for the paper, was so taken with the play that he wrote a highly favorable review.

Hobson's accolade brought Pinter to the attention of Michael Codron, a young London producer, who asked the young actor if he had any other works he'd like to see produced. Pinter sent Codron *The Birthday Party* and *The Dumb Waiter.* The producer staged the former, which opened on April 28, 1958, to generally unfavorable reviews. Hobson, however, reviewed the play in the *Sunday Times* four days after opening night, stating that, based on the evidence of this play, "Mr. Pinter possesses the most original, disturbing, and arresting talent in theatrical London." Despite such strong praise, it was too late to save that production of *The Birthday Party* and the show soon closed. *The Dumb Waiter* later had its first English production, coupled with *The Room,* at the Hampstead Theatre Club in 1960.

By the late 1950s, Pinter was becoming a playwright in increasing demand. The British Broadcasting Corporation (BBC) commissioned Pinter to write a radio drama, a piece he called *Something in Common,* which was not produced. The BBC then commissioned another sixty-minute play, *A Slight Ache* (1959), the first of Pinter's many (produced) plays written for radio or television. Also in 1959, Pinter wrote a series of comic sketches that were included in popular revues. In 1960, Pinter had his first major theatrical success with *The Caretaker.* Pinter, now recognized as an important writer, worked prolifically on his dramas, producing such works as *Night School* (1960), *The Dwarfs* (1960), *The Collection* (1961), *The Lover* (1963), *The Tea Party* (1965), and *The Basement* (1967). He also began working in the medium of film, writing the screenplays for *The Servant* (1963) and *The Pumpkin Eater* (1964), which both received major awards.

The Homecoming, Pinter's third full-length play, was first produced at the New Theatre in Cardiff, Wales, in 1965. Under the auspices of the Royal Shakespeare Company, it moved to the Aldwych Theatre in London later that year. In 1967 the production made its American debut on Broadway at the Music Box Theatre. The play became a sensational success and established Pinter as a significant dramatist in the United States.

Throughout the 1960s, 70s, 80s, and 90s, Pinter has continued to flourish in theatre as a playwright, director (of both his own works and those by other playwrights), and occasionally as an actor. He also continues to write for films, including *The Last Tycoon, The French Lieutenant's Woman* (adapted from the book by John Fowles), and *Turtle Diary,* as well as adaptations of his own plays (including *The Birthday Party, Betrayal,* and *The Homecoming*).

Pinter and Merchant had one child, a son named Daniel, before divorcing in 1980. He remarried later that year, taking the writer Lady Antonia Fraser as his wife. Pinter's work has spanned five decades, and he remains one of the worlds most respected and widely produced playwrights.

PLOT SUMMARY

The Homecoming is set in a large room in an old house in working-class North London. This is the home of Max, a retired butcher; Sam, his brother, who drives for a car-hire (cab) service; and two of Max's sons: Lenny, a successful pimp, and Joey, a dullard who works on a demolition crew during the day while trying to become a professional boxer.

Act I , scene 1

The play opens with Lenny reading the newspaper. Max enters looking for scissors and is ignored by Lenny. Max talks about his late wife Jessie and his late friend MacGregor. He speaks of Jessie with both fondness and shocking disapproval: "She wasn't such a bad woman. Even though it made me sick just to look at her rotten stinking face, she wasn't such a bad bitch." Max also talks of his special understanding of horses. Lenny tells Max to shut up and then says that Max's cooking is fit only for dogs. Sam enters and Max insults him about his driving and the fact that he is not married. Joey enters from a workout at the gym, and Max turns on him, saying that his trouble as a boxer is that he doesn't know how to attack or defend himself. Max also threatens to throw Sam out when he is too old to pay his way. Sam pointedly reminds Max that Mac and Jessie were very close friends. The scene ends in blackout.

Act I, scene 2

The next scene, a few hours later, opens with Teddy and Ruth standing at the threshold to the room. Teddy is Max's eldest son, a Ph.D. who teaches philosophy at an American university. Ruth is his wife of six years about whom the rest of the family know nothing. They have been on a trip to Europe, and Teddy has brought her to meet the family. Ruth, though at first claiming to be tired, decides to go out for a walk. After Ruth leaves, Lenny enters. The reunion between the two brothers is civil but without any sense of warmth. Teddy goes to bed and Lenny goes and gets a clock that he suspects of disturbing his sleep.

Ruth enters and after some surprising small talk, says that she is Teddy's wife. Lenny pays no attention to that. He launches into a long story which ends with his beating up a whore, whom he would have killed except for the bother of getting rid of the body. He then tells another long story that ends with his beating up an old woman, Whether true or not, these tales are obviously meant to intimidate Ruth. They do not. There follows a wonderfully theatrical power play with Ruth dominating Lenny by using a glass of water to taunt him with sexual favors. Ruth goes to bed leaving Lenny alone. Max enters and Lenny turns on him asking about the night he was conceived. Max spits at him and says he will drown in his own blood.

Act I, scene 3

The next scene opens at six-thirty the next morning. Joey is working out. Max enters complaining that Sam is in his kitchen. He calls Sam into the room and belittles him. Teddy and Ruth enter, and Max calls Ruth a "smelly scruffer," a "stinking pox-ridden slut," and says that there hasn't been a whore in the house since Jessie died. Ruth seems to be unfazed by this verbal abuse. Joey apologizes for Max, saying he is an old man. Max hits Joey in the stomach with all his might. Joey staggers across the room, and Max begins to collapse with the exertion; Sam tries to help Max, and Max hits him in the head with his cane. Max then asks Ruth if she is a mother, seems pleased when she says she has three boys, and asks Teddy for a cuddle. Teddy accepts.

Act II, scene 1

It is just after dinner on the same day. Ruth serves coffee, and the men smoke cigars. Max praises Ruth and tells her that Jessie was the backbone of the family, that she taught the boys "all the morality they know . . . every single bit of the moral code they live by." Max then berates Sam and complains that he has worked hard all his life to support his brother and his own family—"three bastard sons, a slutbitch of a wife"—and even claims to have suffered the pains of childbirth. After further abusing Sam, Max turns to Teddy and gives his marriage his blessing, saying that Ruth is a charming woman. Sam leaves.

Lenny tries to engage Teddy in philosophical speculation about a table. Teddy refuses to be drawn in. Ruth points out that when she moves her leg her underwear moves with her and that perhaps the fact that her lips move is more important than the words which come through them. After a silence Joey, Max, and Lenny leave to go to the gym. Teddy suggests to Ruth that it is time to return home to America. Ruth seems uninterested. Teddy goes to pack. Lenny enters, and he and Ruth talk about the weather. Then Ruth says that before she went to America she had been a "model for the body," and she seems to have a longing for that life again. Teddy enters.

Lenny and Ruth dance slowly and kiss. Max and Joey enter and Joey delightfully says Ruth is a tart. He grabs her and starts to make love to her on the sofa. Max makes small talk with Teddy and praises Ruth in extremely sentimental terms. Ruth suddenly pushes Joey away, stands up, and demands a drink. She further demands food, that the record be turned off, and that she be given a particular kind of glass. She then asks if the family have read Teddy's critical works. Teddy says that they wouldn't understand them.

Harold Pinter in New York, 1967, the year The Homecoming *won the Tony Award for best drama*

Act II, scene 2

The following scene takes place that evening and opens with Teddy in his coat sitting dejectedly with his suitcases beside him. Sam asks if Teddy remembers MacGregor and says that Teddy was always his mother's favorite. When Lenny enters,

Sam leaves. Lenny accuses Teddy of stealing his sandwich and is outraged when Teddy admits that he did. Joey enters: he has been in his room with Ruth for two hours but he didn't get "all the way." Max and Sam enter and Max demands, "Where's the whore?" Max commiserates with Joey and says that it might be good to have Ruth stay with them. Teddy says that she should go home to her children. The problem of supporting Ruth is discussed, and Lenny suggests that she could pay her own way by working as a whore. Max, Joey, and Lenny agree that this is a good idea.

When Ruth enters, Teddy explains what the family has in mind. Ruth says, "How very nice of them." Her demands, however, are very specific: a flat with three rooms and a bath, a maid, complete wardrobe, and that the original outlay must be viewed as a capital investment. She demands a contract to be signed before witnesses. All is agreed to. Sam then bursts out with the information that MacGregor had Jessie in the back of Sam's cab as he drove them along. He collapses. No one helps him. Teddy complains that he had counted on Sam to drive him to the airport and leaves to find a cab. Ruth sits in Max's chair, Joey sits on the floor and puts his head in her lap. Max complains that he will be left out, that she thinks he is an old man, and he collapses. As Max crawls toward Ruth, asking her for a kiss, Lenny sullenly stands watching.

CHARACTERS

Jessie

Jessie is Max's late wife and the mother of Teddy, Lenny, and Joey. Though she never appears in the play, she is mentioned frequently and her presence is felt throughout. She is praised by Max in saintly terms as being "the backbone of the family" and also condemned by him as a "slutbitch." She had a close relationship with Max's friend MacGregor.

Joey

Joey is a rather stupid man in his mid-twenties and the youngest of the three sons. He wants to be a professional boxer and to that end works out in a gym. His regular job is as a demolition laborer. Joey is delighted when he sees Ruth and Lenny dancing and kissing and immediately takes Ruth to the sofa where he begins to "make love" to her. Later, he spends two hours with Ruth alone in his room but does not "get all the way," and he seems content with that. At the end of the play, Joey sits at Ruth's feet like a child, with her stroking his head like a pet.

Lenny

Lenny is in his early thirties and is the second son. He is a successful pimp with a string of prostitutes. Lenny is the first of the sons introduced in the play, and he seems to dominate the household with a cold, quick wit. He is also the first of the family to meet Ruth, and he immediately attempts to dominate her. He tells two long stories, one about being propositioned by a prostitute by the harbor front and the other about going to help an old lady; both end with his beating the women. Ironically, Lenny seems to be sexually as well as emotionally impotent; Ruth almost instinctively recognizes this and turns it against him. Lenny later suggests setting up Ruth as a prostitute so she can pay her own way while "staying with the family." At the end of the play, Lenny is standing to one side as Joey sits at Ruth's feet and Max crawls towards her begging for a kiss.

Mac

See MacGregor

MacGregor

MacGregor, now dead, was a ruffian friend of Max. Together they were "two of the worst hated men in the West End." Like Jessie, he never appears in the play but is often referred to and figures prominently in Max's memory. Metaphorically, MacGregor's ghost haunts Max because of Mac's "close relationship" with Max's wife Jessie.

Max

Max is the seventy-year-old father of the household. He is a shrewd, crude, brutish retired butcher. He attempts to maintain household dominance with threats and the evidence of his past as a hard-working man who supported his wife and sons. He also invokes his past reputation as a violent thug who was feared by everyone. His initial confrontation with Lenny at the beginning of the play ends with the father backing down from his threats. He later physically assaults both his son Joey and his brother Sam. Although he is viciously insulting upon first meeting Ruth, calling her a "smelly scrubber" and a "pox-ridden slut," he later speaks of her in sentimentally glowing terms. He is astute enough to recognize, near the end of the play, that it is Ruth who will ''make use of us,'' rather than the other way around.

Ruth

Ruth is Teddy's wife and the mother of their three boys. She is the agent for change in the power struggle of the all-male household. Her marriage is apparently rocky at best. When she first appears in the second scene of the play, she immediately displays her independence. She uses semantic quibbles to undermine her husband's authority. It is nearly midnight and although she says she is tired and asks if she can sit, when Teddy tells her to sit she refuses to do so. When he suggests they go to bed she decides to go for a walk. Throughout the play she is able to take control from each of the men, beginning with a wonderfully understated theatrical scene with Lenny. She charms Sam and uses sex to dominate Joey. When the family suggests that she stay with them and help pay her way by spending a couple of hours a night in a West End flat, she knows immediately what they are proposing. She treats the offer purely as a business proposition and proves a tough negotiator. The men agree to all of her demands, and she agrees that it is a very attractive idea. At the end of the play she has chosen to stay with the family.

Sam

Sam is Max's brother and co-owner of the house. He works as a chauffeur for a car rental service. Sam is the only one who does not attempt to control Ruth. He seems to be a gentle, sensitive, and even gallant man. He is gracious with Ruth, and he tries to console Teddy by telling him that he was always his mother's favorite. There are many indications that he is not interested in sex at all, something that is used against him by Max. However, Sam has survived in this household; in his own quiet way, he is tough. Near the end of the play he attempts to undermine Max by blurting out what everyone has always suspected, that MacGregor had Jessie in the back seat of his cab and thus may be the father of at least one of the boys.

Teddy

Teddy, in his mid-thirties and the eldest son, is a Ph.D. who teaches philosophy at a university in America. He married Ruth just before leaving for America six years before the play begins. He has never told his family he was married, and, as the play begins, he is bringing Ruth home to meet them for the first time. It is soon obvious that the marriage is a dry and loveless one. Teddy is able to see what is happening in the dynamics between Ruth and the men of his family, but he is either unable or unwilling to put a stop to it. He has narrowed his intellectual focus in order to objectify others in an apparent attempt to avoid emotional involvement and thus to protect himself from pain. He says that he can see what others do, that it is the same things that he does, but that he won't be involved in it. He relates the family's proposition to Ruth and does not try to dissuade her when she accepts it. He says that he and their boys can manage until she comes back to America.

MEDIA ADAPTATIONS

- *The Homecoming* was made into a film in 1973 for the American Film Theatre production series. It was directed by Sir Peter Hall and featured the original Royal Shakespeare Company cast: Vivian Merchant as Ruth, Michael Jayston as Teddy, Paul Rogers as Max, Cyril Cusack as Sam, Ian Holm as Lenny, and Terrence Rigby as Joey.

THEMES

Alienation and Loneliness

A family lives in the same house and though they live side-by-side physically, their emotional alienation and consequent loneliness is palpable. Perhaps the most alienated of all the characters are Teddy and Ruth. They seem to have *chosen* to remain emotionally separate from the others. Teddy very clearly states this when talking about his ''critical works.'' He says that it is a question of how far one can operate *on* things and not *in* things. He has chosen not to be emotionally involved with anyone and apparently has chosen to specialize in a very arcane branch of philosophy in order to maintain what he calls his ''intellectual equilibrium''; more likely this field allows him to work with little contact with others. Teddy says his relatives are just

TOPICS FOR FURTHER STUDY

- Pinter believes that social violence is due to resentment. Research the break-up of the former Yugoslavia (Bosnia-Herzegovina), or other areas of late–twentieth century civil strife (such as Rwanda). Consider what part long–standing resentments played in the events. Compare them to the personal strife that occurs in Pinter's play.
- Research the feminist movement of the 1960s and after. Does Ruth answer the feminist definition of a free woman? Or is she a man's (Pinter's) idea of a free woman?
- "Subtext" is usually defined as "the action beneath the words," or as "the words *not* spoken." In *The Homecoming,* compare what is being talked about, *how* it is being talked about, and the subtext in the first scene of Act II.
- There are many instances of events that are remembered in *The Homecoming,* such as Ruth's memories of her past profession as a model, Lenny's memories of meeting a woman down by the docks, and Max's memories of Jessie. How accurately do you think these memories reflect the past and how are they used to affect the current situation?
- Ruth in *The Homecoming* and Kate in *Old Times* both end up in control of their situations. Compare and contrast how they achieve these positions of power. What part does "selective memory" play in these power struggles?

---

objects and, "You just . . . move about. I can observe it. I can see what you do. It's the same as I do. But you're lost in it. You won't get me being. . . . I won't be lost in it." Teddy displays a near complete apathy to the events that unfold during his visit. Despite losing his wife to his father and brothers (not to mention a life of prostitution), despite watching his uncle collapse in front of him, he remains passionless and isolated from an emotional tie to these events.

Ruth also chooses to treat others as "objects" to be controlled. She agrees to work as a prostitute, which by nature requires a lack of emotional involvement, and at the same time she agrees to "take on" the men of the family. She shows no hesitation or sense of loss when she chooses not to return to her three sons and her home in America. She even calls Teddy "Eddy" when telling him not to become a stranger as he leaves for America.

Anger and Hatred

Anger abounds in *The Homecoming.* The play opens with Max looking for scissors and Lenny ignoring him. Lenny then responds with, "Why don't you shut up, you daft prat?" Throughout the first scene, as the family of men are introduced, anger and hatred seem to be the main traits of their relationships and their preferred modes of conduct. Lenny calls Max a "stupid sod," and Max responds with, "Listen! I'll chop your spine off, you talk to me like that!" Even when talking about the past, Max recalls that he and his late friend Mac (MacGregor) were two of the "worst hated men in the West End"; even something like nostalgia, which is typically happy and fond, is tainted with loathing.

None of the relationships in the play are warm and caring. When Max's brother Sam comes home from work, Max taunts him, and the seemingly gentle Sam retorts with innuendoes about Max's late wife Jessie and his friend Mac—a sore spot that has obviously been picked at many times before. In fact, the smoldering anger over the suspicion of what took place between Jessie and Mac is a weapon often used against Max by both Sam and Lenny. When Joey, Max's dullard younger son, returns home from the gym, Max turns on him and belittles his dreams of becoming a professional boxer. Joey is too slow witted to respond and simply retreats from the room. The attempt to escape from this seething anger and vicious attacks was probably what drove Teddy to retreat into a narrow intellectual discipline, to marry without telling his family, and to move to America.

Appearance and Reality

Although there are flare ups of anger and even violence, most of the brutality in *The Homecoming* is covered with a seemingly sophisticated veneer. When the actual physical violence does erupt, it seems comic. Lenny's stories about the tart down by the harbor and the old woman that he beat up are told in an almost off-hand way. The violence is contained in the subtext, the threat of violence to Ruth or any woman for whom Lenny takes a disliking. Ruth also behaves with outward decorum which belies her inner fire and sexuality.

Act II starts out with the whole family having after-dinner coffee and cigars. They exchange pleasantries about the meal, the coffee, and family chat about how proud Jessie would be of her fine sons and how much she would like to see her grandchildren. It seems to be a warm family gathering. Seething beneath the surface, however, is a violent dominance game in which there is a constant fight for control of the family. One of the rules of the family seems to be that when a blow is delivered the one who is attacked must not show his hurt. Even after Ruth has decided to stay and become a prostitute, Teddy's leave taking is comically conventional. He tells Max how good it has been to see him, there is advice on how best to get to the airport, and Max gives him a picture of himself to show the grandchildren. This surface conventionality helps to make the emotionally violent reality stand out as even more grotesque.

Doubt and Ambiguity

Pinter's plays are filled with ambiguity. He does not spell things out clearly and the viewer must often construct the past out of small hints, which may or may not be true. Lenny's stories about beating up women may be true or he may be lying to bolster his image as a tough pimp. It isn't revealed where in America Teddy teaches or if he truly does have teaching post. It isn't clear what Ruth means when she tells Lenny she had been a ''model for the body.'' There's further doubt regarding Sam's sexuality, Joey's boxing career, and Max's younger days (though it is revealed that he and Mac were something of a fearsome pair).

Perhaps most striking is the dichotomy in Mac's recollections of his wife, Jessie (he refers to her as both a ''slutbitch'' and as a warm, giving mother and wife). It is unclear which of his recollections best summarized his wife—or if they are both accurate. When Sam says that he knows that Mac and Jessie had had sexual relations, he immediately collapses with an apparent heart attack or stroke and yet no one pays any attention to what, again, may or may not be the truth. Part of what Pinter is saying is that life itself is mostly ambiguous and that people must often navigate their lives without satisfactory knowledge or guidance; the truth may set you free but good luck finding it.

Language and Meaning

Language in *The Homecoming* is used by the characters to attain tactical advantage. The language is seemingly a very accurate reproduction of normal speech. However, it is very carefully selected and, while still seeming ''realistic,'' it reflects the fact that people think at different speeds, use language to evade confrontation, and think and speak in metaphors. Frequently people seem to misunderstand one another when they actually don't want to understand or to be seen to understand. Language, in Pinter's hands, is a weapon. Put into the mouths of characters like Lenny and Max, it seeks to hurt others. By belittling and verbally abusing the other characters, Lenny and Max can keep them off guard, control them. While this has been an effective tool in the past, the presence of Ruth upsets the balance. Not only can she match or better the men's verbal skills, she has nonverbal sexual skills which she uses to ultimately gain the upper hand.

Morals and Morality

One of the things that bothered some critics about *The Homecoming* is the complete lack of a moral framework. Although none of the characters seems to have any moral scruples at all, Pinter does not condemn any of them. That is part of the viewer's astonishment at Ruth's deciding to stay and ''service'' the family while also working as a prostitute. Equally astonishing is the calm with which Teddy accepts her decision. Pinter includes no hint of his personal feelings toward these characters actions. Their fates are stated objectively; it is up to the audience to decide what is moral and what is not.

Politics

At the time *The Homecoming* was written, many young British playwrights were writing plays with overt political messages. While Pinter addresses no political system in his play, *The Homecoming* does deal with politics: the psychic politics of the family and of the sexes. This play very powerfully shows these dynamics at work. By extension the audience is able to relate these politics to the wider arenas of organizations and even states. A viewer can easily extrapolate the relationship between Max and his sons to that between a politician and his constituents. Ruth's ascension to family dominance is, likewise, similar to a rebel force arriving in a capital and toppling the old regime in a coup.

Sex

The Homecoming is rife with sex, although none of it seems to have anything to do with love and little has to do with lust or pleasure. In most cases, sex in the play is another weapon used for gaining control. Jessie, the mother of Teddy, Lenny, and Joey, is viewed both as a nurturing figure and as a whore, a role that Ruth overtly takes over at the end of the play. Jessie's sexual relations with Max's friend MacGregor is a theme that is alluded to frequently throughout the play.

Ruth blatantly uses sex and Lenny's apparent fear of sex in order to dominate him in their first encounter. Later she again uses sex to dominate Lenny while they dance. Immediately after that she begins foreplay with Joey in full view of the rest of the family, including her husband. Later she spends two hours in Joey's room leading him on without "going all the way," and he is enthralled with her. She agrees to be a prostitute as a business proposition. Teddy seems to accept her sexual activity as somehow separate from her role as mother in their family of boys. Even Sam's lack of sexual interest is used as a weapon against him. When Joey and Lenny relate a story of their sexual escapade with two girls, it is really a story about having the power to frighten away the girls' escorts and then to have the girls in the rubble of a demolition site. Sex for these people is a matter of power and domination.

Sex Roles

Max has become the "mother" of the household in charge of the cooking. The men see women as objects to be dominated and to use for sexual gratification. Lenny runs a string of prostitutes; upon first meeting Ruth, Max assumes she is a prostitute; when Joey sees her dancing and brushing lips with Lenny in Act II, he exclaims, "She's a tart. Old Lenny's got a tart in here.... Just up my street!" Ruth is also the mother of three boys, as was Jessie. Part of what Pinter is dealing with, and part of what some members of the audience find astonishing and upsetting, is the fact that Ruth encompasses both of the stereotypical polar extremes assigned to women by men: Madonna and whore.

Sexism

The whole family of men assumes that women are there to be used. Teddy sees Ruth as a mother and helpmate. Max and Lenny immediately assume she is a whore. Moreover, Max attempts to lower the other men, attacking their maleness by calling them "bitches" or other derogatory terms usually used to refer to women. Ruth, too, uses sexism to emasculate Lenny. After toying with Joey she abruptly stands and demands a drink: when Lenny asks if she wants it on the rocks, she says, "Rocks? What do you know about rocks?" Her double entendre is not lost on Lenny. In fact, the whole play can be read as an attempt to keep women "in their place," and the victorious revolt against that effort by Ruth. She takes complete control. She escapes from a dead, arid marriage, and she takes control of the business negotiations and demands a contract based on firm economic principles. She will use her body as she sees fit in order to gain what she wants and without any concern for what others, including her husband, think. As Pinter said in a conversation with Mel Gussow of the *New York Times,* "Ruth in *The Homecoming*—no one can tell her what to do. She is the nearest to a free woman that I've ever written—a free and independent mind."

STYLE

Setting

The setting of *The Homecoming* is realistic. It consists of a large room with a window, an archway upstage where a wall has been removed, stairs up to a second floor, a door leading to outside and a hallway leading to interior rooms. The furnishings, too, are realistic: two armchairs, a large sofa, sideboard with a mirror above it, and various other chairs and small tables. The set stays the same throughout.

Plot

The play takes place over a period of approximately twenty hours and there is one basic plot with no subplots. Here are all the requisite unities of time, place, and action that Aristotle put forth as the ideals for constructing a tight, powerful drama. Why, then, were audiences, including many critics, disturbed not only by the content but also by the form of the play? Part of the answer is in the audience's expectation that they will somehow be told about the characters in clear-cut exposition. In the realistic tradition—still overwhelmingly predominant in 1965—audiences expected to be informed of character background which would lead them to accept as ultimately logical and reasonable the responses of the characters at the point of climax and the falling action.

Viewers also expect the play to advance to its resolution in a logical cause-and-effect progression. In *The Homecoming* the exposition is slight and not always reliable because characters frequently constructs fictitious pasts in order to gain advantage in the present, as Lenny does when telling stories about brutalizing women when seeking to dominate Ruth at their first meeting. And, at first glance, most audiences are shocked and stunned when Ruth decides to abandon her husband and three sons to work as a prostitute and ''service'' the rest of the family. The denouement consists of Teddy departing for the airport and Ruth sitting in a chair with Joey at her feet, Max crawling and begging for a kiss, and Lenny in the background looking on. There is no further explanation for the action. The logical progression is there, but it is not blatantly put forth and explained as it would be in a realistic play such as Henrik Ibsen's *A Doll's House.* The audience is left to sift the action for clues as to how this outcome could possibly make sense.

Language

Another of the disturbing elements of Pinter's plays is his use of language. Pinter's characters speak with the all the hesitations, evasions, and non sequiturs of everyday speech. Moreover, the characters do not respond to questions with obviously logical answers, as would happen in a ''realistic'' play. Pinter's characters do not use language to communicate directly and logically; they use language to attack, defend, and stall while seeking out the motive rather than the direct meaning of the question.

Language for Pinter is never divorced from tactical maneuvering. He very carefully catches the rhythms of thought and language, and he structures these rhythms partly through his use of pauses and silences written into the script. These rhythms are also integral to the situation and relationships. While a great deal has been written about the use of these devices, they are not really mysterious to the astute actor: they are part of the thought processes. Pinter put it very succinctly in his conversation with Gussow when he said, ''The pause is a pause because of what has just happened in the minds and guts of the characters. They spring out of the text. They're not formal conveniences or stresses but part of the body of the action. . . . And a silence equally means that something has happened to create the impossibility of anyone speaking for a certain amount of time—until they can recover from whatever happened before the silence.'' Nevertheless, to an audience used to hearing rationally logical conversations in plays of the realistic style, the more elusive—and more ''real''—dialogue of Pinter's plays caused confusion.

Action

The answer to the problem of dramatic irony is that the audience must tune in to the action that is taking place on the subtextual level. Pinter's characters may seem to know more about what is going on than the audience because those characters are constantly involved in a battle for dominance or at the very least survival in the savage world in which they live. Even though on the surface the dialogue may seem to be about a sandwich or an ashtray or a glass of water, the characters are fully aware that the real action is about leverage, a battle which they can ill afford to lose. For Pinter, the shifting of an ashtray or the drinking of a glass of water is a large theatrical gesture. The characters know that, and the audience comes to recognize it as well.

HISTORICAL CONTEXT

While *The Homecoming* is grounded in the specifics of setting and family relationships, there is very little reference to the world at large. Nevertheless, the strife within the play's family reflects a turbulent time in the world in the year of its debut, 1965. The United States was being sucked deeper and deeper into the war in Vietnam. U.S. bombers pounded North Vietnam in February of 1965, and on March 8, U.S. Marines landed at Da Nang in the first deployment of U.S. combat troops in Vietnam.

COMPARE & CONTRAST

- **1965:** The feminist movement is getting underway, making demands for positive, concrete steps towards social equality and equality in the work-place for women.

  Today: While there is greater consciousness about women's issues and many advances have been made, there is still inequality for women in many facets of contemporary society. There has been some backlash to the more radical and strident of feminists.

- **1965:** The Sexual Revolution has begun, with sexual freedom being exhorted for both men and women. Concepts such as "Free Love" are advocated to free both mind and body.

  Today: Society is more open regarding issues of sex. Sexual freedom in society is prevalent. Sexual issues are talked about and displayed in popular media that were unmentionable in 1965.

- **1965:** Sexual promiscuity is prevalent, with many people having multiple sex partners. Sexually-transmitted diseases, such as syphilis, are easily treatable.

  Today: There is broad recognition that promiscuity and casual sex can lead to incurable ailments such as herpes. The outbreak of AIDS in the 1980s brings the realization that sex can kill.

- **1965:** The United States, which has never lost a war, is one of two superpowers and is engaged in a "cold war" with the Soviet Union. The United States is also being drawn deeper and deeper into the war in Vietnam.

  Today: The United States went through a major trauma because of wide-spread opposition to the war in Vietnam, a war which the country lost. Nevertheless, the collapse of the Soviet Union in the late-1980s has left the United States as the only superpower in the world.

On June 28 the first full-scale combat offensive by U.S. troops began.

America in 1965 reflected the turmoil of the military escalation. Anti-war rallies were held in four American cities and the term "flower power" was introduced by poet Allen Ginsberg to describe nonviolent protest. The Hell's Angels motorcycle gang attacked marchers calling them "un-American." University enrollments swelled as young Americans took advantage of draft deferrals for college students to escape the expanding war in Vietnam and campuses were tense with unrest. Still more young men evaded the draft outright, fleeing to Canada to escape combat duty.

Civil rights activist Malcolm X was assassinated on February 21, 1965, in the Harlem area of New York City. The Voting Rights Act became law on August 10, and federal examiners began registering black voters in Alabama, Louisiana, and Mississippi. In Alabama, civil rights marchers were attacked by Alabama state police using tear gas, whips, nightsticks, and dogs. President Lyndon Johnson sent three thousand National Guardsman and military police to protect the civil rights marchers. In Chicago, police arrested 526 anti-segregation demonstrators in June. The Watts section of Los Angeles had violent race riots beginning August 12. Over ten thousand blacks burned and looted an area of five hundred square blocks and destroyed an estimated forty million dollars worth of property. Fifteen thousand police and National Guardsmen were called in, thirty-four people were killed and nearly four thousand arrested. More than two hundred businesses were totally destroyed.

In other parts of the world, Rhodesia (now Zimbabwe) unilaterally declared independence from Britain. London called the declaration illegal and treasonable and declared economic sanctions against the country. There were demonstrations outside Rhodesia House in London. Despot Nicolae

Ceausescu succeeded as head of state in Romania, where he would rule until 1989. There was a coup in the Independent Congo Republic and General Joseph Mobuto made himself president and proceeded to rule as dictator.

Despite such strife (and perhaps because of it), the United States was in a period of economic growth and prosperity during the mid-1960s. In his State of the Union speech, President Johnson outlined programs for a "Great Society" that he hoped would eliminate poverty in America. Across the Atlantic things were less rosy, as Britain froze wages, salaries, and prices in an effort to check inflation in that country.

The Federal Aid to the Arts Act was signed by President Johnson in September, 1965. This established the National Endowment for the Arts and the Humanities. The United States was the last of the industrialized societies to provide direct aid to the arts. In New York City, the Vivian Beaumont Theatre opened in Lincoln Center. Pop Art, as exemplified by Andy Warhol's Campbell's Tomato Soup Can painting, and "Op" art became fashionable. The Rolling Stones gained huge success with their song "(I Can't Get No) Satisfaction." The Grateful Dead had its beginnings with "acid-rock" in San Francisco. The mini-skirt appeared in London. The English Stage Company at the Royal Court Theatre declared itself a "club theatre" in order to evade preproduction censorship for the production of playwright Edward Bond's *Saved,* which deals with moral malaise and violence in working-class London. Off- off-Broadway theatres, founded as an alternative to commercial theatre, were growing in number and showing themselves willing to fight for freedom of speech and artistic expression.

In Hackney, a working-class neighborhood in North London just beyond the boundaries of the Cockney area of the East End, life continued much as it had for generations. In an unpublished autobiographical memoir quoted by Michael Billington in *The Life and Work of Harold Pinter,* Pinter vividly describes the Hackney of his youth: "It brimmed over with milk bars, Italian cafes, Fifty Shilling tailors and barber shops. Prams and busy ramshackle stalls clogged up the main street—street violinists, trumpeters, match sellers. Many Jews lived in the district, noisy but candid; mostly taxi drivers and pressers, machinists and cutters who steamed all day in their workshop ovens. Up the hill lived the richer, the "better-class" Jews, strutting with their mink-coats and American suits and ties. Bookmakers, jewelers and furriers with gownshops in Great Portland Street."

CRITICAL OVERVIEW

When *The Homecoming* opened in London on June 3, 1965, Harold Pinter was already considered a major playwright in England, and his new play was eagerly awaited. Harold Hobson, critic for the *Sunday Times,* who alone had championed Pinter's debut *The Room* and his 1958 *The Birthday Party,* had said then that "Mr. Pinter . . . possesses the most original, disturbing and arresting talent in theatrical London," and he predicted then that Pinter would make his mark in theatre. The great success of *The Caretaker* in 1960, radio plays such as *A Slight Ache,* and short stage and television plays had fulfilled Hobson's predictions, and the word "Pinteresque" had already been coined to denote the playwright's style.

The Homecoming is a deeply disturbing play and the critics' reception reflected the drama's turmoil. B. A. Young of the *Financial Times* called the play "stark and horrible" but also said that it is "monstrously effective theatre." Although Young did not think Pinter to be an *important* playwright, he pointed out that "he has this enormous capacity for generating tension among his characters in which the audience becomes irresistibly involved." Bernard Levin in the *Daily Mail,* while crediting Pinter's "dazzling dramatic legerdemain," was negative and saw no point to the play. Philip Hope-Wallace of the *Guardian* objected strongly (and longly) about the lack of dramatic irony—in which the audience knows more than the characters on stage—and the fact that it was the actors (characters?) who seemed to know more than the audience. The critic seemed to be completely baffled by the play and said that it "leaves us feeling cheated."

Hobson wrote in the *Sunday Times* that he liked the play but was deeply disturbed by the lack of a moral stand by the author, saying "I am troubled by the complete absence from the play of any moral comment whatsoever. To make such a comment does not necessitate the author's being conventional or religious; it does necessitate, however, his having made up his mind about life.'' Penelope Gilliatt in the *Observer* called the opening of *The Homecoming* ''an exultant night . . . it offered the stirring spectacle of a man in total command of his talent.''

British audiences responded positively and the play had an eighteen-month run at the Aldwych Theatre in London before moving to New York on January 3, 1967, after a brief pre-Broadway run in Boston. It also quickly had other productions around the world: Paris, Berlin, Geneva, Gothenburg, Munich, Bremerhaven, Amsterdam, Copenhagen, Helsinki, Stockholm, and Sydney, Australia.

The Broadway reviews were mixed but predominantly positive. Norman Nadel in the *World Journal Tribune* called it a ''nightmare play'' and a ''fascinating but unfathomable comedy'' and thought it would appeal only to more adventurous theatregoers. Martin Gottfried, the powerful critic of *Women's Wear Daily,* found it ''a fascinating and bizarre comedy'' that ''is so deep-veined with implication and so consistently provocative, controlling and comic that it not only demands respect but, more important, it wins attention and thought. The play . . . carries theatre life and with it the workings of a probing and creative mind.'' John Chapman of the *Daily News* did not like the play and, while he said that Pinter created interesting characters, comedy, and suspense, the playwright lacked the important ingredient needed to be an important dramatist—''good taste.'' The most devastating review came from Walter Kerr of the *New York Times,* who said that *The Homecoming* consists of ''a single situation that the author refuses to dramatize until he has dragged us all, aching, through a half-drugged dream.'' He did find the final twenty minutes of the play to be interesting as Pinter ''broke apart our preconditioned expectations to the situations'' and ''the erratic energies onstage display their own naked authority by forcing us to accept the unpredictable as though it were the natural shape of things.'' The general message from Kerr, however, was that the play dragged and needed ''a second situation'' to give it life.

The Homecoming managed to overcome the negative aspects of the reviews, went on to a long run, and established Pinter on Broadway. It won the Drama Critics' Circle Award, a Tony Award, and the Whitbread Anglo-American Theatre Award as best play of the year. It has been produced throughout the world and continues to achieve both critical and popular success in major revivals, such as that at the Royal National Theatre, London, in 1997. Pinter continues to be one of the most written-about playwrights working today, and *The Homecoming* is by general consensus held to be one of his most important works-by many accounts his masterpiece.

CRITICISM

Terry Browne

Browne is a noted drama authority. In this essay he discusses the power of Pinter's language as action and weapon.

Harold Pinter has stated unequivocally many times that ''I do not write theses: I write plays.'' He says that his personal judgments are reserved for the ''shape and validity'' of his work. He is concerned with expressing his vision in a way that communicates *directly* to the audience. Audiences in 1965 (and to a large degree even today) were used to realism with its specific biographical facts, implicit or explicit judgements on characters and situations, summary speeches, and neatly wrapped denouement. The audience may then agree or disagree with the author's view or conclusions, but at least the author's stance was clearly delineated. That is not so with Pinter, and this is profoundly disturbing to many critics and viewers. Pinter banishes the notion of the omniscient, moral author and makes no judgements about his characters or their situations. The characters are defined by their actions rather than judged by their author. This technique puts the perception—and moral judgement—of these characters squarely in the hands of the audience.

Like many plays *The Homecoming* presents us with a solidly realistic grounding in a particular place. There is an almost uncanny reproduction of real life in the characters' language. The story is simple: a man brings his wife of six years home to meet his family for the first time. There is a struggle for control of the family in which the new wife is first the target of domination and ultimately the victor. In this battle for supremacy, the character resort to their basest instincts for survival, casting most accoutrements of civility aside. While these people reveal themselves as vicious creatures, little information is given as to what specific events in their lives made them this way. This ambiguity in their backgrounds, especially Ruth's, adds to both

WHAT DO I READ NEXT?

- Two of Pinter's early plays provide background to *The Homecoming: The Birthday Party* (1958), Pinter's first full-length play, contains all the hallmarks of Pinter's style and concerns; *The Caretaker,* which opened April 17, 1960, at the small Arts Theatre Club in London, explores loneliness and power struggles among three men. Centered on a tramp who is given a place to stay by a mentally damaged man, this play was Pinter's first major commercial success.
- Pinter's *Old Times* (1970), delves into time and memory, which Pinter finds to be fluid and uncertain. It also further explores the inability of a man to fully know a woman or to possess her. It is a move away from the more realistic *The Homecoming.*
- *Glengarry Glen Ross* by David Mamet shows the influence of Pinter, especially in the use of language, on the younger American playwright. The play was first produced in 1983 at the Royal National Theatre, London, at Pinter's suggestion.
- *Endgame* by Samuel Beckett was first produced in 1957 in French at the Royal Court Theatre, London. This play has some of the qualities and concerns seen in *The Homecoming:* mutual interdependence of characters, hate, an enclosed environment, and the use of spare language and lack of specific background information. Beckett is an acknowledged influence on Pinter.
- *Sexual Power* by Carolyn Johnston, published by Alabama University Press in 1992, gives a feminist perspective on the American family from the seventeenth century to the present.

the allure and repulsive nature of Pinter's characters. While the play is grounded in a specific reality, it also provides a sense of mystery that lends itself to many valid interpretations. *The Homecoming* offers its audiences a powerful glimpse into the darkness of human nature but it also leaves character motivation and history open to interpretation.

Most of the "action" in *The Homecoming* is contained in the language and works on a psychological level. Language for Pinter is never devoid of tactical purpose. His characters do not speak in a logical question-response manner; they constantly probe the other's assumed intentions, cover-up their own intentions, counter-strike, and intentionally evade. They are constantly using language to create a reality in which they can dominate the others. This leads to very powerful and constant action on the subtextual level. Ruth may seem to be talking about a glass of water when she says to Lenny, "Have a sip. Go on. Have a sip from my glass. . . . Sit on my lap. Take a long cool sip. . . . Put your head back and open your mouth," but Lenny and the audience know that she is making an overt sexual proposal. Did Ruth have a job in her past that equipped her to deal with men on this level, or did she acquire this skill from her six years with Teddy? Another puzzle for the viewer. In another instance, Sam seems to be gently praising Jessie when he tells Max that he would "Never get a bride like you had, anyway. Nothing like your bride . . . going about these days. Like Jessie." In reality he is reminding Max that Jessie was, at best, a loose woman who had an affair with Max's best friend MacGregor. And Max understands the real meaning in Sam's words.

Despite their ambiguous histories, Pinter creates wonderful characters. In fact, he has been "accused" by some critics of merely writing characters that actors like to play, as though that were a fault in his writing. He does write fascinating characters. Max is a gem of contradictions: sly, clever, charming, vicious, violent, and ultimately vulnerable and pitiful. Ruth is sexually seething beneath her cool, polite exterior. Lenny is all cool polish and wit over his inner fears and weaknesses. Even gentle Sam has the weapons that have allowed him

Ruth (Jane Lowe) is surrounded by her husband's family, (left to right) Max (John Savident), Joey (Terence Rigby), and Lenny (playwright Pinter taking a turn at acting)

to survive in this savage household. These are luminous, multifaceted characters, the kind that actors define as "meaty" and crave for their challenging nature. They are always active and they always have the capacity to surprise us. And despite their often revolting behavior, these are characters that an audience seeks out as well. They offer a vicarious ride into humanity's lower depths and a tangible mystery of human nature.

Moreover, Pinter is able to make us laugh at the brutish behavior of his characters. As Harold Clurman put it in his review of *The Homecoming* in the *Nation:* "The mask is one of horror subdued in glacial irony." We are constantly surprised by the incongruity between what we expect in these family relationships and what is actually expressed. The brutality and crudity of feeling that break through the veneer of civility constantly surprises us. For example, the opening scene of Act II might come from a "drawing room" comedy—those polite, witty staples of British theatre for decades before Pinter. In *The Homecoming* the family is having after-dinner coffee and the chit-chat about family life and Max's late wife, Jessie, is quickly recognized as hypocritical sentimentality to the point of parody.

So, too, the first psycho-sexual duel between Ruth and Lenny has the power to provoke laughter as we watch Lenny nonchalantly weave his stories of violence to women in order to intimidate and dominate Ruth, only to have Ruth turn the tables on him with sexual innuendo. She easily demolishes Lenny, and we delight in seeing him calling after her, "Is that supposed to be some kind of proposal?" as she climbs the stairs totally victorious. Even the overtly physical violence seems almost like slapstick comedy. When Max knocks Joey, the aspiring boxer, to the floor with one punch, then hits Sam, and finally collapses himself, it is, on the surface at least, funny. When Sam collapses from an apparent stroke after blurting out that "Mac had Jessie in the backseat of my cab as I drove them along," it is funny because of the reaction of Max, who says, "What's he done? Dropped dead?. . . A corpse on my floor? Get him out of here." In her comical nonchalance, Ruth seems not even to have noticed.

Pinter's humor is often categorized as black humor for its ability to draw laughter out of what are commonly regarded as serious events or situations. Much of this dark comedy is drawn from actual events in Pinter's life. The basic idea for *The Homecoming* comes from the fact that one of his boyhood friends, Morris Wernick, did in fact marry without telling his family and immediately moved to Canada. He kept up the pretense of being unmarried for ten years before taking his whole family to meet his father. His father provided the inspiration for Max, and Wernick also had an uncle who was a cab driver—much like Sam in the play. All this means that the basic situation, which served as a springboard for Pinter's imagination, is grounded solidly in reality. Nevertheless, Michael Billington in his study of early drafts of the play discovered that the play grows from the image of a man and a woman who are in discord. From that start, Pinter seems to be able to tap directly into his subconscious. He draws on his own obsessions and inner tensions, and he has the ability to make those inner dreams concrete on the stage.

In spite of the fact that Pinter does not consciously write to illustrate a theme, his plays do communicate, and communicate directly, to an audience. Part of the power of *The Homecoming* is the

"THE CHARACTERS IN *THE HOMECOMING* ARE DEFINED BY THEIR ACTIONS RATHER THAN JUDGED BY THEIR AUTHOR."

fact that, like all potent drama, the play does lend itself to many interpretations.

The play has been held to be a very particular Jewish domestic drama—a view that Pinter is quick to dispel by pointing out that audiences from Italy to Japan respond to it. It could also be seen as a simple study of the loss of human sensitivity, of emotional impotence in which all human warmth has been smothered. Certainly the play shows life to be a ceaseless struggle in which language is used as a negotiating weapon to attack or cover-up and defend. In this view, all the characters are doomed to isolation and profound loneliness. It has even been suggested that the whole thing is a hoax perpetrated by Teddy. In this view, Teddy has hired a prostitute and orchestrated the whole thing to wreak revenge on his cruel family.

Martin Esslin builds a solid case for an Oedipal interpretation of *The Homecoming* in which Ruth, taking on the dual roles of Madonna and whore, is the object of the sons' lust as well as an avenging angel who dethrones and utterly humiliates the father. Another interpretation of the Oedipus myth that fits the play is the ritual sacrificing of the old king, Max, so that there may be rejuvenation of the social body. Unlike the myth, however, a new king does not rise from the ranks of young men to assume the throne; the heir apparent Lenny is denied his ascension. From almost all perspectives, the new "king" is Ruth.

In his book *The Life and Work of Harold Pinter,* Billinton, while appreciating other views, finds *The Homecoming* to be "less that of Oedipal wish-fulfillment than of female triumph over a male-power structure." There is no doubt in my mind that Ruth does triumph. From her introduction she makes it clear that she will not act just because others tell her to do so; she makes her own decisions for very specific reasons. Ruth shows a distinct talent for bending the men to her will. And she is able to tailor her interaction with them to best manipulate their individual personalities.

When Lenny refuses to accept that she is in fact married to Teddy and attempts to intimidate her with stories of his brutality towards women, she is unmoved. When he tries to physically threaten her by repeatedly moving her ashtray and attempting to take a waterglass from her, she turns the tables on him by using the glass of water as a metaphor for sex. She defuses Max by calmly *not* responding to his taunts of ''pox-ridden slut'' and ''whore.'' She is genteel to Sam, and she openly seduces Joey. She takes control of the negotiations concerning the conditions under which she will work as a prostitute, and she drives a hard bargain. She ends up enthroned in an armchair, probably Max's, with the men around her like tamed animals. Joey is at her feet like a puppy, Max is crawling towards her begging for a kiss, Sam lies comatose on the floor, and Lenny is sulkily standing off to the side, denied his chance to rule. Ruth is queen of this jungle.

Source: Terry Browne, for *Drama for Students,* Gale, 1998.

Maggie Gee

Gee reviews a 1997 London production of Pinter's play. Praising both the text and the new performance, the critic contends that thirty-two years afters its debut, the play ''still has the power to shock.''

A beautiful, elegant woman, Ruth, sprawls on a sofa in a drab working-class front room which contains five men: her husband, Teddy, her husband's two brothers, her elderly father-in-law and his brother. Her husband's youngest brother, Joey, lies heavily on top of her, grinding his pelvis into her in a simulation of intercourse, while the other brother caresses her hair and the two older men watch, transfixed. Soon her husband, who loves her, will stand by passively, as his family (whom she has only just met) concoct a scheme to set her up as a prostitute in the West End, servicing them at home in the evenings.

Thirty-two years after its London premiere in 1965, *The Homecoming,* in Roger Michell's intelligent new production, still has the power to shock. It drags out of the darkness the forbidden sexual desires of fathers for their sons' wives and brothers for their brothers', showing life in an all-male family as a cauldron of anger, competition, lust and loneliness, which boils over when a woman finally arrives. The superficially unlikely, even laughable, code of behaviour by which this particular family operates is also disturbing at a deep level, because the fantasies and drives underlying it are universally recognizable.

Harold Pinter's best work draws deeply on the unconscious—he says he is aware of ''Images, characters, insisting upon being written''. This is not done showily, in the manner of Theatre of the Absurd; rather, everything is contained by an apparently neat and orderly reality which soon begins to fray at the edges. According to the playwright, ''what happens in my plays could happen anywhere, at any time, in any place''. Here, what happens is that the clever son, Teddy, returns home unexpectedly from America to introduce his wife to his family, in a mood of blind optimism—''They're very warm people, really''—and everything goes wrong. It is a family of men, for Teddy's mother, Jessie, alternately described as a paragon of motherhood and ''slut-bitch'' by the father, Max, is dead. In a sense, the whole play is about her absence, echoing the hinted absence of Max's own bedridden mother before her, and culminating in her transgressive replacement by a nubile daughter-figure, Ruth.

Max's father is an exaggeratedly sentimental, bullying patriarch, but Pinter makes Max unique by sharpening the familiar shifts between physical violence and demonstrative tenderness, anger and maudlin sorrow. David Bradley gives a riveting performance, transforming himself to terrifying effect at the end of the first act from a pathetic old boaster into a man who can lay out brother and son almost simultaneously, commanding the otherwise silent theatre afterwards with a low growl and a gargoyle stare. But extremes, and quick movement between extremes, always make for comic possibility, since laughter is based on surprise, and the text of this dark and sinister play is full of comic moments which this excellent ensemble cast exploits to the full. There's some inventive witty language, too. Accused by his brother of not going the whole hog with Ruth, inarticulate Joey explains that sometimes you can be happy ''without going any 'og''. When her husband finally leaves in disgust, Ruth manages the priceless ''Don't become a stranger''.

The Homecoming shows men and women deeply divided. The men are all dogs, a woman's worst nightmare of what men might be. Max growls like a dog; his son says they eat like dogs, they boast of having raped two women on a bomb-site like dogs;

they sniff round Ruth and try to mount her like dogs. Pinter does not often write good parts for women—*Old Times, Betrayal* and *A Kind of Alaska* are exceptions—and this play's only woman, Ruth, is a compendium of stereotypes from cool Madonna to promiscuous "tart". But she is also, as Teddy hints once or twice, "ill"—mentally ill—which makes her behaviour just about plausible in realistic terms. Lindsay Duncan adds depth and mystery to this very difficult role, and at the end brings real pathos to the interesting gloss Michell's production puts on Pinter's text, introducing overtly maternal tenderness to Pinter's ambivalent image of reconciliation between men and women. The play is neither feminist nor misogynist, but turns instead on two contradictory truths about men who lack mothering—their brutalization and their child-like need for tenderness.

Source: Maggie Gee, review of *The Homecoming* in the *Times Literary Supplement,* Number 4896, January 31, 1997, p. 17.

Charles A. Carpenter

Carpenter discusses the nature of absurdity in Pinter's play, concluding that most critics ignore the work's true power in trying to penetrate the meaning of the playwright's absurdist touches.

Pinter's *Homecoming* may be the most enigmatic work of art since the Mona Lisa, an image its main character, Ruth, evokes. At the turning point of the play, Ruth's professor-husband, Teddy, watches intently as she lies on the living-room couch with one of his brothers while the other strokes her hair. His father, Max, claiming he is broadminded, calls her "a woman of quality," "a woman of feeling." Shortly after Ruth frees herself she asks Teddy, out of the blue: "Have your family read your critical works?"

This provokes the smug Ph.D. to a slightly manic assertion: "To see, to be able to *see!* I'm the one who can see. That's why I can write my critical works. Might do you good . . . have a look at them . . . see how certain people can view . . . things . . . how certain people can maintain . . . intellectual equilibrium." His reaction to this intensely disconcerting moment parallels that of Pinter critics who, like Teddy, refuse to let themselves be "lost in it." This is, of course, the natural reaction for people whose public image depends upon maintaining their intellectual equilibrium. But it is hardly the appropriate reaction either for Teddy, who restricts his protestations to eating his pimp–brother Lenny's

" *THE HOMECOMING* SHOWS MEN AND WOMEN DEEPLY DIVIDED. THE MEN ARE ALL DOGS, A WOMAN'S WORST NIGHTMARE OF WHAT MEN MIGHT BE."

cheese–roll, or for people genuinely experiencing a Pinter play.

Whatever else this response may involve, it must surely involve letting oneself be "lost in it." The jolt to one's intellectual equilibrium—what Bert States has dubbed "the shock of nonrecognition" [see his essay "Pinter's *Homecoming* The Shock of Nonrecogmtion," *Hudson Review,* Autumn 1968]—must be acknowledged as a validly evoked response. The urge for rational illumination that so often follows—the nose-tickle crying for a sneeze—must be regarded as an integral second stage of that evoked response. In experiencing these repeated "Pinteresque" moments, we are put precisely in the dilemma of Camus's "absurd man" described in *The Myth of Sisyphus.* We are confronted with bewilderment, disruption, chaos, what Beckett referred to as "this buzzing confusion." In response, we involuntarily reach out for clarity, understanding, Godot: the little explanation that is not there. We become like Ionesco's Detective in *Victims of Duty,* who lays its underpinnings bare: "I don't believe in the absurd. Everything hangs together; everything can be comprehended . . . thanks to the achievements of human thought and science." Camus's hero, the true believer in absurdity, acknowledges this recurring double take as a poignant byproduct of the absurd human condition, and in so doing, Camus says, reveals his "lucidity." Moreover, he becomes capable of reveling in the actual impact of the situation: the rich dark comedy of it, if you will. Sisyphus grows happy with his stone.

At these moments, in life or at a Pinter play, bizarre actions and reactions, churning with apparent meaning but inherently unexplainable, trigger the automatic desire for explanation built into us. An earlier pivotal incident in *The Homecoming* puts the idea in the form of a graphic enigma. Before her outright defection, Ruth invites her all–male audi-

"PINTER'S *HOMECOMING* MAY BE THE MOST ENIGMATIC WORK OF ART SINCE THE MONA LISA."

ence to watch her as she moves her leg, but warns them that even though their minds may stray to the underwear that moves with it, all she is doing is moving her leg. She continues: "My lips move. Why don't you restrict . . . your observations to that? Perhaps the fact that they move is more significant . . . than the words which come through them." What do Ruth's words mean? Be strict phenomenologists! Pay no attention to the inadvertently moving underwear, on which I have taken pains to rivet your attention; consider what I am saying insignificant—though I have made it surge with significance. Her words are of course absurd, since they cancel themselves out logically. But can we resist taking the lure and, on impulse, groping for the significance so deviously implied? Only the dull or jaded could. What we can try to avoid, however, is blurring the moment by detaching ourselves from the play in a face–saving quest for comprehension.

Glance at a more flagrant example. Soon after Ruth meets Lenny in Act I, he abruptly asks her if he can hold her hand. She asks why, and he says, "I'll tell you why." He then spins an involved story about being approached under an arch by a lady whose chauffeur, a friend of the family, had tracked him down. Deciding she was "falling apart with the pox," he spurned her advances, "clumped her one," and stopped short of killing her only because of the inconvenience. "So I just gave her another belt in the nose and a couple of turns of the boot and sort of left it at that." A baffling reason for wanting to hold Ruth's hand! If at this point we care more about recovering our intellectual aplomb than about letting the play carry us along in its inexorable absurd flow, we will wrench ourselves away from its grip on us; assume the pose of the Critic-Detective; and forget that the scene, in spite of its spray of beckoning clues (partly because of them, in fact), will finally defy comprehension, and that the play, by its nature, is chuckling at our knee-jerk response to one of its more transparent brain–teasers. In Camus's terms, the extent to which we avoid the role of public explainer and acknowledge the way the play has "caught" us becomes the genuine measure of our lucidity.

That avoidance and acknowledgement also give us a much better chance to enjoy the play—to relish the delectable, audacious absurdity of such moments. The distinctive power of *The Homecoming* derives largely from the bizarrely disconcerting quality of the things that happen to characters depicted as real people in the real world. Think of what typical first–nighters probably tell their friends about the play: a professor visits his grubby home after several years abroad and brings his wife, about whom he has not even told his family. The repulsive father calls her a whore, and the two repulsive brothers treat her like one. She does not seem to mind, and after a little bargaining accepts a deal to stay on as the family pet. The husband stands by complacently, smirk on his face, and finally leaves. If these spectators get around to elaborating on the play, they probably recall more and more incidents that involve "absurd" actions and a dazzling variety of reactions: Ruth making Lenny "some kind of proposal" soon after she meets him; Max lurching from extreme to extreme in his treatment of Ruth; Joey emerging after two hours of "not going any hog" with Ruth upstairs; Lenny getting the bright idea of putting her "on the game" in a Greek Street flat and Ruth raising the ante extravagantly before accepting; everyone ignoring uncle Sam's traumatic revelation—and prone body—at the end. Untutored spectators are not apt to lose sight of what makes the play so eccentric and electric; as they reflect rather idly on their experience, they are more than likely to keep focusing on those bizarre moments that amused, shocked, fascinated, and above all puzzled them.

But what can trained literary analysts do that "mere" playgoers cannot? Some will warp and deface this perspective; others will develop and refine it. Those who take the latter path may begin simply by noting more or less covert instances of bizarre behavior which have to be perceived to be appreciated: when Teddy chats with Lenny in scene one, for example, he does not mention the existence of Ruth (who has gone for a 1:00 a.m. stroll), and he goes to bed before Ruth returns, in effect leaving her to Lenny. An especially profitable avenue is open for critics with a penchant for close analysis: focus on details that lend themselves readily to facile interpretation, such as Max's stick or Lenny's comment to Teddy that his cigar has gone out, and demonstrate their immunity to interpretation.

Ruth's enigmatic farewell to her husband, ''Eddie. . . . Don't become a stranger,'' is a manageable example. As Bernard Dukore notes, the fact that Ruth calls him Eddie suggests that ''Teddy'' is meant as a nickname not for Theodore but for Edward—a suggestion which invites comparisons to the similarly cuckolded stuffed shirt named Edward in *A Slight Ache.* But she may also be symbolically withdrawing from him by muffing his name; or she may be knocking the ''Theo''—the divinity—out of what is left of him; or she may be hinting he is no longer her teddy bear—or Teddy boy, for that matter. The rest of her statement, ''Don't become a stranger,'' must be easier; the heavy odds are that she means the opposite of what she says. Or, after all, does she still want to keep a line open to her own children, even though she now has a new set? Or is her pleasantry, as a scholar sitting beside me in the British Museum once assured me, the way a London prostitute says, ''So long—come again'' to her clients? Surely the play's obtrusive ''homecoming'' metaphor must be hiding in there somewhere. Or does Ruth mean, Teddy, don't make yourself becoming to a stranger! It must be more sensible to grant the incomprehensibility of such conundrums than to flail for ''the solution'' and thus flout their essential nature. In a play like this, we know—to a certain extent—that we cannot know.

A full–fledged analysis concentrating on the play's bizarre and disconcerting effects, or at least trying not to dissipate them, might well aim to project what Kelly Morris has deftly termed [in her essay ''*The Homecoming,*'' *Tulane Drama Review,* Winter 1966] ''the suction of the absurd.'' As the play progresses, characters and audience alike get caught up in this suction. Take as a central example Lenny's victimization—or manhandling, if you prefer—by Ruth. In Act I she toys frivolously with him, countering his macho moves with audacities that throw him off kilter. From his lightly mocking ''You must be connected with my brother in some way. . . . You sort of live with him over there, do you?'' and his leering offer to relieve her of her drink, he is reduced by a little seductive bullying to shouting: ''What was that supposed to be? Some kind of proposal?'' No doubt he is conscious to some degree of having been manipulated, and alert spectators will have observed the Venus' flytrap in action, so that both he and the audience have a chance to shake off the disconcerting effect of Ruth's bizarre behavior.

Relief gets harder as the ''suction'' intensifies in Act II. When Teddy is present, Ruth joins Lenny in ruffling his proud feathers enough to convince him that he had better grab Ruth and flee if he is to avoid being ''lost'' in the situation. After Lenny prompts him to absurd evasions of a few philosophical basics (''What do you make of all this business of being and not–being?''), Ruth calls attention to the elegant reality of her leg. Then she declares Teddy's adopted land full of rock, sand, space, and insects. Lenny may believe he has gained an ally, or even a potential filly for his stable, since he pretends to leave with Max and Joey but reappears the instant Teddy goes upstairs to pack. In sharp contrast to his first encounter with Ruth, this time he is low–keyed and conciliatory. Again he digresses about a lady, but he gave this one a flowery hat instead of ''a short–arm jab to the belly.'' When Ruth reminisces dreamily about her life as a nude model (I assume) before she went off to America, Lenny seems to read her behavior as confirmation that she is making him ''some kind of proposal.''

Whether or not Lenny does, when Teddy comes downstairs to take Ruth home, he steps into the most bizarre auction scene in all domestic drama, and it is engineered by Lenny. The jaunty pimp puts on some jazz, asks Ruth for ''just one dance'' before she goes, receives full compliance, kisses her a few times, hands her over to Joey for a bit of mauling, parts them with a touch of his foot, and pours drinks for all to celebrate the realignment. Though it is Teddy who visibly strains against the pressure of absurdity at this moment, Lenny has actually set himself up for a subtle comic downfall. Ruth's siege of deep–felt nostalgia—not about ''working'' as any kind of sex object but about posing for photographers at a genteel country estate—was entirely introspective and self–directed. To put it graphically, Lenny may have gathered that she was showing him her underwear when she was really just moving her leg. By the time she responds to his advances, he is deceived into thinking he has her pegged and will endure no more tremors from her behavior. He is thus a prime candidate for a shake–up.

Ruth administers the shake–up in two salvos, turning Lenny's cockiness as a shrewd exploiter of women into the sullen acquiescence of a man conned by one. It would be misleading to represent this as a conscious plot on her part, however; view it rather as the effect of her disturbing actions, whatever their roots. First, she somehow manages to play mother–beloved instead of whore to Joey, the test case client Lenny has arranged. Lenny covers up his anxiety quite well when he learns this, but is clearly jolted by the realization that Ruth may be a mere tease. Joey snorts that he can be happy "without going any hog," but what will the paying customers say? Second, Ruth responds to the idea of paying her way as a prostitute by making exorbitant demands that Lenny thought he could handle but cannot. He had said to the men: "I know these women. Once they get started they ruin your budget." Ruth reduces him to:

> LENNY. We'd supply everything. Everything you need. [Note the qualification—everything you *need*]
> RUTH. I'd need an awful lot. Otherwise I wouldn't be content.
> LENNY. You'd have everything. [Qualification dropped.]

Lenny does not squirm perceptibly during his public humiliation, even when it also becomes clear that Ruth will most probably refuse to "pull her weight" inside the house (no homecoming for Max and Lenny either). But as the final tableau implies, Ruth has effectively thrust him into the background shadows, big bear–enforcer Joey at her side. Whether Lenny becomes a cover–up–at–all–costs stoic or he is rendered catatonic as this barrage of the unmanageable shatters his delusion of firm control, he is certainly caught up in the "suction of the absurd"—no less than Teddy, in fact, and Teddy can at least escape. The audience, caught in the same suction (though with the cushion of aesthetic distance), leaves with heads buzzing: no escape but in the critics' explanations. Why Ruth carries out these strikingly unexpected acts of apparent self–gratification, by the way, is a wide–open question, but her spate of nostalgia for the best moments of the old life may have served vaguely as the impetus. Or perhaps it was simply her way of thanking Teddy for offering her the opportunity to help him with his lectures when they return.

This brief essay does not pretend to be a fully developed interpretive argument about *The Homecoming.* It is meant to exemplify the direction that might be taken by critical analysis which tries to be faithful to the genuine absurd experience of the play as it unfolds. The finely crafted progression of bizarre and disconcerting events might be approached from many other points of view. Mine, for example, completely neglects the two crucial offstage presences, Jessie and MacGregor, and fails to address Sam's important role. Nor does it do justice to one of the most prominent effects on that average first–nighter on whom I stake so much: the raunchy, ugly, gorgeous vulgarity of the piece. "What I mean," Lenny twits Teddy, " . . . you must know lots of professors, heads of departments, men like that. They pop over here for a week at the Savoy, they need somewhere they can go to have a nice quiet poke. And of course you'd be in a position to give them inside information. . . . You could be our representative in the States." This excites Max: "Of course. We're talking in international terms! By the time we've finished Pan American'll give us a discount." There. I haven't neglected that.

It seems unfortunate as well as symptomatic that few critics in the past fifteen years have taken an approach that accepts and even relishes the absurdity of Pinter's depicted world. Precious few have resisted the urge to chase the will–o'–the–wisp of a solution to the mind–bending indeterminacies *The Homecoming* in particular exudes. The gradual drift of criticism away from the reality of the play is marked by the actual titles of three early studies: the earliest, "Puzzling Pinter" [Richard Schechner, *Tulane Drama Review,* Winter 1966]; the others, "A Clue to the Pinter Puzzle" [Arthur Ganz, *Educational Theatre Journal,* Vol. 21, 1969]; and "Not So Puzzling Pinter" [Herbert Goldstone, *Theatre Annual,* Vol. 25, 1969]. Ionesco's Detectives have been at work. What they have accomplished often seems dazzling in its perception and profundity. Some of it even seems inevitable when one is immersed in it. But if it violates the inherent nature of the play by trying to defuse its stunningly absurd time bombs, then what it is doing is busily explaining away the chief source of the play's power and of its richly deserved stature.

Source: Charles A. Carpenter, "'Victims of Duty'? The Critics, Absurdity, and '*The Homecoming* '" in *Modern Drama,* Vol. XXV, no. 4, December, 1982, pp. 489–95.

SOURCES

Elsom, John. *Postwar British Theatre Criticism,* Routledge & Kegan Paul, 1981, pp. 155-60.

Gottfried, Martin. Review of *The Homecoming* in *Women's Wear Daily,* January 6, 1967.

Grecco, Stephen. "Harold Pinter" in *Concise Dictionary of British Literary Biography,* Volume 8: *Contemporary Writers, 1960 to the Present,* Gale (Detroit), 1992, pp. 315-36.

Kerr, Walter. "The Theatre: Pinter's *Homecoming*" in the *New York Times,* January 6, 1967.

Nadel, Norman. ''*Homecoming* Unfathomable'' in *World Journal Tribune,* January 6, 1967.

Salem, Daniel. ''The Impact of Pinter's Work'' in *Ariel: A Review of International English Literature,* Vol. 17, no. 1, January, 1986, pp. 71-83.

Taylor, John Russell. Review of *The Homecoming* in *Plays and Players, 1953-1968,* edited by Peter Roberts, Methuen, 1988, p. 196.

Watts, Richard. ''Hospitality of a London Family'' in the *New York Post,* January 6, 1967.

FURTHER READING

Billington, Michael. *The Life and Work of Harold Pinter,* Faber & Faber, 1996.
This is by far the best and most complete biography of Pinter. The commentary on the plays is extremely useful. Billington has been the theatre critic for the *Guardian* newspaper since 1971.

Burkmann, Katherine H. and John L. Kundert Gibbs, editors. *Pinter at Sixty,* Indiana University Press, 1963.
This is a collection of essays by scholars and critics and gives a variety of views on Pinter's work as a whole.

Esslin, Martin. *Pinter: The Playwright,* Methuen, 1982.
First published in England under the title *The Peopled Wound,* Esslin's book covers all of Pinter's plays through *Victoria Station* (1982), and includes a short section on the screenplays. Esslin provides great insight and a thoroughness of knowledge about European theatre that is matched by none.

Gussow, Mel. *Conversations with Pinter,* Grove Press, 1994.
This short book gives valuable insights into Pinter's working methods and his views on playwriting and life in general through a series of conversations with Gussow of the *New York Times* from 1971 to 1993.

Knowles, Ronald. *Understanding Harold Pinter,* University of South Carolina Press, 1995.
Part of the ''Understanding Contemporary Literature'' series, this book offers criticism and interpretation and includes biographical references.

Lear

EDWARD BOND

1971

Edward Bond's *Lear* was first produced at the Royal Court Theatre in London in 1971. Bond's 1965 play *Saved* had already established his position as an important new playwright, and some believe early reviewers of *Lear* did not fully understand the play but were reluctant to condemn it, largely because of Bond's reputation. Many did find fault with the play, however, and much attention was focused on *Lear*'s tremendous violence. Some were critical of that violence, while others defended its extremity as essential to the playwright's purpose. As with Bond's other plays, the violence in *Lear* remains a subject of critical debate to this day.

Another focus of attention on *Lear* is its relationship to William Shakespeare's play *King Lear.* As the playwright has noted, it is important to note that Bond's *Lear* be seen not simply as an adaptation of Shakespeare's play but as a comment on that drama. In various interviews, Bond has said that current audience reaction to Shakespeare's *King Lear,* which focuses on the artistic experience of the play, is far removed from the way Shakespeare's audience would have responded. Bond's purpose is to make Shakespeare's play more politically effective, more likely to cause people to question their society and themselves, rather than simply to have an uplifting aesthetic experience. As a socialist playwright, Bond writes plays that are not meant merely to entertain but to help to bring about change in society.

Lear has been called the most violent drama ever staged as well as the most controversial of Bond's plays. It has been revived a number of times since its original production, and its reputation has grown as more critical attention has been paid to Bond's work. Although it is clear that *Lear* is an important work among Bond's plays, its full effect on contemporary drama remains to be seen.

AUTHOR BIOGRAPHY

Edward Bond was born on July 18, 1934, to working class parents in Holloway, a North London suburb in England. When World War II began in 1939, Bond, like many children, was evacuated to the countryside. Even so, he was exposed to the violence of the war, the bombings, the continual sense of danger, all of which helped to shape Bond's image of the world as a violent place. Bond's education was interrupted by the war, and he left school for good at fifteen. He worked in factories and offices and served for two years in the British army. In his early twenties, he began writing plays.

At this time, in the 1950s, a new generation of playwrights was beginning to revolutionize British drama. These playwrights included John Osborne (*Look Back in Anger*), Arnold Wesker (*Chicken Soup with Barley*), and Harold Pinter (*The Homecoming*). As a group, they moved away from the predictable, even insipid, British post-war theater to create drama, often political, that was new and vibrant. Bond eventually became one of this group of new playwrights.

Bond wrote a number of plays before his first staged work, *The Pope's Wedding,* was produced in 1962. Although that play contained some violence, it was not until the production of *Saved* (1965), a play that includes an onstage depiction of the stoning of a baby, that Bond became notorious for the extreme violence of his work. The Lord Chamberlain, a public official responsible at the time for maintaining moral standards in British theater, heavily censored the original script. The eventual production of the play, in its entirety in 1965 at the Royal Court, resulted in the theater being prosecuted and fined.

Bond's next play, *Early Morning,* produced in 1968, featured cannibalism. It was the last play banned by the Lord Chamberlain before censorship in the British theater was abolished that same year. Other important plays by Bond include *Lear* (1971), *Bingo* (1971), and *Restoration* (1968). He has also written two volumes of poetry and a number of screenplays, including *Walkabout* (1971), directed by Nicolas Roeg.

In his later work, Bond continues to be noted for the violence in his writing. A socialist and atheist, he is also known for the highly political content of his plays, and by the 1990s was considered a major voice in the British theater.

PLOT SUMMARY

Act I

Lear opens at the site of a wall King Lear is having built in order to keep enemies out of his kingdom. Two workers carry a dead laborer onstage just before Lear enters with Lord Warrington and Lear's daughters, Bodice and Fontanelle, among others. When Lear sees the dead man, his primary concern is with the resulting delay to the building of the wall, and he shoots the worker who accidentally caused the man's death. Bodice and Fontanelle object to Lear's violence and reveal their own plans to marry Lear's enemies, the Duke of North and the Duke of Cornwall, respectively. Lear's daughters believe their marriages will lead to peace, but Lear believes that only the wall can protect his people. After Lear and the others leave, Bodice and Fontanelle reveal the plans they share with their husbands to attack Lear's armies. In Scene 2, as Lear prepares for war, Warrington informs him that each daughter has written separately, each asking Warrington to betray Lear, then the other daughter. In Scene 3, each of the daughters complains about her husband and reveals plans to have him killed.

In Scene 4, the audience discovers that the sisters' armies have been victorious, but Bodice and Fontanelle each has failed at having her husband killed. Warrington, now a prisoner whose tongue has been cut out, is brought before the sisters. Bodice calmly knits while Warrington is tortured by her soldiers. Fontanelle calls for increased violence against Warrington, then deafens him by poking Bodice's knitting needles into his ears. Warrington is taken out by a soldier.

In Scene 5, Lear, in the woods, finds bread on the ground and eats it. Warrington, crippled, and for whom the bread is intended, sneaks up behind Lear with a knife but leaves when the Gravedigger's Boy

Edward Bond

arrives with bread and water for Lear. The Boy asks Lear to stay with him and his wife. Scene 6 takes place at the Boy's house, where Lear finds out how the Boy lives. The Boy has two fields and his pregnant wife, Cordelia, keeps pigs. When Lear goes out with the Boy, Warrington returns with a knife, and the Boy's wife calls out, saying that the Wild Man has returned. While Lear sleeps, Warrington returns with a knife, attacks Lear, then leaves.

In Scene 7, the Boy complains to Lear about the king who caused so much suffering for the workers building his wall, but asks Lear to stay. A sergeant and three soldiers come on stage looking for Lear. Warrington's body is discovered plugging the well. The soldiers kill the Boy, rape Cordelia, and kill the pigs. The Carpenter arrives and kills the soldiers. Lear is taken prisoner.

Act II

In the first scene, saying Lear is mad, Bodice and Fontanelle bring him before a judge. When asked about Bodice and Fontanelle, Lear denies that they are his daughters. Bodice has her mirror given to Lear, as she believes that madmen are frightened of themselves. Lear sees himself in the mirror as a tortured animal in a cage. He is found mad and taken away. Bodice tells Fontanelle that there are malcontents in the kingdom and that there will be a civil war. Fontanelle replies that the rebels are led by Cordelia.

In Scene 2, the Gravedigger's Boy's Ghost appears to Lear in his cell. Lear asks the Ghost to bring him his daughters. The apparitions that appear are of Bodice and Fontanelle as young girls. Lear and his daughters talk as the two girls sit with their heads on his knees. Lear asks the daughters to stay, but they leave him. The Ghost reappears and asks Lear if he can stay with him. Lear agrees, saying they will be comforted by the sound of each other's voices.

In Scene 3, Cordelia appears with her soldiers, one of whom was wounded in a skirmish with Bodice and Fontanelle's troops. The Carpenter arrives. A soldier captured by Cordelia's men asks to join their forces, but Cordelia has him shot because he does not hate. The others go offstage, leaving the wounded soldier to die alone. In Scene 4, Bodice and Fontanelle, talking at their headquarters, reveal that their husbands have tried to desert. Fontanelle is given Lear's death warrant by Bodice and signs it. The Dukes of North and Cornwall arrive and are told they are to be kept in cells unless there is a need for them to be seen in public. Left alone, Bodice reveals that she started to have the wall pulled down, but that she needed the workers as soldiers.

In Scene 5, Cordelia's soldiers, who appear leading Lear and other prisoners, have lost their way. Lear says that he only wants to live to find the Ghost and help him. Fontanelle is brought in, a prisoner also. In Scene 6, Lear and the other prisoners, including Fontanelle, are in their cell. The Ghost arrives. He is cold and thin. Lear says he wishes he'd been the Ghost's father and looked after him. Fontanelle tells Lear that if he helps her, she will protect him if Bodice is victorious. At the Carpenter's command, a soldier shoots Fontanelle. A medical doctor who is also a prisoner arrives to perform an autopsy on Fontanelle. Lear is awed by the beauty of the inside of her body, in contrast to her cruelty and hatred when alive.

Bodice arrives as a prisoner, indicating that Cordelia's forces have defeated the last remnants of the daughters' regime. Lear tells his daughter that he destroyed Fontanelle. Bodice too has been sentenced to death. The soldiers stab her with a bayonet three times. Cordelia, now the Carpenter's wife, has asked that Lear not be killed. Using a "scientific device," the doctor removes Lear's eyes. In terrible pain, Lear leaves the prison with the Ghost. In Scene 7, Lear meets a family of farmers by the wall. They reveal that the father will go to work on the wall and the son will become a soldier. Lear feels pity and tells them to run away. Lear says that Cordelia does not know what she is doing and that he will write to tell her of the people's suffering.

Act III

In Scene 1, Lear is living in the Boy's old house with Thomas, his wife Susan, and John, all of whom care for Lear in his blindness. A deserter from Cordelia's wall arrives; the Ghost wants him to leave for the sake of everyone else's safety. Soldiers arrive, looking for the deserter, but Lear hides the fugitive. Unable to find him, the soldiers leave. The others want the deserter to leave as well, but Lear insists that he—and all escapees who come to the house—can stay.

Scene 2 occurs some months later. At the Boy's house, Lear tells a group of people a fable. The audience learns from Thomas that hundreds gather to hear Lear's public speeches, but Thomas believes it is dangerous for Lear to continue speaking out against the government. An officer arrives with Lear's old Councilor and accuses Lear of hiding deserters. The deserter from Scene 2 is taken away to be hanged. The Councilor tells Lear that Cordelia has tolerated Lear's speaking, but now he must stop. The Councilor and those who came with him leave. Lear complains that he is still a prisoner; there is a wall everywhere. The Ghost enters; he is thinner and more shrunken. The Ghost suggests that he poison the well so the others will leave; he will take Lear to a spring to drink. Lear sleeps, and John tells Susan that he is leaving and asks her to come with him. John leaves, Thomas enters, and Susan, crying, asks Thomas to take her away from Lear. Thomas tells Susan to come into the house.

In Scene 3, Lear is alone in the woods. The Ghost arrives; he is deteriorating rapidly and appears terrified. The Ghost believes he is dying and weeps because he is afraid. Cordelia and the Carpenter enter. Cordelia speaks of how the soldiers killed her husband and raped her and of the way in which her new government is creating a better way of life. The Ghost watches his former wife, wishing he could speak to her. Cordelia asks Lear to stop working against her. Lear tells Cordelia she must pull the wall down, but she says the kingdom will be attacked by enemies if she does. When Lear continues saying he will not be quiet, Cordelia says he will be put on trial, then leaves.

The Ghost is gored to death by pigs that have gone mad. In Scene 4, Lear is taken to the wall by Susan. He climbs up on the structure in order to dig it up. The Farmer's Son, now a soldier, shoots Lear, injuring him. Lear continues to shovel. The Farmer's Son shoots Lear again, killing him. Lear's body is left alone onstage.

CHARACTERS

Ben

Ben is an orderly in the prison who is kind to Lear. When Ben, pursued by soldiers, later appears at the Gravedigger's Boy's house, Lear takes him in despite the danger in doing so.

Bishop

The Bishop appears briefly in the first act, blessing Lear's army. He tells Lear that God will support him, not the women who act against him.

Bodice

Bodice is Lear's daughter and Fontanelle's sister. In the first scene, she objects to her father's cruelty in killing one of his workmen, but when she marries the Duke of North and leads a successful rebellion against her father, she becomes more cruel than he was, even coolly planning her own husband's murder. Although in many ways she is quite similar to her sister, Bodice is the more cold and calculating of the two. While Warrington is being tortured, Bodice calmly knits, and her concentration on her knitting throughout this horrid scene is so extreme that it becomes darkly comic. As the play progresses, Bodice's desire for power grows, and she imprisons her husband and speaks of eventually killing her sister. She is, however, the more introspective of the two sisters, and in a monologue speaks of her own feeling that all of her power traps her and makes her its slave. When Bodice is finally imprisoned, she is as calculating as ever. She is killed by Cordelia's soldiers while in prison, and it is clear that she has learned nothing.

Carpenter

The Carpenter is first seen at the home of the Gravedigger's Boy and his wife, Cordelia. The Gravedigger's Boy says that the Carpenter comes to their home often because of his love for Cordelia. Shortly after soldiers kill the Gravedigger's Boy and rape Cordelia, the Carpenter comes on stage and kills the soldiers. He and Cordelia marry. Although his killing of the soldiers seems to be a noble act, when Cordelia gains power, he becomes a part of her corrupt government.

Cordelia

The audience first sees Cordelia, the Gravedigger's Boy's Wife, at home with her husband when Lear comes seeking shelter. She is not as compassionate as the Gravedigger's Boy and wants Lear to leave. After her husband is killed by the soldiers who cruelly rape her, Cordelia marries the Carpenter and leads a rebellion against Bodice and Fontanelle. Her rebellion is successful, but once in power, she is every bit as cruel as those she fought against. It is Cordelia who leaves her own wounded soldier to die alone, who orders the executions of Bodice and Fontanelle, and the blinding of Lear. She allows Lear to live but tries to stop his public speaking. It is one of her soldiers who finally kills Lear.

Duke of Cornwall

The Duke of Cornwall begins as an enemy of Lear's kingdom, but Fontanelle says that by marrying him, she can bring peace between him and her father. Instead, he becomes a part of Fontanelle and Bodice's revolution against Lear. Fontanelle quickly tires of him and attempts to have him killed. He survives, but Fontanelle later has him imprisoned. As a character, he is virtually interchangeable with the Duke of North.

Duke of North

Initially an enemy of Lear's kingdom, the Duke of North marries Bodice, supposedly in order to bring peace, but then supports Bodice and Fontanelle's revolution. Bodice, however, soon grows tired of him and tries to have him killed. Although that attempt fails, she eventually succeeds in having him imprisoned. There is little difference between the Duke of North and the Duke of Cornwall, Fontanelle's husband.

Farmer

The Farmer appears by Lear's wall with his wife and son shortly after Lear is released, blinded, from prison. When Lear asks to rest in his home, the Farmer explains that he has lost everything due to the madness of the king and his obsession with building the wall. Lear begins to see the real effects of what he has done and to feel compassion for the people of the kingdom.

Farmer's Son

The Farmer's Son appears with his mother and father at Lear's wall. At the time Lear meets him, he is being conscripted into Cordelia's army. Lear begs him not to go, but to run away instead. In the final scene, it is the Farmer's Son, now a soldier, who shoots and kills Lear.

Farmer's Wife

The Farmer's Wife appears at Lear's wall with her husband and son. She is resigned to the dark fate of her family.

Firing Squad Officer

The Firing Squad Officer commands the firing squad that is supposed to shoot one of Lear's workers at his command. When they are not quick enough, Lear shoots the man himself.

Fontanelle

Fontanelle is Lear's daughter and Bodice's sister. In the first scene, her objection to her father's killing of a workman makes her seem compassionate, but when she and Bodice lead the rebellion against Lear, it becomes clear that she is immensely cruel. Fontanelle plans the murder of her husband, an effort which fails, but is shown at her cruelest during the torture of Warrington, when she becomes so excited about Warrington's suffering that the result is a sort of black humor. Her extreme pleasure in the torture contrasts with Bodice's calm state. Although Fontanelle and Bodice are supposedly working together, they are not loyal to one another; Fontanelle has her own spies. Fontanelle is finally imprisoned by Cordelia and executed. Afterwards, she is autopsied onstage and Lear is moved by the beauty of the inside of her body. In viewing Fontanelle's autopsy, Lear becomes aware of his responsibility in the formation of his children's characters. Although she learns nothing herself, in death Fontanelle contributes to Lear's clearer understanding of his own cruelty.

Ghost

See Gravedigger's Boy

Gravedigger's Boy

The Gravedigger's Boy plays a strong part in teaching Lear about compassion. When he first meets Lear, the Gravedigger's Boy is living in a pastoral setting with his pregnant wife, Cordelia. The simplicity of his life and his kindness bring about the beginning of Lear's change. After the Gravedigger's Boy is murdered by soldiers, he later appears to Lear in his prison cell, now as a Ghost. As the Ghost, he continues to teach Lear as he tries to help him, but the Ghost himself is in a state of continuing deterioration. He is slowly dying and is afraid. Lear, calling the Ghost his boy, becomes his protector, but is unable to save the Ghost from his decline. Meanwhile, the Ghost continues in his protective attitude toward Lear. The two learn to help and teach each other and to show one another true kindness and compassion. Finally, however, the Ghost is mauled to death by maddened pigs, and Lear feels the pain of his second death.

Gravedigger's Boy's Wife

See Cordelia

John

John lives with Thomas, Susan, and Lear at the Gravedigger's Boy's house. He is more critical of Lear and eventually leaves for the city, asking Susan to leave Thomas and come with him. She stays with Thomas and Lear.

Judge

The Judge, who is clearly under the control of Bodice and Fontanelle, presides at Lear's trial and concludes that Lear is mad.

Lear

Lear is the play's title character. The action revolves largely around his growth as an individual. When he first appears on stage, it is as a cruel king bent on building a wall around his kingdom, supposedly to protect his people. His actions, however, soon show his indifference to their lives, as he kills a workman who has accidentally killed another and thus delayed the completion of the wall. When Lear is deposed by his daughters, Bodice and Fontanelle, he begins to suffer and to change through that suffering. When the rebellion first begins, Lear denies that he even has daughters, but he eventually takes responsibility for his part in building their characters. His relationship with the Gravedigger's Boy, and subsequently with the Gravedigger's Boy's Ghost, also changes him as he begins to see the possibility of true kindness. Much of Lear's change, in fact, comes because of his relationships with other people. As he sees the world through their eyes, he develops compassion and is finally willing to give his own life because of the good it might do others. His final act, an attempt to dig up his own wall, shows the extent of his transformation. It is this transformation that is the center of the play.

Officer

The Officer comes to the Gravedigger's Boy's house while Lear is living there with Thomas, Susan, and John. He accuses Lear of harboring deserters and takes the Small Man away to be executed.

Old Councilor

The Old Councilor is loyal to whatever regime is in power. He begins as a minister of Lear's, supports Bodice and Fontanelle when they are in power, and eventually works for Cordelia.

Prisoners

Four Prisoners appear with Lear in a prison convoy. One of them is also the Prison Doctor who performs the autopsy on Fontanelle and later blinds Lear.

Small Man

The Small Man is a deserter pursued by soldiers. He asks Lear, Thomas, Susan, and John to hide him. Lear tries to protect him, but he is eventually found by the soldiers and taken away to be executed.

Soldiers

Fourteen soldiers have speaking parts in the play, and others appear on stage. These soldiers are a frequent presence throughout the play and are usually seen in the act of killing or torturing people. They are in the service of the various corrupt regimes.

Susan

Susan is Thomas's wife and lives at the Gravedigger's Boy's house with Thomas, John, and Lear. Like Thomas, she is concerned that Lear's compassion for others will endanger the household, but it is she who leads Lear to his wall so that he can commit his defiant final act.

Thomas

Thomas, his wife Susan, and John live with Lear at the Gravedigger's Boy's house after Lear has been blinded and released from prison. Thomas is compassionate, but unlike Lear, he is reluctant to endanger the household by helping those pursued by Cordelia's army. He is also concerned that Lear's public speaking will bring trouble. Yet he says he wants to fight for the good of the people. Susan and John want him to leave Lear, but he refuses.

Warrington

Warrington is loyal to Lear. He is captured and brutally tortured under the direction of Lear's daughters when they first rebel against their father. The daughters decide not to kill Warrington and for a time he lives in the woods and is referred to as "the wild man" by the Gravedigger's Boy and his wife. He drowns in their well.

Wild Man

See Warrington

Workmen

The three workmen appear in the first scene, where they are seen building Lear's wall. Their only value to Lear is in their ability to work on the wall. When one is accidentally killed, Lear's only concern is for the resulting delay in building the wall.

Wounded Rebel Soldier

The Wounded Rebel Soldier was injured fighting in Cordelia's army. She, the Carpenter, and the other rebel soldiers abandon him to die alone.

THEMES

Parents and Children

In *Lear* Bond provides a picture of a family that has disintegrated. In the very first scene of the play, Bond portrays hostility between Lear and his daughters. Bodice and Fontanelle reveal to their father that they will marry his enemies, the Duke of North and the Duke of Cornwall, then tear down Lear's wall. Lear responds in kind, telling them he has always known of their maliciousness. When Lear leaves the stage, Bodice and Fontanelle reveal their plans to attack their father's army. Lear and his daughters are literally at war with one another; when presented with Lear's death warrant, Fontanelle eagerly signs it. At his trial Lear seems to reject his children altogether, saying he has no daughters.

Yet in prison, Lear shows a desire for a relationship with his children. Lear asks the Ghost to bring him his daughters who, he now says, will help him. Apparitions of the daughters as young girls appear, and the audience is given the sense of happier, more peaceful times. The daughters are afraid of being in prison, but Lear comforts them. When they say they must leave, Lear begs them to stay. Lear realizes that at some point in the past his daughters were kind, lovable people. Later, when Fontanelle is killed and autopsied, the procedure reveals to Lear that his daughter is flesh and bone and not some evil beast in human guise.

Lear is awed by the beauty and purity of the inside of Fontanelle's body. He sees no maliciousness, no evil, there, just base human matter. He says that if he had known how beautiful Fontanelle was, he would have loved her. "Did I make this—and destroy it?" he asks. It is only at the autopsy that Lear realizes that he is responsible for the evil in his daughters. He has shaped their personalities and behavior. They learned all of their cruelty, greed, and thirst for power from him. There is an inherent connection between the children and the parent who nurtured their development, and Lear can no longer see himself as simply the victim of his daughters' evil. Lear and his daughters are inextricably bound together. By the time Lear realizes this, however, it is too late. Both daughters are dead, and he cannot change the past. The disintegrated family cannot be rebuilt. Lear must live with his guilt.

Violence and Power

In his preface to *Lear* Bond states, "I write about violence as naturally as Jane Austen wrote about manners." For Bond, violence is an integral part of contemporary society; writing about modern culture means writing about violence. *Lear* begins and ends with violence. In the first scene, Lear shoots a worker who has accidentally caused another worker's death; in the last scene, a soldier shoots and kills Lear. In between, there are numerous acts of brutality. Warrington's tongue is cut out, he is tortured, and knitting needles are shoved into his ears. The innocent Gravedigger's Boy is shot, and his wife is raped. Even as a Ghost, the Gravedigger's Boy suffers a second violent death, this time an

TOPICS FOR FURTHER STUDY

- Discuss the difference between William Shakespeare's *King Lear* and Bond's *Lear.* In what ways has Bond changed Shakespeare's play? What might be the significance of those changes? Consider especially Bond's characterizations of Lear and Cordelia.
- Compare Lear to Oedipus in Sophocles's play *Oedipus Rex.* Compare the blinding of Oedipus to that of Lear. How does blindness work as a metaphor in each play?
- Using Machiavelli's *The Prince* as a resource, discuss the nature of political power. How is power obtained and maintained? Is it possible to seek power in an ethical manner? How do individuals seek and secure power today?
- Research Bertolt Brecht's concepts of epic theater and the alienation effect. How does Bond employ Brecht's concepts in *Lear?*
- While some critics consider Lear's final act of digging up his wall futile, others have seen purpose in it. Given that Lear knows that he cannot destroy the wall and that he almost certainly will die if he tries, what could be his purpose in the attempt? Is anything achieved by Lear's defiance?

attack by pigs. Fontanelle is shot and Bodice is gored by soldiers. Numerous minor characters also die violent deaths.

Aside from the violence, there are scenes depicting graphic gore. The autopsy of Fontanelle and the blinding of Lear are among the most horrifying scenes in recent literature. As traumatic as watching Bond's violent scenes may be for the audience, however, it is important to note that these scenes are not mere titillation or sensationalism; Bond uses the violence in *Lear,* as well as in his other plays, to highlight the violence of modern society. His interest is not simply in the violence itself, but in the circumstances that provoke such savagery in both reality and fiction.

Most of the violence in *Lear* is directly related to the desire for power. When the first worker is shot in Act I, the audience immediately realizes a connection between Lear's power and the violence that has repeatedly been used in the formation of his regime. Supposedly horrified by Lear's violence, Bodice and Fontanelle revolt against their father, but once in power, they are every bit as violent as he. One might expect Cordelia, originally one of the oppressed masses, to also govern without violence, but, once in power, she is as ruthless as Lear and his daughters. Although the rulers change, their policies of governing through violence remain the same. The very structure of this society is violent. It is Bond's intention that the audience see the violence of Lear's society as a reflection of its own time. Through recognition of its own savagery, society may change.

Transformation

Lear begins the play as a violent man, a ruthless king. His rancor is immediately highlighted when he shoots one worker who has accidentally killed another. The crime, in Lear's view, is not in taking an innocent life, but in delaying the building of the wall. Although the king, when he talks of his people in the abstract, speaks of his duty to protect them, as individuals their lives mean nothing to him. As the play progresses—and his circumstances change—Lear begins to perceive things differently. When his daughters' revolution succeeds, he flees to the countryside, where he meets the Gravedigger's Boy, who generously feeds him and gives him sanctuary.

Lear witnesses the human ability to forgive when the Boy tells him of the subjects' suffering caused by the building of the wall and yet allows the deposed king to stay. Lear's education in suffering is continued when he sees the Boy killed, his wife raped, and their livestock killed. His imprisonment by his daughters also teaches him about pain. In prison, Lear develops feelings of protectiveness toward the Ghost. Also in prison, Lear's observation of Fontanelle's autopsy helps him to further see the damage for which he is responsible. At this point, when he is beginning to see, Lear is blinded.

The blind Lear is released and meets the farmer, his wife, and their son; Lear now truly sees their suffering and longs to end it. He begins to live among the people and endangers his own life by offering sanctuary to all who need it and by speaking out against Cordelia's regime. Lear's last act is his attempt to tear down the wall, an attempt that will clearly fail, and he dies in this symbolic act. Violence and evil still reign. Yet, in Lear's transformation and virtuous final act, an example for positive change has been presented.

STYLE

Epic Theater/Alienation Effect

Twentieth-century playwright Bertold Brecht (*The Threepenny Opera*) developed the modern concept of the epic theater for use in his political dramas. Unlike conventional drama, epic theater develops from a sequence of many scenes, as in *Lear,* that often take place over a considerable time period and employ a large number of characters. The continuous movement from scene to scene is meant to keep the audience from becoming too emotionally involved with the characters. This lack of emotional involvement is also developed through Brecht's alienation effect, which occurs when the audience is continuously made aware that it is not watching reality but a play.

In *Lear* characters periodically speak to the audience rather than to one another. This sort of speech is called an ''aside'' and contributes to the alienation effect. When Warrington is tortured, the darkly comic comments of Bodice and Fontanelle remind the audience that this is an exaggerated fiction removed from reality. This is part of the alienation effect as well. The purpose of this method is to force the audience to use its intellect rather than its emotions in considering the themes and action of the play. Brecht believed that focusing on reason, not emotion, would be more effective in conveying the motives of political drama.

Anachronism

An anachronism is an object or idea that is from a time period different from the one in which a work of literature is set; it is something that is clearly out of context with the rest of the work's environment. The modern workers building Lear's wall are an anachronism, as is the futuristic ''scientific device'' used to blind Lear. Anachronisms can have two major effects. They are sometimes used to make a story more universal—to illustrate that the story is not only about the time in which it is set but that it uses themes and ideas that apply to all times. Anachronisms can also contribute to the alienation effect, creating a sense of the surreal that reinforces the unreality of the proceedings. In *Lear,* Bond's anachronistic technique serves both purposes.

Allusion

An allusion refers to something outside of the play, usually a literary work. By using allusion, the playwright is able to enrich the audience's experience of the drama. Though a complete story in itself, Bond's entire play is an allusion to William Shakespeare's *King Lear.* Because the play is about Shakespeare's text, familiarity with *King Lear* will deepen the audience's understanding of Bond's interpretation. Bodice's knitting in times of mayhem is an allusion to Charles Dickens's *A Tale of Two Cities,* a novel about the French Revolution in which the character Madame Defarge, one of the revolutionaries, knits a list of aristocrats who must die into a scarf.

Setting

Bond's play takes place in a year numbered 3100, presumably in ancient Britain, although Bond fills his story with modern devices, indicating that the action may be taking place in some distant future. Read in this manner, Bond could be condemning the phenomenon of history repeating itself. If the play is set in the future, then the events are a recreation of the original Lear legend that took place centuries before.

The action of the play takes place in a multitude of locations, but there are some that reappear within the play. Although the audience does not actually see Lear's wall until the final scene, the play opens near the wall, which becomes a pervasive symbolic presence throughout the play. Frequent references to the wall cause the audience to sense a feeling of enclosure and claustrophobia that is representative of the oppression caused by the different regimes throughout the play. Paradoxically, in the final scene the audience is shown the wall, and thus the possibility of a future on the outside; the inspiration for freedom is deepened by Lear's insistence that the structure, and all that it symbolizes, be destroyed.

The Gravedigger's Boy's house is also an important location. It is in this more pastoral setting that Lear experiences the possibility of change and the depth of human kindness. It is to this house that the blind Lear returns and establishes a sanctuary for fugitives from the regime. The house represents the chance of happiness and freedom, an idyll from oppression. Another important location is the prison, where Lear learns of his own responsibility for the suffering of others. Imprisoned with his daughters, he becomes aware that their evil is a reflection—and creation—of his own capacity for such behavior.

Metaphor

A metaphor is a word or phrase whose literal meaning is subverted to represent something else. The wall, the play's greatest metaphor, is a presence which pervades the play even when it is not seen. It is representative of the oppression and control of various corrupt regimes. Bodice and Fontanelle as well as Cordelia initially see the wall as something that must be dug up. Yet whoever ascends to power realizes that the wall is a means to preserve their authority. At the same time, the people see the wall as the source of their misery. Because of the massive effort put into constructing the wall, their farms are lost and the men sicken and die. The structure is also a metaphor for the ''wall'' that Lear has figuratively built between himself and his adult daughters, as well as between himself and the emotional needs of his subjects. Lear's final attempt to dig up the wall represents his realization that such oppressive structures must be demolished to advance humanity.

The blinding of Lear is also metaphoric. In literature blindness is often associated with greater insight. Tiresias, the mythological Greek prophet, is blind as is the character of Oedipus. Lear is blinded just as he begins to realize his own responsibility for the pain of others. In these cases, physical blindness enables greater insight into the human condition. It is also symbolic of an epiphany or great self-reflection. As with the legend of Oedipus (who unwittingly killed his father, married his mother, and, upon learning what he had done, blinded himself), Lear's blinding occurs at the moment that he gains full realization of his life's atrocities.

HISTORICAL CONTEXT

British writers of Bond's generation were profoundly influenced by World War II and its aftermath. German leader Adolf Hitler's intense bombing of London, known as the ''blitz,'' brought the horrors of war home to British soil. At the end of the war, the discovery of the Nazi concentration camps (in which millions were put to death for their perceived threat to the German regime) revealed a previously unimagined evil. The American use of the atomic bomb at the end of the war led to new fears about the future of the planet, fears which were exacerbated when Britain tested its first hydrogen bomb in 1954.

For the British people, the violence of war was very real. At the close of the conflict, Britain began to lose its status as a nation. It had once been said that the sun never set on the British empire. Now that same empire was gradually dismantled as former colonies such as India and Africa regained their autonomy. The Suez crisis of 1956, in which Britain tried to gain control of the Suez Canal in Egypt and was subsequently condemned for its military interference, caused great disillusionment with the government. After the United Nations condemned Britain's action, troops were forced to withdraw, and the prime minister resigned. Equally sobering for leftist causes was the Soviet Union's invasion of Hungary in 1956 and its subsequent invasion of Czechoslovakia in 1968. Socialism, seen by many as a hope for the future, was revealed to be as aggressive, dictatorial, and violent as any other political system.

The postwar years in England also saw the development of the Welfare State, in which responsibility for the poor would rest largely on the government. In 1946, the National Insurance Act and the National Health Service Act were passed. The National Assistance Act of 1948 was designed to provide government relief for the poor. Many

COMPARE & CONTRAST

- **1971:** Advances in science and technology create fears that humankind is tragically abandoning its bucolic past. Contemporary problems such as overpopulated urban areas and vast unemployment are blamed on technological advances that replace humans with machines.

  Today: Computers have revolutionized business, education, and personal lives in developed countries but are also criticized for leading to alienation and an escape from ''real'' life. The successful cloning of sheep leads to questions about medical ethics.

- **1971:** American intervention in Vietnam and British military presence in Northern Ireland make the horrors of war real as American and British young men die in violent altercations with the results being televised. Four student protesters are killed at Kent State University in Ohio, leading to a further sense of violence at home.

  Today: Wars continue, including those in the Balkan regions and the Persian Gulf, but public protests against these conflicts are less visible. Concern about violence focuses more on gang wars and other types of urban crime.

- **1971:** Focus on helping the poor is primarily evidenced in legislation and government assistance, but there is some movement toward abolishing Britain's welfare state as Education Minister Margaret Thatcher ends the free milk program in schools.

  Today: Many government social programs of the 1960s and 1970s have been dismantled. There are still efforts at governmental assistance to the poor, but people in general are more skeptical that government can make such programs work. Focus is on the assistance of the private sector and there is a greater emphasis on volunteerism.

- **1971:** Despite the oppression of socialist regimes, such as those of the Soviet Union and East Germany, socialism is romanticized, particularly by the young. In Britain especially, socialism is considered a viable alternative form of government.

  Today: The Soviet Union has been dismantled and the Berlin Wall torn down. Socialism is rarely romanticized as it was. There are comparatively few socialists in the United States, but the movement still has some strength in Britain. This is particularly evident on the British stage.

---

believed that through the government's actions, poverty and unemployment would be abolished, a line of reasoning that was quickly proven false. The belief in the need for government assistance for the poor, however, continued into the late 1960s and early 1970s. In these later years, government policies also became increasingly liberal. Homosexuality, previously illegal, was now considered outside of government jurisdiction. The National Health Service began to fund contraception and abortions for the poor. Women and members of minority groups began to agitate for their rights. The Lord Chamberlain's power to censor the theater was abolished.

In his preface to *Lear* Bond writes, ''We can see that most men are spending their lives doing things for which they are not biologically designed. We are not designed for our production lines, housing blocks, even cars; and these things are not designed for us.'' Bond's suspicion of technology is a reflection of his times. During this period the idyllic pastoral life depicted at the home of *Lear* 's Gravedigger's Boy was fast disappearing as farms became more industrialized. There was also the sense that the increase in technology, because of the resulting displacement of workers, was a large contributor to the problems of unemployment and, thus, poverty. Medical advances were also under suspicion. When the first heart transplant was performed in England in 1967, some compared that breakthrough to the depiction of biological technology (and the creation of a monster) in Mary Shelley's novel *Frankenstein.*

The time in which Bond wrote *Lear* was also a time of violence. In 1968 alone the Soviets invaded Czechoslovakia, Martin Luther King and Robert Kennedy were both assassinated, and the Six Day War was fought in Israel. During these years, the war in Vietnam was escalating, and British troops were sent into Northern Ireland to quell unrest over that country's sovereignty. Students became deeply involved in politics and there were mass demonstrations. It also became clear, however, that the students could turn violent as well. In 1970, three members of the radical American group ''The Weathermen'' were killed when the bomb they were building for terrorist purposes exploded. It was this type of destruction, this kind of violence, that is dramatized in *Lear,* a play in which all governments and all revolutions are shown to be violent and, ultimately, alike in their ruthless cruelty and disregard for human life.

CRITICAL OVERVIEW

The pervasive violence of Bond's *Lear* has been a focus of criticism since the play's premiere in 1971. By that time, Bond was well known for the graphic nature of his 1965 play *Saved,* which features a scene in which a baby in a carriage is stoned to death. That play, in part because of its intense savagery, received many negative reviews, but its importance in British theater was virtually unquestioned by the time of *Lear*'s debut six years later. Richard Scharine, in *The Plays of Edward Bond,* quoted the *Lear*'s assistant director, Gregory Dark, on the influence of *Saved*'s reputation on early reviews of Bond's 1971 work: ''On the whole, we felt that the critics were scared of giving an outright condemnation—they had been caught out that way with *Saved*—but obviously did not like the play, so they chose a middle road which satisfied nobody, and really meant nothing.'' Critic Benedict Nightingale, quoted by Scharine, managed criticism and qualified praise of *Lear* at the same time: ''I must admit that the more seats around me emptied, the more the play impressed me, albeit against many of my instincts and much of my judgement.'' Nightingale also offered mild criticism of Bond's violence, saying that ''The play's horrors . . . have their perhaps overemphatic place.''

In *Bond on File* Philip Roberts quoted early reviews by Irving Wardle and Helen Dawson, both of whom defend Bond's graphic depictions while acknowledging their profoundly disturbing nature. Wardle wrote, ''At first glance [Bond] seems totally lacking in common humanity. But what passes for common humanity in other writers can mean that they share our own compromising attachments.'' Dawson noted that ''the violence is not at all gloating; it hurts, as it is meant to do, but there is no relish in it. As a result, *Lear,* despite its unflinching brutality, is not a negative work.''

When the play was revived in 1983, twelve years after its original production, Anthony Masters, also quoted by Roberts, wrote, ''What is unbearable about seeing Edward Bond's greatest . . . play again . . . is not the horrors and bleakness of war, the bayonetings and mutilations . . . and the other brutalities that had members of Thursday night's audience carried out in seizures of shock.'' For Masters, what was truly horrible was ''the knowledge that [the play] is even more topical now and will become more so as man's inhumanity gains subtle sophistication with the twenty-first century's approach.'' For Masters, it was not so much the violence itself that was upsetting, but what Bond was saying by the portrayal of such violence. According to Masters, ''the reality of the violence was the true horror.''

Nonetheless, for most later critics, it is the violence that remains disturbing and continues to dominate discussion of the play. David L. Hirst, in his book *Edward Bond,* wrote that ''it may be that the excessive amount of realistic violence in the play—far greater than in any of Bond's previous dramas and never equaled in any play since—considerably alienated reviewers and public alike when the play was first performed.'' The violence, according to Hirst, creates two problems for the audience member: ''There is an escalating violence in the play which makes very tough demands on the audience; and there is no apparent escape from it.'' However, this is not necessarily negative for Hirst. He saw *Lear* as part of a tradition of twentieth century drama, an example of Bertolt Brecht's concept of the alienation effect. For Brecht, because drama is supposed to teach, it is important that theater audiences not simply have feelings about the play's characters, but that they think. Such tremendously disturbing scenes of brutality can overwhelm

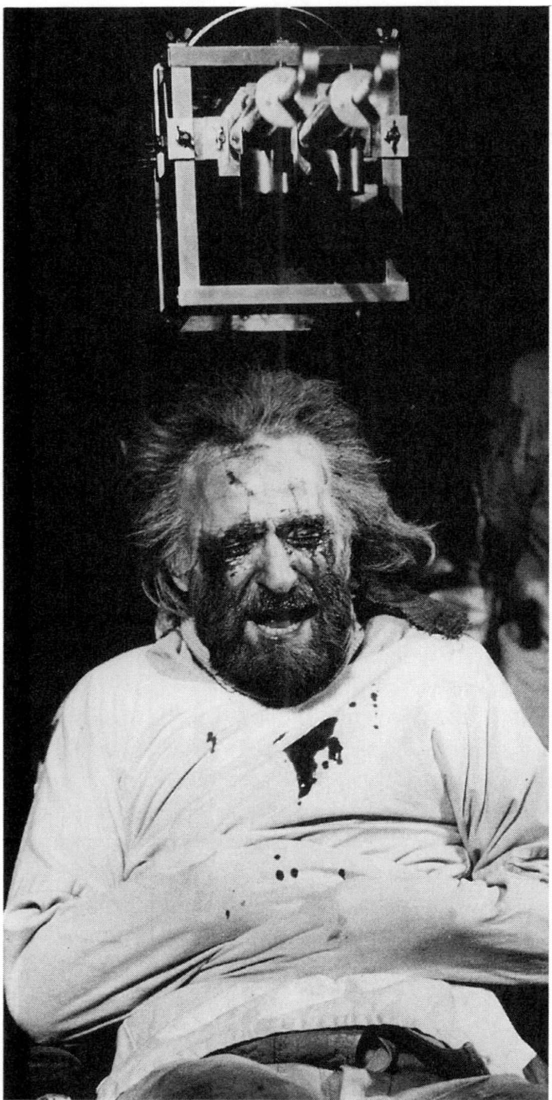

Lear*'s graphic portrayals of violence were a frequent topic for critics. Here, Lear (Robert Peck) is blinded by a futuristic torture device in a Royal Shakespeare Company production*

the audience so greatly that viewers disengage themselves from identifying with the characters and are able to view the violence in a more distant way, to examine it. In that sense, audience alienation is a desirable effect as it enables the audience to go beyond emotion to thought.

On the other hand, Jenny S. Spencer in her book, *Dramatic Strategies in the Plays of Edward Bond,* saw the savagery in *Lear* as intended to have the opposite effect. Spencer referred to the violent scenes in the play as ''akin to terrorist tactics, depend[ing] upon a certain amount of shock, and play[ing] upon the audience's socially conditioned fears.'' For Spencer, ''Bond calls on his audience to 'witness' and 'suffer' the full force of the characters' actions . . . one must *feel* the urgently unacceptable nature of events before desiring to change them.'' According to this viewpoint, what Bond intends is not alienation, but identification. The audience is not meant to feel distance from the characters, but, through its shock and horror, to empathize.

Despite differing viewpoints on *Lear's* violence, few critics now simply condemn the play, as earlier critics condemned *Saved,* for its excesses. The focus of most criticism is to consider, not the violence itself, but Bond's purpose in portraying such severity. The question is not whether such intensity is appropriate, but what Bond is trying to show and whether the violence of *Lear* ultimately serves its purpose.

CRITICISM

Clare Cross

Cross is a Ph.D. candidate specializing in modern drama. In this essay she discusses the moral development of Lear in Bond's play.

In his play *Lear,* Edward Bond focuses on the moral development of the title character, a king in ancient Britain. Although Lear begins the play as an old man, his behavior is that of a child; he is totally absorbed in himself and his own security and needs. He is literally building a wall to keep others out. As the play progresses, however, Lear loses his position of power and is forced to move outside of his self-absorbed sphere and into the society he helped to create. As he suffers along with his former subjects, Lear begins to mature, realizing that others are human beings with needs and desires of their own. For the first time, Lear truly sees other people, and this leads him to recognize the consequences of his own actions and to take responsibility for what he has done. His moral growth, however, is only complete when he turns his understanding into action. It is only then that he becomes a morally mature human being.

When the audience first meets Lear, he is morally a child, seeing nothing beyond his own

WHAT DO I READ NEXT?

- *King Lear,* a play written by William Shakespeare in about 1605, is the original source of Bond's adaptation. In essence, Bond's play is not a rewriting of Shakespeare's play but a reaction to that text, particularly to Shakespeare's portrayal of King Lear and his three daughters.
- *Saved,* Bond's 1965 play, also focuses on the violence of today's culture. As in *Lear,* Bond's use of onstage violence is extreme, but his focus this time is on the contemporary working class.
- *Mother Courage and Her Children,* a play written by Bertolt Brecht in 1939, also focuses on the horrors of war. As in *Lear,* the fact that the ruling regime changes does not matter. The people continue in their poverty and degradation. Like Lear, the character of Mother Courage suffers greatly, but she does not change because of her suffering.
- *The Wall* (1979) is a concept album by the group Pink Floyd. Its story deals with a disillusioned rock star who, through various events in his life, constructs an imaginary wall between himself and the rest of the world. Within his mind the wall becomes a real barrier that he must destroy to once again join humanity. The work was also adapted as a film by director Alan Parker.
- *The Prince,* by Renaissance philosopher Nicolo Machiavelli, is a classic discourse on the proper way to rule, marked by its emphasis on the need for a ruler to maintain power by all means necessary, including violence and cruelty.

---

needs and desires. He is obsessed with the building of his wall, which he claims will benefit his people. It is clear from the beginning, however, that Lear has a callous disregard for others. He complains about the workers leaving wood in the mud to rot, then almost immediately turns to complaints about the living conditions of the men. Bond makes it clear, however, that Lear's complaints do not arise from true concern for his workers. His dissatisfaction about their living conditions is, in fact, parallel to his complaint about the wood. ''You must deal with this fever, '' he tells the Foreman. ''When [the men] finish work they must be kept in dry huts. All these huts are wet.'' Like the wood, the men are being left to rot. Lear goes on to tell the Foreman, ''You waste men,'' a statement that shows that to Lear, the workers are simply more materials to be used in building the wall.

Bond makes Lear's attitude even more clear when Lear's primary concern with the accidental death of a worker is that it will cause delay in building the wall. Lear insists, over the protests of his two daughters, Bodice and Fontanelle, that the worker who inadvertently caused the death be executed. Here Bond contrasts Lear's spoken concern for his people with his actions. When his daughters say they will tear down the wall, Lear says, ''I loved and cared for all my children, and now you've sold them to their enemies!'' Immediately after this statement, Lear shoots the worker who caused the death; it is Lear who is the true enemy of his people.

What Lear's wall actually protects is not so much his subjects but his position as their king. When his daughters reveal their plans to take over the kingdom, Lear turns on them as well, saying, ''I built my wall against *you* as well as my other enemies.'' In his book *The Art and Politics of Edward Bond,* Lou Lappin pointed out that Lear's wall also functions as a glorification of himself. Lear says, ''When I'm dead my people will live in freedom and peace and remember my name, no—venerate it.'' Lappin called the building of Lear's wall ''a self-absorbed gesture, an act of solipsism that seeks to ennoble itself in a cult of personality.'' Like a child, Lear thinks only of himself.

In his book *The Plays of Edward Bond,* Richard Scharine wrote, ''When Lear is overthrown, he is propelled into the society he created like a baby being born.'' Scharine went on to say, however, that ''the mere fact of his being overthrown does not teach Lear moral maturity.'' At the Gravedigger's Boy's house, Lear is still very much a child. Physically, he depends on the Gravedigger's Boy and his wife to feed and shelter him. ''You've looked after me well,'' says Lear. ''I slept like a child in the silence all day.'' Like a child, Lear retains his self-absorption. When he glimpses the tortured Warrington, Lear's emphasis is not on Warrington's pain, but on the effect of that sight on himself: ''I've seen a ghost. I'm going to die. That's why he came back. I'll die.'' When Cordelia, the Gravedigger's Boy's Wife, tells Lear he must go, his response resembles a child's tantrum: ''No, I won't go. He said I could stay. He won't break his word. . . . No, I won't be at everyone's call! My daughters sent you! *You* go! It's you who destroy this place! We must get rid of you!'' It is only when the soldiers arrive, killing the Gravedigger's Boy and raping Cordelia, that Lear shows some recognition of the pain of others when he says to the soldiers: ''O burn the house! You've murdered the husband, slaughtered the cattle, poisoned the well, raped the mother, killed the child—you must burn the house!'' Yet as Jenny S. Spencer pointed out in her book *Dramatic Strategies in the Plays of Edward Bond,* Lear's cry of horror is ''ironically underscored'' by Lear's ''unrecognized responsibility for the soldier's brutality.'' Lear has begun to see outside of himself, but he still does not recognize that the pain he sees is the consequence of his own actions.

Lear's lack of insight continues in the courtroom scene. As Scharine noted, Lear ''still does not understand that he himself is the architect of his prison.'' Not only does he not realize his responsibility for his daughters' actions, he denies that he has daughters at all. In his madness, he sees himself in the mirror as an animal in a cage, but in viewing himself as an animal, he also sees himself primarily as the victim of others and an object of pity. ''Who shut that animal in that cage?'' he asks. ''Let it out.'' Yet at the same time, Lear's view of himself as an animal implies a greater connection with those around him. ''No, that's not the king,'' he says. He is not above the others. In fact, Lear shows the mirror around to those in the courtroom, letting them see the animal, an act that equates the others with himself. In a sense, all are victims. Lear can now see pain outside of himself. However, his moral growth is still incomplete. He still does not take responsibility for his actions, still does not see his own guilt.

It is in his prison cell, after the Gravedigger's Boy's Ghost appears to him and brings him his daughters as young children, that Lear begins to see a connection between his daughters and himself. In the courtroom he says, ''My daughters have been murdered and these monsters have taken their place.'' Yet when Bodice and Fontanelle appear as young girls, Lear shows that they are, in fact, his daughters. The apparitions sit next to Lear with their heads on his knees, and he strokes their hair. When they finally leave, he asks them not to go. At this point, Lear begins to see what he has done, saying, ''I killed so many people and never looked at one of their faces.'' When the Ghost, already deteriorating, asks to stay with Lear, Lear responds for the first time with real compassion: ''Yes, yes, Poor boy. . . . I'll hold you. We'll help each other. Cry while I sleep, and I'll cry and watch while you sleep. . . . The sound of the human voice will comfort us.'' Lear recognizes not only that the Ghost can help him but also that he can help the Ghost. Later, when walking with the other prisoners, Lear expresses even more concern, saying ''I don't want to live except for the boy. Who'd look after him?'' In his relationship with the Ghost, Lear also begins to develop a sense of his own responsibility, saying of the Ghost: ''I did him a great wrong once, a very great wrong. He's never blamed me. I must be kind to him now.'' Lear is now moving toward moral maturity, toward the recognition that he needs to practice compassion, responsibility and action.

With Fontanelle's autopsy, Lear's responsibility becomes even more clear to him. When he sees the inside of her body, he says, ''She was cruel and angry and hard. . . . Where is the beast?'' He is surprised to find there is no monster inside of Fontanelle. ''I am astonished,'' he continues. ''I have never seen anything so beautiful.'' Unlike the Ghost, Fontanelle had done Lear wrong, so he could continue to see her as a monster, separate from himself, but at this point Lear understands his responsibility in forming her character. ''Did I make this,'' he asks, ''and destroy it?'' Earlier, when the Ghost had tried to take Lear away from the jail, Lear answered, ''I ran away so often, but my life was ruined just the same. Now I'll stay.'' Lear continues now in his desire to face reality. He says, ''I must open my eyes and see.''

Lear's desire to finally see is followed almost immediately by his blinding. Scharine quoted Bond as saying, "blindness is a dramatic metaphor for insight, that is why Gloucester, Oedipus, and Tiresias are blind." Once blinded, Lear is released into the countryside. Near the wall, he meets the Farmer, the Farmer's Wife, and their son, all of whom describe how the lives they had known were destroyed by Lear's wall. Lear now sees that he has harmed not only isolated individuals but all of his society, and he is horrified. Falling on his knees, in a posture that asks forgiveness, Lear begs the Farmer's Son not to go into the army, but his efforts are fruitless. As Scharine pointed out, "The society that Lear created has been perfected. Cordelia's subjects are socially moralized and go to their consumption by the social order without questioning." Lear cannot unmake the society he has created, and he sees the depths of his guilt.

In the third act, Lear is seen living at the Gravedigger's Boy's former house with Susan, Thomas, and John. In a sense, this is an attempt to return to the idealized, pastoral life that he glimpsed while living with the Boy and Cordelia—the life he lead in his child-like phase. Lear, however, has changed. He is no longer the self-absorbed child, simply seeking the help of others. Now it is Lear who shows compassion, even as the others, including the Ghost, are concerned that Lear is endangering himself by helping those the government considers enemies. When Lear is told to protect himself, to tell those who come to him that they must leave, Lear insists that all can stay: "I won't turn anyone away. They can eat my food while it lasts and when it's gone they can go if they like, but I won't send anyone away."

Lear is not only taking people in, however; he is also speaking out against the government he helped to create. Lear's former Councilor appears, telling him he must end his public life: "In future you will not speak in public or involve yourself in any public affairs. Your visitors will be vetted by the area military authorities. All these people must go." Knowing that he cannot defeat Cordelia's regime, Lear despairs. He is trapped. "There's a wall everywhere," he says. "I'm buried alive in a wall. Does this suffering and misery last forever?. . . I know nothing, I can do nothing. I am nothing."

After Cordelia tells Lear that he will be tried and executed, however, Lear is again able to move beyond himself and his own despair to his final act, an attempt to dig up and destroy the wall he created.

"LEAR'S ATTACK ON THE WALL CARRIES SYMBOLIC WEIGHT, FOR THE BARRIER HE SEEKS TO DESTROY IS NOT ONLY THE PHYSICAL WALL HE HAS BUILT BUT THE METAPHORIC WALL HE HAS CONSTRUCTED BETWEEN HIMSELF AND OTHERS."

In their book, *Playwrights' Progress,* Colin Chambers and Mike Prior saw Lear's final act as "so random and so futile that it seems an almost meaningless choice except in terms of the individual conscience." For Chambers and Prior, "Lear's final nod towards the continuing existence of a will to resist is . . . a gesture."

Yet Malcolm Hay and Philip Roberts, in their book *Bond: A Study of His Plays,* disagreed. "The gesture he makes is neither final nor futile," they wrote. "It is the demonstration of Lear's integrity to those he leaves behind that action is both necessary and responsible." Knowing that he will die soon anyway, Lear uses his death to show the need, not only for compassion and responsibility, but also for action. No longer the child who hides behind his wall, Lear has reached a position of moral maturity and even an ability to teach others. In the final scene, as the workers leave Lear's body on stage, one looks back, showing that others can learn from Lear's death, that there is purpose in his moral journey, that his final act is not futile.

Lear's attack on the wall also carries symbolic weight, for the barrier he seeks to destroy is not only the physical wall he has built but the metaphoric wall he has constructed between himself and others. In gaining compassion for his former subjects—and human life in general—Lear completes his transformation by seeking to eradicate both of these walls. Yet where he fails to destroy the physical wall, he more importantly succeeds in tearing down the wall within himself.

Source: Clare Cross, for *Drama for Students,* Gale, 1998.

James C. Bulman

In this excerpt, Bulman discusses how Bond related the themes of Shakespeare's King Lear *to his belief that playwrights "must be morally responsible to their societies," the result being his own version of the classic play.*

Edward Bond thinks that playwrights must be morally responsible to their societies. Their plays ought not only to analyze history—how societies became what they are—but also to suggest ways in which societies can better themselves. Too often, he believes, theater is immoral. It encourages playwrights who have no political awareness; it fosters uncritical attitudes toward plays that have become classics. Such plays, he argues, may have been moral enough in their days. But they have outlived their historical moments and entered the realm of myth; and because myth codifies and perpetuates the values of the old order, it is dangerous. Bond wants his audiences to "escape from a mythology of the past, which often lives on as the culture of the present," and thus be free to correct injustices: theater therefore must commit itself to political reform if it is to be moral instead of frivolous. Its aesthetic cannot be divorced from that commitment.

Not surprisingly, then, Bond has turned repeatedly to our most revered cultural myths as subjects for his plays. By doing so, he has been able to feed on fables of proven theatrical power, yet, by revising them, to attack their social and political presuppositions. The myth of King Lear haunted Bond most of all. Why Lear? Bond replies: "I can only say that Lear was standing in my path and I had to get him out of the way. (*Theatre Quarterly,* Vol. 2, No. 5, 1972)" For Bond, Lear epitomized all that was best and worst in Western culture. Lear was authoritarian, his rule was socially oppressive, he was blind to the needs of common humanity, and he resorted to violence. And yet the old king learned to see: he acquired the power to penetrate the myths of the civilization he had made—belief that tyranny can be just, that despotism can be benevolent, that violence can preserve peace. Bond loved the old king for his insight, loathed him for neglecting to act on it. Likewise, Bond admired Shakespeare's *King Lear* for its potent critique of the human condition; but insofar as Shakespeare elected to focus on Lear's *personal* suffering rather than on the society that Lear had tyrannized, Bond condemned the play as a dangerous product of its age, bound in by the very myths it exposed.

Perhaps "condemned" is too strong a word. In *The Activist Papers,* Bond explains that the Elizabethan aesthetic was different from ours: in soliloquy, Hamlet and Lear spoke not merely through their own consciousnesses, but through "the consciousness of history itself." Their voices were at once personal and universal:

> When Shakespeare wrote the court had political power and the rulers were a private family as well as a state institution. This meant that Shakespeare didn't need to distinguish clearly between public and private, political and personal. He could handle the two things together so that it seemed as if political problems could have personal solutions.

That is, the problems of Lear's world could be purged within the confines of Lear's own imagination.

What was true for the Elizabethans, however, is not true for us. Bond suggests that by maintaining a fascination with the personal at the expense of the political, with the individual at the expense of the social, modern drama has devolved into absurdity; and he rejects the theater of the absurd on moral grounds:

> Now society can no longer be expressed politically and morally in terms of the individual and so soliloquies don't work in the same way. The individual is no longer a metaphor for the state and his private feelings can no longer be used to express cause in history or will in politics. Changes in social and political relations make a new drama urgently necessary. . . . The bourgeois theatre clings to psychological drama and so it can't deal with the major dramatic themes. Hamlet's soliloquy has withered into the senile monologue of Krapp's last tape.

This in part explains, I think, why Bond felt compelled to revise *King Lear*—to rip it from the embrace of bourgeois psychology where our modern sensibilities are wont to lock it and to address more clearly the moral issues it raises; to make it the public play that Bond thought it had the potential to become. Bond's model for such revision was Brecht. He had seen the Berliner Ensemble when it visited London in 1956, and his work with George Devine and his successor William Gaskill in the Royal Court Writers' Group educated him more formally in Brecht's methods. *Lear,* which he began in 1969 and which opened at the Royal Court in 1971, represents Bond's first significant attempt at epic drama. In it, he presents a series of scenes (equivalent to Brecht's *gestus*) that offer social and moral perceptions of the world: he disavows coherent psychological motivation of characters and eschews conventional notions of dramatic causality.

A few instances will illustrate how Bond has transformed Shakespeare's original into a Brechtian critique of contemporary culture. For example, he does not allow Lear a loving Cordelia to forgive him his sins and entice him into the antisocial resignation of ''Come, let's away to prison. We two alone will sing like birds i' the' cage.'' Such *contemptus mundi* finds no sympathy in a socialist bent on reforming *this* world. In fact, Bond regarded Shakespeare's Cordelia as ''an absolute menace—a very dangerous type of person.'' I suspect he felt this way for two reasons. First, by fighting a war on her father's behalf, Cordelia presumes to use violence to protect the ''right''; and ''right'' to her means returning society to what it was—reinstituting a patriarchy. And second, by defending her father, by ignoring his past iniquities and assuring him that he has ''No cause, no cause'' to feel guilt, she reduces the play to a melodrama about a poor old man who has been mightily abused. Bond abstracted those qualities of Cordelia that seemed to him politically most significant—her self-righteous militarism and her willingness to overlook Lear's social irresponsibility—and divided them between two characters in his own play: the new Cordelia (no longer Lear's daughter) and her husband, the Gravedigger's Boy.

Bond's Cordelia is a victim of the war that Lear wages against his daughters and that his daughters wage against each other. She hears soldiers slaughter her pigs; she watches soldiers brutally murder her husband; then she herself is raped. These atrocities prompt her to take revenge. She becomes a kind of guerrilla leader bent on reform who, once victorious, attempts to make her country safe by rebuilding a wall to protect it. She thus repeats Lear's error of building the wall in the first place. Lear himself has come to understand the folly of it. Walls only bring woe; and so, as a blind prophet at the end of act three—a British Oedipus at Colonus—he speaks against them. Cordelia defends herself with the myth that one needs walls to keep out enemies; and when he protests: ''Then nothing's changed! A revolution must at least reform!'', she replies: ''Everything *else* is changed.'' Through Cordelia, Bond dramatizes what he regards as the major flaw in our conception of a humane society: defensiveness.

Against this self-destructive Cordelia, Bond pits the Gravedigger's Boy, who embodies the more charitable instincts of Shakespeare's Cordelia—someone who would allow the king to retreat from self-knowledge and live out his old age in ignorance of what he has done. Rather like Lear's Fool,

" BOND WANTS HIS AUDIENCES TO 'ESCAPE FROM A MYTHOLOGY OF THE PAST, WHICH OFTEN LIVES ON AS THE CULTURE OF THE PRESENT,' AND THUS BE FREE TO CORRECT INJUSTICES."

the Boy attempts to talk sense to the poor old king—to calm the storm raging within—when the king comes to him unhoused. Later, when he returns as a ghost, the Boy tempts Lear, in the words of Simon Trussler, ''towards an easeful rather than a useful death''—with a vision of idyllic retreat such as Shakespeare's Cordelia offered her father. But Bond's Lear knows he must resist the temptation, because it would mean turning his back on political responsibility; and Bond's Lear has learned, as Shakespeare's had not, that to reform society, to build it into something more humane, one must acknowledge the loss of innocence and then act on that loss by tearing down the wall that separates men from other men, not merely suffer in guilty silence. Together, then, Cordelia and the Gravedigger's Boy represent the Scylla and Charybdis, married in opposition, of political defensiveness and private retreat between which Lear must sail if he is to become a genuinely moral man. . . .

Source: James C. Bulman, ''Bond, Shakespeare, and the Absurd,'' in *Modern Drama,* Volume XXIX, no. 1, 1986, pp. 60–70.

Alan Sinfield

Sinfield uses the occasion of concurrent productions of Shakespeare's and Bond's similar works to compare Bond's modern version with that of its classical inspiration. He concludes that, despite criticism to the contrary, Bond's play is not a satire or ''hostile critique'' of Shakespeare's work but merely employs the story to relate themes both universal and contemporary.

King Lear is a great play. By itself, the proposition seems harmless enough, and I don't mean to dispute it, but its ramifications in English culture are considerable. The 1982 production by the Royal Shakespeare Company at their main theatre in Stratford and the concurrent presentation of Edward Bond's *Lear* at The Other Place provoke fundamental questions about the way we use Shakespeare.

Since its first production at the Royal Court in 1971 Bond's play has been regarded, in the main, with horror and respect as a modern gloss on *King Lear.* What critics have found it difficult to say outright, because of this matter of greatness, is that Bond's *Lear* amounts to a systematic and hostile critique of Shakespeare's play, at least as it is usually understood.

King Lear suggests that loosening the conventional bonds of authority in society gives rein to all manner of violent disturbance. Bond believes the opposite: that the State, as we have developed it, is the main source of injustice, cruelty and misery: "Your Law always does more harm than crime, and your morality is a form of violence." We need not regard this just as Bond's act of faith; the same conclusions are reached by Richard Leakey through his palaeoanthropological research (see Richard Leakey and Roger Lewin, *People of the Lake,* London, 1979). By making his Cordelia the leader of an insurrection which, when successful, re-establishes most of the repressive apparatus of the government it has overthrown, Bond draws attention to the fact that in *King Lear* Cordelia seeks to redress the wrongs committed by her sisters by having her army fight their army. In other words, at the level of the State and its readiness to take and to sacrifice the lives of ordinary people, *King Lear* does not envisage the need for an alteration in principle. Shakespeare's king perceives that the State has perpetuated injustice: "Take physic, Pomp;/ Expose thyself to feel what wretches feel,/That thou mayst shake the superflux to them," but pomp is not called upon to revise its authority, only to distribute superfluity. Albany's final proposal is that Kent and Edgar should "the gor'd state sustain." Bond's point, in relation both to *King Lear* and to certain modern ideas about revolution and social change, is that you cannot expect to modify the repressive Lear society without challenging its fundamental structures.

Shakespeare's and Bond's attitudes are dependent finally upon divergent views of human nature. When Shakespeare's Lear demands, "Then let them anatomise Regan, see what breeds about her heart. Is there any cause in nature that make these hard hearts?," there is no reply. It seems that we must refer the answer to the gods, who are not as systematically concerned for humanity as Lear once thought. The autopsy on Fontanelle in Bond's play leads Lear to appreciate the potential beauty and goodness of humanity: "She sleeps inside like a lion and a lamb and a child. The things are so beautiful. I am astonished. I have never seen anything so beautiful." For Shakespeare the problem begins when authority is weakened. That is why there is no prior motivation for Lear and his daughters: established hierarchy guarantees order and no remoter source is in question, except perhaps the gods. Bond, however, shows that his characters have been socialised into paranoia and violence. Shakespeare's Lear spends most of the play discovering what the world is, essentially, like; Bond's Lear discovers that things do not have to be the way they are.

The positive force in Shakespeare's play is the personal loyalty of Cordelia, Kent and Edgar. It is shown to transcend the punitive ethic assumed by the king:

> I know you do not love me; for your sisters Have, as I do remember, done me wrong: You have some cause, they have not. No cause, no cause.

But the play knows no way of relating this generosity of spirit to the structure of State authority. That is why it is difficult to reconcile Cordelia's initial legalism with her subsequent magnanimity: one belongs to the endorsement of formal order in the play, the other to the interpersonal ethic which responds to the collapse of order. Shakespeare, with great integrity, makes his inability to relate the two apparent when he has Cordelia's army defeated. The interpersonal ethic remains as a subversive intuition of another way of relating, but the reconstitution of the State over the dead body of Cordelia is offered as the most satisfactory attainable conclusion.

The most provocative aspect of Bond's *Lear,* conversely, is the repudiation of merely personal solutions. The Gravedigger's Boy represents a pastoral withdrawal which is destroyed, initially, through Lear's selfish intrusion. His ghostly presence helps Lear to recover his sanity through the experience of personal affection (the combined role of the Fool and Cordelia in Shakespeare's play). But Bond makes his Lear realise that this is not enough. Whereas Shakespeare allows Lear to rejoice in the prospect of imprisonment with Cordelia and the selfishness of this sentiment is not foregrounded, the Boy's notion that Lear should withdraw from political engagement, put a wall around them and accept the demands of the State, is recognised as a temptation. So Lear allows him to die and sets out to begin dismantling the wall. Individual "redemption" through interpersonal love is not enough, the State must be confronted.

In August 1982 Bond's *Lear* seemed relevant enough, with the Falklands, Lebanon and Poland in mind. Without necessarily agreeing with Bond, we can see that he has engaged with major political issues. The RSC production by Barry Kyle was excellent. The epic mode of the play is not immediately suited to a small space with the audience on three sides, and it may be that this staging altered the implications of the violence in the play, bringing it into our homes (as it were) rather than keeping it out there in the political arena where it belongs. But perhaps this corresponds to the effect of TV—the medium through which most of us experience political violence—and is therefore appropriate. Barry Kyle made strong use of diagonal lines where a conventional stage would have permitted depth, and managed to establish stylisation and allusion—for instance, taking the clothes-line behind which the Gravedigger's Boy is killed diagonally, and the final interview between Cordelia and Lear, with the Boy behind him, at right angles to that line. Bob Peck was massive as Lear; it became quite excruciating to follow his weary, painful limbs in movement. Mark Rylance was both gruesome and winning as the Boy and his interaction with Lear was physical and moving. It falls to these two actors to repudiate any imputation that Bond is deficient in positive human feeling—to show that the rejection of the interpersonal pastoral is grounded in sufficient awareness of what is sacrificed. To my mind they achieved this.

Adrian Noble, who produced *King Lear,* was evidently conscious of the main lines of Bond's critique. Bob Crowley's set, a towering, bleak imperial facade (the back of which was torn out when Lear is exposed on the heath) was reminiscent of the wall which dominates the Bond set; many of the costumes were the same—rough, clumsy greatcoats, the gear of an army on the march, exposed to danger, accustomed to discomfort. Some of the casting of the two plays overlapped significantly, and Bob Peck looked like Michael Gambon, who was Shakespeare's Lear. I am about to make a number of intricate and critical points about this interpretation of *King Lear,* so it should be established at the start that Gambon's performance was an extraordinary achievement: entirely convincing, broad in scope, moving though not in the expected places, inventive but not quirky.

"BOND'S *LEAR* AMOUNTS TO A SYSTEMATIC AND HOSTILE CRITIQUE OF SHAKESPEARE'S PLAY, AT LEAST AS IT IS USUALLY UNDERSTOOD."

As a member of the International Shakespeare Conference I had the advantage of a question and answer session with Noble, so I know that it was his intention to bring out a contemporary political dimension in *King Lear.* He said that the effect of concurrent work on Bond's play was like a steady drip of cold water, preventing them from keeping *King Lear* in a separate historical pocket; that the country was at war when the play was in rehearsal, that he wanted to show "the potential for violence which you get within an absolute State," and that they had felt the events and value system of the play to be relevant constantly in the current political climate.

In many ways this was a triumphantly political interpretation. "We did want to put a war on stage," Noble remarked, and the sense of unnamed people moving about a recalcitrant terrain, menaced by each other, was strong; and the sense that they had to lift really heavy objects, had trouble keeping warm, keeping going. The great achievement was the refusal or suppression of the transcendence which is usually assumed to be the goal of certain episodes. In this production Edmund, Goneril and Regan are not evil incarnate (nor is there any attempt to make them seem justified, as in Peter Brook's version). Edmund (Clive Wood) is butch, sulky and scornful; Goneril (Sara Kestelman) is like an obsessive landlady, tidying up the set, who goes on to accosting the lodgers in the hallway. They are cruel and selfish, but they are people. The account of Cordelia shaking "The holy water from her heavenly eyes" is all but smothered by soldiers humping sandbags around the stage; "Ripeness is all" is shouted, desperately, over the drum of the preparing army in turbulent lighting. Frequently lighting is used to disconfirm the centrality of the main protagonists: it refuses to focus them but, instead, moves independently, so that they come in and out of it. When Edgar flees, the spotlight rakes the stage and the audience, as if from a watchtower in a prison camp.

The whole effect is to quell the commonest interpretation of the play as "tragedy," wherein the king, especially, transcends events by the intensity of his inner experience. So Noble reserves attention for the range of characters and for the power of political relations. Gambon's Lear is not inward-looking: he does not discover reality in the depths of himself. He is mad for much less of the time than is commonly supposed, so that there is far less pitiful raving, far less sense that the essential struggle, the essential reality, is inside his head. In the disputes with Goneril and Regan he retains the unwavering baleful glare with which he began; his anger is rarely uncontrolled, he is frail but determined, nobody's fool. In particular, he is rational at the Dover meeting with Gloucester, so that "A dog's obey'd in office" comes through as powerful analysis. This scene was most effective: there was little courting of expressionist significance, but two old men seeing the way the world goes, nodding, chuckling and crying together. Again, when Lear wakes with Cordelia, the whole impression is of a bemused old man, and of physical frailty: it is a human incident, and the visual key is given by pyjamas rather than the customary flowing white robes of an Old Testament prophet/penitent. "Come, let's away to prison" is spoken matter of factly, flatly, as a clear perception of the kind of life that may be left to them; and at the end Lear is sane, though he has trouble coping with a stage full of people. At every point in the latter part of the play Noble and Gambon prevent Lear becoming an ultimate representative of "man."

This assault on the transcendence often ascribed to the "tragic hero" is expressed most importantly in the treatment of the blind/sight imagery—"I stumbled when I saw." The production is very physical throughout: Lear is ready to strike anyone, and also to hug anyone—he hugs Goneril, the Fool, Kent, Edgar, Gloucester. "I see it feelingly," Gloucester says. The production takes this up, and so disqualifies the whole dichotomy of mundane versus transcendent vision. The point is not insight into a further reality, there is no further reality—just the material world in which people and systems do things to you, and you respond to it most fully through the sense of touch. Touch is both more basic (in Platonic thought sight is the highest sense, touch the lowest) and more communicative, more to do with human interaction. For this Lear, the chaos and threat is not, finally, inside him; the precision of Gambon's acting is all directed towards responding to other people. This is a Lear of reaction, not distraction.

We have, then, a production which turns one eye towards Bond, which is aiming at a political awareness relevant to the problems of the world today. At the same time, in the middle of the production, there is an alternative, incompatible conception, equally powerfully realised. This split exposes with almost brutal clarity the uses to which Shakespeare is put by the RSC and English culture at large.

The issue is focused by the storm, which is brilliantly staged with flashing lights, billowing smoke, and noises which were those of the elements but which also (several people remarked) led one to think of an air raid on Beirut (the current international horror). This was a tour de force, a kind of infernal discotheque. And perched above it all, on a platform on a pole fifteen feet above the stage, were Lear (looking like a Blakean deity) and the Fool clinging to him. But all this magnificent effect worked against a socio-political understanding of what was going on. A society in dissolution was transformed into the universe in apocalypse. The idea is in the text—"Is this the promis'd end?"—but Doomsday is not a socio-political concept.

Noble said that his idea in staging the storm was to show "what it's like inside that head . . . what it's like when the horizon tilts." Fine, but this is suddenly to transform the action into the interior monologue which in other respects it is not. The presentation of real human relations, with all the disparities of power, suffering and understanding, and their implied ramifications in society at large, could well continue through the scenes on the heath. But Noble is tempted into another manner—he mentioned Jan Kott's essay "King Lear or Endgame."

The Beckettian aspect is developed through the Fool, who is played with great agility, inventiveness and conviction by Antony Sher. Initially his relationship with Lear is played realistically: he tries to cheer Lear up but cannot avoid mentioning the source of Lear's disquiet. But the manner of the professional clown is already hinting at a more abstract notion of the Fool's role. When he and Lear crouch at the front of the stage and peer desperately at each other, their shadows thrown monstrously on to the back wall, and when the Fool, left for once to himself, goes off like a spring released, cavorting manically round the stage and shaking his fist at the sky, we begin to suspect that the Fool is supposed to stand for something, perhaps an aspect of Lear's psyche. Adrian Noble in fact confirmed that this was his conception: this is why, in the most striking innovation of the production, *Lear kills the Fool.*

Lear is anatomising Regan—plucking handfuls of feathers out of a pillow (a few are still in the air in the closing scenes of the play); he flings the pillow across the stage, sending a light swinging, and the Fool, who has jumped in fright into a large dustbin (*Endgame*) catches it; Lear stabs the pillow, and the Fool through it; Lear never realises what he has done. Noble meant this to be Lear killing his conscience, that of which he is ashamed. I didn't think of this at the time, and I don't see how Lear is supposed to manage without a conscience in the second part of the play (he seems to have it at the reunion with Cordelia).

Two general reflections arise from the confusion in this production—three if we begin, as we should, by granting without reserve its sheer professional competence, intelligence and power to provoke thought. The first concerns the RSC. In the 1960s it was a spearhead, in some ways more important than the Royal Court, of a left-liberal movement in the theatre and ultimately in the country. By the end of the decade, this movement had become established—had become an establishment. In theatre, it had purpose and committed audiences when the West End was floundering; it successfully challenged censorship; it had the endorsement of national subsidy; it gave birth to the National Theatre. The dominant influences were Brecht, representing political concern; and Beckett/ Artaud, representing a sense that the human condition is fundamentally absurd and violent. Together, these influences destroyed the assumptions of naturalism and opened the way to vital developments in theatrical stylisation, but, finally, they are incompatible. The first is materialist and optimistic about humanity, tracing our ills to changeable political structures. The second is essentialist and nihilistic, discovering in the depths of personality inexorable tendencies towards cruelty, alienation and self-destruction. Their co-occurrence in the work of Peter Brook for the RSC, including his *King Lear* of 1962 (much influenced by Jan Kott), *The Marat—Sade* and *US*, rendered this work powerful but politically and artistically incoherent. The same conjunction informs the 1982 production of *King Lear.*

But the original movement, contradictory as it was, was of its time. These were new, exciting influences, and the confused and compromised political stance was characteristic of other institutions in the period. Bond's use of violence to shock us into awareness also shows signs of Artaud. What we must ponder now is how far the RSC is living off the manner which served it before, how far it is depending on the thought of an earlier generation rather than assessing, clarifying and challenging that thought. Two pieces of evidence are quite disconcerting. One is Noble's appeal to Jan Kott ("one has to read Kott")—Lear even leaves his boots at the front of the stage, like Estragon. The other is the programme. The RSC pioneered the intellectual programme, but this one is all design, a production job, in which pictures and quotations from the most diverse prestigious intellectual sources are jumbled together in an evocative collage (including Auden, Dylan Thomas, Keats, Kozintsev and Dostoyevsky); and, in particular, we find the political awareness of Orwell and Bond ("Our world is not absurd—our society is") alongside the apocalyptic transcendentalism of Ecclesiastes and Yeats. It seems, at least, that the RSC is in danger of parodying its former achievements.

However, and this is my second general reflection, it is probably not fair to blame this gifted company for problems which may be traced much further back, namely to our whole conception of Shakespeare and his "greatness." Since *King Lear* is a great play—I think this is the underlying argument—it must speak to our condition. And if our condition seems to involve brutally destructive political systems and profound inner compulsions which threaten a general apocalypse, then the play must be seen to address such issues. The text as we have received it tends to encourage certain ways of seeing the world and to inhibit others and does not, of course, envisage modern society. Therefore the play and current concerns must, by one means or another, be brought into line.

Hence the extraordinary conventions which govern contemporary productions. In the attempt to get the play to "work" as the director wants, almost anything may be cut, almost any "business" may be added to affect the significance of the words and, increasingly, words may be altered or added. But all these developments are mashed together so that only the expert can see what has been done, and the impression that we are "really" seeing Shakespeare is preserved. For an excellently detailed and discriminating description of such practices, see Stanley Wells's account in *Critical Quarterly* of two productions of *Measure for Measure.* Of one production he concludes: "Some of the ways in which it departed from tradition were entirely legitimate. Others required textual tinkering. The resulting play may be more sentimental, and happier, than that suggested by the script that has come down to us, but in its own terms it worked.'' But Dr. Wells still speaks, throughout, of ''the play:'' it is assumed that we remain, importantly, in the presence of Shakespeare's original genius.

My objective is not a theoretical discussion of at what point this or that production becomes no longer ''the same'' play; nor is it a complaint that Shakespeare's text is being tampered with (it is still there for another day). I am trying to identify the cultural assumptions, based on a conception of Shakespeare's greatness, which hold that we can and should ventriloquise contemporary significance through the plays, and the manipulations of presentation which ensue.

In part directors are trying to cope with the fact that most people in the audience don't understand the language: part of the greatness is that Shakespeare speaks to us even across such barriers of comprehension. Hence the business which breaks up a conversation or a line unexpectedly, making a joke unanticipated in a straightforward reading (it is called ''making the scene work''). But also, the cutting and business are designed to wrest the text away from what seem to be its dominant concerns and into a preferred dimension of meaning, using every slightest cue, nuance, crux and hiatus to develop an ''interpretation.'' If, instead, the company reworked the play explicitly, the interpretation would lose the apparent authority of Shakespeare, and Shakespeare's basically conservative oeuvre would lose the apparent authority of speaking to all conditions. This is the great collusion in which most productions of Shakespeare have become involved. The shuffles commonly conducted maintain both these dubious authorities, and more adventurous treatments—like Bond's and Charles Marowitz's—become objects of suspicion.

It is these pressures that lie behind the kinds of efforts the RSC makes to achieve relevance. This production pushes the conventions of interpretation to the limit by having Lear kill the Fool and by omitting (as Brook did) Edmund's attempt to save Cordelia and Lear. The first is designed to develop Lear's inner experience in a way barely suggested by the text; the second is designed to suppress issues of good, evil and the perversity of fortune and to leave the responsibility for failing to secure the safety of Lear and Cordelia with Albany who (Noble says) is preoccupied with the feud in his own family—so that the theme of the damage done by arbitrary rule is sustained to the end. In so far as these intentions are (as I have argued) contradictory, they witness to a theatrical mode which is in danger of ossification. By offering extreme instances of the conventions of presentation which accompany that mode, they draw attention to their artificiality. Noble leads his audience (or those to whom I spoke) to ask whether this is *really* Shakespeare.

The questions which should be asked, however, are whether any production which aspires to modern relevance is really Shakespeare; whether our conception of the greatness of *King Lear*—meaning capable of speaking positively to all conditions—is honest; and whether attempts to ventriloquise a modern political stance through the play will inevitably be confused by countervailing implications in the text. It may be that the only way to produce a more definite political theatre (or criticism) is not to interpret *King Lear* but, as Edward Bond sees, to quarrel with it.

Source: Alan Sinfield, ''*King Lear* versus *Lear* at Stratford,'' in *Critical Quarterly,* Volume 24, no. 4, Winter, 1982, pp. 5–14.

SOURCES

Hay, Malcolm and Philip Roberts. *Bond: A Study of His Plays,* Eyre Methuen, 1980, p. 103.

Lappin, Lou. *The Art and Politics of Edward Bond,* Peter Lang, 1987, p. 129.

Roberts, Philip, Editor. *Bond on File,* Methuen, 1985, pp. 23-24.

Scharine, Richard. *The Plays of Edward Bond,* Bucknell, 1975, pp. 184-209.

FURTHER READING

Chambers, Colin and Mike Prior. *Playwrights' Progress: Patterns of Postwar British Drama,* Amber Lane, 1987.

This book is a good general introduction to British drama after World War II. It includes individual chapters on Bond and a number of his contemporaries.

Hirst, David L. *Edward Bond,* Macmillan, 1985.

This is a general introduction to Bond's work.

Sked, Alan, and Chris Cook. *Post-War Britain: A Political History,* Penguin, 1990.

This book provides a history of politics in Great Britain from World War II through the 1980s, including a detailed look at the 1970s, when *Lear* was first produced.

Spencer, Jenny S. *Dramatic Strategies in the Plays of Edward Bond,* Cambridge, 1992.
Spencer's book provides strong analyses of many of Bond's plays, including *Lear.*

Trussler, Simon, Editor. *New Theatre Voices of the Seventies,* Eyre Methuen, 1981.
This book contains sixteen interviews with contemporary British playwrights, including Bond, reprinted from *Theatre Quarterly.* In his interview, Bond discusses *Lear.*

Major Barbara

GEORGE BERNARD SHAW

1905

George Bernard Shaw's *Major Barbara* has been called the most controversial of Shaw's works. The play was first produced at the Royal Court Theatre in London in 1905, and early reviews were decidedly mixed. Shaw's seeming criticism of Christianity caused some to accuse him of blasphemy, while others defended what they saw as Shaw's realistic presentation of religion. Critics complained about the violence of the play, particularly in the second act, saying it was so excessive as to be beyond realism. Others disagreed, saying that the depiction of that violence, if unrealistic, was so only because the violence was subdued. Whatever the opinion of the critics, however, the play was a success with the public. It remains popular and has enjoyed numerous revivals, including an adaptation to film in 1941. Today it is considered a very important work, not only among Shaw's plays but also in the history of modern drama.

Many of Shaw's plays are known for their involved arguments and *Major Barbara* is no exception. Shaw himself called the play ''a discussion in three long acts,'' and much of the play's ''action'' consists, in fact, of words. When the play was published in 1907, Shaw added, as with many of his works, a lengthy preface, contributing further discussion about the play itself. In addition, the play is noted for its unconventional attitudes toward morality as well as its irony and humor. Given the serious nature of the issues examined in the play—wealth and poverty, business and religion, cynicism

and idealism—it is sometimes easy to overlook the fact that *Major Barbara* is, in fact, a comedy. Shaw uses the play to entertain his audience, to make people laugh, while examining issues that are as important today as they were when the play was first written.

AUTHOR BIOGRAPHY

George Bernard Shaw was born in Dublin, Ireland, on July 26, 1856. His father was an alcoholic and unsuccessful businessman, and his mother a genteel woman interested in music and art. The family was poor and, when Shaw was six, moved in with another family to save expenses; his early experience of poverty is speculated to have affected the decidedly unromantic view of the poor shown in many of his plays, including *Major Barbara.* Shaw's formal education was brief, and he began work in a land agent's office before he was sixteen.

In 1876 Shaw moved to London, joining his mother and sisters, who had arrived from Dublin the previous year. Working as a writer focusing on music criticism, short fiction, and drama, Shaw initially was unable to earn his own living and relied on his mother's earnings as well as an inheritance in order to make ends meet. His attempts at writing fiction were unsuccessful. It was not until the 1880s that Shaw achieved some success and was able to support himself. By this time he had made some significant changes in his life, including becoming a vegetarian and devoting his political energies to the cause of socialism. Shaw joined the Fabian Society, a group of socialists whose credo held that changes in government could not be successfully accomplished quickly by revolutionary means. Rather, the Fabians held that lasting change could only be wrought by sensible, gradual change.

As a member of the new Fabian Society (which was formed in England in 1884), Shaw was often called upon to speak, and he became a skilled orator as well as a noteworthy essayist. He also wrote book reviews and art criticism and became a well-regarded music and theater critic. During this period, Shaw became an admirer of Norwegian playwright Henrik Ibsen (*A Doll's House*), whose dramas, known for their realism and focus on important social issues, were to become a major influence on Shaw's own writing. In 1895, Shaw became a theater critic for the *Saturday Review* and used his column to criticize the artificiality and hypocrisy of the English stage.

Shaw had been writing drama since the 1880s when his first play, *Widowers' Houses* was produced in 1892, followed by the writing of *The Philanderer* (1893) and *Mrs. Warren's Profession* (1893), neither of which was produced for over a decade. Shaw's literary output was enormous, and he gradually gained fame as a dramatist. In the next few decades he completed numerous works, including *Arms and the Man* (1894), *Candida* (1894), *Major Barbara* (1905), and *Pygmalion* (1914), his best-known work which became the inspiration for the 1956 musical *My Fair Lady.* When World War I broke out in 1914, Shaw temporarily ceased writing drama and turned instead to expounding on his pacifist views, which were extremely unpopular until public opinion shifted later in the war. After the war ended, he continued to write; his post-war plays include *Heartbreak House* (1916-1917) and *St. Joan* (1923).

In 1898, Shaw married Charlotte Payne-Townshend, an heiress, also interested in socialism, who had admired Shaw's writing. The marriage ended with Charlotte's death in 1943. Shaw won the Nobel Prize for literature in 1925, and he continued to write plays until his death at ninety-four on November 2, 1950. Known for his wit, social commentary, and brilliant dialogue, Shaw has often been called the greatest English dramatist since William Shakespeare.

PLOT SUMMARY

Act I

Major Barbara opens with Lady Britomart in the library of her house in London, England, as her son Stephen, whom she has summoned, enters. She has asked to see him, she reveals, because of her concern about his future financial well-being, as well as that of his sisters, Sarah and Barbara. The audience learns that her daughter Sarah is engaged to Charles Lomax, who will not be able to support her until he receives his inheritance. It is also revealed that her other daughter, Barbara, who has joined the Salvation Army, is engaged to Adolphus Cusins, a Greek scholar who also has an insufficient income and who, Lady Britomart believes, only pretends to be a Salvationist because he is in love with Barbara. Stephen as well should soon seek a wife and will need to provide for his own family.

George Bernard Shaw at his desk in 1928

For this additional monetary support, Lady Britomart tells Stephen that she must turn to the children's father, Andrew Undershaft, a wealthy munitions manufacturer from whom she has been separated for many years.

Lady Britomart also reveals that Stephen will not inherit his father's business because each heir to the Undershaft enterprise must be a foundling and must, when he dies, leave the business to another foundling. Stephen, horrified by his father's profession, does not wish to take his father's money and is upset when he discovers that Undershaft is expected at Lady Britomart's house almost immediately.

Barbara, Sarah, Cusins, and Lomax, who have also been summoned, enter the library. Barbara is enthusiastic about seeing her father because he has a soul to be saved. Undershaft is shown into the room and introduced to his children. He expresses an interest in the Salvation Army, saying that their motto, ''Blood and Fire,'' could be his as well. While the others are clearly uncomfortable with Undershaft's profiting from war, he reveals that he is not at all ashamed.

When Barbara invites him to her Salvation Army shelter, he agrees to come the next day provided she will come the day after to his munitions factories. Barbara, hoping to convert her father, agrees to this arrangement, while he says that he may in fact convert her. When Lady Britomart decides to ring for prayers, Undershaft says that he will only stay for a service conducted by Barbara, and Barbara agrees to conduct one. All leave for the service in the drawing room, except for Stephen who, still disgusted by his father, remains in the library.

Act II

This act opens the following day at Barbara's Salvation Army shelter where Snobby Price, an unemployed workman, and Rummy Mitchens, a poverty-stricken woman, are seated at a table, eating the Army's standard meal of bread and milk. Both admit to confessing sins they never committed in order to please the Salvationists, on whom they depend for assistance. Jenny Hill, a young Salvationist, enters with Peter Shirley, also unemployed. Bill Walker, a rough young man, enters and accuses Hill of taking his girlfriend, whom Barbara later reveals has been ''saved,'' into the Army. In his anger, Walker pushes Hill, strikes Mitchens, then strikes Hill as well. Barbara enters and, by her frank manner, lack of anger, and persistent talk of God's love, arouses feelings of shame, compounded also by Hill's forgiveness, in Walker.

Undershaft enters and observes as Barbara continues to work on Walker, who becomes more and more uncomfortable, finally leaving to seek his girlfriend at another shelter. Barbara exits, leaving Cusins to converse with Undershaft, who reveals that he considers money and gunpowder necessary to salvation, for without them, one cannot afford such niceties as honor, truth, and love. Cusins reveals that he has indeed become a Salvationist for love of Barbara, and the two men discover that their love for Barbara is what they have in common. Undershaft says he will convert Barbara to preaching his gospel and, to reach that end, will buy the Army, an organization that he finds useful because it causes workers to be honest and happy, and thus less likely to form unions or become socialists.

When Barbara returns, Undershaft offers her money, but she refuses, believing his money to be tainted because of his profession. At this point, Walker returns and offers Hill a pound because of his ill treatment of her. She refuses, suggesting the money be given to Mitchens, whom he also hurt, but he will only give it to Hill, as Mitchens met his violence with threats of her own. Hill suggests some of the money be given to the Army, but Barbara refuses; what she wants is Walker's soul, which she hopes to save.

Mrs. Baines, the Army Commissioner, enters, saying she has wonderful news. A Lord Saxmundham will give the Army five thousand pounds if five other men will each meet his donation. Undershaft reveals that this benefactor owns Bodger's Whiskey, a fact that does not dissuade Mrs. Baines, who asks Undershaft for five thousand as well. When Undershaft agrees, Barbara is incredulous that the Army will take his money or the money from Bodger's Whiskey; she believes that businesses such as her father's and the whiskey company are harmful to a humane, Christian society. Cusins suggests that Mrs. Baines, Undershaft, and himself march immediately to the coming meeting, but Barbara refuses to attend. After the others leave, Walker, who has returned, taunts the defeated Barbara for saying the Army will not be bought. When Walker leaves, Barbara states that she will no longer work for the army and offers to take Shirley to tea. The act ends with the two of them leaving together.

Act III

This act opens in Lady Britomart's library, where Lady Britomart and Sarah are seated along with Barbara, who is now out of uniform. Lomax enters, followed by Cusins, who has spent the night drinking with Undershaft. Undershaft arrives to take the family to see his factories and Perivale St. Andrews, the model town he has built in which his workers live. Lady Britomart sends the children out of the room. Alone with her husband, she immediately tells Undershaft what income Barbara and Sarah will need, and he agrees to provide it. She once again appeals to Undershaft to leave his business to Stephen, but he refuses and, when Stephen enters, Stephen says he does not want his father's business. Barbara, Sarah, Cusins, and Lomax then enter the room and leave for their tour of Undershaft's empire.

The scene shifts to Undershaft's factories and town, where Barbara stands as Cusins, Stephen, Sarah, and Lomax enter, each in turn exclaiming over the beauty of Perivale St. Andrews. Undershaft then enters, followed by Lady Britomart who, also praising the town, suggests the business be left, not to Stephen, but to Cusins and thus Barbara. When Undershaft responds that he must leave his factories to a foundling, Cusins reveals that his parents are related and that their marriage, while accepted in Australia, is not legal in Britain. Undershaft replies that Cusins can indeed succeed him. Cusins proceeds to bargain for a high salary, while Barbara comments that he is selling his soul. When she speaks of how her own beliefs have been shattered, Undershaft tells her she must seek a new religion, that he saw only poverty and misery at her shelter, in contrast to the material comfort of his own workers, whom he has saved from the horror of poverty. Asking Cusins to decide about succeeding him, Undershaft leaves with the others to see the gun cotton shed, and Barbara and Cusins are left alone.

Cusins tells Barbara he will accept Undershaft's offer, to which she replies that, if he had not, she would marry the man who would choose to succeed her father. Barbara has decided that she must have the town, that she must save the souls of those who cannot be bribed with bread or Heaven, that now she has found her work. When the others come out of the shed, Barbara asks her mother to help her choose one of her father's houses for herself and Cusins.

CHARACTERS

Mrs. Baines

Mrs. Baines, a Salvation Army Commissioner, accepts the Undershaft money that Barbara has

MEDIA ADAPTATIONS

- *Major Barbara* was adapted as a film in 1941, with additional scenes and characters added by Shaw. The film was directed by Gabriel Pascal and starred Wendy Hiller, Robert Morley, Rex Harrison, and Robert Newton.

turned down, then reveals that the Army has also accepted money from Lord Saxmundham of Bodger's Whiskey. Her willingness to accept money from those who cause so much harm disillusions Barbara and results in Barbara's leaving the Army.

Major Barbara

See Barbara Undershaft

Cholly

See Charles Lomax

Adolphus Cusins

Cusins is engaged to Barbara. Shaw describes him as "capable possibly of murder, but not of cruelty or coarseness." A professor of Greek, he pretends to be a Salvationist because of his love for Barbara, though he tells Andrew Undershaft that he has a genuine interest in religion. He shares some of Barbara's idealism and is revolted by Undershaft's cynical religion of money and gunpowder; in fact, he frequently calls Undershaft the devil or Mephistopheles. Yet he is also persuaded to some extent by Undershaft's arguments and agrees to succeed Undershaft in his armaments business. Nonetheless, he brings some of his own idealism to that business, initially telling Undershaft that he will sell arms only to whom he wishes, while Undershaft insists he sell to everyone. Finally, citing his own socially acceptable but morally questionable acts, he agrees to accept Undershaft's offer, but leaves the audience with the impression that he and Barbara will try to do good through a business based on evil.

Dolly

See Adolphus Cusins

Jenny Hill

Jenny is a sincere Salvationist who takes Mitchens and Price's insincere religious posturings at face value. When Walker strikes her, her unending forgiveness and compassion cause him to feel tremendous guilt.

Charles Lomax

Charles is engaged to Sarah. He is a flighty young man whose lack of intelligence and inappropriate comments make him a source of humor in the play.

Rummy Mitchens

Mitchens is seen at the Salvation Army shelter. Worn down by poverty, she appears to be elderly but is probably middle-aged. She appreciates the kindness of the Salvation Army workers but knows that to make them happy, she must confess a multitude of sins. When Walker strikes her, she repays him with anger and threats, in contrast to Jenny Hill, who treats the brute with kindness and forgiveness.

Snobby Price

Price is an unemployed workman who admits to confessing sins he never committed in order to please the Salvationists. He shows two faces to the audience: the cynicism he displays with Mitchens and the exaggerated religious demeanor he puts on in front of Barbara and Jenny.

Peter Shirley

Shirley is a forty-six-year-old worker who is ashamed of accepting help from the Salvation Army. He has recently lost his job because his streak of gray hair makes him look like an old man. He tells Undershaft that he and those like him are poor because they work to make Undershaft and his kind rich.

Andrew Undershaft

Undershaft, Barbara's father, has become a wealthy man through the manufacture of armaments. Money and gunpowder form the basis of his religion, and he says that the Salvation Army's slogan, ''Blood and Fire,'' could be his own. Though others are horrified by his profession, he is unapologetic, and his motto is ''unashamed.'' Life as an arms manufacturer has kept him from what is believes is the greatest sin—poverty. There are numerous references to him as the devil throughout the play, and Barbara's description of how she has imagined his workplace fits in with stereotypical images of hell. Yet his workplace is not a hell; his workers are well fed and live in clean, comfortable houses. There is, however, a certain cynicism in all this; if his workers are satisfied, they will be better employees, less likely to form unions, more likely to be reliable. Undershaft's love for Barbara is genuine, and he wishes to convert her to his point of view. The play's ending appears to leave him triumphant, but Barbara remains a reformer. She has seen the reality of what her father says and does, but she has not adopted his cynicism.

Barbara Undershaft

Barbara is the title character of the play. Born into a well-to-do family, she becomes a major in the Salvation Army, dismissing her servant and sharply curtailing her spending. Her primary focus is on doing what she believes to be the work of God. Shaw describes her as jolly and energetic and these attributes show in her work at the Salvation Army shelter, where her religious devotion and quiet persistence gradually begin to break the defenses of even the rough Bill Walker. Barbara is engaged to Adolphus Cusins. The play is set in motion when Barbara, meeting her father for the first time, asks him to come to her shelter, and he agrees, providing she comes to see his foundry and model town. Barbara's idealism is dashed when her father comes to the shelter and the Army eagerly accepts his money, which Barbara considers tainted. She abandons the Army, not knowing what she will now do with the rest of her life.

When she sees the beauty of Perivale St. Andrews, Barbara becomes convinced that it is better to save those souls which cannot be bribed with bread or heaven. As Cusins accepts the proposition that he succeed Undershaft, Barbara gains a new sense of purpose. She has grown wise, but retains a sense of idealism in her plan to transform her father's model town.

Lady Britomart Undershaft

Lady Britomart is Barbara's mother and Andrew Undershaft's estranged wife. At the beginning of the play she has summoned Undershaft to discuss with him how he will provide for his adult children. She is particularly concerned about their son Stephen. She initially separated from Undershaft because of his intention of leaving his business to a foundling instead of to Stephen. By the end of the play, she is satisfied with Undershaft leaving the business to Barbara through Cusins.

Sarah Undershaft

Sarah is Barbara's sister. She is more superficial than Barbara. Shaw describes her as ''slender, bored, and mundane.'' She is engaged to Charles Lomax.

Stephen Undershaft

Stephen is the .twenty-five-year-old son of Andrew Undershaft and Lady Britomart. He is a serious young man, initially horrified by his father's line of work and, unlike his siblings, rejects Undershaft from the beginning. But seeing his father's foundry and the city Perivale St. Andrews, he comes to admire and respect his father's work.

Bill Walker

Walker is a rough young man who comes to the shelter looking for a fight and eventually strikes both Mitchens and Hill. Because Mitchens responds with anger, he is not ashamed of striking her, but Hill's forgiveness provokes strong feelings of guilt within him. When he tries to pay money for his misdeed, Barbara tells him that the Army cannot be bought. But when Mrs. Baines accepts Undershaft's money, Walker taunts Barbara, saying his money was only turned down because it wasn't enough.

THEMES

Parent and Child

In the opening act of *Major Barbara,* Barbara meets her father, whom she cannot remember ever knowing. Although she has been raised solely by her mother, the two do not seem close, and Lady Britomart is clearly unhappy with—even uncomprehending of—Barbara's interest in the Salvation Army. Barbara is not close to either her mother or her father, but in the Army she has found a sort of

TOPICS FOR FURTHER STUDY

- Research the place of women in the late nineteenth and early twentieth centuries. How does Barbara rebel against traditional feminine roles?
- In view of Shaw's socialism, what might have been his purpose in making Andrew Undershaft's armaments factory and the adjacent town a model of success? In what ways does Shaw manage to show the negative side of Undershaft's achievement?
- Compare Barbara and Cusins to the character Dr. Faustus in Christopher Marlowe's play *The Tragical History of Dr. Faustus.* Given that Undershaft is frequently referred to as a Satanic character, does Cusins sell his soul to the Devil? Does Barbara sell hers?
- Compare Andrew Undershaft to Mother Courage in Bertolt Brecht's play *Mother Courage and Her Children,* which was first produced during World War II. How might the intervening years of war account for differences between the two characters and between the two plays?
- Read Henry David Thoreau's essay ''Civil Disobedience.'' Discuss whether or not the characters in *Major Barbara* live according to their consciences. What does Shaw say about the relationship between individual action and society?

surrogate parent, a fact that is emphasized when Barbara later says that there are no orphans in the Army.

When Undershaft enters, however, the importance of the relationship between Barbara and her father becomes immediately apparent. Barbara sees him as a soul in need of salvation; he wishes to convert her to his view of life. While showing the importance of Barbara's relationship with her father, Shaw also establishes some tension between Lady Britomart and Undershaft as parents when, as Undershaft leaves the room with the children at the end of Act I, Lady Britomart expresses dismay over the possibility of the children changing their loyalty from the mother who raised them to the father who initially cannot remember their names or even exactly how many children he has.

As the play progresses, Barbara becomes disillusioned with her surrogate parent, the Salvation Army, because of its acceptance of her father's tainted money. At first she believes she has lost everything important to her, but after touring the Undershaft factories and town, she begins to see her father's point of view and to become closer to him. Because Cusins has been chosen as Undershaft's successor, Barbara has, in essence, become her father's heir. Her drawing closer to her father is concurrent with a newfound dependence on her mother. As the play closes, Barbara is seen calling out for her mother and clinging to her skirts like a child. Asking her mother to help her choose a home in her father's city, Barbara has finally become closer to both of her parents, though she also retains her own sense of self.

God and Religion

Through Barbara's involvement with the Salvation Army, Shaw offers an examination of Christianity in general and the Salvation Army in particular. Barbara's initial focus is on doing the work of God. Act II gives the audience a chance to look at the practical implications of this work, as seen through the eyes of its targeted beneficiaries. Through the conversation of Rummy Mitchens and Snobby Price, Shaw reveals that, while grateful for the material assistance the Army gives them, Mitchens and Price essentially earn this assistance by lying. Both talk about the Salvation Army meetings in which they are expected to ''testify'' about their conversions. Price prides himself on convincing the Army of his former evil. ''I know wot they like,'' he says. "I'll tell 'em how I blasphemed and gambled and wopped my old mother." Mitchens bemoans the unfairness to women; their confessions cannot be loudly proclaimed but "'az to be whispered to one lady at a time."

The audience discovers the Army's manipulation as well in Barbara's treatment of Bill Walker. In order to try to save his soul, Barbara works incessantly on Walker's feelings of guilt about striking Mitchens and Jenny Hill. In addition, Barbara believes the Army to be hypocritical when it takes money from Bodger Whiskey and her father's munitions business, both of whom seem to embody the very evil the Salvation Army wants to eliminate. In the end, it is Undershaft's religion that feeds, houses, and clothes people.

Yet Shaw is not simply maligning the Army or Christianity. There is sincerity in Jenny Hill "turning the other cheek." And Barbara's intentions, though possibly misguided, are pure. In the end, though Barbara has abandoned the Army, she still speaks of saving souls but now without the Army's bribes of bread and heaven. She sees her new mission as "the raising of hell to heaven and of man to God, through the unveiling of an eternal light in the Valley of the Shadow." Though Shaw reveals problems in the Army's techniques, the play does not dismiss the search for God.

A Salvation Army volunteer bangs a drum in a production of Major Barbara

Good vs. Evil

Shaw throws the traditional concept of good and evil into question throughout *Major Barbara.* In the beginning of the play, it seems fairly obvious that Barbara, who lives on little money so she can work feeding and sheltering the poor as well as trying to save their souls, is doing good. At the same time, Undershaft, who has become a rich man selling armaments to combatants regardless of the morality of their causes, and who believes poverty to be the only sin, is evil. Barbara's Salvation Army seems to be doing only good while Undershaft's factories, which initially horrify most of the play's major characters, are inherently evil. Yet in the second act, good and evil become interconnected as it is revealed that the Salvation Army is glad to accept funding from Undershaft's armaments as well as Bodger's Whiskey. Barbara, who sees good and evil as entirely separate entities, is horrified to discover that the Army takes this tainted money, so horrified, in fact, that she abandons the Army altogether. The sense of interconnection between good and evil is continued in the third act, where the audience discovers the results of Undershaft's evil—clean, well-kept homes for Undershaft's employees. Through his armaments, Undershaft has saved his workers from the evil of poverty; he has succeeded where the Army has failed. Through the success of her father's morally questionable business, Barbara is finally able to see the moral complexity of the concepts of good and evil.

Growth and Development

Barbara begins the play as an innocent who believes she has discovered the one right path in the Salvation Army. Moral issues are simple for her. The Army's mission of materially assisting the poor as well as working to save their souls is the work of God. Undershaft's munitions and Bodger's Whiskey are the work of the Devil. As the play progresses, however, Barbara discovers that the Salvation Army, dependent on the funding of Undershaft, Lord Saxmundham, and others like them, is not as morally pure as she believed. Unable to accept the fact that the work of God is being done with the Devil's money, she abandons her idealism as well as the Army itself. Barbara says, ''I stood on the rock I thought eternal; and without a word of warning it reeled and crumbled under me.'' Undershaft identifies her confusion as growth, saying to her, ''You have learnt something. That always feels at first as if you had lost something.''

Losing her faith in the Army, Barbara finally comes to see that eliminating poverty is in itself a good deed and that, because of the material success of Undershaft's workers, she can no longer bribe them with bread or heaven; she is free to work, unencumbered, on saving their souls. Despite this sense of Barbara reaching a sort of maturity at the end of the play, Shaw presents Barbara's growth as a paradox. The audience's final view of Barbara is of her calling for her mother, seeking her guidance. Thus Shaw complicates the concept of growth and development, leaving the audience with the sense that Barbara has matured and yet is still, in some ways, a child.

STYLE

Plot and Subplot

Critics have noted at least four possible plots in *Major Barbara:* the conversion struggle between Barbara and her father, the question of how Lady Britomart will secure incomes for her children, the question of whether Barbara and Cusins will marry, and Barbara's battle for Bill Walker's soul. Although each are distinct plots, all are intertwined throughout the course of the play. The ''good vs. evil'' contest between Barbara and her father is most often seen as the main plot, as the action of the play revolves around its development. The others can be considered subplots. Although they are important, their main function is to support the main plot thread and their resolution is subordinate to that of the primary storyline.

Setting

Since Shaw did not specify a time period for the action in *Major Barbara,* the action can be assumed to take place around 1905, the year of the first production. The action takes place in three locations: Lady Britomart's library, Barbara's Salvation Army shelter, and Undershaft's factory and model town of Perivale St. Andrews. The depiction of these three locations highlights the conflict between Barbara and Undershaft. They meet first on neutral ground, then in her territory, then in his, which also becomes Barbara's by the end of the play. The stage is used to illustrate the opulence of Lady Britomart's way of life in Act I, the poverty and degradation of the shelter in Act II, and the clean, modest comfort of Undershaft's place of business in Act III. Also in Act III, however, the mutilated dummy soldiers serve as mute testimony to the horrors of Undershaft's business, undermining some of Perivale St. Andrew's beauty.

Allusion

An allusion is an indirect reference, usually to another literary work. Being familiar with an author's allusions leads to a deeper understanding of his or her work. In *Major Barbara,* references to Undershaft as the Devil and Mephistopheles as well as the selling-and saving-of souls are allusions to the Faust legends, in which Faust sells his soul to the Devil. The best known English-language retelling of this tale is Christopher Marlowe's *The Tragical History of Dr. Faustus* (1594). Another well-known version is Johann Wolfgang von Goethe's *Faust* (Part I, 1808, Part II, 1832). There are also numerous references in *Major Barbara* to Dionysus, the Greek god of wine, and to Euripides, whose play *The Bacchae* (406 B.C.) is about the worship of Dionysus.

Symbolism

A symbol is a person, object, or action that suggests something else. Barbara's Salvation Army uniform and brooch are symbols of her faith in the Salvation Army. When she loses her faith, she no longer wears either. The mutilated dummy soldiers that appear in Act III are symbols of the violence of both war and capitalism.

Comedy

The word comedy can refer to a play that is light and entertaining and has a happy ending. It can also be used to mean a play that deals with serious topics in a light or satirical manner. *Major Barbara* is both. There are many humorous moments throughout the play: Undershaft's inability to remember the names of his children; Lomax's stupidity, illustrated by his numerous inane comments and by his smoking in the explosives shed, nearly blowing up the Undershaft business; Lady Britomart's control of her controlling husband. Shaw satirizes the Salvation Army by showing the recipients of its largesse gain this Christian organization's assistance by deceit. He also satirizes the violence of capitalism by juxtaposing the beauty of Perivale St. Andrews with the horror of the work done there. The play also has a happy ending. The heroine Barbara has found her work and, as occurs in numerous comedies, the play ends with a decision to marry.

Dialogue

Dialogue is an important aspect of *Major Barbara,* which has been criticized for what is sometimes seen as an excessive emphasis on verbal argument. Much of the ''action'' of the play, in fact, is actually in the dialogue, as characters' discussions move the drama forward. For instance, Cusins' decision to succeed Undershaft is preceded by lengthy arguments about moral issues. Shaw himself referred to the plays as ''a discussion in three long acts.''

HISTORICAL CONTEXT

The early 1900s saw an increasing interest in socialism (which advocates government ownership and/or control of the production and distribution of goods and services) worldwide, with Russian workers revolting against the Czar in 1905. In the United States, Upton Sinclair's novel *The Jungle* depicted the horrifying working conditions of immigrant laborers in the meat packing plants of Chicago and called for a socialist solution. Sinclair inadvertently attracted more attention to the impurity of the meat products Americans were consuming than the plight of the workers, but the resulting passage of the Pure Food and Drug Act of 1906 was nevertheless a victory of sorts over unbridled capitalism.

Over the course of the nineteenth century, England had changed from a primarily agricultural society to an industrial nation, and many people had moved from the country to the towns. The rise in industry brought an increasing amount of worker unrest and unemployment, which rose between 1900 and 1904. At the time, the government began to take more responsibility for the unemployed. With the passage of the Unemployed Workmen Act of 1905, committees to assist the unemployed were established by the government, yet unemployment remained a major problem, working conditions were far from ideal, and laborers remained dissatisfied. There were a large number of strikes, and membership in trade unions doubled between 1900 and 1914.

In this climate, the socialist Fabian Society, of which Shaw was a member, gained influence. The Fabians believed in changing society through participation in government—as opposed to overthrowing governments through revolutions—and members were elected to a variety of positions. The Fabian Society was only one of many organizations aimed at bringing about social reform. A number of individuals became known for their own efforts as well. Late Victorian and Edwardian England had begun to see poverty as the result of unemployment rather than the immorality of the poor, and so people were open to efforts at reform. This new attitude toward the poor is reflect in *Major Barbara,* which depicts poverty as an unnatural (even immoral) state for humankind.

Religion was an important force in England at this time, and churches were a major influence on efforts at social reform. In 1890, Salvation Army founder William Booth published *In Darkest England and the Way Out,* in which he argued that England, with the horrors of its own poverty, could not consider itself superior to Africa. Booth called for major changes in society in order to eliminate poverty. Shaw was greatly impressed by Booth's work, and its influence, particularly Booth's perception of poverty, can be seen in *Major Barbara.*

Although the importance of churches at this time cannot be ignored, there was also a rise in agnosticism, the belief that it is impossible to know whether or not there is a God. The term ''agnostic,'' in fact, was coined by British naturalist Thomas Huxley in 1869. In 1859, Charles Darwin had published *The Origin of Species,* in which he presented his theories of evolution and natural selection. Darwin's theories shocked Victorians, as it cast doubt on traditional religious beliefs (most notably the belief that man was divinely created rather than evolved from lower primates as Darwin's work suggested), and religious people still

COMPARE & CONTRAST

- **1905:** Interest in socialism grows with the development of many socialist organizations and an attempt at revolution in Russia. Although this revolution initially fails, hopes among socialists for future revolutions are high.

  Today: The collapse of the governments of the Soviet Union and East Germany serves to create strong doubts about the possible viability of any socialist regime (many argue that, like Russia's system, a socialist government cannot function without becoming a communist dictatorship). Although there are still socialist organizations, their beliefs are now well outside the mainstream of society.

- **1905:** Women struggle for basic rights, including the right to vote, which is not granted in England until 1926.

  Today: In the United States and England, women have earned legal rights equal to those of men, but many believe that much progress remains to be made, particularly in non-Western countries.

- **1905:** Christianity is a major force, affecting all aspects of society, but interest in agnosticism continues to grow. In Western nations, members of non-Christian religions are subject to discrimination.

  Today: Christianity remains viable, though its influence on society as a whole is lessened. Interest in non-Christian religions increases, and adherents of those religions face less prejudice. Agnosticism and atheism are acceptable—and increasingly popular—options.

- **1905:** The government becomes more involved in social programs. Individuals and organizations make major efforts at social reform.

  Today: Many people believe that the government cannot effectively solve social problems, and the governments of England and the United States have cut spending on social programs, resulting in a greater emphasis on volunteerism and privately-funded organizations such as Greenpeace and Amnesty International.

- **1905:** Charles Darwin's theories continue to cause debate. Much scientific progress is made, including Einstein's publication of his paper on the theory of relativity, but many question the good of rapid scientific and technological advances.

  Today: The theories of natural selection and evolution are accepted by most educated people, but there is an increase in the search for scientific evidence for creationism (the belief that man was created, fully-formed, by God). The cloning of sheep raises serious ethical questions. The astronomical increase in the use of computers causes some debate over advancing technology's effect on the quality of life.

---

felt threatened by Darwin's theories in the late nineteenth and early twentieth centuries.

For many, this period was a time of doubt as scientific progress seemed to call the truth of religion into question. In general, the good of increasing developments in science and technology was itself doubted. Early in the nineteenth century, the Luddites, who considered advancing technology to be an evil, had literally smashed the machines of the Industrial Revolution. This mistrust of scientific and technological progress, which continued into the next century, is reflected in *Major Barbara* when Undershaft delights in the development of more advanced weapons technology, which is ''better'' because it can kill people more efficiently.

Another area of much disagreement was the subject of women's rights. The struggle for women's suffrage (or the right to vote) in England began in the 1870s and continued, without success, until 1926, when women were finally allowed to vote. At the time *Major Barbara* was produced, it had only recently been decided that women had the legal right to own property. And in *Major Barbara,* when Lady Britomart wants the Undershaft business to go to Barbara, this is accomplished by naming Cusins, Barbara's future husband, as Undershaft's successor. The place of women in society, however, was changing. The term ''new woman,'' probably coined in 1894, came into prominence. The new woman was a member of a new, more liberated, generation. She believed in women's suffrage as well as education for women and the end of the sexual double standard. The character of Barbara, who gains the masculine title of Major and who looks for fulfillment and duty outside of the home but who by the end of the play clearly embraces domestic life and the world of her mother as well, reflects the changing roles of women in Shaw's time.

CRITICAL OVERVIEW

In the second volume of his biography, *Bernard Shaw,* Michael Holroyd writes of early reactions to *Major Barbara*'s first production, focusing on the fact that, as Holroyd puts it, ''The critics were impressively divided.'' Holroyd quotes one reviewer who spoke of the play's ''religious passion,'' as well as another who called Shaw ''destitute of the religious emotion,'' and a third who suggested that *Major Barbara*'s ''offences against good taste and good feeling'' should have resulted in the play's censorship. Shaw, Holroyd writes, was accused of ''deliberate perversity'' and praised for his ''sense of spiritual beauty.'' He was called ''a high genius'' as well as ''a writer whose absence of feeling makes him a very unsafe guide.'' While the play no longer faces charges of blasphemy or immorality, it continues to be controversial. Much of that controversy revolves around the seeming ambiguity of Shaw's purpose. As Harold Bloom writes in his introduction to *George Bernard Shaw's Major Barbara,* ''the drama moves finally in a direction equally available for interpretation by the extreme Left or the extreme Right.''

Writing in 1905, reviewer William Archer, quoted in Margery Morgan's compilation *File on Shaw,* said that ''The play is one long discussion between Barbara . . . and Undershaft; and to Undershaft Mr. Shaw resolutely gives the upper hand.'' Some critics have continued to follow Archer's lead, seeing Undershaft as the clear winner in the play's central conflict, as he supports realism over Barbara's idealism. Pat M. Carr in *Bernard Shaw* refers to Undershaft as Barbara's ''mentor,'' saying that he contributes to her growth with ''his greater realistic knowledge of the ways of the world.'' Undershaft, says Carr, is ''the devil's advocate who has all the sensible lines.''

Other critics, however, have focused on the complexity of Shaw's ending. In *Bernard Shaw, Playwright: Aspects of Shavian Drama,* Bernard F. Dukore notes that Undershaft has a ''more viable morality than [Cusins and Barbara], since it fits the facts of life.'' But Dukore goes on to point out that Cusins and Barbara will ultimately change Perivale St. Andrews ''from paternalistic capitalism to presumably socialist democracy.'' Although Undershaft's model city can be seen as heaven, according to Dukore, ''it is a potential heaven, or . . . a hell that may be raised to heaven.'' Barbara Bellow Watson, in her essay ''Sainthood for Millionaires,'' in *George Bernard Shaw's Major Barbara* acknowledges that the apparent victory is Undershaft's. He achieves ''the reversal of all the stubbornly held opinions of his opponents,'' but Watson adds that Undershaft's seeming victory is ''paradoxical only if we expect a socialist author to render simplistic fantasies in which virtue (poverty) triumphs over vice (money and power), or suffers in the right way.'' In other words, Shaw does not abandon his own socialism in this play; Undershaft only seems to be victorious. Shaw's criticism of capitalism is subtle; Watson refers, for example to ''the products of Capitalism being miserably on display in Act II,'' which takes place at the shelter. In the end, Watson says, ''Christianity may be vanquished, but materialism has not triumphed.'' Alfred Turco, Jr., in his essay ''Shaw's Moral Vision'' (also in *George Bernard Shaw's Major Barbara*) also writes that Undershaft is not the clear winner, but, in Turco's opinion, the important point is not that Undershaft has failed to wholly convert Barbara, but, in fact, that each has succeeded, in part, in converting the other. Turco writes, ''Barbara and Cusins 'give up' the Salvation Army by accepting the cannon factory, and Undershaft gives up his cannons by placing the power they represent at the service of the religious impulse.'' Neither side has lost and ''The respective 'professions' of Barbara and Undershaft will now develop in meaningful relation to each other instead of in isolation.'' The resolution of the play is in the syntheses of Barbara and Undershaft's convictions.

Margery M. Morgan, in her essay "Skeptical Faith," argues, however, that no such synthesis exists, but the play must be seen in a larger context. Morgan says the ending "implies a recognition . . . that the true resolution of socialist drama belongs not in the work of art but outside it in society." She acknowledges that, within the play, there is a resolution of plot in Cusin's acceptance of Undershaft's offer, but "as a total structure of ideas the play remains a paradox in which antitheses retain their full value and cannot be resolved away." Within the play, for Morgan, there is no resolution. In his essay "Shaw's Own Problem Play," J. Percy Smith argues that at least part of the problem in *Major Barbara*'s interpretation lies in "the ambivalence of Shaw's attitude to the central moral question that [the play] raises. In other words, the ending remains unclear because Shaw himself never decided who really triumphs.

In spite of continued argument over the play's ending, most critics writing today agree that *Major Barbara* is one of Shaw's greatest works, and the play's importance in modern drama is virtually unchallenged. For many, the complications and seeming paradox of the play's final act only add to *Major Barbara*'s complexity and richness as well as Shaw's reputation as one of the twentieth century's greatest playwrights.

CRITICISM

Clare Cross

Cross is a Ph.D. candidate specializing in modern drama. In this essay she discusses the development of Barbara's identity as it relates to her involvement with family and work.

In his play *Major Barbara,* Shaw focuses on the development of identity in his lead character, Barbara Undershaft. Although Barbara has a strong sense of self at the beginning of the play, Shaw shows that her identity is not fixed and simple but fluid and complex. Her identity is composed of many factors that, initially, seem at odds. She is the daughter of wealthy parents whose lifestyles she rejects. Instead she chooses to work for the Salvation Army, accepting the tiny sum of a pound a week as salary. While her allegiance at the play's outset lies almost wholly with the Army, Barbara will come to realize that her family may enable her to better perform the work of God. This realization will bring her closer to God, closer to her parents and family, and, ultimately, bring her to a true concept of her identity within the world in which the play is set.

From the beginning of the play, Barbara has, in essence, three parents: Lady Britomart, Andrew Undershaft, and her heavenly Father, God, whom she serves through her work in the Salvation Army. Act One establishes the positions of these three parents in Barbara's life. As the play begins, the audience discovers that Barbara has been entirely brought up by her mother and does not even know her biological father. Although her mother has raised her, it soon becomes clear that Barbara has rejected Lady Britomart's way of life. Before Barbara even walks on stage, her mother expresses disappointment in the path Barbara has taken: "I thought Barbara was going to make the most brilliant career of all. . . . And what does she do? Joins the Salvation Army; discharges her maid; lives on a pound a week; and walks in one evening with a professor of Greek whom she has picked up in the street."

Barbara has clearly forsaken the opulence of her mother's life as well as Britomart's idea of an appropriate career for a respectable society woman. Yet, there is another way to see Barbara's relationship with her mother. As feminist critic J. Ellen Gainor remarked in her book *Shaw's Daughters: Dramatic and Narrative Constructions of Gender,* "The first half of the play . . . stresses Barbara's maternal resemblance, which Shaw notes in several stage directions as well as in a wonderfully comic speech by her mother." The speech Gainor referred to is that in which Lady Britomart complains about Barbara's "propensity to have her own way and order people about" and adds, "I'm sure I don't know where she picks it up," when it is, in fact, obvious that Barbara's behavior resembles that of no one so much as Lady Britomart herself. In addition, while Barbara has rejected the luxury of her mother's lifestyle, she continues to live in her mother's house; her autonomy and austere lifestyle are supported by a safety net in the form of her mother's wealth. In spite of her verbal declarations of independence, Barbara is reliant on her mother's way of life and still very much Lady Britomart's daughter.

Undershaft's initial relationship with Barbara is also established in the first act. Barbara's name is Undershaft, and she has been raised on her father's fortune (though her determination to live on "a

WHAT DO I READ NEXT?

- *Mrs. Warren's Profession,* a play written by Shaw in 1898, is also concerned with the morality of avoiding poverty by doing what may be considered immoral work. Shaw's original title for *Major Barbara* was *Andrew Undershaft's Profession.*
- *Mother Courage and Her Children,* a play written by Bertolt Brecht in 1939, seems to have been influenced by *Major Barbara.* Mother Courage, like Undershaft, is dependent on war to make her living but at a severe cost to her children and herself.
- *The Tragical History of Dr. Faustus* by Christopher Marlowe, probably first performed in 1594, is a retelling of the legend of Faust, who sells his soul to the Devil. In *Major Barbara,* Undershaft is sometimes called Mephistopheles, the name of the Devil in Marlowe's play.
- "Civil Disobedience," published in 1849, is an essay by Henry David Thoreau, who spent time in prison for refusing to pay taxes to support what he believed to be an immoral war. In this essay, Thoreau argues for following one's conscience, even if it means disobeying the law.
- *A Doll's House,* a play by Henrik Ibsen, published in 1879, is also about the question of whether a seemingly immoral act can, in fact be the right thing to do. The play's lead character, Nora, is an early example of the strong independent woman of the late Victorian stage. Shaw was greatly influenced by Ibsen's work.
- *The Jungle,* socialist Upton Sinclair's 1906 novel, reveals the horrors of workers' conditions in the Chicago meat-packing plants of that time. In his preface to *Major Barbara,* Shaw writes about Sinclair's novel showing the position in which a capitalist society places the poor.

pound a week'' symbolically rejects that wealth). But in his introduction to the critical collection *George Bernard Shaw's Major Barbara,* Harold Bloom points out that in the course of their initial discussion, Barbara and Undershaft are ''[bonded] against the mother, as each stands for . . . religion as the Life force.'' The two also agree on the motto ''blood and fire''—although there is considerable difference in the meaning each takes from the phrase.

At the end of Act One, when Barbara and Undershaft each agree to visit the other's place of work, the bond between father and daughter is again emphasized. After years of absence from their lives, Undershaft arrives and, while not completely winning them over, immediately wins the attentions of his daughters. When Lady Britomart complains about a father who ''steals [the children's] affection away from [the mother],'' Shaw establishes a tension between the paternal and maternal, the masculine and feminine forces in Barbara's life. Gainor saw Barbara as the product of both parents, embracing the masculine as well as the feminine in her work in the Salvation Army. As Gainor pointed out, ''the Army's essential function is more 'feminine': nurturing and concerned with the personal, while its structure is 'masculine': an army with hierarchies of power and financial concerns.''

In spite of the tension between masculine and feminine, the first act presents Barbara as primarily a child of God. It is for her ''heavenly Father'' that Barbara has abandoned her father's money and her mother's concept of a ''brilliant career'' and chosen to do the work of God. When Lady Britomart tells Undershaft that Barbara ''has no father to advise her,'' Barbara replies, ''Oh yes she has. There are no orphans in the Salvation Army.'' God the Father has become Barbara's parent as well as the center of her work. Even Barbara's name and clothes reflect her total absorption into the world of this father. She is no longer Barbara Undershaft but Major Barbara.

Undershaft (holding trombone) visits Barbara at the Salvation Army in an American Repertory Theatre production of Shaw's play

She wears the uniform of the Salvation Army. Despite the resemblance she bears to her father and mother, Barbara sees her identity as fixed. She is the child of God. God's work (as represented by the Army's mission) is her work. Barbara sees no compromise in this; her work with the Army is the ultimate expression of her devotion to God.

In the second act, Shaw shows Barbara Undershaft as Major Barbara, Salvationist, child of God. Although this scene at the shelter shows Barbara in her element, doing the work of her heavenly father, it is also at this point in the play that Undershaft begins to stake his claim on her. In his discussion with Cusins, he reveals that he loves Barbara, revealing his paternal emotions for her. Undershaft identifies Barbara with himself. When Cusins says that "Barbara is quite original in her own religion," Undershaft answers, "Barbara Undershaft would be . . . it is the Undershaft inheritance." He then goes on to say "I shall hand on my torch to my daughter." As Gainor appraised, "The father sees in the daughter an image of himself and intends to develop her capacity to carry on his public functions, as well as convert her to a form of

Undershaft philosopher.'' Undershaft sees himself as Barbara's true father. Bernard F. Dukore wrote in his book *Bernard Shaw: Playwright,* ''Symbolically as well as literally, Undershaft sires Barbara.'' As Barbara's father, Undershaft sees her identity in him and wants her to do his work. Later Barbara will see that being the daughter of Undershaft is indeed a part of her identity. She will also realize that being his daughter enables her to better perform her religious work.

But in Act Two, Barbara still sees Undershaft as the man in opposition to her true father, a man whose business negatively affects her real work. In support of this, Shaw does suggest that that Undershaft is the opposite of God. Throughout *Major Barbara,* Undershaft is referred to as the Devil, the Prince of Darkness, and Mephistopheles. And it is in the second act that Barbara's earthly father reveals the hypocrisy of the Salvation Army. In essence, Undershaft buys the Salvation Army, and Barbara sees her identity as a child of God destroyed. She expresses that loss of identity in the symbolic action of pinning her Salvation Army brooch on Undershaft's collar. In the third act, she will exchange her uniform for ordinary clothes.

Barbara later cries out, ''My God: why hast thou forsaken me?'' In addition to losing God and the Salvation Army, she has also lost her work. ''I'm like you now,'' she says to Peter Shirley. ''Cleaned out, and lost my job.'' She later expresses the importance of this loss: ''I stood on the rock eternal; and without a word of warning it reeled and crumbled under me. I was safe with an infinite wisdom watching me . . . and in a moment . . . I stood alone.'' The identity she saw as permanent seems to be gone altogether.

It is in the third act that Barbara begins to synthesize a new identity out of the fractured parts of her character. At first, when Barbara prepares to leave for Undershaft's factories and model town, the gulf she sees between God and Undershaft is emphasized when she describes her sense of Undershaft's work: ''I have always thought of it as a sort of pit where lost creatures with blackened faces stirred up smoky fires and were driven and tormented by my father.'' Clearly she is describing the traditional Christian imagery of hell with her father as the Devil. But Undershaft is not the devil, and it is in this act that she begins to accept him as a parent. When he tells her, ''You have learnt something. That always feels at first as if you lost something.'' This statement shows Undershaft in an understanding, fatherly role. For her part, Barbara begins to see that her father's work may do some good and that she may be able to learn from him.

"AS BARBARA'S FATHER, UNDERSHAFT SEES HER IDENTITY IN HIM AND WANTS HER TO DO HIS WORK."

It is here that Undershaft tells her he saved her soul from the seven deadly sins: ''Food, clothing, firing, rent, taxes, respectability, and children.'' It is only because of Undershaft, who has provided for Barbara's physical needs her entire life, that Barbara had the means to be able to seek and serve God. Her acceptance of Undershaft as her father is emphasized when, after Cusins decides to succeed her father, Barbara reveals that, had he not, she would have married the man who did. As Dukore pointed out, ''Barbara, marrying Cusins, becomes—since Adolphus takes his new father's name—Mrs. Andrew Undershaft.'' Since Undershaft's successor must take his name, Barbara would have become Mrs. Andrew Undershaft regardless of who became her father's heir. Bloom, taking a Freudian point of view, saw Barbara's acceptance of her father as symbolically incestuous and refers to the pair's ''dance of repressed psychosexual courtship.'' It seems more accurate, however, to see her as becoming fully her father's daughter, retaining, even in marriage, her father's name. In addition, this name is also her mother's, which places her even more strongly with both of her earthly parents.

Despite her disillusionment with the Salvation Army (and her ''deal with the devil'' in becoming Undershaft's heir), Barbara remains her heavenly Father's daughter as well; she has merely exchanged her idealistic view of God's work for one more realistic. She recognizes that poverty is in itself an evil, but her concern is still for saving souls, though no longer ''weak souls in starved bodies. . . . My father shall never throw it in my teeth again that my converts were bribed with bread.'' She will continue to do the work of God but on different terms: ''Let God's work be done for its own sake.''

In addition to accepting both Undershaft and God as fathers, in the final scene Barbara turns again to her mother. ''After all,'' she says, ''my dear old mother has more sense than any of you.'' Although Barbara contrasts her mother's desire for ''the houses and the kitchen ranges and the linen and the china,'' of Perivale St. Andrews with her own focus on ''all the human souls to be saved,'' she still accepts her place as her mother's daughter. At the end of the play, Shaw describes her cry, ''Mamma! Mamma! I want Mamma,'' as childlike, and describes Barbara as ''[clutching] like a baby at her mother's skirt.'' Gainor viewed the reversion of Barbara to a childlike state as her acceptance of her role as a woman in her society. According to Gainor, women at this time ''must . . . be reinscribed within the feminine realm to rationalize or confirm their status.'' She went on to say, ''As Victorian culture associated the child with the feminine, a display of childish behavior affirms the gender of the daughter.'' So Gainor saw Barbara's identity reverting to an earlier association with her mother thus establishing her femininity and subservient place in society.

There is, however, another way to view Barbara's childlike behavior in the final scene. As John A. Bertolini wrote in his book *The Playwrighting Self of Bernard Shaw,* ''Barbara herself is mad with delight for the idea of conversion, especially conversion as a cleansing away of the old self.'' What Barbara experiences in the last scene can also be seen as ''self-renewal through childlike behavior.'' Although the final scene certainly does identify Barbara as her mother's daughter, it also can be seen as indicative of a rebirth. Barbara has become a new person with a new identity which is a combination of all facets of her character.

Barbara's new identity, however, is not solely with mother, father, or God. She has synthesized all three of these influences; she encompasses the masculine, the feminine, the spiritual. Similarly, her work is now also a synthesis, the domestic aspect of her marriage reflecting her mother's influence, her new understanding of the Undershaft business reflecting her father's, her desire to save souls reflecting God's. All are integrated to create a new sense of work, a new sense of family, and a new way of life. Barbara's character loses its fragmentary nature, and she becomes her true self.

Source: Clare Cross, for *Drama for Students,* Gale, 1998.

Dennis Kennedy

Calling Major Barbara *Shaw's ''most successful'' drama, Kennedy provides an overview and background of Shaw's play in this essay.*

Shaw wrote a number of plays concerned with wealth and its distribution, but *Major Barbara* may be the most complex in theme and the most successful as drama. Barbara Undershaft has defied upper-class conventions by becoming a major in the Salvation Army, dedicating herself to the poor of London, who, naturally enough, resist her ministrations whenever they go beyond food and shelter. Adolphus Cusins, a professor of Greek given to quoting Euripides, pretends an equal dedication in order to be near her. Her mother, Lady Britomart—the owner of one of Shaw's most resounding character names—now needs more money for her children's marriages and turns to her long-estranged husband, Andrew Undershaft, a munitions maker of low birth but noble proportions. He is ''fabulously wealthy, because there is always a war going on somewhere''; but the ''Undershaft inheritance,'' which insists that the business must be passed on to another foundling boy, has been the cause of the rupture in their marriage. Andrew Undershaft is at the opposite moral pole from Barbara, yet father and daughter are immediately fascinated with one another and strike a bargain: he will visit her shelter if she will visit his armament works. The shelter is also in financial need and is saved from ruin only by the generosity of Undershaft and a whisky distiller; Barbara, shocked that the Army will accept money from two such manufacturers of evil, loses her faith and resigns her position. But Undershaft's creed, that the worst of all possible crimes is poverty, begins to convert Cusins and Barbara, especially when they see its effects in his utopian company town. When Cusins turns out to be a foundling he is installed as the heir to the Undershaft money, gunpowder, and destruction, with Barbara by his side.

If Shaw had wished to write a simple play he would have made Undershaft an industrialist like Andrew Carnegie, someone whose labor practices may have been questionable but who made contributions to social and economic advancement. Instead Undershaft is made to be a sower of death, like Alfred Nobel, disdaining common morality and the common excuses for his trade, selling munitions to anyone who applies, revelling in the devastation his guns bring. Nobel wished to buy respectability by endowing a prize for peace; Undershaft demands that his contribution to the Salvation Army be treated anonymously. As Cusins notes continually, Undershaft is a Prince of Darkness, a Dionysus in touch with the underside of human existence. Thus the dilemma he presents to Barbara and to readers and audience is enormously complicated. If poverty is the worst of crimes, then anything that eradicates it is good, even if that thing is, itself, normally considered evil. In this extreme of cases, Shaw's play implies, the end not only justifies Undershaft's means, but his means are the only realistic ones that can achieve the end.

A powerful second act in Barbara's West Ham shelter shows that the Salvation Army is an unwitting tool of the status quo: it relieves the effects of poverty just enough to blunt the edge of social revolution, without actually altering the conditions of the classes or attempting to redistribute wealth. The violence and desperation of a bully like Bill Walker cannot be corrected by hot soup and a prayer meeting because they are caused not by moral defects but by social inequities. When Barbara loses her faith in the Army she awakens to the sentimental nature of the Christian promise of salvation; she also slowly awakens to the fact that the Army, dependent upon the largess of capitalists, is therefore part of the capitalist establishment, as much as the Parliament that Undershaft brags is in his pocket. As one of the spiritual and economic unfortunates, Walker knows this truth in his bones. After the Army has accepted Undershaft's money, Walker speaks the cruellest and most incisive line of the play, rubbing salt into Barbara's wounds: ''Wot prawce selvytion nah?''

The cannon is the metaphoric heart of *Major Barbara.* From its mock-military title to its numerous references to actual battles, the play offers glimpses of the destructive impulse; the final scene is literally dominated by a huge cannon center stage. In shifting its attention from Barbara's spiritual dilemma to Undershaft's vision of an orderly universe based on gunpowder, the play seems to promote the strongman as savior, and firepower as the ultimate arbiter. Shaw's Preface, a brilliant essay on the nature of wealth, provides a less disturbing philosophic context by suggesting that public choice need not lie between poverty on the one hand and bombs on the other, since it is capitalism that sanctions both; in a more humane economy both would be eradicated. But the play itself is profoundly ambiguous in its social morality; the diabolic Undershaft is its most gripping character, and even when he is taken ironically *Major Barbara* resists neat categorizing.

"SHAW WROTE A NUMBER OF PLAYS CONCERNED WITH WEALTH AND ITS DISTRIBUTION, BUT *MAJOR BARBARA* MAY BE THE MOST COMPLEX IN THEME AND THE MOST SUCCESSFUL AS DRAMA."

Despite its disturbing theme, its theatrical vitality has been unquestioned since the first performance in 1905. Shaw wrote it for Granville Barker's Court Theatre seasons, his first play designed with a specific company of actors in mind (Barker played Cusins, a role modelled on their mutual friend Gilbert Murray, whose translations of Euripides, which Cusins quotes, were also being performed at the Court). Since its twin subjects of war and money have been the central subjects of the 20th century, it has shown little sign of losing its hold on us.

Source: Dennis Kennedy, ''*Major Barbara*'' in *The International Dictionary of Theater,* Volume 1: *Plays,* edited by Mark Hawkins-Dady, St. James Press, 1992, p. 462.

Michael C. O'Neill

Reviewing a 1987 production of Major Barbara *at that year's Shaw Festival in Ontario, Canada, O'Neill affirms the theatrical power of Shaw's play, calling the production the highlight of the festival.*

Genuine theatrical salvation for *Major Barbara,* perhaps Bernard Shaw's most relentless discussion for the stage, is the chief pleasure of the 1987 Shaw Festival where huge and handsome, if unadventuresome, productions are often the rule. As conceived by Christopher Newton, who also serves as the festival's artistic director, *Major Barbara* finds in the spectacle of its staging a visual accompaniment for the dazzling brilliance of Shaw's ideas.

Major Barbara has been directed with the scope and vision of opera, thereby revealing yet another key to a play in which Shaw, the music critic and great arbiter of the western artistic heritage, provides a symphony of thought articulated

> "MAJOR BARBARA IS PERHAPS BERNARD SHAW'S MOST RELENTLESS DISCUSSION FOR THE STAGE."

and debated in the intellectual duets of Undershaft and Cusins and in the passionate verbal arias of Barbara and the poor she intends to save. The stylized tones and rhythmic variety of the play's language are enriched, as the Salvation Army's activities are, with music: Barbara sings, Lomax is ordered to accompany prayers on the organ, Undershaft plays the trombone, and Cusins beats a huge drum to be near the woman he worships with the fervor of felt religion. These apparent clues to the musical nature of *Major Barbara* march through the production like a Salvation Army hymn, and the motif is completed at the play's end, when, after Barbara and Cusins have agreed to make war on war, ''We're In The Money'' plays softly and cynically as the house lights come up.

Each scene seems to have been orchestrated with comparable insight and choreographed as well with precision of movement and gesture. The curious and outraged Wilton Crescent quartet of Lady Britomart and her children, unable to resist Undershaft's charm, gives way in the second act to a chorus of humiliation in the Salvation Army shelter that crescendos into a lament of hypocrisy and despair. For the grand finale at Perivale St. Andrews, the characters flow effortlessly about Undershaft's stark white utopia, anxious to grasp a new illusion in which the benefits of wealth are an endless song.

These operatic dimensions of the play are boldly stated in the designs of Cameron Porteous, who uses the full height of the Festival Theater stage to dwarf Shaw's principals in settings as elaborate and as meaningful as the ideas they discuss. Lady Britomart's library is a huge, rich room of books, marble, pottery, and dark wood, a small corner of the British Empire exhibiting its wealth. The walls are covered with paper and stained glass depicting the wild growth of the jungle that lies just beneath the polished exterior of those who live there, for these are powerful and rich people who are summoned together to discuss self-preservation through a continuation of their position and wealth. They descend, in Act II, into the hell of the East Ham shelter, a dimly lit, towering grey brick affair with smoke rolling across the littered floor. The nightmarish quality of the setting reinforces the moral quandary of this inferno where an army of angels unwittingly perpetuates the suffering it seeks to assuage, and the devilish Undershaft offers the only hope of an earthly redemption from poverty.

The scenic tour de force, however, occurs in the third act as the library revolves in full view into the foundry of Undershaft and Lazarus, visually suggesting the creative evolution from the former world into the latter that will be effected through the inheritance of Barbara and Cusins. The works themselves are wittily conveyed: a huge, phallic cannon dominates a setting of white marble steps, Greek columns, and dummy soldiers displayed like so many Attic statues. The classicism of Cusins, already incorporated into the enterprise he intends to transform, appears frozen in another time, and thus the setting metaphorically asserts that his real connection to ancient Greece lies in the spirit of Dionysus within himself. That spirit draws him to Barbara and will propel them past her father into a future they envision but do not as yet understand.

Jim Mezon's Cusins, full of a calculated subtlety that grows into confidence by the play's end, emerges as a formidable revival to the properly demonic Undershaft, played by Douglas Rain with great verbal dexterity and just a hint of relief that the life force is indeed doing its work through him as he passes on the foundry to his chosen heirs. Both men bring a sexual edge to their roles, giving further credence to Shaw's contention that the superman is compelling and irresistible. Martha Burns as Barbara is full of confused energy, waiting to be awakened by her father's challenge and Cusins's love. The three form a Shavian love triangle in which the object of their affection is the force they instinctively recognize in one another.

The entire cast seems to have discovered a rich sexual energy in the play that imbues its comic moments with human folly and heightens its philosophical intrigue with unstated tension. Frances Hyland avoids the temptation to play Lady Britomart as a cousin to Lady Bracknell, opting instead to create an aging ingenue who pinches her cheeks to look attractive for Undershaft and sees in Barbara and Cusins a reflection of the feelings for her husband that she still relishes. As performed by Jon Bryden, Bill Walker's attacks on Jenny Hill and

Rummy Mitchens seethe with the potential for rape, whereas Steven Sutcliffe's Stephen seems to wander through the play trying to figure out why anyone would expect him to marry. Lomax and Sarah, played by Michael Howell and Barbara Worthy, serve as effective foils for Cusins and Barbara. In the utter banality of their relationship, they demonstrate Shaw's belief in the power of the intellect to transform and sustain. The most passionate moment of *Major Barbara* occurs, appropriately, when Cusins and Barbara agree to accept Undershaft's challenge. As they embrace in a long, provocative kiss on the steps of the foundry, there is no mistaking that for Shaw the passion of the intellect and passion itself are inseparable.

This is an inspired production, a Shavian masterpiece accorded as little reverence as Undershaft himself gives tradition, yet thoughtful enough to make Shaw's ideas live and breathe through his characters, who, with us since 1903, are now beginning to touch the realm of myth. The result is fresh and very funny, tantalizing the audience with possibilities of the human spirit we already expect will never come to pass.

Source: Michael C. O'Neill, review of *Major Barbara* in *Theatre Journal,* Volume 40, no. 1, March, 1988, pp. 105–06.

SOURCES

Bertolini, John A. *The Playwrighting Self of Bernard Shaw,* Southern Illinois University Press (Carbondale), 1991, pp. 64-65.

Bloom, Harold. Introduction to his *George Bernard Shaw's* Major Barbara, Chelsea House (New York), 1988, pp. 1-11.

Carr, Pat M. *Bernard Shaw,* Frederick Ungar (New York), 1976, pp. 58.

Dukore, Bernard F. *Bernard Shaw, Playwright: Aspects of Shavian Drama,* University of Missouri Press (Columbia), 1973, pp. 86-90.

Gainor, J. Ellen. *Shaw's Daughters: Dramatic and Narrative Constructions of Gender,* University of Michigan Press (Ann Arbor), 1991, pp. 218-24.

Holroyd, Michael. *Bernard Shaw. Volume II: 1898-1918: The Pursuit of Power,* Penguin (London), 1989, pp. 147-48.

Archer, William. *File on Shaw,* edited by Margery M. Morgan, Methuen Drama (London), 1989, p. 54.

Morgan, Margery M. "Skeptical Faith" in *George Bernard Shaw's* Major Barbara, edited by Harold Bloom, Chelsea House (New York), 1988, pp. 49-73.

Smith, J. Percy. "Shaw's Own Problem Play" in *George Bernard Shaw's* Major Barbara, edited by Harold Bloom, Chelsea House, 1988, pp. 133-51.

Turco, Alfred, Jr. "Shaw's Moral Vision" in *George Bernard Shaw's* Major Barbara, edited by Harold Bloom, Chelsea House, 1988, pp. 103-31.

Watson, Barbara Bellow. "Sainthood for Millionaires" in *George Bernard Shaw's* Major Barbara, edited by Harold Bloom, Chelsea House, 1988, pp. 13-31.

FURTHER READING

Bloom, Harold, Editor. *George Bernard Shaw's* Major Barbara, Chelsea House, 1988.

This is a collection of papers by numerous critics on different aspects of Shaw's play.

Briggs, Asa. *A Social History of England,* Weidenfeld and Nicolson (London), 1994.

A study of English society from antiquity to the present, this books contains a lengthy chapter on the Victorian and early Edwardian eras.

Gainor, J. Ellen. *Shaw's Daughters: Dramatic and Narrative Constructions of Gender,* University of Michigan Press, 1991.

This is a study of women in Shaw's plays, focusing on the conception of womanhood in Victorian culture and the image of the daughter in Shaw's plays.

Peters, Sally. *Bernard Shaw: The Ascent of the Superman,* Yale University Press (New Haven), 1996.

This is an extended literary biography of Shaw, discussing his life as well as his works.

Weintraub, Stanley. *Shaw's People: Victoria to Churchill,* Pennsylvania State University Press (University Park), 1996.

This book focuses on Shaw and his relationships with and attitudes toward various people of his time, including Salvation Army founder William Booth. It places Shaw more completely in the context of his society.

Marat/Sade

PETER WEISS

1964

Whether reading or watching a performance, *Marat/ Sade* is neither a comfortable nor an immediately enjoyable play. The work, whose full title is *The Persecution and Assassination of Jean-Paul Marat As Performed by the Inmates of the Asylum of Charenton under the Direction of The Marquis de Sade,* is more commonly known by its truncated name. The play was first performed in West Berlin at the Schiller Theater in 1964 and directed by Konrad Swinarksi. It was not until British director Peter Brook staged an English language version in London, however, that Weiss and his play received wide acclaim. That production, staged in 1964 at the Aldwych Theatre, brought *Marat/Sade* to the attention of the world as critics and audiences hailed the play's unique style and structure.

Swinarksi's direction was tame compared to what Brook would do to the work in London and, the following year, in New York. According to David Richard Jones in *Great Directors at Work: Stanislavsky, Brecht, Kazan, Brook:* ''Most audiences experienced it as powerful. Viewers showed that they were strongly affected by its magnitude, whether they walked out in anger or stayed seated, shaking, at the end. The show usually had a similar impact on critics, other theatre workers, and the actors themselves.''

Audience members did storm out of performances of *Marat/Sade;* some viewers reacted so strongly that they became ill. ''At least one spectator, the German actress Ruth Arrack, died in the auditorium during a performance,'' reported Jones. The fever pitch of the play's emotions, combined with its frank violence and brutality, led many of the play's detractors to label it as nothing more than ''shock theatre.''

Debate existed among critics about the value of the play. Some suggested that the real meaning of the play was perhaps ambiguous. The majority of critics, however, felt that the ambiguity of the play was intentional and a means to force the audience to assess the proceedings and come to their own conclusions. Despite what some perceived as a lack of resolution in *Marat/Sade,* all who viewed the production agreed that it was a spectacle the likes of which the London and New York stages rarely saw.

AUTHOR BIOGRAPHY

Peter Ulrich Weiss was born on November 8, 1916, in Nowawes, a German province near Berlin. A textile merchant, his father was a Hungarian of Jewish descent. His mother, a German Christian, was a former actress. At three, he and his family moved to Bremen, which is the city Weiss associates with childhood and his first rebellion against the wealth and the social pressures of an upper middle class upbringing. In his adolescence the family moved to Berlin, where Weiss began training for a career as a visual artist. His life changed drastically, however, when Adolf Hitler's National Socialist Party (the Nazis) rose to political power in Germany. The Nazis were racial purists who believed that non-Germans were a detriment to society and should be rooted out. Being half Jewish and a Czech citizen Weiss was a particular target for such oppression.

As the Nazi's persecution of Jews became more violent, the Weiss family fled Germany in 1935, settling near London where Weiss was sent to take photography classes, since his family felt that painters couldn't make a decent living. In his spare time, however, he continued to paint, using his attic as a studio. His disavowal of his family's values (and wealth) forced him out on his own, and he pursued his studies as an artist in London. He later studied at the Art Academy in Prague, Czechoslovakia, and struck up a friendship with author Herman Hesse (*Siddartha*), whose work he had been reading for years. Although painting was his major passion, Weiss began writing as well. In 1939, his family moved to Sweden, and Weiss went along, later joining a commune of other German-speaking artists in Sweden.

During this period, Weiss began writing more seriously, publishing his first book in Swedish in 1944. Returning to Germany as a journalist following World War II, he started writing in dramatic form and produced a radio play, *The Tower,* in 1948. Gradually, the majority of his creative work focused on writing, although he also made documentary and feature films. His fiction work included two autobiographical novels, *The Leavetaking* and *Vanishing Point.*

The 1964 production of his play *Marat/Sade* established Weiss as a writer of international acclaim. The play, with its daring style and strong political content, won a number of honors, including a Lessing Preis Award, an Antionette (''Tony'') Perry Award, and the Drama Critics' Circle Award for best play. The drama was produced in London and New York with direction by Peter Brooks, who many credit as much as Weiss with defining the work's unique structure.

Like *Marat/Sade,* later plays by Weiss continued a political vein, these works include *Trotsky in Exile, Vietnam Discourse,* and *The Investigation,* which is about Nazi War Crime trials.

Weiss died in Sweden in 1982 and was posthumously awarded the Georg Buchner Prize for outstanding achievement in German letters. Although some critics have considered his work too heavy in political agenda, Roger Ellis said in *Peter Weiss in Exile: A Critical Study of His Works:* ''Weiss always sought something contemporary in his studies of the past: an understanding of the roots of social violence, of the extent of human influence upon historical development, of the restrictive conditions which bear upon modern artists and how to overcome them, and, most especially, an understanding of the roots of the seemingly paradoxical faith of certain individuals who struggle unsuccessfully to improve apparently hopeless situations.''

Or, in Weiss's own words, ''I myself think that art should be so strong that it changes life; otherwise it is a failure.''

PLOT SUMMARY

Act I

Marat/Sade is set in the bath hall of an insane asylum at Charenton; the time is some years after the French Revolution. The play opens with the Marquis de Sade undertaking some last minute preparations for a play he has written with the parts to be played by inmates of the asylum. Invited to watch this spectacle are members of the French aristocracy, specifically Coulmier, the director of the clinic, and his family. Sade gives a signal and Coulmier and his family enter as the actors, a scraggly lot of patients from the asylum, wait tensely.

Coulmier introduces this play within a play by describing the modern advanced treatment at Charenton, which includes therapy through education and art. The Herald points out the main characters—Sade who is seated in his dais, Jean-Paul Marat who is placed in his bath, and Charlotte Corday. There is also Duperret, who buzzes around Corday trying to get his hands on her, and the radical priest Jacques Roux. The Herald explains each of the characters as well as the story line. Corday is coming to Paris to murder Marat in his bath.

At this point the cast pauses to offer an homage to Marat and engage in a slight discussion of his role. This sequence ends with a refrain that will be repeated throughout the play:

> *Marat, we're poor and the poor stay poor/Marat don't make us wait any more/We want our rights and we don't care how/We want our revolution NOW*

Emotions rise as this is recited and the patients/actors become agitated; the asylum's nurses restrain them. Coulmier complains to Sade about this outburst, calling on him to control what is happening on stage.

At this point Corday is introduced and her role in the play explained further. Marat, cared for by his mistress Simonne in his bathtub, claims, "I am the Revolution." Corday makes her first attempt to contact him, knocking at his door. She is sent away, reminded by Simonne that she must come three times before gaining entrance. The Four Singers then describe Corday's visit to Paris and she responds. Marat, in his bath, attacks the conduct of the ruling class after the revolution, and the patients mime an execution. They play with the severed head, kicking and throwing it about the stage. Coulmier breaks into this play in progress, suggesting that this violence isn't helping the patients. The Herald smooths things over by declaring that of course this play is talking about the past. Then Sade and Marat launch into a conversation about life and death, in which Sade ultimately looks at war and the manner in which anonymous deaths are parceled out. He wonders whether Marat has become an aristocrat because he has questioned Sade's lack of compassion.

Marat makes an indictment against the status quo, including the way the church has been used to keep the poor in place by encouraging them to view suffering as an honor. This statement is too much for Coulmier, who again questions Sade about the cuts in the play that they had supposedly agreed upon. Sade and Marat continue to talk, Sade suggesting that his health may be the most important thing to Marat, who then lashes out at the ruling class, complaining of how oppressed people still are.

Duperret is introduced and talks with Corday about her plans, but he (or the patient playing him) is more interested in touching her body and must have his attention refocused. Sade taunts Marat, questioning the validity of the revolution, pointing out that everything comes down to the personal, to oneself. Roux speaks up and encourages a continued revolution of the masses but is restrained. This is too much for Coulmier and he again protests the events taking place in Sade's play. Roux appeals to Marat and Coulmier demands the scene be cut. Sade continues his conversation with Marat and talks of confronting the criminal in himself while he has Corday beat him. Marat sits in his bath and asks for his pen and paper so he can write down his ideas. He wonders aloud if the revolution that has taken place has improved things. Sade questions Marat's ideology.

Corday makes a second attempt to see Marat and is turned away. Sade taunts Marat about the reasons people join the revolution. Marat is visited by voices from his past and feverishly begs for help in writing down his thoughts. The act ends with the repeated demand from the patient/actors for revolution.

Act II

The second act opens with an imagined scene in the National Assembly where Marat questions the actions of those in power after the revolution, saying they are as bad as before the revolution. His words are received with mixed emotions. Some cheer him on while others question his facts and intentions, including Duperret. Coulmier can take it no longer and jumps up, demanding Sade cut these parts from the play. Roux interrupts and further incites the patients.

Marat, exhausted, is in his bath again, tended to by Simonne. He is once again attempting to commit his thoughts to paper. Sade, to the side, questions the revolutionary's writing, claiming that nothing can be achieved by scribbling. Marat defends himself, saying that he always wrote with action in mind and that it wasn't a replacement for action, only a preparation. But Sade doesn't let up and asks him to look at the sorry state of the revolution. Marat is confused and exhausted.

Corday prepares herself for her final visit to Marat's bath. She takes her dagger in hand, while Duperret suggests she throw it away and give up on this goal. He begs her to go away with him. She refuses and resolutely goes to Marat's door. Sade interjects his idea about sensuality at this point and stirs up the patients to sing "what's the point of a revolution without general copulation." Corday knocks at Marat's door and is invited to enter.

The Herald engages in a brief recitation of history, claiming fifteen glorious years since the revolution and the rise of Napoleon. Marat is killed in his bath by Corday.

Coulmier tries to bring a conclusion, again insisting "we live in far different times." The patients, however, are aroused and march around the stage. Coulmier enlists the nurses to strike them down. As the nurses violently beat the patients, Sade looks on laughing. The play ends.

Peter Weiss in 1966

CHARACTERS

Charlotte Corday

Corday exists in a dream and must at times be ushered to her appointed times and places. She speaks in a sing-song voice, never fully dimensional, but resolute even in her dream-like state. It is not explained whether her behavior is historical or merely the personality traits of the mental patient playing her in Sade's inner play. Like other characters in the play within the play, Corday's ambiguous nature inspires disturbing feelings in the audience.

Corday is going to murder Marat. She comes to Paris, buys the knife, and confers with Duperret, who, at the last minute, tries to dissuade her from committing the murder. She is determined, however, to accomplish this mission. She also interacts with Sade, and in what many consider a startling scene in Brook's production, lashes Sade at his request—not with a whip but with her hair.

Corday approaches the thought of killing Marat with fascination. The manner in which she describes how she will kill him is spiked with eroticism. She views Marat's murder as an act that will free humankind. She once found Marat's ideas appealing, but she is disappointed by the revolution's outcome. She sees his death as the first step in a new revolution. Near the end, Corday envisions her own death at the guillotine.

MEDIA ADAPTATIONS

- A filmed version of Brook's staging of *Marat/Sade* was produced in 1966. The original cast is featured, including Glenda Jackson as Corday. Video is available from Waterbearer Films, Lumivision, and I.S. Productions.
- Caedmon produced a sound recording in 1967 called *Peter Weiss Reading from His Works.* This includes several scenes from *Marat/Sade.*
- An audio recording of the Brook production of *Marat/Sade* was issued by Caedmon and includes original cast members from the early productions by the Royal Shakespeare Company. Available from Caedmon.

Coulmier

Coulmier is the director of the mental asylum, quite smug about the advanced treatment employed by the Charenton asylum; he boasts of the progress they have made using art and music in therapy. He interrupts Sade's play on several occasions, complaining about inciteful sections that should be removed. He also interjects to assure anyone listening that the disgraceful subjects in Sade's play occurred long ago and that things are much better now. His nervousness increases as the patients are aroused and, in the final scene, he orders the nurses to brutally beat down the rioting patients.

Duperret

Duperret is a rather foppish character whose mind is constantly on sex. He takes any opportunity he can to manhandle women, whether it is Corday, who ignores his advances, or the wife and daughter of Coulmier, who at first don't know how to react to him and later merely push him away. He coaxes Corday along on her mission but tries to talk her out of the murder just before she commits it. He entreats her to leave Paris with him.

Like all of the characters in Sade's inner play, Duperret is essayed by an insane actor. His actions are never defined as those of a sane participant in Marat's murder or those of a psychotic patient. His relentless and overt sexual behavior seems to indicate that the personality of the patient is spilling over into the character, however.

Simonne Evrard

She is the mistress of Marat and regularly fusses over him and changes his bandages. She sends Corday away twice but on the assassin's third visit, Simonne allows her to enter.

Four Singers

Like the Herald, these four report what is happening throughout the play, through music and mime. They are partly comic.

Herald

The Herald acts as a kind of chorus, ushering the audience through the play. So there will be no surprises, he announces what is going to happen: Corday will murder Marat; she will have to come to his door three times before she can enter. He frequently interrupts, using coarsely comic language to describe what is happening in the play. He interjects himself into scenes and at times prompts characters on their lines or actions.

Jean-Paul Marat

Marat is a physician and journalist who played a significant role in the French Revolution. As a character in Sade's inner play—which takes place several years after the war—he is a confused man tortured by his memories and the realization that the revolution did not accomplish what he intended. He is plagued by a skin disease and can only find relief by soaking in a bath, which is where he spends his time on stage.

Marat struggles to organize his thoughts, speaking of his ideals for social reform. It is these ideas he defends as he debates with Sade. "I am the Revolution," he claims at one point. He criticizes the ruling class, those who survived the revolution and live to again profit from it, and the church, which has contributed to oppression by convincing the poor that they are blessed. "We invented the Revolution but we don't know how to run it," he says. Sade scolds Marat for hiding behind his words and failing to take action; Marat explains that he never believed the pen alone could destroy institutions. He contends that social injustice demands action and that human beings are called to challenge the status quo and change it.

Marat lacks Sade's eloquence, but he seems to truly believe the ideals of which he speaks. When he writes he does so with action in mind, he says, although he is clearly doing nothing more than sitting in his bathtub. By the play's end he is exhausted and filled with doubt about his words and the revolution they helped inspire. He desperately tries to dictate a call to the people of France when he is stabbed by Corday.

Nurses

These are Coulmier's stooges, who keep the patients in line as needed, and overcome Roux when his speeches become too incendiary. They are brutish men who carry batons to beat down the patients.

Patients

These are the insane who populate the play, lurking in the background. They chant to Marat that they want a revolution "NOW!" As the play concludes, they are incited by Sade and Roux and begin rioting, chanting "Revolution! Copulation!" They are savagely beaten by the Nurses.

Jacques Roux

A former priest, Roux levels strong accusations against the church and interjects his radical ideas during Sade's play; at one point he calls for the churches to be closed and turned into schools. His questions and allegations disturb Coulmier and incite the patients. Although he is in a sort of straightjacket and has limited mobility, his mouth is often running. He is frequently pulled to the side by the asylum attendants to be silenced.

Sade

Sade is the author of the inner play. Interred in the Charenton Asylum, he writes plays for the patients to perform. Sixty-eight-years-old, he is fat and noticeably eccentric. He interacts at times with the characters within the play he is directing. He regularly confronts his lead character, Marat, eloquently debating the French Revolution. He exhibits a fascination with death, especially the painful, tortured variety. He admits to a confusion about his role in his ongoing conversation with Marat, saying, "I do not know if I am hangman or victim."

Sade doesn't believe in idealists, only in himself. He describes his imprisonment in the Bastille in which he confronted the criminal within himself, a criminal that committed desecrations and tortures, acts for which he was whipped. Thirteen years of imprisonment have taught him the depths of his own depravity and allowed him to focus his attention on the body—particularly the concept of sadomasochistic sex. Sade's efforts are heroically honest, wrote Penelope Gilliatt in *Vogue,* "but he is neither an admirable nor an enviable man, being without charity and mad."

Marquis de Sade

See Sade

Sisters

These are athletic looking men who are dressed in light grey. They carry rosaries and attend to Corday.

THEMES

Class Conflict

In this retelling of the French Revolution's aftermath, Weiss raises questions about the struggle between classes, between the aristocracy or privileged class, and the poor, lower class. The picture that he paints is a grim one. The much-needed, much-touted Revolution in France has come. Heads have rolled—literally—and changes in France's government have been introduced. But the question is raised, have things really changed or have the new ruling class adopted the ways of the old aristocracy? The play notes the actions of the ruling class and how the poor are treated. The situation has slightly improved but not enough to merit the loss of life in the revolution.

The church is scrutinized for aiding the ruling class by encouraging those in poverty to turn to God and see merit in suffering. Churches should be made into schools, the play suggests, at least they might then make some positive contribution to society. The lives of the new ruling class are examined, pointing out a basic pattern. Once in power, those who may have started out with good intentions become corrupt. Power corrupts, greed corrupts. The wealth resides with the minority who control society; the pattern is repeated with the rich getting richer, the poor getting poorer.

These messages are couched in the surreal setting of an insane asylum with three major factions (represented by Marat, Sade, and Coulmier) debating the reality of the times and the issues.

TOPICS FOR FURTHER STUDY

- Research the French Revolution of the eighteenth century and the civil rights and antiwar movements in the U.S. in the 1960s. Discuss the similarities and differences in these events and the two time periods.
- Were Sade and Marat insane? Why or why not?
- Research how the Nazis treated artists in the 1930s and 1940s. How may this have influenced Weiss's work?
- Look at the characters of Sade, Marat, and Coulmier. Name three contemporary characters, real or fictional, that seem most similar to them and illustrate how they are alike.

While this occurs, the insane inmates become agitated and threaten the security of the institution. Coulmier, representing the status quo and those in power, continually defends the present, pointing out the improvements; he is the one most threatened by the unruliness of the patients, who represent the poor masses. Weiss uses the similarities between the oppressed poor and the incarcerated patients to show that inequity existed not only in the French Revolution but in all social situations—even ones as microcosmic as the power structure of an insane asylum.

Weiss held many communist sympathies, and he employs socialist ideology to the events he depicts. He illustrates the theory that oppressed people will rise up to better their conditions in life. In the play within the play, the actors/patients praise Marat's efforts in the revolution, yet they also criticize him for not going far enough. They want continued revolt to the point that real change takes place. While these exhortations seem directed at Marat and the circumstances following the revolution, they can just as easily be applied beyond the setting of Sade's play. Criticism is also leveled at the ruling class of the French society that is represented by the audience members visiting the asylum. More succinctly, the patients' calls for change can be focused on the asylum director, whose efforts at progressive therapy are appreciated but who could also do much more to make life in the asylum better.

Body vs. Mind

Yet the major conflict of *Marat/Sade* is not found between the patients and Coulmier. It lies in the contrasting ideas of Sade and Marat. Sade, as the author of the play within the play, gets to confront Marat and his ideology. Their division is the conflict between the physical world and the mind—or inner world.

Marat represents a deep faith in ideas and ideals. He is tortured at times with the ineffectiveness of words but nonetheless defends their power. Words are a representation of ideas. But he insists he has not fallen back on verbiage to avoid action. Clearly the masses are swayed by words but the sympathies of the crowd are fickle; Marat and his ideas can be rejected. While his concepts were inspiring, Marat's theories of revolution did not go far enough to address the potential for history repeating itself; they have not wrought the revolution that was desired. ''We want the revolution NOW,'' demand the patients. The impoverished and disenfranchised demand that Marat get out of his head and bring change through action. Is the pen mightier than the sword? The play presents the pen as basically impotent. Marat's revolution yields a society too similar to the one he sought to vanquish.

Sade argues with Marat about the ineffectiveness of his thoughts and words. He points out the failure of the revolution to bring real change. Sade believes that the revolution failed because its architects failed to address human nature. He tell Marat that change in society cannot be wrought without first changing man's nature, starting with the body and working outward. To this end Sade proposes his theory of pleasure gained through a combination of agony and ecstasy. By pushing the body to its threshold, one will gain complete knowledge of oneself. Only at that point can humankind hope to change the way they interact.

Appearance vs. Reality

Throughout the play, the traditional barriers between the stage and the audience are broken down. Several times during the course of Sade's play, Coulmier interrupts the action to criticize the work's content. Sade also invades the play's action with his own comments, taking the opportunity to engage Marat in debates on mind and body. Perhaps most unsettling and surreal for the actual viewer (as opposed to the onstage audience represented by Coulmier and his family) are the performances of the inmates enacting the various roles in Sade's drama. It is never clear if their actions are dictated by the Marquis's script and direction or by their own, insane motivations. Similarly, the actors' call for revolution is ambiguous. Weiss does not clarify if the call is directed toward the action in Sade's play, toward Coulmier and his class, or to the actual audience. Many have theorized that it is unimportant who the target is as long as the message is understood.

STYLE

Play within a Play

Weiss uses the technique of a play within a play to tell his story. This layers the play and creates a certain distance for the audience while providing the playwright with narration to explain the work. Marat is both a character in the inner play and is pulled to the outer play in debates with Sade. Coulmier exists in the outer play and regularly challenges what Sade, the creator of the inner play, is doing.

This technique had been used fairly extensively prior to *Marat/Sade*—notably in the Rodgers and Hammerstein musical *The King and I.* As with Weiss's play, the inner play in *The King and I* addresses issues that are being discussed in the outer play. The slave girl Tuptim acts out *Uncle Tom's Cabin,* a story that she uses as a thinly disguised critique of the King of Siam, for whom the inner play is being performed, and his policy toward his servants. Plays like *The King and I* used the play within play technique for a small section of the overall play. *Marat/Sade,* however, builds its entire foundation on this conceit.

While some critics complained that Weiss's multiple layers were little more than theatrical gimmickry, the majority felt that it was an effective technique that, while failing to answer all questions raised by the plot, made the play a riveting, thought-provoking experience.

Theatre of Cruelty

Weiss was a proponent of a form of experimental theatre known as the Theatre of Cruelty. This was developed primarily by Antonin Artaud, a French actor and director. Artaud wanted theatre to go far beyond the written script (just as Sade wants life to be beyond thoughts and ideas), so elements such as lighting, sound effects, and other forms of technology do not just flesh out the text but play an active role in its presentation and interpretation. In *Marat/Sade* this is employed through the extensive use of special effects such as the gruesome execution sequence.

Albert Bermel wrote in *Artaud's Theatre of Cruelty* that Artaud "did not care whether his characters won or lost arguments. He wanted to use them in order to expose his audiences to a range of their own feelings that was unconscious and therefore normally inaccessible to them." This is evident in the central conflict between Sade and Marat. While Sade's criticism of Marat leads the audience to believe he will offer a solution that Marat's ideas and thoughts could not, they are confounded in this expectation when Sade offers up the concept of carnality. His alternative does little to solve the problems created by the revolution, but it does offer a glimpse into his psyche. In this sense Weiss provokes the audience to consider the character with whom they most identify and which personality traits are closest to their own.

The concept of cruelty for Artaud was the idea of exposing the audience to danger but then to ultimately free them from it, creating a sort of cleansing transformation. Cruelty, as he was using the idea, did not mean actual physical assault but that the energy of the production made as a sort of attack on the defenses of the viewer; it threatened their concept of normality, exposing them to the fragile nature of human interaction. Theatre of Cruelty seeks to make its audience aware that the balance can topple at any moment and everything can be thrown into utter chaos.

In *Marat/Sade* Weiss employs these ideas by creating an environment that is unruly and unsafe. While he allows the actual audience a degree of distance and safety—putting the audience of the inner play at the greatest physical risk—they will nevertheless identify with the inner audience and empathize with their fearful situation. The inmates are odd, ugly, obviously insane. They seem ready to spill over into riot at any moment.

Weiss creates unease with a number of techniques meant to disturb. The play is written in verse form and has song and dance laced throughout it. The Corday character delivers her lines with a singsong effect, seeming to sleepwalk through her part. This gives her a ghostlike persona that contributes to the surreal effect of watching a play within a play. Added to this is the increasing unrest of the patients, their songs and screams, their threatening behavior. The sum effect of these elements is to unnerve the audience, place them off-balance so that they do not know what to expect. Through this Weiss hoped to confront the audience, make them think, by vicariously putting them through a hellish process he sought to provoke feelings that would not dissipate when the houselights came up.

By many accounts, the impact is significant. The audience may not like it, but they do not forget the experience. As director Brook said of his staging in the introduction to the published version of *Marat/Sade,* "I know of one acid test in the theatre. It is literally an acid test. When a performance is over, what remains? Fun can be forgotten, but powerful emotion also disappears and good arguments lose their thread. When emotion and argument are harnessed to a wish from the audience to see more clearly into itself—then something in the mind burns. The event scorches onto the memory an outline, a taste, a trace, a smell—a picture. It is the play's central image that remains, its silhouette, and if the elements are rightly blended this silhouette will be its meaning, this shape will be the essence of what it has to say."

Brechtian Influence

Weiss readily admitted his debt to Bertolt Brecht, a German dramatist who lived from 1898-1956. Brecht was known for an approach to epic theatre which he used to make social criticism while using a technique called "Alienation." Brook explained this concept in the introduction to *Marat/Sade:* "Alienation is the art of placing an action at a distance so that it can be judged objectively and so that it can be seen in relation to the world—or rather worlds—around it."

HISTORICAL CONTEXT

The History of the Play within the Play

It's important to understand the historical events chronicled in *Marat/Sade.* Although part of Sade's drama is fiction it is based on actual events. Jean-Paul Marat was murdered by Charlotte Corday in 1793. He was a physician and journalist who used his newspaper as a platform for his political beliefs. As a member of the Jacobin party, he played an instrumental part in instigating the French Revolution. The Marquis de Sade was an author living in France during the time of the revolution. He had been imprisoned for his cruel sexual practices (the term "sadism" is a derivation of his name and is used to describe sexual pleasure gained through the causing of pain). He was in residence at the Asylum at Charenton and did write plays while there. He did not know Marat but did give a memorial address at his funeral.

The French Revolution actually took place between 1787 and 1799, with a major climax in 1789, when an outraged mob stormed the Bastille, a fortress and prison. Later the French royal family was forced to flee and the king, Louis XVI, was captured and executed. Leadership in the government thereafter brought about a Reign of Terror in which perceived enemies of the cause were sought out and slaughtered. Later, Napoleon Bonaparte assumed power and built France into a considerable empire. Reasons for the revolution are many, the strongest being the impoverished state of the peasants and the lack of any political power by the middle class. *Marat/Sade* is set in 1808, when the Revolution was over, but the play reenacts an important event from those bloody days—the assassination of Marat, one of the revolutions' key architects.

The Foundation of Weiss's Politics

Weiss experienced three major wars in his lifetime. World War I was in full swing when he was born, the second World War sent his family into exile, and, at the time he was writing *Marat/Sade,* the Vietnam War was escalating into a vicious battle of attrition. Having experienced the cruel effects of dictatorship firsthand, Weiss came to oppose fascist governments of any kind. He found a positive alternative to such oppressive rule in the concepts of communism, which idealizes equality of ownership and government by the people.

At the time he was developing the play, former Nazi leaders were being tried for war crimes committed during World War II. In the United States, the year 1964 was pivotal because it marked the Tonkin Bay incident in Vietnam and the official authorization by Congress to involve U.S. troops in that conflict. The country was recovering from the assassination the year before of President John F. Kennedy.

This timeframe was also the beginning of other significant action in the U.S., most notably the start

COMPARE & CONTRAST

- **1787:** Responding to increasing economic pressures caused by war, poor harvest, inequitable taxation, and the extravagances of the monarchy, Louis the XVI of France convenes the Estates General. Although this seems a victory for the aristocracy, it is really the beginning of the revolution.

  1964: Following the directions put in place by the late President Kennedy, President Lyndon Johnson calls for victory in the "war on poverty" and signs into law The Economic Opportunity Act, creating an Officer of Economic Opportunity. This office was to oversee a myriad of agencies providing services to the poor, ensuring better nutrition, health, and education for the underprivileged.

  Today: Conservative leadership has eroded funding for government programs aiding the poor. Welfare and programs for health and education to inner cities have been severely curtailed or completely phased out. The disparity between the poor and the wealthy grows.

- **1793:** The French Revolution begins, as the poor rise up to overthrow the monarchy in one of the bloodiest wars of the eighteenth century.

  1964: North Vietnamese fire at a U.S. destroyer in the Tonkin Gulf, off the coast of Vietnam. The Tonkin Gulf Resolution is passed giving the President authority to take military action; this essentially launches the Vietnam War, in which U.S. forces fight in South Vietnam, opposing the communist threat from North Vietnam.

  Today: The Communist Party has dissipated with the dissolution of the Soviet Union and Eastern European countries. East and West Germany are reunited. The U.S. continues to wage small military actions, mostly in the Middle East, but where Vietnam was long and bloody, current wars rely on technology and have resulted in minimal loss of American life.

- **1789:** The National Assembly of France introduces the "Declaration of the Rights of Man and the Citizen."

  1964: The Civil Rights Bill is passed after a lengthy and bitter fight by southern senators. The bodies of three civil rights workers are discovered in Mississippi, the victim of white supremacists. Race riots erupt in Harlem and Philadelphia. Atlanta restaurant owner Lester Maddox closes his restaurant rather than be forced to serve blacks. His stance against integration leads him to the governorship of Georgia. Civil rights leader Martin Luther King, Jr. is awarded the Nobel Peace Prize.

  Today: Although schools and neighborhoods have been integrated, racism has not been eliminated. The conservative agenda includes elimination of affirmative action measures which insure fair and even preferential treatment for minorities. Neo-Nazis and other white supremist groups are on the rise. African Americans have attained positions of power, including seats in the U.S. senate and House of Representatives and Supreme Court appointments.

---

of the civil rights movement as well as the women's movement. The civil rights movement was marked by violence and race riots in major cities. The energy of the movement gathered steam and rolled over into the antiwar movement. The 1960s were revolutionary times with a preponderance of both peaceful and violent demonstrations against the government.

But like Weiss's play (Marat's concepts), much of the rhetoric of the 1960s was merely that, and although important issues were addressed, things didn't necessarily change. Or not that much. Those in power within the resistance movement, mostly white males, were reticent to accept women as much other than sex objects. So those who were disenfranchised continued in that state. Gains were made in civil rights but it has become apparent in the decades following that racism cannot be legislated away. These events were hard to ignore and many have speculated that they in some way influenced the themes of *Marat/Sade.*

The Culture of 1960s

In literature, the 1950s produced a generation of beatniks, bohemian artists who lived on the edge of society and actively criticized the government and society. This movement spread and spawned the hippies of the 1960s. One notable poet of the Beat Generation, as it was called, was Allen Ginsberg, whose long diatribes against America were laced with profanity and references to sex and drugs. His *Howl,* which was first published in 1956, started out with this line: "I saw the best minds of my generation destroyed by madness. . . ." Another poem titled *America* starts with this: "America I've given you all and now I'm nothing/America two dollars and twenty-seven cents January 17, 1956/I can't stand my own mind/America when will we end the human war?"

Artists during this time included Andy Warhol who was shocking and questioning artistic values with his silk screens of pop icons done larger than life, including the Campbell soup can and Marilyn Monroe. The Beatles made their first trip to the U.S. in 1964, wedging a chasm between generations of music lovers. The folk music of Bob Dylan and Joan Baez was popular, inspiring musicians to address political and social issues in their compositions. Folk music—and later rock—became a foundation from which to protest such topics as the war and racism.

CRITICAL OVERVIEW

When the work *Marat/Sade* was first produced, it became a bit of a joke to some. A common jibe was often directed at the play's lengthy name: "No, I haven't seen the play, but I've read the title." The first production of the play was staged in West Berlin, Germany, under the direction of Konrad Swinarski. From the start the work was controversial, which is often the best publicity. In its initial run, many critics saw the influence of fellow German Bertolt Brecht on Weiss and his play. Weiss admitted his debt to the great playwright, stating "Brecht influenced me as a dramatist. I learnt most from Brecht. I learnt clarity from him, the necessity of making clear the social question in a play. I learnt from his lightness. He is never heavy in the psychological German way." Of this first production, the London *Times* claimed it was "the most ambitious example of the Theatre of Cruelty yet to appear. Practically every influence current in operation in intellectual high fashion is to be found in this play."

It was the direction of Peter Brook and his London production of the play, however, that brought *Marat/Sade* to the highest level of international critical acclaim. Brook attended rehearsals for the first production in West Berlin and there met Weiss. The two agreed to take the play to London, where Brook would reinterpret it and later move the production to New York. The Brook-directed version made its debut at the Aldwych Theatre in 1964.

As with the German production, the London performances almost immediately sparked controversy, including a verbal attack on the play by a member of the theatre company's executive council. Critics also had a good deal to say about Weiss's work. Millie Painter-Downes of the *New Yorker* called it "a dazzling theatrical experience" and a "stunning production." She ended her favorable review by stating, "It is an electrifying show, which would have been a hit even without the present controversy."

While most reviewers conceded the work's originality, their appraisals were mixed. A critic from *Newsweek* questioned whether Weiss should be considered a revolutionary playwright: "Beneath all the business, all the violence and startling gestures, is a vacuum. Weiss, for all his pretensions, is a conventional socialist and an extremely limited philosopher." The critic went on to say that although the play is impressive, "it establishes a kind of frenetic dance, a choreographed quest for the truths of the imagination, flattering our sense of the fashionable, our desire to be at wicked, important happenings, but offering no light and no resurrection, *Marat/Sade* is to be seen but not believed." A reviewer for *Time* labeled it "inspired sensationalism," while Harold Clurman of the *Nation* called it "fascinating entertainment." Clurman both praised and questioned the work, seeing it as a dialogue with the spirit of the playwright yet he also appraised that the text, when removed from Brook's theatrics, was trite.

One of the most disturbing parts of the Brook production followed the play's proper ending. At the curtain call, the actors would clap back to the audience in a rhythmic pattern which had the effect of shutting up the audience, "dismissing us scornfully as representatives of a public that has evaded its responsibility to recognize the horrendous atrocity of life within us and around us," claimed Henry Hewes in the *Saturday Review.*

While such gestures were startling and unconventional—and many critics found them patently offensive—few could deny the power of such theatrics. While a critical consensus could not be reached regarding the artistic merits of *Marat/Sade,* most agreed that it is a singular work deserving attention. Thirty years after its initial production, Weiss's play is still considered innovative and shocking; it is regarded as a hallmark of progressive theatre.

CRITICISM

Etta Worthington

Worthington is a professional writer who specializes in drama. In this essay she discusses the debate between the play's title characters, the Marquis de Sade and Jean-Paul Marat.

Peter Weiss's *Marat/Sade* presents us with a very bleak world where madness and pessimism prevail. This is a grey world in which range of color is absent and where there seems to be no salvation. Just reading the play, however, makes it difficult to get the full impression, since plays are meant to be seen not merely read. Writing in *Civilization,* playwright Tony Kushner (*Angels in America*) described a recent play he had seen and said reading the text "is an incomplete experience of the work, as reading any play must necessarily be, since a play in book form is a little like an octopus out of water."

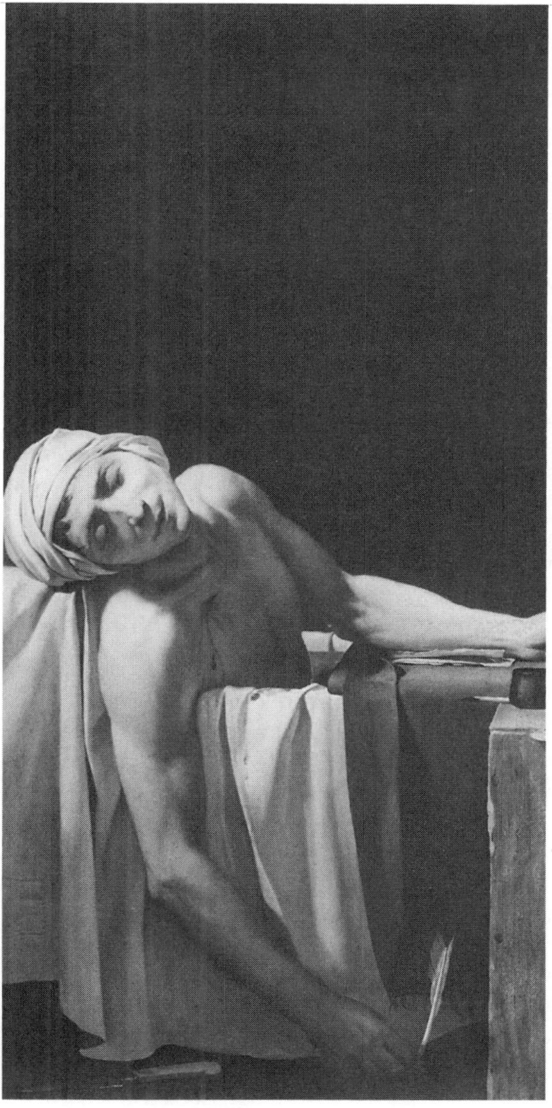

Jacques-Louis David's famous 1793 painting depicting the assassinated Jean-Paul Marat in his tub, pen in hand

Book in hand, we grapple with the text but have a much more distant experience with the action described. In *Marat/Sade,* the background of mentally ill patients on the brink of violence creates a disturbing experience in which we have to deal with the concept of madness while, simultaneously, interpreting the central action as the two main characters duke it out in an intellectual sparring of ideas.

A critic from Newsweek responded to the 1965 New York performance of *Marat/Sade* with a claim that the play appealed to a contemporary audience who wanted to be in on "wicked, important happenings, but offering no light and no resurrection." But both Sade and Marat purport to offer salvation. Marat, on the one hand, stands for revolutionary idealism. Yet it is an idealism that has him locked in his head, swimming in his bath—a critic but not a creator.

Sade is a disillusioned, washed-out old man, cynical and preoccupied with death and pain:

> *Any animal plant or man who dies/adds to Nature's compost heap*

WHAT DO I READ NEXT?

- *Mother Courage and Her Children* (1939) is a well-known and often performed play by Bertolt Brecht. The play is set during the Thirty Years War and is considered a masterpiece.
- Herman Hesse's *Beneath the Wheel* (1906) is a good example of the work of this writer who was a friend and mentor to Weiss. This book looks at the duality of man through a story of two students.
- Martin Esslin wrote a small book titled *Antonin Artaud* (1976). This work offers a quick look at Artaud's ideas about the Theatre of Cruelty.
- Howard Barker's *Scenes from an Execution* (1984) deals with an historical event and is produced in an experimental fashion.
- Written in 1951, *Saint Joan* by George Bernard Shaw looks at the life and ultimate execution of Joan of Arc. Like Weiss's drama, Shaw's work is very political.
- Janet Frame's *Faces in the Water* (1961) is a novel that examines the mentally ill residing in institutions.
- Another German writer who influenced Weiss was Franz Kafka. *Complete Stories and Parables* (1946) is a good introduction to this important writer.

This bleak outlook on human existence is followed by a rhapsody in which Sade speaks of slow, torturous death and complains about anonymous cheapened death. Clearly to Sade, suffering and pain bring significance. And while Sade goes on to question his experience and how anything can be known, a patient prances around claiming "the earth is spread thick with squashed human guts" and then says he is a mad animal.

Although Sade himself is also mad, he sees himself above it all, better than the patients around him. Yet his very dependence on his inner world makes his form of insanity no better than the others. While he says he cannot trust his own experience, he tells Marat that the only thing that is real is his imagination and the world inside his head. He disavows any belief in revolution, claiming to only believe in himself.

But the self in which Sade believes has a distinctly sordid side. He admits to Marat that he sank to the depths during his imprisonment in the Bastille, in which he imagined the worst of society. "I dug the criminal out of me," he claims, "so I could understand him." And the criminal that he discovered both enjoyed creating pain in others and also having discomfort inflicted on himself. But he sees himself flawed because even in finding the criminal inside he could not bring himself to murder "although murder was the final proof of my existence."

Despite being mired in his madness, Sade can still taunt Marat about how useless the revolution has been. This massive social change has not really altered the heart and soul of man. He claims that people join a revolution for reasons quite trivial, quite apart from the ideals of the masterminds. "A poet runs out of poetry and desperately gropes for new images." He along with the man with ill-fitting shoes and the woman with a too-short husband tack their faith on a revolution that will bring them salvation. Sade points out to Marat that the revolution has failed and has only produced a greater evil. Words, he contends are also without value. All that is anything is in the body:

> *Marat forget the rest/there's nothing else/ beyond the body*

And so Sade has distanced himself from the revolution, this beacon, this chance for mankind to be saved. He cannot see worth in anything that does not address man's carnal nature; ''What's a revolution without general copulation,'' he asks.

Marat suffers intense anguish, as does Sade. Part of his suffering is physical, with a skin disease that leaves him fevered and itching, unable to find relief. The disease is a metaphor for the disease of the times, of mankind, a condition which can be eased but never completely cured. Yet Marat professes himself a believer in man's ability to change. He withstands the cynicism of Sade. While Sade has dug into his criminal self, Marat digs into his skin for words to give France a new beginning:

my head's on fire/I can't breath/ There is a rioting mob inside me/I am the Revolution

Marat counters Sade's cynicism about death and the insignificance of the individual by claiming Sade is without compassion. It is his compassion that is tormenting Marat, as he sees people killed, oppressed beneath the wheel, just to support the lifestyles of the aristocracy. Marat agrees with Sade that the revolution hasn't succeeded. ''We're clogged with dead ideas. We stand here more oppressed than when we've begun.'' In his tortured state, he hallucinates. For him, the answer is in his mind because he's determined the soul is in the brain. Salvation then lies in ideas.

But Marat who has been writing feverishly, collapses, defeated, confused now about his ideas. Why is everything so disjointed he questions:

Everything I wrote of spoke/was considered and true/ each argument was sound/And now/doubt/Why does everything sound false

Yet even with this admission of hopelessness Marat digs for his pen, for the words that he can say to save both France and himself. To the end he clings to the belief that the will of the individual is important and can change things:

against Nature's silence I use action/In the vast indifference I invent a meaning. . . ./The important thing is to pull yourself up by your own hair/to turn yourself inside out/to see the whole world with fresh eyes.

The doubts that Marat seems to voice, his confusion, seem to most represent those of the author. Yes, ''*Marat/Sade* is full of doubts, my doubts,'' Weiss admitted. ''The only alternative is that I give my doubts, that I show my situation of doubtfulness and the great difficulties I undergo to find some way out of it. That is the only thing I can reach.''

Certainly Weiss wanted his audience to experience madness. Pandemonium reigns in the back-

MARAT/SADE'S ULTIMATE MESSAGE: NOTHING MAKES SENSE."

ground of this ongoing debate between Sade and Marat, as the play marches forward to its conclusion. It is clear that Weiss is referring to the madness of the times. Although set in the early 1800s, post-Revolutionary times during Napoleon's reign, he laces the text with references to the present (when he was writing the play) and to recent history. There's mention of ''anonymous cheapened death which we could dole out to entire nations on a mathematical basis,'' and the idea of a ''final solution.'' These are both clear references to the Holocaust perpetrated by Nazi Germany.

At the core of the play is the question between Marat and Sade. ''The central question about the debates was, Who wins? Was Marat correct when he said society must change before humanity can change? Or was it more important, as Sade believed, to change the self before changing society?'' Peter Brook asked in the play's introduction, noting that audiences in America were divided in their response. Weiss himself, Brooks asserted, wanted that uncertainty in the play. Brook believes that the words of Sade best describe it:

Before deciding what is wrong and what is right/first we must find out what we are/I/do not know myself

The uncertainty that Sade voices, as the more eloquent of the two debaters, seems to be the message that Weiss is giving his audience. There is no certainty. There is no complete knowledge. Weiss after several productions of *Marat/Sade* placed his sympathy with Marat, but even in tipping the balance in favor of the radical who believes society can change, the play ends in a riot, with insane patients chanting *Revolution Revolution Copulation Copulation* while nurses bludgeon them with sticks.

''Nothing, we feel, could ever stop this riot. Nothing, we conclude, can ever stop the madness of the world,'' said Brook. And that pervasive image of madness stays in the mind of the viewer. All polemics and diatribes aside, the madness is the most memorable aspect of Weiss's work.

Although Weiss may want us to take away some hope for change, it is hard to be a true believer. One may walk away with the thought, "Vanity of vanities, all is vanity," a refrain that runs throughout the book of Ecclesiastics in the Bible, a refrain arrived at by King Solomon, who had done extensive research into life—concluding that none of it really made sense.

And that, in a way, is *Marat/Sade* 's ultimate message: Nothing makes sense. Peter Brook, referring to the New York production, stated that "it wasn't affirming what was good and glorious in life, but something that most spectators would relate to very directly, violence and madness."

This is what Kushner labeled "Difficult Art." He described the concept in *Civilization:* "It insists on its spectators doing some of the work. . . . We are meant to learn that we are born into a world in which what is easy, commonsensical and evident is very often a lie and that labor is required to make sense as much as to make shoes and houses and superhighways."

Source: Etta Worthington for *Drama for Students,* Gale, 1998.

Howard Taubman

In the following review which was originally published on December 28, 1965, Taubman praises director Peter Brooks's production of Weiss's Marat/Sade *for presenting "a fresh, probing sensibility in original stage terms."*

Imagination has not vanished from the stage. Nor intelligence. For proof see Peter Weiss's play, which opened last night at the Martin Beck Theater.

The exceptional length of the play's title is not caprice. The play reverberates with overtones even as its name is crowded with words and syllables: *The Persecution and Assassination of Marat as Performed by the Inmates of the Asylum of Charenton Under the Direction of the Marquis de Sade.*

Mr. Weiss has written a play within a play, and in both there are unexpected resonances of comment and meaning. He has used the techniques of Brechts, invoking verse, music and speeches to the audience to produce an effect of standing apart, but has orchestrated them in his own way. In the end one is involved as one stands apart; one thinks when one should feel and feels when one should think.

There is hardly anything conventional about the play. But Mr. Weiss's novel devices are not employed for the sake of novelty. His primary purpose, if one may dare to isolate one aim as the chief one, is to examine the conflict between individualism carried to extreme lengths and the idea of a political and social upheaval.

Spokesman for this sort of individualism is Sade; the voice of upheaval is Marat. But Mr. Weiss has gone beyond a simple confrontation. He has achieved a remarkable density of impression and impact by locating his conflict, in the course of his play within a play, in a mental institution.

The result is a vivid work that vibrates on wild, intense, murmurous and furious levels. It is sardonic and impassioned, pitiful and explosive. It may put you off at times with its apparent absurdity, or it may shock you with its allusions to violence and naked emotions. But it will not leave you untouched.

As the play begins on the wide, lofty uncurtained stage, furnished with a few planks, benches and several pits, the inmates of Charenton wander in. They wear rough, tattered rags, and some are twisted in body and limbs as well in mind. The director of the asylum and two of his ladies in their elegant clothes arrive, and he explains that he has encouraged Sade to direct the inmates in this play for its therapeutic value.

Mr. Weiss has not invented this point. Sade, who was an inmate at Charenton, did write and stage plays there in the early years of the 19th century. What Mr. Weiss has invented is the play that Sade has chosen to write and direct, though certain details of the Marat story used in Sade's play are facts of history.

The play unfolds in a series of episodes. The basic action involves the events leading up to the slaying of Marat by Charlotte Corday. But the episodes do not follow an ordinary continuity. Songs, scenes that at first view seem irrelevant, the unpredictable movements and sounds of the patients, weave around the main action to provide a remarkable richness of texture.

Marat, his body angry and blotched with a feverish ailment, sits in his bathtub, a bandage on his head and a sheet over his shoulders, but the tormenting pains and memories cannot be appeased. Since Marat is played by a Charenton paranoiac, his fierce outbursts have a deepened anguish. Sade, of course, is Sade, but despite his worn, faded finery, he is also an inmate, and the fury of his worship of self becomes both heightened and oddly pathetic.

They are both rebels. Sade is in revolt against accepted notions because he needs to believe in and explore himself. Marat is the social revolutionary. Their ideas clash, but Mr. Weiss does not choose between them.

He lets passionate, burning truths emerge from their feverish preoccupations. Out of the mouths and actions of other inmates in this madhouse come other insights.

Mr. Weiss, a German who fled Nazism and who now lives in Sweden, has written in a kind of singsong vernacular, which rises often to eloquence. Geoffrey Skelton's English version and Adrian Mitchell's verse adaptation establish the flavor of the playwright's style.

This is a work, that demands all the theater's arts and artifices, and this production by Great Britain's Royal Shakespeare Company, staged with savage brilliance by Peter Brook, translates Mr. Weiss's writing into throbbing theatrical terms.

The images of life in a mental institution are weird and moving. An inmate who raves like a mad animal and utters searing truths is not an oddity; he freezes the blood. Inmates going through a make-believe guillotining and falling pell mell into a pit are horrifying and piteous. A quartet of inmates done up as clowns caper and cavort amusingly and piercingly. Even the whipping of Sade by Charlotte Corday with her long hair, though not literally painful, stings.

Mr. Brook has used sound like a conjurer. There is not only Richard Peaslee's evocative, simple music for the songs and for the band, dressed like inmates and seated in boxes on opposite sides of the house. There are also the clanging of chains, the pounding of boards, the eerie moans of the inmates.

The visitors from Britain are performing Mr. Weiss's play with conviction and intensity, in taut, colorful ensemble. The entire company deserves to be noticed, but there is time only to speak admiringly of Ian Richardson's flaming Marat, Patrick Magee's cold, sinuous Sade, Glenda Jackson's wild Corday, Clifford Rose's elegantly superficial asylum director, and Michael Williams's subtle Herald.

Mr. Weiss's play expresses a fresh, probing sensibility in original stage terms. Like its title, it will give you original stage terms. Like its title it will give you pause, stir your imagination and provoke your mind. It is good to encounter a playwright who dares to challenge the theater and its audience to full participation.

"*MARAT/SADE* IS A VIVID WORK THAT VIBRATES ON WILD, INTENSE, MURMUROUS AND FURIOUS LEVELS. IT IS SARDONIC AND IMPASSIONED, PITIFUL AND EXPLOSIVE."

Source: Howard Taubman, review of *Marat/Sade* (1965) in *On Stage: Selected Theater Reviews from the New York Times, 1920–1970,* edited by Bernard Beckerman and Howard Siegman, Arno Press, 1973, pp. 485–86.

SOURCES

Bermel, Albert. *Artaud's Theatre of Cruelty,* Tallinger, 1977.

Brook, Peter. *The Empty Space,* Avon, 1968.

Brook, Peter. Introduction to *Marat/Sade,* by Peter Weiss, Atheneum, 1965.

Clurman, Harold. Review of *Marat/Sade* in the *Nation,* January 17, 1966.

Ellis, Roger. *Peter Weiss in Exile: A Critical Study of His Works,* UMI Research Press, 1987.

Gilliatt, Penelope. "Peter Brook: A Natural Saboteur of Order" in *Vogue,* January 1, 1966.

Ginsberg, Allen. *Howl and Other Poems,* City Lights Books, 1956.

Hewes, Henry. Review of *Marat/Sade* in the *Saturday Review,* January 15, 1966.

Hilton, Ian. *Peter Weiss: A Search for Affinities,* Oswald Wolff, 1970.

Jones, David Richard. *Great Directors at Work: Stanislavsky, Brecht, Kazan, Brook,* University of California Press, 1986.

Kushner, Tony. "The Art of the Difficult" in *Civilization,* August/September, 1997.

Painter-Downes, Mollie. Review of *Marat/Sade* in the *New Yorker,* September 19, 1964.

Review of *Marat/Sade* in *Newsweek,* January 10, 1966.

Review of *Marat/Sade* in *Time,* January 7, 1966.

FURTHER READING

Cohen, Robert. *Understanding Peter Weiss,* University of South Carolina Press, 1993.

This work provides a good biographical overview of Weiss's life as well as a critical study of his work, including a whole section on *Marat/Sade.*

Connor, Clifford D. *Jean Paul Marat: Scientist and Revolutionary,* Humanities Press, 1993.

This is a biography of Marat, looking at his life both before and after the Revolution.

Schama, Simon. *Citizens: A Chronicle of the French Revolution,* Vintage Books, 1988.

This book provides some insight into the events and significance of the French Revolution. It offers a useful overview of the events depicted in Sade's play within the play.

Weiss, Peter. *Exile: A Novel,* Delacorte, 1968.

This is an English translation of two of Weiss's autobiographical novels, *The Leavetaking* and *Vanishing Point.*

"Master Harold"... and the Boys

ATHOL FUGARD

1982

First produced at the Yale Repertory Theater in 1982, Athol Fugard's *"Master Harold"... and the Boys* is based on the playwright's early life in South Africa. But the play itself is not a simple retelling of an incident from his past. Rather, Fugard has presented a personal experience that extends to universal humanity. If the play were simply a polemic against the policy of apartheid, it would already be outdated now that sweeping change has transformed South Africa. Instead, Fugard wrote a play about human relationships that are put to the test by societal and personal forces.

Because Fugard (critically) focused most of his work on the injustices of the apartheid system of South Africa's government, government officials called many of Fugard's works subversive and several times attempted to prevent publication and/or production of his plays. Much of his early work was presented to small private audiences to avoid government censorship. *"Master Harold" ... and the Boys,* however, played 344 performances on Broadway and was produced in other major cities including London. The play was officially banned by the South African government. Despite the efforts of his native country, the wider world community did not ignore Fugard's work and *"Master Harold" ... and the Boys* earned the Drama Desk Award and Critics Circle Award for best play in 1983, and London's *Evening Standard* Award in 1984. The play has subsequently earned a place in contemporary world drama, enjoying frequent revivals around

the world. It is considered to be one of Fugard's masterpieces and a vital work valued for both its universal themes of humanity and its skilled theater craft.

AUTHOR BIOGRAPHY

Harold Athol Fugard was born June 11, 1932, in Middleburg, Cape Province, South Africa (and later raised in Port Elizabeth, South Africa), to a father who was English and a mother who was Afrikaner (a white South African descended from Dutch settlers). Fugard described his father as a man ''full of pointless, unthought-out prejudices.'' His mother, on the other hand, felt ''outrage and anger over the injustice of [South African] society''—particularly the system of apartheid that established separate, unequal rights for whites and blacks.

Fugard attended Port Elizabeth Technical College and the University of Cape Town, where he studied philosophy. He dropped out in 1953, just prior to graduation, however, and toured the world as a crew member of a tramp steamer bound from the Sudan to the Far East between 1953 and 1955. During this time he attempted to write a novel but, dissatisfied with what he produced, he destroyed the manuscript. A few years later, just about the time of his marriage to South African actress Sheila Meiring in 1956, Fugard developed an interest in writing for the stage.

His first full length plays, *No-Good Friday* (1956) and *Nongogo* (1957) grew out of his experiences in Johannesburg, South Africa, in the late 1950s. Fugard worked there briefly as a clerk in the Native Commissioner's Court, which tried cases against nonwhites (the South African term for black citizens) who had been arrested for failing to carry identification. ''I knew the system was evil,'' Fugard recalled, ''but until then I had no idea of just how systematically evil it was. That was my revelation.'' These initial plays were performed by Fugard and black amateur actors for small private audiences.

After a brief move to England in 1959, Fugard returned to South Africa and completed a novel, *Tsotsi.* Although he attempted to destroy this manuscript as he had an earlier one, a copy survived and was published twenty years later. Fugard's first major theatrical success was *The Blood Knot* (1961), a story about the sense of conflict and harmony between two nonwhite half-brothers. First presented to a private audience in 1961, the play featured Fugard as the light-skinned brother, Morris, and actor Zakes Mokae—who became a close friend and long time Fugard collaborator—as the dark-skinned brother, Zach. In *The Blood Knot,* Fugard dramatizes the racial hatred that infects so many South African relationships. This ambivalence perverts the ''blood knot,'' or common bond of humanity.

In 1983, Fugard earned the Drama Desk Award and the Critic's Circle Award for best play and, in 1984, the *Evening Standard* of London award for *''Master Harold''. . . and the Boys.* Widely considered Fugard's best and most autobiographical play, *''Master Harold''* centers on the relationship of two black waiters, Sam and Willy, to Hally (''Master Harold''), a white teenager embittered by the neglect of his alcoholic, racist father.

In addition to his plays and notebooks, Fugard has also written screenplays for *Boseman and Lena* (based on his play), 1972; *The Guest,* 1976; *Meetings with Remarkable Men,* 1979; *Marigolds in August,* 1980; *Ghandi,* 1982; and *The Killing Fields,* 1984.

PLOT SUMMARY

''Master Harold''. . . and the Boys is a one-act that takes place inside the St. George's Park Tea Room on a wet and windy Port Elizabeth (South Africa) afternoon in 1950. No customers populate the restaurant and most of tables and chairs have been stacked to one side. Two black waiters, Willie and Sam, are on stage as the play begins. Willie is mopping the floor, and Sam is reading comic books at a table which has been set for a meal. Willie wants to improve his dancing skills but appears to have been deserted by his partner after he beat her. Sam offers Willie advice about improving both his dancing technique and his domestic relations.

The son of the tea room's owner, Hally, enters direct from school. He eats a bowl of soup and talks to the two men with whom he appears to have a close relationship. Hally, while displaying obvious affection for the men—especially Sam—takes a pedantic tone, assuming the role of teacher. Yet the nature of their interaction clearly shows Sam as the teacher and Hally as the eager pupil. Their discussion ranges from what Hally has been learning at school about great men of history to reminiscences

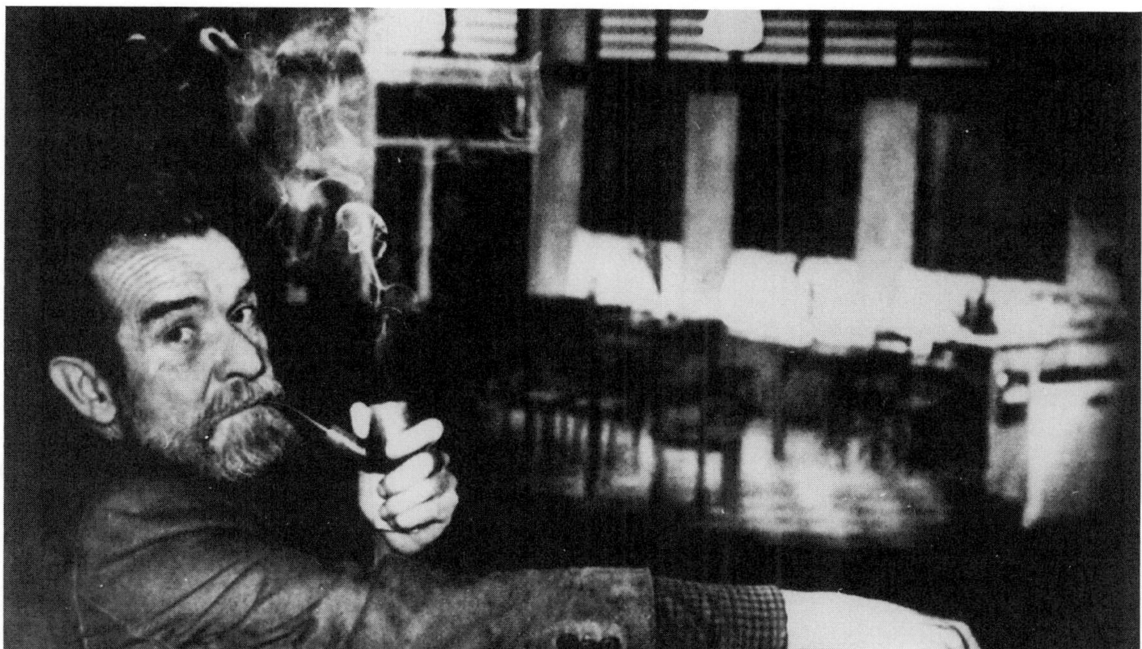

Athol Fugard on the opening night of ''Master Harold'' . . . and the Boys *at Johannesburg's Market Theatre in 1983. It was the play's first performance in Fugard's native South Africa, having been previously banned.*

of the old Jubilee Boarding House, where the young Hally used to hide in Sam and Willie's room. They also talk about the kite that Sam made for Hally and taught him how to fly as well as the art of ballroom dancing.

The recollection of the kite has special significance for Sam and Hally. The kite is a symbol of their deep friendship. An incident from a few years prior is recalled in which Sam had to carry Hally's father, drunken to the point of incoherence, home. The boy was deeply ashamed of his father and greatly depressed by the incident. Sam built him the kite as a symbol of their friendship and to give Hally something to which he could, figuratively and literally, look up, holding his head high (''I wanted you to look up, be proud of something, of yourself . . .'').

From the exchanges between Hally and the two men and two one-sided telephone conversations, it becomes apparent that Hally's crippled and drunken father is to return home from the hospital that day. Hally loves his father but is also ashamed of him and wants him to remain at the hospital. At first the boy pretends that it isn't true, that his father will remain at the hospital indefinitely, preserving the idyllic quality of Hally's recent life. Yet as the realization sinks in, Hally becomes depressed and tells Sam that it might be time to build another kite.

As his father's return becomes imminent, Hally's mood changes drastically. He becomes brutally rude to the two men, insults them with racial slurs, and, in an act of cruel insolence, spits in Sam's face. Sam starts forward as if he means to strike the boy, but Willie restrains him. Sam regains his composure and, removing his white servant's jacket, extends his hand to Hally in a gesture of equality, friendship, and forgiveness. The boy, however, is too ashamed of his cruelty to even look the older man in the face. Hally departs, and Sam and Willie dance together as Sarah Vaughn sings the blues.

CHARACTERS

Hally

Seventeen-year old Hally, the white son of the owners of the St. George's Park Tea Room, is the ''Master Harold'' of the title. Hally appears devoted to Sam, one of two black waiters employed by his family's business. The young man takes great pride

MEDIA ADAPTATIONS

- *''Master Harold'' . . . and the Boys* was adapted as a television film in 1985. Produced by Lorimar pictures and directed by Michael Lindsay-Hogg, this production starred Matthew Broderick as Hally, John Kani as Willie, and longtime Fugard collaborator Zakes Mokae as Sam. It is available on video through Facets Video.

in ''educating'' Sam through brief recapitulations of lessons learned from books and in the classroom. But, in reality, it has been Sam who has been ''educating'' the young man, teaching him the ways of the world. Hally, however, has been affected by both the South African apartheid society of the late 1950s, which has taught him to view nonwhites as second-class citizens, and his drunken father's inability to serve as a parent. When Hally learns that his father is coming home from the alcoholic ward of the local hospital, he is conflicted with feelings of both love and shame. The self-assured young man of the beginning of the play degenerates into an embittered child who lashes out at the nearest target—Sam. At the play's conclusion, the student who had all the answers for his ''pupil'' leaves the tea room confused and in pain.

Fugard himself served as the model for Hally. As he recalled in a 1961 entry in his memoir *Notebooks,* the man whose full name is Harold Athol Lannigan Fugard (he was called Hally as a youth) was ashamed of his father, a lame man with a drinking problem. But, Fugard did not simply retell what happened in his life, choosing instead to embellish and slightly alter the story. For instance, Fugard was fourteen at the time of the play's pivotal episode, but he makes his character Hally three years older. Additionally, the incident where Hally spits in Sam's face did not take place in the cafe but while Hally (Fugard) was bicycling. In the same entry dated March, 1961, Fugard vaguely ''recall[s] shyly haunting the servants' quarters in the well of the hotel . . . a world [he] didn't fully understand.'' He refers in this entry to Sam as ''the most significant, the only friend of [his] boyhood years.''

Master Harold

See Hally

Sam

Sam, a black man in his mid-forties, is a waiter at the St. George Park Tea Room owned by Hally's parents. He has been employed by the family a long time, at least since the days of the Jubilee Boarding House. He has served as a father figure to young Hally while the boy's father spends time in and out of the hospital recovering from bouts of alcoholism. After one particularly humiliating episode for Hally, where Sam carried the boy's drunken father home on his back, Sam made a kite for Hally out of brown paper and tomato-box wood with water and flour for glue. He built the kite because he wanted Hally to ''look up, be proud of something.'' When Hally, in frustration and rage at things beyond his control, spits in his face, Sam offers his young friend a chance at reconciliation. An offer that is refused by Hally.

Not just a servant, Sam is a recognized expert, at least by Willie and Hally, on dance. He offers advice to both his fellow waiter, Willie, as well as Hally on the intricacies and symbolic nature of ballroom dancing. ''There's no collisions out there, Hally. Nobody trips or stumbles or bumps into anybody else. That's what the moment is all about. To be one of those finalists on that dance floor is like . . . like being in a dream about a world in which accidents don't happen . . . it's beautiful because that is what we want life to be like.''

The character of Sam is based on Sam Semela, a Basuto (a tribe of people who live in the Lesotho region of South Africa) who worked for Fugard's family for fifteen years. Fugard's mother fired Sam when he became careless and began arriving late for work. Fugard remembers his mother saying, ''His work went to hell. He didn't seem to care no more.''

Willie

Willie also works at the St. George Tea Room as a waiter. Much of his attention is centered on the upcoming ballroom dancing championships. He takes much good-natured ribbing from Sam about practicing his dancing with a pillow. When Hally arrives, Willie assumes the servant role, referring to

Hally as ''Master Harold.'' Throughout much of the play, Willie observes, but rarely comments on, the exchanges between Sam and Hally. In the pivotal scene where Hally spits in Sam's face, it is Willie who groans (''long and heartfelt'' according to the stage directions); it is Willie who stops Sam from hitting Hally; it is Willie who says that if Hally had spit in his face, he would also want to hit him hard, but would probably just go cry in the back room. Ultimately, Willie crystallizes the emotion of the play: ''Is bad. Is all bad in here now.''

THEMES

Anger and Hatred

''Master Harold''... and the Boys presents in vivid detail what happens in a society constructed in institutional anger and hatred (apartheid). The policies of the South African government in the mid-1950s legislated a certain amount of hatred and anger between whites and blacks. Sam, long a victim of these official and traditional policies, has attempted to transcend the hatred and anger. He acts as a surrogate father to Hally, fortifying the boy's sense of well-being (both through kind acts such as building the kite and through allowing the boy to teach him what he learned in school) and imparting his wisdom to Hally in a series of life lessons (his dance hall metaphors for peaceful coexistence). That a seventeen-year-old can spit in the face of a black man without even the thought of repercussions shines a harsh light onto the institutional policies of hatred that were fostered in South Africa.

Hally must also cope with his own feelings of anger and hatred toward his father, feelings that are conflicted by his simultaneous love for his father. After each of the telephone calls, Hally becomes dark and sullen. The humanitarian affirmations he had been espousing prior to the phone calls evaporate into confusion and anger. Even though Sam is the recipient of the most vicious insult, it is his father who is the true focal point of Hally's rage. Societal taboos and restrictions prevent Hally from telling his father what he really thinks. Those same societal influences allow Hally to redirect his anger and frustration to Sam without fear of consequences. The aftermath, however, is far more destructive than any punishment, as Hally must carry with him the knowledge that he has gravely wronged one of his truest friends.

Human Rights

The South African system of apartheid comes under heavy attack in *''Master Harold''... and the Boys* despite the fact that apartheid is not directly addressed in the play. Instead, it is the society that the system has created that is criticized. It is not merely that racial prejudice is legislated in South Africa. This prejudice weasels its way into every facet of life, so much so that the language begins to reflect the disparity of power where black men are forced by law to be subservient to white children. The young Hally with the appropriately immature nickname transforms into ''Master Harold'' in the context of the prejudicial attitudes promoted by apartheid. On the other hand, Sam, the white boy's mentor and surrogate father, is regarded as the ''boy,'' a second-class citizen who is looked down upon. Yet Sam's maturity and honor are clearly shown in his compassion, humanity, and sense of what is right and wrong.

Within the culture of the play, there is nothing unusual about a white child hitting or degrading a black man. It would have been unheard of for the black man in the South Africa of the 1950s to strike back, however. His anger and frustration could only be released on those even more dispossessed: black women and children. The white child hits the black man, the black man hits the black woman, the black woman hits the black child. It is a system in which violence spirals downward in a hierarchy of degradation, as evidenced in Willie's abusive relationship with his dancing partner.

Rites of Passage

Hally has two courses of action open to him in his journey toward maturity—the loving, reasoned way of Sam or the indifferent, humiliating way of Hally's father and the rest of South African society. Sam offers Hally more than one opportunity to break with institutional forms of racism and embark on a new course. Sam is tempted to strike back after Hally spits in his face but, instead, tries to turn the occasion into a positive learning experience that will guide the boy towards better relationships with his fellow man.

For Sam, the appropriate action is in virtue rather than violence, in reasoning rather than rage. Sam trusts in his capacity to move Hally to shame through exemplary behavior and an appeal to morality. He forgives the white boy who doesn't know any better and behaves like a ''man'' in order to teach Hally the basics of honorable behavior. In a

TOPICS FOR FURTHER STUDY

- Research the South African system of apartheid. Compare that system to the segregated system of ''separate but equal'' that existed in the United States in the 1950s. What differences in the respective governments of the two countries enabled the U.S. to overcome racial inequalities before South Africa?
- Discuss the episode of the kite, particularly in the light of Sam's explanation after Hally has spit in his face.
- Sam discusses the complexities of human relations by using the metaphor of dance. Show how this metaphor works in the context of the play.
- Hally has two one-sided telephone conversations during the play. Discuss his mood after each one. Why is the second call more troubling than the first?
- Almost all of the dialogue in the play is between Sam and Hally. What is Willie's role in this drama? Is it mere observer? Or is his role more significant than that?

challenge to change what has happened through an act of personal transformation, Sam extends his hand toward Hally in a gesture of reconciliation. ''You don't *have* to sit up there by yourself,'' he says, recalling Hally's feeling of isolation on the ''Whites Only'' bench. ''You know what that bench means now and you can leave it any time you choose. All you've got to do is stand up and walk away from it.'' The invitation to ''walk away'' is a chance to leave Hally's past behind, to abandon the ways of apartheid and become an honorable adult. Hally, however, is paralyzed by both shame and the ingrained attitudes fostered by society; he cannot break free of them to begin his journey as a ''man.''

STYLE

Setting

''Master Harold''... and the Boys is a drama set in the St. George's Tea Room on a wet and windy afternoon. The year is 1950 and the location is Port Elizabeth, South Africa. The entire play takes place in the restaurant. While it is a small, enclosed space, the tea room serves as a microcosm of South African society at large. The attitudes and situations that are displayed in the restaurant are variations on what occurred on a daily basis under the system of apartheid.

Realism

''Master Harold''... and the Boys subscribes to the school of realism in that the actions and dialogue of the three characters are very much as they would be in real life. This is not surprising given that the play is based on events from Fugard's own life. Like his titular character, the playwright had the nickname Hally as well as an alcoholic father of whom he was greatly ashamed. Fugard found a surrogate father in a black man who worked at his parents' cafe, a relationship much like the one between Hally and Sam. The play also enacts a historical reality in its portrayal of the actions and attitudes of South Africa at the height of apartheid.

Yet realism in literature is not a mere transcription of actual events; it seeks to use reality as a kind of mirror in which the audience can see themselves. Fugard uses realistic events and settings to strike chords of recognition in his audience. The play may be based on a specific event from his own childhood, but the themes of societal prejudice are universal. By portraying the severe emotional toll that is exacted when inequality is a fundamental concept in society, the playwright hopes to make his viewers aware and hopefully prevent future instances of injustice. The play is not about the history of apartheid politics but more specifically a family history that illustrates the evils of such a prejudiced system.

Symbolism

Two images play prominent roles in this drama: the kite and dancing. Made out of tomato-box slats, brown paper, discarded socks, and glue, the kite represents the soaring hopes for equality between the races and the triumph of human love over prejudice and hatred. Sam made the kite for Hally to lift the boy's spirits. A past incident is recalled in which Hally's father had become so drunk at a local bar that he had soiled himself. Because the mother was not at home, Hally had to go to the bar and ask permission for Sam to enter in order to take his father home. The event greatly disturbed and depressed the boy. Sam tells Hally he made the kite because he ''wanted [him] to look up, be proud of something, of [him]self.'' At the end of the play, after Hally has spit in his face, Sam, in a final attempt at reconciliation, offers Hally the opportunity to ''fly another kite.'' ''You can't fly kites on rainy days,'' says Hally. This exchange illustrates the two characters' personalities and is also reflective of South African culture at large. Sam, like many South Africans, wishes to reconcile, put the past behind him, and work towards a better future. Hally, also like many of his countrymen, realizes what he has done is wrong yet is too programmed to attempt change.

Dancing assumes the role as metaphor for life in the play. From the tribulations of Willie and his partner to Willie and Sam's poignant dance that concludes the play, dancing helps the characters makes sense of a world that seems out of control. Describing his idea of a perfect ballroom—metaphorically an ideal world—Sam tell Hally, ''There are no collisions out there.... Nobody trips or stumbles or bumps into anybody else . . . like being in a dream about a world in which accidents don't happen.''

HISTORICAL CONTEXT

Separate and Unequal

In the mid-twentieth century, the country of South Africa was dominated by the policy of apartheid, a separation and segregation based on race. Strict policies prohibited and governed such issues as intermarriage, land ownership, and use of public facilities. In *''Master Harold'' . . . and the Boys,* Sam illustrates the division quite clearly: ''I couldn't sit down there and stay with you,'' referring to a ''Whites Only'' bench upon which Hally sat. The laws deliberately set out to humiliate people of color, even to the point of determining who could sit on a particular bench. Errol Durbach explained the psychopathology of apartheid in *Modern Drama:* ''It is not that racial prejudice is *legislated* in South Africa. It insinuates itself into every social sphere of existence, until the very language of ordinary human discourse begins to reflect the policy that makes black men subservient to the power exercised by white children.''

Fugard's Underground Theater

Many of Fugard's early plays were performed for small private audiences rather than in public theaters; apartheid laws forbade white actors appearing on stage with black actors. In the 1960s, Fugard helped to start the Serpent Players, an all-black theater group made up of residents of New Brighton, the black township of Fugard's hometown of Port Elizabeth. Despite frequent harassment from the police, the Serpent Players continued to perform, and Fugard's involvement with the group did much to establish black South African theater.

In Fugard's first major theatrical success, *The Blood Knot,* Fugard appeared as a light-skinned nonwhite half brother, a commentary on a individual's search for freedom in a country that denied such independence. In this play, Fugard dramatized the ambivalence and racial hatred that infected many South African relationships, perverting the ''blood knot,'' or common bond of humanity. Despite voicing the concerns of the country's black majority, Fugard's drama was considered rebellious by the white ruling minority. Because it so implicitly criticized the way of life for many Afrikaners, his work was often banned or heavily censored. It was not until *''Master Harold'' . . . and the Boys,* which had its debut outside of South Africa, that the rest of the world became aware of Fugard's work. With endorsements from critics and audiences in New York and London, *''Master Harold''*'s message was being heard, despite a South African ruling banning performance or publication of the play.

The End of Apartheid

The culture of racism that was promoted by apartheid continued virtually unchecked throughout the 1950s and well into the next three decades. By 1982, apartheid was recognized in much of the free

COMPARE & CONTRAST

- **1950s:** In South Africa, the system of apartheid legislates the separation of the races. Black people are forced to live in designated areas and may only use designated public facilities.

  1980s: The world condemns the policy of apartheid. Many people across the globe protest the involvement of businesses in South Africa and demonstrate for divestiture of investments in that country.

  Today: The government of South Africa has officially renounced the policy of apartheid and has elected a black leader, Nelson Mandela.

- **1950s:** In America, pre-World War II race restrictions (Jim Crow laws) are discarded. Black people assert their civil rights with marches, demonstrations, sit-down strikes, and boycotts. The Supreme Court strikes down the doctrine of ''separate but equal'' in the landmark *Brown v. the Board of Education* decision. In the ensuing decade, the Civil Rights Movement will reach a fever pitch, creating sweeping legislation to promote equality among races.

  1980s: While race relations in the U.S. have improved since the 1950s and 1960s, there is still considerable inequality to be addressed. These disparities are trivial compared with the plight of South African blacks, however. Expanding public knowledge of apartheid renews many Americans commitment to racial harmony and equality in their own country.

  Today: The U.S. has instituted policies that forbid discrimination based on race or color in the areas of employment, housing, and access to government services. Despite the obvious benefits of such policies, many conservative politicians seek to eradicate such practices as Affirmative Action, claiming that it denies qualified whites equal opportunity.

world as a dire injustice against humanity. Activist organizations such as Amnesty International fought for the eradication of such an inherently racist society, going to great lengths to publicize South Africa's criminal treatment of its black majority. Along with the human rights violations of communist China, South Africa's policies were considered among the gravest.

Blacks who spoke out against the government's policies were routinely arrested and imprisoned. The most famous activist/prisoner in the South African penal system was Nelson Mandela, whose public campaigns for equality resulted in a sentence of life imprisonment. At the time of *''Master Harold''*'s first production in 1982, Mandela was one of the best-known political prisoners in the world. Despite the efforts of the South African government, Mandela's message was being heard across continents. In 1987, while still a prisoner, he was awarded the Nobel Peace Prize. In 1990, then president F. W. de Klerk ordered Mandela's release, after twenty-seven years of incarceration. Soon after, de Klerk dissolved the system of apartheid and agreed to open elections that would allow blacks to both run for office and freely vote. In 1991, Mandela was elected the president of South Africa and his party, the African National Congress, took control of the government. After decades of subordination, South Africa's black majority finally had an equal voice in their country.

CRITICAL OVERVIEW

The summary of *''Master Harold''*'s action cannot begin to suggest its emotional intensity or its impact on an audience. Many who saw the play in its debut were greatly troubled by the society it depicted. Since that time *''Master Harold''* has continued to provoke critics and audiences alike.

Errol Durbach, writing in *Modern Drama,* asserted that *''Master Harold''... and the Boys* is not an overtly political play, but a depiction of ''a personal power-struggle with political implications.'' The only definition that the South African system can conceive of in the relationship of White to Black is one that humiliates black people. This definition ''insinuates itself into every social sphere of existence, until the very language of ordinary human discourse begins to reflect the policy that makes black men subservient to the power exercised by white children.'' In the society depicted by Fugard White equals ''Master'' and Black equals ''boy.'' It is an equation, continued Durbach, that ignores the traditional relationship of labor to management or of paid employee to paying employer.

During the course of the drama, Hally rapidly realigns the components of his long-standing friendship with Sam into the socio-political patterns of master and servant. Hally changes from intimate familiarity with his black companions to patronizing condescension to his social inferiors. It is an exercise of power by Hally, himself a ''boy'' who feels powerless to control the circumstance of his life and therefore seeks some measure of autonomy in his interaction with Sam and Willie.

Robert Brustein, in a review in the *New Republic,* described *''Master Harold''... and the Boys* as the ''quintessential racial anecdote,'' and ascribed to Fugard's writing ''a sweetness and sanctity that more than compensates for what might be prosaic, rhetorical, or contrived about it.'' There is a suggestion that Fugard's obsession with the theme of racial injustice may be an expression of his own guilt and act of expiation. As Brian Crow noted in the *International Dictionary of Theatre,* ''biographical information, however, is not needed in order for the play to make its full impact in the theatre. This is achieved primarily through an audience's empathy with the loving relationship between Hally and Sam and its violation through Hally's inability to cope with his emotional turmoil over his father, and its expression in racism. If to what extent the play manages ... to transmute autobiographical experience into a larger exploration or analysis of racism in South Africa is arguable; what seems quite certain is its capacity to involve and disturb audiences everywhere.''

Yet not all critical reaction to Fugard's work has been positive. Failing to see the play's wider message on racism, Stephen Gray saw *''Master Harold''* as nothing more than a play about apartheid. In a 1990 *New Theatre Quarterly* article, Gray noted that South Africa's dissolution of apartheid has made the play obsolete, stating that it ''feels like a museum piece today.'' Other negative criticism found the play's black characters to be falsely represented. As Jeanne Colleran reported in *Modern Drama,* ''To some black critics, the character of Sam is a grotesquerie. His forbearance and forgiveness, far from being virtues, are embodiments of the worst kind of Uncle Tom-ism.'' Such reproach prompted Fugard to clarify his intentions during the Anson Phelps Stokes Institute's Africa Roundtable. As Colleran reported, Fugard stated that his intention was to tell a story: ''I never set out to serve a cause.... The question of being a spokesman for Black politics is something I've never claimed for myself.''

Such criticism for *''Master Harold''* was sporadic, however. The majority of critics and audiences embraced the play as important and thought-provoking. Commenting on Fugard's ability to fuse theatricality with strong political issues, Dennis Walder wrote in *Athol Fugard,* ''Fugard's work... contains a potential for subversion, a potential which, I would suggest, is the hallmark of great art, and which qualifies his best work to be called great.''

CRITICISM

William P. Wiles

In this essay Wiles examines Fugard's play as a political drama, taking into account the dissolution of the apartheid system in South Africa and how that affects contemporary perceptions of the work. He concludes that the play is still relevant as a chronicle of human relations.

What happens to the overall effect of a play when the societal forces that shaped it have changed to the point where the playwright himself says: ''[A] political miracle has taken place in my time.''? Such might appear to be the case for Athol Fugard and his play *''Master Harold''... and the Boys.* The South African system of apartheid—legislated separation of the races—has been dismantled; free and open elections have been held; a black man, Nelson Mandela, has been elected president of the country. The power of whites, regardless of their age or station, to subjugate and humiliate blacks

Willie (Ramolao Makhene) and Sam (John Kani) listen to Hally (Duart Sylwain) recount his lessons in a 1983 National Theatre production

with the full blessing of the government and society at large has evaporated. The question that begs to be asked, then, is: What *is* this play about if not about political struggle?

By focusing attention on the adolescent antagonist Hally, Fugard creates a more personal drama—a drama rooted in the uncertainties of a youth who attends a second-rate school and whose parents own and operate a third-rate cafe. Displaying ''a few stale cakes,'' ''a not very impressive display of sweets,'' and ''a few sad ferns in pots,'' the St. George's Park Tea Room hardly seems the seat of power. And, the arrival of Hally, in clothes that are ''a little neglected and untidy'' and drenched from the heavy rains that keep customers away, does little to prepare the audience for the play's explosive confrontation.

When Hally enters the cafe, it appears that he is glad for the lack of patrons so that he and Sam and Willie can have a ''nice, quiet afternoon.'' There is the implication that both he and the two men have enjoyed these types of days in the past. Hally's world, however, begins to crumble when Sam informs him that his mother has gone to the hospital to

WHAT DO I READ NEXT?

- *Selected Stories,* a collection of short stories by Nobel-Prize winning author Nadine Gordimer. A white South African like Fugard, Gordimer brings her characters and the African landscape they inhabit to life.
- *Hamlet,* one of William Shakespeare's classic tragedies, was written in approximately 1603. It concerns a young man who has unresolved issues with both his father and his uncle. His inability to articulate his feelings causes him to lash out at people he loves with serious consequences.
- *To Kill a Mockingbird* (1960), a novel by Harper Lee that examines the events of a American town in the South during the Depression. The novel confronts issues of racism and power through the story a black man on trial for the rape of a white woman and the white lawyer who defends him.
- *Black like Me* (1961) a memoir written by John Howard Griffin, recounts the adventures of a white man who changed the pigment of his skin to resemble a black man in the 1950s in the American South. The books offers a unique perspective on the treatment of African Americans during a pivotal time in the history of civil rights.

bring his father home. Hally's annoyance at the comic books piled on the table—''intellectual rubbish''—changes into fury when Willie throws a slop rag at Sam, misses, and hits Hally. Hally swears and tells both Willie and Sam to ''stop fooling around.'' Hally calls Sam back to have him explain what Hally's mother said before she left for the hospital. He convinces himself that his father is not coming home, that Sam heard wrong, and that the world he has created for himself will continue undisturbed.

His willingness to shift the discussion to the varieties of textbook learning and then to the more important learning gleaned from the servants quarters at the old Jubilee Boarding House under the tutelage of Sam and Willie, indicate Hally's inability to accept that his life is about to change once again. Hally returns to the comfort of the historical past, discussing Joan of Arc, World War I, Charles Darwin, Abraham Lincoln, and William Shakespeare with Sam. He also returns to his own familiar past and the flying of a homemade kite that Sam made for him.

It is the kite that provides Hally with the defining moment of his young life—a black man and a young white boy enjoying each other's company and a shared accomplishment. Hally says ''I don't know how to describe it, Sam. Ja! The miracle happened!'' Hally appears to want to return to the safety of their shared past when he mentions to Sam that ''[i]t's time for another one, you know.'' The uncertainties of adolescence challenge Hally's place, not only in the world at large but in his family as well. Of his time spent with Sam he summarizes: ''It's just that life felt the right size in there . . . not too big and not too small. Wasn't so hard to work up a bit of courage. It's got so bloody complicated since then.''

Hally's violent reaction to the news that his father is indeed returning home (the stage directions describe Hally as ''seething with irritation and frustration'') clearly illustrate the complications Hally must now face. ''Just when things are going along all right, without fail someone or something will come along and spoil everything. Somebody should write that down as a fundamental law of the Universe. The principle of perpetual disappointment.'' Hally's attack on Willie's backside with a ruler and the ''I-allow-you-a-little-freedom-and-what-do-you-do-with-it'' speech show that Hally resists acknowledging the changes and accompanying complications that will inevitably take place when his father returns home.

"WHAT *IS 'MASTER HAROLD'... AND THE BOYS* ABOUT IF NOT ABOUT POLITICAL STRUGGLE?"

In the ensuing ballroom dancing discussion (Fugard himself was a dancing champion in his teens), Sam describes the dance finals ''like being in a dream about a world in which accidents don't happen.'' Sam's view of the world as dance floor contrasts sharply with Hally's nostalgic view of life as the right size in the old Jubilee Boarding house. Hally wants things to remain static, to never change. Sam, on the other hand, wants the world ''to dance like champions instead of always being a bunch of beginners at it.'' There are no collisions in Sam's view because the participants have discovered ways of moving around the dance floor without bumping into one another; symbolically, this is Sam's hope that the world can live together peacefully without prejudice or inequality. Hally appears momentarily convinced at the end of this discussion: ''We mustn't despair. Maybe there is hope for mankind after all.'' But then the phone rings and Hally's world shatters with the news that his mother will be bringing his father home.

At this point, Hally's demeanor becomes ''vicious'' and ''desperate,'' and at the end of the conversation Hally is ''desolate.'' He slams books and smashes the bottle of brandy his mother had told him to get for his father. With reckless words and ugly laughter, Hally mocks his crippled father, insinuating him into the dance metaphor as the ones who are ''out there tripping up everybody and trying to get into the act.'' His childhood world is now smashed beyond recognition as Hally swears at Sam and chastises him for meddling in something he knows nothing about.

Hally's adolescent posturing leads him to demand that Sam call him ''Master Harold, like Willie [does].'' Because he cannot control the events surrounding his father's homecoming, Hally lashes out at the convenient targets of Willie and Sam, people he feels he *can* control. The youth's petulance manifests itself with a vengeance. Hally lets fly with a racist comment and compounds the ugliness of the offense by insisting that it is a ''bloody good joke.'' Hally's final act of naked cruelty is to spit in Sam's face. For Hally, the bond with Sam is forever broken. The demarcation between master and servant is clearly defined.

Although sorely tempted to repay violence with violence, Sam remains the gentle father, the true friend, the moral teacher. Having removed the symbol of servitude (the white servant's jacket) that distinguishes him as a ''boy,'' Sam presents the *personal* rather than *political* response to Hally's indignities—an extended hand and the offer to try again and ''fly another kite.'' But Hally has shamed himself beyond compassion and cannot respond to Sam's final lesson.

Errol Durbach wrote in *Modern Drama* that the final dramatic images—the rain of despair, the wind where no kites fly, the hopelessness of relationships ripped apart by racist attitudes, the comforting music that elicits compassion for children who are a victims of their own upbringing, and ''the image of a world where 'Whites Only' leave two black men dancing together in an act of solidarity''—represent Fugard's movement between hope and despair, qualified only by the realization that '''Master Harold' grows up to be Athol Fugard and that the play itself is an act of atonement to the memory of Sam and 'H.D.F.' [Harold David Fugard]—the Black and White fathers to whom [the play] is dedicated.''

So, then, back the original question—what is the play about if not political struggle? It is a play about fathers and sons, and how those roles can be both supportive and destructive. It is a play that illustrates how relationships can be strained by factors beyond the participants. It is a play that offers suggestions and gestures for forgiveness and compassion. It is a play ultimately about race. Not black, or white, or red, or yellow, or brown, but human.

Source: William P. Wiles, for *Drama for Students,* Gale, 1998.

Brian Sutton

Sutton's article addresses the symbolism of Fugard's characters looking up and down—both visually and metaphorically through language—within the play. He uses several examples to illustrate the characters various states of optimism and pessimism.

Many writers have noted the conflict between idealism and reality in Athol Fugard's *Master Harold...*

and the Boys. Dennis Walder, for example, describes a ''gap between the . . . harsh, even violent reality'' that the play's characters endure, and the ''ideal world imagined by Sam'' with his ''idea of dancing as a paradigm of universal harmony'' [*Athol Fugard,* Macmillan, 1984]. Others have noted a second, closely related conflict: that between self-esteem and self-loathing. Frank Rich observes, ''Fugard's point is simple enough: before we can practice compassion . . . we must learn to respect ourselves'' [*New York Times,* May 5, 1982]. But no writer has pointed out that both conflicts are neatly summarized within the play by one more conflict: that between looking up and looking down.

This last conflict is especially suited to a play, because the audience can *see* characters looking up or down. And Fugard, who usually directs the premieres of his plays, is especially sensitive to the theatre's physical possibilities, as other writers have observed. In his published notebooks, Fugard states, ''Only a fraction of my truth is in the words,'' adding that the rest resides in ''the carnal reality of the actor in space and time'' (171). Thus, it is no surprise that the conflict between looking up and looking down in *Master Harold* emerges through visual elements as well as through dialogue.

Fugard begins establishing the significance of looking down the moment the play begins. As the curtain rises, the audience sees Sam and Willie, two black servants working in a restaurant in the apartheid South Africa of 1950. Willie is on his knees, scrubbing the restaurant floor. This task forces him to look down, and as Russell Vandenbroucke notes, his image ''is an inescapable reminder of the role blacks are expected to play'' in his society [*Truths the Hand Can Touch: The Theatre of Athol Fugard,* Theatre Communizations Group, 1985]. Thus, looking down is associated with an oppressive reality.

Fugard then begins associating looking up with achieving the ideal world symbolized by dance. Just seconds into the play, Willie rises from scrubbing the floor, begins practicing a dance step, and asks Sam for pointers. Part of the advice Sam gives is ''Don't look down!'' Sam tells Willie that dancing should ''look like romance,'' which he defines as a ''love story with happy ending.'' In the widely available videotape of the play, Sam looks upward as he says, ''It must look like romance.'' Significantly, the actor playing Sam on the videotape, Zakes Mokae, previously played the role on Broadway under Fugard's direction.

"THE CONFLICT BETWEEN LOOKING UP AND LOOKING DOWN IN *MASTER HAROLD* EMERGES THROUGH VISUAL ELEMENTS AS WELL AS THROUGH DIALOGUE."

After Sam's comment, Fugard further establishes the conflict between ideal and real. Willie counters Sam's idealistic vision by describing his own reality: Hilda, his girlfriend and dance partner, has no teeth; she has told authorities that he is behind in child support payments to her; he suspects that she has been sleeping with other men and that her child is not really his son; she cannot keep up with the beat when they dance; and because he has beaten her in frustration, she now refuses to come near him, thus leaving him not only estranged from his lover, but also without a partner for the upcoming ballroom dance competition. Facing this reality, Willie has trouble looking up toward an idealistic vision.

Soon Hally, the restaurant owner's teenage son, enters. His superior position is immediately established visually, as Willie jokingly springs to attention and salutes him. But when the ensuring dialogue reveals Hally's indifference to his exams and Sam's subtle strategies to help him pass them, we realize that Hally lacks self-esteem and that Sam tries to improve the boy's self-image.

Fugard then associates high self-esteem with looking up, as Hally recalls the time that Sam made him a kite. Typically, Hally had assumed that the project would fail, as he states, ''I thought, 'Like everything else in my life, here comes another fiasco.''' But the kite did fly and, Hally recalls, ''I was so proud of us! . . . I had a stiff neck the next day from looking up so much.''

Not until late in the play does Sam reveal why he made the kite, in the process revealing one reason for Hally's low self-esteem. He reminds Hally of the time Hally's father passed out in a bar and had to be carried home by Sam—with Hally, still a child, forced to accompany Sam to enable him to enter the whites-only bar. With Hally following behind, Sam had carried the father home past crowds of staring people, and then had to clean him up from having ''messed in his trousers.'' Sam adds,

> After we got him to bed you came back with me to my room and sat in a corner and carried on just looking down at the ground. And for days after that! You hadn't done anything wrong, but you went around as if you owed the world an apology for being alive. I didn't like seeing that!. . . If you really want to know, that's why I made you that kite. I wanted you to look up, be proud of something, of yourself. . . .

But by this point, the hope the Hally will look up has faded, for he has subjected Sam to a vicious attack climaxed by his spitting in the black man's face. Thus, Hally has destroyed his relationship with his best friend and surrogate father; he has turned away from Sam's vision of universal cooperation; and he has increased his own burden of shame, thus lowering his self-esteem still further.

At the end it is Willie, not Hally, who begins to look up and share Sam's vision. He states that he will apologize to Hilda, promise not to beat her anymore, and ''romance with her from beginning to end.'' Then he plays the restaurant's juke box and asks Sam to dance, saying, ''Let's dream. . . . You lead, I follow.''

Although the stage directions do not specify it, in performance the men's gazes undoubtedly reflect the reversal that has taken place involving Willie and Hally. Because Willie has finally internalized the lessons Sam has been teaching, during the final dance sequence he surely cannot violate Sam's earlier injunction, ''Don't look down!'' In contrast, because Hally is repeatedly described as ashamed of his outburst, at the end he is surely avoiding Sam's eyes, looking at the floor just as he did after his father passed out in the bar. The actor who played Willie on the videotape, longtime Fugard associate John Kani, never lets his gaze drift downward during the closing dance sequence; while Matthew Broderick, as Hally, looks down almost constantly during the final portion of the play.

Because of Hally's actions, audiences are utterly harrowed by the play's end. But if we look beyond the play to the reality behind it, there is hope. Since the play is based on actual events from Fugard's childhood, we know that in real life, the boy who spat in the face of a black man named Sam outgrew his anger and racism, and even used the incident to create a play celebrating a vision of universal cooperation. And South Africa has not only abolished apartheid, but has elected a black man as its president. Perhaps things, and people, are finally looking up.

Source: Brian Sutton, ''Fugard's *Master Harold . . . and the Boys*'' in the *Explicator,* Volume 54, no. 2, Winter, 1996 , pp. 120–23.

Errol Durbach

In this essay, Durbach discusses the personal manner in which Fugard's play examines the South African system of apartheid.

In this play, dredged out of Athol Fugard's painful memories of a South African adolescence, at least one event stands out in joyous recollection: the boy's exhilarating, liberating, and ultimately transcendent experience of flying a kite made out of tomato-box slats, brown paper, discarded stockings, and string. From the scraps and leavings of the depressingly mundane, the boy intuits the meaning of a soul-life; and he responds to the experience as a ''miracle.'' ''Why did you make that kite, Sam?'' he asks of the black servant whose gift it was—but the answer is not given until much later in the play. Nor can Hally recollect the reason for Sam's failure to share in the experience of high-flying delight:

> HALLY . . . You left me after that, didn't you? You explained how to get it down, we tied it to the bench so that I could sit and watch it, and you went away. I wanted you to stay, you know. I was a little scared of having to look after it by myself.
> SAM (*Quietly*) I had work to do, Hally.

In the final moments of the play Sam provides the simple explanation: the kite had been a symbolic gift to console the child against the degrading shame of having to cope with a drunken and crippled father—an attempt to raise his eyes from the ground of humiliation:

> That's not the way a boy grows up to be a man!. . . But the one person who should have been teaching you what that means was the cause of your shame. If you really want to know, that's why I made you that kite. I wanted you to look up, be proud of something, of yourself . . .

The second question has an answer more readily understood by one familiar with apartheid's so-called ''petty'' operations:

> I couldn't sit down there and stay with you. It was a ''Whites Only'' bench. You were too young, too

> excited to notice then. But not anymore. If you're not careful . . . Master Harold . . . you're going to be sitting up there by yourself for a long time to come, and there won't be a kite in the sky.

This, in essence, is the psychopathology of apartheid. Growing up to be a ''man'' within a system that deliberately sets out to humiliate black people, even to the point of relegating them to separate benches, entails the danger of habitual indifference to the everyday details that shape black/white relationships and, finally, pervert them. It is not merely that racial prejudice is *legislated* in South Africa. It insinuates itself into every social sphere of existence, until the very language of ordinary human discourse begins to reflect the policy that makes black men subservient to the power exercised by white children. Hally, the seventeen-year-old white boy whose affectionately diminutive name is an index of his social immaturity, is ''Master Harold'' in the context of attitudes fostered by apartheid. And the black man who is his mentor and surrogate father is the ''boy''—in all but compassion, humanity, and moral intelligence.

This, finally, is the only definition that the South African system can conceive of in the relationship of White to Black; and Hally, with the facility of one habituated to such power play, saves face and forestalls criticism by rapidly realigning the components of friendship into the socio-political patterns of mastery and servitude. Like quicksilver, he shifts from intimate familiarity with his black companions, to patronising condescension to his social inferiors, to an appalling exercise of power over the powerless ''boys'' simply by choosing to play the role of ''baas'':

> HALLY Sam! Willie! (*Grabs his ruler and gives* WILLIE *a vicious whack on the bum*) How the hell am I supposed to concentrate with the two of you behaving like bloody children! [. . .] Get back to your work. You too, Sam. (*His ruler*) Do you want another one, Willie?
>
> (SAM *and* WILLIE *return to their work.* HALLY *uses the opportunity to escape from his unsuccessful attempt at homework. He struts around like a little despot, ruler in hand, giving vent to his anger and frustration*)

Within the culture portrayed in the play there is nothing particularly remarkable about a white child hitting a black man. It would have been unheard of on the other hand for a black man, in the South Africa of the 1950s, to strike back. *His* anger and

"IT WOULD CLEARLY BE MISLEADING TO CLAIM THAT *'MASTER HAROLD'. . . AND THE BOYS* ADDRESSES THE GROWING COMPLEXITY OF APARTHEID POLITICS IN THE SOUTH AFRICA OF 1987. IT IS A 'HISTORY' PLAY AS AN EXORCISM OF THE TORMENTED GHOSTS OF FUGARD'S CHILDHOOD"

frustration could be unleashed only upon those even more pitifully dispossessed of the human rights to dignity and respect. The white child hits the black man, and the black man hits the black woman. It is a system in which violence spirals downwards in a hierarchy of degradation—as Fugard shows in Willie's relationship with his battered dancing partner who can no longer tolerate the abuse.

A very simple racial equation operates within apartheid: White = ''Master''; Black = ''Boy''. It is an equation which ignores traditional relationships of labour to management, of paid employee to paying employer, or contractual relationships between freely consenting parties. And Sam's attempt to define the nature of his employment in conventional terms is countermanded by Hally's application of the equation:

> HALLY You're only a servant here, and don't forget it. [. . .] And as far as my father is concerned, all you need to remember is that he's your boss.
>
> SAM (*Needled at last*) No, he isn't. I get paid by your mother.
>
> HALLY Don't argue with me, Sam!
>
> SAM Then don't say he's my boss.
>
> HALLY He's a white man and that's good enough for you.

What needles Sam is the thought of being paid for his work by a bigot who shows him none of the simple human respect that is everyone's most urgent *need* in Fugard's world—the white child's in a family that shames him, and the black man's in a culture that humiliates him. It is the common denominator that Sam and Hally share; and the ultimate goal of ''Master'' Harold's power-play is to secure his own desire for self-respect at the expense of a man whose native dignity proves all but impervious to these attempts to ''boy'' him. It is a self-defeating and self-destructive ploy, imposed by threat and blackmail upon a relationship which has all the potential for mutual comfort, support, and love. It is the human content of their shared affection that Hally is about to petrify into the equation of apartheid:

> HALLY To begin with, why don't you also start calling me Master Harold, like Willie.
> SAM [. . .] And if I don't?
> HALLY You might lose your job.
> SAM (*Quietly and very carefully*) If you make me say it once, I'll never call you anything else again. [. . .] You must decide what it means to you.
> HALLY Well, I have. It's good news. Because that is exactly what Master Harold wants from now on. Think of it as a little lesson in respect, Sam, that's long overdue. [. . .] I can tell you now that somebody who will be glad to hear I've finally given it to you will be my Dad. Yes! He agrees with my Mom. He's always going on about it as well. ''You must teach the boys to show you more respect, my son.''

''Teaching respect'' loses all semantic value in the context of apartheid. It means coercion by threat, just as ''showing respect'' means acquiescence through enforced abasement. It is easy to teach Willie respect—one does it with the stick, and with impunity because Willie lacks the necessary sentiment of self-regard to oppose such treatment. His predictable response is to insist that Hally whack Sam as well—the sole comfort of the wretched being to recognise fellow-sufferers in distress. But Hally cannot *command* Sam's respect; and if he cannot *win* it, his only recourse is to humiliate Sam to the point where, by default, his own pathetic superiority supervenes. Finally, the only power left to Hally is the wounding power of bigotry supported by a system in which ''black'' is, *ipso facto,* base. Echoing his father's words, associating himself with the very cause of his shame, he spreads the ''filth'' he has been taught in a racist joke—the penultimate weapon in his arsenal of power. It is a crude pun about a ''nigger's arse'' not being ''fair''; and one senses, in the numb incredulity of the two black men, an irreversible redefinition of their relationship with their white charge. In the ensuing silence, he belabours the pun—the double meaning of ''fair'' as light in colour *and* just and decent—and is ensnared in the moral implications of his bid for respect through insult and abuse:

> SAM You're really trying hard to be ugly, aren't you? And why drag poor Willie into it? He's done nothing to you except show you the respect you want so badly. That's also not being fair, you know . . . and *I* mean just or decent.

And to underscore the embarrassment that Hally has brought upon himself, Sam performs an action of rebuke through self-abasement that reveals both the reality and the vulnerability of the ''nigger's arse''—the thing that the Master feels at liberty to mock at and kick: ''*He drops his trousers and underpants and presents his backside for HALLY's inspection.*'' His nakedness is clearly no laughing matter. It calls in question the justice and decency and fairness of an entire system which can encourage a child so to humiliate a man. Its indictment is Dostoievskian in its power to shame.

Hally's countermeasure is to exercise his power to degrade with impunity: he spits in Sam's face, saving his own by fouling another's and, in so doing, placing Sam forever in the role of ''boy'' to his ''Master''. It is a gesture of contempt and angry frustration, the adolescent's protest against his own sense of degradation—horribly misdirected against the wrong source, as Sam instantly realises: ''The face you should be spitting in,'' he says, ''is your father's . . . but you used mine, because you think you're safe inside your fair skin . . . and this time I don't mean just or decent.'' It is Hally's ''white'' father who ensures the ''principle of perpetual disappointment'' in the boy's life—the crippled alcoholic who must be dragged out of bars fouled in his own excrement, whose chamber pots must be emptied by the boy, and whose imminent return from the hospital provokes in Hally the thought of further humiliating servitude. But it is Hally's black ''father'' who must bear the brunt of his anguish and his shame. Sam has become his ''spitting boy'' just as Willie had been his ''whipping boy'', the recipient of a contempt which he cannot reveal to his father whom he both loves and despises. This is the moment, Fugard admitted in an interview, ''which totally symbolised the ugliness, the potential ugliness waiting for me as a White South African.''

The overwhelming shame of the actual event is recorded in the section of Fugard's *Notebooks* dealing with his childhood memories of growing up in Port Elizabeth. But he sets the play five years later, in 1950, that *annus mirabilis* of Apartheid legislation; and Fugard's political point of view is nowhere more clearly revealed than in his location of the encroaching ugliness of South Africa's destiny in a *personal* rather than a *national* failure of moral decency. Despite the statutory enforcement of racist laws in the 1950s, apartheid (like charity) is seen to begin *at home,* in the small details of everyday existence. There is no sense, in the play, of the Nationalist Government's Population Registration Act of 1950 with its racial system of classification by colour, the Group Areas Act of 1950 which demarcated the areas of permissible domicile for the races and controlled the ownership of property in those areas, the 1950 Amendment to the Immorality Act which prohibited sexual contact across the colour bar, or the Suppression of Communism Act of 1950 which empowered the minister of Justice to ban suspect individuals without trial or right of appeal—indeed, without even notifying the detainee of the nature of his offence. There is nothing of Kafka's nightmare about Fugard's world, nothing of the political absurdity of Vaclav Havel's vision of man's soul under totalitarianism. Nor does he invoke the ridiculous terms of the Separate Amenities Act which, in 1953, would subject a black man sitting on a ''Whites Only'' bench (''reserved for the exclusive use of persons belonging to a particular race or class, being a race or class to which he does not belong'') to a fine not exceeding fifty pounds or imprisonment not exceeding three months, or to both.

Fugard's is not a drama of political protest nor an expose of a corrupt regime entrenched in its position of power. His detractors on the militant Left call him bitterly to task for failing to fight against the system, just as his Right-wing detractors point to the obsolescence of his political vision—to the disappearance of ''Whites Only'' signs on South African benches in the 1980s. Plays like *Statements after an Arrest under the Immorality Act* or *Sizwe Bansi is Dead* may, indeed, seem anachronistic after the rescinding of the Immorality Act and the Pass laws with which they deal. But the psychopathology of apartheid in Fugard's drama is quite distinct from Government policy. There is no guarantee, when the letter of all the 1950's legislation has passed into oblivion, that the *attitudes* which informed its spirit will disappear as well. The Laws are crucial historical background to Fugard's world, but these attitudes are the substance of his most insistent misgivings about apartheid's operation upon human relationships.

In the absence of explicit political comment, it might seem tendentious to equate the social awkwardness of a troubled teenager with government policy. Hally's condescending attitude towards his ''boys'', his failure to share with them any of the chocolate and cake and ice-cream that he is constantly consuming—these may be evidence of an ingrained arrogance and selfishness rather than a culturally conditioned attitude to an ''inferior'' race. But these unobtrusive details underscore the more overt acts of insulting racism in the play. Having whacked one ''boy'' with a ruler and spat in the other's face, his last shamefaced act is to remove the wretched day's takings from the cash register—essentially small change—and tell Willie to lock up for him. One entrusts the ''boy'' with the keys to the tearoom, but not with the few coins which might tempt him to play the juke-box or take the bus home. One may *give* a ''boy'' some cake or chocolate, but never *offer* it. Every social gesture, within the South African context, becomes an affirmation or a negation of the principle of apartheid; and every act is more or less political.

Against the petty and unconscious cruelties of Hally, Fugard juxtaposes the magnanimity of Sam: the compassionate father, the good friend, the moral teacher. He offers a solution to the predicament, again in *personal* rather than *political* terms—a response so lacking in revolutionary fervour as to alienate, once again, the new generation of post-Sowetan critics of Athol Fugard's drama. Mastering his violence and the desire to strike Hally for spitting at him, Sam carefully considers the strategy of aggression with Willie, and they both agree to suffer the indignity in stoical resignation:

> WILLIE [. . .] But maybe all I do is go cry at the back. He's little boy, Boet Sam. Little *white* boy. Long trousers now, but he's still little boy.
>
> SAM (*His violence ebbing away into defeat as quickly as it flooded*) You're right. So go on, then: groan again, Willie. You do it better than me.

Though struck to the quick, they endure the insult with weeping and groaning rather than striking back. There is no revolution in the St. George's Park Tearoom—but not because the black man is culturally conditioned to patience, nor for fear of putting his job in jeopardy. In Fugard's world, as in Prospero's, the rarer action is in virtue than in vengeance, in humane reasoning rather than fury; and Sam trusts, once again, to his capacity for moving Master Harold to shame through moral suasion and exemplary behaviour. He forgives the little white boy who knows no better, and behaves like a ''man'' in order to teach him the rudiments of ''manly'' behaviour. Turning the other cheek may not be politically expedient as a response to apartheid, but where problems are engendered at the personal level it is only at the personal level that they may be resolved.

''I oscillate,'' says the precocious Hally early in the play, ''between hope and despair for this world.... But things will change, you wait and see.'' On the whole, Sam's politics are ranged on the side of hope—the hope born, initially, of a naive vision of reform and racial harmony but modulating, in the final scenes, to the more sombre hope of salvaging the scrap of value remaining in his relationship with the little white master. He dreams of a world transformed by some benevolent reformer—a saviour like Napoleon for whom all men were equal before the law, or another Abraham Lincoln who fought for the oppressed, or a Tolstoy, or Gandhi, or Christ; and he envisions life as a celestial ballroom in which no accidents occur, in which powers are harmoniously aligned on the global dance floor. But, like Hally, he is forced to acknowledge the harsh reality of things: we go on waiting for the ''Man of Magnitude'', he admits, bumping and colliding until we're sick and tired. All that remains is the small gesture, the little act of decency that may turn a fragment of the dream into something real. This, finally, is what he hopes for. He takes off his servant's jacket and returns in clothes that no longer distinguish him as a ''boy''; he addresses Hally by the affectionate diminutive once again; and he offers, very simply, the chance to ''fly another kite.'' ''You can't fly kites on rainy days,'' says Hally—and the rain and the wind squalling beyond the windows of the tearoom assume the depressing and hopeless condition of the entire South African situation. Better weather tomorrow? No one is sure.

At this point in the Yale Repertory production of the play, the excellent Zakes Mokae playing Sam extends his hand tentatively towards Hally in a gesture of appeal and reconciliation as important to his well-being as to the boy's; and he challenges him to change the situation through an act of personal transformation which flies in the face of his cultural and political conditioning: ''You don't *have* to sit up there by yourself,'' he says, recalling the boy's isolation on the ''Whites Only'' bench. You know what that bench means now, and you can leave it any time you choose. All you've got to do is stand up and walk away from it.'' But ingrained attitudes die hard. Paralysed by shame but incapable of extending himself towards the black man, Hally hesitates and then walks out into the rain as Sam's hand crumples in its gesture.

If anyone has learned a lesson from this bleak afternoon of moral instruction it is the simple, inarticulate Willie who, in his effort to comfort Sam, endorses his dream-ideal of life as a ballroom. He vows never to beat up his partner again, and slips his bus fare into the juke-box which ''*comes to life in the gray twilight, blushing its way through a spectrum of soft, romantic colours.*'' ''Let's dream,'' he says. And the two men sway through the room to Sarah Vaughan's melancholy lullaby to an unhappy child—''Little man you're crying.'' The final dramatic image is suffused with the ambiguous tonalities typical of Fugard's best work: the rain of despair beyond the windows, the wind in which no kites fly, the hopelessness of a situation where people are driven apart by racist attitudes, the consoling music which evokes our compassion for children who are casualties of their upbringing, the hope that shame and embarrassment might induce change in a morally receptive child, the delusory political vision of racial harmony on the South African dance floor, and the image of a world where ''Whites Only'' leave two black men dancing together in an act of solidarity. It is a typically Fugardian oscillation between hope and despair, qualified only by the realisation that ''Master Harold'' grows up to be Athol Fugard and that the play itself is an act of atonement and moral reparation to the memory of Sam and ''H.D.F.''—the Black and the White fathers to whom it is dedicated.

It would clearly be misleading to claim that *''Master Harold'' . . . and the boys* addresses the growing complexity of apartheid politics in the South Africa of 1987. It is a ''history'' play—a *family* ''history'' written, like O'Neill's *Long Day's Journey into Night,* as an exorcism of the tormented ghosts of his childhood; but it is also a phase of South African ''history'', an anachronistic backward glace to a time when black men in their stoical optimism still dreamed of social change and when white boys might have been able to grasp the implications of ''Whites Only'' benches and choose to walk away from them. It deals with a rite of passage clumsily negotiated, a failure of love in a personal power-struggle with political implications. Alan Paton, writing in the same time-frame of history, projects a similar vision of tenuous hope for racial harmony—and also the dreadful consequences of its deferment. Msimangu, the black priest in *Cry, the Beloved Country,* speaks the powerful subtext beneath the action of Fugard's play:

> But there is only one thing that has power completely, and that is love. Because when a man loves, he seeks no power, and therefore he has power. I see only one hope for our country, and that is when white men and black men, desiring neither power nor money, but desiring only the good of their country, come together to work for it.
>
> He was grave and silent, and then he said sombrely, I have one great fear in my heart, that one day when they are turned to loving, they will find we are turned to hating.

Source: Errol Durbach, ''*Master Harold . . . and the Boys:* Athol Fugard and the Psychopathology of Apartheid'' in *Modern Drama,* Volume XXX, no. 2, December, 1987, pp. 505–13.

SOURCES

Brustein, Robert. Review of *''Master Harold''* in the *New Republic,* Vol. 186, No. 25, June 23, 1982, pp. 30-31.

Colleran, Jeanne. *Modern Drama,* Vol. XXXIII, no. 1, March, 1990, pp. 82-92.

Crow, Brian. ''*Master Harold . . . and the Boys*'' in *International Dictionary of Theatre,* Vol. 1: *Plays,* edited by Mark Hawkins-Dady, St. James Press, 1992.

Durbach, Errol, ''*'Master Harold'. . .and the Boys:* Athol Fugard and the Psychopathology of Apartheid'' in *Modern Drama,* Vol. XXX, no. 4, December 1987, pp. 505-13.

Gray, Stephen. *New Theatre Quarterly,* Vol. VI, no. 21, February, 1990, pp. 25-30.

FURTHER READING

Brians, Paul. ''Athol Fugard: *'Master Harold' . . . and the Boys''* at http://www.wsu.edu:8080/~brians/anglophone/fugard.html.

A website containing notes to the Penguin Plays edition of *''Master Harold'' . . . and the Boys* (1984); organized by page number.

Mallaby, Sebastian. *After Apartheid: The Future of South Africa,* Times Books, 1992.

Polarized by decades of apartheid, black and white South Africans now face the challenges of racial coexistence and economic growth in a new, multiracial nation. This incisive examination of the radical consequences of apartheid's demise offers a penetrating look at South Africa on the brink of racial and historic change.

''Underdog's South African Independent Film Site'' at http://www.safilm.org.za/.

A home page with links to Film Festivals, Film Schools, Showdata's SA Film Site, and other independent South African media artists.

Walder, Dennis. *Athol Fugard,* Macmillan, 1984.

Walder is a South African educator and critic. His book offers analysis of Fugard's career up through 1984 and includes considerable discussion of *''Master Harold.''*

Private Lives

NOEL COWARD

1930

Private Lives is considered a prime example of the sophisticated comedies of Noel Coward, one of the most-prominent dramatists of his era. An overwhelming critical and commercial success when it was first produced in 1930, *Private Lives* remains a standard of repertory and non-professional theatre companies everywhere and has entertained audiences for well over half a century.

The action of the play concerns a divorced couple, Elyot and Amanda, who meet on their respective honeymoons to second spouses. They realize that they are still in love with each other and should never have divorced; they abandon their new spouses and run off together, though they are soon caught up in the same violent arguments that originally plagued their stormy marriage. This simple, somewhat contrived situation provides all the structure Coward requires to display his eccentric wit and deft comedic stagecraft, which are considered the main strengths of the play. The protagonists lampoon the hypocrisies and pretensions of modern manners and social conventions and seek true love regardless of the cost to their reputations. Once they free themselves from the ''outside world,'' however, their inner passions and jealousies (their ''private lives'') consume them, leaving them trapped in an inescapable cycle of love and hate.

Expressed in such terms, the plot resembles that of a tragedy, but Coward (who acted the role of Elyot himself in the early productions) fashions

from it a fast-paced comedy, moving from misfortune to full-blown absurdity before tragedy has time to take hold. Prone to cynicism and irreverence, his glamorous upper-class characters seem incapable of taking much of anything seriously for long—a condition which usually proves contagious for the audience as well. Often accused of wasting his evident talent on superficial entertainments, Coward firmly believed the theatre existed for people's amusement, not to teach or reform them. On these terms, *Private Lives* is considered one of the enduring successes of modern comedic theatre.

Noel Coward as he prepares to leave his home for a royal function at St. James's Palace, London, 1937

AUTHOR BIOGRAPHY

Noel Peirce Coward is celebrated as one of the most prominent and prolific talents of the modern British theater. His witty, sophisticated comedies were immensely popular in the early part of the twentieth century and have been widely performed ever since. A theatrical jack-of-all-trades, Coward made his mark not only as a playwright but as an actor, director, producer, songwriter, and lyricist; he also wrote novels, short stories, screenplays, and several volumes of autobiography, as well as being a popular night-club entertainer. In a career that spanned over a half-century, he was associated with most of the leading personalities of the London stage. A show business legend and renowned *raconteur* (a person skilled in telling amusing stories or anecdotes), Coward was known to his contemporaries as much for his off-stage personality as for his many professional accomplishments.

Born on December 16, 1899, in Teddington-on-Thames, Middlesex, England, Coward was drawn to the stage in early childhood. Encouraged by his parents, he made his professional acting debut at the age of twelve and had begun writing plays and songs by the time he was twenty. In 1925, his reputation as a playwright was established by the hit comedy *Hay Fever.* Over the next twenty years he produced a string of critical and commercial successes, including *Bitter Sweet* (1929), *Private Lives* (1930), *Design for Living* (1933), *Tonight at Eight-Thirty* (1936), *Blithe Spirit* (1941), and *Present Laughter* (1942).

While the majority of Coward's work consists of satiric "comedies of manners" (dramatic works that poke fun at the manners and fashions of a particular social class) and musical revues, his style also encompassed elements of melodrama, modern psychological theatrics, and social drama. During World War II, he wrote two plays celebrating British nationalism and ideals (*This Happy Breed* [1943] and *Peace in Our Time* [1947]) and the film *In Which We Serve,* a tribute to the British Royal Navy, which he co-directed with noted film director David Lean (*Lawrence of Arabia, The Bridge on the River Kwai*).

After the War, Coward's popularity faded somewhat, due in part to changing tastes among audiences and critics; though he remained a prominent figure in the theatrical world, his slightly-darker stage comedies of this period (including *South Sea Bubble* [1951] and *Nude with Violin* [1956]) failed to elicit the same enthusiasm as his lighter pre-war triumphs. While his work for the stage diminished, he continued to write short fiction, and his 1960 novel, *Pomp and Circumstance,* was a bestseller. His published diaries and reminiscences also found a wide audience, particularly an early autobiography, *Present Indicative* (1937) and its sequel, *Future Indefinite* (1954).

Coward died of a heart attack on March 26, 1973, in Blue Harbor, Jamaica. Among his many honors, he was given the New York Drama Critics Circle Award (Best Foreign Play, 1942, for *Blithe Spirit*), a Special Academy Award from the Academy of Motion Picture Arts and Sciences (1942, for *In Which We Serve*), and a Special Tony Award from the League of American Theatres and Producers in 1970. Coward was knighted in 1970 and memorialized in Westminster Abbey in 1984.

PLOT SUMMARY

Act I

The setting is the terrace of an elegant hotel on the French Riviera; two separate suites open onto it, from either side of the stage. This simple situation contains a number of remarkable coincidences, as the audience quickly learns in a series of brief, mirror-image episodes. Each suite is occupied by a honeymooning couple, fresh from the altar: Elyot and Sibyl Chase on one side, and Victor and Amanda Prynne on the other. Elyot and Amanda were each previously married, a matter of some anxiety to their new spouses; in fact, they happen to have been married to each other, a three-year union they both describe as an intolerable round of violent arguments and passionate jealousies. Five years after their divorce, each is starting off on a new life, with what seems to be a more stable and manageable partner. Adding to the coincidence, they happen to have married at the same time . . . and to have chosen the same hotel for their honeymoon . . . and to have been assigned adjoining suites.

Each couple makes an appearance on the terrace, then goes back inside, in a series of alternating episodes and near-misses that establishes the complex situation. The honeymoons are not starting well, for Sibyl and Victor each persist in asking about their new spouses' first marriages. Annoyed, Elyot and Amanda both profess to be far happier with their new mates but also give indications of already becoming bored by them. Finally, Amanda and Elyot notice each other, without coming face-to-face, and react with panic. They rush to their spouses, each demanding to leave the hotel immediately, but neither Sibyl nor Victor will agree to such a sudden change in their honeymoon plans. The result is each new couple's "first quarrel," with Victor stalking off to the bar and Sibyl to the hotel casino. Left alone, Elyot and Amanda finally confront each other again.

Sharing the cocktails their spouses have abandoned, they behave coolly, making civil small talk, inquiring about the new spouses, toasting each other's happiness, and light-heartedly reminiscing over their disastrous marriage. The hotel orchestra (playing in the garden below the terrace) strikes up an old love song, and Amanda sings along while Elyot watches her intently. Their reactions suggest that it had been "their song" when they were a couple; when the music ends, Amanda is fighting back tears. After an awkward moment, their reminiscences grow more regretful. They ascribe their marital fireworks to having been "ridiculously over in love." "To hell with love," Amanda vows; love had led them into "selfishnessness, cruelty, hatred, possessiveness, petty jealousy." And yet, she observes, here they are, "starting afresh with two quite different people. In love all over again, aren't we?" Elyot fails to answer at first, then gives the answer she doesn't want to hear: "No. . . . We're not in love all over again, and you know it." Saying goodnight, he turns abruptly back toward his suite.

Amanda is panic-stricken, and calls him back. The moment, the music, and the memories have clearly rekindled their former passion, but she refuses to face that fact, asking him to divert her with small talk until she can pull herself together. The effort fails miserably, however, and they soon confirm that they are—and have always been—in love. After some negotiations, they agree to elope immediately, abandoning the people they have just married and escaping to an apartment Amanda keeps in Paris. Worried that they will soon ruin their love all over again with their arguing, Amanda insists on a promise "never to quarrel again," to be enforced by a code-phrase, "Solomon Isaacs." When they feel a fight developing, one or the other will say "Solomon Isaacs," a signal for two minutes of silence ("with an option of renewal") in which to cool down. Agreeing to the pact, they escape. The act ends with the jilted Victor and Sibyl returning to the terrace, discovering their common plight, and trying to absorb it all as they drink the cocktails Elyot and Amanda have left behind.

Act II

A few days later, the scene picks up the fugitive couple in Amanda's well-appointed Paris flat, savoring their sudden happiness. They have sent the maid home and are relaxing in cozy domestic bliss. Throughout this Act, their rambling conversations reveal the mixed emotions of their situation. The ever-shifting flow of talk runs into three alternating streams: the exchange of romantic endearments, coupled with witty banter that parodies aristocratic manners; the revival of ''old scores'' from their marriage, leading to arguments that are only headed off by the invocation of Solomon Isaacs (who is soon abbreviated to ''Sollocks'' for economy's sake); and anxious speculation about the future—what to do when Victor and Sibyl catch up to them—and whether they will make their love work out this time around. Soon Elyot grows passionately romantic, but Amanda is not in the mood. His resentment at her refusal escalates into a battle that is just barely contained with an urgent ''triple Sollocks.''

In the calm following this storm, Elyot sits down to the piano and begins playing idly. Amanda joins him and they sing several old songs together, concluding with ''their'' song from the terrace scene. The sudden ring of the telephone breaks their reverie. Although it turns out to be a wrong number, their first, terrified thought is that it is Victor and Sibyl. ''What shall we do if they suddenly walk in on us?,'' Elyot asks; ''Behave exquisitely,'' Amanda replies airily. But the phone call has shaken her composure; as she grows somber (speculating that happiness like theirs cannot last), Elyot earnestly tells her not to be serious. He urges her to ''be flippant'' and ''laugh at everything''—including themselves, their love, and the inevitability of death. ''Let's be superficial and pity the poor philosophers,'' he rhapsodizes; ''Let's blow trumpets and squeakers, and enjoy the party as much as we can, like very small, quite idiotic school-children.''

A tender moment follows but soon another ''skeleton'' from the past is being tossed around, an affair Elyot had suspected during their marriage. Tempers rise quickly, until Amanda calls him a ''ridiculous ass,'' and turns on the record-player to shut him out. Elyot turns it off, and a battle for the machine ensues. Elyot hastily calls for the truce of ''Sollocks,'' but this time the skirmish will not be contained. ''Sollocks yourself,'' Amanda cries furiously, smashing the phonograph record over his head. ''You spiteful little beast,'' he answers, slapping her in the face. They settle down to a full-scale brawl, with lamps and vases flying, furniture overturned, unrestrained verbal assaults, and slapstick choreography. As they roll on the floor in what Coward describes as ''paroxysms of rage,'' Victor and Sibyl enter through the front door, and gape at the combatants in silent shock. The struggle continues until Amanda knocks Elyot down, rushes through a side door, and slams it behind her. He jumps up, runs into the room opposite hers, and slams the door. As Victor and Sibyl creep inside and sink wordlessly onto the sofa, the curtain falls.

Act III

At 8:30 the next morning, amid the debris from last night's battle, Victor sleeps on a sofa blocking the doorway to Amanda's room, while Sibyl is similarly encamped at Elyot's door. Louise, the maid, arrives for work, waking the jilted spouses. Amanda soon emerges from her room with a packed suitcase and heads for the door; cut off from escape, she is ''gracefully determined to rise above the situation.'' Acting the role of the perfect hostess, she arranges for Louise to bring breakfast out. Elyot completes the group and is upbraided by Victor for his ''flippant'' attitude towards the situation; soon they are on the verge of coming to blows, and Amanda and Sibyl withdraw to another room. Elyot refuses to fight, however; he argues that it would prove nothing and would only satisfy the ''primitive feminine instincts'' of the women, who want to be fought over. Victor tries to discuss the legal details of their situation, but Elyot storms off to his room, calling him a ''rampaging gas bag.''

Sibyl soon joins Elyot in his room, leaving Victor and Amanda to negotiate a settlement. At first, they agree that Victor will sue for divorce immediately while Amanda exiles herself in some foreign country. Victor soon softens his position, however, offering to live apart but delay a formal divorce to protect her reputation. Sibyl and Elyot emerge and announce that they have reached a similar decision: she will not divorce him for a year.

Louise brings breakfast, and the four settle down awkwardly to dine. Amanda makes light conversation in an effort to smooth over the discomfort, but Elyot will not play along: he mocks her ''proper'' manners, and soon disrupts her composure. As she ''chokes violently,'' Victor again assails

Elyot's flippancy, while Sibyl defends her husband. Soon Victor and Sibyl are arguing lustily; for three days they've been getting on each other's nerves and their anger now comes spilling out, as Elyot and Amanda watch in amazement. As the argument escalates, they laugh to themselves, and Elyot blows Amanda a kiss across the table. Their spouses don't even notice as they rise and walk silently to the front door, hand-in-hand. Sibyl slaps Victor, he shakes her violently, and Elyot and Amanda, with their suitcases, go smilingly out the door, as the curtain falls.

CHARACTERS

Elyot Chase

The witty and cynical Elyot is the male lead, whose love/hate relationship with Amanda forms the centerpiece of *Private Lives.* Though his occupation (if any) is unidentified, he is wealthy and fashionable, accustomed to luxury, and self-indulgent. In conversation, his habit is to ''be flippant'' and mock traditional social conventions; if he has a philosophy, it lies in his refusal to ever be serious, in defiance of ''all the futile moralists who try to make life unbearable.'' He holds to no Great Truths; everything is ''nonsense'' in the long run, nothing is eternal, and the intelligent response is to live for the moment and savor all pleasures, to ''be superficial and pity the poor philosophers'' who search for higher meanings and moral truths.

For all his eloquent rebellion, however, Elyot has his insecurities, and is not unaffected by social expectations. At the play's beginning, he has willingly entered into a conventional marriage; though it appears doomed and promises to be unfulfilling for him, he is resigned (before meeting Amanda again) to acting out the shallow role of husband. Confronted by Victor in Act III, he doesn't defend his actions, admitting that he is completely in the wrong, and that his flippancy is meant ''to cover a very real embarrassment.'' Though he is wise to its hypocrisies, Elyot is not immune to society's demands—just as he is not immune to his attraction for Amanda, despite the bitter history of their marriage, and the violent jealousies they inspire in each other.

Sibyl Chase

Sibyl is Elyot's second wife, seven years younger than her husband; but although she is the newlywed ''Mrs. Chase,'' she is quickly thrown together with Victor Prynne by their shared fate. From the end of the first Act, she and Victor become a kind of ''couple,'' traveling together as they seek justice from their wandering spouses. As a couple, they balance the central pairing of Elyot and Amanda, and while they are the ''wronged parties,'' they are meant to receive little sympathy from the audience. As Coward has sketched them, they contrast unfavorably in every sense with the passionate, witty couple at the heart of the action.

In comparison to Amanda, Sibyl is shallow, inexperienced, and unreflective, dutifully acting out her social roles with a false, exaggerated femininity. As the blushing bride, she is bubbly and romantic, deferring to her husband and denying any intention to ''manage'' or run his life. Cast as the abandoned wife, she gives way to dramatic tears and self-pity, while demonstrating an ability to ''manage'' both Victor and Elyot in order to get her way. Coward leaves her character relatively undeveloped; like Victor, she is a superficial foil for the sophisticated protagonists, Elyot and Amanda.

Louise

Louise is the maid at Amanda's Paris flat, a minor character; she appears briefly in Act III, primarily to serve breakfast to the four protagonists.

Amanda Prynne

As Coward's heroine, Amanda is sharp-witted and glamorous, strong-willed and passionate. By abandoning Victor (and by being sexually active while unmarried), she defies the conventional, reserved, and subordinate role for her gender—especially as dictated by the society of the first half of the twentieth century. Her relationship with Elyot, though hopelessly plagued by their hateful bickering, also offers a more equal—and honest—alliance than that with the stodgy Victor: she and Elyot are intellectual equals and comfortable companions, at least in the moments between their violent conflicts.

Though she and Elyot mock the formalities of aristocratic manners, Amanda is well-versed in social conventions and their power to smooth over conflicts. If Elyot's philosophy is to ''be flippant,'' hers is to ''behave exquisitely''; like Elyot's, Amanda's strategy serves to cover the embarrassment of facing the consequences of their actions and to distance herself from the uncomfortable realities of their volatile relationship.

Victor Prynne

Steadfastly conventional and self-consciously masculine, Victor is the conservative counterpart to Elyot's rebellious flippancy. Habitually ''serious,'' proper, and moderate in all things, he is paternally protective of Amanda; yet his formal, dignified posturing seems to cover a bland and passionless nature. When he confronts Elyot in Act III, he strikes a belligerent pose, but Elyot sees through his blustering threats, calling him ''all fuss and fume, one of these cotton-wool Englishmen''; unable to defend his own position, Elyot nonetheless expresses contempt for Victor: ''[I]f you had a spark of manliness in you, you'd have shot me.'' In defense of his and Sibyl's ''honor,'' Victor presents a caricature of manly chivalry, which evaporates completely when it is confronted and questioned by Elyot: his violence is easily neutralized by Elyot's clever argumentation, but when his temper is roused, he is not above striking the woman he claims to defend. Like Sibyl, he is an underdeveloped character, a dull stereotype who serves as a background to highlight the brilliance of the unconventional protagonists.

THEMES

Public vs. Private Life

As a ''comedy of manners,'' *Private Lives* deals with the conventions and social rituals by which a person presents their ''public'' self to the world—and with the ''private'' passions and motivations that lie beneath the veneer of etiquette and respectability. The title comes from a speech Amanda makes early in the first Act. ''I think very few people are completely normal, deep down in their private lives,'' she muses. ''It all depends on a combination of circumstances;'' given the right conditions, ''there's no knowing what one mightn't do.'' She soon illustrates the point by impulsively running off with Elyot, in contradiction to law, social taboo, and the marriage vows she has just taken—yet in accordance with her personal needs and private desires.

MEDIA ADAPTATIONS

- A film adaptation of *Private Lives* was released in December, 1931, by Metro-Goldwyn-Mayer. It starred Norma Shearer and Robert Montgomery as Amanda and Elyot, with Reginald Denny and Una Merkel as Victor and Sibyl. While it retained most of Coward's story and dialogue, director Sidney Franklin also made significant alterations: extending the ''set-up'' in Act I while compressing the action of Acts II and III; and having the lovers escape not to a Paris flat but to a Swiss chalet. The film is available on videocassette through MGM/UA Home Video.

Victor and Sibyl represent the traditional, ''normal'' modes of behavior for their gender-roles. He is conservative and reliable, moderate in all things, and paternally protective of his bride; she is bubbly and romantic, given to dramatic emotional displays, expecting (and needing) to be ''taken care of'' by her man. Coward sketches them as shallow, comic exaggerations of their types: Victor is a stodgy, blustering charade of ''rugged grandeur,'' while Sibyl is a coquettish ''flapper,'' flighty, empty-headed, and demanding. Neither appears capable of an original thought, and the sympathies of the audience are clearly meant for Elyot and Amanda, in their rebellion against the restrictive bonds of convention. Glamorous and witty, Elyot and Amanda lampoon ''respectable'' manners mercilessly and dare to follow their hearts, regardless of the social consequences.

These appealing ''social outlaws'' do not live happily ever after, however. Once free to ''be themselves,'' they are soon fighting like animals, despite their best intentions and the great love they have for each other. On one side, Coward presents social conventions as silly and restrictive, causing people to repress their ''private lives'' or urges and behave hypocritically. But he also suggests that they have an important, and necessary, ''civilizing'' effect; without them, the worst of human nature

TOPICS FOR FURTHER STUDY

- Choose an episode of a television "situation comedy," and compare its dialogue to that of *Private Lives.* In what ways do they differ? How is the humor in Coward's play achieved in contrast to the humor of the sitcom?
- Coward is often compared to an earlier British dramatist known for his satiric wit, Oscar Wilde. Read Wilde's *The Importance of Being Earnest* (1895) and compare and contrast it with *Private Lives.*
- Assume that Victor and Sybil divorce their spouses after the play ends and marry each other. Write a brief description of their lives together. Try to employ dialogue similar to that between Elyot and Amanda in Act II.
- What do you think of Coward's view of marriage? What are your personal opinions on the subject? Support your arguments with examples of married couples you have known.

arises and people become slaves to violent passions and petty jealousies. Manners and rules give life a structure, helping to manage and mediate the inevitable conflicts that arise when people interact.

For all their rebellion and mockery, Elyot and Amanda are fluent in social ritual and deploy it strategically throughout the play: in their pact that the magic words "Solomon Isaacs" will halt their quarreling, for example, and in Amanda's resolve to "behave exquisitely" when Victor and Sibyl catch up with them. In Act III, she does exactly that, acting the perfect hostess amid the debris of her brawl with Elyot, who admires her cool ability to "carry off the most embarrassing situation with such tact, and delicacy." Confronted at last by Sybil and Victor, Elyot observes that the four of them have "no prescribed etiquette to fall back upon"; in such a case, his habitual response is cynical "flippancy," while Amanda relies on the very social conventions they have both been ridiculing. In the end, the wronged-but-ridiculous spouses are beaten at their own game; the outlaws escape the (public) consequences of their transgressions, at least temporarily, while their conventional counterparts descend to the same savage passions that have plagued Elyot and Amanda's stormy love.

Love and Passion

Like the protagonists in a sentimental romance, Elyot and Amanda seem meant for each other, drawn together by a deep, inescapable love that overrides all other concerns (and common sense). Coward uses them, however, to refute the conventions of romantic love: instead of bringing contentment and fulfillment, "True Love" has the couple locked in a passionate death-grip, tossing them helplessly between the extremes of love and hate, pleasure and pain.

Having married for love and found it a disaster, Amanda and Elyot try to make "safer" choices in their second marriages; each envisions a steadier, if less-passionate alliance, with a more-manageable, less-sophisticated partner. Elyot tells Sibyl that love should be "kind, and undramatic. Something steady and sweet, to smooth out your nerves when you're tired. Something tremendously cozy; and unflurried by scenes and jealousies." Similarly, Amanda assures Victor that their love will last, because she loves him more "calmly" than she loved Elyot. But the spark of the old couple's reunion instantly reveals these platitudes as pure self-deception: very often, love is not "calm" or easily-managed but an uncontrollable force that disarms self-control, dispels reason, and sweeps people away with the force of its passion. As embodied by Amanda and Elyot, love can be both a blessing and a curse; it intoxicates and elates but can just as quickly lead to "selfishness, cruelty, hatred, possessiveness, [and] petty jealousy." "To hell with love," Amanda vows—just before she risks everything for it, once again. She and Elyot are veterans in the battle of the sexes, wise to love's traps and minefields, but their wisdom fails to bring them the least bit of immunity from the pitfalls of love.

STYLE

While Coward is known for his witty dialogue, his work is relatively short on quotable "punch-lines" or one-liners, the kind of which define the comedic style of writers like playwright Neil Simon (*The Odd Couple*) and filmmaker Woody Allen (*Annie Hall*). The humor of *Private Lives* depends greatly on its expert stagecraft and carefully-balanced construction. In his introduction to the anthology *Play Parade,* Coward modestly describes the play as ''a reasonably well-constructed duologue for two experienced performers, with a couple of extra puppets thrown in to assist the plot and provide contrast.'' This self-deprecating assessment points to two of the playwright's strengths: his awareness of the abilities of the ''experienced performers'' with whom he worked, and his attention to contrast and symmetry.

Coward used actors he knew; he often tailored his fictional characters to match his thespians personalities and physical traits, and he paced his dialogue to fit these actors' timing and delivery. (*Private Lives* was specifically written for Gertrude Lawrence, who essayed Amanda, and Coward himself; the pair had worked together often before starring in the play's first production.) As Enoch Brater noted in the *Dictionary of Literary Biography,* Coward's language ''is not by itself inherently funny; what makes it effective on stage is the way it has been designed as a cue for performance.'' The shifting moods and volatile chemistry of Elyot and Amanda's relationship are carefully orchestrated through their conversation. While their clever dialogue ''works'' reasonably well on the page, it is difficult to read the text without also envisioning the give-and-take of gestures, expressions, and voice inflections (not to mention the broad physicality of the slapstick fights) that mark its performance. These are large, ''meaty,'' and demanding roles, characters meant to capture and hold the attention of the audience; for all the ''literary'' nature of their conversation, their every nuance has been fashioned with an eye toward the visual, toward a realization on the living stage.

Coward freely acknowledged that the play's secondary characters, Sibyl and Victor, were relatively insubstantial (''little better than ninepins,'' he wrote in *Play Parade,* ''lightly wooden, and only there at all in order to be knocked down repeatedly and stood up again.'') Although they are the hapless ''butts'' of Coward's humor and never threaten to outshine the protagonists, their deployment is crucial to the play's success. Their conventional notions of marriage provide a contrast to the risky, emotional alliance between Elyot and Amanda; in turn, the protagonists' passion, glamour and intelligence are heightened by the bland personalities of their counterparts.

In the tightly-scripted first Act, Coward achieves another kind of balance, through the individual scenes of the two newlywed couples, which lead up to Elyot and Amanda's reunion. In alternating appearances, the couples are presented as mirror-images of one another, separately enacting the same scenarios with an exaggerated symmetry, down to the pacing and content of their dialogue. The audience is quickly cued to the similarities between Sibyl and Victor—and between Amanda and Elyot. Long before they switch partners, each pair (Sibyl/Victor, Amanda/Elyot) is revealed as a kind of ''couple,'' having more in common with each other than they do with their new spouses. The jilting of Sibyl and Victor is a ''scandal,'' but Coward has already enlisted the audience's sympathy for it; dramatically speaking, the rearranged ''couples'' make far more sense, and their re-shuffling allows each character to escape from what would clearly have been a disastrous mismatch.

A comparable symmetry marks the play's ending: as Elyot and Amanda sneak off together (echoing their sudden disappearance in Act I), their conventional, ''respectable'' spouses are locked in an escalating argument, which mirrors Elyot and Amanda's fireworks in Act II. Thrown together by circumstances, Sibyl and Victor have truly become a ''couple,'' however temporary, and their fight serves to make that fact official. Given a few years, they might become well-matched, veteran combatants, like their wayward spouses. Their argument, and Elyot and Amanda's sly escape, may each be humorous in themselves, but the juxtaposition heightens the effect considerably, making a comic moment resonate with the themes Coward has developed throughout the play.

HISTORICAL CONTEXT

Throughout the 1920s, and particularly during the Great Depression of the 1930s, many of the most popular plays and films were light comedies set

COMPARE & CONTRAST

- **1930:** Astronomers at the Lowell Observatory in Flagstaff, Arizona, discover a ninth planet in the solar system and name it Pluto. It is the first ''new'' planet since Neptune was sighted in 1846. The discovery is made with mankind's most-advanced tool for space exploration: a telescope.

  Today: Humans have walked on the moon, first landing in 1969. Unmanned spacecraft have explored the outer reaches of the solar system, mapping the surfaces of planets known only as points of light in 1930. The satellite-mounted Hubbell telescope was launched into space in the mid-1990s, providing astronomers with the most in-depth space pictures to date. No probes have yet made close observations of Pluto, though in 1978, the planet was discovered to have a moon, named Charon.

- **1930:** The world's population reaches two billion, with the great majority of people living in rural areas.

  Today: Global population passed the five billion mark during the 1980s, and continues to grow; more than fifty percent of the populace now live in towns and cities.

- **1930:** In India, Mahatma Ghandi begins a civil disobedience campaign in protest of British colonial rule, by leading his followers on a 165-mile march.

  Today: Ghandi's efforts drew worldwide attention to the cause of Indian independence, which was finally achieved in 1947. His doctrines of passive resistance and civil disobedience helped inspire the strategies employed by the American civil rights movement of the 1950s and 1960s, and influenced the philosophy of Dr. Martin Luther King, Jr. Such peaceful practices continue to be employed by contemporary protesters.

---

among the wealthy, privileged members of ''high society.'' When such works are associated with the Depression, their appeal is usually ascribed to the audience's need for escape from their grim circumstances, if only briefly, and only in imagination: they offered glamorous fantasies of unimaginable luxury, to audiences who were struggling to secure the bare necessities. Given its upper-class setting and its appearance in the year after the 1929 New York stock market crash, *Private Lives* might appear to be such a work of Depression-era ''escapism.'' Yet when the play was written, the full and lasting effects of the economic crisis were not yet widely recognized, either in Europe or America. While it may be classed as light entertainment, intended more for diversion than enlightenment, *Private Lives* belongs to an earlier tradition, associated with the social transformations of the ''Roaring Twenties.'' In this tradition, the escapades of the ''idle rich'' were not only glamorous and amusing but provided a way to address ongoing controversies over manners and morals.

The 1920s are usually characterized, both in Europe and in America, as a turbulent decade in which established truths of all kinds came under question and the traditional bounds of social conduct were widely challenged. After the unprecedented destruction of World War I, with its enormous toll in human life, many felt disillusioned with ''the old order.'' Many felt that the common practices of the nineteenth century yielded years of senseless slaughter and economic hardship. At the same time, science was increasingly seen as a challenge to traditional religious beliefs (a fact borne out by the Scopes Monkey Trial, which pitted the theories of divine human creation and evolution against each other). Rapid technological advances (a continuance of the industrial revolution that was begun in the latter half of the 1800s) were changing

A scene from a 1940 production of Private Lives starring Gertrude Lawrence as Amanda, Coward as Elyot, Adrienne Allen as Sibyl, and Lawrence Olivier as Victor

daily life in many ways, suggesting that a new, ''modern'' world was coming into being—one that would require new values and new standards of behavior.

While the United States had outlawed the sale and consumption of alcohol in 1920 (the eighteenth amendment to the Constitution, often referred to as simply Prohibition), the law was widely defied. Criminal elements rose to supply the illegal commodity so many citizens demanded. Many historians credit the birth of powerful organized crime in the U.S. to the illicit alcohol trade; crime bosses came to significant prominence and wealth during this period, the most notable being Al Capone. Too late to curb the tide of organized crime or the American public's increasing pleasure in moderate disobedience, prohibition was repealed in 1933.

Social standards of the Victorian era were also challenged on several fronts, particularly in regard to the changing status of women, who were demanding and taking on public roles traditionally denied them, including voting, land ownership, and careers. The alleged immorality of ''the younger generation'' became a matter of intense scrutiny, centered on behaviors ranging from smoking, drinking, and dancing to sexual promiscuity; the image of amoral ''flaming youth,'' celebrated in F. Scott Fitzgerald's bestselling novel, *This Side of Paradise* (1920), was the subject of public controversy throughout the early Twenties. The stereotypes of the young female ''flapper'' (young women who dressed suggestively and indulged in excessive socializing) and the illicit underworld ''speakeasy'' (establishments that served contraband liquor) suggested a revolution in public attitudes and a momentous change in moral standards. Depending on one's viewpoint, such sensations in popular culture represented either a long-overdue liberation from obsolete, restrictive standards, or the catastrophic decline of civilization itself.

One of Fitzgerald's most famous aphorisms is that ''the very rich are different from you and I''; that difference apparently creates a dual fascination in the larger culture, a mix of envious admiration and moralistic disapproval. ''You and I'' seem to enjoy fantasizing about the conspicuous luxury of the upper classes, while still cherishing the belief that a moderate lifestyle is more safe and secure; wealth cannot truly buy happiness—and may even be an obstacle to personal fulfillment. In their pursuit of fashionable sensation and self-indulgent consumption, the ''idle rich'' seem immune from traditional moral codes: they can afford to risk public disapproval by defying convention, though they are often made to pay for their excesses in the long run. Thus, the world of the wealthy can serve as a ''safe'' stage for the consideration of moral questions, for it presents a ''special case,'' distanced from the conditions of the everyday; the wealthy are licensed to behave in ways that might be unacceptable for characters with whom the audience identified more closely.

While Amanda and Elyot's casual attitude toward divorce and marital fidelity may seem unremarkable to modern audiences, it represented a controversial ''new morality'' in its time. Audience members could either admire their liberated, ''progressive'' outlook, or else enjoy the crisis and conflict that result from their ''immoral'' actions. Though Coward presents them as glamorous and sophisticated, their faults are also apparent, and they pointedly do not ''live happily ever after''; regardless of one's moral standards, it is difficult to either idolize or demonize them without reservations.

While its sexual references are few and quite indirect, *Private Lives* was considered somewhat suggestive, though well within the accepted standards of the day. In terms of the prevailing morality, it was both mildly titillating and ultimately reassuring. Had Elyot and Amanda been working- or middle-class characters, their attitudes would have been more controversial, and their story would seem less a proper subject for light-hearted entertainment. In the alluring, unreal world of ''high society,'' however, audiences could approach themes that might otherwise have hit uncomfortably close to home.

CRITICAL OVERVIEW

Private Lives was a runaway hit when it debuted in 1930, and the play has remained popular in revivals ever since. In the initial production, Coward himself starred as Elyot opposite Gertrude Lawrence's Amanda. The play was produced at London's Phoenix Theatre, opening in September, 1930, after preview runs in Edinburgh, Birmingham, Manchester, and Southsea. The *Daily Mail* reported that tickets to the three-month engagement were in great demand, ''though the piece is meant neither to instruct, to improve, nor to uplift.'' In the *New York Times,* drama critic Charles Morgan called the play ''a remarkable tour de force,'' despite a story that was ''almost impudently insubstantial. . . . The speed, the impudence, the frothiness of [Coward's] dialogue are his salvation, and his performance is brilliant.'' After its New York debut, at the Times Square Theater in January of 1931, J. Brooks Atkinson of the *New York Times* found the essence of the play to be its ''well-bred petulance'' and ''cosmopolitan fatigue.'' ''Mr. Coward's talent for small things remains unimpaired,'' Atkinson reported; ''[he] has an impish wit, a genius for phrasemaking, and an engaging manner on the stage.'' Metro-Goldwyn-Mayer (MGM) quickly acquired the film rights to Coward's international sensation and had a feature adaptation (starring Robert Montgomery and Norma Shearer in the leads) in theaters by the end of 1931.

Subsequent critical assessments (both of *Private Lives* and of Coward's work in general) tend to follow the tone of these early reviews. While noting a lack of substance, of ''big ideas'' or grand themes, critics nonetheless acknowledge an abundance of style, wit, and comedic pacing; the result is taken not as ''Immortal Drama,'' but as highly-entertaining dramatic spectacle. Producing such work was

Coward's conscious intention; he once said he had "no great or beautiful thoughts" to express, and no particular desire to include such thoughts in his plays if he did have them. "The primary and dominant function of the theatre is to amuse people," he believed, "not to reform or edify them." His "smart" humor is prized for its eccentricity; as Atkinson observed of *Private Lives,* "Mr. Coward's wit is not ostentatious. He tucks it neatly away in pat phrases and subtle word combinations and smartly bizarre allusions." While satiric humor is a staple of his work, he is not usually considered to present any unified critique of society, or to advance a consistent, identifiable philosophy. For this reason, his characters and situations are often considered to be superficial, even trivial. His wit, however, is nearly always classed as "sophisticated," and his dialogue is praised for its intelligence and cleverness. Disdaining "high-brow" conceptions of art, Coward claimed not to be writing for posterity; yet his "talent for small things" has shown a remarkable staying-power, and his work has delighted audiences for several generations.

Private Lives remains a popular standard for repertory companies everywhere. After more than a half-century, it evidently retains its appeal for a wide audience. Major London revivals were staged in 1944, 1963, 1969 (a 70th birthday tribute for Coward at the Phoenix Theater), and 1980, marking its 50th anniversary. Tammy Grimes won a Tony Award for her performance as Amanda in a 1970 Broadway revival, and a 1983 production featured Richard Burton and Elizabeth Taylor.

CRITICISM

Tom Faulkner

Faulkner is a professional writer with a B.A. in English from Wayne State University. In this essay, he examines Coward's treatment of gender-roles and marriage.

As Noel Coward repeatedly insisted, *Private Lives* is a light comedy, intended to amuse and captivate its audience, rather than to teach moral lessons or advance a particular ideology. It is exactly the sort of popular work scholars may "murder to dissect:" to over-analyze its "deeper meanings" is to risk blinding ourselves to its glittering surfaces or sacrificing the light-hearted pleasures its author has carefully provided. Nonetheless, the lasting popularity of *Private Lives* indicates that it *does* have "something to say" beneath its eccentric, entertaining banter, something that has appealed to audiences for several generations now. Its many intriguing qualities include Coward's cynical perspective on the eternal "battle of the sexes" and an exploration of traditional gender-roles that can be seen to anticipate the social and sexual transformations of more recent years.

In this reading, Victor and Sibyl are cartoonish representatives of the traditional male and female roles: he is stolid and conservative, paternally wishing to "look after" his new wife; she is emotional and sentimental, fully expecting to be taken care of by her husband. Coward intentionally sketches these characters as dull and two-dimensional, thoroughly predictable in their blind embrace of society's expectations. In contrast, Elyot and Amanda are alluring rebels, who mock convention and follow their individual desires, despite the social disapproval they invite.

In historical terms, Coward can be said to dramatize the opposition between Victorian moral codes and such "modernist" doctrines as "free love," "companionate marriage," guilt-free divorce and female equality. These were among the catch-phrases of a widespread moral controversy at the time *Private Lives* was written; in different words, similar concerns have appeared in more recent debates over feminism, sexuality, and "family values" (a debate that reached a high point with former vice president Dan Quayle criticizing the sitcom *Murphy Brown* for a plotline that involved the title character becoming a single mother). Amanda and Elyot clearly represent the "progressive" moral position, in opposition to restrictive traditions. Yet in another sense they are firmly traditional; while they defy conventional notions of social respectability, they remain faithful to the dictates of another convention, that of romantic love. When Elyot and Amanda escape the legal bonds of their new marriages it is not to pursue a promiscuous lifestyle or to make a philosophical statement but to follow the stronger love between themselves: they are romantics following their own hearts regardless of the consequences, not revolutionaries who seek to overthrow all conventions.

Victor and Sibyl embrace the sterile, unequal terms of traditional marriage. Coward implies that, unlike their worldly and sophisticated partners, they lack the imagination to feel restricted by the artifi-

WHAT DO I READ NEXT?

- If you enjoy one play by Coward, the next logical step is to investigate his other works. *Design for Living* (1933), about a "progressive" romantic triangle, and *Blithe Spirit* (1941), about a man who is haunted by the meddling ghost of his first wife, share much of the style and sensibility of *Private Lives.*
- Frederick Lewis Allen's *Only Yesterday: An Informal History of the 1920s* (1931) and *Since Yesterday: The 1930s in America* (1940) are lively, readable histories of the twenties and thirties, respectively, written by a contemporary historian. They provide a useful survey of the major events of the years during which Coward achieved his widest fame.
- *The Amazing Mr. Noel Coward* (1933), by Peter Braybrooke, written soon after *Private Lives* appeared, is an enthusiastic celebration of Coward's talents. While far from objective, it vividly reflects the towering stature Coward attained in the popular theatre of the 1930s.

cial confines of their stereotypical gender-roles or the self-awareness to notice any conflict between their private desires and the public images they strive to maintain. It may be that they simply cannot conceive of any alternatives to the parts they have always expected to play. Amanda and Elyot, on the other hand, are too intelligent and self-aware to be satisfied for long in the confinement of a conventional marriage—even though they were both willing to enter into such an alliance before their youthful passion was rekindled. Their impulsive decision is a courageous (if selfish) search for a more fulfilling alternative, which allows them more equal roles. The traditional marriage represented by Victor and Sibyl is an unbalanced equation: either the man has full authority over his submissive wife or she "runs" him surreptitiously, bending him to her will while maintaining a dependent pose. Though it is marked by violent strife, Amanda and Elyot's precarious relationship is distinctly more honest and equal than the second marriages they had anticipated and truer to their individual "private lives" or desires.

"Private lives," however, turn out to be messy and volatile, requiring boundaries of some sort to keep from breaking out in primitive, passionate conflict. While this psychological truth is evident in Elyot and Amanda's love/hate relationship, it applies equally to Victor and Sibyl, whose repressed passions come spilling out at the end of Act III, echoing the wild skirmishes between the play's central couple. Confused and distraught, lacking a "prescribed etiquette to fall back upon," they drop their "respectable" poses, and soon engage in the very behavior which they found so shocking and reprehensible in Elyot and Amanda. As Amanda observes in the play's signature speech, few of us are "completely normal" beneath our public roles, even those like Sibyl and Victor who seem most tediously normal; when "the right spark is struck, there's no knowing what one mightn't do."

By traditional standards, Elyot and Amanda's previous marriage and divorce, as well as their troubled reunion, are proof that they are "incompatible" as marriage partners. Yet they seem to be made for each other and to be far more compatible as a couple than they are with their new spouses. The problem with their first marriage, they agree, was that they loved each other too much; their romantic passion brought out other passions, and they became "two violent acids bubbling about in a nasty little matrimonial bottle." In their second marriages, they have overcompensated for their bitter experience, seeking to avoid the problem by marrying people with whom they are clearly *not* in love. Apparently, they have convinced themselves that these unions can last, precisely because they feel no passionate attachment to their partners: there is utterly no danger of loving too much.

When Amanda and Elyot's passion for each other is awakened, however, such a safe, lukewarm relationship is no longer an acceptable compromise—though a satisfying, long-term marriage seems no more possible than it was their first time around. Early in Act II, Amanda offers a different diagnosis of their troubles, targeting not love but marriage itself: "I believe it was just the fact of our being married, and clamped together publicly, that wrecked us before." Marriage is claustrophobic, a "nasty little bottle" that contains passion under pressure, building until it explodes. To Coward's sensibility, it is love and marriage that are incompatible. His protagonists may have one or the other but not both.

Amanda and Elyot begin their second tryst with a number of advantages on their side. They are not only lovers but old friends and, intellectually, kindred spirits. They hold no surprises for each other, yet remain strongly attracted. Their disastrous experience has made them aware of the pitfalls of marriage, and they are consciously determined to avoid repeating their mistakes. A marriage counselor would likely consider such a couple well-prepared for partnership and rate their chances of success high. But their good intentions and hard-earned wisdom are little, if any, help, and they are soon caught up in the same jealousies and resentments that had made their life together intolerable.

Overall, this amounts to a severely pessimistic view of the prospects for men and women. While the conventional marriages are unacceptably hollow and passionless, Elyot and Amanda's efforts to live their love prove no more workable; their commitment to their passion only dooms them to endless cycles of love and hate. When they sneak off together at the final curtain, it is clear that their escape is temporary and provisional and their happiness momentary and precarious. They have triumphed and regained their equilibrium but nothing is guaranteed. Though the audience may wish them well, their future together is questionable. They easily outsmart and outmaneuver Victor and Sibyl and presumably can do so indefinitely, for the weaker characters are clearly no match for them. Unfortunately, they are *too* good a match for each other, too alike and too evenly-matched for one to successfully "manage" the other. Worse yet, they both seem incapable of managing themselves. Marriage is quite possible, Coward seems to be saying—but not among two people who share so many personality traits—and not in the presence of passionate love.

" *PRIVATE LIVES*'S MANY INTRIGUING QUALITIES INCLUDE COWARD'S CYNICAL PERSPECTIVE ON THE ETERNAL 'BATTLE OF THE SEXES' AND AN EXPLORATION OF TRADITIONAL GENDER-ROLES THAT CAN BE SEEN TO ANTICIPATE THE SOCIAL AND SEXUAL TRANSFORMATIONS OF MORE RECENT YEARS."

Drama often dictates that the people and events it portrays are larger than life. In this sense Amanda and Elyot's relationship can be seen as an exaggerated case of marital ups and downs. Marriage is very often hard work for the two people who try to maintain it, for every happiness there is often matched sorrow or disappointment. Through his protagonists, who represent an extreme of the precariousness of relationships, Coward is making the humorous statement that sharing your life with another is not always easy and true romance does not always end "happily ever after."

Source: Tom Faulkner, for *Drama for Students,* Gale, 1998.

Brendan Gill

In this review of a 1968 revival performance of Private Lives, *Gill offers the opinion that this work is Coward's finest and a prime example of skilled farce. The critic also states that the enduring appeal of the play is a fitting birthday present for Coward, whose seventieth anniversary was marked by the new production.*

Four of the most fruitful days of 1929 were surely those that Noel Coward, on a lazy holiday trip around the world, spent writing *Private Lives.* The first act of the play, which I don't hesitate to call as nearly flawless a first act for a comedy as any in the language, is said to have been jotted down overnight—formidable proof of the fact, repugnant to

"COWARD IS THE GREATEST OF ENGLISH THEATRICAL FIGURES IN THE MULTIFARIOUSNESS OF HIS GIFTS."

puritans, that time and effort have no necessary connection with achievement in the arts. Neither, for that matter, does age—Coward was twenty-nine when he wrote *Private Lives,* and he was never to surpass it. (Indeed, he had already composed, at twenty-five, its only possible rival for comic excellence, *Hay Fever.*) The play had its world premiere in Edinburgh, in 1930, starting Gertrude Lawrence (who had inspired it) as Amanda and Coward as Elyot, with Laurence Olivier and Adrianne Allen in supporting roles. The sun has long since set on the British Empire that Coward made such fun of and later glorified, but I doubt if it has ever set, or ever *will* set, on *Private Lives.* Now the play has bobbed up here, at the Billy Rose Theatre, in an APA production sponsored by David Merrick. The production is an admirable one and will serve nicely to help celebrate the occasion of Coward's seventieth birthday, on Tuesday next. As a small sprig to add to the laurels being heaped up in honor of that day, I will repeat an opinion that I have often expressed, with a gravity not quite wholly based on a desire to irritate certain friends of mine in Academe—that Coward is the greatest of English theatrical figures in the multifariousness of his gifts. Who but he has written his own plays and musical comedies, directed them, acted in them, danced in them, and sung in them songs of his own composition? Poor Shakespeare, after all (and I have been waiting a long time to set down the words "poor Shakespeare"), merely wrote, acted, and composed the lyrics of a few songs in his plays. As far as I know, there isn't much likelihood that when he played the Ghost in "Hamlet" he broke out into song and dance, though the idea is an appealing one and somebody is bound to make use of it sooner or later.

Simple as it may seem in the reading, *Private Lives* is extremely hard to act well; the lines of the play turn out to matter less than the silences between the lines, and the duration of these silences must be calculated to the millisecond. The director of the present production, Stephen Porter, has performed these calculations with exemplary skill. He is aware that much of our pleasure in the play comes from our being allowed to know, from moment to moment, more than the characters themselves are allowed to know. Our laughter springs as much from the sudden glory of anticipation fulfilled as from the witty expression of any ordinary human feeling or—perish the thought!—thought. The first act has a symmetry of word and deed so exact as to be almost uncanny; the two newlywed couples in the swagger hotel in Deauville are made to move through a series of discomfitures as neatly introduced, exhibited, and dismissed as so many magic hoops, cards, coins, and colored handkerchiefs. In the second act, the prestidigitator risks losing control by losing momentum. We perceive that he has time to kill on his way to a third act (in the twenties, a playwright who plotted a comedy in two acts would no doubt have been accused of shortchanging his audience), and we come dangerously close to seeing Amanda and Elyot for what they are—in real life, two of the least delightful people imaginable, with nothing to do but eat, drink, bicker, make love, and congratulate themselves on their isolation from a world unworthy of them. In the third act, the prestidigitator is again in full control; after a flurry of slapstick physical encounters, he rings down the curtain on a breakfast scene that is at once consummately trivial and just the right size.

Amanda and Elyot are played by Tammy Grimes and Brian Bedford. I wouldn't have guessed that Miss Grimes, whose voice to my ears is like chalk on slate, could bring off the role of a pretty, willful English girl of those distant flapper days, but she does, she does, and Brian Bedford is appropriately clipped of accent and selfish of purpose as Elyot. David Glover plays the staunch and obtuse ninny who has just become Amanda's second husband, and Suzanne Grossmann, looking a trifle jaded for the part, plays Elyot's bewildered twenty-three-year-old bride. The amusing Art-Deco settings and the lighting are by James Tilton and the costumes are by Joe Eula.

Source: Brendan Gill, "Happy Birthday, Dear Noel," in the *New Yorker,* Volume XLV, no. 43, December 13, 1969, pp. 115–16.

Brooks Atkinson

In this review of the original Broadway production—which starred playwright Coward in the lead role of Elyot—Atkinson gives a favorable appraisal of the play's comedic offerings.

Noel Coward's talent for little things remains unimpaired. In *Private Lives,* in which he appeared at the Times Square last evening, he has nothing to say, and manages to say it with competent agility for three acts. Sometimes the nothingness of this comedy begins to show through the dialogue. Particularly in the long second act, which is as thin as a patent partition, Mr. Coward's talent for little things threatens to run dry. But when the time comes to drop the second act curtain his old facility for theatrical climax comes bubbling out of the tap again. There is a sudden brawl. Mr. Coward, in person, and Gertrude Lawrence, likewise in person, start tumbling over the furniture and rolling on the floor, and the audience roars with delight. For Mr. Coward, who dotes on pranks, has an impish wit, a genius for phrase-making, a subtlety of inflection and an engaging manner on the stage. Paired with Miss Lawrence in a mild five-part escapade, he carries *Private Lives* through by the skin of his teeth.

Take two married couples on their respective honeymoons, divide them instantly, and there—if the two leading players are glamorous comedians—you have the situation. As a matter of fact, it has a little more finesse than that. For Elyot Chase, who feels rather grumpy about his second honeymoon, and Amanda Prynne, who feels rather grumpy about hers, were divorced from each other five years ago. When they see each other at the same honeymoon hotel in France, they suddenly realize that they should never have been divorced. Their new marriages are horrible blunders. Their impulse is to fly away together at once. They fly. How rapturously they love and quarrel in a Paris flat, and how frightfully embarrassed they are when their deserted bride and bridegroom finally catch up with them, is what keeps Mr. Coward just this side of his wits' end for the remaining two acts.

For the most part it is a duologue between Mr. Coward and Miss Lawrence. Jill Esmond, as the deserted bride, and Laurence Olivier, as the deserted bridegroom, are permitted to chatter foolishly once or twice in the first act, and to help keep the ball rolling at the end. After the furniture has been upset. Therese Guadri, as a French maid, is invited to come in, raise the curtains and jabber her Gallic distress over unseemly confusion. But these are

"MR. COWARD'S WIT IS NOT OSTENTATIOUS. HE TUCKS IT AWAY NEATLY IN PAT PHRASES AND SUBTLE WORD COMBINATIONS AND SMARTLY BIZARRE ALLUSIONS."

ultitarian parts in the major tour de force of Mr. Coward and Miss Lawrence cooing and spatting at home.

Be it known that their passion is a troubled one. They coo with languid pleasure. But they are also touchy, and fly on the instant into feline rages. Mr. Coward's wit is not ostentatious. He tucks it away neatly in pat phrases and subtle word combinations and smartly bizarre allusions. Occasionally he comes out boldly with a flat statement of facts. "Certain women should be struck regularly like gongs," he declares. Acting just as he writes, he is crisp, swift and accurate. And Miss Lawrence, whose subtlety has not always been conspicuous, plays this time with rapidity and humor. Her ruddy beauty, her supple grace and the russet drawl in her voice keep you interested in the slightly wind-blown affairs of a scanty comedy. If Mr. Coward's talent were the least bit clumsy, there would be no comedy at all.

Source: Brooks Atkinson, "Mr. Coward Still Going Along" (1931) in *On Stage: Selected Theater Reviews from the New York Times, 1920–1970,* edited by Bernard Beckerman and Howard Siegman, Arno Press, 1973, pp. 122–23.

SOURCES

Atkinson, Brooks. Review of *Private Lives* in the *New York Times,* January 28, 1931; May 14, 1931.

Brater, Enoch. "Noel Coward" in the *Dictionary of Literary Biography,* Volume 10: *Modern British Dramatists, 1900-1945,* edited by Stanley Weintraub, Gale, 1982.

Coward, Noel. Introduction to *Play Parade,* Doubleday, 1933, p. xiii.

London *Daily Mail,* reprinted in the *New York Times,* September 25, 1930.

Morgan, Charles. Review of *Private Lives* in the *New York Times,* October 12, 1930.

FURTHER READING

Castle, Charles. *Noel,* Doubleday, 1972.

One of several fond tributes to Coward, Castle's book is drawn from the reminiscences of friends and theatrical colleagues, as well as Coward's own observations.

Coward, Noel. *Present Indicative,* Doubleday, 1937; and *Future Indefinite,* Doubleday, 1954.

Coward's two major volumes of autobiography provide glimpses of his legendary personality and storytelling ability. *Present Indicative* includes more detail from the period in which *Private Lives* was written and first produced.

Hoare, Philip. *Noel Coward: A Biography,* Simon & Schuster, 1995.

A extensively-researched biography, written with the cooperation of Coward's estate, Hoare's volume draws on previously-unavailable source material to produce a thorough account of the playwright's life and times.

Levin, Miller. *Noel Coward,* Twayne, 1968.

A concise survey of Coward's long career, it includes a biographical essay and a critical assessment of each of his major works.

True West

SAM SHEPARD

1980

Sam Shepard's very successful playwrighting career began in the mid-1960s when his often bizarre and anti-realistic plays were produced in experimental off- off-Broadway theatres such as La Mama and Theatre Genesis at St. Mark's Church in-the-Bowery. The launching of Shepard's playwrighting career is generally attributed to a 1967 review by Michael Smith in the *Village Voice.* Smith's enthusiastic appraisal of the first two of Shepard's early plays—*Cowboys* and *The Rock Garden* (both 1964)—brought the playwright to the attention of mainstream critics and audiences. By 1976, Shepard had more than thirty of these mostly one-act plays to his credit and had become an established cult figure.

With *Curse of the Starving Class* (1977) and *Buried Child* (1978), Shepard began producing what are now considered his major plays, works defined by a clear focus on such topics as dysfunctional families and social fringe dwellers. These plays, in contrast to his earlier work, also display a more conventional approach to plot and character. His popularity broadened and by the time *True West* appeared in 1980, many critics felt that Shepard was at the forefront of new American playwrights and, along with other dramatists such as David Mamet, Marsha Norman, and Beth Henley, was defining a new decade of theatre.

While *True West* represents a continued movement in Shepard's drama toward realistic charac-

terization, plot, setting, and dialogue, the play also has touchstones in his experimental days, retaining a number of unusual, fantastical elements—such as the grotesque violence and the startling transformations of its two main characters. Some commentators refer to these later plays as examples of ''magical realism'' (a literary genre defined by the works of such writers as Jorge Luis Borges and Federico Garcia Lorca) because they begin with realistic characters and situations but gradually acquire more bizarre qualities until they finally seem to fuse realism and fantasy. In many circles *True West* was hailed as a breakthrough for Shepard, a work in which experimental drama was successfully melded with the more conventional elements of modern theatre. Though *True West* is one of Shepard's most accessible dramas, it retains the unmistakable signature of his earlier adventurous work.

AUTHOR BIOGRAPHY

Sam Shepard was born Samuel Shepard Rogers, Jr., in Fort Sheridan, Illinois, on November 5, 1943. Because his father was in the military, Shepard's family moved frequently during his childhood (including one move to the South Pacific island of Guam) before settling in Southern California. As he related in an interview in *Theatre Quarterly,* Shepard's adult perception of his early life, especially ''that particular sort of temporary society that you find in Southern California,'' has led in many of his plays to investigations of the feeling ''that you don't belong to any particular culture.'' This sense of rootlessness has led Shepard to explore (and often fuse) two facets of the American experience: the mythical West and the American family.

Noted for his bleak portrayal of American family life, Shepard's own upbringing was complicated by a very strict alcoholic father. Shepard left home while still a teenager, eventually arriving in New York City in 1963, a period in which the burgeoning and experimental off- off-Broadway theatre movement was experiencing a jolt of energetic creativity. Shepard had gone to New York to pursue a career as a rock musician and perhaps try his hand at acting; he knew very little about theatre. But living in the artistically-charged atmosphere of the Lower East Side, Shepard was soon writing plays that were produced and received enthusiastically by the small, non-commercial off- off-Broadway theatre houses.

Too unconventional in his early plays and still a commercial risk with his off-beat later plays, Shepard is the most successful and respected American playwright never to have had a play premiere on Broadway. (Though a 1996 revival of *Buried Child* [1978] was directed by noted actor and experimental impresario Gary Sinise, a founder and the creative director of the influential Steppenwolf theatre company in Chicago, and enjoyed moderate success on Broadway.) Shepard's plays continue to be popular off-Broadway and in regional, educational, and experimental theatres around the country, and he has won numerous awards and honors for his work. *Buried Child* won the Pulitzer Prize for drama in 1979, and he has received eleven Obie Awards as well as a New York Drama Critics Circle Award for *A Lie of the Mind* (1985).

In 1974, after returning to America from a three-year stay in England, Shepard launched another successful career as a movie actor and has appeared in many films. Among his better-known performances are roles in director Terence Mallick's *Days of Heaven* (1978) and Phillip Kaufman's *The Right Stuff* (1983), a film that gained him an Academy Award nomination for his portrayal of test pilot Chuck Yeager. He has also appeared in such popular films as *Steel Magnolias* (1989), *Thunderheart* (1992), and *The Pelican Brief* (1993), among others. He is also a successful screenwriter and film director, having adapted and/or directed many of his own works, including *Fool for Love* (1983) and *Silent Tongue* (1994).

Following the popularity *True West* in 1980 he again found success with *Fool for Love* and mixed successes with *A Lie of the Mind* (1985), *States of Shock* (1991), and *Simpatico* (1994). In the 1990s Shepard expanded his writing focus to include prose with the 1996 collection *Cruising Paradise: Tales.*

In Shepard's personal life, he married actress O-Lan Johnson Dark on November 9, 1969. Before their divorce, that union yielded a child, Jesse Mojo. During his acting work on the film *Frances* in 1982, Shepard became involved with his costar Jessica Lange. Though never married, the couple have maintained a longstanding personal and working relationship. They have two children, Hannah Jane and Samuel Walker.

PLOT SUMMARY

Scene 1

True West takes place in a kitchen and in the adjoining breakfast alcove area of a well-kept Southern California suburban home about forty miles east of Los Angeles. The alcove is filled with house plants, mostly Boston ferns hanging in planters. In the first scene, it is night and crickets are chirping outside while Austin, a neatly dressed man in his early thirties, is seated at the glass breakfast table in the alcove writing in a notebook. He is working by candlelight while moonlight streams through the alcove windows. His older brother, Lee—dressed in a filthy, white T-shirt, tattered overcoat, and baggy pants—reclines against the kitchen sink, mildly drunk, a beer in his hand.

Austin and Lee are together for the first time in five years, and it is clear that Lee is jealous because his mother chose Austin to take care of the house while she vacationed in Alaska. He is also intimidated by Austin's status and refinement. Lee's conversation, with its subdued hostility, bothers Austin, who is trying to write, but Austin remains polite. Lee has just returned from the Mojave Desert, where he visited with their father. When Austin asks how long Lee plans to stay, the older brother reveals that he intends to burglarize the houses in the neighborhood. He requests the use of Austin's car, and when Austin objects and seems too condescending, Lee grabs and shakes him violently, demonstrating his superior physical strength.

Scene 2

On the morning of the next day, Austin is misting his mother's plants and Lee is sitting at the alcove table drinking beer. He reports that he went out the night before on foot and scouted houses to burgle. Austin informs Lee that the movie producer he is writing for is coming to visit and Lee agrees to leave for a few hours if he can take Austin's car.

Scene 3

It is afternoon and Austin is meeting with Saul Kimmer, Hollywood movie producer, who loves the "great story" that Austin has described for him and only needs a synopsis to convince studio executives to bankroll Austin's screenplay. Lee returns prematurely, carrying a stolen television set. After introductions Lee ingratiates himself with Kimmer and persuades the producer to go golfing with him the next morning. As Austin maneuvers Saul out the door, Lee tells Kimmer he has an idea for a contemporary Western movie; the producer suggests having Austin write an outline for consideration.

Sam Shepard

Scene 4

It is night, coyotes bark in the distance, and Lee is dictating his story to Austin, who is reluctantly typing an outline. Austin finds Lee's story preposterous, "not enough like real life," but Lee is desperate to finish and subtly threatens Austin if he doesn't help. Lee has begun to have visions of a steady income and a life filled with middle-class amenities and says to Austin, "I always wondered what'd be like to be you." Austin responds by saying he used to envy the excitement of Lee's life: "you were always on some adventure."

Scene 5

The next morning, Lee is at the table with a set of golf clubs discussing the early morning round of golf he has just finished with Saul Kimmer. He claims that Saul liked the outline so much he gave Lee a set of clubs as an advance. Austin takes a bottle of his mother's champagne to celebrate and then learns that he is to write the script of Lee's outline rather than work on his own script. Austin is angry and calls Lee's story the "dumbest" he has ever heard in his life. At the height of their argument, Lee threatens Austin with a golf club.

Scene 6

That afternoon, Kimmer joins them and admits that he prefers Lee's story to Austin's, adding that he likes Lee's plan to use some of the money from the sale of the script to set up a trust fund for the brother's father. Austin refuses to write the script, even though Saul says the deal is worth three hundred thousand dollars for the first draft alone. The producer claims that Lee has ''raw talent,'' that his story about the ''real West'' has ''the ring of truth.'' Austin shouts that ''there's no such thing as the West anymore! It's a dead issue!''

Scene 7

It is night again, and throughout this and the following scene, the dog-like yapping of coyotes intensifies into a frenzy as their pack grows in numbers, perhaps luring and killing pets from suburban yards. Lee is at the typewriter, struggling to type with one finger while Austin sits on the kitchen floor, drunk and singing. Lee complains that he needs quiet to concentrate, and Austin suggests that maybe he will try his hand at burglary now that Lee has taken up screenwriting. Lee scoffs at this, saying Austin couldn't steal a toaster. Meanwhile Lee is angrily getting tangled up in the typewriter ribbon but calms down to beg Austin to help him get his story down on paper. Austin interrupts to tell Lee the ''true to life'' story about how their father lost his false teeth.

Scene 8

Just before sunrise the next morning, Austin has reappeared with numerous toasters stolen from neighborhood houses and Lee has methodically smashed the typewriter with a golf club and is burning pages of the script. Both men are now drunk and the house is a shambles. All of the house plants are dead and drooping from lack of water. Austin starts making toast and Lee tries to phone a woman he knows in Bakersfield, California. Austin tells Lee he wants to come with him to live in the desert. Lee agrees to take him if Austin will write what he dictates of his story.

Scene 9

At mid-day, in blazing heat, the house is covered with debris—bottles, toasters, the smashed typewriter, a ripped out telephone, etc. It is like a desert junk yard at high noon in intense yellow light. Austin is scribbling in a notebook while Lee, shirtless and beer in hand, is slowly walking around the room, picking his way through the objects on the floor. When Austin reads back what Lee has dictated, it sounds cliched and ''stupid'' to Lee and he denies dictating it.

Their mother enters, having returned early from her vacation to Alaska. She is taken aback by the mess in the house, especially her dead plants, but she seems more interested in telling her sons that the famous artist, Pablo Picasso, is in town to visit the museum. Austin informs her that Picasso is dead and that he and Lee are leaving for the desert. But Lee insists that he's going alone, that he's giving up on the screenplay, and that he needs to borrow his mother's china, something ''authentic,'' to take with him to the desert.

Austin attempts to stop Lee from leaving by strangling him with a piece of phone cord. His mother, meanwhile, calmly insists that Austin should not kill his brother and exits, saying she's going to check into a motel, that she doesn't recognize her house any more. When Austin releases the tension on the cord around Lee's neck it appears that Lee is dead, but after a few moments Lee leaps to his feet and the two brothers square off as a single coyote is heard in the distance and moonlight falls across the room.

CHARACTERS

Austin

At the beginning of the play, Austin is the apparently conventional brother dressed in a light blue sports shirt, a light tan cardigan sweater, clean blue jeans, and white tennis shoes. In his early thirties, he is neat and organized, clearly a responsible adult. He appears to be an accomplished writer and, in fitting with his accountable nature, has been chosen by his mother to take care of her house while she is on vacation in Alaska. In the first half of the play he tries hard to be polite and understanding with his apparently less-refined older brother, Lee, and is dominated by Lee's violence and superior strength. In the second half of the play, however, Austin's behavior begins to reflect his brother's, becoming coarse and sloppy in his demeanor and appearance. By the end of the play, Austin is profoundly drunk, has stolen numerous toasters from the neighborhood, and is on the verge of strangling his brother to death. As evidenced by Lee's increasing seriousness and new dedication to writing—traits that Austin displayed at the play's outset—it is clear that the brothers have exchanged significant aspects of their personalities. Austin, for his part, reveals a desire to emulate his brother's wilder tendencies, to live a less-structured, more adventurous life.

Saul Kimmer

Saul Kimmer is a slick Hollywood movie producer in his late forties who comes to the house to discuss business with Austin but ends up playing golf with Lee and agreeing to back Lee's screenplay rather than Austin's. He is cartoonishly dressed in a pink and white flower print sports coat with matching polyester slacks and black and white loafers. While a significant device in shifting the action of the play—sparking pivotal changes in each brothers' behavior—the character of Kimmer is little more than a stereotype of a fast-talking, soulless Hollywood executive. It is clear that he cares little about the artistic merits of either brother's screenplay but is merely interested in which film will make him more money.

Lee

Lee is Austin's older brother and something of a social misfit. He is in his early forties and, at the beginning of the play, appears completely uncivilized. He is dressed in a filthy T-shirt, a pink suede belt, a tattered brown overcoat, and shoes with holes in the soles; he is a poster child for careless slobs. Lee has come to visit Austin following a reunion with the brothers' estranged father, who lives in the desert. Obviously lacking in financial security and social graces, Lee is jealous of his little brother's success and refinement. Initially, he swills beer, talks aggressively, plans burglaries in his mother's neighborhood, and bullies Austin. When Hollywood producer Saul Kimmer arrives, Lee butts in and deflects Kimmer's interest away from Austin's screenplay by proposing his own idea for a film set in the "true West." While Lee appears close to a successful screenwriting deal, he becomes very anxious about success and the prospect of actually writing the script. With no writing—let alone typing—skills, he needs Austin's help. Just as the older brother is seeing the benefits of emulating his brother's discipline, however, Austin has become

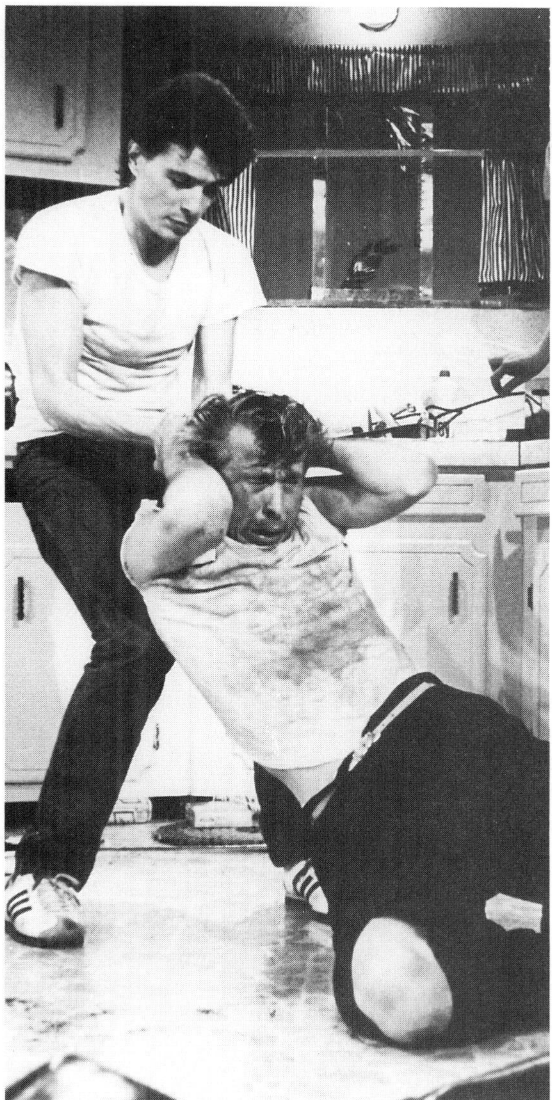

Amidst the debris of the totaled kitchen, Austin attempts to strangle Lee

too drunk to help him. As Austin has become infatuated with the idea of living Lee's wild and free life, Lee has glimpsed the possibilities that honest success offers.

Mom

The mother of Austin and Lee appears at the end of the play, returning from her vacation in Alaska to discover her house in shambles. In her early sixties, she is a small woman dressed in a conservative white skirt and matching jacket with a red shoulder bag and two pieces of matching lug-

MEDIA ADAPTATIONS

- The Steppenwolf production of *True West* at the Cherry Lane Theatre in New York City with John Malkovich as Lee and Gary Sinise as Austin was recorded for the Public Broadcasting System's *American Playhouse* series and then released as a feature film in 1987. This 110 minute film can be rented at selected video stores or purchased from Academy Home Entertainment, Shelburne, Vermont, or through Critics' Choice Video. It is also available in laser disk format from LaserVision.
- An amateur production of the play directed by Charles Doolittle at Moraine Valley Community College in Palos Hills, Illinois, in December of 1988 was taped on videocassette, and the college also preserved a series of twenty-two slides featuring selected scenes from the play.

gage. Her response to the disaster is eccentrically muted. She speaks softly, chastising her sons in a tone that makes her seem relatively unconcerned, even while Austin seems to be strangling Lee to death. Having read that a Picasso exhibit was coming to the museum in her home town, she thinks it means that Picasso himself will be there, unaware that Picasso has already died. While appearing a trifle odd, Mother's reaction to the carnage her sons have wrought indicates that she has grown accustomed to such behavior and no longer feels a need to respond to it. Her detached attitude toward her sons' irrational actions suggests that this incident is not unique in the brothers' relationship.

THEMES

Change and Transformation

Central to a thematic analysis of *True West* is the exchange of personality traits between brothers Austin and Lee as their conflict over screenplays develops. In the beginning, they are polar opposites, as the clean-cut and conventional Austin confidently prepares his script for the Hollywood producer, Saul Kimmer, and the ill-kept and anti-social Lee announces his plans to burglarize the neighborhood. By the end of the play, however, Lee and his movie idea have won Kimmer's favor, and Lee is attempting to be industrious while Austin has assumed Lee's habits of heavy drinking and petty crime.

The catalyst for this transformation is the Hollywood producer Saul Kimmer and the opportunities he represents for each of the brothers. In the beginning, Austin seems to be relatively accomplished and confident as a writer, but Kimmer is offering Austin his "big break," his opportunity for fame and fortune within the framework of his conventional life. Austin seems to be a steady, middle-class family man. He has a wife and children "up north," an Ivy League education, and a determination to gain fame and fortune through hard work in the highly competitive entertainment industry. But when Kimmer rejects Austin's movie idea in favor of his crass brother's script proposal, Austin loses his sense of superiority. He is transformed as he loses the connection with his familiar concept of self. Confronted with the possibility that his intelligence, drive, and talent may not be enough to attain his dreams, Austin suffers an identity crisis. He is left a hollow shell (as he says in the play "there's nothing real down here, Lee! Least of all me!"). In this state of mind, Austin tries out Lee's identity to see how it suits him; he adopts an irresponsible attitude, steals toasters, and talks of ditching his conventional existence for an adventurous life of crime and travel.

For Lee, Kimmer represents more than a chance for fame and fortune; he represents an opportuni-

TOPICS FOR FURTHER STUDY

- Research the importance of music in Shepard's life and the way this interest gets reflected in his plays, especially his early work.
- Research the statistics of domestic violence in America to see how accurate Lee is when he says, ''you go down to the L.A. Police Department there and ask them what kinda' people kill each other the most. . . . Family people. Brothers. Brothers-in-law. Cousins. Real American-type people. They kill each other in the heat mostly. In the Smog-Alerts. In the Brush Fire Season.'' Is this statement an accurate one of domestic violence, explain how closely it reflects (or does not reflect) real violence between family members.
- Research the subject of dysfunctional families in America and compare some of the more ''common'' dysfunctional features with the family in *True West.*
- Research the rise of the off- off-Broadway theatre movement and read several of Shepard's early plays to see how they derived from and accurately represented that vibrant atmosphere of New York City in the early 1960s.

ty for parity with—or even genuine superiority over—Austin as well as legitimacy in the eyes of the conventional world. Initially, Lee approaches Kimmer as a con artist, just as he has approached so many other people in his life, but when Lee sees an opportunity for respectability, he is transformed into a comically desperate man struggling to gain what he has disdained most of his life: a comfortable, middle-class existence.

The simplest explanation for putting his characters through these reversals is that Shepard is demonstrating that things are often not as they seem. Reality is complex and slippery, maybe even hopelessly elusive, and the man who seems to be a steady middle-class provider for his family might not be quite as stable as he appears. Shepard is also suggesting that a violent, animal-like nature might lie just below the surface of all human beings, waiting only sufficiently trying circumstances to crack the shell of a public persona and reveal the capacity for horror underneath.

Ultimately, Shepard is suggesting that what is attributed as personality, character, and a sense of identity might be little more than public role playing that, upon close inspection, does not come close to revealing the true nature of the person. This can be extrapolated to infer that a person engaged in this role playing may even convince themselves that their identity is what they have created. When confronted with the possibility that this role may not be their true self, the realization can often be traumatic—as it is for Austin.

In Lee's case, the persona he exhibits at the beginning of the play is most likely his true self. He has learned not to care what others think of his behavior and, as a result, has become free to act on any impulse that occurs to him. When his idea for a film receives serious consideration from Kimmer, however, Lee begins to understand the benefits that can be reaped from playing a role. As Austin did at the play's outset, he learns to control his baser instincts in the service of attaining respect and wealth.

Identity: the Search for Self

At the beginning of the play, Austin and Lee, like most human beings, take their identities for granted and would consider those identities stable and unchanging if they thought of them at all. Austin is a little more self-assured about himself, confidently feeling ''in charge,'' even in the face of Lee's threatening behavior. But after Kimmer rejects his movie idea in Scene 6, Austin's sense of identity is shattered. He repeats the personal pronoun ''I'' as a way of trying to hold on to his old sense of himself—"I drive on the freeway every day. I swallow the smog. I watch the news in color. I shop in the Safeway. I'm the one who's in touch! Not him!"

But in the next scene, Austin is only in touch with the alcohol he consumes as his hazy mind gropes for a new sense of identity. Set adrift from his old persona, he tries Lee's on for size: "well, maybe I oughta' go out and try my hand at your trade. Since you're doing so good at mine." He also decides that he's going to live in the desert, like Lee, because he's now decided "there's nothin' down here for me. There never was. . . . I keep finding myself getting off the freeway at familiar landmarks that turn out to be unfamiliar." Perhaps most significantly, he even begins to taunt Lee physically, testing the idea that he might be able to hold his own with Lee in terms of brute strength. This idea gets evaluated at the end of the play when he seems to have overcome and strangled Lee.

At the beginning of the play, Lee is much more defensive about his self-image. To some extent convinced that Austin's sophistication is enviable, Lee fakes sophistication of his own: "you got coffee?. . . Real coffee? From the bean?" Stung by his mother's preference for Austin as a house-sitter, Lee asserts his competence in domestic matters: "she might've just as easily asked me to take care of her place as you. . . . I mean I know how to water plants." However, it is as a natural man, as a desert survivor, that Lee most confidently defines his sense of self. But after Kimmer tempts Lee with the hope of becoming more conventional and sophisticated, Lee temporarily discards his desert-rat identity and tries to assume a new one: "I'm a screenwriter now! I'm legitimate." But when this new identity fails, Lee shouts, "here I am again in a desperate situation! This would never happen out on the desert. I would never be in this kinda' situation out on the desert."

The resolution of these two identity crises comes at the very end of the play when Lee rises from the floor with the phone cord around his neck and it's clear that Austin has not defeated Lee physically. Lee is still the physically stronger of the two, as well as the more cunning. Lee has given up his attempt to adjust his sense of self and is going back to the desert, though he plans to bring with him "something authentic" so he can feel more "civilized." As for Austin, the future is less clear, but he will also probably carry with him a more complex sense of self than he had before.

In a 1980 interview with Robert Coe in the *New York Times Magazine,* Shepard said that in *True West* he "wanted to write a play about double nature, one that wouldn't be symbolic or metaphorical or any of that stuff. I just wanted to give a taste of what it feels like to be two-sided. It's a real thing, double nature. I think we're split in a much more devastating way than psychology can ever reveal. . . . It's something we've got to live with."

STYLE

Realism

Shepard's story of two brothers contending for superiority as screenwriters begins in a realistic style, a style that Shepard rejected in the early phase of his playwrighting career. The realistic style as a conscious literary movement began in the 19th century as a reaction to romantic melodramas. These melodramas were an approach to story telling that offered outlandish situations, characters, and dialogue in the hopes of thrilling and entertaining an audience (and at the expense of presenting believable works of fiction). Mark Twain's essay, "Fenimore Cooper's Literary Offenses (1895)," is a classic example of the outraged response that realists had to this exaggerated form of storytelling.

As realism gained wider acceptance among readers and critics, however, it became evident that this form also had artistic limitations. Not the least of these limitations is presenting a reader or audience with characters and situations that bear little difference to those that they might encounter in their everyday life; the risk being that such commonplace material could easily be perceived as boring or dull. In addressing this pitfall, writers have embraced, among myriad other styles, the disciplines of both fantastic melodrama and hard realism. Many twentieth century authors have incorporated extravagant elements into their otherwise realistic writing to expand evocative possibilities and express what cannot be so easily suggested in a realistic framework. In *True West* Shepard has it both ways as he begins the play in a realistic style and gradually introduces bizarre elements to achieve a mythic dimension in his story.

Shepard's realism begins with a detailed description at the beginning of the play text of what the characters should wear and what the stage set should look like. Shepard's uncharacteristic attention to such detail includes specifications for costume colors and fabrics and for set detail as specific as "Boston ferns hanging in planters at different levels." Some of the specifications could be considered significant in themselves, like "the floor of the alcove is composed of green synthetic grass," but most of the realistic detail is designed to simply create a neutral backdrop for the evolution of character and situation on stage. In a prefatory "note on set and costume" Shepard specifies that "the set should be constructed realistically with no attempt to distort its dimensions, shapes, objects, or colors" because "if a stylistic 'concept' is grafted onto the set design it will only serve to confuse the evolution of the characters' situation, which is the most important focus of the play."

In this realistic setting, the characters speak casual dialogue filled with realistically elliptical speech like "you keepin' the plants watered?" and simple, monosyllabic answers like "yeah." Shepard specifies dialogue style with orthographic spellings of informal speech—"ya' got crickets anyway. Tons a' crickets out there." As early as 1974, in an interview in *Theatre Quarterly* with Kenneth Chubb, Shepard announced that "I'd like to try a whole different way of writing now, which is very stark and not so flashy and not full of a lot of mythic figures and everything, and try to scrape it down to the bone as much as possible. . . . it could be called realism, but not the kind of realism where husbands and wives squabble and that kind of stuff." By starting in a realistic style and gradually adding nonrealistic elements, Shepard was able to satisfy his characteristic interest in mythic qualities but in a much subtler way than in his earlier plays.

The Grotesque

The grotesque refers to aspects of a story that are so exaggerated and strange that they call attention to themselves as unreal. By the end of *True West* Austin and Lee are less like the plausible characters who began the play and more like primal savages as they square off against one another in the final scene. The incongruous qualities that Shepard almost imperceptibly introduces into *True West* gradually modify the impression of the two brothers and their situation until Austin and Lee become more mythic and evocative than two squabbling brothers could realistically be.

The first hint of the grotesque is Lee's matter-of-fact announcement that he's going to burglarize the neighborhood. This, combined with his extremely slovenly appearance and his eccentric assertion, "I don't sleep," at the end of the first scene, suggest that he is almost supernatural. Increasing violence also accentuates the play's separation from the normal, from Lee's menacing of Austin with a golf club in the fifth scene to his methodical destruction of the typewriter, burning of the film script, trashing of the kitchen, and ripping of the telephone off the wall in Scene 8. Austin adds to the grotesquerie in the opening of Scene 7 when, completely drunk, he shocks the audience with his drastic transformation. Furthermore, his "real" story of his father's false teeth is so surreal that it adds significantly to the play's distorted atmosphere.

In this same scene, the sound of the coyotes begins to build beyond natural levels. At the beginning of the play, the sound of the crickets and coyotes is environmental noise and a realistic part of the play's western setting. However, as the brothers begin their transformations and their situations become increasing bizarre, the coyotes' howls become nearly oppressive, a clamorous expression of the turmoil each brother feels. The encroaching coyote howls also signal the transformation of the house from a normal suburban dwelling to a wilder, more primitive environment.

In visual terms this is represented by the outrageous mess that Austin and Lee make of their mother's home. By the last scene of the play, the debris has created a "sea of junk," in "intense yellow light," as if the house were "a desert junkyard at high noon." According to Shepard's textual directions, by the end of the play "the coolness of the preceding scenes is totally obliterated" and the set is no longer a domestic home. It is now a mythic battlefield. Quite unrealistically, the house plants that have only been without water for a day and a half are now all dead. Austin and Lee's peculiar mother doesn't recognize the home as hers and leaves to check into a motel. And finally, "the figures of the brothers now appear to be caught in a vast desert-like landscape." Austin and Lee have become elemental forces in a mythic struggle and not merely brothers competing for screenwriting honors.

HISTORICAL CONTEXT

The Persistence of Frontier Ideals in American Culture

The title of Shepard's play, *True West,* is significant in many ways but one clear reference is to the American frontier West as an ideal of masculine

COMPARE & CONTRAST

- **1980:** *Double Fantasy,* an album by former Beatles member John Lennon and his wife Yoko Ono, is released in 1980, and on December 8 Lennon is fatally shot by a deranged fan with a handgun outside his New York City apartment building. Lennon's death increases support for laws controlling handguns, but president-elect Ronald Reagan rejects gun control legislation. U.S. handguns kill an average of twenty-nine people a day and fifty-five million handguns are believed to be in circulation.

  Today: Largely due to an assassination attempt on President Reagan in 1981 where his Press Secretary James Brady was shot and severely paralyzed for life, the ''Brady Bill'' requires a five-day waiting period before the sale of a handgun can be completed. Gun violence continues to be an alarming part of American culture, and as Lee says in Scene 4 of *True West,* ''you go down to the L.A. Police Department there and ask them what kinda' people kill each other the most. . . . Family people. Brothers. Brothers-in-law. Cousins. Real American-type people.'' Lee's remark has significance in that a large part of handgun violence occurs between family members—often children playing with their parents' weapons.

- **1980:** Ted Turner's Cable News Network (CNN) goes on the air on June 1 among predictions from many that there can be no reliable audience for a 24 hour-a-day news channel.

  Today: CNN, ESPN, and a host of proliferating cable networks have become international institutions. Nearly everywhere in the world where there is a television set there is CNN reporting the news. In the United States, the cable revolution has succeeding in nearly eclipsing the big-three networks—ABC, CBS, and NBC—that used to rule the airwaves.

- **1980:** On July 2, the U.S. Supreme Court rules in Richmond Newspapers versus Virginia that the press has a right to attend criminal trials.

  Today: The most publicized and publicly monitored trial in history, the televised O. J. Simpson murder trial, has left many people wondering if jurisprudence is well-served by making criminal cases into media events.

forcefulness and independence. Though cowboys and gunslingers have disappeared, the ideal of rough and ready men continues to persist in America. The characters of Austin and Lee are defined by their relation to the myth of the old West. Austin is a sophisticated city boy, an Ivy League egghead with little apparent aptitude for survival skills or physical force. Lee, on the other hand, is someone who can survive in the desert—who knows the land and can make things happen with his instinct and physical prowess. He, for instance, knows the difference between urban and rural coyotes—''they don't yap like that on the desert. They howl. These are city coyotes here''—and his movie idea is for a true-to-life, contemporary Western. When Austin has his identity crisis, he wants to leave his wife and children and live on the desert to get in touch with a more elemental self, and when Lee rejects the temptations of civilization it is to the desert (which serves as the closest thing to the unsettled frontier of the old West) he will return.

All through 1980, the year that Shepard introduced his play, the U.S. was engaged in a hostage crisis in Tehran, the capital of Iran. Parts of that situation illustrate the persistence of masculine, frontier ideals in American culture. In November of 1979, anti-American demonstrators goaded by Iran's Ayatollah Khomeini had marched on the U.S. Embassy in Tehran, seized control, and taken sixty diplomats as hostages. Khomeini eventually threatened to put these hostages on trial and execute them as spies. They would not be freed until January of

1981, 444 days later. Throughout 1980, this unprecedented takeover of a U.S. Embassy brought howls of protest from the American public and contributed significantly to President Jimmy Carter's loss in the 1980 election. The American public demanded action, reprisals, or a rescue, and the government's inability to immediately answer this direct challenge to American sovereignty was perceived as an insult to American honor.

Then, on the evening of April 24, 1980, a ninety-man commando group with eight helicopters and six transport planes took off from Egypt and the Arabian Sea to rendezvous in the Iranian desert in an attempt to rescue the hostages. But numerous problems culminated in the collision of one of the helicopters with a transport plane and eight men were killed and five others were injured. The ignominy of this failed mission was perhaps the greatest blow to American pride during the 1980 hostage crisis. Unlike their counterparts in Western folklore, the calvary (the U.S. government and its soldiers) had failed to arrive and rescue the settlers (the hostages) from the villains (the Iranian terrorists).

The U.S. Elects a President from Hollywood

Another important ingredient in *True West* is the apparent criticism of Hollywood values. By 1980 Shepard was a fairly successful actor and screenwriter. While his work in Hollywood contributed to his monetary success and allowed him the freedom to pursue his theatre art, many speculate that Shepard's experience in the movie industry also made him cynical about the business. In *True West* he is at least somewhat critical of what Hollywood represents.

While the character of Kimmer can be perceived as neither good nor evil, the description of his garish clothes and his dialogue make him sound quite showy and suggest a lack of genuine taste. And his world is obviously a world of shallow commerce rather than of art. When Lee asks Kimmer ''what kinda' stuff do ya' go in for?,'' Kimmer says, ''oh, the usual. You know. Good love interest. Lots of action.'' Austin eventually calls Kimmer a ''hustler'' and theirs is an unashamed language of business as they refer to ''projects,'' ''seed money,'' and ''commercial potential.'' And perhaps most importantly, the accountability entailed in their ''deals'' is as ludicrous as Kimmer's clothes. They sell movies on a mere synopsis or outline of the plot and demand $300,000 up front for a simple first draft. As Kimmer says so succinctly through Lee, ''in this business we make movies, American movies. Leave the films to the French.''

In the 1980 Presidential election, America's tolerance for Hollywood values, shallow or otherwise, was demonstrated in its election of Ronald Reagan as the country's fortieth president. Before entering politics, the sixty-nine-year-old conservative, who also served two terms as the Governor of California, had a long and successful career as a Hollywood actor. In the 1980 Presidential campaign, Reagan made a large impact with slick television commercials that exploited his style over substance cinematic image. Public opinion polls also revealed that he probably gained votes with an impressive showing in the televised presidential debate with Jimmy Carter in October. In November, Reagan won in a landslide, gaining fifty-one percent of the popular vote (43 million) to Carter's forty-one percent (35 million). The electoral vote was even more lopsided, with Reagan winning 489 to 49 and Carter taking only six states and the District of Columbia.

Many political commentators suggested that Reagan's overwhelming victory was facilitated by the increasing impact that television charisma was having on American politics. Confronted with a campaign where television presence was perhaps the most important political quality, Reagan's twenty-year career as an actor in over fifty Hollywood films enabled him to exploit the medium brilliantly. Others speculated that Reagan's success was strongly rooted in his (or his publicists') ability to extrapolate his good guy screen persona (which often took the form of a virtuous cowboy) into the arena of world politics. Much as the heroic Hollywood cowboys were able to solve complex problems with simple, manly actions, Reagan's political style was built around a return to basic decency and noble values. While these attributes performed wonderfully in films, the real world often presented situations in which good and bad were difficult to distinguish and which required complex solutions. Nevertheless, following a declining economy and the rigors of the Iran hostage crisis, the strong, frontiersman image that Reagan offered proved irresistible to American voters for eight years.

The American public's desire for the simplicity of times such as those in the old West found fulfillment in a president such as Ronald Reagan. In Shepard's play, Austin also expresses a desire to return to a more basic way of life—although his motivation is based on a different set of circumstances. Given the public climate at the time that *True West* was written and produced, Shepard had probably encountered more than a few individuals who, for any number of reasons, wanted to return to the true West.

CRITICAL OVERVIEW

True West has had an interesting production history that suggests the secret to the play's success might lie in its sense of humor. *True West* was first performed in July of 1980 at the Magic Theatre in San Francisco, where Shepard had for six years served as the playwright in residence. Directed by Robert Woodruff, this production was performed with well-known local actors and was very well-received. Reviewing the play for the journal *Theatre,* William Kleb noted that "the comic elements in *True West* were stressed" in this initial production.

Because of Shepard's rising status (he had won a Pulitzer Prize in 1979 for *Buried Child*), the play was then brought to New York City where, in the words of the *Village Voice*'s Don Shewey, the play "had become a media event, breathlessly anticipated as the latest work by 'the hottest young playwright in America.'" In December the play officially opened off-Broadway at Joseph Papp's Public Theatre, but by that time a rancorous conflict between Papp and director Woodruff over casting and artistic differences had become public and was dominating the critical response to the play. New York movie actors Tommy Lee Jones and Peter Boyle had taken over the roles of Austin and Lee, but the stars were feuding, the official opening had been twice postponed, and after disastrous preview performances the dissatisfied Woodruff resigned from the production. Papp replaced Woodruff as director, thereby alienating Shepard, who joined Woodruff in denouncing and disowning the production (though Shepard never came to New York City to see it because he was working on a movie at the time). Papp insisted that he altered little in Woodruff's staging, but the controversy succeeded in overshadowing the production itself. Frank Rich, writing for the *New York Times,* praised Shepard's play but denounced Papp's production, saying that the production was "little more than a stand-up run-through of a text that remains to be explored." Focusing on the Papp controversy, Rich asserted, "this play hasn't been misdirected; it really looks as if it hasn't been directed at all." He added that "you know a play has no director when funny dialogue dies before it reaches the audience." Rich concluded by saying "it's impossible to evaluate a play definitively when it hasn't been brought to life on stage."

Some reviewers agreed in part with Rich. T. E. Kalem, writing for *Time,* said that "certain errors of perception and direction are quite evident, but enough of the true Shepard is here to do him honor. Papp has certainly retained Shepard's singular gift for lunging simultaneously at the jugular and the funny bone." Other reviewers, however, dismissed Shepard's play as well as Papp's production. Douglas Watt of the *Daily News* found the play "simplistic," though he noted that "oddly, most of the first half of 'True West' is exceedingly funny." Writing for *Newsweek,* Jack Kroll found the play "an unfortunate mess" saying that "the new actors, Peter Boyle and Tommy Lee Jones, are sometimes effective and funny, but they seem distant from the play and uncertain about the effects they're trying for." *Christian Science Monitor* critic John Beaufort found the production "tedious" and the humor "harsh and abrasive." *New York Times* critic Walter Kerr simply found the play filled with "pretentiousness," its thematic issues recycled and unconvincing. The Public Theatre production of *True West* closed after only fifty-two performances.

However, the critical reputation and vitality of Shepard's play was saved two years later by a Chicago-based production. The small Steppenwolf Theatre, founded in 1976 and led by fledgling actors Gary Sinise and John Malkovich, produced a widely praised rendition of the play that emphasized Shepard's sense of humor. It sold out in Chicago for a six-week run and then ran twelve more weeks in a larger, more commercial Chicago theatre. This production then transferred to the off-Broadway, Cherry Lane Theatre in New York City in October of 1982. Sinise performed double duty, both directing the production and playing Austin while Malkovich's energetic portrayal of Lee astounded audiences. The two actors later went on to considerable movie stardom but were both making their New York debuts in the Cherry Lane production. Mel Gussow of the *New York Times* called the production "an act of theatrical restitution and restoration." The critic exclaimed that now one could see that "it was the [1980] production not the play that was originally at fault." In the Steppenwolf version, the play was "rambunctious and spontaneous," as well as "uproarious," with a performance by Malkovich that

Gussow called "a comic original." Shewey echoed this sentiment in the *Village Voice,* calling the play "a rip-roaring comic production . . . featuring the beyond-*Animal House* performance of John Malkovich." According to Gussow, Malkovich was "amusing and menacing at the same instant." Gussow observed that with this production "no one forgets that the playwright means to be playful." Gussow ended his review prophetically by saying "'True West,' revivified, should now take its rightful place in the company of the best of Shepard." The Steppenwolf production ran for 762 performances, at the time a New York record for a Shepard play. The production was subsequently videotaped and broadcast on the Public Broadcasting System's *American Playhouse* series in January of 1984. This version was also released as a feature film in 1986.

CRITICISM

Terry Nienhuis

Nienhuis is an associate professor of English at Western Carolina University. In this essay he examines the nature of myth as it pertains to Shepard's play. Nienhuis also discusses the abundant humor in the work.

As critic Frank Rich pointed out in his *New York Times* review of the original Off-Broadway production of Shepard's play, "*True West* is a worthy direct descendant of Mr. Shepard's *Curse of the Starving Class* and *Buried Child.* Many of his persistent recent themes are present and accounted for—the spiritual death of the American family, the corruption of the artist by business, the vanishing of the Western wilderness and its promising dream of freedom." Critics and scholars have since elaborated on these and related themes, pointing out, for example, that Lee represents the vanishing "old" West and Austin the plasticized, overdeveloped "new" West of Hollywood and its adjacent suburbs. It has been further stated that American myths such as the legendary American West or the tradition of the stable family not only fail to sustain contemporary Americans but often, in their elusiveness, delude and frustrate them.

The investigation of such themes has also suggested that *True West* is Shepard's most personal and autobiographically revealing play—that Austin and Lee's desert-dwelling father is inspired by Shepard's own absent parent and that Austin and Lee represent divided aspects of Shepard himself. Henry Schvey, writing in *Modern Drama,* suggested that "Austin, the successful Hollywood screenwriter, clearly represents the side of Shepard that has accommodated itself to material success, the aspects that have moved him from his counterculture roots in the off- off-Broadway theatre movement of the sixties to a commercially successful career as a film star. Lee, although presented as Austin's brother in the play, is in fact his alter-ego, the part of Shepard's divided self that is rough and crude, lives outside the law, and is drawn toward the elusive image of his father. The play, then, is not so much a bout between two brothers as it is an externalized metaphor of the dialectic between the dual aspects of Shepard's psyche." Or, as actor John Malkovich has so succinctly and colorfully put it, "Lee is the side of Shepard that's always been strangled but never quite killed."

However interesting and fruitful these investigations might be, it is possible that such close attention to Shepard's serious themes has often blinded critics, audiences, and readers to the richly subtle and irreverently unconventional humor in Shepard's play. Certainly, the production history of *True West* suggests that it can be disastrous to overlook the play's sense of humor. Contrasting the 1980 Public Theatre and the 1982 Steppenwolf/Cherry Lane Theatre productions of the play, *New York Times* critic Mel Gussow remembered that the original "seemed, for the freewheeling Mr. Shepard, uncharacteristically heavy-handed." And when critic Douglas Watt reviewed the first New York production of the play in the *Daily News,* he confidently proclaimed that Austin's monologue about his father's false teeth was "phonier" than Lee's movie idea. Watt also disapproved of the mother's departure at the end of the play, calling it "symbolism [that] hits you on the head like a 2-wood." Perhaps sensitivity to Shepard's sense of humor is important to the viewer or reader of *True West* because without it the play will seem "heavy-handed" or pretentious rather than an effective exploration of Shepard's persistent themes—and a biting satire of modern life in the West.

Much of the humor in *True West* plays off the very serious sense of menace that Lee brings to the action. The earliest manifestation of humor, for example, is a form of comic relief. In the first scene, Lee's menacing quality has been clearly established when he "suddenly lunges at Austin, grabs him violently by the shirt and shakes him with tremen-

WHAT DO I READ NEXT?

- *The Rock Garden* (1964) is a one-act play that, along with *Cowboys,* launched Shepard's playwrighting career. A series of strange conversations between a teenage boy and his mother and father, the play ends with a sexually explicit speech from the boy that some have considered obscene. Shepard says that "*Rock Garden* is about leaving my mom and dad."
- *The Tooth of Crime* (1972) is a very unconventional two-act play with music that has often been called Shepard's "masterpiece." It portrays a battle for dominance in the popular music industry between an established country music idol and the newest rock singer sensation. Their battle resembles a Western "shoot-out," as well as urban "turf wars," and investigates our culture's need for celebrity status.
- *Angel City* (1976) is a two-act play by Shepard that even more clearly than *True West* attacks the Hollywood film industry and the way it can corrupt the artistic spirit.
- Henry Nash Smith's *Virgin Land: The American West As Symbol and Myth* (1950) is a very well-known work of historiography that analyzes the concept of the West in American history and how it translates into elements of modern culture.
- William Goldman's *Adventures in the Screen Trade: A Personal View of Hollywood and Screenwriting* (1983) is an autobiographical expose of the Hollywood film industry. Goldman is a highly successful screenwriter and the author of *Butch Cassidy and the Sundance Kid, All the President's Men,* and *The Princess Bride,* among other well-known films.
- *In the Jungle of Cities* (1923) by the great German playwright, Bertolt Brecht, portrays a mythic conflict between a timber merchant and a librarian. In an interview with Kenneth Chubb in 1974, Shepard said that Brecht was his favorite playwright and that *In the Jungle of Cities* is a conflict, "a bout, between these two characters, taken in a completely open-ended way, the bout is never defined as being anything but metaphysical."

dous power." Austin placates Lee with an apology, there is a "long pause," and then Lee makes a drastic and comical shift in subject—"those are the most monotonous fuckin' crickets I ever heard in my life." This line has been set up by Lee's implied appreciation of the cricket sound at the very beginning of the play—"ya' got crickets anyway. Tons a' crickets out there." And the relatively small laugh from his profane second reference to crickets is simply a preparation for a much bigger laugh in Scene 4 when an exasperated Lee is arguing with Austin over the validity of the chase scene in Lee's movie: (Lee turns violently toward windows in alcove and throws beer can at them, screaming) "goddamn these crickets! (yells at crickets) Shut up out there! (pause, turns back toward table) This place is like a fuckin' rest home here. How're you supposed to think!"

Much of the humor in the play comes from Lee's annoyance. We all feel annoyed in our lives but are often embarrassed by the obvious triviality of it, so we enjoy identifying with Lee's exasperation, especially when it is expressed in clever ways ("now who in the hell wants to eat offa' plate with the State of Idaho starin' ya' in the face. Every time ya' take a bite ya' get to see a little bit more."). In part, we laugh at Lee's annoyance because he freely expresses feelings that most people are too embarrassed or self-conscious to state aloud. Consequently, the more trivial the causes for Lee's annoyance, the funnier it is for the audience. For example, in Scene 7, the irritated Lee, the adept desert survivor, struggles with something as ordinarily manageable as a typewriter ribbon. Furthermore, Lee's annoyance is humorous because it comes from the silly attempt to assume an overnight competence in the complex art of screenwriting. His newfound sense of filmmaking expertise makes him funny: "I'm trying to do some screenwriting here!!"

Saul Kimmer is another source of humor in *True West* because he is so ridiculously slick and shallow. Thus, it is funny when Lee can manipulate Kimmer (one con man conning another) even though Lee can't get Kimmer's name right. From his "inadvertent" early entrance with the stolen television set to Saul's unctuous exit line, "I'll give you a ring," Lee's triumph over the pretentiously self-important Saul Kimmer is our own joyful and risible triumph over the phonies who surround us in our daily lives.

Beyond Kimmer, however, the movie industry itself is treated humorously for the ridiculous practices it routinely employs. For example, Lee's description for Kimmer of the pathos in the ending of the film, *Lonely Are the Brave,* is simply the beginning of hilarious send-ups of movie ideas. When Lee is outlining his story for Austin in Scene 4, for example, it is obvious that he is making the story up as he goes along:

> Lee: . . . And number three—
> Austin: I thought there was only two.
> Lee: There's three. There's a third unforeseen realization.

As Austin later says, "it's the dumbest story I ever heard in my life."

True West, of course, focuses on transformations, and transformations of many kinds are funny when we see them as postured, opportunistic, and insincere—especially when the transformation is drastic. In Shepard's play, Lee's attempt to transform himself into a legitimate screenwriter, though perhaps ultimately pathetic, is funny because he has made such a pretense earlier of disdaining Austin's comfortable and conventional materialism. Thus, when Lee adopts new and temporary ambitions, his aspirations look pathetically adolescent and ridiculous: "a ranch? I could get a ranch?" An even more subtle example occurs in Scene 5, when Lee suddenly becomes a responsible momma's boy and says to Austin, "you shouldn't oughta' take her champagne, Austin. She's gonna' miss that."

It is perhaps a toss-up as to whether Austin's or Lee's transformation is funnier. Lee's is funny because of his desperation, and we laugh at it out of relief because his desperation is not ours. Lee probably reaches his comic peak in the last scene when he has lost touch with whatever instinctive quality he might have had as a storyteller and in a new and

> "AMERICAN MYTHS SUCH AS THE LEGENDARY AMERICAN WEST OR THE TRADITION OF THE STABLE FAMILY NOT ONLY FAIL TO SUSTAIN CONTEMPORARY AMERICANS BUT OFTEN, IN THEIR ELUSIVENESS, DELUDE AND FRUSTRATE THEM."

false hypersensitivity to language rejects a perfectly colloquial line like, "I know this prairie like the back a' my hand." Then, when the inebriated Austin suggests as an alternative the ludicrous, "I'm on intimate terms with this prairie," Lee says, "that's good. I like that. . . . Sounds original now."

Austin's transformation, on the other hand, is funny because it is a liberation, and we laugh because we would sometimes like to "let go" ourselves. But after Austin becomes liberated through too much drink in Scene 7, much of the humor comes from the irony this liberation creates. Specific lines are funny when they work as ironic echoes from the beginning of the play—now it is Austin who says, "don't worry about me. I'm not the one to worry about."

Perhaps the main benefit from examining the humor in *True West* is that it can explain some aspects of the text that have consistently presented problems for audiences, critics, and readers. Perhaps foremost among these is Austin's story about his father's false teeth. Initially the story is jarring because it is so specifically mundane and bizarre, but the story can have a wonderful pathos if it is performed or read with a feeling for its sense of humor. It is delivered, one must remember, by someone who is very drunk, and much of the humor comes from Austin presenting the story as profound when he has temporarily lost his sense of judgment. However, if the story is presented to the audience without its sense of dark humor, it will sound pretentious and even silly rather than twistedly hilarious and, at moments, even profound and moving.

A similar problem occurs with the appearance of Austin and Lee's mother, which will seem unrealistic or arbitrary unless it's played as humorous. Laughter often comes from the incongruous and unexpected and the Mother's understated response to the phenomenal mess in her house certainly fits this description. But the unexpectedly calm response from the mother is also disturbing to audiences and readers because it is the culmination of the play's gradual shift from the realistic to the grotesque. Her comically limpid response to the devastation helps to assure that the play will end in a grotesque rather than a realistic style. Realistic responses to such a mess would probably include rage or sorrow, but when she explains her reason for returning early from Alaska (''I just started missing all my plants'') it's clear that she is not a realistic, conventional mother, for as soon as she sees that all her plants are dead she exhibits a sense of acceptance (''oh well, one less thing to take care of I guess'') that immediately contradicts her stated reason for returning home.

This discord that Shepard creates with his bizarre mother figure is so extreme that it perhaps tests the limits of humor, but taking her comically is necessary to mute the very real violence that is taking place between Austin and Lee as the play closes. In her disconnected frame of mind, the mother sees her sons' violence as a commonplace occurrence, a little boy's tussle, saying ''you boys shouldn't fight in the house. Go outside and fight.'' Thus, Shepard's eccentric portrayal of violence is perfectly complemented by her comic obliviousness: she says the right words but doesn't feel the meaning behind them—''you're not killing him are you? You oughta' let him breathe a little bit.'' The humor is certainly dark, but to not see the mother as humorous is to risk an excessively heavy-handed reading of a rich comic line like, ''that's a savage thing to do.''

Source: Terry Nienhuis, for *Drama for Students,* Gale, 1998.

Jeffrey D. Hoeper

In this essay, Hoeper outlines the parallels between Shepard's True West *and the biblical parable of Cain and Abel, comparing the two tales of sibling rivalry.*

''Myth speaks to everything at once, especially the emotions,'' writes Sam Shepard (*American Dreams: The Imagination of Sam Shepard,* edited by Bonnie Maranca, [New York], 1981). Acting on this indirect authorial invitation, critics have understandably devoted much attention to the mythic elements in Shepard's work. Most notably, Tucker Orbison has exposed three levels of mythic response in *True West:* the mythic West of the cowboy; the mythic ''mystery of the artist'' in which the writer delves into the self to explore archetypal conflicts ''fraught with the terrors of nightdreaming''; and finally the mythic conflict of the doppelganger, the ''second self,'' as revealed in the role reversal of Lee and Austin at the play's crisis.

Important as these three levels of mythic response are, the play explores yet another—and arguably a more important—myth through its biblical allusions and parallels. The play's plot harks back to the archetypal story of Cain and Abel—in the Byronic variant in which Cain, the peaceful tiller of the soil, is a sympathetic figure, while Abel, the smug slaughterer of sheep, is inexplicably favored by a bloodthirsty deity. As in Genesis, the action takes place to the east of Eden. Shepard sets his play ''*in a Southern California suburb, about 40 miles east of Los Angeles.*'' Lee describes the suburban homes as being ''Like a paradise'' and Austin subsequently comments, ''This is a Paradise down here. . . . We're livin' in a Paradise.''

Granted, these references to Paradise have the informality of a cliché and the sibling rivalry between Austin and Lee is a fairly hackneyed literary motif; nevertheless, the biblical story of Cain is part of our common cultural heritage, and any story of fraternal battle recalls it in some measure. Further, the more closely one looks at Shepard's play, the more reminders there are of the pre-Christian conflict between Cain and Abel. One fairly common interpretation of the story in Genesis is that it was part of an effort by the invading Hebrews to discredit the matriarchal worship of the indigenous Canaanites. According to this interpretation, the story of the Fall is at heart a symbolic exploration of the problem of evil. How does a patriarchal society that assumes the existence of a beneficent masculine creator account for evil? It lays the burden of original sin at the feet of the first woman. And her first offspring is Cain, the original murderer.

By discrediting women and those who serve women or worship women, the ancient patriarchs may have sought to combat the matriarchal worship of the Triple Goddess in her many manifestations as Astarte, Ishtar, Isis, Artemis, Aphrodite, Demeter, Diana, and others. Before the invasion of the Hebrews, the Canaanites worshipped a variety of gods, but fertility rites were central to their religion and the triple goddesses Asherah, Anath, and Astarte were worshipped with special fervor as life-bringers and harvest-givers. As Pamela Berger has noted, "Almost every major excavation of middle Bronze Age through early Iron Age sites (2000–600 BC) has produced terra-cotta plaques impressed with the nude female holding plant forms and standing in such a position that she can be identified as a goddess" (*The Goddess Obscured: Transformation of The Grain Protector from Goddess to Saint,* [Boston], 1985). The springtime planting of seed, the summer-long ripening, the fall harvest, the wintery decline into the soil, and the subsequent resurrection were seen as mirroring female fecundity and as most appropriately revered by offering the fruits of the soil in libations and cakes of wheat. Cain's ritual offerings of grain and libations were characteristic of the worship of the Goddess. Abel's bloody sacrifice of a sheep from his fold was characteristic of early Hebraic devotion. The symbolic conflict between matriarchal and patriarchal worship in Genesis is complemented by the more directly historical account in the book of Joshua of the efforts to destroy the worship of the Goddess.

At the beginning of *True West* there are hints of this pre-Christian conflict between the patriarchal and matriarchal orders. The play is set in the mother's home. Her neighborhood is like Paradise. Her home is filled with vegetation:

> *The windows look out to bushes and citrus trees. The alcove is filled with all sorts of house plants in various spots, mostly Boston ferns hanging in planters at different levels. The floor of the alcove is composed of green synthetic grass.*

Her plants are being served by a dutiful son. Her name is given as "mother" or "Mom," nothing more.

In coming down from the lush north to write a romantic screenplay, Austin may be said to be acting in the service of love (or Aphrodite) and his earnings will be used to support his wife and children. His decision to write by candlelight reflects his attempt to establish a romantic mood appropriate to the story he is striving to create. Like Cain, Austin is associated with vegetation; in his mother's absence, he has vowed to lend her flourishing house plants. The first lines in Scene 1 underscore that duty, and Scene 2 opens with Austin "*watering plants with a vaporizer.*" Like Abel, however, Austin is the younger of two brothers and he is clearly the better brother—kind, industrious, and moral.

In contrast, Lee comes up from the desert, like the nomadic Hebrews at the end of their exodus and the beginning of their conquest of Canaan. Somewhere in that vast desert Lee has communed with

"MOTHERS, FATHERS, GODS, AND GODDESSES ARE ALL EQUALLY COMIC, TRIVIAL, INSIGNIFICANT, AND INSANE IN THE TRUE WEST OF SAM SHEPARD'S *TRUE WEST.*"

the "old man"—the father, whom Austin in his prosperity has apparently abandoned. Lee is Austin's sinister opposite, and his questionable character is clearly suggested by his appearance:

> *filthy white t-shirt, tattered brown overcoat covered with dust, dark blue baggy suit pants from the Salvation Army, pink suede belt, pointed black forties dress shoes scuffed up, holes in the soles, no socks, no hat, long pronounced sideburns, "Gene Vincent" hairdo, two days' growth of beard, bad teeth.*

Lee is an outcast who prefers the company of the snakes in the desert to that of other men. A virtual illiterate, he makes his living by theft. For Lee, the candlelight by which Austin works is reminiscent of the "old guys," "The Forefathers." Most directly, the allusion is to the first settlers of the West, but the somewhat odd phrasing, the repetition, and the capitalization draw our attention to the masculinity of these Forefathers and may recall the Hebrew patriarchs. Like those patriarchs and like Abel, Lee is associated with the sacrifice of animals. In Scene 1 he brags to Austin: "Had me a Pit Bull there for a while but I lost him . . . Fightin' dog. Damn I made some good money off that little dog. Real good money."

In Genesis blood sacrifice is required by the patriarchal deity Yahweh, and in *True West* Lee is clearly allied with the masculine and violent values of this deity. Even Lee's vocabulary associates him with blood sacrifices. When Austin innocently offers to give him money, Lee furiously rejects the gift, calling it "Hollywood blood money" and accusing Austin of attempting to use that money to "buy off" the "Old Man." Throughout much of the play, references to the father, who is (like the mother) left unnamed, prompt in Lee a sense of reverence and pride, while in Austin such references provoke an outbreak of hostility, guilt, or disgust. Thus, in the play, as in Genesis, the patriarchal and matriarchal systems clash.

In the Americanized mythology of *True West,* however, the biblical story of Cain and Abel undergoes ironic and comic revisions that undermine both the patriarchal values of Lee and the matriarchal values of Austin. The true American deity is Success, and Austin is initially that deity's favored child. The deity's agent is a Hollywood producer named Saul Kimmer, who has promised Austin a lucrative movie contract for the love story he is writing.

In contrast, Lee offers Saul a Western about a man's confrontation with his wife's lover and involving a bizarre chase in which two horses are taken by trailer to the Texas panhandle and then ridden into the desert at night. Lee seeks Austin's creative assistance in writing an outline of the plot, but he angrily rejects the notion that Austin's contribution is important or inspired: ''Favor! Big Favor! Handin' down favors from the mountain top.'' The implication is that Austin is not like God handing down the tablets to Moses; what Austin hands down, Lee is quite prepared to reject. Clichéd as Lee's story is, it holds out the promise of a bloody duel at the end, the blood offering that Abel presented to Yahweh. As one might predict, the god of Hollywood eventually rejects Austin's comparatively wholesome love story and smiles on Lee's Western, just as the Old Testament deity accepted Abel's blood sacrifice and threw down the altar of Cain.

In Genesis, Saul is the king of the Hebrews who proves himself incapable of controlling the Philistines (I Samuel 31). The allusion works well within *True West.* With the rejection of Austin's script, Saul abandons all efforts to control the Philistines in American culture, whose indifference to refinement and art is well illustrated by their taste in movies. While Austin had been initially pleased to hear Lee refer to his romantic screenplay as ''art,'' Lee desires no esthetic (i.e., feminine) qualities in his Western. He approvingly quotes Saul as saying, ''In this business we make movies, American movies. Leave the films to the French.'' Further, when Saul promises to produce a movie based on Lee's story, Lee arranges to have ''a big slice'' of his profits (perhaps a tithe?) turned over to the father.

In the second half of the play, Austin becomes more and more embittered and increasingly similar to his evil brother. Having in a sense been failed by the matriarchal deity, Austin neglects her rites. He lets his mother's plants go unwatered, forgets about returning to his wife and children, and begs Lee to take him into the desert.

Meanwhile Lee, the creature of night, the desert, and the patriarchy, begs for Austin's creative assistance. Despite Austin's chiding that Lee is creating only ''illusions of characters'' drawn from ''fantasies of a long lost boyhood,'' Lee's optimism about his story remains strong until Scene 7, when Austin tells him about his last encounter with their father. Lee's confidence is apparently shattered after he hears Austin's ludicrous description of their patriarch as a toothless, drunken beggar staggering from one bar to another and searching for the doggie bag of Chop Suey that contains his false teeth.

Scene 8 opens upon a tableau of defeatism and desolation, framed by their mother's ''dead and drooping'' house plants. That this opening tableau is symbolic and imbued with the irrationality characteristic of myth is borne out by the chronology of the play, which suggests that only forty-eight hours have passed since Austin was watering the flourishing house plants in Scene 2. Both brothers have lost faith in themselves and in the values that had allowed them to define themselves. Austin has transformed himself into a pale imitation of Lee by stealing toasters instead of TVs. Meanwhile Lee has become an even more frustrated writer than Austin had been in Scene 1. He stands before us smashing a golf club into Austin's typewriter with the regularity and impassivity of a metronome. Allen Ramsey aptly points out that this scene presents us with ''the symbolic destruction of the West called Hollywood, with Shepard's three symbols of that world—the golf club, the typewriter, and the manuscript''(*Publications of the Arkansas Philological Society,* fall, 1989). For both brothers Hollywood has proven to be no Paradise.

Brutal and insensitive by nature, Lee is incapable of writing a screenplay for the same reason that he is incapable of treating women with tenderness or concern. Claiming that he needs a woman, he fumbles through his collection of scribbled telephone numbers, desperately dials the operator, and rips the telephone from the wall when even she hangs up on him. Clearly, Lee is no favorite of many-named Astarte. Just as clearly, Austin hasn't got the hang of male machismo. Having lost faith in the power of romance, Austin assures Lee that ''A woman isn't the answer. Never was,'' but Austin is too wrapped up in his conscience and too concerned about his victims to be a self-satisfied liberator of small appliances. Nor can he treat women as casual sex objects; when Lee asks if he knows any women, Austin can only answer, ''I'm a married man.''

As this penultimate scene unfolds, Austin's strangely devotional attitude towards toast becomes the primary focus of dramatic concern. Lee finally demands angrily, ''What is this bullshit with the toast anyway! You make it sound like salvation or something.'' And Austin replies, ''Well it is like salvation sort of.'' Lee then concludes, ''so go to church why don't ya.'' In a comic and incongruous fashion, the scene presents a veiled allusion both to the ritual offering of grain in matriarchal religion and to the breaking of bread in Christianity. The contrast between the two brothers, as well as the matriarchal and patriarchal systems of belief, is summarized by their own synopses: Austin loves beginnings (birth, creativity); Lee counters that he has ''always been kinda' partial to endings'' (death, conclusions, conquest). The conflict between the brothers reaches a new level of intensity as Lee knocks away Austin's neatly slacked plate of bread and then methodically crushes each piece of toast. Finally, their temporary alliance in creating a script about mortal battle in the desert is ratified in a parody of communion when Lee ''takes a huge crushing bite'' of toast while staring raptly into his brother's eyes.

The final scene presents a mockery of matriarchal religion to balance the dismissal of the patriarchy in Scene 7 and the parody of communion in Scene 8. First, we see the comic ineptitude of both brothers as writers. They argue over the clichéd line ''I know this prairie like the back a' my hand''—eventually changing it to ''I'm on intimate terms with this prairie'' even though they are aware of the sexual connotation of the words. Is it too fanciful to see in this sentence a parody of matriarchal religion, with its emphasis on the planting of seed in the soil of Mother Earth? Perhaps. But then Mom arrives like a *deus ex machina* at the very moment that Lee repeats, '''He's on intimate terms with this prairie.' Sounds real mysterious and kinda' threatening at the same time.'' Yet if Mom is Mother Earth amid her wilted plants, hasn't she become trivial, irrelevant, comic, and a little mad?

Mom says she has come back from Alaska because she ''just started missing all [her] plants.'' The greatest power of the Goddess was the ability to bring the dead back to life—possibly as an emblem of the annual rebirth of life in the spring. Thus, Isis resurrects her husband Osiris and is ''responsible for the rebirth of vegetation.'' Similarly, in the ancient Ugaritic mythology of Canaan, Anath brings about the resurrection of her brother/lover Baal. Although the plants remain dead in *True West,* Mom does announce a resurrection of sorts. She claims that ''Picasso's in town. Isn't that incredible?'' When Austin points out that Picasso is dead, she merely reiterates, ''No, he's not dead. He's visiting the museum. . . . We have to go down there and see him. . . . This is the chance of a lifetime.'' With the patriarch rendered toothless and the matriarch demented, both brothers seem lost. The play concludes with Lee and Austin warily circling each other ''in a vast desert-like landscape'' while a single coyote yaps for the kill.

True West is, of course, Shepard's attempt to synthesize the characteristics of the ''true West''—a West that is represented neither by the love story of Austin nor by the implausible chase sequence of Lee, but rather by the play itself, in which good is warped until it is indistinguishable from evil and craftsmanship of any kind is scorned in the pursuit of popularity. Later, in *A Lie of the Mind,* Shepard will begin toying with a synthesis of the masculine and feminine into what Beth calls a ''woman-man.'' In *True West,* however, mothers and fathers, as well as matriarchy and patriarchy, are equally irrelevant to modern life. The modern West is a place guided by false materialistic gods who misjudge the efforts of men and set them at each others' throats. Mothers, fathers, gods, and goddesses are all equally comic, trivial, insignificant, and insane in the true West of Sam Shepard's *True West.*

Source: Jeffrey D. Hoeper, ''Cain, Canaanites, and Philistines in Sam Shepard's *True West,*'' in *Modern Drama,* Vol. 36, No. 1, March, 1993, pp. 76–81.

Frank Rich

In this review of True West*'s Broadway debut, Rich offers a mixed assessment of the play, praising Shepard's text yet lamenting the shortcomings of this particular production.*

Some day, when the Warring parties get around to writing their memoirs, we may actually discover who killed *True West,* the Sam Shepard play that finally opened at the Public Theater last night. As the press has already reported, this failure is an orphan. Robert Woodruff, the nominal director, left the play in previews and disowned the production. Mr. Shepard has also disowned the production, although he has not ventured from California to see it. The producer Joseph Papp, meanwhile, has been left, holding the bag. New Year's will be, here

"*TRUE WEST* SEEMS TO BE A VERY GOOD SHEPARD PLAY—WHICH MEANS THAT IT'S ONE OF THE AMERICAN THEATER'S MOST PRECIOUS NATURAL RESOURCES."

shortly, and one can only hope that these talented men will forgive and forget.

At least their battle has been fought for a worthwhile cause. *True West* seems to be a very good Shepard play—which means that it's one of the American theater's most precious natural resources. But no play can hold the stage all by itself. Except for odd moments, when Mr. Shepard's fantastic language rips through the theater on its own sinuous strength, the *True West* at the Public amounts to little more than a stand-up run-through of a text that remains to be explored. This play hasn't been misdirected; it really looks as if it hasn't been directed at all.

You know a play has no director when funny dialogue dies before it reaches the audience. Or when two lead actors step on each other's lines and do "business" rather than create characters. Or when entrances and scene-endings look arbitrary rather than preplanned. Or when big farcical sequences—an avalanche of Coors beer cans, for instance—clatter about the stage creating confusion rather than mirth. Or when an evening's climax—the mystical death embrace of two fratricidal brothers—is so vaguely choreographed it looks like a polka. All these things and more happen at the Public.

It's a terrible shame. *True West* is a worthy direct descendant of Mr. Shepard's *Curse of the Starving Class* and *Buried Child.* Many of his persistent recent themes are present and accounted for—the spiritual death of the American family, the corruption of the artist by business, the vanishing of the Western wilderness and its promised dream of freedom. If the playwright dramatizes his concerns in fantastic flights of poetic imagery, that imagery always springs directly from the life of the people and drama he has invented. Mr. Shepard doesn't graft symbols onto his plays. He's a true artist; his best works are organic creations that cannot be broken down into their constituent parts.

The brothers of *True West* are both hustlers, or, if you will, modernday cowboys who have lost their range. Lee (Peter Boyle) is a drifter and petty burglar, and the younger Austin (Tommy Lee Jones) is a screenwriter. The play is about what happens when the two men reunite in their mother's ticky-tacky suburban Los Angeles home. By the end of the evening, they have stolen each other's identities and destroyed the house, and yet they can never completely sever the ties that bind. Like the heroes in the "True life" Hollywood movie western they write during the course of the play, Lee and Austin are "two lamebrains" doomed to chase each other eternally across a desolate, ever-receding frontier.

Mr. Shepard is an awesome writer. When Lee and Austin lament the passing of the West they loved (and that maybe never existed), they launch into respectively loopy, nostalgic monologues about the film *Lonely Are the Brave* and the now-extinct neighborhood of their youth. Amusing as they are, these comic riffs are also moving because they give such full life to Mr. Shepard's conflict between America's myths and the bitter, plastic reality that actually exists: Lee can no longer distinguish the true West from the copy, he finds in a movie; Austin discovers that his childhood memories are inseparable from the vistas he sees on cheap post cards. Looking for roots, Mr. Shepard's characters fall into a void.

The playwright also provides motifs involving dogs, crickets, desert topography, cars, household appliances (especially toasters and television sets) and the brothers' unseen, destitute father. As the play progresses, these images keep folding into one another until we are completely transported into the vibrant landscape of Mr. Shepard's imagination. Such is the collective power of this playwright's words that even his wilder conceits seem naturalistic in the context of his play. We never question that Lee would try to destroy a typewriter with a golf club or that the family patriarch would lose his false teeth in a doggie bag full of chop suey.

True West slips only when Mr. Shepard, a master of ellipses, tries to fill in his blanks. Does he really need lines like, "There's nothing real here now, least of all me," or, "There's no such thing as the West anymore"? The movie-industry gags, most of which involve a producer in gold chains

(Louis Zorich), are jarring as well. Mr. Shepard's witticisms about development deals and agents have been written funnier by Woody Allen and Paul Mazursky, and they bring *True West* down to earth.

Still, these judgments must be tentative. It's impossible to evaluate a play definitively when it hasn't been brought to life on stage. There's nervous energy at the Public, but it leads nowhere. Mr. Boyle, a loping, illshaven figure in baggy clothes, is engagingly sleazy for a while, but his performance trails off into vagueness and repetition just as it should begin to build. Mr. Jones is kinetic and finally frantic as he tries and fails to get a handle on the screenwriter. We never believe that these actors are mirror-image brothers locked into a psychological cat-and-mouse game. Theatergoers who venture to the Public must depend on their own imaginations to supply the crackling timing and the violent tension that are absent. Who's to blame? Please address your inquiries to the Messrs. Shepard, Woodruff and Papp. And while you're writing, demand restitution. These men owe New York a *true True West.*

Source: Frank Rich, review of *True West,* in the *New York Times,* Vol. 130, No. 44807, December 24, 1980, p. C9.

SOURCES

Beaufort, John. Review of *True West* in the *Christian Science Monitor,* December 31, 1980.

Chubb, Kenneth. Interview with Sam Shepard in *Theatre Quarterly,* Vol. IV, no. 15, August-October, 1974, pp. 3-16.

Coe, Robert. Interview with Sam Shepard in the *New York Times Magazine,* November 23, 1980.

Gussow, Mel. ''Brothers and Rivals'' in the *New York Times,* October 17, 1982.

Kalem, T. E. ''City Coyotes Prowling the Brain'' in *Time,* January 5, 1981.

Kerr, Walter. ''Of Shepard's Myths and Ibsen's Man'' in the *New York Times,* Vol. 50, no. 3, January 11, 1981.

Kroll, Jack. ''California Dreaming'' in *Newsweek,* January 5, 1981.

Rich, Frank. ''Shepard's *True West*'' in the *New York Times,* December 24, 1980.

Watt, Douglas. ''*True West* Moves Shepard in the Right Direction'' in the *Daily News,* December 24, 1980.

FURTHER READING

Grant, Gary. ''Shifting the Paradigm: Shepard, Myth, and the Transformation of Consciousness'' in *Modern Drama,* Vol. 36, no. 1, March, 1993, pp. 120-30.

One of several valuable essays in this special issue devoted in large part to Shepard, Grant asserts that Shepard's dramatic style is a ''new way of seeing'' that is similar to the experience of listening to jazz or rock and roll music.

Hart, Lynda. *Sam Shepard's Metaphorical Stages,* Greenwood Press, 1987.

In addition to a valuable section on *True West,* Hart's book contains an interesting descriptive essay of Shepard's film career and an excellent biographical sketch of the playwright's life.

Hoeper, Jeffrey D. ''Cain, Canaanites, and Philistines in Sam Shepard's *True West*'' in *Modern Drama,* Vol. 36, no. 1, March, 1993, pp. 76-82.

Examines *True West* as a biblical allegory. Hoeper compares Austin and Lee to the biblical figures of Cain and Abel, the combative sons of Adam and Eve.

Holstein, Suzy Clarkson. '''All Growed Up' in the True West, or Huck and Tom Meet Sam Shepard'' in *Western American Literature,* Vol. 29, no. 1, Spring, 1994, pp. 41-50.

Citing similarities between Mark Twain's character Huck Finn and Lee and Twain's Tom Sawyer and Austin, Holstein suggests that Shepard's brothers could be understood as adult versions of these young literary characters.

Kleb, William. ''Sam Shepard'' in *American Playwrights since 1945,* edited by Philip C. Kolin. Greenwood Press, 1989.

Kleb's long essay in this valuable reference guide to American theatre provides an assessment of Shepard's reputation and a detailed and fascinating summary of the production histories of Shepard's plays, including the controversial production history of *True West.* The essay includes several very useful bibliographies.

Kleb, William. ''Theatre in San Francisco: Sam Shepard's *True West* '' in *Theatre,* Vol. 12, no. 1, Fall-Winter, 1980, pp. 65-71.

This review essay of the original production of the play in San Francisco suggests in its conclusion that *True West* may be Shepard's self-dramatization of divided identity and his most subjective and personal play.

Orbison, Tucker. ''Mythic Levels in Shepard's *True West* in *Modern Drama,* Vol. 27, no. 4, December, 1984, pp. 506-19.

A thorough and detailed examination of what is meant when critics and scholars say that Shepard writes ''mythic'' drama.

Rosen, Carol. '''Emotional Territory': An Interview with Sam Shepard'' in *Modern Drama,* Vol. 36, no. 1, March, 1993, pp. 1-11.

In his first extensive interview in a decade, Shepard discusses his themes, his methods of working, and many other interesting topics.

Schvey, Henry I. ''A Worm in the Wood: The Father-Son Relationship in the Plays of Sam Shepard'' in *Modern Drama,* Vol. 36, no. 1, March, 1993, pp 12- 26.

The fathers in Shepard's plays, including the father in *True West,* are based on the relationship Shepard had with his own father. The presence of the father lingers in the son ''like a worm in the wood.''

Shewey, Don. ''The True Story of 'True West''' in the *Village Voice,* November 30, 1982, p. 115.

A review of the 1982 Cherry Lane Theatre production by Gary Sinise's Steppenwolf company. In addition to providing a review of the performance, this piece offers an analysis of the controversy that surrounded the original production two years earlier at Joseph Papp's Public Theatre.

Waiting for Lefty

CLIFFORD ODETS

1935

Clifford Odets's *Waiting for Lefty* is a vigorous, confrontational work, based on a 1934 strike of unionized New York cabdrivers. Explicit political messages dominate the play, whose ultimate goal was nothing less than the promotion of a communist revolution in America. Appearing at the height of the Great Depression, the play's original 1935 production was a critical and popular sensation. *Waiting for Lefty* was widely staged throughout the country and brought Odets sudden fame. While its dramatic style has long since fallen out of fashion (along with the idealistic politics that inspired it), it is considered a prime example of a *genre* known as ''revolutionary'' or ''agitprop'' theatre. (The latter term is a combination of ''agitation'' and ''propaganda.'') The idealistic practitioners of agitprop sought to harness the power of drama to a specific political cause and create a ''people's theatre'' for the new world that would follow the revolution.

A one-act play in eight episodes, *Waiting for Lefty* is composed of two basic stagings. The main setting is a union hall, where the members wait to take a hotly-contested strike vote. While the corrupt union leader Harry Fatt arrogantly tries to discourage the members from walking out, support for a strike is high, and the workers nervously await the arrival of the leader of the strike faction, Lefty Costello. As they wait, members of the strike committee address the workers, each telling the story of how he came to be involved in the union and convinced of the necessity for a strike. These indi-

vidual stories are sketched in a series of vignettes, played out in a small spotlit area of the stage. Each is a story of unjust victimization, mirroring Fatt's heavy-handed attempts to control the union meeting. The building tension and emotion reaches a climax when the news arrives that Lefty has been murdered, and the meeting erupts in a unanimous demand to "Strike! Strike!"

Modern audiences may find *Waiting for Lefty*'s style and dogmatic politics strange and unfamiliar; it is rarely produced and is often characterized as an historical curiosity. More than most dramas, it is the product of a particular time and place—for its overriding concern was to influence that time and place, not to create "immortal art," and certainly not to create diverting, light-hearted entertainment. It faced its grim times squarely and offered its audience a stirring vision of hope. In this sense *Waiting for Lefty* is seen as an important dramatic work that offers historical evidence of the social power and aspirations of theatre.

AUTHOR BIOGRAPHY

Clifford Odets is best-known for his early, Depression-era dramas, particularly *Waiting for Lefty,* an overt work of propaganda that tells a story of working-class struggle, intended to promote a socialist revolution. His later works were more conventional in style and content and seldom preached a political message. Though his later work often met with critical and commercial approval, he never regained the prominence he enjoyed in the 1930s. He is primarily associated with the left-wing "agitprop" (a term defined as political propaganda as proffered through literature, drama, art, and music) theatre of that time.

Odets was born July 18, 1906, in Philadelphia, Pennsylvania, the son of Russian Jewish immigrants. He moved with his family to the Bronx at the age of six. Though he would associate himself with the political causes of the working-class and downtrodden, his early circumstances were decidedly middle-class. Odets rebelled against his father's strong wish that he enter the family printing business, aspiring instead to become an actor. He dropped out of high school in 1923 and entered into a succession of minor jobs in the theatrical world, eventually finding his way to the Group Theater in 1930.

As its name suggests, the Group Theater was a collective, whose members embraced socialist principles and saw their theatrical work as an expression of their political values. Disdaining the "star-system" and commercialism of Broadway, their ideal was to be a community of equals, working selflessly together to produce works that would serve to help transform society itself by dramatizing the political realities of the times and inspiring audiences to join the struggle for change. Odets was asked to submit plays for the troupe, and the productions of his work began to attract wide critical attention. When *Waiting for Lefty* debuted in 1935, it proved immensely popular and drew high praise from drama critics, securing for its author a sudden, national reputation. The play won both the Yale Drama Prize and the New Theatre League award for 1935 and was widely produced across the country.

Odets began receiving offers from Hollywood and from the "big-time," mainstream (Broadway) theatres and production companies. Though he continued to work with the Group Theater, he also pursued these more commercial opportunities, with the justification that the income they produced would subsidize the continuing efforts of the Group. In 1937 he wrote *Golden Boy,* the tale of a troubled prizefighter; it became his greatest commercial success, and the sale of the movie rights for $75,000 provided much-needed capital for the collective. Like most of Odets's subsequent work, its style is more conventional than that of *Waiting for Lefty,* and it lacks an overt political message. As Odets rose to prominence and mainstream approval, many left-wing contemporaries accused him of "selling out," abandoning his principles to enhance the commercial appeal of his work. Eventually he broke with the Group Theatre and the agitprop style.

Odets became a Hollywood screenwriter and continued to write for the theatre. In 1952 he was called before a Congressional subcommittee investigating "un-American activities" and asked to testify about his previous left-wing agitation efforts. This experience, part of the infamous anti-communist "witch hunts" of the McCarthy era (named for Senator Joseph McCarthy, who spearheaded the persecution), appears to have had a devastating impact on Odets. He had already renounced many of his earlier political beliefs, but his very association with left-wing causes left him vulnerable to being ''blacklisted'' (prohibited from working) as a ''security risk.'' Many people in his position were forced to either abandon their careers or testify against their former associates—who would then become targets of the same sort of persecution.

While Odets did not technically ''name names'' in his subcommittee appearance (each of the people he mentioned had already come to the attention of the committee), he did cooperate enough to remove himself from further suspicion. He later expressed guilt and ''repulsion'' for his testimony and apparently was tormented by the matter for the rest of his life. He continued to write screenplays, teleplays, and dramas but his production dropped off after 1952, and he never regained his earlier prominence. He was honored with an Award of Merit Medal from the American Academy of Arts and Letters in 1961. Odets died two years later on August 14, 1963, in Los Angeles, California.

Clifford Odets in 1956

PLOT SUMMARY

Prologue: The Strike Meeting

The curtain rises on a union meeting, already in progress. Harry Fatt, the union leader, is addressing a group of workers seated before him. A six- or seven-man committee sits in a semicircle behind him. Fatt speaks forcefully against a proposed strike, noting the failure of several recent strikes, and arguing that such tactics are both unproductive and unnecessary. He expresses confidence that the President is ''looking out for our interests,'' and suggests that those who wish to strike are communists (''reds''), out to destroy everything Americans hold dear. Despite his confidence and heated rhetoric, Fatt's message is not well-received. Throughout his speech the voices of workers rise in opposition and defiance, while the ominous presence of a ''gunman,'' who menaces the hecklers, suggests that Fatt's leadership has less than honest democratic origins.

From the workers comes an enthusiastic call for Lefty, the (elected) chairman of the strike committee, who is mysteriously absent from the meeting. Fatt suggests that Lefty has abandoned the workers. The workers demand to hear from the other members of the strike committee. Unable to calm the crowd, Fatt ''insolently'' gives way to Joe Mitchell, a committee member. Joe denies that he is a ''red,'' offering his war wounds as evidence of his patriotism, and defends Lefty's courage and conviction. He speaks to the workers of their own poverty and exploitation, arguing that a strike is the only way they might achieve ''a living wage.'' Joe tells the workers they must each make up their own minds on the issue; as for himself, ''[m]y wife made up my mind last week.'' As he begins to relate the experience, the stage lights fade out.

Scene I: Joe and Edna

A spotlight creates a small playing space within the meeting; the workers remain ''dimly visible in the outer dark,'' occasionally commenting on the action. Joe, a cabdriver, comes home from a long and unprofitable day's work to a desperate household. The furniture has just been repossessed, the rent is two months past due, the children have gone to bed without dinner, and his wife, Edna, is in a sullen and bitter mood. Exasperated by their poverty, Edna taunts and challenges Joe, finally threatening to leave him for her old boyfriend, Bud Haas.

Edna makes it clear that she doesn't directly blame Joe for their condition but rather the bosses who set the terms of his employment. She resents her husband for passively accepting his lot. "For God's sake, do something, Joe," Edna pleads, "get wise. Maybe get your buddies together, maybe go on strike for better money." Joe first argues that "strikes don't work" but later admits that the union leaders are "racketeers" who rule by force without consulting the workers—standing up to them could cost his life. Edna replies that she'd rather see him dead if he won't fight for his family. Once more she urges him to take action by helping organize the union cabbies to "[s]weep out those racketeers," to "stand up like men and fight for the crying kids and wives." This time, her argument wins Joe over; he jumps up, kisses her passionately, and rushes out to find Lefty (who apparently has already begun organizing within the union). As Edna stands in triumph, the stage lights come up and the scene returns to the union meeting, where Joe concludes his speech by calling for a strike.

Continuing the workers' stories, Miller is called upon to relate the circumstances that brought him to the strike meeting.

Scene II: Lab Assistant Episode

After a blackout, the scene finds Miller, a lab assistant, in the luxurious office of his employer, the industrialist Fayette. Fayette compliments Miller's work, gives him a twenty-dollar raise, and tells him he's being transferred to a new project working under a "very important chemist," Dr. Brenner. Miller's gratitude for the promotion gradually dissolves as the particulars of the project are revealed. He will have to live at the lab full-time throughout the project, working in utmost secrecy. His job will be to develop chemical weapons for the military in preparation for the "new war" Fayette considers imminent. Having lost a brother and two cousins in the last war, Miller expresses reservations about the nature of the work. Fayette appeals to Miller's self-interest: the project will mean advancement in his career and personal exemption from military service. Fayette believes that the consequences of the work are "not our worry," and that business can never be "sentimental over human life." Finally, he asks Miller to provide him with "confidential" reports on Brenner throughout the project—to, in effect, spy on his colleague. Miller refuses indignantly, saying that he's "not built that way." Fayette offers a larger raise, appeals to Miller's patriotism, and eventually threatens to fire him, all to no avail: Miller stands firm in his decision, is fired by Fayette, and concludes the interview by punching his (former) boss "square in the mouth."

Scene III: The Young Hack and His Girl

In another domestic scene, Florrie and her brother Irv argue about her boyfriend, Sid, who is coming to take her out dancing. She and Sid are in love and want to marry. But like Joe, Sid is a cabdriver and doesn't earn enough to support a family. Moreover, Florrie and Irv's mother is bedridden, and the family has been struggling. They depend on her for the care and housework she provides as well as the income from her job as a store clerk. Irv recognizes that Sid is serious in his intentions but intentions aren't enough: Florrie's duty is to her family and it's simply "no time to get married." Irv demands that she stop seeing Sid and even threatens to beat the boyfriend up. While she asserts the right to a life of her own, she agrees that she and Sid need to have a serious talk.

Sid arrives, and the lovers soon begin to confront their situation together. Despite their love, they can find no way around the economic facts. They've been engaged for three years now, but Sid is no closer to being able to provide for her and sees no prospects for the future. His brother Sam, despite the advantage of a college education, has just joined the navy because he was unable to find a job. Sid feels like "a dog," unable to "look the world straight in the face, spit in its eye like a man should do"—though perhaps, with Florrie beside him, he might. "But something wants us to be lonely like that," she answers, "crawling alone in the dark. Or they want us trapped." Sid identifies that "something" as "the big-shot money men" in power, who keep people like themselves in poverty and send people like Sam off to war. Reluctantly, he concludes that they must separate ("If we can't climb higher than this together—we better stay apart.") After a last, passionate dance to a phonograph record, he tries to leave but is unable. Florrie bursts into tears, Sid falls to his knees and buries his face in her lap. The scene blacks out.

Scene IV: Labor Spy Episode

The action returns to the union meeting. Fatt argues once again that a strike won't succeed. He introduces a speaker with "practical strike experience" to help persuade the workers of that fact: Tom Clayton from Philadelphia, the veteran of a failed taxi strike some three months ago. This "thin, modest individual" tells his fellow-cabbies that Fatt is right, but he is soon shouted down by a "Clear Voice" in the crowd who claims that "Clayton" is an impostor, a company spy named Clancy. Over Fatt's objections, the Voice details Clancy's long career as a strike-breaker. Fatt demands proof, and "Clayton" calls his accuser a liar, claiming never to have seen him before. At this point the "voice" identifies himself—as the traitor's own brother. As the impostor "Clayton" flees down the center aisle, Fatt pretends to have been ignorant of the deception.

Scene V: The Young Actor

An unemployed actor named Philips waits in the office of a theatrical producer, Grady, making conversation with Grady's secretary—who is clearly not an admirer of her boss. She reveals that Grady is luxuriating in a perfumed bath while he makes Philips wait. She advises Philips to lie about his experience, since Grady "wouldn't know a good actor if he fell over him in the dark." Philips confides to her that he is desperate for a job. She offers him a dollar. He answers that it won't help much: his wife is expecting their first child in a month, and he must find a way to support them.

Grady (played by Fatt) enters, asks his secretary to call the hospital to "see how Boris is," and conducts a gruff job interview. He soon catches Philips in a lie about his resume and abruptly decides he can't use the actor; he has an opening for the part of a soldier and needs a bigger man. Philips protests that he has military experience and is sure he can act the role. He guarantees a fine performance, telling the producer that he's an "artist." But Grady is a businessman with investments to protect, and the safe course is to cast for physical type, not to take chances on unknown actors. "What do I care if you can act it?," he asks Philips, "Your face and height we want, not your soul, son." Philips pleads for any work, however small, but Grady has nothing to offer. As he concludes the interview, the secretary reports that "Boris" is doing fine.

After Grady leaves, the secretary tells Philips that "Boris" is Grady's dog, in the hospital to be castrated. "They do the same to you, but you don't know it!," she says, then advises, "In the next office, don't let them see you down in the mouth." As he starts to leave, thanking her for treating him "like a human being," she offers the dollar again, telling him it will buy him ten loaves of bread—or nine loaves and "one copy of The Communist Manifesto." "What's that?," he asks, taking the dollar; she promises to give him a copy, describing the document, in biblical terms, as the revelation of "a new earth and a new heaven" and of a world where the *militant,* not the meek, will inherit the earth. "Come out in the light, Comrade," she says, as the scene dissolves in blackout.

Scene VI: Intern Episode

Dr. Barnes, an elderly hospital administrator, angrily finishes a phone call, referring to a decision he had opposed involving a Dr. Benjamin. He is about to pour himself a drink when Benjamin arrives at his office. Hiding the bottle, he invites the young doctor into his office. Benjamin reports that he has just been replaced on one of his "charity cases" by an incompetent surgeon who happens to be a Senator's nephew; the case is serious, and he fears the patient's life is in danger. Barnes tries to evade the issue but soon lets down his guard: "God damn it, do you think it's my fault?," he despairs. Benjamin apologetically starts to leave, but Barnes calls him back.

Gradually, Barnes reveals that the hospital will be undergoing several changes—decisions he has fought against and is ashamed to carry out. Because of budget cutbacks, a charity ward is being closed and several staff members will be laid off. Benjamin has shown great promise and is considered "top man here"—yet he is to lose his job while less qualified doctors keep theirs. Barnes confirms that Benjamin is a victim of anti-Semitism, despite the presence of several wealthy Jews on the hospital's board of directors. He remarks that he sees little difference "between wealthy Jews and rich Gentiles" and bitterly complains that "doctors don't run medicine" in this "rich man's country."

A phone call interrupts Barnes with the news that Benjamin's patient has died on the operating table; it is the emotional "last straw" for both men. Benjamin had doubted radical political doctrines before but now sees them confirmed by his experience: "you don't believe theories until they happen to you." Barnes encourages his colleague's outrage and new-found determination. He is too old for the cause (a "fossil" who must yet provide for an invalid daughter), but he exhorts the younger man to fight the system that has victimized him. Benjamin considers emigrating to Russia for "the wonderful opportunity to do good work in their socialized medicine,'' but he chooses instead to stay and work for change in America. He will find a working-class job (''maybe drive a cab'') and join the proletarian struggle. He raises high a clenched fist as the scene blacks out.

Conclusion: Strike Meeting

Back at the union meeting, an old worker named Agate Keller offers a rambling speech. He seems eccentric and suggests that he ''ain't been right'' since falling out of the cradle in infancy. Yet Keller also shows a passionate attachment to the working-class cause. As an eleven-year-old factory worker, he lost an eye in an industrial accident; he mentions that there was a union in that factory but that its officers were corrupt and did nothing for the members. Fatt and his supporters object loudly, but Keller demurs that he was merely speaking of ''unions in general'' and expresses confidence that ''our officers is all aces.''

Keller goes on to tell about being unable to wear his union button today: it seems that, when he reached for his coat, he found the button was on fire—''blush[ing] itself to death,'' out of shame. Fatt again tries to shout him down and the gunman approaches menacingly, but Keller breaks away and continues. A group of workers forms protectively around him, and, with rising emotion, he declares that their lives are on the line, that the choice is between ''slow death and war.'' ''What are we waiting for?,'' he cries. ''Don't wait for Lefty! He might never come.'' A worker breaks in with the sudden news that Lefty has been found, shot dead—presumably by the ''racketeers'' in the union leadership. In tears, Keller exhorts the crowd to sacrifice their very lives to create ''a new world.'' Addressing the audience, he demands, ''Well, what's the answer?'' The workers provide that answer-''Strike!''—in a triumphant chant that swells as the curtain falls.

CHARACTERS

Dr. Barnes

In Scene VI, Barnes is a hospital administrator torn between his convictions and his professional obligations. He deplores the ruthless, discriminatory policies of the hospital's wealthy board of directors, especially their dismissal of the talented young Dr. Benjamin; but he is also powerless to change these decisions, and sees no choice but to carry them out. Because of his advanced age, and the fact that he must provide for an invalid daughter, he feels unable to participate directly in the workers' struggle. Yet he is a passionate believer in the cause and exhorts the younger man to take up the fight he wishes he could join, encouraging Benjamin to fire a shot ''for old Doc Barnes.''

Dr. Benjamin

A talented and dedicated young surgeon, Dr. Benjamin learns in Scene VI that he is losing his job because of the discriminatory policies of his hospital's directors. The experience persuades him of the truth of communist theory and fires his determination to fight the capitalist system. He is tempted to emigrate to Russia, in order to work under a system of socialized medicine but decides to stay in America even though this means giving up the medical career for which his parents sacrificed so much to provide him. He takes a job as a cab driver and becomes a member of the strike committee.

Clancy

See Tom Clayton

Tom Clayton

The ''labor spy'' in Scene IV, ''Tom Clayton'' poses as a ''brother'' cabbie from Philadelphia. Having participated in a failed taxi strike there a few months ago, he offers that bitter experience to convince the members that a strike is useless. But a ''clear voice'' from the crowd—which turns out to be that of his own brother—exposes him as a strikebreaker named ''Clancy,'' who has long been employed by industrialists to undermine militant union organizers. His charade exposed, the deceitful ''Clayton'' flees the wrath of the workers.

''Clear Voice'' (Clancy's brother)

Unidentified at first, this ''voice'' emerges from the crowd in Scene IV to denounce ''Tom Clayton'' as a labor spy. His knowledge of ''Clayton'' is irrefutable, for the traitor he detests is ''my own lousy brother.'' Like many other characters, the ''voice'' has discovered where his true loyalties lie; in this case, his commitment to the working class far outweighs the bonds of family.

Lefty Costello

Though he is the title character, Lefty never appears on stage; nonetheless, he is a heroic figure, in direct contrast to Fatt's villainy. A dedicated union organizer (and presumably a communist), he enjoys the confidence of the workers and seems to be their true leader, the driving force behind the strike effort. He has been elected chairman of the strike committee, and his absence at the meeting is troubling; it seems the members are counting on his leadership to stand up to Fatt and make the eagerly-awaited strike a reality.

Lefty recalls other heroic, martyred organizers of union lore, like the legendary folk-singer Joe Hill. Though their loss is deeply felt, such figures are never considered irreplaceable, for their cause is one of mass action. The play's climax comes when the workers *stop* waiting for Lefty and take responsibility for their own struggle. Though they have depended on him, they do not need a leader to give them power; they need only seize the collective power they had always had, by standing together in defiance.

Harry Fatt

Harry Fatt, the corrupt union leader, is the play's most obvious villain and the primary focus of its outrage—a stereotypical ''fat cat,'' driven by a ruthless greed and a hunger for power. He is unmoved by the desperate poverty of the workers he claims to serve. He is purposely exaggerated, a constant force of pure evil. Odets intended the audience to see him as ''an ugly menace,'' hovering over the lives of all the characters. Though Fatt pays lip-service to democratic principles and rails against the ''anti-American'' nature of communism, he is a tyrant and ''racketeer,'' imposing his will on the union by force and intimidation. The union members overwhelmingly support a strike, and the play's political logic demands one. Yet Fatt is determined to prevent it and to maintain control by any possible means, including murder.

In his production notes, Odets leaves no doubt about the character's significance: ''Fatt, of course, represents the capitalist system throughout the play.'' An industrialist like Fayette (in Scene II) might seem a more logical representative; but Fatt is equally a ''boss'' and enemy of the workers, for his corrupt leadership subverts their struggle for a better life. Whether or not he is directly employed by wealthy capitalists (and the ''Labor Spy Episode'' implies that he is), he serves their cause well, for his actions work as surely as theirs to secure the corrupt system. Like theirs, his power is based on the workers' continued exploitation. In Scene V, Odets emphasizes this connection by having Fatt act the role of Grady, the wealthy theatrical producer. No other character has such a dual function; the roles of ''labor boss'' and ''business executive'' are shown to be literally interchangeable. Like other bosses, Fatt can be defeated only by the collective action of the workers, who rise triumphantly against him as the curtain falls.

Fayette

The head of a large industrial corporation, Fayette is clearly in the ''capitalist'' camp. In Scene II, he offers his employee, the lab assistant Miller, an attractive but unsavory proposition: a generous raise and promotion if he will only agree to help develop fearsome chemical weapons and also agree to spy on his fellow scientists. Fayette is untroubled by the ethical concerns that consume Miller; his only principles seem to be profit and self-interest. ''If big business went sentimental over human life,'' he asserts, ''there wouldn't be big business of any sort!'' Like other ''bosses'' in the play, he is an enemy of the working class. When he pays for his transgressions with a solid punch in the mouth, the audience is meant to feel that it is richly-deserved.

Florence

In Scene III, Florrie and her boyfriend Sid are tragic lovers, unable to marry because of their poverty. Their situation resembles that of Joe and Edna in Scene I; however, their scene is not a confrontation but an emotional *tableaux* (a staged depiction, often without words) of shared misery. They see that they are victims of ''the money men'' whose system keeps them ''lonely'' and ''trapped''—"highly insulting us,'' as Florrie says. The pathos of their reluctant parting is only leavened by the suggestion that his heartbreak leads Sid to join the union cause, the only possible hope of changing their circumstances.

Florrie

See Florence

Mr. Grady

Played by the same actor that plays Harry Fatt, Grady represents the capitalist system in Scene V. He plays a wealthy theatre producer from whom Philips seeks an acting job. He is extravagantly rich, thoroughly self-indulgent, and all but blind to the suffering of others. Though he is an important part of a ''creative'' profession, Grady is a hard-headed businessman; he bases his decisions on economics not art. Though he has the power to relieve Philips's plight, his decision is automatic and inflexible: not even ''Jesus Christ'' would get a part from him if he didn't fit the type. Unable to ignore the young actor's misery, he offers a perfunctory ''I'm sorry'' and ''good luck''—but he expresses far more concern for the health of ''Boris''—his pet wolfhound.

Gunman

The Gunman is Harry Fatt's ''muscle'' and enforcer. Though he has few lines, he is as sinister a figure as Fatt himself, a constant menace. He ''keeps order'' at the union meeting by moving in to silence anyone who challenges Fatt's rule. Though the question is left open, it is possible that he (or another of Fatt's ''henchmen'') is Lefty's murderer. In political terms, he represents all the various forces of violence (military, police, or reactionary gangs) at the disposal of those in power. His kind is used to bully the workers into submission and crush any threat to the establishment. In the final scene, both Fatt and the Gunman try to physically restrain Agate Keller—and, significantly, are unable to do so. Keller's comrades form a human shield, protecting him as he exhorts the meeting to defiance.

Henchman

See Gunman

Irv

Irv appears briefly in Scene III, arguing with his sister Florrie over her relationship with Sid. He knows they are in love but reminds Florrie of the economic facts: Sid doesn't make enough to support her, and Florrie is needed at home, to care for their ailing mother. He adopts a stern, paternal tone (perhaps taking the role of their absent father), urging her to break off the affair and threatening Sid with violence if he persists in his attentions.

Agate Keller

Agate Keller is the last strike-committee member to address the meeting, and he leads the workers in the final call for a strike. He seems eccentric at first and deferential to the corrupt union leaders; but this turns out to be a sly pose, enabling him to criticize Fatt's regime by indirect means. As he continues, and receives the support of his comrades, his speech grows more lucid, plain-spoken, and passionate. Keller is proud to come from ''deep down in the working class,'' and he is bitterly resentful of ''the boss class,'' whose luxuries are paid for with the blood of workers. With growing enthusiasm, he tells the union members they have a simple choice: ''slow death or fight.'' When Lefty's death is announced, he leads the group (and the theatre audience) into a declaration of war, exhorting the ''stormbirds of the working class'' to offer their lives in order to ''make a new world.''

Miller

A scientist working in the research department of a large industrial corporation, Miller is the ''lab assistant'' of Scene II and a strike-committee member. His conversion to the movement grows out of a crucial career decision. His boss, the powerful industrialist Fayette, offers him an attractive promotion and a chance to work with a renowned chemist. But the ''opportunity'' has several strings attached: he must sacrifice his home life, even spy on his colleague—and his job will be to develop chemical weapons, to be used in the ''new war'' Fayette assures him is coming. Miller has seen a brother and two cousins killed in the last war (World War I), possibly by poison gas; he is haunted by their memory and by his mother's belief that their deaths served no ''good cause.'' His principles will not allow him to do Fayette's bidding. He refuses the job and is promptly fired. His pacifism does not prevent him, however, from punching Fayette ''square in the mouth.''

Edna Mitchell

In Scene I, Edna provides the motivation for her husband Joe to become active in the strike movement. Fed up with the family's desperate poverty, she bitterly vents her frustration and finally threatens to leave Joe for her old boyfriend. As she admits, her behavior is that of a ''sour old nag,'' but Odets makes clear that this is a result of her circumstances, not her character—and that her ''nagging'' includes the truth Joe needs to understand what he must do. Edna loves Joe and knows that he is not to blame for their condition. She also knows, however, that their condition is truly desperate and this knowledge provokes her to consider desperate measures. When Joe finally decides to enlist in the union struggle, Edna is ''triumphant'' and drops all thought of breaking up the family.

Joe Mitchell

A member of the strike committee, Joe is the first to rise and speak in Lefty's place. He is not motivated by political abstractions but by the hard facts of life: the hopeless poverty that engulfs his family and the families of his fellow workers. In Scene I, he is goaded into action by his long-suffering wife, Edna. Though he works hard, they are falling further behind, and he feels powerless to change things. Edna demands that he ''do something,'' and ''get wise'' to the way he and the others are being exploited. She nags, pleads, and finally threatens to leave him; at last, her desperation breaks through his denial, opening his eyes to the fact that only a strike can force the cab companies to pay a living wage. He chooses to stand and fight for his family, and that decision is what keeps his family together.

Philips

The ''young actor'' in Scene V, Philips becomes politicized through his inability to find a job and the intervention of Grady's communist stenographer. Devoted to his art and desperate to provide for his pregnant wife, he finds that his ''market value'' depends on his physical appearance, not his acting ability or his creative ''soul.'' Under the system (represented by the wealthy, self-indulgent Grady), art must make a profit and its ''creative decisions'' (such as the casting of a play) are based on iron-clad business principles. Disillusioned, feeling less-than-human in his defeat, Philips is ready for the message of the Communist Manifesto and the hope of revolution. Introduced to communism by the secretary, he goes on to serve as a member of the strike committee.

Sid

The ''young hack'' in scene III, Sid is forced to break off his engagement to Florrie, because he cannot earn enough to support her. Humiliated and heartbroken, he feels like ''a dog,'' not a man—for that is how he feels ''the money men'' treat people like him. But he can also see a day when ''all the dogs like us will be down on them together—an ocean knocking them to hell and back.'' Though he does not speak at the meeting, he is presumably a member of the strike committee and a part of the ''ocean'' that rises at the play's climax.

Stenographer

In Scene V, Grady's nameless stenographer recruits the young actor Philips to the workers' cause by introducing him to communist theory. In private, she freely expresses her contempt for her boss and for all that he stands. Though she works ''within the system,'' she is passionately committed to its eventual destruction. In anti-communist works, such subversive agents are primary villains (like the Fatt/Grady character here); they seduce their unwitting victims into ruthless service for an evil cause. But Odets's ''Comrade'' is humane, as her concern for Philips demonstrates. He is touched that she treats him ''like a human being,'' and desperately in need of the nourishment she offers, both for his body (the bread her dollar will buy) and his soul (the promise of liberation). Her devotion to the cause mirrors religious fervor, and she speaks of the Communist Manifesto in biblical terms, leaving no doubt that it contains a truth that will set him free.

THEMES

Class Conflict

Odets wrote *Waiting for Lefty* while a member of the Communist Party and intended it as a work of propaganda to promote the cause of a socialist revolution in America (much like the one that took place in Russia on November 6, 1917). Given that Marxist theory (based in a work called the Communist Manifesto by Karl Marx, from which leftist political philosophies derive) focuses on the economic conflict among social classes, it is perhaps inevitable that this is an intensely ''class-con-

TOPICS FOR FURTHER STUDY

- Compare Odets's working-class characters to the ways blue-collar workers are presented in three to four contemporary works of your own selection (sources can include movies, television, or books, as well as plays.) In your analysis, try to determine whether the differences you find are a function of: historical changes in the popular image of ''the working class''; differences in the authors' intentions or beliefs; or differences of style and genre.
- Research the 1934 New York taxi strike (the incident on which *Waiting for Lefty* is based). How closely does Odets follow the historical facts? What were the consequences of the real-life strike? Considering his purposes in the play, try to determine the reasons for any changes Odets made in adapting these ''current events'' for his fictional production.
- Research the Communist Manifesto and outline its main arguments. Then, study the dialogue in *Waiting for Lefty* to find specific instances in which the characters advance that document's principles or echo its slogans. Write an essay that reports and analyzes your findings.
- The counterculture of the 1960s revived the notion of using drama as a means for political change in ''street theatre'' performances by groups like the San Francisco Mime Troupe and the staging of propaganda plays. Research this development, in newspapers and periodicals of that time. How does the radical theatre of the 1930s compare to its 1960s counterpart? In what, if any, significant ways did it change?

---

scious'' play. Characters are clearly identified by class, and these classes are presented in vivid opposition: on the one hand, virtuous and long-suffering members of the working class; on the other, the greedy, inhumane capitalists who exploit them at every turn. Despite the realistic conventions and dialogue that characterize the domestic relationships in Scenes I (''Joe and Edna'') and III (''The Young Hack and his Girl''), the larger struggle between ''workers'' and ''capitalists'' is painted in broad strokes of black and white. The villainous Harry Fatt is a purposely exaggerated stereotype, and even the heroic workers border on cartoonishness in their constant, one-dimensional nobility.

The effect of all this is far from subtle and may tempt modern readers to consider the work beyond all credibility. But given its specific, highly political purposes aimed at a specific moment in time, it may be unfair to evaluate *Waiting for Lefty* by traditional critical standards. Odets sought to dramatize Marxism—a notoriously dry and complex theory whose expressions are often mired in specialized jargon and clinical abstractions. Its logic is that of the ''dialectic,'' rooted in the dynamic of competing, opposing forces (including, of course, the classes of Capital and Labor).

Odets applies Marx's insights to individual experience, replacing abstract theories with the gritty and affecting stuff of human lives. As Dr. Benjamin (played by Odets himself in some early productions) says, ''you don't believe theories until they happen to you.'' Here the playwright shows theory happening to people as the individual characters come to realize how their misery has been engineered by the ''bosses'' and ''money men.'' Individually, they are powerless to change their lot, but collectively—working as a class in response to those in power—they are able to triumph.

The wide variety of characters, and the diversity of paths they follow to the strike meeting, cuts across many traditional boundaries of class. Impoverished blue-collar workers like Joe and Sid, for example, are often considered to inhabit a different world from that of salaried, relatively-privileged professionals like Dr. Benjamin or the lab assistant Miller—yet they all belong to the strike committee, and the union is presumably stronger for the combination of their talents and backgrounds, the confluence of various classes working together. Had Miller and Dr. Benjamin continued to serve their capitalist bosses, of course, they would have remained "class enemies" to the workers; but their experience has shown them that they are affected by the machinations of power no less than the working class; their interests cannot be separated from those of "common laborers." They have realized that their ultimate loyalty is to "the people," transcending any personal distinctions among comrades.

The diversity of "types" also increases the chances that an individual audience member will find at least one character with whom to identify—and, since each character's story points to the same, class-based enemy, it makes no practical difference which character that may be. Together, their stories demonstrate the many, insidious ways the system sustains itself and abuses those dependent upon it for their livelihood. The characters' shared determination eclipses their differences; solidarity against the capitalist class outweighs all other private loyalties, including self-interest (the prestige and money Miller turns down) and even family (the "lousy" brother Clancy who is exposed as a strikebreaker). Class struggle, according to Marx, is the primary fact of economic existence, and Odets holds to it as a central theme, though his work unfolds in a radically different form. By the time Agate Keller cries, "Well, what's the answer?," the play's logic allows only one possible response; the individual reader/viewer response to the play depends largely on our answer to another question: "Which side are you on?"

STYLE

Staging

Odets specifies that *Waiting for Lefty* is enacted on "a bare stage." Whether the setting is a union hall, an office, or an apartment, there are no furnishings to help establish the scene. The full stage—extending into the audience—represents the strike meeting. For the "flashback" scenes that tell the stories of various individuals, simple lighting effects are used to create small, intimate playing spaces onstage. Such stark, relatively undefined staging is not uncommon, and "minimalist" dramatists often choose it for various aesthetic reasons. In the case of *Waiting for Lefty,* however, it is clear that Odets's intentions were not *merely* artistic. As an overtly propagandistic work of "proletarian theatre" ("proletariat" meaning the lowest class in a society), his play was meant not only for the formal, professional theatre (with its largely upper- and middle-class audience) but for any group of workers, anywhere, who wished to stage it. The simplified stagecraft thus reflects practical considerations, for it enables the work to be produced in any large meeting-hall, cheaply and with a minimum of technical sophistication.

The lack of formal scenery also tends to blur the distinction between the space of the stage and that of the audience; in effect, the entire theatre becomes the "union hall," and audience members are made to feel part of the action. The rows of seated workers facing the speaker's platform extend into rows of seated customers watching the play, and remarks from the platform are directed to both "crowds." Keller's climactic question, "Well, what's the answer?," is asked not of the workers but of the audience itself. The heckling "voices" of workers often come from actors seated within the audience, and when the "labor spy" in Scene IV is exposed, he flees off the stage and down the center aisle. Such effects are traditionally considered to make the action more vivid and immediate to the audience, to involve them on a visceral, emotional level—these goals are consistent with the play's crusading spirit. They also tend to erode the traditional distinction between drama and "real life"—sometimes to the discomfort of theatregoers who don't expect or appreciate the "invasion" of their space. *Waiting for Lefty* was not meant to be viewed with detachment, as an abstract literary fantasy, but to be experienced directly with the urgency of a real-life crisis.

None of the action takes place in a clearly enclosed space; in the personal vignettes, a spotlit area loosely defines an apartment or office, but the "outside world" of the strike meeting constantly intrudes on these private dramas. Odets directs that the "workers" onstage remain visible at the fringes of the light, milling about, often commenting directly on the action in the manner of a classical Greek chorus. Above all, the villainous figure of Harry Fatt is never absent, hovering over these small tragedies as an ''ugly menace:'' ''Perhaps he puffs smoke into the spotted playing space,'' the playwright suggests in his production notes; ''perhaps during the action of a playlet he might insolently walk in and around the unseeing players.'' In its various forms, the capitalist system he represents has brutalized each of the protagonists, but in the larger space of the strike meeting, their collective strength enables them to defy, and ultimately defeat, their oppressor. The blurring of the stage/audience ''boundary'' encourages a similar response to the play itself: inviting the individual viewer to feel he is a part of the collective ''struggle'' surrounding him and connecting the dramatized strike within the theatre to the larger, real-life drama outside. In more ways than one, Odets intended *Waiting for Lefty* as a play of the people.

HISTORICAL CONTEXT

Waiting for Lefty was inspired by a 1934 taxi strike in New York City, an event that would still have been fresh in the minds of its original, 1935 audience. But while it was sparked by a single historic incident, the play's ambitions extend much further—in fact, they reach far beyond the traditionally accepted terms of entertainment and dramatic art. Odets and his colleagues in the Group Theatre were dedicated political activists and saw their work in the theatre as the means to a much greater purpose: promoting a mass movement for a socialist revolution in America. A popular sensation in its day, the play and its politics have since fallen out of fashion—to the point that today's students may well wonder what all the fuss was about. For this reason, any attempt to appreciate Odets's achievement must be rooted in an understanding of *Waiting for Lefty*'s cultural and historical context.

The 1930s in America are remembered as ''hard times'' of poverty and despair, dominated by the continuing crisis of the Great Depression. Banks and businesses had failed, millions of people were without work—and, for several years following the stock market crash of 1929, the efforts of business and government leaders to manage the situation had done little to stem the tide of human suffering. The ''temporary'' crisis of 1929 began to appear permanent, and many Americans saw this as evidence that the country's economic and political system was intrinsically flawed: it had failed completely and could no longer be fixed by traditional remedies. In this context, political ideas that had previously seemed ''radical'' or ''un-American'' to the majority took on a new appeal. Activist movements of many kinds sprang up and enjoyed wide popularity—some resembling the right-wing fascist movements rising in Europe (particularly those found in Nazi Germany). Other movements adopted a left-wing (communist or socialist) orientation. Leftist philosophies found a particular appeal among industrial workers as well as a great many young artists and intellectuals—including Clifford Odets, who joined the American Communist Party in 1934. Though his party membership lasted only eight months, it included the period in which *Waiting for Lefty* was written.

American communists saw the Depression as bitter proof of Karl Marx's socioeconomic theories and of the betrayal of traditional American ideals. They did not consider themselves ''unpatriotic'' (as communists would soon be widely portrayed by the McCarthy ''witch hunts'' of the 1950s). Rather, by seeking power for ''the people'' against the power of a wealthy minority, they believed they served the true realization of patriotic ideals—which had been hijacked in the service of capital by its agents, the politicians and business leaders who were failing ''the people'' so completely.

The revolution Odets and his ''comrades'' hoped for was an American one, a quest for equality and justice. To promote its realization, they felt, was a noble and idealistic cause. The Group Theatre, then, did not produce ''art of art's sake'' but for the sake of the revolution. Its productions were overtly political and propagandistic—intended not to amuse but to educate and to inspire the audience to mass action. Group members did not hope to produce an evening's light entertainment or a rarefied aesthetic experience. They considered themselves above such motivations as profit for the producers or fame and fortune for the actors. They were revolutionaries, no less than soldiers on the front line, and their ''weapon'' was the theatre. They would harness its emotional power to spread the word and to raise the spirits of the struggling masses.

COMPARE & CONTRAST

- **1935:** The United Automobile Workers (UAW) holds its first convention in Detroit, Michigan. After a long, bitter, and often violent struggle between union organizers and corporate management, climaxed by a celebrated ''sit-down'' strike at a General Motors plant in Flint, Michigan, one of the nation's biggest and most important industries is unionized.

  Today: Once vilified as a subversive threat, the UAW remains one of the country's largest trade unions. After World War II, the powerful American Federation of Labor and Congress of Industrial Organizations (AFL-CIO) federation (of which the UAW was a member) removed communists and their ''sympathizers'' from its governing board, as the trade union movement was caught up in the rising tide of anticommunist fervor. During the post-war economic boom, while auto sales rose steadily, the UAW adopted more cooperative strategies toward management, and negotiated contracts that secured a high standard of living for a generation of autoworkers, until declining sales in the 1970s weakened the industry as a whole.

- **1935:** An Iowa statistician named George Gallup founds the American Institute of Public Opinion and develops a procedure to measure reader reaction to newspaper stories. The ''Gallup Poll'' initiates a new industry: the sampling and packaging of public opinion.

  Today: Polling is a pervasive part of American life, as the computer revolution has facilitated ''instant'' surveys and the retention of vast stores of information. Sophisticated statistical analyses play an important role in the decision-making of businesses from television networks to diaper manufacturers, who rely on polling not just to measure the preferences of customers but to anticipate their responses to products still under development. The similar use of polling by media savvy politicians and by trial attorneys in jury selection has inspired wide controversy.

- **1935:** On May 11, President Roosevelt establishes the Rural Electrification Administration (REA) to facilitate the spread of electricity to sparsely populated areas. Of the thirty million Americans living in rural areas, only 10% have access to electricity. The REA not only provides valuable utilities to numerous homes, it creates numerous jobs for out of work tradesman and engineers.

  Today: Virtually all of the country has electricity. Within fifteen years of the establishment of the REA, only 10% of U.S. farms were *without* electricity. Electricity provides rural communities with access to the same technological advances as urban areas.

In *Waiting for Lefty,* Odets *dramatizes* communist theory, translating politics to the level of the personal. The emotional ''playlets'' depict the effects of capitalism not in intellectual abstractions but in stark human realities, as individuals ranging from blue-collar workers to salaried professionals are each destroyed by the same, heartless ''system.'' Each finds the same answer in mass action against the bosses. The ''crowd scenes'' which bring them together are staged to make audience members feel that they, too, are part of the strike meeting. Presumably, they will also be caught up in the final call to ''Strike!'' and feel the thrill and power of collective participation.

Odets conceived the work as ''people's theatre,'' something closer to folk art than Broadway glamour. He designed it to be adaptable for informal performance by small, nonprofessional groups. And for several years *Waiting for Lefty was* produced as a popular fundraiser by leftist political organizations and union factions throughout the country. For

Odets and his colleagues, the success of their work would not be measured in box office receipts nor critical approval but in the number of people it inspired in the struggle to transform society.

By 1935, Franklin Delano Roosevelt had been the American president for three years and his ''New Deal'' programs to stimulate the economy were beginning to take effect. Despite encouraging signs, the New Deal, which enacted government-sponsored work programs to put people back to work, was highly controversial. Roosevelt's conservative critics called the program communistic, while leftists felt it conceded far too much to the ''evil'' forces of capital.

To workers, the New Deal gave government support to the movement for industrial unionization—which had long been an arena for leftist organizers. Many saw hope in this flowering of unionism, for it seemed to be just the sort of working-class, mass action that communism advocates. However, several of the new industrial unions were tainted by charges of corruption, of dictatorial leaders, ties to organized crime, or collusion with management to limit worker's demands and prevent strikes. To communists, union corruption was a betrayal of the workers' hopes, and the amoral ''labor boss'' was as much an enemy of the people as the stereotyped ''greedy industrialist.'' As the cabdrivers in *Waiting for Lefty* learn, they cannot count on leaders to give them justice—not even a heroic communist martyr like Lefty. Workers must maintain control of their own movement, and stand united to ensure that their will is carried out.

In the Cold War years following World War II, many who had been Depression-era radicals were persecuted in an anticommunist backlash through the infamous ''witch-hunts'' of Senator Joseph McCarthy and his supporters in the House Committee on Un-American Activities. Those in the entertainment industry were particularly vulnerable; in Hollywood, any past connection with a left-wing organization could cause one's name to appear on a privately circulated ''blacklist'' as an alleged ''security risk.'' Industry executives caved in to right-wing pressure; to be blacklisted was to be unemployable and perhaps to be the subject of a congressional investigation. Those associated with causes like the Group Theatre often faced the choice of giving up their careers or compromising their principles in hopes of getting off the list. Commonly, they would be asked to swear a loyalty oath, renounce their past leftist associations, and testify freely about the activities of their colleagues.

Odets had been writing screenplays since 1941 and was called before the House Committee on Un-American Activities in 1952. He testified about his activities in the 1930s, evidently enough to satisfy the subcommittee and remove himself from further suspicion. While he didn't provide the names of anyone who hadn't already been mentioned to the committee, Odets later expressed guilt and ''revulsion'' over his testimony. He is said to have been tormented by the matter until his death in 1963, and he produced relatively little writing, for stage or screen, after his 1952 subcommittee appearance.

CRITICAL OVERVIEW

Since its opening, *Waiting for Lefty* has been considered a prime example of the dramatic genre known as agitprop (and also known as revolutionary theatre and proletarian drama, among other labels). The play is often considered *the* definitive example of this genre. How one feels about that type—widely popular in its time but unfashionable in recent years—seems to have a great deal to do with one's critical reaction.

Waiting for Lefty's original production in 1935 was a critical success and a popular hit. Reviewing it for the *New York Times,* Brooks Atkinson praised it as not only ''one of the best working-class dramas that have been written'' but as ''one of the most dynamic dramas of the year in any department of our theatre.'' He stressed its realism and intensity: ''the characters are right off the city pavements; the emotions are tender and raw, and some of them are bitter.'' Remaining neutral on the play's political message, Atkinson stressed its social importance as well as its relevance to the troubled moment in history it portrays: ''People who want to understand the times through which they are living,'' he wrote, ''can scarcely afford to ignore it.'' Harold Clurman, a founder of the Group Theatre, recalled of an early performance that the audience joined spontaneously and enthusiastically in the climactic call to ''Strike! Strike!'' As he recalled in *The Fervent Years: The*

Story of the Group Theatre and the Thirties, Clurman considered their reaction both "a tribute to the play's effectiveness" and "a testimony of the audience's hunger for constructive social action. It was the birth cry of the thirties. Our youth had found its voice." By July of 1935 (within six months of its debut), *Waiting for Lefty* had been produced in thirty cities across the country. For several years, productions of the play were staged as fundraisers and morale boosters by a variety of left-wing organizations.

While he produced one of its most celebrated works, Odets wrote little else in the agitprop vein. His later dramas and screenplays are far more conventional, with little emphasis on overt political messages. For this reason—coupled with his commercial success on Broadway and in Hollywood—many of his revolutionary comrades accused him of selling out the cause and betraying his principles. Odets clearly changed his thinking in some ways and came to renounce his Communist Party membership. Other critics, however, question whether he experienced any abrupt reversal in his earlier conceptions of drama. In this view, *Waiting for Lefty* is a one-of-a-kind effort, produced in a burst of idealistic exuberance, and its political crusading is atypical of Odets's usual concerns, before and after its composition. As a whole, his writing bears more resemblance to this play's intimate domestic sketches than to the high drama of the raucous strike meeting. In such works as *Awake and Sing!, Golden Boy,* and *The Big Knife,* Odets's strengths are generally considered to include his realistic characterization and dialogue as well as his deft exploration of personal and domestic conflicts.

Waiting for Lefty was not written "for the ages," to stand as an immortal work of art but for a specific time and culture to advance particular social and political aspirations. In that light, it may be somewhat irrelevant that, by most accounts, the play no longer inspires the admiration and enthusiasm it sparked in the 1930s. To modern tastes, it typically appears as an anachronism, obsolete in both style and substance. Its slogan laced dialogue seems forced and unnatural, while its broad characterizations seem simplistic and melodramatic. Its moralizing tone is far less palatable today, when preaching of any kind is unfashionable, and its "party-line" analysis seems dogmatic and unsophisticated.

Most importantly, the solution it offers—a communist revolution—appears in a radically different light for modern audiences. During the Depression, it appeared as a viable and desirable alternative; true believers thought they could glimpse it on the horizon. But after decades of tense Cold War geopolitics followed by the rapid decline of world communism in the late-1980s, to even consider such a revolution *possible* requires an imaginative leap. It is certainly possible to appreciate a work for its formal qualities, or its treatment of universal human themes, apart from its specific "message" and historical context—but for a play like *Waiting for Lefty,* the message was its entire reason for being, and its ability to influence audiences in that crucial moment of history was its greatest measure of success.

CRITICISM

Tom Faulkner

Faulkner is a professional writer with a B.A. in English. In this essay he discusses the ways in which Odets infuses his play with traditionally "American" values and imagery, effectively combating the negative stereotypes regarding communism.

If you approached Clifford Odets in 1935 and told him that his celebrated play *Waiting for Lefty* was a work of communist propaganda, he would not likely have been insulted or alarmed. He would probably consider it an accurate description of his drama, exactly what he had intended to create. A few years later, however, the same phrase could only be taken as a vicious accusation, equivalent to being called traitor: the propagandist was no less than an enemy to his own country, preaching an evil gospel that threatened all our cherished American ideals. The infamous work of the House Un-American Activities Committee to root out "communist infiltrators" during the 1950s helped solidify the popular image of communist revolution as the antithesis of the American Dream. But to Odets and his leftist contemporaries in 1935, the two sets of ideals were not necessarily contradictory; rather, they appeared as differing formulations of the same basic human longings. In their embrace of communism, leftist activists sought to realize the promise an American Dream they believed had long been

The climactic scene of Waiting for Lefty, *in which the cast exhorts the audience to ''Strike! Strike!! Strike!!!''*

deferred by the tyranny of capitalism. *Waiting for Lefty* thus presents a curious spectacle to the modern imagination: an all-American communist uprising.

The ''un-American'' stereotype of communism was not an invention of the Cold War. After the Russian revolution in 1917, Marxism (communism) was widely portrayed in America as a ''foreign'' or ''alien'' philosophy, inconsistent with such native ideals as individual freedom and equal opportunity. With its resistance toward organized religion and private property rights, communism was seen as an assault on America's fundamental institutions. While the deprivations of the Great Depression made leftist ideas more attractive to many Americans, the stereotype remained in circulation, and it was a staple of anticommunist agitation.

A close reading of *Waiting for Lefty* reveals that Odets sought to counter this widespread perception by presenting revolutionaries whose actions were grounded firmly in the American mainstream. Such an approach makes the philosophical ''medicine'' more palatable; audience members who had considered themselves ''100% Americans'' (and therefore uninterested in anything that even resembled com-

WHAT DO I READ NEXT?

- Odets's other works provide for interesting comparisons with *Waiting for Lefty* and reveal the full range of his talents and concerns. Two works from his time with the Group Theatre, *Awake and Sing!* (1935) and *Paradise Lost* (1935), each make political points by relating the story of an American family but they do so in very different ways. *Awake and Sing!* is a realistic account of the struggles of a working-class Jewish family, akin to the domestic vignettes in *Waiting for Lefty. Paradise Lost* concerns a declining middle-class family and relies heavily on symbolism, with each family member representing a particular middle-class value.
- *The Big Knife,* written by Odets in 1949, deals with the personal and professional conflicts of a movie actor named Charlie Castles, who ultimately commits suicide. It can be seen as a reflection of the difficulties Odets encountered while working for Hollywood and might even be said to foreshadow the turmoil he would experience during the McCarthy era.
- Odets's contemporaries in Depression-era political drama provoke insightful comparison. John Howard Lawson's *Marching Song* details the conflict between a union and a gang of vicious strikebreakers; *Black Pit,* by Albert Maltz, concerns the struggles of a group of West Virginia coal miners. While their themes and goals closely resemble those of *Waiting for Lefty,* each play has its own, unique voice—an indication of the wide spectrum of participants and philosophies within the radical theatre movement.
- *Hard Times,* by Studs Terkel (1970) is a rich oral history of the Depression, culled from hundreds of interviews with people from all walks of life. Their first-hand accounts combine to paint a vivid picture of those times, with an intensity seldom found in traditional historical accounts.

munism) might be led to rethink their positions. While Odets is often accused of presenting an oversimplified, ''black and white'' picture of society (in which one is either a noble worker or an evil capitalist), he also depicts a political landscape that breaks down the familiar opposition between communism and Americanism.

As the unqualified villain of the play, the arrogant union boss Harry Fatt provides a reliable barometer of how *not* to interpret the action. Early in the opening scene, he trumpets the traditional stereotype, vilifying the ''reds'' within the union who want to call a strike as enemies of everything that Americans hold dear. Fatt paints an alarmist, clearly exaggerated picture of a communist takeover: ''They'll have your wives and sisters in the whorehouses, like they done in Russia. They'll tear Christ off his bleeding cross. They'll wreck your homes and throw your babies in the river.'' His view is soon contradicted by Joe Mitchell, who supports the strike and defends the honor of the communist organizer, Lefty Costello. ''You boys know me,'' he tells his fellow workers. ''I ain't a red boy one bit! Here I'm carryin' a shrapnel that big I picked up in the war.'' Joe has risked his life for his country; his patriotism is beyond question. He thus provides ''living proof'' that supporting mass action by workers is not the same as advocating the ruin of everything good and decent. Fatt's appeal to patriotic ideals is shown to be a piece of deceptive rhetoric, an undeserved slur directed at those who oppose his will.

Fatt's false, apocalyptic vision of a revolution is echoed, however, in language describing the *real* effects of the capitalist system on the lives of the workers. In Scene I, Edna charges that Joe's boss is ''giving [our] kids that fancy disease called the rickets'' (by paying him so little that he cannot afford a proper diet for them) and is actively breaking up their marriage (for Edna, Joe's boss is

WAITING FOR LEFTY PRESENTS A CURIOUS SPECTACLE TO THE MODERN IMAGINATION: AN ALL-AMERICAN COMMUNIST UPRISING."

''putting ideas in my head a mile a minute. . . . He's throwing me into [her old boyfriend] Bud Haas's lap.'') Similar ''bosses'' prevent the lovers Sid and Florrie from building a life together, and (figuratively) castrate the young actor Philips. If there is a threat to the sanctity of the American family, the audience is meant to find it not in the specter of socialist revolution but in the deprivations required by the capitalist system.

Representatives of capital in the play behave in ways that offend traditional democratic ideals of equality and fair play. The hospital's board of directors is infected with the ''virus'' of anti-Semitism as surely as Adolf Hitler's Nazi Germany was; they fire the gifted Dr. Benjamin because he is Jewish and replace him with the murderously incompetent (but politically well-connected) Dr. Leeds. They also close down a charity ward because it fails to turn a profit. While doctors like Barnes and Benjamin are pledged to relieve human suffering, the board's policy grants their services only to those who can pay.

The industrialist Fayette lets ethnic stereotypes and prejudice drive his employment policies: he prefers that his skilled workers refrain from alcohol, but he states that ''Pollacks and niggers, they're better drunk—keeps 'em out of mischief.'' Similarly, the theatrical producer Grady calls for ''the nigger boy'' to bring him a hangover remedy. Throughout the play, the notion that ''all men are created equal'' seems to be an ''alien'' philosophy to these alleged defenders of Americanism—but a fundamental principle of the workers' struggle.

The individual workers we meet in Odets's play are steeped in traditional values: hard-working, devoted to family life, and dedicated to fairness and equal rights. In standing up to the corrupt, exploitative ''bosses,'' they also stand for *true* Americanism. When Fayette asks Miller to abandon his principles by agreeing to work on a sinister military contract, the scientist answers that he'd ''rather dig ditches first.'' ''That's a job for foreigners,'' Fayette replies; to which Miller demands, ''But sneaking—and making poison gas—that's for Americans?'' The ''subversive'' worker again displays a deeper commitment to national ideals than the capitalist, who uses them only to justify actions that are thoroughly ''un-American.''

Dr. Barnes provides the rationale of communist ''Americanism'' when he ties the proposed workers' revolution to the cause of the Founding Fathers. In his anger at the hospital board he rails: ''Out of a revolutionary background! Spirit of '76! Ancestors froze at Valley Forge! What's it all mean? Slops! The honest workers were sold out then , in '76. The Constitution's for rich men, then and now. Slops!'' Barnes has no quarrel with the ideals of the American Revolution, only with the idea that they have been achieved. By including laws that enforced the rights of capital, at the expense of individual rights, he sees the Constitution as having subverted the ''Spirit of '76.'' He feels he lives in a land that celebrates government ''of, for, and by the people,'' but works to keep power in the hands of a propertied few. The new revolution he urges Benjamin to fight for will be just as ''American'' as the first—but it will be a *successful* revolution, one which truly establishes the noble ideals that have been perverted by the rule of capitalism.

Finally, Odets offers a counterpart to the stereotype of a propagandist in the character of the stenographer who recruits the young actor Philips to the workers' cause. In anticommunist lore, such figures are primary villains, the lowest of the low. They serve a Godless, treasonous cause, employing any devious means to seduce their unwitting victims. Though she is sarcastic in her contempt for her boss, the nameless secretary responds humanely to Philips's desperate plight, offering him a dollar and advising him on the fine points of job hunting. In contrast to Grady, she treats Philips ''like a human being.'' (Capitalists consistently treat workers like ''dogs,'' but Grady goes further, showing markedly less concern for Philips than he has for his pet dog Boris.) When she speaks of the Communist Manifesto, the stenographer uses the language of the Bible—implying that it *is* a kind of bible: a revelatory text, offering a truth that will set Philips free, a vision of heaven, and an inspiring message of hope. The ''comrade'' who surreptitiously circulates propaganda is commonly cast as an unprincipled spy, luring the innocent to destruction with cool calculation. Instead, the audience is given a character very much like an evangelist, selflessly devoted to the saving of lost souls.

Through such devices, Odets sought to give his play a wider appeal and to make communist ideals resonate with the familiar elements of the American Dream. He was not only ''preaching to the converted'' (directing the work to those who already supported the cause) but trying to reach new converts as well. In his deployment of traditional American imagery, he sought to overcome the popular stereotype of the Left by showing communists who were also true Americans and contrasting them with villains who speak the language of patriotism but ''walk the walk'' of tyranny.

Source: Tom Faulkner, for *Drama for Students,* Gale, 1998.

John Simon

Simon reviews a revival of Waiting for Lefty *directed by actress Joanne Woodward. The critic gives an enthusiastic appraisal of the production and explains why dramas such as Odets's merit periodic rekindling. He calls* Waiting for Lefty *the ''strongest agitprop play written in America.''*

There are plays whose historic interest justifies their periodic revival, especially if that interest covers both political and theatrical history. Such is the case of Clifford Odets's *Waiting for Lefty* (1935), the strongest agitprop play written in America. ''An essentially lusty outcry, informed with the enthusiasm of a cheering grandstand,'' as Harold Clurman called it, the work was inspired by an unsuccessful strike of New York's taxi drivers. Though a product of Odets's Communist period, it is happily free from doctrinaire Marxism.

As revived by the Blue Light Theater Company under Joanne Woodward's unfussy direction, the production profits from arena staging as it plants both workers and goons among the audience surrounding an essentially bare platform, and effectively simulates a labor meeting. We are alternatingly in that rented hall and in evoked domestic or workplace situations that conjure up the backgrounds of these destitute cabbies whom the corrupt union boss and his henchmen would prevent from striking. This allows us, in the end, to join in the climactic shouts of ''Strike! Strike!! Strike!!!''

WAITING FOR LEFTY IS THE STRONGEST AGITPROP PLAY WRITTEN IN AMERICA."

The dramatic memory vignettes are simple, almost schematic, but they work. To quote Gerald Weales's *Clifford Odets, Playwright,* lack of psychological depth is no problem where ''characters are not thin realistic figures but thickened-out agitprop cartoons.'' Yet these Depression-starved workers and their exploiters get at the essential issues in high-voltage, vaulting verbiage: We believe them as we believe a piece of electrifying newspaper reportage. A stark platform with a stool or two becomes the home of assorted human miseries: We relive the original audiences' involvement in the call to strike, their mingling with the cast as they emerged into the street charged with revolutionary ardor. Miss Woodward prefaces the short play with the actors' singing period songs of a similarly activist nature, and the device works rousingly. The performers are all solidly in character, which means that they play boldly but not hysterically. And then there is Marisa Tomei.

Although Miss Tomei blends smoothly into the ensemble, the actress, here playing two very different but equally well-etched parts, proves again what charm can do for an artist when she has it in spades. Good as Miss Tomei is in movies, it is on the stage that we need her: We must follow up that concluding ''Strike! Strike!! Strike!!!'' with a ''Stay! Stay!! Stay!!!'' especially for her.

Source: John Simon, ''A More Perfect Union'' in *New York,* Volume 30, no. 20, May 26, 1997 , pp. 78–79.

Frederick C. Stern

Stern reviews a 1975 collegiate production of Odets's drama. While he finds that the play contains some stirring dramatic moments, the critic concludes that the play lacks pertinence to late-twentieth century America.

East Chicago, Indiana, is not one of the great theatre centers of the United States. Driving towards Calu-

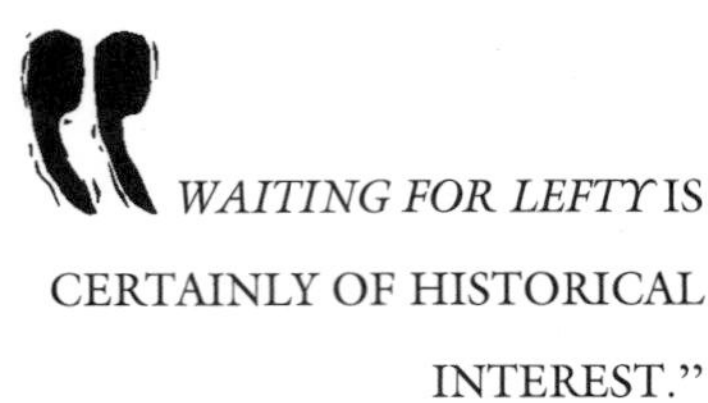

WAITING FOR LEFTY IS CERTAINLY OF HISTORICAL INTEREST."

met College's playhouse one is aware of the fires from steel mills and the smell of the oil refineries, of homes owned by steelworkers and oilworkers, of a city far from lovely but alive. One is also conscious that this is a union town. What better place than Calumet College for a production of *Waiting for Lefty?* This play, in this locale, at this moment, is also appropriate because much that it portrays is, still and again, with us. Though hard times are felt a little less sharply in steel and oil centers than in auto towns, hard times are here. No wonder that the audience for this play was involved and interested.

Calumet College's theatre is a converted house, decorated in black and lack-of-paint, showing loving care but little money. On entering, recorded union songs provide a musical background; posters from the thirties are plastered everywhere. The first "act" of the play is not the play at all, but a live concert by five musicians of labor songs, held together by a narrative which tells each song's history. The audience sings along, claps, joins, enjoys. The cast members, in the meantime, have seated themselves on stage and in the audience, distinguishable only by their thirties clothing. Then there is an intermission.

When the play begins, the audience is prepared for the union-hall setting, and seems to have little trouble accepting the convention of the cab drivers telling their stories by acting out scenes from their lives. Joe shows us how his wife Edna's insistence turned him militant; Sid demonstrates why he and Florie cannot marry under these economic circumstances. Between these scenes there is the union-hall strike talk, the exposure of the labor spy, and, dominating everything, the figure of Fatt, the labor racketeer.

But director Walter Skiba makes a serious mistake. Instead of letting the scenes from the workers' lives and the union hall scenes follow one another, thus leading to the climax at which Lefty's killing is announced and the strike is called, Skiba interrupts the action. After each scene, the musicians perform another song, while slides of labor struggles of the thirties and of more recent years are projected onto an upstage screen. The screen is too small for the images to be seen clearly and, although the pictures final the sixties and seventies make an apt political point, they are too obviously anachronistic, distracting from the play's milieu of the thirties.

The actors are earnest and serious about their work, though they are certainly not professionals, and not even of the caliber one might find at a college with a highly developed theatre department. It hardly matters. There are moving moments in this play, moving because one is aware of the reality outside the theatre, moving because one senses that Odets' passion has been communicated to these actors who are steel and oil workers and the sons and daughters of steel and oil workers. Even the most obvious of Odets' scenes have about them an earnestness which is often the most engaging aspect of "committed" art by a competent artist. In that sense, the play holds up, and the Calumet College Theater performs a real service in producing it.

The play lacks depth, however, as it simplifies, in the most blatant way, both the problem and the solution. It is meant to bring people into struggle, but its shallowness becomes most apparent when one realizes that, by 1935, Brecht had already written *The Measures Taken, The Mother, The Baden Play for Learning,* and *The Deadly Sins of the Petty Bourgeois.* The comparison exposes not only problems in the American radical theatre, but also problems for American political radicalism—perhaps the very problems that made it impossible for so many leftists of the thirties, in and out of the theatre, to retain their radical ideology. Brecht's awareness of both political and moral complexity is such that commitment come with open eyes and aware mind, while Odets' play can only lead to an emotional charge. The charge can only last so long, perhaps for the length of a play or of a strike, but not long enough for a lifetime of radical activity. It may be unfair to ask Odets' play to carry the weight of such a comparison. He was writing, after all under the influence of "agit-prop" and, for "agit-prop" purposes, his play works well, even here in this college theatre.

Waiting for Lefty is certainly of historical interest, and in this setting has relevance. It would have been easier to judge the play, forty years after it was first produced, if we could have seen it without the interruption of music, without the forced and failed effort to "update" it by using slides from labor struggles of more recent vintage. I saw the play on the last night of its run. The audience—students and faculty, families of cast members, some area radicals and liberals—seemed excited by the play and highly appreciative of it. I found myself disturbed by the technical problems I have described and both saddened and politically trouble by the shallowness of the play. Perhaps ask too much of the theatre, of the play, and of the playwright. Perhaps those in the audience who simply let the emotions flow are right—but I really don't think so.

Source: Frederick C. Stern, review of *Waiting for Lefty* in *Educational Theatre Journal,* Volume 27, no. 3, October, 1975, pp. 411–12.

Joseph Wood Krutch

In this review of the original production of Waiting for Lefty, *Krutch praises Odets for creating a political drama that entertains without compromising its political goals. As the critic describes it, Odets's play is "a very effective dramatic equivalent of soap-box oratory."*

A new production by the Group Theater supplies the answer to a question I asked in this column three weeks ago. Mr. Clifford Odets, the talented author of *Awake and Sing,* has come out for the revolution and thrown in his artistic lot with those who use the theater for direct propaganda. The earlier play, it seems, was written some three years ago before his convictions had crystallized, and it owes to that fact a certain contemplative and brooding quality. The new ones—there are two on a double bill at the Longacre—waste no time on what the author now doubtless regards as side issues, and they hammer away with an unrelenting insistency upon a single theme: Workers of the World Unite!

Waiting for Lefty, a brief sketch suggested by the recent strike of taxi drivers, is incomparably the better of the two, and whatever else one may say of it, there is no denying its effectiveness as a tour de force. It begins *in media res* on the platform at a strikers' meeting, and "plants" interrupting from the audience create the illusion that the meeting is actually taking place at the very moment of repre-

"THERE IS NO DENYING *WAITING FOR LEFTY'S* EFFECTIVENESS AS A TOUR DE FORCE."

sentation. Brief flashbacks reveal crucial moments in the lives of the drivers, but the scene really remains in the hall itself, and the piece ends when the strike is voted. The pace is swift, the characterization is for the most part crisp, and the points are made, one after another, with bold simplicity. What Mr. Odets is trying to do could hardly be done more economically or more effectively.

Cold analysis, to be sure, clearly reveals the fact that such simplicity must be paid for at a certain price. The villains are mere caricatures and even the very human heroes occasionally freeze into stained-glass attitudes, as, for example, a certain lady secretary in one of the flashbacks does when she suddenly stops in her tracks to pay a glowing tribute to "The Communist Manifesto" and to urge its perusal upon all and sundry. No one, however, expects subtleties from a soap-box, and the interesting fact is that Mr. Odets has invented a form which turns out to be a very effective dramatic equivalent of soap-box oratory.

Innumerable other "proletarian" dramatists have tried to do the same thing with far less success. Some of them have got bogged in futuristic symbolism which could not conceivably do more than bewilder "the worker"; others have stuck close to the usual form of the drama without realizing that this form was developed for other uses and that their attempt to employ it for directly hortatory purposes can only end in what appears to be more than exceedingly crude dramaturgy. Mr. Odets, on the other hand, has made a clean sweep of the conventional form along with the conventional intentions. He boldly accepts as his scene the very platform he intends to use, and from it permits his characters to deliver speeches which are far more convincing there than they would be if elaborately worked into a conventional dramatic story. Like many of his fellows he has evidently decided that art is a weapon, but unlike many who proclaim the doctrine, he has the full courage of his conviction. To others he leaves the somewhat nervous determination to prove that direct exhortation can somehow be made compatible with "art" and that "revolutionary" plays can be two things at once. The result of his downrightness is to succeed where most of the others have failed. He does not ask to be judged by any standards except those which one would apply to the agitator, but by those standards his success is very nearly complete.

Waiting for Lefty is played upon what is practically a bare stage. It could be acted in any union hall by amateur actors, and the fact accords well with the intention of a play which would be wholly in place as part of the campaign laid out by any strike committee. Indeed, it is somewhat out of place anywhere else for the simple reason that its appeal to action is too direct not to seem almost absurd when addressed to an audience most of whose members are not, after all, actually faced with the problem which is put up to them in so completely concrete a form. The play might, on the other hand, actually turn the tide at a strikers' meeting, and that is more than can be said of most plays whose avowed intention is to promote the class war. . . .

Source: Joseph Wood Krutch, "Mr. Odets Speaks His Mind" in the *Nation,* Volume 140, no.3640, April 10, 1935 , pp. 427–28.

SOURCES

Atkinson, Brooks. Review of *Waiting for Lefty* in the *New York Times,* March 27, 1935.

Clurman, Harold. *The Fervent Years: The Story of the Group Theatre and the Thirties,* Knopf, 1945, reprinted, Harcourt, 1975.

FURTHER READING

Brenman-Gibson, Margaret. *Clifford Odets, American Playwright: The Years from 1906 to 1940,* Atheneum, 1982.
This is an extensive, thoroughly researched account of Odets's early career, and contains a detailed treatment of his years with the Group Theatre.

Goldstein, Malcolm. *The Political Stage: American Drama and Theatre of the Great Depression,* Oxford, 1974.
Goldstein presents a full history of Depression-era political drama, covering not only the Group Theatre but many similar organizations, including the Theatre Guild, Theatre Union, and the "Living Newspaper" productions of the Federal Theatre Project.

Goodman, Walter. *The Committee: The Extraordinary Career of the House Committee on Un-American Activities,* Farrar, Strauss & Giroux, 1968.
Goodman offers a thorough history of the Congressional committee that was at the center of the Cold War anticommunist crusade, including the appearances of Odets and several of his 1930s contemporaries.

Mendelsohn, Michael J. *Clifford Odets: Humanitarian Dramatist,* Everett/Edwards, 1969.
Mendelsohn provides a concise biography of the playwright, including a critical analysis of each of his works.

Smiley, Sam. *The Drama of Attack: Didactic Plays of the American Depression,* University of Missouri Press, 1972.
This work of literary scholarship closely analyzes a wide range of politically concerned plays of the 1930s, including works by Odets, John Howard Lawson, George Sklar, Albert Maltz, Paul Perkins, and Elmer Rice.

Who's Afraid of Virginia Woolf?

EDWARD ALBEE

1962

Who's Afraid of Virginia Woolf?, Edward Albee's first full-length play and his first to appear on Broadway, is considered by many to be his greatest dramatic achievement, as well as a central work in the contemporary American theatre. *Virginia Woolf* focuses on an embittered academic couple who gradually draw a younger couple, freshly arrived from the Midwest, into their vicious games of marital love-hatred. The play is a dramatic bloodsport fought with words rather than weapons—''verbal fencing,'' wrote Ruby Cohn in *Edward Albee,* ''in the most adroit dialogue ever heard on the American stage.'' The play premiered October 13, 1962, at New York's Billy Rose Theatre and starred, in the roles of the battling husband and wife, Arthur Hill as George and Uta Hagen as Martha. The acclaimed production ran for 664 performances and led almost immediately to other successful productions throughout the United States and the world; the play has continued to be revived frequently.

Virginia Woolf garnered an impressive collection of awards, including the New York Drama Critics' Circle Award, the Foreign Press Association Award, two Antoinette Perry (''Tony'') Awards, the *Variety* Drama Critics' Poll Award, and the *Evening Standard* Award. For the play, Albee was additionally selected as the most promising playwright of the 1962-63 Broadway season by the New York Drama Critics' organization. When Albee did not receive the Pulitzer Prize for his widely-acclaimed play because one of the trustees objected to

its sexual subject matter, drama advisors John Gassner and John Mason Brown publicly resigned from the jury in protest.

AUTHOR BIOGRAPHY

Edward Albee, numbered among the United States's most acclaimed and controversial playwrights, was born March 12, 1928. As the adopted son of Reed and Frances Albee, heirs to the fortune of American theater manager Edward Franklin Albee, he had an early introduction to the theatre. He began attending performances at the age of six and wrote a three-act sex farce when he was twelve. Albee attended several private and military schools and enrolled briefly at Connecticut's Trinity College from 1946-47. He held a variety of jobs over the next decade, working as a writer for WNYC-radio, an office boy for an advertising agency, a record salesman, and a messenger for Western Union. He wrote both fiction and poetry as a young man, achieving some limited success, and at the age of thirty returned to writing plays, making an impact with his one-act *The Zoo Story* (1959). Over the next few years Albee continued to satirize American social values with a series of important one-act plays: *The Death of Bessie Smith* (1960), the savagely expressionistic *The Sandbox* (1960), and *The American Dream* (1961).

Albee came fully into the national spotlight with his first full-length play, *Who's Afraid of Virginia Woolf?* (1962). The play quickly developed a reputation as one of the most challenging works of the contemporary American theatre, even if some critics faulted it as morbid and self-indulgent. Albee has yet to make as large an impact with any of his subsequent plays, many of which have failed commercially and elicited scathing reviews. At the same time, however, the playwright has been commended for his commitment to theatrical experimentation. Albee's 1966 play *A Delicate Balance,* in which a troubled middle-aged couple examine their relationship during a prolonged visit by two close friends, earned him a Pulitzer Prize which many felt was a belated attempt by the Pulitzer committee to honor Albee for *Virginia Woolf.* Albee won a second Pulitzer for his 1975 play *Seascape,* in which two couples—one human, the other a pair of intelligent lizard-like creatures that have been driven from the sea by the process of evolution—discuss the purpose of existence. Albee has also continued to write experimental one-acts, including the paired plays *Box* and *Quotations from Chairman Mao Tse-Tung* (1968), and his 1977 work *Listening: A Chamber Play.* He received a third Pulitzer Prize in 1994 for his play *Three Tall Women.*

Albee has also adapted many works of fiction for the stage, including the novels *The Ballad of the Sad Cafe* by Carson McCullers, *Breakfast at Tiffany's* by Truman Capote, and *Lolita* by Vladimir Nabokov. Early in his career, he also collaborated on the opera *Bartleby,* based on a story by Herman Melville. Albee has applied his theatrical talents to directing productions of his own plays and has also served as co-producer at the New Playwrights Unit Workshop, co-director of the Vivian Beaumont Theatre, founder of the William Flanagan Center for Creative Persons in Mountauk, NY, and member of the National Endowment for the Arts grant-giving council. He has lectured extensively at college campuses and visited Russia and several Latin American countries on cultural exchanges through the U.S. State Department.

PLOT SUMMARY

Act I: "Fun and Games"

The play takes place one late night on the campus of a small New England college, in the home of a childless, middle-aged couple. Martha is the daughter of the college president and George, her husband, a professor of history whose career has stalled. The two stumble in from a faculty party where it is obvious that they have already been drinking a great deal. Their conversation is disjointed, Martha making jokes that George ignores or appears not to understand. She chastises him for his behavior at the party: "you never *do* anything; you never *mix.* "

Martha has apparently invited a young couple, "what's-their-name," over to continue the festivities. Neither George nor Martha can remember much about their guests, to whom "Daddy said we should be nice." When George expresses frustration at Martha always springing such things on him, Martha pokes fun at his sulking and sings to him the "Virginia Woolf" song, apparently a joke she heard earlier at the party. The doorbell chimes, but

Edward Albee outside of the Colonial Theatre in Boston, where he directed a 1976 production of Who's Afraid of Virginia Woolf?

George and Martha continue scrapping (with George warning Martha "don't start in on the bit 'bout the kid"), until George finally flings the door open just at the moment that Martha lets out a rousing "SCREW YOU!" Nick and Honey (much to George's delight) are clearly taken aback by Martha's outburst, but although their entrance is awkward they do not turn back.

After some uncomfortable exchanges regarding Martha's father and Nick's job at the college, Martha takes Honey to show her around the house and lead her to the "euphemism" (bathroom). George provokes Nick with more or less "trick" questions, until Nick snaps out, "All right . . . what do you want me to say?" When the talk turns to children, Nick comments awkwardly that he and Honey have none, and George is coy, stating that the information is "for me to know and you to find out." Honey returns on her own, and in talking to George reveals that Martha told her about their son. Martha then returns, having changed into a more voluptuous outfit, and as the talk turns to bodies and exercise routines, her tone with Nick grows more flirtatious. The two couples discuss George and Martha's son and Martha's devotion to her father. Martha's story of her courtship with George leads her into another tirade about his professional failure. Especially angry at having this all played out in front of the company, George smashes a liquor bottle on the bar and attempts to drown out Martha's story. Honey runs out of the room feeling nauseous, and Nick follows her. The act ends as it began, with Martha's expletive, "Jesus!"

Act II: "Walpurgisnacht"

[*The subtitle of this act "Walpurgisnacht," means "Walpurgis night" and is commonly known as the "eve of May." It is a holiday of German origin held after midnight on April 30 (May 1). During this event, witches gather in the Hartz Mountains to meet with the Devil and plot evil.*]

Nick and George are alone. In light of Martha's attacks and his situation in general, George tries to gain sympathy from Nick but is rebuffed: "I just don't see why you feel you have to subject *other* people to it." The mood is tense between them, but Nick opens up to tell George the circumstances of his marriage with Honey (a false pregnancy), and they share a laugh over Nick's observation, "She blew up, and then she went down." George tells Nick a story of an early drinking adventure with his friends, including a boy who had accidentally shot his mother and then, the following summer, had an automobile wreck in which his father also died. Nick admits that money in his wife's family was also a factor in his marrying Honey, and George sympathizes with the situation.

They seem to be enjoying each other's company now, as they joke about the ''inevitability'' of Nick taking over the college through a strategy of ''plowing pertinent wives.'' Nick grows nervous, however, when he can no longer tell to what extent George is joking about the professional value of committing adultery with Martha. Honey and Martha return, Nick paying close attention to his wife as George and Martha go at one another again, using their son as a weapon. Martha claims that George made the child throw up all the time, and George counters that the boy ''ran away from home all the time because Martha here used to corner him.''

Music is put on and the couples dance, Martha flirting heavily with Nick as an affront to George. As she dances, Martha tells Nick another story from the past, about a book that George wrote which her father refused to allow him to publish. Martha's father had thought the manuscript was ''a novel all about a naughty boychild who killed his mother and father dead,'' but George revealed to him (as Martha is doing for the guests) that the story was true and had happened to him. As Nick makes the connection to the story George had told him earlier, George is furious, his hands on Martha's throat as he yells ''YOU SATANIC BITCH!''

Everyone calms down as George observes that, having played ''Humiliate the Host,'' they need a new party game. He suggests ''Hump the Hostess,'' but Nick is genuinely a bit frightened by George's tone. George proposes ''Get the Guests'' as a game and plays it by retelling the story of Nick and Honey's courtship. Honey is upset that Nick told George their own secrets, and she runs out of the room, Nick following. Martha for a moment is somewhat perversely impressed by George's angry performance. ''It's the most . . . life you've shown in a long time,'' she observes. Quickly, however, they are once again threatening each other. Nick returns, reporting that Honey is lying peacefully on the bathroom floor.

As George goes off to get ice for the drinks, Martha and Nick come together in a long kiss. George sees this going on when he returns and settles down to read a book. The incongruity of this action drives Martha crazy, as George obviously knows what is going on between her and Nick but does not seem to care. Martha sends Nick off to the kitchen and then follows him there. George flings his book away, hitting the door chimes, the noise of which rouses Honey. Honey's insistence that someone was ringing at the door gives George an idea—to pretend there had been someone there, with terrible news about the death of their son.

Act III: ''The Exorcism''

Martha enters, alone, amusing herself with her own prattle but also frustrated at not being able to find the others. As Martha stands there, saying ''clink!'' to the jiggling ice in her glass, Nick enters, convinced everyone in the house has gone mad. Martha upbraids Nick for his poor sexual performance, calling him a ''flop.'' She actually speaks fondly of George, although the extent to which her comments are genuine is difficult to gauge. As Martha continues to mock Nick, the doorbell rings, and Nick opens the door to admit George, who carries a large bouquet of snapdragons and calls out ''*flores para los muertos.*'' Martha is gleefully amused at this performance, and although she and George continue to argue all the while, they appear to be in allegiance against Nick, who they have taken to calling their ''houseboy.'' Nick observes with frustration, ''Hell, I don't know when you people are lying, or what.''

George summons Honey for ''one more game, and then beddie-bye.'' He appears at his strongest in the course of the play, warning Martha ''I'm going to knock you around, and I want you up for it.'' Nick returns with Honey, who has ''decided I don't remember anything'' about the evening. George builds up to his game slowly, prompting Martha to speak fondly about their son as she has throughout the evening. He then performs a ceremony of exorcism, first in Latin text as a counterpoint to Martha's speeches, then announcing at last, ''our son is . . . dead.'' Martha is hysterical at first, screaming at George ''YOU CANNOT DO THAT!'' and bursting into tears. Gradually, however, she grows more calm. Nick, finally understanding the reality of the situation—that the ''son'' is a fictional creation—is more baffled than ever about George and Martha's relationship. At last he and Honey make their exit. A tender moment follows, as dawn begins to break. George explains the necessity of putting their lie behind them, and Martha appears to understand.

Martha (Elizabeth Taylor) berates Nick (George Segal) in a scene from the 1966 film adaptation. Taylor's performance won her an Academy Award for best actress

For once she is comfortable enough to admit that she feels real human fear.

CHARACTERS

George

George is Martha's husband. He is forty-six-years-old and a professor of history who has amassed a record of academic mediocrity. He married Martha, daughter of the college president, early in his career but has failed to live up to the overwhelming expectations of his wife and her father, who hoped George would succeed him. George, as Martha is fond of saying, is a bog in the history department; after many years he is not yet even the departmental chair.

As a result of his professional frustration, George feels threatened by up-and-coming young faculty members like Nick and tries to compensate through showy displays of intellectual superiority. George appears to have been responsible for the deaths of

MEDIA ADAPTATIONS

- A sound recording of *Who's Afraid of Virginia Woolf?* with the original Broadway cast was released by Columbia in 1963 (catalog number CDOS 687); though out of print, it is available in some libraries.
- The play was also adapted into a highly acclaimed film in 1966, directed by Mike Nichols and released by Warner Bros. The film won the Academy Awards for Best Actress (Elizabeth Taylor as Martha) and Best Supporting Actress (Sandy Dennis as Honey), as well as three technical awards in the black and white division (Art Direction, Costume Design, and Cinematography). The film additionally received nominations for Best Picture, Best Director, Best Actor (Richard Burton as George), Best Supporting Actor (George Segal as Nick), and Best Screenplay based on material from another medium (Ernest Lehman, for his adaptation of Albee's play).

both of his parents, in two separate accidents which Martha claims were intentional. He is clearly traumatized by this fact, and tells Nick the story as if it had happened to someone else. While George's ''killing'' of the invented son is planned as an act of revenge for Martha's having humiliated him, it comes off more as a mercy gesture, a necessary step to free both him and Martha from destructive illusion.

Honey

A twenty-six-year-old blond girl, ''rather plain.'' Like her husband, Nick, Honey is from the Midwest, striving with her husband to make their way in new surroundings. Honey is not depicted as particularly bright, but she is capable of exerting her will. She is afraid of bearing a child, and as George suspects, she has avoided pregnancy without Nick's knowledge. The circumstance of her marriage to Nick, a false pregnancy, is a source of discomfort to both of them (Honey apparently either genuinely believed herself to be—or pretended to be—pregnant). She changes her mind later in the play, announcing abruptly, ''I want a child.'' While the conversion seems scarcely credible it does appear sustained through the play's conclusion.

Martha

''A large, boisterous woman, 52, looking somewhat younger. Ample, but not fleshy.'' A traditional view of gender roles would depict Martha as ''manlike,'' for her loud, coarse ways, and domineering treatment of George, against whom she has waged for years a war of attrition. Martha had dreams of power which she feels were defeated by George's lack of ambition. As susceptible as George is to Martha's relentless ridicule over his professional failure, Martha is very sensitive to George's criticisms—of her heavy drinking, her sometimes lascivious behavior, and her ''braying'' laugh. George also attempts to pass himself off as her intellectual superior.

Martha is also very well educated, however, if not graduate degreed, and much of the struggle between the couple takes place on intellectual terms (even if it occasionally degenerates to a string of insults in French). During the course of the play, Martha violates the most important rule of the game-playing province she inhabits with George: that their invented son never be mentioned to anyone. George's act of revenge is to ''kill'' the son, which has a profound effect on Martha, breaking through her obstinate strength. The play's closing moment is perhaps the most tender in the entire play, as Martha is able to let her guard down enough around George to admit, for once, being subject to real human fear.

Nick

Nick is described as blond and good-looking, around thirty-years-old. He is a young biology professor who represents a threat to George on a number of different fronts, with his youth, his good looks and sexual energy, and his ambition and willingness to prostitute himself for professional advancement. In short, he seems capable of achieving the promise to which George never lived up. (Although, significantly, the result of his encounter with Martha is impotency, and sexual and professional success are closely linked in the play.) Nick is emotionally empty, a state of being Albee associates (as he does in other plays) with a Midwestern upbringing. As a scientist, Nick's duty is to avoid surprise and establish predictable order. George, meanwhile, is fascinated by the unpredictability of history and seizes on this essential difference in their intellectual pursuits. Further distancing himself from Nick, George essentially accuses the biomedical profession of plotting to turn humankind into a genetically engineered, homogenous species. Critics have suggested that Nick represents to George the threat of voracious totalitarianism, insinuated by the similarity between his name and that of the Russian leader Nikita Khrushchev. (This is not so much a direct allegory as just one aspect to the depth of characterization in the play.)

THEMES

Absurdity

Literally meaning "out of harmony," absurd was the existentialist Albert Camus's designation for the situation of modern men and women whose lives lack meaning as they drift in an inhuman universe. *Virginia Woolf* probes the question of what happens to human beings when they no longer have recourse to the illusions which had previously given their lives meaning. The theme of absurdity is a prevalent one in Albee's plays, as is suggested by the frequent references to the theatre of the absurd in analyzing his writing. Albee describes the philosophical notion of absurdity as "having to do with man's attempt to make sense for himself out of his senseless position in a world which makes no sense . . . because the moral, religious, political and social structures man has erected to 'illusion' himself have collapsed." Perhaps the most articulate and sustained expression of the absurdity of existence is found in George's speech near the beginning of the second act, in which he concludes that despite all "the trouble to construct a civilization," when the last trumpet sounds, "through all the sensible sound of men building," the message to humanity will be, simply: "Up yours."

American Dream

Albee's early plays all express discontent with the optimism and conformity of the 1950s with the materialist ideals that prospered in America during the economic boom following World War II. Albee's early play *The American Dream,* as one would suspect from the title, is a much more explicit treatment of the theme, but in *Virginia Woolf,* Albee also parodies the ideals which in western civilization are supposed to give life meaning. The historical resonance with the Washingtons (George and Martha) is not meant to go unnoticed, as the play attacks the edifice of dreams and self-deceptions that constitute American mythology as Albee sees it. The decline of the American Dream (and of the country in general) resonates throughout *Virginia Woolf.* George observes, for example: "We drink a great deal in this country, and I suspect we'll be drinking a great deal more, too . . . if we survive."

Fear

As suggested by the title, the emotion of fear is a central thematic component of the play. To be afraid of "Virginia Woolf," as Martha says she is at the play's conclusion, is to admit a very human fear about the lack of inherent meaning in one's existence. In order to feel fear, one has to have shed all of the illusions which had previously seemed to give life meaning. Thus, the play presents Martha's fear (and George's, which he acknowledges by nodding silently in response to her) as a life-affirming phenomenon. Better to acknowledge the fear and work through it, the play suggests, than to continue living a lie.

Revenge

The will for revenge appears to be a major force in George and Martha's life. Each seems eternally to be seeking retribution for some past slight or insult. George's "killing" of the invented son is planned as the ultimate act of revenge, for a series of humiliations public and private, and especially for Martha's having broken a fundamental rule of their relationship, by mentioning the son to Honey. In the end, however, killing the son comes off more as a gesture of mercy, a necessary step to free both him and Martha from a destructive illusion.

TOPICS FOR FURTHER STUDY

- What do you feel is the significance of each character's name in this play? What effects did Albee achieve by not giving either couple a last name?
- Discuss in depth the subtitles Albee gave to each act: "Fun and Games," "Walpurgisnacht," and "The Exorcism" (which was Albee's working title for the play as a whole). What do you feel is the significance of each of these subtitles to the plot and themes of the play?
- Research the physical and emotional effects of alcohol. Does heavy drinking appear to be a factor in the behavior of the characters in this play? How do you think it affects George and Martha's marriage?
- Discuss some of the significant puns or plays on words in *Who's Afraid of Virginia Woolf?* (including the one found in the title). What does Albee achieve by using them, in terms of humor, dramatic themes, and character development?

Science and Technology

The play hints strongly at a mass progress towards impotence and depersonalization by the declining western world, which George at least, as a historian and a humanist, blames on scientific advancement. He concocts a doomsday scenario upon which many of his attacks against Nick, the biologist, are based: through genetic technology, "All imbalances will be corrected, sifted out. . . . We will have a race of men . . . test-tube bred . . . incubator-born . . . superb and sublime. . . . *But!* Everyone will tend to be rather the same. . . . Alike." One could argue whether or not George's perspective is reflected in the play as a whole, but as American culture at the time was growing more culturally homogenous through technological inventions like television (which portrayed ideals for how people should look and behave), Albee's resistance to such a process shows through in his play.

Truth and Falsehood

Martha comments to George "Truth and illusion . . . you don't know the difference," and his reply is, "No; but we must carry on as though we did." The growth of these characters through the course of the play rests in the attempt to cease "carrying on," and to attack falsehood on a number of levels, in the hopes of finding something true. Many deep secrets are revealed in the process, forcing the characters to confront the consequences. The primary "exorcism" in the play is the killing of Martha and George's imaginary son, but other explosive confrontations with realities past and present abound in the play, for example: Nick's confession of his material motives for marrying Honey, Honey's revelation of her fear of bearing a child, and George's trauma at having caused (if even accidentally) the deaths of his parents. At one point, George observes about his relationship with Martha: "accommodation, malleability, adjustment . . . those do seem to be in the order of things, don't they?" Throughout the play, characters go through the more difficult process of peeling off layer after layer of pretense and artificiality. The play seems to suggest that even at the naked core of an individual there are destructive illusions, and the pain of losing them is staggering.

STYLE

A good part of the reason *Who's Afraid of Virginia Woolf?* appeared so vibrantly new, so challenging, to theatergoers in 1962 is the novel and often surprising manner in which its author combined different theatrical styles and techniques. In particular, Albee straddled a divide between a predominantly naturalistic American playwriting tradition of social criticism, and what was beginning to be called the "Theater of the Absurd" (Martin Esslin published a landmark study with that same title in 1961). Philosophically almost all of Albee's dramatic writing is aligned with the absurdist idea that human existence is essentially pointless. In describing Albee's mature work, traditional terms such as realism, surrealism, expressionism, absurdism, and naturalism have limited value (especially given that terms like absurdism and expressionism have often been removed from their historically specific context and expanded to mean essentially any form of modern theatre that does not appear realistic).

The divergent aspects of Albee's style are highlighted by the wide-ranging list of dramatic influences usually ascribed to him: Eugene O'Neill (*Long Day's Journey into Night*), most predominantly, accompanied both by American realists Arthur Miller (*The Crucible*) and Tennessee Williams (*Cat on a Hot Tin Roof*) and absurdists like Eugene Ionesco (*The Bald Prima Donna*) and Samuel Beckett (*Waiting for Godot*)—indeed, for the American premiere of *The Zoo Story* Albee's play was paired on the bill with Beckett's *Krapp's Last Tape.*

Albee does not usually take issue with the conjectures of critics regarding his influences but at the same time dismisses the singular importance of any one name. "I've been influenced by everybody, for God's sake," he stated in *Newsweek.* "Everything I've seen, either accepting it or rejecting it. I'm aware when I write a line like Williams. I'm aware when I use silence like Beckett." Trying, with other playwrights of the early 1960s, to prevent theatre in the United States from retreating into lethargy, Albee turned toward Europe for new forms with which to experiment, as O'Neill had done in an earlier generation. The nature of human experience to Albee could not be represented either by a straightforward realism or a casual departure from it.

Who's Afraid of Virginia Woolf? is realistic in form and structure: it is located in a recognizable setting, the plot unfolds in linear progression, and the characters are fully-realized individuals. Albee, however, does not write in a strictly realist vein; Cohn commented in *Edward Albee* that "the play has been viewed as realistic psychology. But credible motivation drives psychological drama, and Albee's motivation is designedly flimsy." Albee challenges audience expectations about genre with elements out of place in a strictly realistic environment, such as the play's almost unbelievably merciless sense of humor.

Played at such an intense psychological level, *Virginia Woolf* almost resembles expressionist drama (meaning that there is a more pronounced expression of the unconscious, rather than character only being revealed through outward action). The *Nation*'s Harold Clurman, for instance, observed that the play "verges on a certain expressionism." The interior, psychological element of the play is a heavy presence, for even while the plot moves forward in real time, it also digs deeply into the past and into the psyche of each of its characters. (Perhaps the strongest example of this tendency is the central importance of the invented—and constantly shifting—history of Martha and George's son.)

While the play is "a volcanic eruption," wrote Howard Taubman in the *New York Times,* one might as well call it "an irruption, for the explosion is inward as well as outward." Realistic drama usually unfolds by presenting a conflict, then resolving it with each event in the plot connecting to the others in a cause-and-effect manner, but in *Virginia Woolf,* the most dramatic conflicts and their potential resolutions seem to lie deep within the minds of the characters.

Theatrical elements of the absurd are much more pronounced in Albee's experimental one-acts like *The Sandbox* and *The American Dream.* Nevertheless, Albee's writing, *Virginia Woolf* included, shares with the absurdists certain philosophical concepts "having to do," in Albee's words, "with man's attempt to make sense for himself out of his senseless position in a world which makes no sense . . . because the moral, religious, political and social structures man has erected to 'illusion' himself have collapsed." In illustrating the collapse of such meaning-endowing structures, Albee also to some extent affirms as a spiritual necessity the need to search for transcendent meaning. Therefore, his work differentiates itself from the utterly nihilistic vision found in much absurdist theatre (nihilism refers to a philosophical doctrine that all values are baseless and nothing is truly knowable or can be communicated). Albee has never liked the phrase Theatre of the Absurd applied to describe his plays, finding negative connotations in the term. To Albee (as he expressed in a 1962 article in the *New York Times Magazine*), the "absurd" theatre is the Broadway, commercial one, in which a play's merits are judged solely by its economic performance.

Just as the challenge of Albee's stems from the fact that it closely resembles realism in form and structure while departing from it in important ways, so the language of the play reflects this same dichotomy. Albee's characters talk not in fully ''realistic'' dialogue, ''but a highly literate and full-bodied distillation of common American speech,'' as Clurman described it. The speech manages to sound real within its context but the language is also heightened, and one almost cannot believe what one is hearing. Albee himself observed in *Newsweek,* ''It's not the purpose of any art form to be just like life. . . . Reality on stage is highly selective reality, chosen to give form. Real dialogue on stage is impossible.''

Who's Afraid of Virginia Woolf? has been described as a blood sport whose ''weapons are words—vicious, cruel, unspeakably humiliating, unpredictably hilarious—the language of personal annihilation'' (*Time*). Albee's ability to use the incongruity of little-child talk for dramatic effect has also been widely noted as a strength of his theatrical language. First appearing in *The Zoo Story,* the technique became even more of a satiric weapon in his subsequent plays, especially *Who's Afraid of Virginia Woolf?,* his first full-length work.

HISTORICAL CONTEXT

In 1962, the year *Who's Afraid of Virgina Woolf?* premiered on Broadway, the major shakeup of American society in the late 1960s was still several years away. But already civil rights protests and riots over desegregation at such educational institutes as the University of Mississippi were showing Americans that the unprecedented optimism and economic growth following the second World War was far from a reality for many. Meanwhile, certain artists and other individuals began expressing a dissatisfaction with the social conformity of the 1950s. For the most part, however, American society continued to revel in a complacent idealism, and would do so until President John F. Kennedy's assassination in November, 1963.

Economically and socially, America was being homogenized through planned suburbs, fast food, and shopping centers; a conformity of thought was strongly encouraged by the social politics of the Cold War. Dissenting voices like Albee's registered discontent with what they saw as the corrupt and/or empty values of American society; to such a perspective, past notions of objective reality were no longer reliable guidelines.

Free expression (particularly in the area of political thought) in American society was not as sharply curtailed as it had been during the era of the McCarthy hearings on ''un-American activities'' (the McCarthy proceedings sought to ''root out'' communist elements in American society), but several circumstances contributed to a consolidation of political opinion around an aggressive national stance toward the communist Soviet Union. The first had been the launch of the satellite *Sputnik* on October 4, 1957, which suddenly undermined, technologically and psychologically, America's unquestioned position as the world's superpower.

The Soviet conquest of space castrated the American psyche, and the perceived threat presented by *Sputnik* and the Soviet's subsequent success in launching a human being into space cannot be underestimated. In 1962 an upswing in American self-image followed the success of astronaut John Glenn in completing the first U.S. Earth orbits on February 7. (The successful launching of the American satellite *Telstar I* followed on July 12.) Still, political anxiety over the spread of communism throughout the world did not abate, and in the brewing civil conflict in South Vietnam it prompted increased American support toward the elimination of communist Vietcong guerrillas, in the form of money, arms, and field observers (America's support of democratic forces in Vietnam would soon escalate to full military involvement). Meanwhile, with the Cold War seemingly dividing global politics into only two massive spheres, American (democracy) and Soviet (communist), 1962 also saw the establishment of an independent organization of African states and national independence for Jamaica, Algeria, Trinidad and Tobago, Western Somoa, Uganda, and Tanganyika.

The Cold War also focused attention on the island nation of Cuba in 1962. President Kennedy on February 3, ceased all U.S. trade with Cuba as punishment towards the communist government established there by dictator Fidel Castro's coup in 1959. U.S. surveillance photographs revealed the presence of Soviet missiles in Cuba, prompting Kennedy to order an air and sea ''quarantine'' of Cuba to prevent any further shipments of arms to Castro. Soviet Premiere Nikita Khrushchev offered to remove the missiles if the U.S. would withdraw

COMPARE & CONTRAST

- **1962:** The Cuban missile crisis in October makes the threat of global nuclear war seem an imminent possibility.

  Today: The Cold War over, the United States no longer faces the consolidated military strength of a communist rival. The Berlin Wall, a powerful symbol of Cold War division, fell in 1989. The fear of nuclear war is no longer as great, although there exists widespread concern about the spread of nuclear technology to terrorist groups or so-called "rogue states."

- **1962:** Cold War competition with the Soviet Union affects many aspects of American life. In space, prior Soviet achievements are matched by the U.S. this year, as Col. John Glenn achieves the first U.S. Earth orbit and the U.S. launches its first satellite, *Telstar.*

  Today: The Soviet Union no longer exists as such, first withdrawing its control over the Eastern Bloc countries, and then fragmenting into independent states. While several other countries maintain economic influence of a par with the United States, the U.S. is widely recognized since the fall of the Soviet Union as the world's only remaining "superpower." The U.S. space program, NASA, is the world leader, with regular successful launches of space shuttles.

- **1962:** Institutions of higher education enjoy substantial levels of federal funding and increased enrollments which are the legacy of the post-war Baby Boom and grant programs like the G.I. Bill. College teaching is a secure and expanding profession in most academic fields.

  Today: Under severe economic crises, colleges and universities are "downsizing" their faculties, increasing class sizes, and relying more heavily on part-time and adjunct instructors rather than tenured faculty. The inability to advance in academia that George demonstrates would not be viewed today so much as a personal failure as an economic factor of radically shrinking professional opportunities.

- **1962:** The Broadway theatre is in decline as a force in American culture, both economically, and, more acutely, in qualitative terms. Producers are increasingly unwilling to take a chance on any new work which might not succeed commercially.

  Today: The decline of Broadway has continued. Fewer new productions than ever are mounted each year and fewer people look to Broadway as the indicator of the American theatre. The majority of new productions are large-scale commercial spectacles such as Andrew Lloyd Weber's *Phantom of the Opera.* In addition to the alternatives presented off-Broadway, new work prospers in important regional theatres across the county.

---

its own missiles from Turkey. President Kennedy rejected the offer, and for several days, during what became known as the Cuban Missile Crisis, the threat of nuclear confrontation loomed large. The situation was quietly diffused and both the Soviet missiles in Cuba and the U.S. missiles in Turkey were removed. Yet the standoff left a permanent scar on the American psyche; the plausibility of nuclear weapons would subsequently be viewed with greater fear and skepticism in the coming decades.

Culturally, the American theatre in 1962 continued a downward trend in creative energy. Some large musical productions did well during the year, but Broadway continued its protracted decline—both economically and especially in artistic terms. While theaters across Europe were typically staging challenging plays of ethical significance (in 1962, for example, Friedrich Durrenmatt's *The Physicist,* and Eugene Ionesco's *Exit the King*), American theatre was becoming progressively safer. Producers were increasingly unwilling to take a chance on any new work which might not succeed commercially. In terms of new Broadway productions, the fifty-four plays in the 1962 season were only six more than the all-time low up to that point. By bridging the gap from the experimental off-Broadway (where Arthur Kopit's *Oh, Dad, Poor Dad, Mama's Hung You in the Closet and We're Feeling So Sad* was another success of the year) to Broadway, Albee breathed new life into the mainstream of American theatre.

CRITICAL OVERVIEW

Upon the premiere of *Who's Afraid of Virginia Woolf?* some critics praised virtually every aspect of the play, while others faulted it as too long, too vulgar, or too pessimistic; almost everyone, however, saw in the play the potential to breathe new life into a Broadway theatre that was no longer the creative force it had been. ''An exciting play,'' after all, ''is good antidote for what ails Broadway theater,'' Taubman noted in the *New York Times.* Whether they admire or detest the play, Taubman observed, ''theatergoers cannot see it and shrug it off. They burn with an urge to approve or differ.''

A reviewer for *Time* claimed that Albee's play ''has jolted the Broadway season to life.'' Similarly, a reviewer for *Newsweek* called the play a ''brilliantly original work of art—an excoriating theatrical experience, surging with shocks of recognition and dramatic fire. It will be igniting Broadway for some time to come.'' Although he found *Virginia Woolf* important in the context of the Broadway season, Harold Clurman of the *Nation* called the play ''a minor work within the prospect of Albee's further development.'' (In this his opinion differs greatly from the popular notion that *Virginia Woolf* was the high point of Albee's creative career.)

Critics praised the density of Albee's writing, the challenge presented by his complex merging of multiple theatrical elements. Henry Hewes in the *Saturday Review* observed that *Virginia Woolf* contained some of the same complex Freudian psychology of Albee's earlier plays but that the new work ''is more recognizably real and self-generating than were its predecessors.'' While the play also has a ''sense of the ridiculous . . . things are hardly exaggerated enough to be called 'Theatre of the Absurd,' either.'' John Gassner commented in *Dramatic Soundings: Evaluations and Retractions Culled from Thirty Years of Drama Criticism* that ''Mr. Albee has written a terrifying thing—perhaps *the* negative play to end all negative plays, yet also a curiously compassionate play.'' The powerful sense of recognition inspired in audiences by the play rested, most critics observed, in the speech of Albee's characters, what Cohn called ''the most adroit dialogue ever heard on the American stage.'' Clurman wrote that the dialogue ''is superbly virile and pliant; it also *sounds.*''

Reviewers who were generally positive about the quality and importance of *Virginia Woolf,* however, criticized certain aspects of Albee's technique. Taubman in the *New York Times* expressed mild reservations about a key plot device and whether Martha and George are ''believable all the way.'' The *Time* reviewer, meanwhile, found the plot resolution ''woefully inadequate and incongruous, rather like tracing the source of the Niagara to a water pistol.'' The review also found the play ''needlessly long . . . repetitious, slavishly, sometimes superficially Freudian, and given to trite thoughts about scientific doom.''

And, as with any work of art, there were those who, despite overwhelmingly positive reception, found little to praise in *Virginia Woolf.* The *New Yorker* review thought Albee imitative of O'Neill ''without having much to talk about,'' and though granting him ''a certain dramatic flair,'' found it ''ill-directed . . . in the present enterprise.''

In the nearly four decades since the premiere of *Who's Afraid of Virginia Woolf?,* not only has the play remained luminous in the minds of critics and other theatergoers (as well as generations of readers), but so much so that almost the entire rest of Albee's career has seemed tarnished in comparison. While Albee went on to win three Pulitzer Prizes and other high honors, he has also occasionally been plagued by negative criticism and commercial failure of his productions. Richard Amacher wrote in his 1969 book *Edward Albee* that the playwright has earned a great deal of criticism precisely because he continues to experiment rather than shape his work to commercial taste or repeat his past successes, because he ''does attempt a more difficult, a more deeply penetrating, view of reality than some of the older dramatists, who by comparison seem merely to scratch the surface of illusion.''

But if such total artistic, critical, and commercial success never again coalesced around one single work for Albee, as it did around *Virginia Woolf,*

Real-life husband and wife Elizabeth Taylor and Richard Burton as Albee's fictional couple Martha and George in the film version

his new work in subsequent decades has nevertheless had an impact. *Virginia Woolf,* meanwhile, continues to draw close interest and is continuously revived, extensively read and studied, and widely written about; the play's richness shows itself in the variety of topics of inquiry. Many writers have explored it as a social phenomenon, a challenge to corrupted values particular to its time. Psychological readings of the play have also been quite popular—both Freudian readings of the psyches of the characters, and studies of external behavior and modes of communication using other psychological models. Joy Flasch, in her *Modern Drama* analysis of the play inspired by Eric Berne's study *Games People Play,* saw the conclusion of the play as an "attempt to put aside the destructive Games which have taken the place of true Intimacy. It will be difficult, perhaps impossible."

The differing perspectives the work has inspired, in addition to the pure entertainment value that it provides, have made *Who's Afraid of Virginia Woolf?* a hallmark of contemporary American theatre. That new ideas and fresh perspectives continue to be discovered within the play's text—and that multiple generations have found merit in the work—is a testament to the depth of Albee's creation.

CRITICISM

Christopher G. Busiel

Busiel is a Ph.D. candidate with a specialty in drama. In this essay he examines the bond between George and Martha; while their relationship may be antagonistic, Busiel proposes that it may be love that keeps them together.

The complexity of the marital relations between Martha and George is one of the central strengths of Albee's technique in *Who's Afraid of Virginia Woolf?* Audiences and critics alike were often repelled by the depth of George and Martha's viciousness toward one another. *Time* magazine commented that for Eugene O'Neill "marriage had its serpents, but they were invaders in Eden. To Albee, marriage seems to be a no-exit hell in which the only intimacy is a hopeless common damnation." Some criticism of the play suggested that it constitutes a critique of heterosexual relationships from a gay perspective (Albee has never acknowledged or denied being gay). This is one eminent possibility, yet it is only one level on which the play functions.

WHAT DO I READ NEXT?

- *The Zoo Story,* Albee's first play written as an adult. The one-act premiered in 1959 and suggests the future elements of Albee's work (especially the idea suggested in the title that beneath the illusion of civilization, human beings are essentially animals capable of startling viciousness). In the play, Jerry, an embittered outsider, confronts the conformist Peter on a park bench, inducing him to listen to much of Jerry's life story and then provoking him into defending himself and his way of life.
- *A Delicate Balance.* Albee won his first Pulitzer Prize for this 1966 play, but many considered the award merely belated recognition for *Virginia Woolf.* This play revolves around similar elements (two couples in a living room engaged in a crisis, the death of a child, the failures of educated and well-intentioned people), causing critics to variously see it either as a compelling counterpoint to Albee's earlier work, or as repetitive imitation of it.
- *Oh, Dad, Poor Dad, Mama's Hung You in the Closet and We're Feeling So Sad* by Arthur Kopit, a theatrical parody of the Oedipus complex. This is the best-known play by an experimental dramatist whose work first appeared around the same time as Albee's, and who (along with Jack Gelber) is often discussed in relation to Albee.
- *Long Day's Journey into Night,* one of Eugene O'Neill's dramatic masterpieces. O'Neill is regularly evoked by critics as an influence upon Albee's style, especially this realistic, autobiographical play which unfolds over a long night of emotionally intense dialogue. Albee has joked that critics might only be observing superficially that both plays ''have four characters and they talk a great deal and nothing happens,'' but deeper connections definitely exist. Both O'Neill and Albee, despite their experimentation with a wide variety of styles, remain best known for their more realistic, psychologically complex dramas.

While George and Martha's marriage seems utterly destructive, the play is especially captivating because the couple nevertheless appear inextricably bound to one another. Given the richness of Albee's dialogue and the depth of characterization in the play, George and Martha's marriage cannot be summed up easily as a ''love-hate relationship'' or even as a sadomasochistic need to inflict hurt upon one another. Audiences in 1962 found Martha and George's marriage perplexing, and subsequent years, rather than revealing its mystery, have only highlighted its enduring complexity.

The cruelty of George and Martha's fun and games is not gratuitous but borne out of thwarted passion (one thinks not only of their childless marriage but moments like Martha's invitation to George to ''give your Mommy a big sloppy kiss,'' which he is too preoccupied to reciprocate). There is a loving bond between them which persists even in their assaults: ''You're going bald,'' Martha tells George; ''so are you,'' he replies, after which they pause and ''both laugh.'' They seem particularly close when, after so many years, one of them manages to surprise the other. Martha is delighted by George's trick with the shotgun which produces a Chinese parasol, laughing heartily and asking, ''Where'd you get that, you bastard?''

The incongruity is readily apparent, for the joke only functions because the characters (and perhaps the audience) believe for just a moment that George might actually shoot Martha for having once again humiliated him publicly. While the marriage appears so destructive, it may exert its greatest damage on outsiders who do not understand the mutual affection that runs as an undercurrent to George and Martha's most outrageous attacks on one another.

Ruby Cohn observed in *Edward Albee* that the play offers repeated ''views of the togetherness of George and Martha, and during the three acts each is visibly tormented by the extended absence of the other. However malicious they sound, they *need* one another—a need that may be called love.'' Other critics view the relationship quite differently; Harold Clurman, for example, commented in the *Nation* that ''Martha and George, we are told, love each other after all. How?. . . What interests—even petty—do they have or share?''

Clearly, one interest they share is the verbal fencing which tests their inventive minds; each genuinely admires the other's mental agility. While they occasionally hurt one another, they both seem to live to play the sport. This point is made explicitly by Martha, who chastises George for going too far after his game of ''Get the Guests'' has driven Honey and Nick from the room. George tries to rationalize his behavior in terms of Martha's treatment of him throughout the evening. ''[Y]ou can humiliate me, you can tear me apart . . . ALL NIGHT . . . and that's perfectly all right . . . that's OK.'' The exchange which follows is one of the most revealing in the play:

MARTHA: You can stand it!

GEORGE: I cannot stand it!

MARTHA: You can stand it!! You married me for it!! (*silence*)

GEORGE: (*Quietly*) That is a desperately sick lie.

MARTHA: Don't you know it, even yet?

George continues to deny the validity of Martha's point, as have some critics. Clurman suggested that Martha merely ''rationalizes her cruelty to George on the ground that he masochistically enjoys her beatings.'' In the context of the play, however, Martha's observation has the ring of truth. George, as she points out to Nick, is stronger than he appears, and the possibility exists that he enjoys the verbal sport on a level which far exceeds masochism.

That George and Martha may ultimately respect one another despite virtually ceaseless verbal abuse is suggested by the fact that each passes up the opportunity to blame their lack of children on the other. When Nick realizes that Martha and George's son is a fantasy, he asks George: ''you couldn't have . . . any?'' If Martha is barren, George could have taken advantage of this opportunity for revenge, but he responds, ''*We* couldn't.'' The same opportunity exists for Martha if George is infertile, but she, too, asserts, ''*We* couldn't.'' George and Martha have ruthlessly exposed other equally humiliating facts about each other during the course of the evening, yet their mutual sadness over the issue of children constitutes a basis for mutual support.

"THE COMPLEXITY OF THE MARITAL RELATIONS BETWEEN MARTHA AND GEORGE IS ONE OF THE CENTRAL STRENGTHS OF ALBEE'S TECHNIQUE IN *WHO'S AFRAID OF VIRGINIA WOOLF?*"

Martha seems to regret much of what has passed between her and George in a speech at the beginning of the third act, after her failed sexual encounter with Nick. Perhaps it is only the disappointment of the moment (and Albee challenges the audience whether or not to believe a woman's tender words about a husband on whom she has just attempted to cheat), but Martha does seem to regret her treatment of George throughout the years: ''George who is good to me, and whom I revile . . . who keeps learning the games we play as quickly as I can change the rules . . . who has made the hideous, the hurting, the insulting mistake of loving me and must be punished for it. . . . Some day . . . hah! Some *night* . . . some stupid, liquor-ridden night . . . I will go too far . . . and I'll either break the man's back . . . or push him off for good . . . which is what I deserve.'' Of course, the night she speaks of has arrived (as the audience is aware, but Nick does not seem to acknowledge). The irony of her observation is that, indeed, George's back will not be broken, but rather he will take an action that not only assures his ''victory'' in the evening's games but will force the couple to reconstitute the basis of their marriage.

While George's ''killing'' of the invented son is planned as an act of revenge, the ultimate rebuke to Martha, it comes off more as an act of mercy. George and Martha recognize at the end of the play that continuing to live with this particular illusion is destructive to both of them (''It was time to do it,'' George says simply). Cohn observed that George and Martha ''have cemented their marriage with the fiction of their child,'' but they learn that ''such lies must be killed before they kill.'' George's difficult action brings about perhaps the most tender moment of the entire play, as Martha is able to let her guard down enough around George to admit, for once, being subject to real human fear:

GEORGE: Who's afraid of Virginia Woolf. . . .

MARTHA: I . . . am . . . George. . . . I . . . am. . . .

(*GEORGE nods, slowly*)

There is an absence of love in a marriage which has had its unconfronted truths covered over; once the veneer has been removed, could we say George and Martha do seem to love one another by the end of the play? In the dawn breaking at play's end there is renewal, an affirmation of the strength gained from mutual support and the abandonment of a lie. C. N. Stavrou observed in the *Southwest Review,* ''A splinter of light is discernible amid the gloaming of nihilism's smog.'' Certainly, the conclusion of *Virginia Woolf* constitutes a fundamental break with the spirit of the play to that point. For some, this transition does not ring true; *Modern Drama*'s Richard Dozier, for example, found George and Martha's ''sentimental reconciliation'' to be ''hardly in keeping with the rest of the play.''

Ultimately, the question of whether Martha and George love one another is not clearly resolved for the audience; indeed, the answer may depend most upon one's own definition of love. Despite their destructive behavior, the couple has a close bond, a mutual dependency that has sustained them through the years. Dependency is not widely considered a healthy substitute for love, however, and one may view George and Martha's need for one another as sadomasochistic desire or unhealthy obsession rather than love. Indeed, that such dependency passes for love in the modern age may constitute part of Albee's larger critique of martial relationships. Clearly, however, Martha and George's relationship moves into a new phase at the conclusion of the play. If they do truly love one another, the ''exorcism'' of the illusionary son provides their best opportunity to rebuild their marriage on a new basis. Whether they will be willing and able to take advantage of this opportunity, however, the audience is merely left to ponder.

Source: Christopher G. Busiel, for *Drama for Students,* Gale, 1997.

Steven Carter

In this brief article, Carter explains how the play's religious imagery and its wordplay interact.

Most critics of Edward Albee's *Who's Afraid of Virginia Woolf?* are mindful of the play's rich array of religious signifiers, from Martha's deified father (George: ''He's a god, we all know that,'' 26 [New American Library edition of *Who's Afraid of Virginia Woolf?,* 1962]), to the sacrificial son (Martha: ''Poor lamb,'' 221); from George's Requiem Mass (''Domine: et lux perpetua luceat eis,'' 227), to the Sabbath denouement (George: ''Sunday tomorrow; all day,'' 239), and so forth.

The self-reflexivity of the play's language has also served as a *point d'appui* for critical inquiry. Similar words and phrases bounce back and forth throughout all three acts:

Martha. George and Martha, sad, sad, sad. (191)
Nick. George and Martha, sad, sad, sad. (191)
Honey .. . . and so they were married. . . .
George.. . . and so they were married. . . . (146)
Nick. Lady, please. . . . (232)
Honey. Lady . . . please. . . . (233)

What has gone unnoticed, so far as I know, is the conjoining of these two essential motifs. This linkage occurs during two critical moments in the play: one at the beginning of act 1, the other at the conclusion of act 3.

It is Martha who utters the play's first word: ''Jes*us.*'' Terribly shaken at the very end of the play by the death of the imaginary son, she echoes this initial line: ''Just . . . us?'' On both occasions, she and George are alone on stage (3, 241). This subtle play on the off-rhymes ''Jes*us*'' and ''Just . . . us?'' accomplishes three things: It links up the aforementioned motifs of religion and language, making of them in effect a single, overarching motif; it brings Martha, the uncertain atheist who is also scared of being alone, to a crossroads; and it refreshes, in a single homophone, the audience's collective memory of the play's central conflict among George, Martha, and the son.

The transcendent son brings a double-edged sword to George and Martha's relationship. He gives them something to share above and beyond the disillusionments and recriminations of a tortured marriage. Ironically, however, the son also provides them with a doomsday weapon to use in their ''total war'' against each other (159). Martha's line, ''He's not completely sure it's his own kid,'' simultaneously wounds George and reinforces the notion of Immaculate Conception. George's line, ''He is dead. Kyrie, eleison . . .'' shatters Martha and reprises the Requiem Mass earlier in act 3 (71,

Martha (Diana Rigg) and George (David Suchet) share a rare tender moment in a 1996 production staged at the Almeida Theatre in London

223). From Martha's ''Jes*us*'' to her ''Just . . . us?'' Albee's play *between* words foregrounds this tragic duality.

The italicized ''us'' in ''Jes*us*'' is, in short, a mnemonic clue to the play's ultimate irony: The cherished son must be sacrificed in order to redeem the *us,* the barren marriage of George and Martha. Put another way, in tones meant to be spoken ''very softly, very slowly,'' George and Martha transubstantiate the atonement of act 1 to the at*one*-ment of act 3 (239). The audience should now understand why Nick's question, ''You couldn't have . . . any?'' prompts George and Martha's '' *We* couldn't,'' a mutual response, which is accompanied by Albee's stage direction, *A hint of communion in this* (238).

Source: Steven Carter, review of *Who's Afraid of Virginia Woolf?,* in the *Explicator,* Volume 55, no. 2, Winter, 1997, pp. 102–03.

Orley I. Holtan

Holtan offers evidence that Albee's play, while a riveting character study, is also an allegory for the history of America, beginning with George Washington and the American Revolution.

Near the end of the second act of *Who's Afraid of Virginia Woolf?* George, the professor of history, is left alone onstage while Martha, his wife, and Nick are playing the preliminary rounds of "hump the hostess" in the kitchen. Attempting to control his hurt and anger he reads aloud from a book he has taken from the shelf, "And the West, encumbered by crippling alliances and burdened with a morality too rigid to accommodate itself to the swing of events must—eventually—fall." George is clearly encumbered with a crippling alliance—his marriage to Martha—and does seem to be burdened with a kind of morality that makes it difficult for him to respond in kind to her vicious attacks. At the same time, this observation on the movements of history, read in connection with the events of George's personal history, is a splendid example of how Albee has managed to endow the events of the family drama with a deeper significance, suggestive of larger events and movements. Various critics have noted a number of possible interpretations and levels of meaning in the play. I feel that one of the most profitable ways of looking at *Who's Afraid of Virginia Woolf?* is to see it as an allegory for the American historical experience.

Indeed, Albee had previously used the domestic setting in just such an allegorical way, though not so subtly or successfully. *The American Dream,* produced off-Broadway in 1961, depicted a symbolic couple, Mommy and Daddy, who had mutilated and emasculated their adopted son when he showed signs of independence and who threaten to send Grandma, with her pioneer toughness and independence, off to a home. In replying to the attacks of certain critics on the play Albee remarked that it was "a stand against the vision that everything in this slipping land of ours is peachy keen." (preface to *The American Dream,* [New York], 1960) Similarly, in talking about *Who's Afraid of Virginia Woolf?,* Albee told Michael Rutenberg that George and Martha were deliberately named after George and Martha Washington and that the imaginary child could represent the uncompleted revolutionary spirit of this country.

My argument is further strengthened by the fact that history figures so prominently in the play. The word or a variant of it runs like a leitmotif through the entire play, being used twenty-eight times in the first act alone. George is a professor of history who does not run the history department, Nick's timetable is history, Martha's father had a sense of history and, in the second act after the "get the guests" sequence, George remarks, "the patterns of history." It would seem appropriate then, before the play is examined at length, briefly to consider the special significance of history in American thought and experience.

One of the principal myths on which this country was founded was the notion that America was a New Eden, a second chance ordained by God or Providence in which man could begin all over again, freed from the accumulated sin and corruption of Western history. Not only could the American become a New Adam and found upon the unspoiled continent an ideal human polity, but this new way of life and new order of society could serve as a shining example to redeem erring Europe from her own sinfulness. America had established a covenant with God or with Nature (the myth had its beginnings with the Puritan settlements and became secularized as time went on) and could remain free of the vicissitudes of history provided she kept the terms of the covenant, retained her simplicity, shunned European complexity and sophistication and avoided the twin temptations of urbanization and industrialization. Unfortunately, such a dream of perfection could not find realization in an imperfect world; the troubles and complexities Americans thought they had left behind began to invade the New World. Yet so strong was the myth that the tendency of American thinkers and historians was to locate the causative factor not in the nature of man nor the impossibility of the dream but in the failure of the new nation to keep the covenant, and to look backward to a golden age in the past before Americans had allowed themselves to be seduced by alien complexities and affectations. Thus the majority of American historians, says David Noble, have been Jeremiahs, decrying America's involvement within the transitory patterns of European history and calling Americans back to their duties and obligations. Having started with such a dream of innocence and perfection, much of the American experience has involved a deeply felt sense of loss and failure.

As one looks at the attitudes of George and Martha one is immediately struck by the fact that the orientation of both characters is to the past and is coupled with an acute sense of failure which, furthermore, has often involved a loss of innocence. When George was first courting Martha, for example, she had liked "real ladylike little drinkies." Now her taste runs to "rubbing alcohol." Over the years she has learned that alcohol "pure and simple" is for the "pure and simple." The adjectives applied to Martha are ironic for whatever she may have been in the days of their courtship she is now obviously neither pure nor simple. The note of past failure is struck even more clearly a few minutes later in a scene between George and Nick:

> NICK: . . . you . . . you've been here quite a long time, haven't you?
> GEORGE: What? Oh . . . yes. Ever since I married . . . uh, what's her name . . . uh, Martha. Even before that. Forever. Dashed hopes and good intentions. Good, better, best, bested. How do you like that for a declension, young man? Eh?

Through this scene, of course, the play remains on a comparatively realistic level. Martha's changed drinking habits and George's sense of failure in his career need not be taken allegorically. In the second act, however, matters become more complex. Shortly after the beginning of the act George tells a long story about a boy who had ordered "bergin" in a speakeasy (an error growing out of innocence and unworldliness). He is described as having been blonde with the face of a cherub and as laughing delightedly at his own error. Yet this "cherub" had killed his mother with a shotgun some time before, "completely accidentally, without even an unconscious motivation," and later, when he learned that he had killed his father also, in an automobile accident, he went mad and has spent the last thirty years in an asylum. George follows the story with an observation about insane people. They don't age in the usual sense; "the underuse of everything leaves them quite whole." Martha later indicates that the story came from George's unpublished novel and that George himself may have been the boy in question. The facts of the case are never clear. They are specifically contradicted in the third act; furthermore, George has obviously not spent the last thirty years in a literal asylum. The issue is clouded even further by the suggestion that even the unpublished novel may be an invention, another of the "games" with which the couple keeps themselves occupied. In the light of the confusion over the "facts" an allegorical interpretation almost forces itself upon us. George, in fact, gives the audience a nudge in that direction when talking about his "second novel"; "it was an allegory really, but it could be read as straight cozy prose."

Allegorically, then, how is the story to be taken? Clearly it is the passage from innocence to guilt and madness. America had begun as a fresh, unspoiled continent, convinced that it was unique in human history in its opportunity to create a perfect society. In cutting itself off from its European tradition and history it had, in effect, killed its "parents." Yet one cannot escape history. Even if one kills one's parents, literally or symbolically, one cannot wipe out the objective fact of their having existed nor destroy the genetic and environmental influences they have given one. Only by retreating into madness can one escape the vicissitudes of history and live completely in one's own world. It is clear that George envies those (the mad) who have remained untouched by life's experience; he would like to escape from reality, from aging, from history but he has been unable to do so. Both George and Martha indicate at various points that "back there," "in the beginning," "when I first came to New Carthage," there might have been a chance for them. That chance was lost and now their "crippling alliance" exacts its toll from both of them.

> "IN THIS PLAY ALBEE HAS CREATED A RICH AND TROUBLING ALLEGORY FOR THE AMERICAN HISTORICAL EXPERIENCE, THE STORY OF A NATION THAT BEGAN IN BOUNDLESS OPTIMISM AND FAITH IN ITS OWN POWER TO CONTROL THE FUTURE AND THAT HAS HAD TO COME TO GRIPS NOT ONLY WITH EXTERNAL CHALLENGES BUT WITH ITS OWN CORRUPTION, COMPROMISE AND FAILURE, THAT HAS REACHED THE POINT WHERE IT MUST CAST AWAY ITS COMFORTING DREAMS AND LOOK REALITY IN THE FACE."

George's failure to run first the history department and then the college fits well into this line of argument. The college seems to comprise the universe within which the two exist: it surrounds and encompasses them. The outside world rarely enters into the action or dialogue. Martha's father is president of the college and there are allusions, though admittedly subtle ones, to "Daddy's" divinity ("He's a God, we all know that,''; ''The old man is not going to die,''; ''I worshipped that guy. I absolutely worshipped him.'' Furthermore, Daddy had a sense of dynastic history. It was his idea that George should take over the history department, then eventually step into his place and take over the college. George was to be the heir apparent. Daddy, however, watched for a couple of years and came to the conclusion that George lacked leadership potential, that he was not capable of filling the role. George failed and Martha has never let him forget that failure.

Rutenberg has suggested that the six-year age differential between George and Martha may actually be six centuries (again there are subtle suggestions of this in the script), and that Martha, therefore, represents Mother Church while George stands for the new spirit of Protestantism. While Albee agreed that the interpretation was ingenious, he discounted it. If the play is regarded as an allegory of the American historical experience, however, there is another way in which the six-century age differential can be applied. Europe took the first steps toward her long climb out of the Middle Ages in approximately the eleventh century. This was the century of the Viking discovery of America (1000 A.D.), the Norman Conquest (1066) and the First Crusade (1095). The first settlement in North America (Virginia) was in 1607 and the founding of Plymouth Colony and the Massachusetts Bay Colony occurred in 1620 and 1630 respectively. Thus, there is a difference of not quite six centuries from the dawning of national consciousness in Europe to the colonizing of North America. If we date backward from the ratification of the Constitution in 1787 to the signing of the Magna Carta in 1215, we have five hundred and seventy-two years, again almost six centuries. Thus, George came, bright-eyed and bushy tailed as Martha describes him, into the history department and Martha, six years older, fell for him. Similarly, America, full of promise and hope for the future burst upon the scene of history and Europe did fall for America. The idea of America as a New Eden originated, after all, among Europeans who either looked toward or came to America. As George fell short of Martha's expectations, so perhaps did Albee's America fall short of the expectations of Europe and of Providence. Interestingly enough, George did run the history department for a period of four years during the war, but when everybody came back he lost his position of leadership. In the same way America's position of world leadership went virtually unchallenged during World War II but once the war ended and the recovery of Europe became a fact that leadership began to decline. By the time *Who's Afraid of Virginia Woolf?* was produced in 1962, America was trying to exercise her hegemony over increasingly recalcitrant followers.

When all these threads are pulled together one can see that George's marriage and his career can be read as analogues for the American historical experience. America had begun by feeling that she could escape from history, control her own destiny and preserve her innocence, but that fond hope soon met with failure. The American dream—the child which was to be given birth upon the new continent—never really materialized; the paradise on earth was not founded. Instead America was increasingly caught up in the same corruptions, compromises and failures as the rest of the world. That failure may have been all the more painful because America was the victim of her own idealism, unable to escape the realities of history but simultaneously unable to play the game of power politics with the same unscrupulousness as the older nations—''encumbered by crippling alliances and burdened with a morality too rigid to accommodate itself to the swing of events.''

Within the contexts of the play there are two possible ways of dealing with this failure. One is to pretend that it never occurred, to create the child out of the imagination and stubbornly to insist, as does Martha, that ''everything is fine.'' The other is to look backward, recognizing that something has gone wrong but rather than trying to rectify it or questioning the validity of the dream itself, merely to mourn its passing and try to place the blame on something or somebody else. It may be that Albee sees these two modes of dealing with the failure of the dream as characteristic of American behaviour.

But if, in Albee's opinion, America's attempt to escape from or to control history has proved to be a failure, other forces in the contemporary world have not learned her lesson. These other forces are represented by the young biologist, Nick. Albee was asked if Nick were named after Nikita Khruschev. He answered yes, in the same way that George and Martha were named after the Washingtons, but went on to assert that that fact was not very significant. Yet an examination of Nick's function in the play reveals a number of connections if not explicitly with Communism at least with the idea that history can be ''scientifically'' organized and controlled. George accuses Nick of seeking to alter the chromosomes and to sterilize the unfit, thus creating a new super-civilization of scientists and mathematicians, all "smooth, blonde and right at the middleweight limit." In such a world history will have no relevance, diversity will vanish, and a condition of social, intellectual and biological uniformity will be imposed upon the world. Nick makes light of the accusation at first, later is angered by it, but never denies it. In fact, smarting under George's attack he sarcastically avers that he is going to be "the wave of the future." In the second act, with his guard somewhat lowered by George's confidences, he discloses his career plans:

> NICK: . . . What I thought I'd do is . . . I'd sort of insinuate myself generally, play around for a while, find all the weak spots, shore 'em up, but with my own name plate on 'em . . . become sort of a fact, and then turn into a . . . a what?
>
> GEORGE: An inevitability.
>
> NICK: Exactly . . . an inevitability.

Historical inevitability, a term George later twice applies to Nick, is, of course, one of the catch phrases of communism and it is possible to see the post World War II policy of the Soviet Union as a process of insinuating itself and shoring up weak spots. Furthermore, if we conclude for the sake of the argument that Martha represents a Europe originally enraptured but ultimately disillusioned with America, Nick's wooing of her (and hers of him) coincides once again with the patterns of history. Out of his own bitter experience George tries to warn Nick of the folly of trying to control history but Nick, young, brash, and overconfident merely replies, "up yours." This interpretation clarifies George's two puzzling speeches, that in which he declares, "I will not give up Berlin" and that about "ice for the lamps of China." This latter line, especially coming as it does on the heels of Nick's wooing of Martha, suggests the presence in the world of the third force, in the face of which the seduction of Europe by the Soviet Union (or vice-versa) may be futile.

Yet in the "get the guests" sequence George manages to damage Nick heavily and later, when Nick gets Martha off to bed, he proves to be impotent. Indeed, Nick has provided George with the very ammunition that the latter uses against him, the revelation of the compromise and subterfuge on which his marriage is based. Honey has trapped him with a false pregnancy and he has used Honey and her father's money as "a pragmatic extension of the big dream"; her wealth will help him attain his goals. Pursuing the allegorical interpretation, then, in what sense has the Soviet Union compromised? One fact that comes immediately to mind is her perversion of Marx's understanding of the evolution of communism. The state, in the Soviet Union, has not withered away but has become even stronger than it was in the days of the Czars. Furthermore, Russia has had, to some degree, to adopt some of the methods of Western capitalism which she affects to despise. It is interesting in this context, that both couples are barren. George and Martha have an imaginary child; Honey has had at least one false pregnancy. If the communist revolution was to usher in the land of milk and honey, that dream, too, has been stillborn, as surely as the dream of perfection which was to be brought forth on the American continent has failed to materialize. Nick's impotence might suggest that neither the Soviet Union nor the United States is capable of controlling history. Nick simply does not understand the forces with which he is dealing. Devoted to his own ideology—his own "scientific" understanding of the world—he fails to see that no matter how foolish or feeble George may look he is not yet defeated. Nor does he realize the full implications of his attempted affair with Martha. In courting her in order to further his own ambitions he has got himself into a position from which he cannot easily extricate himself. As a matter of fact, in the third act Nick is put through exactly the same paces as was George in the first. He is ridiculed for his failure, taunted with his lack of knowledge, and ordered to answer the door. Far from being in control of the patterns of history he too has become their victim, as George had warned him he would.

The exorcism of the third act functions also within this context. George first forces Martha to recount the tale of the imaginary son—the birth, the innocent childhood, the attempt to bring him up, with its failures and corruptions, but he will not allow her to stick to the pretence that everything is fine. He forces her to acknowledge the failure, to accept her part of the blame and at last "kills" the son. This act seems to create a sense of peace and the beginnings of communion between them and seems also to have a beneficent effect on Nick and Honey. If, as Albee has suggested, the child is taken to represent the notion inherent in the American dream that the new nation could escape from history and the failings of human nature and create a perfect society, that belief is shown to be an illusion which must be destroyed if the couple and the nation are to face the future realistically. The future is, of course, uncertain; there is no guarantee that once illusion is cast away success and happiness will automatically follow—thus the lingering fear of "Virginia Woolf." However, so long as George and Martha, and symbolically America, persist in living in dreams and in refusing to recognize that there is anything wrong, they cannot hope to survive. The end of the play is therefore ambiguous but perhaps guardedly hopeful.

In order for the illusion to be destroyed, however, a night of carnage and chaos has been required. It is undoubtedly significant that the name of the town in which the college is located is New Carthage, with its echoes of the struggle between two great powers, one destroying the other in the interests of Empire, and then destroyed in its turn.

Many critics may object to an analysis of this type. They may argue that the work of art is meant to have immediate impact in the theatre, primarily on the emotional level. Production of *Who's Afraid of Virginia Woolf?* does, I think, fulfill that criterion, but it does something else. Like Ibsen's *The Wild Duck* or *The Master Builder,* for example, it teases the mind of the spectator and will not easily be erased from the consciousness. Albee once remarked that the trouble with most modern plays is that the only thing the spectator is thinking about when he leaves the theatre is where he parked the car. One cannot say that about the spectator of *Who's Afraid of Virginia Woolf?* In this play Albee has created a rich and troubling allegory for the American historical experience, the story of a nation that began in boundless optimism and faith in its own power to control the future and that has had to come to grips not only with external challenges but with its own corruption, compromise and failure, that has reached the point where it must cast away its comforting dreams and look reality in the face.

Source: Orley I. Holtan, "*Who's Afraid of Virginia Woolf?* And the Patterns of History" in *Educational Theatre Journal,* Volume 25, no. 1, March, 1973, pp. 46–52.

SOURCES

Amacher, Richard E. *Edward Albee,* Twayne (Boston), 1969.

"Blood Sport" in *Time,* October 26, 1962, p. 84.

Clurman, Harold. Review of *Who's Afraid of Virginia Woolf?* in the *Nation,* October 27, 1962, pp. 273-74.

Dozier, Richard J. "Adultery and Disappointment in *Who's Afraid of Virginia Woolf?*" in *Modern Drama,* Vol. 11, 1969, pp. 432-36.

"First Nights: Game of Truth" in *Newsweek,* October 29, 1962, p. 52.

Flasch, Joy. "Games People Play in *Who's Afraid of Virginia Woolf?*" in *Modern Drama,* Vol. 10, 1967, pp. 280-88.

Gassner, John. *Dramatic Soundings: Evaluations and Retractions Culled from Thirty Years of Drama Criticism,* Crown, 1968.

Gilman, Richard. *Common and Uncommon Masks: Writings on Theatre 1961-1970,* Random House, 1971.

Hewes, Henry. "Who's Afraid of Big Bad Broadway" in the *Saturday Review,* October 27, 1962, p. 29.

"Long Night's Journey into Daze" in the *New Yorker,* October 20, 1962, pp. 85-86.

Quinn, James P. "Myth and Romance in Albee's *Who's Afraid of Virginia Woolf?*" in the *Arizona Quarterly,* Vol. 30, 1974, pp. 197-204.

Stavrou, C. N. "Albee in Wonderland" in the *Southwest Review,* Winter, 1975, pp. 46-61.

Taubman, Howard. "Cure for Blues" in the *New York Times,* October 28, 1962, sec. 2, p. 1.

FURTHER READING

Cohn, Ruby. *Edward Albee,* University of Minnesota Press (Minneapolis), 1969.

Early, significant assessment of Albee's work, not long but an excellent study of Albee's plays through its year of publication.

Contemporary Literary Criticism, Gale (Detroit): Volume 1, 1973; Volume 2, 1974; Volume 3, 1975; Volume 5, 1976; Volume 9, 1978; Volume 11, 1979; Volume 13, 1980; Volume 25, 1983; Volume 53, 1989; Volume 86, 1995.

The listed volumes of this reference series compile selections of criticism; it is an excellent beginning point for a research paper about Albee. The selections in these ten volumes span Albee's entire playwriting career through 1995. For an overview of Albee's life, also see the entry on him in the *Concise Dictionary of American Literary Biography* (Gale, 1987) and Volume 7 of the *Dictionary of Literary Biography* (Gale).

Esslin, Martin. *Theatre of the Absurd,* Doubleday, 1961.

This is a work on the style of theatre associated with Existentialist ideas about the absurdity of human existence, expressed in an aberrant dramatic style meant to mirror the human situation. Esslin discusses Albee's early plays in the context of playwrights such as Beckett, Ionesco, Genet, and Pinter. While a play like *Who's Afraid of Virginia Woolf?* is less absurdist in form than some of Albee's other work, many critics agree that it expresses a similar philosophical perspective but in a realistic form.

Giantvalley, Scott. *Edward Albee: A Reference Guide,* G. K. Hall (Boston), 1987.

An extensive annotated bibliography of primary and secondary sources by and about Albee. Except for incidental mentions of Albee and some foreign items, this book encompasses most of the listings in previous bibliographies such as *Edward Albee at Home and Abroad* (Amacher and Rule, 1973); *Edward Albee: An Annotated Bibliography 1968-1977* (Charles Lee Green, 1980); and *Edward Albee: A Bibliography* (Richard Tyce, 1986). The guide is organized by year, with extensive cross-listing of topics in the index.

McCarthy, Gerry. *Edward Albee,* St. Martin's (New York), 1987.

Considers selected plays of Albee's from a performance perspective.

Roudane, Matthew C. Who's Afraid of Virginia Woolf?: *Necessary Fictions, Terrifying Realities,* Twayne, 1990.

The first full-length study of Albee's play, which Roudane says "did nothing less than reinvent the American theater." The author places *Who's Afraid of Virginia Woolf?* within the context of modern drama as a whole while also examining its historical and political backdrop. Beneath the animosity, he finds in the play an animating principle which makes it, he asserts, Albee's most life-affirming work.

Rutenberg, Michael E. *Edward Albee: Playwright in Protest,* Avon, 1969.

Rutenberg sees Albee as a writer of effective plays of social protest; he applies psychological and sociological thought to his explications of Albee's plays through *Box/Mao.* The book includes two interviews.

Wattis, Nigel, Producer and Director. *Edward Albee,* London Weekend Television, 1996.

A one-hour documentary distributed through Films for the Humanities and Sciences. Includes interviews with Albee and extracts from performances of his work.

Glossary of Literary Terms

A

Abstract: Used as a noun, the term refers to a short summary or outline of a longer work. As an adjective applied to writing or literary works, abstract refers to words or phrases that name things not knowable through the five senses. Examples of abstracts include the *Cliffs Notes* summaries of major literary works. Examples of abstract terms or concepts include ''idea,'' ''guilt'' ''honesty,'' and ''loyalty.''

Absurd, Theater of the: See *Theater of the Absurd*

Absurdism: See *Theater of the Absurd*

Act: A major section of a play. Acts are divided into varying numbers of shorter scenes. From ancient times to the nineteenth century plays were generally constructed of five acts, but modern works typically consist of one, two, or three acts. Examples of five-act plays include the works of Sophocles and Shakespeare, while the plays of Arthur Miller commonly have a three-act structure.

Acto: A one-act Chicano theater piece developed out of collective improvisation. *Actos* were performed by members of Luis Valdez's Teatro Campesino in California during the mid-1960s.

Aestheticism: A literary and artistic movement of the nineteenth century. Followers of the movement believed that art should not be mixed with social, political, or moral teaching. The statement ''art for art's sake'' is a good summary of aestheticism. The movement had its roots in France, but it gained widespread importance in England in the last half of the nineteenth century, where it helped change the Victorian practice of including moral lessons in literature. Oscar Wilde is one of the best-known ''aesthetes'' of the late nineteenth century.

Age of Johnson: The period in English literature between 1750 and 1798, named after the most prominent literary figure of the age, Samuel Johnson. Works written during this time are noted for their emphasis on ''sensibility,'' or emotional quality. These works formed a transition between the rational works of the Age of Reason, or Neoclassical period, and the emphasis on individual feelings and responses of the Romantic period. Significant writers during the Age of Johnson included the novelists Ann Radcliffe and Henry Mackenzie, dramatists Richard Sheridan and Oliver Goldsmith, and poets William Collins and Thomas Gray. Also known as Age of Sensibility

Age of Reason: See *Neoclassicism*

Age of Sensibility: See *Age of Johnson*

Alexandrine Meter: See *Meter*

Allegory: A narrative technique in which characters representing things or abstract ideas are used to convey a message or teach a lesson. Allegory is typically used to teach moral, ethical, or religious lessons but is sometimes used for satiric or political purposes. Examples of allegorical works include Edmund Spenser's *The Faerie Queene* and John Bunyan's *The Pilgrim's Progress.*

Allusion: A reference to a familiar literary or historical person or event, used to make an idea more easily understood. For example, describing someone as a ''Romeo'' makes an allusion to William Shakespeare's famous young lover in *Romeo and Juliet.*

Amerind Literature: The writing and oral traditions of Native Americans. Native American literature was originally passed on by word of mouth, so it consisted largely of stories and events that were easily memorized. Amerind prose is often rhythmic like poetry because it was recited to the beat of a ceremonial drum. Examples of Amerind literature include the autobiographical *Black Elk Speaks,* the works of N. Scott Momaday, James Welch, and Craig Lee Strete, and the poetry of Luci Tapahonso.

Analogy: A comparison of two things made to explain something unfamiliar through its similarities to something familiar, or to prove one point based on the acceptedness of another. Similes and metaphors are types of analogies. Analogies often take the form of an extended simile, as in William Blake's aphorism: ''As the caterpillar chooses the fairest leaves to lay her eggs on, so the priest lays his curse on the fairest joys.''

Angry Young Men: A group of British writers of the 1950s whose work expressed bitterness and disillusionment with society. Common to their work is an anti-hero who rebels against a corrupt social order and strives for personal integrity. The term has been used to describe Kingsley Amis, John Osborne, Colin Wilson, John Wain, and others.

Antagonist: The major character in a narrative or drama who works against the hero or protagonist. An example of an evil antagonist is Richard Lovelace in Samuel Richardson's *Clarissa,* while a virtuous antagonist is Macduff in William Shakespeare's *Macbeth.*

Anthropomorphism: The presentation of animals or objects in human shape or with human characteristics. The term is derived from the Greek word for ''human form.'' The fables of Aesop, the animated films of Walt Disney, and Richard Adams's *Watership Down* feature anthropomorphic characters.

Anti-hero: A central character in a work of literature who lacks traditional heroic qualities such as courage, physical prowess, and fortitude. Anti-heros typically distrust conventional values and are unable to commit themselves to any ideals. They generally feel helpless in a world over which they have no control. Anti-heroes usually accept, and often celebrate, their positions as social outcasts. A well-known anti-hero is Yossarian in Joseph Heller's novel *Catch-22.*

Antimasque: See *Masque*

Antithesis: The antithesis of something is its direct opposite. In literature, the use of antithesis as a figure of speech results in two statements that show a contrast through the balancing of two opposite ideas. Technically, it is the second portion of the statement that is defined as the ''antithesis''; the first portion is the ''thesis.'' An example of antithesis is found in the following portion of Abraham Lincoln's ''Gettysburg Address''; notice the opposition between the verbs ''remember'' and ''forget'' and the phrases ''what we say'' and ''what they did'': ''The world will little note nor long remember what we say here, but it can never forget what they did here.''

Apocrypha: Writings tentatively attributed to an author but not proven or universally accepted to be their works. The term was originally applied to certain books of the Bible that were not considered inspired and so were not included in the ''sacred canon.'' Geoffrey Chaucer, William Shakespeare, Thomas Kyd, Thomas Middleton, and John Marston all have apocrypha. Apocryphal books of the Bible include the Old Testament's Book of Enoch and New Testament's Gospel of Peter.

Apollonian and Dionysian: The two impulses believed to guide authors of dramatic tragedy. The Apollonian impulse is named after Apollo, the Greek god of light and beauty and the symbol of intellectual order. The Dionysian impulse is named after Dionysus, the Greek god of wine and the symbol of the unrestrained forces of nature. The Apollonian impulse is to create a rational, harmonious world, while the Dionysian is to express the irrational forces of personality. Friedrich Nietzche uses these terms in *The Birth of Tragedy* to designate contrasting elements in Greek tragedy.

Apostrophe: A statement, question, or request addressed to an inanimate object or concept or to a nonexistent or absent person. Requests for inspiration from the muses in poetry are examples of apostrophe, as is Marc Antony's address to Caesar's corpse in William Shakespeare's *Julius Caesar*: ''O, pardon me, thou bleeding piece of earth, That I am meek and gentle with these butchers!. . . Woe to the hand that shed this costly blood!. . . ''

Archetype: The word archetype is commonly used to describe an original pattern or model from which all other things of the same kind are made. This term was introduced to literary criticism from the psychology of Carl Jung. It expresses Jung's theory that behind every person's ''unconscious,'' or repressed memories of the past, lies the ''collective unconscious'' of the human race: memories of the countless typical experiences of our ancestors. These memories are said to prompt illogical associations that trigger powerful emotions in the reader. Often, the emotional process is primitive, even primordial. Archetypes are the literary images that grow out of the ''collective unconscious.'' They appear in literature as incidents and plots that repeat basic patterns of life. They may also appear as stereotyped characters. Examples of literary archetypes include themes such as birth and death and characters such as the Earth Mother.

Argument: The argument of a work is the author's subject matter or principal idea. Examples of defined ''argument'' portions of works include John Milton's *Arguments* to each of the books of *Paradise Lost* and the ''Argument'' to Robert Herrick's *Hesperides.*

Aristotelian Criticism: Specifically, the method of evaluating and analyzing tragedy formulated by the Greek philosopher Aristotle in his *Poetics.* More generally, the term indicates any form of criticism that follows Aristotle's views. Aristotelian criticism focuses on the form and logical structure of a work, apart from its historical or social context, in contrast to ''Platonic Criticism,'' which stresses the usefulness of art. Adherents of New Criticism including John Crowe Ransom and Cleanth Brooks utilize and value the basic ideas of Aristotelian criticism for textual analysis.

Art for Art's Sake: See *Aestheticism*

Aside: A comment made by a stage performer that is intended to be heard by the audience but supposedly not by other characters. Eugene O'Neill's *Strange Interlude* is an extended use of the aside in modern theater.

Audience: The people for whom a piece of literature is written. Authors usually write with a certain audience in mind, for example, children, members of a religious or ethnic group, or colleagues in a professional field. The term ''audience'' also applies to the people who gather to see or hear any performance, including plays, poetry readings, speeches, and concerts. Jane Austen's parody of the gothic novel, *Northanger Abbey,* was originally intended for (and also pokes fun at) an audience of young and avid female gothic novel readers.

Avant-garde: A French term meaning ''vanguard.'' It is used in literary criticism to describe new writing that rejects traditional approaches to literature in favor of innovations in style or content. Twentieth-century examples of the literary *avant-garde* include the Black Mountain School of poets, the Bloomsbury Group, and the Beat Movement.

B

Ballad: A short poem that tells a simple story and has a repeated refrain. Ballads were originally intended to be sung. Early ballads, known as folk ballads, were passed down through generations, so their authors are often unknown. Later ballads composed by known authors are called literary ballads. An example of an anonymous folk ballad is ''Edward,'' which dates from the Middle Ages. Samuel Taylor Coleridge's ''The Rime of the Ancient Mariner'' and John Keats's ''La Belle Dame sans Merci'' are examples of literary ballads.

Baroque: A term used in literary criticism to describe literature that is complex or ornate in style or diction. Baroque works typically express tension, anxiety, and violent emotion. The term ''Baroque Age'' designates a period in Western European literature beginning in the late sixteenth century and ending about one hundred years later. Works of this period often mirror the qualities of works more generally associated with the label ''baroque'' and sometimes feature elaborate conceits. Examples of Baroque works include John Lyly's *Euphues: The Anatomy of Wit,* Luis de Gongora's *Soledads,* and William Shakespeare's *As You Like It.*

Baroque Age: See *Baroque*

Baroque Period: See *Baroque*

Beat Generation: See *Beat Movement*

Beat Movement: A period featuring a group of American poets and novelists of the 1950s and 1960s—including Jack Kerouac, Allen Ginsberg, Gregory Corso, William S. Burroughs, and Lawrence Ferlinghetti—who rejected established social and literary values. Using such techniques as stream of consciousness writing and jazz-influenced free verse and focusing on unusual or abnormal states of mind—generated by religious ecstasy or the use of drugs—the Beat writers aimed to create works that were unconventional in both form and subject matter. Kerouac's *On the Road* is perhaps the best-known example of a Beat Generation novel, and Ginsberg's *Howl* is a famous collection of Beat poetry.

Black Aesthetic Movement: A period of artistic and literary development among African Americans in the 1960s and early 1970s. This was the first major African-American artistic movement since the Harlem Renaissance and was closely paralleled by the civil rights and black power movements. The black aesthetic writers attempted to produce works of art that would be meaningful to the black masses. Key figures in black aesthetics included one of its founders, poet and playwright Amiri Baraka, formerly known as LeRoi Jones; poet and essayist Haki R. Madhubuti, formerly Don L. Lee; poet and playwright Sonia Sanchez; and dramatist Ed Bullins. Works representative of the Black Aesthetic Movement include Amiri Baraka's play *Dutchman,* a 1964 Obie award-winner; *Black Fire: An Anthology of Afro-American Writing,* edited by Baraka and playwright Larry Neal and published in 1968; and Sonia Sanchez's poetry collection *We a BaddDDD People,* published in 1970. Also known as Black Arts Movement.

Black Arts Movement: See *Black Aesthetic Movement*

Black Comedy: See *Black Humor*

Black Humor: Writing that places grotesque elements side by side with humorous ones in an attempt to shock the reader, forcing him or her to laugh at the horrifying reality of a disordered world. Joseph Heller's novel *Catch-22* is considered a superb example of the use of black humor. Other well-known authors who use black humor include Kurt Vonnegut, Edward Albee, Eugene Ionesco, and Harold Pinter. Also known as Black Comedy.

Blank Verse: Loosely, any unrhymed poetry, but more generally, unrhymed iambic pentameter verse (composed of lines of five two-syllable feet with the first syllable accented, the second unaccented). Blank verse has been used by poets since the Renaissance for its flexibility and its graceful, dignified tone. John Milton's *Paradise Lost* is in blank verse, as are most of William Shakespeare's plays.

Bloomsbury Group: A group of English writers, artists, and intellectuals who held informal artistic and philosophical discussions in Bloomsbury, a district of London, from around 1907 to the early 1930s. The Bloomsbury Group held no uniform philosophical beliefs but did commonly express an aversion to moral prudery and a desire for greater social tolerance. At various times the circle included Virginia Woolf, E. M. Forster, Clive Bell, Lytton Strachey, and John Maynard Keynes.

Bon Mot: A French term meaning "good word." A *bon mot* is a witty remark or clever observation. Charles Lamb and Oscar Wilde are celebrated for their witty *bon mots.* Two examples by Oscar Wilde stand out: (1) "All women become their mothers. That is their tragedy. No man does. That's his." (2) "A man cannot be too careful in the choice of his enemies."

Breath Verse: See *Projective Verse*

Burlesque: Any literary work that uses exaggeration to make its subject appear ridiculous, either by treating a trivial subject with profound seriousness or by treating a dignified subject frivolously. The word "burlesque" may also be used as an adjective, as in "burlesque show," to mean "striptease act." Examples of literary burlesque include the comedies of Aristophanes, Miguel de Cervantes's *Don Quixote,*, Samuel Butler's poem "Hudibras," and John Gay's play *The Beggar's Opera.*

C

Cadence: The natural rhythm of language caused by the alternation of accented and unaccented syllables. Much modern poetry—notably free verse—deliberately manipulates cadence to create complex rhythmic effects. James Macpherson's "Ossian poems" are richly cadenced, as is the poetry of the Symbolists, Walt Whitman, and Amy Lowell.

Caesura: A pause in a line of poetry, usually occurring near the middle. It typically corresponds to a break in the natural rhythm or sense of the line but is sometimes shifted to create special meanings or rhythmic effects. The opening line of Edgar Allan Poe's "The Raven" contains a caesura following "dreary": "Once upon a midnight dreary, while I pondered weak and weary. . . ."

Canzone: A short Italian or Provencal lyric poem, commonly about love and often set to music. The *canzone* has no set form but typically contains five or six stanzas made up of seven to twenty lines of eleven syllables each. A shorter, five- to ten-line "envoy," or concluding stanza, completes the poem. Masters of the *canzone* form include

Petrarch, Dante Alighieri, Torquato Tasso, and Guido Cavalcanti.

Carpe Diem: A Latin term meaning "seize the day." This is a traditional theme of poetry, especially lyrics. A *carpe diem* poem advises the reader or the person it addresses to live for today and enjoy the pleasures of the moment. Two celebrated *carpe diem* poems are Andrew Marvell's "To His Coy Mistress" and Robert Herrick's poem beginning "Gather ye rosebuds while ye may. . . ."

Catharsis: The release or purging of unwanted emotions—specifically fear and pity—brought about by exposure to art. The term was first used by the Greek philosopher Aristotle in his *Poetics* to refer to the desired effect of tragedy on spectators. A famous example of catharsis is realized in Sophocles' *Oedipus Rex,* when Oedipus discovers that his wife, Jacosta, is his own mother and that the stranger he killed on the road was his own father.

Celtic Renaissance: A period of Irish literary and cultural history at the end of the nineteenth century. Followers of the movement aimed to create a romantic vision of Celtic myth and legend. The most significant works of the Celtic Renaissance typically present a dreamy, unreal world, usually in reaction against the reality of contemporary problems. William Butler Yeats's *The Wanderings of Oisin* is among the most significant works of the Celtic Renaissance. Also known as Celtic Twilight.

Celtic Twilight: See *Celtic Renaissance*

Character: Broadly speaking, a person in a literary work. The actions of characters are what constitute the plot of a story, novel, or poem. There are numerous types of characters, ranging from simple, stereotypical figures to intricate, multifaceted ones. In the techniques of anthropomorphism and personification, animals—and even places or things—can assume aspects of character. "Characterization" is the process by which an author creates vivid, believable characters in a work of art. This may be done in a variety of ways, including (1) direct description of the character by the narrator; (2) the direct presentation of the speech, thoughts, or actions of the character; and (3) the responses of other characters to the character. The term "character" also refers to a form originated by the ancient Greek writer Theophrastus that later became popular in the seventeenth and eighteenth centuries. It is a short essay or sketch of a person who prominently displays a specific attribute or quality, such as miserliness or ambition. Notable characters in literature include Oedipus Rex, Don Quixote de la Mancha, Macbeth, Candide, Hester Prynne, Ebenezer Scrooge, Huckleberry Finn, Jay Gatsby, Scarlett O'Hara, James Bond, and Kunta Kinte.

Characterization: See *Character*

Chorus: In ancient Greek drama, a group of actors who commented on and interpreted the unfolding action on the stage. Initially the chorus was a major component of the presentation, but over time it became less significant, with its numbers reduced and its role eventually limited to commentary between acts. By the sixteenth century the chorus—if employed at all—was typically a single person who provided a prologue and an epilogue and occasionally appeared between acts to introduce or underscore an important event. The chorus in William Shakespeare's *Henry V* functions in this way. Modern dramas rarely feature a chorus, but T. S. Eliot's *Murder in the Cathedral* and Arthur Miller's *A View from the Bridge* are notable exceptions. The Stage Manager in Thornton Wilder's *Our Town* performs a role similar to that of the chorus.

Chronicle: A record of events presented in chronological order. Although the scope and level of detail provided varies greatly among the chronicles surviving from ancient times, some, such as the *Anglo-Saxon Chronicle,* feature vivid descriptions and a lively recounting of events. During the Elizabethan Age, many dramas—appropriately called "chronicle plays"—were based on material from chronicles. Many of William Shakespeare's dramas of English history as well as Christopher Marlowe's *Edward II* are based in part on Raphael Holinshead's *Chronicles of England, Scotland, and Ireland.*

Classical: In its strictest definition in literary criticism, classicism refers to works of ancient Greek or Roman literature. The term may also be used to describe a literary work of recognized importance (a "classic") from any time period or literature that exhibits the traits of classicism. Classical authors from ancient Greek and Roman times include Juvenal and Homer. Examples of later works and authors now described as classical include French literature of the seventeenth century, Western novels of the nineteenth century, and American fiction of the mid-nineteenth century such as that written by James Fenimore Cooper and Mark Twain.

Classicism: A term used in literary criticism to describe critical doctrines that have their roots in ancient Greek and Roman literature, philosophy, and art. Works associated with classicism typically exhibit restraint on the part of the author, unity of design and purpose, clarity, simplicity, logical organization, and respect for tradition. Examples of literary classicism include Cicero's prose, the dramas of Pierre Corneille and Jean Racine, the poetry of John Dryden and Alexander Pope, and the writings of J. W. von Goethe, G. E. Lessing, and T. S. Eliot.

Climax: The turning point in a narrative, the moment when the conflict is at its most intense. Typically, the structure of stories, novels, and plays is one of rising action, in which tension builds to the climax, followed by falling action, in which tension lessens as the story moves to its conclusion. The climax in James Fenimore Cooper's *The Last of the Mohicans* occurs when Magua and his captive Cora are pursued to the edge of a cliff by Uncas. Magua kills Uncas but is subsequently killed by Hawkeye.

Colloquialism: A word, phrase, or form of pronunciation that is acceptable in casual conversation but not in formal, written communication. It is considered more acceptable than slang. An example of colloquialism can be found in Rudyard Kipling's *Barrack-room Ballads:* When 'Omer smote 'is bloomin' lyre He'd 'eard men sing by land and sea; An' what he thought 'e might require 'E went an' took—the same as me!

Comedy: One of two major types of drama, the other being tragedy. Its aim is to amuse, and it typically ends happily. Comedy assumes many forms, such as farce and burlesque, and uses a variety of techniques, from parody to satire. In a restricted sense the term comedy refers only to dramatic presentations, but in general usage it is commonly applied to nondramatic works as well. Examples of comedies range from the plays of Aristophanes, Terrence, and Plautus, Dante Alighieri's *The Divine Comedy,* Francois Rabelais's *Pantagruel* and *Gargantua,* and some of Geoffrey Chaucer's tales and William Shakespeare's plays to Noel Coward's play *Private Lives* and James Thurber's short story ''The Secret Life of Walter Mitty.''

Comedy of Manners: A play about the manners and conventions of an aristocratic, highly sophisticated society. The characters are usually types rather than individualized personalities, and plot is less important than atmosphere. Such plays were an important aspect of late seventeenth-century English comedy. The comedy of manners was revived in the eighteenth century by Oliver Goldsmith and Richard Brinsley Sheridan, enjoyed a second revival in the late nineteenth century, and has endured into the twentieth century. Examples of comedies of manners include William Congreve's *The Way of the World* in the late seventeenth century, Oliver Goldsmith's *She Stoops to Conquer* and Richard Brinsley Sheridan's *The School for Scandal* in the eighteenth century, Oscar Wilde's *The Importance of Being Earnest* in the nineteenth century, and W. Somerset Maugham's *The Circle* in the twentieth century.

Comic Relief: The use of humor to lighten the mood of a serious or tragic story, especially in plays. The technique is very common in Elizabethan works, and can be an integral part of the plot or simply a brief event designed to break the tension of the scene. The Gravediggers' scene in William Shakespeare's *Hamlet* is a frequently cited example of comic relief.

Commedia dell'arte: An Italian term meaning ''the comedy of guilds'' or ''the comedy of professional actors.'' This form of dramatic comedy was popular in Italy during the sixteenth century. Actors were assigned stock roles (such as Pulcinella, the stupid servant, or Pantalone, the old merchant) and given a basic plot to follow, but all dialogue was improvised. The roles were rigidly typed and the plots were formulaic, usually revolving around young lovers who thwarted their elders and attained wealth and happiness. A rigid convention of the *commedia dell'arte* is the periodic intrusion of Harlequin, who interrupts the play with low buffoonery. Peppino de Filippo's *Metamorphoses of a Wandering Minstrel* gave modern audiences an idea of what *commedia dell'arte* may have been like. Various scenarios for *commedia dell'arte* were compiled in Petraccone's *La commedia dell'arte, storia, technica, scenari,* published in 1927.

Complaint: A lyric poem, popular in the Renaissance, in which the speaker expresses sorrow about his or her condition. Typically, the speaker's sadness is caused by an unresponsive lover, but some complaints cite other sources of unhappiness, such as poverty or fate. A commonly cited example is ''A Complaint by Night of the Lover Not Beloved'' by Henry Howard, Earl of Surrey. Thomas Sackville's ''Complaint of Henry, Duke of Buckingham'' traces the duke's unhappiness to his ruthless ambition.

Conceit: A clever and fanciful metaphor, usually expressed through elaborate and extended comparison, that presents a striking parallel between two seemingly dissimilar things—for example, elaborately comparing a beautiful woman to an object like a garden or the sun. The conceit was a popular device throughout the Elizabethan Age and Baroque Age and was the principal technique of the seventeenth-century English metaphysical poets. This usage of the word conceit is unrelated to the best-known definition of conceit as an arrogant attitude or behavior. The conceit figures prominently in the works of John Donne, Emily Dickinson, and T. S. Eliot.

Concrete: Concrete is the opposite of abstract, and refers to a thing that actually exists or a description that allows the reader to experience an object or concept with the senses. Henry David Thoreau's *Walden* contains much concrete description of nature and wildlife.

Concrete Poetry: Poetry in which visual elements play a large part in the poetic effect. Punctuation marks, letters, or words are arranged on a page to form a visual design: a cross, for example, or a bumblebee. Max Bill and Eugene Gomringer were among the early practitioners of concrete poetry; Haroldo de Campos and Augusto de Campos are among contemporary authors of concrete poetry.

Confessional Poetry: A form of poetry in which the poet reveals very personal, intimate, sometimes shocking information about himself or herself. Anne Sexton, Sylvia Plath, Robert Lowell, and John Berryman wrote poetry in the confessional vein.

Conflict: The conflict in a work of fiction is the issue to be resolved in the story. It usually occurs between two characters, the protagonist and the antagonist, or between the protagonist and society or the protagonist and himself or herself. Conflict in Theodore Dreiser's novel *Sister Carrie* comes as a result of urban society, while Jack London's short story ''To Build a Fire'' concerns the protagonist's battle against the cold and himself.

Connotation: The impression that a word gives beyond its defined meaning. Connotations may be universally understood or may be significant only to a certain group. Both ''horse'' and ''steed'' denote the same animal, but ''steed'' has a different connotation, deriving from the chivalrous or romantic narratives in which the word was once often used.

Consonance: Consonance occurs in poetry when words appearing at the ends of two or more verses have similar final consonant sounds but have final vowel sounds that differ, as with ''stuff'' and ''off.'' Consonance is found in ''The curfew tolls the knells of parting day'' from Thomas Grey's ''An Elegy Written in a Country Church Yard.'' Also known as Half Rhyme or Slant Rhyme.

Convention: Any widely accepted literary device, style, or form. A soliloquy, in which a character reveals to the audience his or her private thoughts, is an example of a dramatic convention.

Corrido: A Mexican ballad. Examples of *corridos* include ''Muerte del afamado Bilito,'' ''La voz de mi conciencia,'' ''Lucio Perez,'' ''La juida,'' and ''Los presos.''

Couplet: Two lines of poetry with the same rhyme and meter, often expressing a complete and self-contained thought. The following couplet is from Alexander Pope's ''Elegy to the Memory of an Unfortunate Lady'': 'Tis Use alone that sanctifies Expense, And Splendour borrows all her rays from Sense.

Criticism: The systematic study and evaluation of literary works, usually based on a specific method or set of principles. An important part of literary studies since ancient times, the practice of criticism has given rise to numerous theories, methods, and ''schools,'' sometimes producing conflicting, even contradictory, interpretations of literature in general as well as of individual works. Even such basic issues as what constitutes a poem or a novel have been the subject of much criticism over the centuries. Seminal texts of literary criticism include Plato's *Republic,* Aristotle's *Poetics,* Sir Philip Sidney's *The Defence of Poesie,* John Dryden's *Of Dramatic Poesie,* and William Wordsworth's ''Preface'' to the second edition of his *Lyrical Ballads.* Contemporary schools of criticism include deconstruction, feminist, psychoanalytic, poststructuralist, new historicist, postcolonialist, and reader- response.

D

Dactyl: See *Foot*

Dadaism: A protest movement in art and literature founded by Tristan Tzara in 1916. Followers of the movement expressed their outrage at the destruction brought about by World War I by revolting against numerous forms of social convention. The Dadaists presented works marked by calculated madness and flamboyant nonsense. They stressed total freedom of expression, commonly through primitive displays of emotion and illogical, often senseless, poetry. The movement ended shortly after the war, when it was replaced by surrealism. Proponents of Dadaism include Andre Breton, Louis Aragon, Philippe Soupault, and Paul Eluard.

Decadent: See *Decadents*

Decadents: The followers of a nineteenth-century literary movement that had its beginnings in French aestheticism. Decadent literature displays a fascination with perverse and morbid states; a search for novelty and sensation—the "new thrill"; a preoccupation with mysticism; and a belief in the senselessness of human existence. The movement is closely associated with the doctrine Art for Art's Sake. The term "decadence" is sometimes used to denote a decline in the quality of art or literature following a period of greatness. Major French decadents are Charles Baudelaire and Arthur Rimbaud. English decadents include Oscar Wilde, Ernest Dowson, and Frank Harris.

Deconstruction: A method of literary criticism developed by Jacques Derrida and characterized by multiple conflicting interpretations of a given work. Deconstructionists consider the impact of the language of a work and suggest that the true meaning of the work is not necessarily the meaning that the author intended. Jacques Derrida's *De la grammatologie* is the seminal text on deconstructive strategies; among American practitioners of this method of criticism are Paul de Man and J. Hillis Miller.

Deduction: The process of reaching a conclusion through reasoning from general premises to a specific premise. An example of deduction is present in the following syllogism: Premise: All mammals are animals. Premise: All whales are mammals. Conclusion: Therefore, all whales are animals.

Denotation: The definition of a word, apart from the impressions or feelings it creates in the reader. The word "apartheid" denotes a political and economic policy of segregation by race, but its connotations—oppression, slavery, inequality—are numerous.

Denouement: A French word meaning "the unknotting." In literary criticism, it denotes the resolution of conflict in fiction or drama. The *denouement* follows the climax and provides an outcome to the primary plot situation as well as an explanation of secondary plot complications. The *denouement* often involves a character's recognition of his or her state of mind or moral condition. A well-known example of *denouement* is the last scene of the play *As You Like It* by William Shakespeare, in which couples are married, an evildoer repents, the identities of two disguised characters are revealed, and a ruler is restored to power. Also known as Falling Action.

Description: Descriptive writing is intended to allow a reader to picture the scene or setting in which the action of a story takes place. The form this description takes often evokes an intended emotional response—a dark, spooky graveyard will evoke fear, and a peaceful, sunny meadow will evoke calmness. An example of a descriptive story is Edgar Allan Poe's *Landor's Cottage,* which offers a detailed depiction of a New York country estate.

Detective Story: A narrative about the solution of a mystery or the identification of a criminal. The conventions of the detective story include the detective's scrupulous use of logic in solving the mystery; incompetent or ineffectual police; a suspect who appears guilty at first but is later proved innocent; and the detective's friend or confidant—often the narrator—whose slowness in interpreting clues emphasizes by contrast the detective's brilliance. Edgar Allan Poe's "Murders in the Rue Morgue" is commonly regarded as the earliest example of this type of story. With this work, Poe established many of the conventions of the detective story genre, which are still in practice. Other practitioners of this vast and extremely popular genre include Arthur Conan Doyle, Dashiell Hammett, and Agatha Christie.

Deus ex machina: A Latin term meaning "god out of a machine." In Greek drama, a god was often lowered onto the stage by a mechanism of some kind to rescue the hero or untangle the plot. By extension, the term refers to any artificial device or coincidence used to bring about a convenient and simple solution to a plot. This is a common device in melodramas and includes such fortunate circumstances as the sudden receipt of a legacy to save the family farm or a last-minute stay of execution. The *deus ex machina* invariably rewards the virtuous and punishes evildoers. Examples of *deus ex machina* include King Louis XIV in Jean-Baptiste Moliere's *Tartuffe* and Queen Victoria in *The Pirates of Penzance* by William Gilbert and Arthur Sullivan. Bertolt Brecht parodies the abuse of such devices in the conclusion of his *Threepenny Opera.*

Dialogue: In its widest sense, dialogue is simply conversation between people in a literary work; in its most restricted sense, it refers specifically to the speech of characters in a drama. As a specific literary genre, a "dialogue" is a composition in which characters debate an issue or idea. The Greek philosopher Plato frequently expounded his theories in the form of dialogues.

Diction: The selection and arrangement of words in a literary work. Either or both may vary depending on the desired effect. There are four general types of diction: ''formal,'' used in scholarly or lofty writing; ''informal,'' used in relaxed but educated conversation; ''colloquial,'' used in everyday speech; and ''slang,'' containing newly coined words and other terms not accepted in formal usage.

Didactic: A term used to describe works of literature that aim to teach some moral, religious, political, or practical lesson. Although didactic elements are often found in artistically pleasing works, the term ''didactic'' usually refers to literature in which the message is more important than the form. The term may also be used to criticize a work that the critic finds ''overly didactic,'' that is, heavy-handed in its delivery of a lesson. Examples of didactic literature include John Bunyan's *Pilgrim's Progress,* Alexander Pope's *Essay on Criticism,* Jean-Jacques Rousseau's *Emile,* and Elizabeth Inchbald's *Simple Story.*

Dimeter: See *Meter*

Dionysian: See *Apollonian and Dionysian*

Discordia concours: A Latin phrase meaning ''discord in harmony.'' The term was coined by the eighteenth-century English writer Samuel Johnson to describe ''a combination of dissimilar images or discovery of occult resemblances in things apparently unlike.'' Johnson created the expression by reversing a phrase by the Latin poet Horace. The metaphysical poetry of John Donne, Richard Crashaw, Abraham Cowley, George Herbert, and Edward Taylor among others, contains many examples of *discordia concours.* In Donne's ''A Valediction: Forbidding Mourning,'' the poet compares the union of himself with his lover to a draftsman's compass: If they be two, they are two so, As stiff twin compasses are two: Thy soul, the fixed foot, makes no show To move, but doth, if the other do; And though it in the center sit, Yet when the other far doth roam, It leans, and hearkens after it, And grows erect, as that comes home.

Dissonance: A combination of harsh or jarring sounds, especially in poetry. Although such combinations may be accidental, poets sometimes intentionally make them to achieve particular effects. Dissonance is also sometimes used to refer to close but not identical rhymes. When this is the case, the word functions as a synonym for consonance. Robert Browning, Gerard Manley Hopkins, and many other poets have made deliberate use of dissonance.

Doppelganger: A literary technique by which a character is duplicated (usually in the form of an alter ego, though sometimes as a ghostly counterpart) or divided into two distinct, usually opposite personalities. The use of this character device is widespread in nineteenth- and twentieth- century literature, and indicates a growing awareness among authors that the ''self'' is really a composite of many ''selves.'' A well-known story containing a *doppelganger* character is Robert Louis Stevenson's *Dr. Jekyll and Mr. Hyde,* which dramatizes an internal struggle between good and evil. Also known as The Double.

Double Entendre: A corruption of a French phrase meaning ''double meaning.'' The term is used to indicate a word or phrase that is deliberately ambiguous, especially when one of the meanings is risque or improper. An example of a *double entendre* is the Elizabethan usage of the verb ''die,'' which refers both to death and to orgasm.

Double, The: See *Doppelganger*

Draft: Any preliminary version of a written work. An author may write dozens of drafts which are revised to form the final work, or he or she may write only one, with few or no revisions. Dorothy Parker's observation that ''I can't write five words but that I change seven'' humorously indicates the purpose of the draft.

Drama: In its widest sense, a drama is any work designed to be presented by actors on a stage. Similarly, ''drama'' denotes a broad literary genre that includes a variety of forms, from pageant and spectacle to tragedy and comedy, as well as countless types and subtypes. More commonly in modern usage, however, a drama is a work that treats serious subjects and themes but does not aim at the grandeur of tragedy. This use of the term originated with the eighteenth-century French writer Denis Diderot, who used the word *drame* to designate his plays about middle- class life; thus ''drama'' typically features characters of a less exalted stature than those of tragedy. Examples of classical dramas include Menander's comedy *Dyscolus* and Sophocles' tragedy *Oedipus Rex.* Contemporary dramas include Eugene O'Neill's *The Iceman Cometh,* Lillian Hellman's *Little Foxes,* and August Wilson's *Ma Rainey's Black Bottom.*

Dramatic Irony: Occurs when the audience of a play or the reader of a work of literature knows something that a character in the work itself does not know. The irony is in the contrast between the intended meaning of the statements or actions of a character and the additional information understood by the audience. A celebrated example of dramatic irony is in Act V of William Shakespeare's *Romeo and Juliet,* where two young lovers meet their end as a result of a tragic misunderstanding. Here, the audience has full knowledge that Juliet's apparent ''death'' is merely temporary; she will regain her senses when the mysterious ''sleeping potion'' she has taken wears off. But Romeo, mistaking Juliet's drug-induced trance for true death, kills himself in grief. Upon awakening, Juliet discovers Romeo's corpse and, in despair, slays herself.

Dramatic Monologue: See *Monologue*

Dramatic Poetry: Any lyric work that employs elements of drama such as dialogue, conflict, or characterization, but excluding works that are intended for stage presentation. A monologue is a form of dramatic poetry.

Dramatis Personae: The characters in a work of literature, particularly a drama. The list of characters printed before the main text of a play or in the program is the *dramatis personae*.

Dream Allegory: See *Dream Vision*

Dream Vision: A literary convention, chiefly of the Middle Ages. In a dream vision a story is presented as a literal dream of the narrator. This device was commonly used to teach moral and religious lessons. Important works of this type are *The Divine Comedy* by Dante Alighieri, *Piers Plowman* by William Langland, and *The Pilgrim's Progress* by John Bunyan. Also known as Dream Allegory.

Dystopia: An imaginary place in a work of fiction where the characters lead dehumanized, fearful lives. Jack London's *The Iron Heel,* Yevgeny Zamyatin's *My,* Aldous Huxley's *Brave New World,* George Orwell's *Nineteen Eighty-four,* and Margaret Atwood's *Handmaid's Tale* portray versions of dystopia.

E

Eclogue: In classical literature, a poem featuring rural themes and structured as a dialogue among shepherds. Eclogues often took specific poetic forms, such as elegies or love poems. Some were written as the soliloquy of a shepherd. In later centuries, ''eclogue'' came to refer to any poem that was in the pastoral tradition or that had a dialogue or monologue structure. A classical example of an eclogue is Virgil's *Eclogues,* also known as *Bucolics.* Giovanni Boccaccio, Edmund Spenser, Andrew Marvell, Jonathan Swift, and Louis MacNeice also wrote eclogues.

Edwardian: Describes cultural conventions identified with the period of the reign of Edward VII of England (1901-1910). Writers of the Edwardian Age typically displayed a strong reaction against the propriety and conservatism of the Victorian Age. Their work often exhibits distrust of authority in religion, politics, and art and expresses strong doubts about the soundness of conventional values. Writers of this era include George Bernard Shaw, H. G. Wells, and Joseph Conrad.

Edwardian Age: See *Edwardian*

Electra Complex: A daughter's amorous obsession with her father. The term Electra complex comes from the plays of Euripides and Sophocles entitled *Electra,* in which the character Electra drives her brother Orestes to kill their mother and her lover in revenge for the murder of their father.

Elegy: A lyric poem that laments the death of a person or the eventual death of all people. In a conventional elegy, set in a classical world, the poet and subject are spoken of as shepherds. In modern criticism, the word elegy is often used to refer to a poem that is melancholy or mournfully contemplative. John Milton's ''Lycidas'' and Percy Bysshe Shelley's ''Adonais'' are two examples of this form.

Elizabethan Age: A period of great economic growth, religious controversy, and nationalism closely associated with the reign of Elizabeth I of England (1558-1603). The Elizabethan Age is considered a part of the general renaissance—that is, the flowering of arts and literature—that took place in Europe during the fourteenth through sixteenth centuries. The era is considered the golden age of English literature. The most important dramas in English and a great deal of lyric poetry were produced during this period, and modern English criticism began around this time. The notable authors of the period—Philip Sidney, Edmund Spenser, Christopher Marlowe, William Shakespeare, Ben Jonson, Francis Bacon, and John Donne—are among the best in all of English literature.

Elizabethan Drama: English comic and tragic plays produced during the Renaissance, or more narrowly, those plays written during the last years of and few years after Queen Elizabeth's reign. William Shakespeare is considered an Elizabethan dramatist in the broader sense, although most of his work was produced during the reign of James I. Examples of Elizabethan comedies include John

Lyly's *The Woman in the Moone,* Thomas Dekker's *The Roaring Girl, or, Moll Cut Purse,* and William Shakespeare's *Twelfth Night.* Examples of Elizabethan tragedies include William Shakespeare's *Antony and Cleopatra,* Thomas Kyd's *The Spanish Tragedy,* and John Webster's *The Tragedy of the Duchess of Malfi.*

Empathy: A sense of shared experience, including emotional and physical feelings, with someone or something other than oneself. Empathy is often used to describe the response of a reader to a literary character. An example of an empathic passage is William Shakespeare's description in his narrative poem *Venus and Adonis* of: the snail, whose tender horns being hit, Shrinks backward in his shelly cave with pain. Readers of Gerard Manley Hopkins's *The Windhover* may experience some of the physical sensations evoked in the description of the movement of the falcon.

English Sonnet: See *Sonnet*

Enjambment: The running over of the sense and structure of a line of verse or a couplet into the following verse or couplet. Andrew Marvell's "To His Coy Mistress" is structured as a series of enjambments, as in lines 11-12: "My vegetable love should grow/Vaster than empires and more slow."

Enlightenment, The: An eighteenth-century philosophical movement. It began in France but had a wide impact throughout Europe and America. Thinkers of the Enlightenment valued reason and believed that both the individual and society could achieve a state of perfection. Corresponding to this essentially humanist vision was a resistance to religious authority. Important figures of the Enlightenment were Denis Diderot and Voltaire in France, Edward Gibbon and David Hume in England, and Thomas Paine and Thomas Jefferson in the United States.

Epic: A long narrative poem about the adventures of a hero of great historic or legendary importance. The setting is vast and the action is often given cosmic significance through the intervention of supernatural forces such as gods, angels, or demons. Epics are typically written in a classical style of grand simplicity with elaborate metaphors and allusions that enhance the symbolic importance of a hero's adventures. Some well-known epics are Homer's *Iliad* and *Odyssey,* Virgil's *Aeneid,* and John Milton's *Paradise Lost.*

Epic Simile: See *Homeric Simile*

Epic Theater: A theory of theatrical presentation developed by twentieth-century German playwright Bertolt Brecht. Brecht created a type of drama that the audience could view with complete detachment. He used what he termed "alienation effects" to create an emotional distance between the audience and the action on stage. Among these effects are: short, self- contained scenes that keep the play from building to a cathartic climax; songs that comment on the action; and techniques of acting that prevent the actor from developing an emotional identity with his role. Besides the plays of Bertolt Brecht, other plays that utilize epic theater conventions include those of Georg Buchner, Frank Wedekind, Erwin Piscator, and Leopold Jessner.

Epigram: A saying that makes the speaker's point quickly and concisely. Samuel Taylor Coleridge wrote an epigram that neatly sums up the form: What is an Epigram? A Dwarfish whole, Its body brevity, and wit its soul.

Epilogue: A concluding statement or section of a literary work. In dramas, particularly those of the seventeenth and eighteenth centuries, the epilogue is a closing speech, often in verse, delivered by an actor at the end of a play and spoken directly to the audience. A famous epilogue is Puck's speech at the end of William Shakespeare's *A Midsummer Night's Dream.*

Epiphany: A sudden revelation of truth inspired by a seemingly trivial incident. The term was widely used by James Joyce in his critical writings, and the stories in Joyce's *Dubliners* are commonly called "epiphanies."

Episode: An incident that forms part of a story and is significantly related to it. Episodes may be either self- contained narratives or events that depend on a larger context for their sense and importance. Examples of episodes include the founding of Wilmington, Delaware in Charles Reade's *The Disinherited Heir* and the individual events comprising the picaresque novels and medieval romances.

Episodic Plot: See *Plot*

Epitaph: An inscription on a tomb or tombstone, or a verse written on the occasion of a person's death. Epitaphs may be serious or humorous. Dorothy Parker's epitaph reads, "I told you I was sick."

Epithalamion: A song or poem written to honor and commemorate a marriage ceremony. Famous examples include Edmund Spenser's "Epithalamion'' and e. e. cummings's ''Epithalamion.'' Also spelled Epithalamium.

Epithalamium: See *Epithalamion*

Epithet: A word or phrase, often disparaging or abusive, that expresses a character trait of someone or something. ''The Napoleon of crime'' is an epithet applied to Professor Moriarty, arch-rival of Sherlock Holmes in Arthur Conan Doyle's series of detective stories.

Exempla: See *Exemplum*

Exemplum: A tale with a moral message. This form of literary sermonizing flourished during the Middle Ages, when *exempla* appeared in collections known as ''example-books.'' The works of Geoffrey Chaucer are full of *exempla.*

Existentialism: A predominantly twentieth-century philosophy concerned with the nature and perception of human existence. There are two major strains of existentialist thought: atheistic and Christian. Followers of atheistic existentialism believe that the individual is alone in a godless universe and that the basic human condition is one of suffering and loneliness. Nevertheless, because there are no fixed values, individuals can create their own characters—indeed, they can shape themselves—through the exercise of free will. The atheistic strain culminates in and is popularly associated with the works of Jean-Paul Sartre. The Christian existentialists, on the other hand, believe that only in God may people find freedom from life's anguish. The two strains hold certain beliefs in common: that existence cannot be fully understood or described through empirical effort; that anguish is a universal element of life; that individuals must bear responsibility for their actions; and that there is no common standard of behavior or perception for religious and ethical matters. Existentialist thought figures prominently in the works of such authors as Eugene Ionesco, Franz Kafka, Fyodor Dostoyevsky, Simone de Beauvoir, Samuel Beckett, and Albert Camus.

Expatriates: See *Expatriatism*

Expatriatism: The practice of leaving one's country to live for an extended period in another country. Literary expatriates include English poets Percy Bysshe Shelley and John Keats in Italy, Polish novelist Joseph Conrad in England, American writers Richard Wright, James Baldwin, Gertrude Stein, and Ernest Hemingway in France, and Trinidadian author Neil Bissondath in Canada.

Exposition: Writing intended to explain the nature of an idea, thing, or theme. Expository writing is often combined with description, narration, or argument. In dramatic writing, the exposition is the introductory material which presents the characters, setting, and tone of the play. An example of dramatic exposition occurs in many nineteenth-century drawing-room comedies in which the butler and the maid open the play with relevant talk about their master and mistress; in composition, exposition relays factual information, as in encyclopedia entries.

Expressionism: An indistinct literary term, originally used to describe an early twentieth-century school of German painting. The term applies to almost any mode of unconventional, highly subjective writing that distorts reality in some way. Advocates of Expressionism include dramatists George Kaiser, Ernst Toller, Luigi Pirandello, Federico Garcia Lorca, Eugene O'Neill, and Elmer Rice; poets George Heym, Ernst Stadler, August Stramm, Gottfried Benn, and Georg Trakl; and novelists Franz Kafka and James Joyce.

Extended Monologue: See *Monologue*

F

Fable: A prose or verse narrative intended to convey a moral. Animals or inanimate objects with human characteristics often serve as characters in fables. A famous fable is Aesop's ''The Tortoise and the Hare.''

Fairy Tales: Short narratives featuring mythical beings such as fairies, elves, and sprites. These tales originally belonged to the folklore of a particular nation or region, such as those collected in Germany by Jacob and Wilhelm Grimm. Two other celebrated writers of fairy tales are Hans Christian Andersen and Rudyard Kipling.

Falling Action: See *Denouement*

Fantasy: A literary form related to mythology and folklore. Fantasy literature is typically set in nonexistent realms and features supernatural beings. Notable examples of fantasy literature are *The Lord of the Rings* by J. R. R. Tolkien and the Gormenghast trilogy by Mervyn Peake.

Farce: A type of comedy characterized by broad humor, outlandish incidents, and often vulgar subject matter. Much of the ''comedy'' in film and television could more accurately be described as farce.

Feet: See *Foot*

Feminine Rhyme: See *Rhyme*

Femme fatale: A French phrase with the literal translation "fatal woman." A *femme fatale* is a sensuous, alluring woman who often leads men into danger or trouble. A classic example of the *femme fatale* is the nameless character in Billy Wilder's *The Seven Year Itch,* portrayed by Marilyn Monroe in the film adaptation.

Fiction: Any story that is the product of imagination rather than a documentation of fact. characters and events in such narratives may be based in real life but their ultimate form and configuration is a creation of the author. Geoffrey Chaucer's *The Canterbury Tales,* Laurence Sterne's *Tristram Shandy,* and Margaret Mitchell's *Gone with the Wind* are examples of fiction.

Figurative Language: A technique in writing in which the author temporarily interrupts the order, construction, or meaning of the writing for a particular effect. This interruption takes the form of one or more figures of speech such as hyperbole, irony, or simile. Figurative language is the opposite of literal language, in which every word is truthful, accurate, and free of exaggeration or embellishment. Examples of figurative language are tropes such as metaphor and rhetorical figures such as apostrophe.

Figures of Speech: Writing that differs from customary conventions for construction, meaning, order, or significance for the purpose of a special meaning or effect. There are two major types of figures of speech: rhetorical figures, which do not make changes in the meaning of the words, and tropes, which do. Types of figures of speech include simile, hyperbole, alliteration, and pun, among many others.

Fin de siecle: A French term meaning "end of the century." The term is used to denote the last decade of the nineteenth century, a transition period when writers and other artists abandoned old conventions and looked for new techniques and objectives. Two writers commonly associated with the *fin de siecle* mindset are Oscar Wilde and George Bernard Shaw.

First Person: See *Point of View*

Flashback: A device used in literature to present action that occurred before the beginning of the story. Flashbacks are often introduced as the dreams or recollections of one or more characters. Flashback techniques are often used in films, where they are typically set off by a gradual changing of one picture to another.

Foil: A character in a work of literature whose physical or psychological qualities contrast strongly with, and therefore highlight, the corresponding qualities of another character. In his Sherlock Holmes stories, Arthur Conan Doyle portrayed Dr. Watson as a man of normal habits and intelligence, making him a foil for the eccentric and wonderfully perceptive Sherlock Holmes.

Folk Ballad: See *Ballad*

Folklore: Traditions and myths preserved in a culture or group of people. Typically, these are passed on by word of mouth in various forms—such as legends, songs, and proverbs—or preserved in customs and ceremonies. This term was first used by W. J. Thoms in 1846. Sir James Frazer's *The Golden Bough* is the record of English folklore; myths about the frontier and the Old South exemplify American folklore.

Folktale: A story originating in oral tradition. Folktales fall into a variety of categories, including legends, ghost stories, fairy tales, fables, and anecdotes based on historical figures and events. Examples of folktales include Giambattista Basile's *The Pentamerone,* which contains the tales of Puss in Boots, Rapunzel, Cinderella, and Beauty and the Beast, and Joel Chandler Harris's Uncle Remus stories, which represent transplanted African folktales and American tales about the characters Mike Fink, Johnny Appleseed, Paul Bunyan, and Pecos Bill.

Foot: The smallest unit of rhythm in a line of poetry. In English-language poetry, a foot is typically one accented syllable combined with one or two unaccented syllables. There are many different types of feet. When the accent is on the second syllable of a two syllable word (con- *tort*), the foot is an "iamb"; the reverse accentual pattern (*tor* - ture) is a "trochee." Other feet that commonly occur in poetry in English are "anapest", two unaccented syllables followed by an accented syllable as in in-ter-*cept*, and "dactyl", an accented syllable followed by two unaccented syllables as in *su*-i- cide.

Foreshadowing: A device used in literature to create expectation or to set up an explanation of later developments. In Charles Dickens's *Great Expectations,* the graveyard encounter at the beginning of the novel between Pip and the escaped convict Magwitch foreshadows the baleful atmosphere and events that comprise much of the narrative.

Form: The pattern or construction of a work which identifies its genre and distinguishes it from other genres. Examples of forms include the different genres, such as the lyric form or the short story form, and various patterns for poetry, such as the verse form or the stanza form.

Formalism: In literary criticism, the belief that literature should follow prescribed rules of construction, such as those that govern the sonnet form. Examples of formalism are found in the work of the New Critics and structuralists.

Fourteener Meter: See *Meter*

Free Verse: Poetry that lacks regular metrical and rhyme patterns but that tries to capture the cadences of everyday speech. The form allows a poet to exploit a variety of rhythmical effects within a single poem. Free-verse techniques have been widely used in the twentieth century by such writers as Ezra Pound, T. S. Eliot, Carl Sandburg, and William Carlos Williams. Also known as *Vers libre.*

Futurism: A flamboyant literary and artistic movement that developed in France, Italy, and Russia from 1908 through the 1920s. Futurist theater and poetry abandoned traditional literary forms. In their place, followers of the movement attempted to achieve total freedom of expression through bizarre imagery and deformed or newly invented words. The Futurists were self-consciously modern artists who attempted to incorporate the appearances and sounds of modern life into their work. Futurist writers include Filippo Tommaso Marinetti, Wyndham Lewis, Guillaume Apollinaire, Velimir Khlebnikov, and Vladimir Mayakovsky.

G

Genre: A category of literary work. In critical theory, genre may refer to both the content of a given work—tragedy, comedy, pastoral—and to its form, such as poetry, novel, or drama. This term also refers to types of popular literature, as in the genres of science fiction or the detective story.

Genteel Tradition: A term coined by critic George Santayana to describe the literary practice of certain late nineteenth- century American writers, especially New Englanders. Followers of the Genteel Tradition emphasized conventionality in social, religious, moral, and literary standards. Some of the best-known writers of the Genteel Tradition are R. H. Stoddard and Bayard Taylor.

Gilded Age: A period in American history during the 1870s characterized by political corruption and materialism. A number of important novels of social and political criticism were written during this time. Examples of Gilded Age literature include Henry Adams's *Democracy* and F. Marion Crawford's *An American Politician.*

Gothic: See *Gothicism*

Gothicism: In literary criticism, works characterized by a taste for the medieval or morbidly attractive. A gothic novel prominently features elements of horror, the supernatural, gloom, and violence: clanking chains, terror, charnel houses, ghosts, medieval castles, and mysteriously slamming doors. The term ''gothic novel'' is also applied to novels that lack elements of the traditional Gothic setting but that create a similar atmosphere of terror or dread. Mary Shelley's *Frankenstein* is perhaps the best-known English work of this kind.

Gothic Novel: See *Gothicism*

Great Chain of Being: The belief that all things and creatures in nature are organized in a hierarchy from inanimate objects at the bottom to God at the top. This system of belief was popular in the seventeenth and eighteenth centuries. A summary of the concept of the great chain of being can be found in the first epistle of Alexander Pope's *An Essay on Man,* and more recently in Arthur O. Lovejoy's *The Great Chain of Being: A Study of the History of an Idea.*

Grotesque: In literary criticism, the subject matter of a work or a style of expression characterized by exaggeration, deformity, freakishness, and disorder. The grotesque often includes an element of comic absurdity. Early examples of literary grotesque include Francois Rabelais's *Pantagruel* and *Gargantua* and Thomas Nashe's *The Unfortunate Traveller,* while more recent examples can be found in the works of Edgar Allan Poe, Evelyn Waugh, Eudora Welty, Flannery O'Connor, Eugene Ionesco, Gunter Grass, Thomas Mann, Mervyn Peake, and Joseph Heller, among many others.

H

Haiku: The shortest form of Japanese poetry, constructed in three lines of five, seven, and five syllables respectively. The message of a *haiku* poem usually centers on some aspect of spirituality and provokes an emotional response in the reader. Early masters of *haiku* include Basho, Buson,

Kobayashi Issa, and Masaoka Shiki. English writers of *haiku* include the Imagists, notably Ezra Pound, H. D., Amy Lowell, Carl Sandburg, and William Carlos Williams. Also known as *Hokku.*

Half Rhyme: See *Consonance*

Hamartia: In tragedy, the event or act that leads to the hero's or heroine's downfall. This term is often incorrectly used as a synonym for tragic flaw. In Richard Wright's *Native Son,* the act that seals Bigger Thomas's fate is his first impulsive murder.

Harlem Renaissance: The Harlem Renaissance of the 1920s is generally considered the first significant movement of black writers and artists in the United States. During this period, new and established black writers published more fiction and poetry than ever before, the first influential black literary journals were established, and black authors and artists received their first widespread recognition and serious critical appraisal. Among the major writers associated with this period are Claude McKay, Jean Toomer, Countee Cullen, Langston Hughes, Arna Bontemps, Nella Larsen, and Zora Neale Hurston. Works representative of the Harlem Renaissance include Arna Bontemps's poems ''The Return'' and ''Golgotha Is a Mountain,'' Claude McKay's novel *Home to Harlem,* Nella Larsen's novel *Passing,* Langston Hughes's poem ''The Negro Speaks of Rivers,'' and the journals *Crisis* and *Opportunity,* both founded during this period. Also known as Negro Renaissance and New Negro Movement.

Harlequin: A stock character of the *commedia dell'arte* who occasionally interrupted the action with silly antics. Harlequin first appeared on the English stage in John Day's *The Travailes of the Three English Brothers.* The San Francisco Mime Troupe is one of the few modern groups to adapt Harlequin to the needs of contemporary satire.

Hellenism: Imitation of ancient Greek thought or styles. Also, an approach to life that focuses on the growth and development of the intellect. ''Hellenism'' is sometimes used to refer to the belief that reason can be applied to examine all human experience. A cogent discussion of Hellenism can be found in Matthew Arnold's *Culture and Anarchy.*

Heptameter: See *Meter*

Hero/Heroine: The principal sympathetic character (male or female) in a literary work. Heroes and heroines typically exhibit admirable traits: idealism, courage, and integrity, for example. Famous heroes and heroines include Pip in Charles Dickens's *Great Expectations,* the anonymous narrator in Ralph Ellison's *Invisible Man,* and Sethe in Toni Morrison's *Beloved.*

Heroic Couplet: A rhyming couplet written in iambic pentameter (a verse with five iambic feet). The following lines by Alexander Pope are an example: ''Truth guards the Poet, sanctifies the line,/ And makes Immortal, Verse as mean as mine.''

Heroic Line: The meter and length of a line of verse in epic or heroic poetry. This varies by language and time period. For example, in English poetry, the heroic line is iambic pentameter (a verse with five iambic feet); in French, the alexandrine (a verse with six iambic feet); in classical literature, dactylic hexameter (a verse with six dactylic feet).

Heroine: See *Hero/Heroine*

Hexameter: See *Meter*

Historical Criticism: The study of a work based on its impact on the world of the time period in which it was written. Examples of postmodern historical criticism can be found in the work of Michel Foucault, Hayden White, Stephen Greenblatt, and Jonathan Goldberg.

Hokku: See *Haiku*

Holocaust: See *Holocaust Literature*

Holocaust Literature: Literature influenced by or written about the Holocaust of World War II. Such literature includes true stories of survival in concentration camps, escape, and life after the war, as well as fictional works and poetry. Representative works of Holocaust literature include Saul Bellow's *Mr. Sammler's Planet,* Anne Frank's *The Diary of a Young Girl,* Jerzy Kosinski's *The Painted Bird,* Arthur Miller's *Incident at Vichy,* Czeslaw Milosz's *Collected Poems,* William Styron's *Sophie's Choice,* and Art Spiegelman's *Maus.*

Homeric Simile: An elaborate, detailed comparison written as a simile many lines in length. An example of an epic simile from John Milton's *Paradise Lost* follows: Angel Forms, who lay entranced Thick as autumnal leaves that strow the brooks In Vallombrosa, where the Etrurian shades High over-arched embower; or scattered sedge Afloat, when with fierce winds Orion armed Hath vexed the Red-Sea coast, whose waves o'erthrew Busiris and his Memphian chivalry, While with perfidious hatred they pursued The sojourners of Goshen, who beheld From the safe shore their floating carcasses And broken chariot-wheels. Also known as Epic Simile.

Horatian Satire: See *Satire*

Humanism: A philosophy that places faith in the dignity of humankind and rejects the medieval perception of the individual as a weak, fallen creature. "Humanists" typically believe in the perfectibility of human nature and view reason and education as the means to that end. Humanist thought is represented in the works of Marsilio Ficino, Ludovico Castelvetro, Edmund Spenser, John Milton, Dean John Colet, Desiderius Erasmus, John Dryden, Alexander Pope, Matthew Arnold, and Irving Babbitt.

Humors: Mentions of the humors refer to the ancient Greek theory that a person's health and personality were determined by the balance of four basic fluids in the body: blood, phlegm, yellow bile, and black bile. A dominance of any fluid would cause extremes in behavior. An excess of blood created a sanguine person who was joyful, aggressive, and passionate; a phlegmatic person was shy, fearful, and sluggish; too much yellow bile led to a choleric temperament characterized by impatience, anger, bitterness, and stubbornness; and excessive black bile created melancholy, a state of laziness, gluttony, and lack of motivation. Literary treatment of the humors is exemplified by several characters in Ben Jonson's plays *Every Man in His Humour* and *Every Man out of His Humour.* Also spelled Humours.

Humours: See *Humors*

Hyperbole: In literary criticism, deliberate exaggeration used to achieve an effect. In William Shakespeare's *Macbeth,* Lady Macbeth hyperbolizes when she says, "All the perfumes of Arabia could not sweeten this little hand."

I

Iamb: See *Foot*

Idiom: A word construction or verbal expression closely associated with a given language. For example, in colloquial English the construction "how come" can be used instead of "why" to introduce a question. Similarly, "a piece of cake" is sometimes used to describe a task that is easily done.

Image: A concrete representation of an object or sensory experience. Typically, such a representation helps evoke the feelings associated with the object or experience itself. Images are either "literal" or "figurative." Literal images are especially concrete and involve little or no extension of the obvious meaning of the words used to express them. Figurative images do not follow the literal meaning of the words exactly. Images in literature are usually visual, but the term "image" can also refer to the representation of any sensory experience. In his poem "The Shepherd's Hour," Paul Verlaine presents the following image: "The Moon is red through horizon's fog;/ In a dancing mist the hazy meadow sleeps." The first line is broadly literal, while the second line involves turns of meaning associated with dancing and sleeping.

Imagery: The array of images in a literary work. Also, figurative language. William Butler Yeats's "The Second Coming" offers a powerful image of encroaching anarchy: Turning and turning in the widening gyre The falcon cannot hear the falconer; Things fall apart. . . .

Imagism: An English and American poetry movement that flourished between 1908 and 1917. The Imagists used precise, clearly presented images in their works. They also used common, everyday speech and aimed for conciseness, concrete imagery, and the creation of new rhythms. Participants in the Imagist movement included Ezra Pound, H. D. (Hilda Doolittle), and Amy Lowell, among others.

In medias res: A Latin term meaning "in the middle of things." It refers to the technique of beginning a story at its midpoint and then using various flashback devices to reveal previous action. This technique originated in such epics as Virgil's *Aeneid.*

Induction: The process of reaching a conclusion by reasoning from specific premises to form a general premise. Also, an introductory portion of a work of literature, especially a play. Geoffrey Chaucer's "Prologue" to the *Canterbury Tales,* Thomas Sackville's "Induction" to *The Mirror of Magistrates,* and the opening scene in William Shakespeare's *The Taming of the Shrew* are examples of inductions to literary works.

Intentional Fallacy: The belief that judgments of a literary work based solely on an author's stated or implied intentions are false and misleading. Critics who believe in the concept of the intentional fallacy typically argue that the work itself is sufficient matter for interpretation, even though they may concede that an author's statement of purpose can be useful. Analysis of William Wordsworth's *Lyrical Ballads* based on the observations about poetry he makes in his ''Preface'' to the second edition of that work is an example of the intentional fallacy.

Interior Monologue: A narrative technique in which characters' thoughts are revealed in a way that appears to be uncontrolled by the author. The interior monologue typically aims to reveal the inner self of a character. It portrays emotional experiences as they occur at both a conscious and unconscious level. images are often used to represent sensations or emotions. One of the best-known interior monologues in English is the Molly Bloom section at the close of James Joyce's *Ulysses.* The interior monologue is also common in the works of Virginia Woolf.

Internal Rhyme: Rhyme that occurs within a single line of verse. An example is in the opening line of Edgar Allan Poe's ''The Raven'': ''Once upon a midnight dreary, while I pondered weak and weary.'' Here, ''dreary'' and ''weary'' make an internal rhyme.

Irish Literary Renaissance: A late nineteenth- and early twentieth-century movement in Irish literature. Members of the movement aimed to reduce the influence of British culture in Ireland and create an Irish national literature. William Butler Yeats, George Moore, and Sean O'Casey are three of the best-known figures of the movement.

Irony: In literary criticism, the effect of language in which the intended meaning is the opposite of what is stated. The title of Jonathan Swift's ''A Modest Proposal'' is ironic because what Swift proposes in this essay is cannibalism—hardly ''modest.''

Italian Sonnet: See *Sonnet*

J

Jacobean Age: The period of the reign of James I of England (1603-1625). The early literature of this period reflected the worldview of the Elizabethan Age, but a darker, more cynical attitude steadily grew in the art and literature of the Jacobean Age. This was an important time for English drama and poetry. Milestones include William Shakespeare's tragedies, tragi-comedies, and sonnets; Ben Jonson's various dramas; and John Donne's metaphysical poetry.

Jargon: Language that is used or understood only by a select group of people. Jargon may refer to terminology used in a certain profession, such as computer jargon, or it may refer to any nonsensical language that is not understood by most people. Literary examples of jargon are Francois Villon's *Ballades en jargon,* which is composed in the secret language of the *coquillards,* and Anthony Burgess's *A Clockwork Orange,* narrated in the fictional characters' language of ''Nadsat.''

Juvenalian Satire: See *Satire*

K

Knickerbocker Group: A somewhat indistinct group of New York writers of the first half of the nineteenth century. Members of the group were linked only by location and a common theme: New York life. Two famous members of the Knickerbocker Group were Washington Irving and William Cullen Bryant. The group's name derives from Irving's *Knickerbocker's History of New York.*

L

Lais: See *Lay*

Lay: A song or simple narrative poem. The form originated in medieval France. Early French *lais* were often based on the Celtic legends and other tales sung by Breton minstrels—thus the name of the ''Breton lay.'' In fourteenth-century England, the term ''lay'' was used to describe short narratives written in imitation of the Breton lays. The most notable of these is Geoffrey Chaucer's ''The Minstrel's Tale.''

Leitmotiv: See *Motif*

Literal Language: An author uses literal language when he or she writes without exaggerating or embellishing the subject matter and without any tools of figurative language. To say ''He ran very quickly down the street'' is to use literal language, whereas to say ''He ran like a hare down the street'' would be using figurative language.

Literary Ballad: See *Ballad*

Literature: Literature is broadly defined as any written or spoken material, but the term most often refers to creative works. Literature includes poetry, drama, fiction, and many kinds of nonfiction writing, as well as oral, dramatic, and broadcast compositions not necessarily preserved in a written format, such as films and television programs.

Lost Generation: A term first used by Gertrude Stein to describe the post-World War I generation of American writers: men and women haunted by a sense of betrayal and emptiness brought about by the destructiveness of the war. The term is commonly applied to Hart Crane, Ernest Hemingway, F. Scott Fitzgerald, and others.

Lyric Poetry: A poem expressing the subjective feelings and personal emotions of the poet. Such poetry is melodic, since it was originally accompanied by a lyre in recitals. Most Western poetry in the twentieth century may be classified as lyrical. Examples of lyric poetry include A. E. Housman's elegy ''To an Athlete Dying Young,'' the odes of Pindar and Horace, Thomas Gray and William Collins, the sonnets of Sir Thomas Wyatt and Sir Philip Sidney, Elizabeth Barrett Browning and Rainer Maria Rilke, and a host of other forms in the poetry of William Blake and Christina Rossetti, among many others.

M

Mannerism: Exaggerated, artificial adherence to a literary manner or style. Also, a popular style of the visual arts of late sixteenth-century Europe that was marked by elongation of the human form and by intentional spatial distortion. Literary works that are self-consciously high-toned and artistic are often said to be ''mannered.'' Authors of such works include Henry James and Gertrude Stein.

Masculine Rhyme: See *Rhyme*

Masque: A lavish and elaborate form of entertainment, often performed in royal courts, that emphasizes song, dance, and costumery. The Renaissance form of the masque grew out of the spectacles of masked figures common in medieval England and Europe. The masque reached its peak of popularity and development in seventeenth-century England, during the reigns of James I and, especially, of Charles I. Ben Jonson, the most significant masque writer, also created the ''antimasque,'' which incorporates elements of humor and the grotesque into the traditional masque and achieved greater dramatic quality. Masque-like interludes appear in Edmund Spenser's *The Faerie Queene* and in William Shakespeare's *The Tempest.* One of the best-known English masques is John Milton's *Comus.*

Measure: The foot, verse, or time sequence used in a literary work, especially a poem. Measure is often used somewhat incorrectly as a synonym for meter.

Melodrama: A play in which the typical plot is a conflict between characters who personify extreme good and evil. Melodramas usually end happily and emphasize sensationalism. Other literary forms that use the same techniques are often labeled ''melodramatic.'' The term was formerly used to describe a combination of drama and music; as such, it was synonymous with ''opera.'' Augustin Daly's *Under the Gaslight* and Dion Boucicault's *The Octoroon, The Colleen Bawn,* and *The Poor of New York* are examples of melodramas. The most popular media for twentieth-century melodramas are motion pictures and television.

Metaphor: A figure of speech that expresses an idea through the image of another object. Metaphors suggest the essence of the first object by identifying it with certain qualities of the second object. An example is ''But soft, what light through yonder window breaks?/ It is the east, and Juliet is the sun'' in William Shakespeare's *Romeo and Juliet.* Here, Juliet, the first object, is identified with qualities of the second object, the sun.

Metaphysical Conceit: See *Conceit*

Metaphysical Poetry: The body of poetry produced by a group of seventeenth-century English writers called the ''Metaphysical Poets.'' The group includes John Donne and Andrew Marvell. The Metaphysical Poets made use of everyday speech, intellectual analysis, and unique imagery. They aimed to portray the ordinary conflicts and contradictions of life. Their poems often took the form of an argument, and many of them emphasize physical and religious love as well as the fleeting nature of life. Elaborate conceits are typical in metaphysical poetry. Marvell's ''To His Coy Mistress'' is a well-known example of a metaphysical poem.

Metaphysical Poets: See *Metaphysical Poetry*

Meter: In literary criticism, the repetition of sound patterns that creates a rhythm in poetry. The patterns are based on the number of syllables and the presence and absence of accents. The unit of rhythm in a line is called a foot. Types of meter are classified according to the number of feet in a line. These are the standard English lines: Monometer, one foot; Dimeter, two feet; Trimeter, three feet; Tetrameter, four feet; Pentameter, five feet; Hexameter, six feet (also called the Alexandrine); Heptameter, seven feet (also called the ''Fourteener'' when the feet are iambic). The most common English meter is the iambic pentameter, in which each line contains ten syllables, or five iambic feet, which individually are composed of an unstressed syllable followed by an accented syllable. Both of the following lines from Alfred, Lord Tennyson's ''Ulysses'' are written in iambic pentameter: Made weak by time and fate, but strong in will To strive, to seek, to find, and not to yield.

Mise en scene: The costumes, scenery, and other properties of a drama. Herbert Beerbohm Tree was renowned for the elaborate *mises en scene* of his lavish Shakespearean productions at His Majesty's Theatre between 1897 and 1915.

Modernism: Modern literary practices. Also, the principles of a literary school that lasted from roughly the beginning of the twentieth century until the end of World War II. Modernism is defined by its rejection of the literary conventions of the nineteenth century and by its opposition to conventional morality, taste, traditions, and economic values. Many writers are associated with the concepts of Modernism, including Albert Camus, Marcel Proust, D. H. Lawrence, W. H. Auden, Ernest Hemingway, William Faulkner, William Butler Yeats, Thomas Mann, Tennessee Williams, Eugene O'Neill, and James Joyce.

Monologue: A composition, written or oral, by a single individual. More specifically, a speech given by a single individual in a drama or other public entertainment. It has no set length, although it is usually several or more lines long. An example of an ''extended monologue''—that is, a monologue of great length and seriousness—occurs in the one-act, one-character play *The Stronger* by August Strindberg.

Monometer: See *Meter*

Mood: The prevailing emotions of a work or of the author in his or her creation of the work. The mood of a work is not always what might be expected based on its subject matter. The poem ''Dover Beach'' by Matthew Arnold offers examples of two different moods originating from the same experience: watching the ocean at night. The mood of the first three lines—The sea is calm tonight The tide is full, the moon lies fair Upon the straights. . . . is in sharp contrast to the mood of the last three lines—And we are here as on a darkling plain Swept with confused alarms of struggle and flight, Where ignorant armies clash by night.

Motif: A theme, character type, image, metaphor, or other verbal element that recurs throughout a single work of literature or occurs in a number of different works over a period of time. For example, the various manifestations of the color white in Herman Melville's *Moby Dick* is a ''specific'' *motif,* while the trials of star-crossed lovers is a ''conventional'' *motif* from the literature of all periods. Also known as *Motiv* or *Leitmotiv.*

Motiv: See *Motif*

Muckrakers: An early twentieth-century group of American writers. Typically, their works exposed the wrongdoings of big business and government in the United States. Upton Sinclair's *The Jungle* exemplifies the muckraking novel.

Muses: Nine Greek mythological goddesses, the daughters of Zeus and Mnemosyne (Memory). Each muse patronized a specific area of the liberal arts and sciences. Calliope presided over epic poetry, Clio over history, Erato over love poetry, Euterpe over music or lyric poetry, Melpomene over tragedy, Polyhymnia over hymns to the gods, Terpsichore over dance, Thalia over comedy, and Urania over astronomy. Poets and writers traditionally made appeals to the Muses for inspiration in their work. John Milton invokes the aid of a muse at the beginning of the first book of his *Paradise Lost:* Of Man's First disobedience, and the Fruit of the Forbidden Tree, whose mortal taste Brought Death into the World, and all our woe, With loss of Eden, till one greater Man Restore us, and regain the blissful Seat, Sing Heav'nly Muse, that on the secret top of Oreb, or of Sinai, didst inspire That Shepherd, who first taught the chosen Seed, In the Beginning how the Heav'ns and Earth Rose out of Chaos. . . .

Mystery: See *Suspense*

Myth: An anonymous tale emerging from the traditional beliefs of a culture or social unit. Myths use supernatural explanations for natural phenomena. They may also explain cosmic issues like creation and death. Collections of myths, known as mythologies, are common to all cultures and nations, but the best-known myths belong to the Norse, Roman, and Greek mythologies. A famous myth is the story of Arachne, an arrogant young girl who challenged a goddess, Athena, to a weaving contest; when the girl won, Athena was enraged and turned Arachne into a spider, thus explaining the existence of spiders.

N

Narration: The telling of a series of events, real or invented. A narration may be either a simple narrative, in which the events are recounted chronologically, or a narrative with a plot, in which the account is given in a style reflecting the author's artistic concept of the story. Narration is sometimes used as a synonym for "storyline." The recounting of scary stories around a campfire is a form of narration.

Narrative: A verse or prose accounting of an event or sequence of events, real or invented. The term is also used as an adjective in the sense "method of narration." For example, in literary criticism, the expression "narrative technique" usually refers to the way the author structures and presents his or her story. Narratives range from the shortest accounts of events, as in Julius Caesar's remark, "I came, I saw, I conquered," to the longest historical or biographical works, as in Edward Gibbon's *The Decline and Fall of the Roman Empire,* as well as diaries, travelogues, novels, ballads, epics, short stories, and other fictional forms.

Narrative Poetry: A nondramatic poem in which the author tells a story. Such poems may be of any length or level of complexity. Epics such as *Beowulf* and ballads are forms of narrative poetry.

Narrator: The teller of a story. The narrator may be the author or a character in the story through whom the author speaks. Huckleberry Finn is the narrator of Mark Twain's *The Adventures of Huckleberry Finn.*

Naturalism: A literary movement of the late nineteenth and early twentieth centuries. The movement's major theorist, French novelist Emile Zola, envisioned a type of fiction that would examine human life with the objectivity of scientific inquiry. The Naturalists typically viewed human beings as either the products of "biological determinism," ruled by hereditary instincts and engaged in an endless struggle for survival, or as the products of "socioeconomic determinism," ruled by social and economic forces beyond their control. In their works, the Naturalists generally ignored the highest levels of society and focused on degradation: poverty, alcoholism, prostitution, insanity, and disease. Naturalism influenced authors throughout the world, including Henrik Ibsen and Thomas Hardy. In the United States, in particular, Naturalism had a profound impact. Among the authors who embraced its principles are Theodore Dreiser, Eugene O'Neill, Stephen Crane, Jack London, and Frank Norris.

Negritude: A literary movement based on the concept of a shared cultural bond on the part of black Africans, wherever they may be in the world. It traces its origins to the former French colonies of Africa and the Caribbean. Negritude poets, novelists, and essayists generally stress four points in their writings: One, black alienation from traditional African culture can lead to feelings of inferiority. Two, European colonialism and Western education should be resisted. Three, black Africans should seek to affirm and define their own identity. Four, African culture can and should be reclaimed. Many Negritude writers also claim that blacks can make unique contributions to the world, based on a heightened appreciation of nature, rhythm, and human emotions—aspects of life they say are not so highly valued in the materialistic and rationalistic West. Examples of Negritude literature include the poetry of both Senegalese Leopold Senghor in *Hosties noires* and Martiniquais Aime-Fernand Cesaire in *Return to My Native Land.*

Negro Renaissance: See *Harlem Renaissance*

Neoclassical Period: See *Neoclassicism*

Neoclassicism: In literary criticism, this term refers to the revival of the attitudes and styles of expression of classical literature. It is generally used to describe a period in European history beginning in the late seventeenth century and lasting until about 1800. In its purest form, Neoclassicism marked a return to order, proportion, restraint, logic, accuracy, and decorum. In England, where Neoclassicism perhaps was most popular, it reflected the influence of seventeenth- century French writers, especially dramatists. Neoclassical writers typically reacted against the intensity and enthusiasm of the Renaissance period. They wrote works that appealed to the intellect, using elevated language and classical literary forms such as satire and the ode. Neoclassical works were often governed by the classical goal of instruction. English neoclassicists included Alexander Pope, Jonathan Swift, Joseph Addison, Sir Richard Steele, John Gay, and Matthew Prior; French neoclassicists included Pierre Corneille and Jean-Baptiste Moliere. Also known as Age of Reason.

Neoclassicists: See *Neoclassicism*

New Criticism: A movement in literary criticism, dating from the late 1920s, that stressed close textual analysis in the interpretation of works of literature. The New Critics saw little merit in historical and biographical analysis. Rather, they aimed to examine the text alone, free from the question of how external events—biographical or otherwise—may have helped shape it. This predominantly American school was named "New Criticism" by one of its practitioners, John Crowe Ransom. Other important New Critics included Allen Tate, R. P. Blackmur, Robert Penn Warren, and Cleanth Brooks.

New Negro Movement: See *Harlem Renaissance*

Noble Savage: The idea that primitive man is noble and good but becomes evil and corrupted as he becomes civilized. The concept of the noble savage originated in the Renaissance period but is more closely identified with such later writers as Jean-Jacques Rousseau and Aphra Behn. First described in John Dryden's play *The Conquest of Granada,* the noble savage is portrayed by the various Native Americans in James Fenimore Cooper's ''Leatherstocking Tales,'' by Queequeg, Daggoo, and Tashtego in Herman Melville's *Moby Dick,* and by John the Savage in Aldous Huxley's *Brave New World.*

O

Objective Correlative: An outward set of objects, a situation, or a chain of events corresponding to an inward experience and evoking this experience in the reader. The term frequently appears in modern criticism in discussions of authors' intended effects on the emotional responses of readers. This term was originally used by T. S. Eliot in his 1919 essay ''Hamlet.''

Objectivity: A quality in writing characterized by the absence of the author's opinion or feeling about the subject matter. Objectivity is an important factor in criticism. The novels of Henry James and, to a certain extent, the poems of John Larkin demonstrate objectivity, and it is central to John Keats's concept of ''negative capability.'' Critical and journalistic writing usually are or attempt to be objective.

Occasional Verse: poetry written on the occasion of a significant historical or personal event. *Vers de societe* is sometimes called occasional verse although it is of a less serious nature. Famous examples of occasional verse include Andrew Marvell's ''Horatian Ode upon Cromwell's Return from England,'' Walt Whitman's ''When Lilacs Last in the Dooryard Bloom'd''—written upon the death of Abraham Lincoln—and Edmund Spenser's commemoration of his wedding, ''Epithalamion.''

Octave: A poem or stanza composed of eight lines. The term octave most often represents the first eight lines of a Petrarchan sonnet. An example of an octave is taken from a translation of a Petrarchan sonnet by Sir Thomas Wyatt: The pillar perish is whereto I leant, The strongest stay of mine unquiet mind; The like of it no man again can find, From East to West Still seeking though he went. To mind unhap! for hap away hath rent Of all my joy the very bark and rind; And I, alas, by chance am thus assigned Daily to mourn till death do it relent.

Ode: Name given to an extended lyric poem characterized by exalted emotion and dignified style. An ode usually concerns a single, serious theme. Most odes, but not all, are addressed to an object or individual. Odes are distinguished from other lyric poetic forms by their complex rhythmic and stanzaic patterns. An example of this form is John Keats's ''Ode to a Nightingale.''

Oedipus Complex: A son's amorous obsession with his mother. The phrase is derived from the story of the ancient Theban hero Oedipus, who unknowingly killed his father and married his mother. Literary occurrences of the Oedipus complex include Andre Gide's *Oedipe* and Jean Cocteau's *La Machine infernale,* as well as the most famous, Sophocles' *Oedipus Rex.*

Omniscience: See *Point of View*

Onomatopoeia: The use of words whose sounds express or suggest their meaning. In its simplest sense, onomatopoeia may be represented by words that mimic the sounds they denote such as ''hiss'' or ''meow.'' At a more subtle level, the pattern and rhythm of sounds and rhymes of a line or poem may be onomatopoeic. A celebrated example of onomatopoeia is the repetition of the word ''bells'' in Edgar Allan Poe's poem ''The Bells.''

Opera: A type of stage performance, usually a drama, in which the dialogue is sung. Classic examples of opera include Giuseppi Verdi's *La traviata,* Giacomo Puccini's *La Boheme,* and Richard Wagner's *Tristan und Isolde.* Major twentieth- century contributors to the form include Richard Strauss and Alban Berg.

Operetta: A usually romantic comic opera. John Gay's *The Beggar's Opera,* Richard Sheridan's *The Duenna,* and numerous works by William Gilbert and Arthur Sullivan are examples of operettas.

Oral Tradition: See *Oral Transmission*

Oral Transmission: A process by which songs, ballads, folklore, and other material are transmitted by word of mouth. The tradition of oral transmission predates the written record systems of literate society. Oral transmission preserves material sometimes over generations, although often with variations. Memory plays a large part in the recitation and preservation of orally transmitted material. Breton lays, French *fabliaux,* national epics (including the Anglo- Saxon *Beowulf,* the Spanish *El Cid,* and the Finnish *Kalevala*), Native American myths and legends, and African folktales told by plantation slaves are examples of orally transmitted literature.

Oration: Formal speaking intended to motivate the listeners to some action or feeling. Such public speaking was much more common before the development of timely printed communication such as newspapers. Famous examples of oration include Abraham Lincoln's "Gettysburg Address" and Dr. Martin Luther King Jr.'s "I Have a Dream" speech.

Ottava Rima: An eight-line stanza of poetry composed in iambic pentameter (a five-foot line in which each foot consists of an unaccented syllable followed by an accented syllable), following the abababcc rhyme scheme. This form has been prominently used by such important English writers as Lord Byron, Henry Wadsworth Longfellow, and W. B. Yeats.

Oxymoron: A phrase combining two contradictory terms. Oxymorons may be intentional or unintentional. The following speech from William Shakespeare's *Romeo and Juliet* uses several oxymorons: Why, then, O brawling love! O loving hate! O anything, of nothing first create! O heavy lightness! serious vanity! Mis-shapen chaos of well-seeming forms! Feather of lead, bright smoke, cold fire, sick health! This love feel I, that feel no love in this.

P

Pantheism: The idea that all things are both a manifestation or revelation of God and a part of God at the same time. Pantheism was a common attitude in the early societies of Egypt, India, and Greece—the term derives from the Greek *pan* meaning "all" and *theos* meaning "deity." It later became a significant part of the Christian faith. William Wordsworth and Ralph Waldo Emerson are among the many writers who have expressed the pantheistic attitude in their works.

Parable: A story intended to teach a moral lesson or answer an ethical question. In the West, the best examples of parables are those of Jesus Christ in the New Testament, notably "The Prodigal Son," but parables also are used in Sufism, rabbinic literature, Hasidism, and Zen Buddhism.

Paradox: A statement that appears illogical or contradictory at first, but may actually point to an underlying truth. "Less is more" is an example of a paradox. Literary examples include Francis Bacon's statement, "The most corrected copies are commonly the least correct," and "All animals are equal, but some animals are more equal than others" from George Orwell's *Animal Farm.*

Parallelism: A method of comparison of two ideas in which each is developed in the same grammatical structure. Ralph Waldo Emerson's "Civilization" contains this example of parallelism: Raphael paints wisdom; Handel sings it, Phidias carves it, Shakespeare writes it, Wren builds it, Columbus sails it, Luther preaches it, Washington arms it, Watt mechanizes it.

Parnassianism: A mid nineteenth-century movement in French literature. Followers of the movement stressed adherence to well-defined artistic forms as a reaction against the often chaotic expression of the artist's ego that dominated the work of the Romantics. The Parnassians also rejected the moral, ethical, and social themes exhibited in the works of French Romantics such as Victor Hugo. The aesthetic doctrines of the Parnassians strongly influenced the later symbolist and decadent movements. Members of the Parnassian school include Leconte de Lisle, Sully Prudhomme, Albert Glatigny, Francois Coppee, and Theodore de Banville.

Parody: In literary criticism, this term refers to an imitation of a serious literary work or the signature style of a particular author in a ridiculous manner. A typical parody adopts the style of the original and applies it to an inappropriate subject for humorous effect. Parody is a form of satire and could be considered the literary equivalent of a caricature or cartoon. Henry Fielding's *Shamela* is a parody of Samuel Richardson's *Pamela.*

Pastoral: A term derived from the Latin word "pastor," meaning shepherd. A pastoral is a literary composition on a rural theme. The conventions of the pastoral were originated by the third-century Greek poet Theocritus, who wrote about the experiences, love affairs, and pastimes of Sicilian shepherds. In a pastoral, characters and language of a courtly nature are often placed in a simple setting. The term pastoral is also used to classify dramas, elegies, and lyrics that exhibit the use of country settings and shepherd characters. Percy Bysshe Shelley's "Adonais" and John Milton's "Lycidas" are two famous examples of pastorals.

Pastorela: The Spanish name for the shepherds play, a folk drama reenacted during the Christmas season. Examples of *pastorelas* include Gomez

Manrique's *Representacion del nacimiento* and the dramas of Lucas Fernandez and Juan del Encina.

Pathetic Fallacy: A term coined by English critic John Ruskin to identify writing that falsely endows nonhuman things with human intentions and feelings, such as "angry clouds" and "sad trees." The pathetic fallacy is a required convention in the classical poetic form of the pastoral elegy, and it is used in the modern poetry of T. S. Eliot, Ezra Pound, and the Imagists. Also known as Poetic Fallacy.

Pelado: Literally the "skinned one" or shirtless one, he was the stock underdog, sharp-witted picaresque character of Mexican vaudeville and tent shows. The *pelado* is found in such works as Don Catarino's *Los effectos de la crisis* and *Regreso a mi tierra.*

Pen Name: See *Pseudonym*

Pentameter: See *Meter*

Persona: A Latin term meaning "mask." *Personae* are the characters in a fictional work of literature. The *persona* generally functions as a mask through which the author tells a story in a voice other than his or her own. A *persona* is usually either a character in a story who acts as a narrator or an "implied author," a voice created by the author to act as the narrator for himself or herself. *Personae* include the narrator of Geoffrey Chaucer's *Canterbury Tales* and Marlow in Joseph Conrad's *Heart of Darkness.*

Personae: See *Persona*

Personal Point of View: See *Point of View*

Personification: A figure of speech that gives human qualities to abstract ideas, animals, and inanimate objects. William Shakespeare used personification in *Romeo and Juliet* in the lines "Arise, fair sun, and kill the envious moon,/ Who is already sick and pale with grief." Here, the moon is portrayed as being envious, sick, and pale with grief—all markedly human qualities. Also known as *Prosopopoeia.*

Petrarchan Sonnet: See *Sonnet*

Phenomenology: A method of literary criticism based on the belief that things have no existence outside of human consciousness or awareness. Proponents of this theory believe that art is a process that takes place in the mind of the observer as he or she contemplates an object rather than a quality of the object itself. Among phenomenological critics are Edmund Husserl, George Poulet, Marcel Raymond, and Roman Ingarden.

Picaresque Novel: Episodic fiction depicting the adventures of a roguish central character ("picaro" is Spanish for "rogue"). The picaresque hero is commonly a low-born but clever individual who wanders into and out of various affairs of love, danger, and farcical intrigue. These involvements may take place at all social levels and typically present a humorous and wide-ranging satire of a given society. Prominent examples of the picaresque novel are *Don Quixote* by Miguel de Cervantes, *Tom Jones* by Henry Fielding, and *Moll Flanders* by Daniel Defoe.

Plagiarism: Claiming another person's written material as one's own. Plagiarism can take the form of direct, word-for- word copying or the theft of the substance or idea of the work. A student who copies an encyclopedia entry and turns it in as a report for school is guilty of plagiarism.

Platonic Criticism: A form of criticism that stresses an artistic work's usefulness as an agent of social engineering rather than any quality or value of the work itself. Platonic criticism takes as its starting point the ancient Greek philosopher Plato's comments on art in his *Republic.*

Platonism: The embracing of the doctrines of the philosopher Plato, popular among the poets of the Renaissance and the Romantic period. Platonism is more flexible than Aristotelian Criticism and places more emphasis on the supernatural and unknown aspects of life. Platonism is expressed in the love poetry of the Renaissance, the fourth book of Baldassare Castiglione's *The Book of the Courtier,* and the poetry of William Blake, William Wordsworth, Percy Bysshe Shelley, Friedrich Holderlin, William Butler Yeats, and Wallace Stevens.

Play: See *Drama*

Plot: In literary criticism, this term refers to the pattern of events in a narrative or drama. In its simplest sense, the plot guides the author in composing the work and helps the reader follow the work. Typically, plots exhibit causality and unity and have a beginning, a middle, and an end. Sometimes, however, a plot may consist of a series of disconnected events, in which case it is known as an "episodic plot." In his *Aspects of the Novel,* E. M. Forster distinguishes between a story, defined as a "narrative of events arranged in their time- sequence," and plot, which organizes the events to a "sense of causality." This definition closely mirrors Aristotle's discussion of plot in his *Poetics.*

Poem: In its broadest sense, a composition utilizing rhyme, meter, concrete detail, and expressive language to create a literary experience with emotional and aesthetic appeal. Typical poems include sonnets, odes, elegies, *haiku,* ballads, and free verse.

Poet: An author who writes poetry or verse. The term is also used to refer to an artist or writer who has an exceptional gift for expression, imagination, and energy in the making of art in any form. Well-known poets include Horace, Basho, Sir Philip Sidney, Sir Edmund Spenser, John Donne, Andrew Marvell, Alexander Pope, Jonathan Swift, George Gordon, Lord Byron, John Keats, Christina Rossetti, W. H. Auden, Stevie Smith, and Sylvia Plath.

Poetic Fallacy: See *Pathetic Fallacy*

Poetic Justice: An outcome in a literary work, not necessarily a poem, in which the good are rewarded and the evil are punished, especially in ways that particularly fit their virtues or crimes. For example, a murderer may himself be murdered, or a thief will find himself penniless.

Poetic License: Distortions of fact and literary convention made by a writer—not always a poet—for the sake of the effect gained. Poetic license is closely related to the concept of "artistic freedom." An author exercises poetic license by saying that a pile of money "reaches as high as a mountain" when the pile is actually only a foot or two high.

Poetics: This term has two closely related meanings. It denotes (1) an aesthetic theory in literary criticism about the essence of poetry or (2) rules prescribing the proper methods, content, style, or diction of poetry. The term poetics may also refer to theories about literature in general, not just poetry.

Poetry: In its broadest sense, writing that aims to present ideas and evoke an emotional experience in the reader through the use of meter, imagery, connotative and concrete words, and a carefully constructed structure based on rhythmic patterns. Poetry typically relies on words and expressions that have several layers of meaning. It also makes use of the effects of regular rhythm on the ear and may make a strong appeal to the senses through the use of imagery. Edgar Allan Poe's "Annabel Lee" and Walt Whitman's *Leaves of Grass* are famous examples of poetry.

Point of View: The narrative perspective from which a literary work is presented to the reader. There are four traditional points of view. The "third person omniscient" gives the reader a "godlike" perspective, unrestricted by time or place, from which to see actions and look into the minds of characters. This allows the author to comment openly on characters and events in the work. The "third person" point of view presents the events of the story from outside of any single character's perception, much like the omniscient point of view, but the reader must understand the action as it takes place and without any special insight into characters' minds or motivations. The "first person" or "personal" point of view relates events as they are perceived by a single character. The main character "tells" the story and may offer opinions about the action and characters which differ from those of the author. Much less common than omniscient, third person, and first person is the "second person" point of view, wherein the author tells the story as if it is happening to the reader. James Thurber employs the omniscient point of view in his short story "The Secret Life of Walter Mitty." Ernest Hemingway's "A Clean, Well-Lighted Place" is a short story told from the third person point of view. Mark Twain's novel *Huck Finn* is presented from the first person viewpoint. Jay McInerney's *Bright Lights, Big City* is an example of a novel which uses the second person point of view.

Polemic: A work in which the author takes a stand on a controversial subject, such as abortion or religion. Such works are often extremely argumentative or provocative. Classic examples of polemics include John Milton's *Aeropagitica* and Thomas Paine's *The American Crisis.*

Pornography: Writing intended to provoke feelings of lust in the reader. Such works are often condemned by critics and teachers, but those which can be shown to have literary value are viewed less harshly. Literary works that have been described as pornographic include Ovid's *The Art of Love,* Margaret of Angouleme's *Heptameron,* John Cleland's *Memoirs of a Woman of Pleasure; or, the Life of Fanny Hill,* the anonymous *My Secret Life,* D. H. Lawrence's *Lady Chatterley's Lover,* and Vladimir Nabokov's *Lolita.*

Post-Aesthetic Movement: An artistic response made by African Americans to the black aesthetic movement of the 1960s and early '70s. Writers since that time have adopted a somewhat different tone in their work, with less emphasis placed on the disparity between black and white in the United States. In the words of post-aesthetic authors such as Toni Morrison, John Edgar Wideman, and Kristin Hunter, African Americans are portrayed as looking inward for answers to their own questions, rather than always looking to the outside world. Two well-known examples of works produced as part of the post-aesthetic movement are the Pulitzer Prize-winning novels *The Color Purple* by Alice Walker and *Beloved* by Toni Morrison.

Postmodernism: Writing from the 1960s forward characterized by experimentation and continuing to apply some of the fundamentals of modernism, which included existentialism and alienation. Postmodernists have gone a step further in the rejection of tradition begun with the modernists by also rejecting traditional forms, preferring the anti-novel over the novel and the anti-hero over the hero. Postmodern writers include Alain Robbe-Grillet, Thomas Pynchon, Margaret Drabble, John Fowles, Adolfo Bioy-Casares, and Gabriel Garcia Marquez.

Pre-Raphaelites: A circle of writers and artists in mid nineteenth-century England. Valuing the pre-Renaissance artistic qualities of religious symbolism, lavish pictorialism, and natural sensuousness, the Pre-Raphaelites cultivated a sense of mystery and melancholy that influenced later writers associated with the Symbolist and Decadent movements. The major members of the group include Dante Gabriel Rossetti, Christina Rossetti, Algernon Swinburne, and Walter Pater.

Primitivism: The belief that primitive peoples were nobler and less flawed than civilized peoples because they had not been subjected to the tainting influence of society. Examples of literature espousing primitivism include Aphra Behn's *Oroonoko: Or, The History of the Royal Slave,* Jean-Jacques Rousseau's *Julie ou la Nouvelle Heloise,* Oliver Goldsmith's *The Deserted Village,* the poems of Robert Burns, Herman Melville's stories *Typee, Omoo,* and *Mardi,* many poems of William Butler Yeats and Robert Frost, and William Golding's novel *Lord of the Flies.*

Projective Verse: A form of free verse in which the poet's breathing pattern determines the lines of the poem. Poets who advocate projective verse are against all formal structures in writing, including meter and form. Besides its creators, Robert Creeley, Robert Duncan, and Charles Olson, two other well-known projective verse poets are Denise Levertov and LeRoi Jones (Amiri Baraka). Also known as Breath Verse.

Prologue: An introductory section of a literary work. It often contains information establishing the situation of the characters or presents information about the setting, time period, or action. In drama, the prologue is spoken by a chorus or by one of the principal characters. In the ''General Prologue'' of *The Canterbury Tales,* Geoffrey Chaucer describes the main characters and establishes the setting and purpose of the work.

Prose: A literary medium that attempts to mirror the language of everyday speech. It is distinguished from poetry by its use of unmetered, unrhymed language consisting of logically related sentences. Prose is usually grouped into paragraphs that form a cohesive whole such as an essay or a novel. Recognized masters of English prose writing include Sir Thomas Malory, William Caxton, Raphael Holinshed, Joseph Addison, Mark Twain, and Ernest Hemingway.

Prosopopoeia: See *Personification*

Protagonist: The central character of a story who serves as a focus for its themes and incidents and as the principal rationale for its development. The protagonist is sometimes referred to in discussions of modern literature as the hero or anti-hero. Well-known protagonists are Hamlet in William Shakespeare's *Hamlet* and Jay Gatsby in F. Scott Fitzgerald's *The Great Gatsby.*

Protest Fiction: Protest fiction has as its primary purpose the protesting of some social injustice, such as racism or discrimination. One example of protest fiction is a series of five novels by Chester Himes, beginning in 1945 with *If He Hollers Let Him Go* and ending in 1955 with *The Primitive.* These works depict the destructive effects of race and gender stereotyping in the context of interracial relationships. Another African American author whose works often revolve around themes of social protest is John Oliver Killens. James Baldwin's essay ''Everybody's Protest Novel'' generated controversy by attacking the authors of protest fiction.

Proverb: A brief, sage saying that expresses a truth about life in a striking manner. ''They are not all cooks who carry long knives'' is an example of a proverb.

Pseudonym: A name assumed by a writer, most often intended to prevent his or her identification as the author of a work. Two or more authors may work together under one pseudonym, or an author may use a different name for each genre he or she publishes in. Some publishing companies maintain ''house pseudonyms,'' under which any number of authors may write installations in a series. Some authors also choose a pseudonym over their real names the way an actor may use a stage name. Examples of pseudonyms (with the author's real name in parentheses) include Voltaire (Francois-Marie Arouet), Novalis (Friedrich von Hardenberg), Currer Bell (Charlotte Bronte), Ellis Bell (Emily Bronte), George Eliot (Maryann Evans), Honorio Bustos Donmecq (Adolfo Bioy-Casares and Jorge Luis Borges), and Richard Bachman (Stephen King).

Pun: A play on words that have similar sounds but different meanings. A serious example of the pun is from John Donne's ''A Hymne to God the Father'': Sweare by thyself, that at my death thy sonne Shall shine as he shines now, and hereto fore; And, having done that, Thou haste done; I fear no more.

Pure Poetry: poetry written without instructional intent or moral purpose that aims only to please a reader by its imagery or musical flow. The term pure poetry is used as the antonym of the term ''didacticism.'' The poetry of Edgar Allan Poe, Stephane Mallarme, Paul Verlaine, Paul Valery, Juan Ramoz Jimenez, and Jorge Guillen offer examples of pure poetry.

Q

Quatrain: A four-line stanza of a poem or an entire poem consisting of four lines. The following quatrain is from Robert Herrick's ''To Live Merrily, and to Trust to Good Verses'': Round, round, the root do's run; And being ravisht thus, Come, I will drink a Tun To my *Propertius.*

R

Raisonneur: A character in a drama who functions as a spokesperson for the dramatist's views. The *raisonneur* typically observes the play without becoming central to its action. *Raisonneurs* were very common in plays of the nineteenth century.

Realism: A nineteenth-century European literary movement that sought to portray familiar characters, situations, and settings in a realistic manner. This was done primarily by using an objective narrative point of view and through the buildup of accurate detail. The standard for success of any realistic work depends on how faithfully it transfers common experience into fictional forms. The realistic method may be altered or extended, as in stream of consciousness writing, to record highly subjective experience. Seminal authors in the tradition of Realism include Honore de Balzac, Gustave Flaubert, and Henry James.

Refrain: A phrase repeated at intervals throughout a poem. A refrain may appear at the end of each stanza or at less regular intervals. It may be altered slightly at each appearance. Some refrains are nonsense expressions—as with ''Nevermore'' in Edgar Allan Poe's ''The Raven''—that seem to take on a different significance with each use.

Renaissance: The period in European history that marked the end of the Middle Ages. It began in Italy in the late fourteenth century. In broad terms, it is usually seen as spanning the fourteenth, fifteenth, and sixteenth centuries, although it did not reach Great Britain, for example, until the 1480s or so. The Renaissance saw an awakening in almost every sphere of human activity, especially science, philosophy, and the arts. The period is best defined by the emergence of a general philosophy that emphasized the importance of the intellect, the individual, and world affairs. It contrasts strongly with the medieval worldview, characterized by the dominant concerns of faith, the social collective, and spiritual salvation. Prominent writers during the Renaissance include Niccolo Machiavelli and Baldassare Castiglione in Italy, Miguel de Cervantes and Lope de Vega in Spain, Jean Froissart and Francois Rabelais in France, Sir Thomas More and Sir Philip Sidney in England, and Desiderius Erasmus in Holland.

Repartee: Conversation featuring snappy retorts and witticisms. Masters of *repartee* include Sydney Smith, Charles Lamb, and Oscar Wilde. An example is recorded in the meeting of ''Beau'' Nash and John Wesley: Nash said, ''I never make way for a fool,'' to which Wesley responded, ''Don't you? I always do,'' and stepped aside.

Resolution: The portion of a story following the climax, in which the conflict is resolved. The resolution of Jane Austen's *Northanger Abbey* is neatly summed up in the following sentence: ''Henry and Catherine were married, the bells rang and every body smiled.''

Restoration: See *Restoration Age*

Restoration Age: A period in English literature beginning with the crowning of Charles II in 1660 and running to about 1700. The era, which was characterized by a reaction against Puritanism, was the first great age of the comedy of manners. The finest literature of the era is typically witty and urbane, and often lewd. Prominent Restoration Age writers include William Congreve, Samuel Pepys, John Dryden, and John Milton.

Revenge Tragedy: A dramatic form popular during the Elizabethan Age, in which the protagonist, directed by the ghost of his murdered father or son, inflicts retaliation upon a powerful villain. Notable features of the revenge tragedy include violence, bizarre criminal acts, intrigue, insanity, a hesitant protagonist, and the use of soliloquy. Thomas Kyd's *Spanish Tragedy* is the first example of revenge tragedy in English, and William Shakespeare's *Hamlet* is perhaps the best. Extreme examples of revenge tragedy, such as John Webster's *The Duchess of Malfi,* are labeled ''tragedies of blood.'' Also known as Tragedy of Blood.

Revista: The Spanish term for a vaudeville musical revue. Examples of *revistas* include Antonio Guzman Aguilera's *Mexico para los mexicanos,* Daniel Vanegas's *Maldito jazz,* and Don Catarino's *Whiskey, morfina y marihuana* and *El desterrado.*

Rhetoric: In literary criticism, this term denotes the art of ethical persuasion. In its strictest sense, rhetoric adheres to various principles developed since classical times for arranging facts and ideas in a clear, persuasive, appealing manner. The term is also used to refer to effective prose in general and theories of or methods for composing effective prose. Classical examples of rhetorics include *The Rhetoric of Aristotle,* Quintillian's *Institutio Oratoria,* and Cicero's *Ad Herennium.*

Rhetorical Question: A question intended to provoke thought, but not an expressed answer, in the reader. It is most commonly used in oratory and other persuasive genres. The following lines from Thomas Gray's ''Elegy Written in a Country Churchyard'' ask rhetorical questions: Can storied urn or animated bust Back to its mansion call the fleeting breath? Can Honour's voice provoke the silent dust, Or Flattery soothe the dull cold ear of Death?

Rhyme: When used as a noun in literary criticism, this term generally refers to a poem in which words sound identical or very similar and appear in parallel positions in two or more lines. Rhymes are classified into different types according to where they fall in a line or stanza or according to the degree of similarity they exhibit in their spellings and sounds. Some major types of rhyme are ''masculine'' rhyme, ''feminine'' rhyme, and ''triple'' rhyme. In a masculine rhyme, the rhyming sound falls in a single accented syllable, as with ''heat'' and ''eat.'' Feminine rhyme is a rhyme of two syllables, one stressed and one unstressed, as with ''merry'' and ''tarry.'' Triple rhyme matches the sound of the accented syllable and the two unaccented syllables that follow: ''narrative'' and ''declarative.'' Robert Browning alternates feminine and masculine rhymes in his ''Soliloquy of the Spanish Cloister'': Gr-r-r—there go, my heart's abhorrence! Water your damned flower-pots, do! If hate killed men, Brother Lawrence, God's blood, would not mine kill you! What? Your myrtle-bush wants trimming? Oh, that rose has prior claims—Needs its leaden vase filled brimming? Hell dry you up with flames! Triple rhymes can be found in Thomas Hood's ''Bridge of Sighs,'' George Gordon Byron's satirical verse, and Ogden Nash's comic poems.

Rhyme Royal: A stanza of seven lines composed in iambic pentameter and rhymed *ababbcc.* The name is said to be a tribute to King James I of Scotland, who made much use of the form in his poetry. Examples of rhyme royal include Geoffrey Chaucer's *The Parlement of Foules,* William Shakespeare's *The Rape of Lucrece,* William Morris's *The Early Paradise,* and John Masefield's *The Widow in the Bye Street.*

Rhyme Scheme: See *Rhyme*

Rhythm: A regular pattern of sound, time intervals, or events occurring in writing, most often and most discernably in poetry. Regular, reliable rhythm is known to be soothing to humans, while interrupted, unpredictable, or rapidly changing rhythm is disturbing. These effects are known to authors, who use them to produce a desired reaction in the reader. An example of a form of irregular rhythm is sprung rhythm poetry; quantitative verse, on the other hand, is very regular in its rhythm.

Rising Action: The part of a drama where the plot becomes increasingly complicated. Rising action leads up to the climax, or turning point, of a drama. The final ''chase scene'' of an action film is generally the rising action which culminates in the film's climax.

Rococo: A style of European architecture that flourished in the eighteenth century, especially in France. The most notable features of *rococo* are its extensive use of ornamentation and its themes of lightness, gaiety, and intimacy. In literary criticism, the term is often used disparagingly to refer to a decadent or over-ornamental style. Alexander Pope's ''The Rape of the Lock'' is an example of literary *rococo.*

Roman a clef: A French phrase meaning ''novel with a key.'' It refers to a narrative in which real persons are portrayed under fictitious names. Jack Kerouac, for example, portrayed various real-life beat generation figures under fictitious names in his *On the Road.*

Romance: A broad term, usually denoting a narrative with exotic, exaggerated, often idealized characters, scenes, and themes. Nathaniel Hawthorne called his *The House of the Seven Gables* and *The Marble Faun* romances in order to distinguish them from clearly realistic works.

Romantic Age: See *Romanticism*

Romanticism: This term has two widely accepted meanings. In historical criticism, it refers to a European intellectual and artistic movement of the late eighteenth and early nineteenth centuries that sought greater freedom of personal expression than that allowed by the strict rules of literary form and logic of the eighteenth-century neoclassicists. The Romantics preferred emotional and imaginative expression to rational analysis. They considered the individual to be at the center of all experience and so placed him or her at the center of their art. The Romantics believed that the creative imagination reveals nobler truths—unique feelings and attitudes—than those that could be discovered by logic or by scientific examination. Both the natural world and the state of childhood were important sources for revelations of ''eternal truths.'' ''Romanticism'' is also used as a general term to refer to a type of sensibility found in all periods of literary history and usually considered to be in opposition to the principles of classicism. In this sense, Romanticism signifies any work or philosophy in which the exotic or dreamlike figure strongly, or that is devoted to individualistic expression, self-analysis, or a pursuit of a higher realm of knowledge than can be discovered by human reason. Prominent Romantics include Jean-Jacques Rousseau, William Wordsworth, John Keats, Lord Byron, and Johann Wolfgang von Goethe.

Romantics: See *Romanticism*

Russian Symbolism: A Russian poetic movement, derived from French symbolism, that flourished between 1894 and 1910. While some Russian Symbolists continued in the French tradition, stressing aestheticism and the importance of suggestion above didactic intent, others saw their craft as a form of mystical worship, and themselves as mediators between the supernatural and the mundane. Russian symbolists include Aleksandr Blok, Vyacheslav Ivanovich Ivanov, Fyodor Sologub, Andrey Bely, Nikolay Gumilyov, and Vladimir Sergeyevich Solovyov.

S

Satire: A work that uses ridicule, humor, and wit to criticize and provoke change in human nature and institutions. There are two major types of satire: ''formal'' or ''direct'' satire speaks directly to the reader or to a character in the work; ''indirect'' satire relies upon the ridiculous behavior of its characters to make its point. Formal satire is further divided into two manners: the ''Horatian,'' which ridicules gently, and the ''Juvenalian,'' which derides its subjects harshly and bitterly. Voltaire's novella *Candide* is an indirect satire. Jonathan Swift's essay ''A Modest Proposal'' is a Juvenalian satire.

Scansion: The analysis or ''scanning'' of a poem to determine its meter and often its rhyme scheme. The most common system of scansion uses accents (slanted lines drawn above syllables) to show stressed syllables, breves (curved lines drawn above syllables) to show unstressed syllables, and vertical lines to separate each foot. In the first line of John Keats's *Endymion,* ''A thing of beauty is a joy forever:'' the word ''thing,'' the first syllable of ''beauty,'' the word ''joy,'' and the second syllable of ''forever'' are stressed, while the words ''A'' and ''of,'' the second syllable of ''beauty,'' the word ''a,'' and the first and third syllables of ''forever'' are unstressed. In the second line: ''Its loveliness increases; it will never'' a pair of vertical lines separate the foot ending with ''increases'' and the one beginning with ''it.''

Scene: A subdivision of an act of a drama, consisting of continuous action taking place at a single time and in a single location. The beginnings and endings of scenes may be indicated by clearing the stage of actors and props or by the entrances and exits of important characters. The first act of William Shakespeare's *Winter's Tale* is comprised of two scenes.

Science Fiction: A type of narrative about or based upon real or imagined scientific theories and technology. Science fiction is often peopled with alien creatures and set on other planets or in different dimensions. Karel Capek's *R.U.R.* is a major work of science fiction.

Second Person: See *Point of View*

Semiotics: The study of how literary forms and conventions affect the meaning of language. Semioticians include Ferdinand de Saussure, Charles Sanders Pierce, Claude Levi-Strauss, Jacques Lacan, Michel Foucault, Jacques Derrida, Roland Barthes, and Julia Kristeva.

Sestet: Any six-line poem or stanza. Examples of the sestet include the last six lines of the Petrarchan sonnet form, the stanza form of Robert Burns's ''A Poet's Welcome to his love-begotten Daughter,'' and the sestina form in W. H. Auden's ''Paysage Moralise.''

Setting: The time, place, and culture in which the action of a narrative takes place. The elements of setting may include geographic location, characters' physical and mental environments, prevailing cultural attitudes, or the historical time in which the action takes place. Examples of settings include the romanticized Scotland in Sir Walter Scott's ''Waverley'' novels, the French provincial setting in Gustave Flaubert's *Madame Bovary,* the fictional Wessex country of Thomas Hardy's novels, and the small towns of southern Ontario in Alice Munro's short stories.

Shakespearean Sonnet: See *Sonnet*

Signifying Monkey: A popular trickster figure in black folklore, with hundreds of tales about this character documented since the 19th century. Henry Louis Gates Jr. examines the history of the signifying monkey in *The Signifying Monkey: Towards a Theory of Afro-American Literary Criticism,* published in 1988.

Simile: A comparison, usually using ''like'' or ''as'', of two essentially dissimilar things, as in ''coffee as cold as ice'' or ''He sounded like a broken record.'' The title of Ernest Hemingway's ''Hills Like White Elephants'' contains a simile.

Slang: A type of informal verbal communication that is generally unacceptable for formal writing. Slang words and phrases are often colorful exaggerations used to emphasize the speaker's point; they may also be shortened versions of an often-used word or phrase. Examples of American slang from the 1990s include ''yuppie'' (an acronym for Young Urban Professional), ''awesome'' (for ''excellent''), wired (for ''nervous'' or ''excited''), and ''chill out'' (for relax).

Slant Rhyme: See *Consonance*

Slave Narrative: Autobiographical accounts of American slave life as told by escaped slaves. These works first appeared during the abolition movement of the 1830s through the 1850s. Olaudah Equiano's *The Interesting Narrative of Olaudah Equiano, or Gustavus Vassa, The African* and Harriet Ann Jacobs's *Incidents in the Life of a Slave Girl* are examples of the slave narrative.

Social Realism: See *Socialist Realism*

Socialist Realism: The Socialist Realism school of literary theory was proposed by Maxim Gorky and established as a dogma by the first Soviet Congress of Writers. It demanded adherence to a communist worldview in works of literature. Its doctrines required an objective viewpoint comprehensible to the working classes and themes of social struggle featuring strong proletarian heroes. A successful work of socialist realism is Nikolay Ostrovsky's *Kak zakalyalas stal* (*How the Steel Was Tempered*). Also known as Social Realism.

Soliloquy: A monologue in a drama used to give the audience information and to develop the speaker's character. It is typically a projection of the speaker's innermost thoughts. Usually delivered while the speaker is alone on stage, a soliloquy is intended to present an illusion of unspoken reflection. A celebrated soliloquy is Hamlet's ''To be or not to be'' speech in William Shakespeare's *Hamlet.*

Sonnet: A fourteen-line poem, usually composed in iambic pentameter, employing one of several rhyme schemes. There are three major types of sonnets, upon which all other variations of the form are based: the ''Petrarchan'' or ''Italian'' sonnet, the ''Shakespearean'' or ''English'' sonnet, and the ''Spenserian'' sonnet. A Petrarchan sonnet consists of an octave rhymed *abbaabba* and a ''sestet'' rhymed either *cdecde, cdccdc,* or *cdedce.* The octave poses a question or problem, relates a narrative, or puts forth a proposition; the sestet presents a solution to the problem, comments upon the narrative, or applies the proposition put forth in the octave. The Shakespearean sonnet is divided into three quatrains and a couplet rhymed *abab cdcd efef gg.* The couplet provides an epigrammatic comment on the narrative or problem put forth in the quatrains. The Spenserian sonnet uses three quatrains and a couplet like the Shakespearean, but links their three rhyme schemes in this way: *abab bcbc cdcd ee.* The Spenserian sonnet develops its theme in two parts like the Petrarchan, its final six lines resolving a problem, analyzing a narrative, or applying a proposition put forth in its first eight lines. Examples of sonnets can be found in Petrarch's *Canzoniere,* Edmund Spenser's *Amoretti,* Elizabeth Barrett

Browning's *Sonnets from the Portuguese,* Rainer Maria Rilke's *Sonnets to Orpheus,* and Adrienne Rich's poem ''The Insusceptibles.''

Spenserian Sonnet: See *Sonnet*

Spenserian Stanza: A nine-line stanza having eight verses in iambic pentameter, its ninth verse in iambic hexameter, and the rhyme scheme ababbcbcc. This stanza form was first used by Edmund Spenser in his allegorical poem *The Faerie Queene.*

Spondee: In poetry meter, a foot consisting of two long or stressed syllables occurring together. This form is quite rare in English verse, and is usually composed of two monosyllabic words. The first foot in the following line from Robert Burns's ''Green Grow the Rashes'' is an example of a spondee: Green grow the rashes, O

Sprung Rhythm: Versification using a specific number of accented syllables per line but disregarding the number of unaccented syllables that fall in each line, producing an irregular rhythm in the poem. Gerard Manley Hopkins, who coined the term ''sprung rhythm,'' is the most notable practitioner of this technique.

Stanza: A subdivision of a poem consisting of lines grouped together, often in recurring patterns of rhyme, line length, and meter. Stanzas may also serve as units of thought in a poem much like paragraphs in prose. Examples of stanza forms include the quatrain, *terza rima, ottava rima,* Spenserian, and the so-called *In Memoriam* stanza from Alfred, Lord Tennyson's poem by that title. The following is an example of the latter form: Love is and was my lord and king, And in his presence I attend To hear the tidings of my friend, Which every hour his couriers bring.

Stereotype: A stereotype was originally the name for a duplication made during the printing process; this led to its modern definition as a person or thing that is (or is assumed to be) the same as all others of its type. Common stereotypical characters include the absent- minded professor, the nagging wife, the troublemaking teenager, and the kindhearted grandmother.

Stream of Consciousness: A narrative technique for rendering the inward experience of a character. This technique is designed to give the impression of an ever-changing series of thoughts, emotions, images, and memories in the spontaneous and seemingly illogical order that they occur in life. The textbook example of stream of consciousness is the last section of James Joyce's *Ulysses.*

Structuralism: A twentieth-century movement in literary criticism that examines how literary texts arrive at their meanings, rather than the meanings themselves. There are two major types of structuralist analysis: one examines the way patterns of linguistic structures unify a specific text and emphasize certain elements of that text, and the other interprets the way literary forms and conventions affect the meaning of language itself. Prominent structuralists include Michel Foucault, Roman Jakobson, and Roland Barthes.

Structure: The form taken by a piece of literature. The structure may be made obvious for ease of understanding, as in nonfiction works, or may obscured for artistic purposes, as in some poetry or seemingly ''unstructured'' prose. Examples of common literary structures include the plot of a narrative, the acts and scenes of a drama, and such poetic forms as the Shakespearean sonnet and the Pindaric ode.

Sturm und Drang: A German term meaning ''storm and stress.'' It refers to a German literary movement of the 1770s and 1780s that reacted against the order and rationalism of the enlightenment, focusing instead on the intense experience of extraordinary individuals. Highly romantic, works of this movement, such as Johann Wolfgang von Goethe's *Gotz von Berlichingen,* are typified by realism, rebelliousness, and intense emotionalism.

Style: A writer's distinctive manner of arranging words to suit his or her ideas and purpose in writing. The unique imprint of the author's personality upon his or her writing, style is the product of an author's way of arranging ideas and his or her use of diction, different sentence structures, rhythm, figures of speech, rhetorical principles, and other elements of composition. Styles may be classified according to period (Metaphysical, Augustan, Georgian), individual authors (Chaucerian, Miltonic, Jamesian), level (grand, middle, low, plain), or language (scientific, expository, poetic, journalistic).

Subject: The person, event, or theme at the center of a work of literature. A work may have one or more subjects of each type, with shorter works tending to have fewer and longer works tending to have more. The subjects of James Baldwin's novel *Go Tell It on the Mountain* include the themes of father-son relationships, religious conversion, black life, and sexuality. The subjects of Anne Frank's

Diary of a Young Girl include Anne and her family members as well as World War II, the Holocaust, and the themes of war, isolation, injustice, and racism.

Subjectivity: Writing that expresses the author's personal feelings about his subject, and which may or may not include factual information about the subject. Subjectivity is demonstrated in James Joyce's *Portrait of the Artist as a Young Man,* Samuel Butler's *The Way of All Flesh,* and Thomas Wolfe's *Look Homeward, Angel.*

Subplot: A secondary story in a narrative. A subplot may serve as a motivating or complicating force for the main plot of the work, or it may provide emphasis for, or relief from, the main plot. The conflict between the Capulets and the Montagues in William Shakespeare's *Romeo and Juliet* is an example of a subplot.

Surrealism: A term introduced to criticism by Guillaume Apollinaire and later adopted by Andre Breton. It refers to a French literary and artistic movement founded in the 1920s. The Surrealists sought to express unconscious thoughts and feelings in their works. The best-known technique used for achieving this aim was automatic writing—transcriptions of spontaneous outpourings from the unconscious. The Surrealists proposed to unify the contrary levels of conscious and unconscious, dream and reality, objectivity and subjectivity into a new level of "super-realism." Surrealism can be found in the poetry of Paul Eluard, Pierre Reverdy, and Louis Aragon, among others.

Suspense: A literary device in which the author maintains the audience's attention through the build-up of events, the outcome of which will soon be revealed. Suspense in William Shakespeare's *Hamlet* is sustained throughout by the question of whether or not the Prince will achieve what he has been instructed to do and of what he intends to do.

Syllogism: A method of presenting a logical argument. In its most basic form, the syllogism consists of a major premise, a minor premise, and a conclusion. An example of a syllogism is: Major premise: When it snows, the streets get wet. Minor premise: It is snowing. Conclusion: The streets are wet.

Symbol: Something that suggests or stands for something else without losing its original identity. In literature, symbols combine their literal meaning with the suggestion of an abstract concept. Literary symbols are of two types: those that carry complex associations of meaning no matter what their contexts, and those that derive their suggestive meaning from their functions in specific literary works. Examples of symbols are sunshine suggesting happiness, rain suggesting sorrow, and storm clouds suggesting despair.

Symbolism: This term has two widely accepted meanings. In historical criticism, it denotes an early modernist literary movement initiated in France during the nineteenth century that reacted against the prevailing standards of realism. Writers in this movement aimed to evoke, indirectly and symbolically, an order of being beyond the material world of the five senses. Poetic expression of personal emotion figured strongly in the movement, typically by means of a private set of symbols uniquely identifiable with the individual poet. The principal aim of the Symbolists was to express in words the highly complex feelings that grew out of everyday contact with the world. In a broader sense, the term "symbolism" refers to the use of one object to represent another. Early members of the Symbolist movement included the French authors Charles Baudelaire and Arthur Rimbaud; William Butler Yeats, James Joyce, and T. S. Eliot were influenced as the movement moved to Ireland, England, and the United States. Examples of the concept of symbolism include a flag that stands for a nation or movement, or an empty cupboard used to suggest hopelessness, poverty, and despair.

Symbolist: See *Symbolism*

Symbolist Movement: See *Symbolism*

Sympathetic Fallacy: See *Affective Fallacy*

T

Tale: A story told by a narrator with a simple plot and little character development. Tales are usually relatively short and often carry a simple message. Examples of tales can be found in the work of Rudyard Kipling, Somerset Maugham, Saki, Anton Chekhov, Guy de Maupassant, and Armistead Maupin.

Tall Tale: A humorous tale told in a straightforward, credible tone but relating absolutely impossible events or feats of the characters. Such tales were commonly told of frontier adventures during the settlement of the west in the United States. Tall tales have been spun around such legendary heroes as Mike Fink, Paul Bunyan, Davy Crockett, Johnny Appleseed, and Captain Stormalong as well as the real-life William F. Cody and Annie Oakley. Literary use of tall tales can be found in Washington Irving's *History of New York,* Mark Twain's *Life on the Mississippi,* and in the German R. F. Raspe's *Baron Munchausen's Narratives of His Marvellous Travels and Campaigns in Russia.*

Tanka: A form of Japanese poetry similar to *haiku.* A *tanka* is five lines long, with the lines containing five, seven, five, seven, and seven syllables respectively. Skilled *tanka* authors include Ishikawa Takuboku, Masaoka Shiki, Amy Lowell, and Adelaide Crapsey.

Teatro Grottesco: See *Theater of the Grotesque*

Terza Rima: A three-line stanza form in poetry in which the rhymes are made on the last word of each line in the following manner: the first and third lines of the first stanza, then the second line of the first stanza and the first and third lines of the second stanza, and so on with the middle line of any stanza rhyming with the first and third lines of the following stanza. An example of *terza rima* is Percy Bysshe Shelley's "The Triumph of Love": As in that trance of wondrous thought I lay This was the tenour of my waking dream. Methought I sate beside a public way Thick strewn with summer dust, and a great stream Of people there was hurrying to and fro Numerous as gnats upon the evening gleam,. . .

Tetrameter: See *Meter*

Textual Criticism: A branch of literary criticism that seeks to establish the authoritative text of a literary work. Textual critics typically compare all known manuscripts or printings of a single work in order to assess the meanings of differences and revisions. This procedure allows them to arrive at a definitive version that (supposedly) corresponds to the author's original intention. Textual criticism was applied during the Renaissance to salvage the classical texts of Greece and Rome, and modern works have been studied, for instance, to undo deliberate correction or censorship, as in the case of novels by Stephen Crane and Theodore Dreiser.

Theater of Cruelty: Term used to denote a group of theatrical techniques designed to eliminate the psychological and emotional distance between actors and audience. This concept, introduced in the 1930s in France, was intended to inspire a more intense theatrical experience than conventional theater allowed. The "cruelty" of this dramatic theory signified not sadism but heightened actor/audience involvement in the dramatic event. The theater of cruelty was theorized by Antonin Artaud in his *Le Theatre et son double* (*The Theatre and Its Double*), and also appears in the work of Jerzy Grotowski, Jean Genet, Jean Vilar, and Arthur Adamov, among others.

Theater of the Absurd: A post-World War II dramatic trend characterized by radical theatrical innovations. In works influenced by the Theater of the absurd, nontraditional, sometimes grotesque characterizations, plots, and stage sets reveal a meaningless universe in which human values are irrelevant. Existentialist themes of estrangement, absurdity, and futility link many of the works of this movement. The principal writers of the Theater of the Absurd are Samuel Beckett, Eugene Ionesco, Jean Genet, and Harold Pinter.

Theater of the Grotesque: An Italian theatrical movement characterized by plays written around the ironic and macabre aspects of daily life in the World War I era. Theater of the Grotesque was named after the play *The Mask and the Face* by Luigi Chiarelli, which was described as "a grotesque in three acts." The movement influenced the work of Italian dramatist Luigi Pirandello, author of *Right You Are, If You Think You Are.* Also known as *Teatro Grottesco.*

Theme: The main point of a work of literature. The term is used interchangeably with thesis. The theme of William Shakespeare's *Othello*—jealousy—is a common one.

Thesis: A thesis is both an essay and the point argued in the essay. Thesis novels and thesis plays share the quality of containing a thesis which is supported through the action of the story. A master's thesis and a doctoral dissertation are two theses required of graduate students.

Thesis Play: See *Thesis*

Three Unities: See *Unities*

Tone: The author's attitude toward his or her audience may be deduced from the tone of the work. A formal tone may create distance or convey politeness, while an informal tone may encourage a friendly, intimate, or intrusive feeling in the reader. The author's attitude toward his or her subject matter may also be deduced from the tone of the words he or she uses in discussing it. The tone of John F. Kennedy's speech which included the appeal to "ask not what your country can do for you" was intended to instill feelings of camaraderie and national pride in listeners.

Tragedy: A drama in prose or poetry about a noble, courageous hero of excellent character who, because of some tragic character flaw or *hamartia*, brings ruin upon him- or herself. Tragedy treats its subjects in a dignified and serious manner, using poetic language to help evoke pity and fear and bring about catharsis, a purging of these emotions. The tragic form was practiced extensively by the ancient Greeks. In the Middle Ages, when classical works were virtually unknown, tragedy came to denote any works about the fall of persons from exalted to low conditions due to any reason: fate, vice, weakness, etc. According to the classical definition of tragedy, such works present the ''pathetic''—that which evokes pity—rather than the tragic. The classical form of tragedy was revived in the sixteenth century; it flourished especially on the Elizabethan stage. In modern times, dramatists have attempted to adapt the form to the needs of modern society by drawing their heroes from the ranks of ordinary men and women and defining the nobility of these heroes in terms of spirit rather than exalted social standing. The greatest classical example of tragedy is Sophocles' *Oedipus Rex.* The ''pathetic'' derivation is exemplified in ''The Monk's Tale'' in Geoffrey Chaucer's *Canterbury Tales.* Notable works produced during the sixteenth century revival include William Shakespeare's *Hamlet, Othello,* and *King Lear.* Modern dramatists working in the tragic tradition include Henrik Ibsen, Arthur Miller, and Eugene O'Neill.

Tragedy of Blood: See *Revenge Tragedy*

Tragic Flaw: In a tragedy, the quality within the hero or heroine which leads to his or her downfall. Examples of the tragic flaw include Othello's jealousy and Hamlet's indecisiveness, although most great tragedies defy such simple interpretation.

Transcendentalism: An American philosophical and religious movement, based in New England from around 1835 until the Civil War. Transcendentalism was a form of American romanticism that had its roots abroad in the works of Thomas Carlyle, Samuel Coleridge, and Johann Wolfgang von Goethe. The Transcendentalists stressed the importance of intuition and subjective experience in communication with God. They rejected religious dogma and texts in favor of mysticism and scientific naturalism. They pursued truths that lie beyond the ''colorless'' realms perceived by reason and the senses and were active social reformers in public education, women's rights, and the abolition of slavery. Prominent members of the group include Ralph Waldo Emerson and Henry David Thoreau.

Trickster: A character or figure common in Native American and African literature who uses his ingenuity to defeat enemies and escape difficult situations. Tricksters are most often animals, such as the spider, hare, or coyote, although they may take the form of humans as well. Examples of trickster tales include Thomas King's *A Coyote Columbus Story,* Ashley F. Bryan's *The Dancing Granny* and Ishmael Reed's *The Last Days of Louisiana Red.*

Trimeter: See *Meter*

Triple Rhyme: See *Rhyme*

Trochee: See *Foot*

U

Understatement: See *Irony*

Unities: Strict rules of dramatic structure, formulated by Italian and French critics of the Renaissance and based loosely on the principles of drama discussed by Aristotle in his *Poetics.* Foremost among these rules were the three unities of action, time, and place that compelled a dramatist to: (1) construct a single plot with a beginning, middle, and end that details the causal relationships of action and character; (2) restrict the action to the events of a single day; and (3) limit the scene to a single place or city. The unities were observed faithfully by continental European writers until the Romantic Age, but they were never regularly observed in English drama. Modern dramatists are typically more concerned with a unity of impression or emotional effect than with any of the classical unities. The unities are observed in Pierre Corneille's tragedy *Polyeuctes* and Jean-Baptiste Racine's *Phedre.* Also known as Three Unities.

Urban Realism: A branch of realist writing that attempts to accurately reflect the often harsh facts of modern urban existence. Some works by Stephen Crane, Theodore Dreiser, Charles Dickens, Fyodor Dostoyevsky, Emile Zola, Abraham Cahan, and Henry Fuller feature urban realism. Modern examples include Claude Brown's *Manchild in the Promised Land* and Ron Milner's *What the Wine Sellers Buy.*

Utopia: A fictional perfect place, such as ''paradise'' or ''heaven.'' Early literary utopias were included in Plato's *Republic* and Sir Thomas More's *Utopia,* while more modern utopias can be found in

Samuel Butler's *Erewhon,* Theodor Herzka's *A Visit to Freeland,* and H. G. Wells' *A Modern Utopia.*

Utopian: See *Utopia*

Utopianism: See *Utopia*

V

Verisimilitude: Literally, the appearance of truth. In literary criticism, the term refers to aspects of a work of literature that seem true to the reader. Verisimilitude is achieved in the work of Honore de Balzac, Gustave Flaubert, and Henry James, among other late nineteenth-century realist writers.

Vers de societe: See *Occasional Verse*

Vers libre: See *Free Verse*

Verse: A line of metered language, a line of a poem, or any work written in verse. The following line of verse is from the epic poem *Don Juan* by Lord Byron: ''My way is to begin with the beginning.''

Versification: The writing of verse. Versification may also refer to the meter, rhyme, and other mechanical components of a poem. Composition of a ''Roses are red, violets are blue'' poem to suit an occasion is a common form of versification practiced by students.

Victorian: Refers broadly to the reign of Queen Victoria of England (1837-1901) and to anything with qualities typical of that era. For example, the qualities of smug narrowmindedness, bourgeois materialism, faith in social progress, and priggish morality are often considered Victorian. This stereotype is contradicted by such dramatic intellectual developments as the theories of Charles Darwin, Karl Marx, and Sigmund Freud (which stirred strong debates in England) and the critical attitudes of serious Victorian writers like Charles Dickens and George Eliot. In literature, the Victorian Period was the great age of the English novel, and the latter part of the era saw the rise of movements such as decadence and symbolism. Works of Victorian literature include the poetry of Robert Browning and Alfred, Lord Tennyson, the criticism of Matthew Arnold and John Ruskin, and the novels of Emily Bronte, William Makepeace Thackeray, and Thomas Hardy. Also known as Victorian Age and Victorian Period.

Victorian Age: See *Victorian*

Victorian Period: See *Victorian*

W

Weltanschauung: A German term referring to a person's worldview or philosophy. Examples of *weltanschauung* include Thomas Hardy's view of the human being as the victim of fate, destiny, or impersonal forces and circumstances, and the disillusioned and laconic cynicism expressed by such poets of the 1930s as W. H. Auden, Sir Stephen Spender, and Sir William Empson.

Weltschmerz: A German term meaning ''world pain.'' It describes a sense of anguish about the nature of existence, usually associated with a melancholy, pessimistic attitude. *Weltschmerz* was expressed in England by George Gordon, Lord Byron in his *Manfred* and *Childe Harold's Pilgrimage,* in France by Viscount de Chateaubriand, Alfred de Vigny, and Alfred de Musset, in Russia by Aleksandr Pushkin and Mikhail Lermontov, in Poland by Juliusz Slowacki, and in America by Nathaniel Hawthorne.

Z

Zarzuela: A type of Spanish operetta. Writers of *zarzuelas* include Lope de Vega and Pedro Calderon.

Zeitgeist: A German term meaning ''spirit of the time.'' It refers to the moral and intellectual trends of a given era. Examples of *zeitgeist* include the preoccupation with the more morbid aspects of dying and death in some Jacobean literature, especially in the works of dramatists Cyril Tourneur and John Webster, and the decadence of the French Symbolists.

Cumulative Author/Title Index

M

N

O

P

R

S

T

V

W

Y

Z

Nationality/Ethnicity Index

Subject/Theme Index

*Boldface terms appear as subheads in Themes section of story.

S

T

U

V

W

Y